*Russian Research Center Studies, 13*

# THE FORMATION OF
# THE SOVIET UNION

# THE FORMATION OF
# THE SOVIET UNION

## COMMUNISM AND NATIONALISM

1917–1923

## Richard Pipes

Revised Edition

**HARVARD UNIVERSITY PRESS**

Cambridge, Massachusetts
and London, England

*Library of Congress Catalog Card Number 64-21284*
*ISBN 0-674-30950-2*
*Printed in the United States of America*

TO MY PARENTS

# PREFACE TO THE REVISED EDITION

This book was originally written in 1948–1953, when the cult of Stalin was most intense, and information on Stalin's role in the shaping of the Soviet Union was hard to come by. I had been forced, therefore, to construct my narrative of the whole critical period 1921–1923 — the years when the principles of the Union were being formulated and carried into practice — from fragmentary and often unreliable evidence. Two years after the book had been published, the Communist Party of the Soviet Union held its Twentieth Congress, at which it condemned the "cult of personality." Shortly afterwards, historical institutes in Russia proper and in the republics began to publish quantities of monographs and collections of documents bearing on the history of the Revolution, Civil War, and establishment of the Union. The purpose of these publications was essentially political and propagandistic: to denigrate Stalin and depict Lenin as the infallible and virtually singlehanded architect of the Soviet multinational state. In so doing, however, they revealed a great deal of information about two vital episodes: the subjugation of Georgia and the formulation of the constitutional principles, because these were issues over which Lenin quarreled and virtually broke off relations with Stalin.

The appearance of this material necessitated a thorough revision of the latter part of my book. I have rewritten for the present edition the section dealing with the conquest of Azerbaijan and Georgia and all of Chapter VI. Nothing published either inside or outside of the Soviet Union on the preceding period (1917–1921) seems to have affected significantly that part of my narrative. The official Soviet interpretation of this period has remained substantially the same as it had been in Stalin's days, and the most important documents bearing on it are still locked up in archives. Hence, I have left Chapters I–IV and most of Chapter V unchanged.

The corresponding sections of the bibliography — the latter part of Chapter V (Azerbaijan and Georgia) and Chapter VI — have been brought up to date to include the most important works used in preparing this edition.

*Richard Pipes*

*January 1964*

# PREFACE TO THE FIRST EDITION

This book deals with the history of the disintegration of the old Russian Empire, and the establishment, on its ruins, of a multinational Communist state: the Union of Soviet Socialist Republics. Its main emphasis is on the national movements in the borderlands, and on the relations between them and the Communist movement. It has as its main objective an analysis of the role which the entire national question played in the Russian Revolution.

The relatively limited span of time which this history covers — from 1917 to 1923 (if one excludes the general introductory chapter concerned with pre-1917 events) — would make it possible to present a coherent chronological account, were it not for the fact that the Revolution ran a somewhat different course in every borderland region, so that a general survey requires numerous digressions in the narrative and shifts from area to area. The author hopes that the reader will tolerate the complexity of the history as a feature of the topic itself.

Insofar as this study is concerned largely with the political aspect of the national question, as distinct from its cultural or economic aspects, peoples without a geographically defined territory of their own, such as the Jews, or those which did not play an important part in the political development of the Soviet state, are not treated, except in passing. Nor does the book discuss those national groups which succeeded in separating themselves from Russia in the course of the Revolution: the Finns, the Baltic peoples, the Poles.

In dealing with foreign words the following general principles are used. Proper names of Russians, Ukrainians, and Belorussians are given in transliteration, except in the case of figures internationally known, where the prevailing English spelling is substituted; thus Trotsky, not Trotskii. Names of persons of Turkic or Caucasian stock are shown in the form which they themselves employed at the time of the Revolution, that is in almost all instances in their Russified form; but, wherever possible, the native one is also given: for example, M. Chokaev (Chokai-ogly). The same rule applies to political parties and institutions: they are given in their Russified form, with the Osmanli Turkish or Arabic equivalents in parentheses. Geographic terms appear in the form current during the period 1917–1923, and where those differ from the terms used in 1952, the latter are also supplied.

Throughout, the Library of Congress system of transliteration of Slavic languages is used, with the ligatures and diacritical marks omitted. This system is shown in the table on pages 291–92.

All the dates for the year 1917 are given according to the Julian calendar, then current in Russia. For 1918, when a calendar reform was introduced, both the Julian and Gregorian dates are used, while for 1919 and the years following all dates are according to the Gregorian calendar. In 1917 the Julian calendar was thirteen days behind the Gregorian one. When the sources were unclear about which calendar was followed, only a single date is given.

I would like to express my gratitude to Professor Michael Karpovich, who originally suggested the subject of this study and who has made many further suggestions in the course of its writing; to the Russian Research Center of Harvard University, and especially to its director, Professor Clyde Kluckhohn, for the most generous assistance; to Professor Robert L. Wolff, for his painstaking critical analysis of the entire manuscript; and to Professor Merle Fainsod for his helpful comments. I would also like to thank the personnel of the Hoover Library and Institute in California for their help in my research. Dr. Franz Schurmann has kindly translated for me most of the Turkish sources; I have also received assistance with the Armenian materials. The maps were prepared by Mr. Robert L. Williams of the Yale Cartographic Laboratory. Mrs. Merle Fainsod and my wife have given much of their time to editing the manuscript, while Mrs. Wiktor Weintraub has assisted me ably in verifying the accuracy of citations and references. Miss Margaret Dalton has been of great assistance in typing the manuscript for publication, and Mrs. James E. Duffy has contributed much experience in the final editing of the book.

*Richard Pipes*

*May 1954*

# CONTENTS

# ILLUSTRATIONS

*Following page 98*

*Volodimir Vinnichenko, 1921 (Ukrainska Vilna Akademiia Nauk SShA,* Volodymyr Vynnychenko, *New York, 1953).*
*Mikhail Hrushevskii (Ukrainian Museum UVAN, New York).*
*Simon Petliura, 1917 (private).*
*Hetman Skoropadski and Kaiser Wilhelm II in Berlin, 1918* (Za velych natsii, *Lwów, 1938).*
*Grigorii Piatakov* (M. Ravich-Cherkasskii, Istoriia Kommunisticheskoi Partii Ukrainy. *Kharkov, 1923).*
*Vladimir Zatonskii (Ravich-Cherkasskii, Istoriia).*
*Khristian Rakovskii (Prozhektor, 31 August 1924).*
*Mykola Skrypnik (Ravich-Cherkasskii, Istoriia).*
*Mehmed Emin Resul-zade, 1951 (photograph by author).*
*Mustafa Chokaev, 1917* (Revue du Monde Musulman, *June 1922).*
*Dzhafer Seidamet and Chelibidzhan Chelibiev, 1917 (private).*
*Zeki Validov (Togan), 1953 (private).*
*Joseph Stalin as Commissar of Nationalities, 1917* (Zhizn' natsional'nostei, *no. 1, 1923).*
*Mirza Sultan-Galiev (Zhizn' natsional'nostei, no. 1, 1923).*
*Said Alim Khan, last Emir of Bukhara (William E. Curtis, Turkestan, New York, 1911).*
*Enver Pasha (Louis Fischer, The Soviets in World Affairs, Princeton, 1952); (reproduced by permission of Princeton University Press and Jonathan Cape, Ltd.).*
*Noi Zhordaniia (private).*
*Irakly Tseretelli, 1917 (private).*
*Akaki Chkhenkeli (private).*
*Budu Mdivani, 1922* (L'Illustration, *no. 4128, 15 April 1922, p. 332).*
*Filipp Makharadze (private).*
*Grigorii Ordzhonikidze (I. Mints and E. Gorodetskii, eds.,* Dokumenty po istorii grazhdanskoi voiny v SSSR, I, *Moscow, 1940).*
*Sergei Kirov (Mints and Gorodetskii, Dokumenty).*
*Stepan Shaumian (Mints and Gorodetskii, Dokumenty).*
*The General Secretariat of the Ukrainian Central Rada, 1917 (private).*
*Mikhail Frunze and Ordzhonikidze at Tiflis, 1924* (USSR in Construction, *April–May 1936).*
*Negotiations between Soviet authorities and Basmachi leaders in the Ferghana region, 1921 (K. Ramzin,* Revoliutsiia v Srednei Azii, *Moscow, 1928).*

## MAPS

## Abbreviations Used in the Notes and Bibliography

IM        *Istorik marksist*
KA        *Krasnyi arkhiv*
LR        *Letopis'* (and *Litopis*) *revoliutsii*
LS        *Leninskii sbornik*
NZ        *Die Neue Zeit*
NV        *Novyi vostok*
PR        *Proletarskaia revoliutsiia*
RN        *Revoliutsiia i natsional'nosti*
SP        *Sovetskoe pravo*
SR        *Sotsialist-Revoliutsioner*
VE        *Vestnik Evropy*
VI        *Voprosy istorii*
VS        *Vlast' sovetov*
ZhN       *Zhizn' natsional'nostei*


CSt-H       Hoover Library and Institute, Stanford, California.
DLC         The Library of Congress, Washington, D.C.
NN          The New York Public Library, New York.
NNC         The Columbia University Library, New York.
Brit. Mus.  The British Museum, London.
Doc. Int.   Bibliothèque de Documentation Internationale Contemporaine, Paris.

# I

# THE NATIONAL PROBLEM

# IN RUSSIA

*The Russian Empire on the Eve of the 1917 Revolution*

The Russian Empire, as it appeared in 1917, was the product of nearly four centuries of continuous expansion. Unlike other European nations, Russia was situated on the edge of the vast Asiatic mainland and knew relatively few geographic deterrents to aggrandizement. This geographically favorable situation was made even more advantageous by the political weakness of Russia's neighbors, who were especially ineffective on the eastern and southern frontiers. Here vast and potentially rich territories were either under the dominion of internally unstable and technologically backward Moslem principalities, or else sparsely populated by nomadic and semi-nomadic groups without any permanent political institutions whatsoever — forces incapable of long range resistance to the pressures of a large and dynamic state. Hence Russia, somewhat like the United States, found outlets for expansive tendencies along its own borders instead of overseas. The process of external growth had been rapid, beginning with the inception of the modern Russian state and developing in close connection with it. It has been estimated that the growth of the Russian Empire between the end of the fifteenth and the end of the nineteenth century proceeded at the rate of 130 square kilometers or fifty square miles a day.*

Almost from its very inception the Moscow state had acquired dominion over non-Russian peoples. Ivan the Terrible conquered Kazan and Astrakhan and brought the state a large number of Turks (Volga Tatars, Bashkirs) and Finns (Chuvashes, Mordvinians) from the region of the Volga River and its tributaries. In the seventeenth century, the

---

* A. Brueckner, *Die Europaeisierung Russlands* (Gotha, 1888), 9. This process slowed down in the century between 1761 and 1856 to a rate of thirty square miles a day. During approximately the same time (1790–1890), the United States expanded at double that rate, or sixty square miles a day; cf. data in the *Encyclopaedia Britannica* (11th ed., 1911), XXVII, 365.

tsars added Siberia, populated by Turkic, Mongol, and Finnish tribes. The left-bank regions of the Dnieper River, with their Cossack population — the forerunners of modern Ukrainians — came under a Russian protectorate in 1654. During the eighteenth century, moving west, Peter the Great conquered from Sweden the eastern shores of the Baltic Sea (today's Estonia and Latvia), while Catherine the Great, as a result of agreements with Austria and Prussia, seized the eastern provinces of the Polish-Lithuanian Commonwealth. Catherine's successful wars with Turkey brought Russia possession of the northern shores of the Black Sea, including the Crimean peninsula. The Transcaucasian Kingdom of Eastern Georgia was incorporated in 1801, Finland in 1809, and the central regions of Poland in 1815. The remainder of Transcaucasia and the Northern Caucasus were acquired in the first half of the century, and Alexander II added most of Turkestan.

The first systematic census, undertaken in 1897, revealed that the majority (55.7 per cent) of the population of the Empire, exclusive of the Grand Duchy of Finland, consisted of non-Russians.[*] The total population of the Empire was 122,666,500. The principal groups were divided, by native language, as follows (the figures are in per cent):[1]

| | |
|---|---:|
| Slavs | |
| Great Russians | 44.32 |
| Ukrainians | 17.81 |
| Poles | 6.31 |
| Belorussians | 4.68 |
| Turkic peoples | 10.82 |
| Jews | 4.03 |
| Finnish peoples | 2.78 |
| Lithuanians and Latvians | 2.46 |
| Germans | 1.42 |
| Caucasian Mountain peoples (*gortsy*) | 1.34 |
| Georgians | 1.07 |
| Armenians | 0.93 |
| Iranian peoples | 0.62 |
| Mongolians | 0.38 |
| Others | 1.03 |

[*] A. I. Kastelianskii, ed., *Formy natsional'nago dvizheniia* (St. Petersburg, 1910), 283. The criterion employed by this census was language, not nationality, that is, all those citizens who considered Russian their native tongue were listed as Russians. Since, however, the Russian language was the *lingua franca* of the Empire and was spoken by many educated non-Russians, the census tended to overestimate the proportion of Russians in the population. The 1926 census, which investigated both the language and the nationality of the inhabitants, revealed that six and one-half million citizens of the Soviet Union (or 4.5 per cent of the entire population) of non-Russian nationality considered Russian their mother tongue. It is not far fetched to suppose, therefore, that the true proportion of non-Russians at the end of the nineteenth century was close to 60 per cent.

One of the anomalies of pre-1917 Russia was the fact that although, to quote one observer, "the Russian Empire, Great Russian in its origin, ceased being such in its ethnic composition," [2] the state, with some exceptions, continued to be treated constitutionally and administratively as a nationally homogeneous unit. The principle of autocracy, preserved in all its essentials until the Revolution of 1905, did not permit — at least in theory — the recognition of separate historic or national territories within the state in which the monarch's authority would be less absolute or rest on a legally different basis from that which he exercised at home. In practice, however, this principle was not always consistently applied. At various times in history Russian tsars did grant considerable autonomy to newly conquered territories, partly in recognition of their special status, partly in anticipation of political reforms in Russia, and in some cases they even entered into contractual relations with subject peoples, thus limiting their own power.

Poland from 1815 to 1831 and Finland from 1809 to 1899 were in theory as well as in practice constitutional monarchies. Other regions, such as the Ukraine from 1654 to 1764, Livonia and Estonia from 1710 to 1783 and from 1795 to the 1800's, enjoyed extensive self rule.[3] But those exceptions were incompatible with the maintenance of the principle of autocracy in Russia itself. Sooner or later, for one reason or another, the privileges granted to conquered peoples were retracted, contracts were unilaterally abrogated, and the subjects, together with their territories, were incorporated into the regular administration of the Empire.

At the close of the nineteenth century, Finland alone still retained a broad measure of self-rule. Indeed, in some respects, it possessed greater democratic rights than Russia proper; Finland under the tsars presented the paradox of a subject nation possessing more political freedom than the people who ruled over it. It was a separate principality, which the Russian monarch governed in his capacity as Grand Duke (*Velikii kniaz'*). The tsar was the chief executive; he controlled the Grand Duchy's foreign affairs; he decided on questions of war and peace; he approved laws and the appointments of judges. The tsar also named the resident Governor General of the Grand Duchy, who headed the Finnish and Russian armies and the police on its territory, and who was responsible for the appointments of the local governors. A State Secretary served as the intermediary between the Russian monarch and the Finnish organs of self-rule. The Finns had complete control over the legislative institutions of the state. They possessed a bicameral legislative body, composed of a Senate and a Seim (Diet). The Senate considered legislative projects and performed the function of the supreme court of the state. The Seim was the highest legislative organ in the country. Called every five years on the basis of nation-wide elections, it initiated and voted on legislation pertaining to its domain. No law could become effective without its approval. Finnish citizens in addition enjoyed other privileges. Every Finnish subject, while in Russia proper, could claim all the rights of Russian citizens, although Russian citizens in Finland were considered foreigners. In every respect, therefore, Finland had a uniquely privileged position in the Russian Empire, which resembled more closely the dominion relationship in existence in the British Empire than the customary colonial relationship prevalent in other parts of Russia.[4] The Finns had originally acquired these privileges from the Swedes, who had ruled their country before the Russian conquest. The tsars preserved them because Finland was acquired by Alexander I, a monarch of relatively liberal views, who, for a time, had thought of introducing a constitutional regime into Russia proper.

Prior to 1917, the Russian Empire also possessed two protectorates, the Central Asian principalities of Bukhara and Khiva. In 1868 and 1873 respectively, these states recognized the sovereignty of the Russian tsar and ceded to him the right to represent them in relations with other powers. They also granted Russians exclusive commercial privileges and were compelled to abolish slavery in their domains. Otherwise, they enjoyed self-rule.

The remaining borderlands of the Empire were administered, in the last decades of the *ancien régime,* in a manner which did not differ essentially — though it differed in some particulars — from that in effect in the territories of Russia proper. Whatever special powers the Imperial Government deemed necessary to grant to the authorities administering these territories were derived not so much from a recognition of the multinational character of the state or from a desire to adapt political institutions to the needs of the inhabitants, as from the impracticability of extending the administrative system of the Great Russian provinces in its entirety to the borderland.

Whereas, for example, Russia was divided into provinces (*gubernie*), administered by governors, most of the borderland areas were grouped into General Gubernie, which included anywhere from a few to a dozen regular provinces, and were headed by governors general, usually high army officers. The distance of the borderlands from the center, the sparsity of population in some and the existence of strong nationalist traditions in others, required that the persons administering such areas be granted greater powers than was necessary in the central provinces of the Empire. The governor general was a viceroy, with extraordinary powers to maintain order and to suppress revolutionary activity. He had a right to employ any means necessary to the performance of his duty, including arrests or expulsions without recourse to courts. In some regions, the governor general also received additional powers, required by local conditions. There were ten such governors general: in Warsaw (with jurisdiction over ten Polish provinces), in Kiev (with jurisdiction over the

Ukraine, or Little Russia, including the provinces of Kiev, Volhynia, and Podolia), in Vilna (today's Lithuania and Belorussia, with the provinces of Vilna, Grodno, and Kovno), two in Central Asia (Turkestan and Steppe), and two in Siberia (the so-called Irkutskoe, and Priamurskoe). The Governor General of Finland, although bearing the title, had in effect very little authority, and could not be classed in the same category as the other governors general. The official heading the administration of the Caucasus, on the other hand, while formally called a viceroy, was for all practical purposes a full-fledged governor general. The city of Moscow, because of its importance and central location, also formed a general gubernia.⁵

Under the governor general were the provincial governors who had to communicate with the central political institutions of the Empire through him, but who, as a rule, were called "military governors" (*voennye gubernatory*), and had both civil and military jurisdiction. The military governors of Turkestan were directly appointed by the Russian Ministry of War.

The gubernie, or provinces, were — as elsewhere in Russia — further subdivided into districts (*okruga,* or less commonly *uezdy*), but in the eastern borderlands such circumscriptions generally embraced much larger territories and had a simpler structure. On the lowest administrative level there existed considerable variety. In some regions, the population was divided into villages or *auly;* in others, where the inhabitants were nomadic, they were organized into tribes; in yet others, they were administered together with the local Russian population.

Russian law also made special provisions for certain groups of non-Russian subjects. Russia, prior to 1917, retained the system of legally recognized classes and class privileges, long since defunct in Western Europe. Within this system there was a social category of so-called *inorodtsy,* a term which has no exact equivalent in English and can best be rendered by the French *peuples allogènes.* The inorodtsy comprised the Jews and most of the nomadic peoples of the Empire, who were subject to special laws rather than to the general laws promulgated in the territories which they inhabited.* For the nomadic inorodtsy, this meant in effect that they possessed the right to self-rule, with their native courts and tribal organization. Their relations with the Russian authorities were limited to the payment of a fixed tribute or tax, usually to an agent of the Ministry of Interior or of State Properties. By settling on land and abandoning nomadic habits, an inorodets changed from his status to that of a regular Russian citizen, with all the duties and privi-

---

* The Russian Code of Law defined *inorodtsy* as subjects belonging to the following groups: the Siberian nomads (which included those of the Steppe General Gubernia of Central Asia), the natives of the Komandorskie Islands, the Samoeds, the nomads of the province of Stavropol, the Kalmyks, the Ordyntsy of the Transcaspian region, the mountain peoples of the Northern Caucasus, and all the Jews.

leges of the class which he had joined; as long as he retained his inorodets status, he gave nothing to the government and received nothing in return.[6] Russian treatment of the nomads was, on the whole, characterized by tolerance and respect for native traditions. Much of the credit for this must be given to the great liberal statesman, M. M. Speranskii, who, at the beginning of the nineteenth century, had laid down the basic principles for their administration.

For the other subgroup of inorodtsy, the Jews, membership in this class entailed stringent restrictions (most of them stemming from eighteenth-century legislation). These forbade them to move out of a strictly defined area in the southwestern and northwestern parts of the Empire, the so-called Pale of Settlement, to purchase landed property, or to settle outside the towns. Such disabilities brought severe social and economic suffering, for the Jews were crowded into towns where they had no adequate basis for livelihood and had to rely heavily on primitive handicraftsmanship and petty trade to survive. By creating abnormal economic conditions in the Jewish communities and preventing them from taking their place in the life of society, the restrictive legislation contributed to the large number of Jews found in radical movements at the beginning of the twentieth century. The Jew could alter his status only by adopting Christianity.*

At no point in its history did tsarist Russia formulate a consistent policy toward the minorities. In the early period of the Empire, approximately from the middle of the sixteenth until the middle of the eighteenth century, the attitude of the government toward its non-Russian subjects was influenced strongly by religion. Where discrimination existed, the principal reason was the desire of the regime to convert Moslems, Jews, and other non-Christians to the Orthodox faith. Toward the end of the eighteenth century, with the secularization of the Russian monarchy, this religious element lost its force, and political considerations loomed ever larger. Thereafter, the treatment of the minorities, as of the Great Russians themselves, was largely determined by the desire on the part of the monarchs to maintain and enforce the principle of autocracy; minority groups which challenged this effort in the name of national rights were treated as harshly as were Russian groups which challenged it in the name of democracy or freedom in general.

The period from the accession of Alexander III (1881) to the outbreak of the 1905 Revolution was that in which persecution of the minorities culminated. The Russian government perhaps for the first time in its entire history adopted a systematic policy of Russification and minority repression, largely in an endeavor to utilize Great Russian national sentiments as a weapon against growing social unrest in the

---

* Exceptions were made only in the case of certain categories of Jews who were either rich merchants or had a higher education.

country. During this period, Finnish privileges were violated through a suspension of the legislative powers of the Seim (1899), the introduction of the compulsory study of Russian in Finnish secondary schools, the subordination of the Finnish Ministry of Post and Telegraphs to the corresponding Russian institution, and other restrictive measures. Polish cultural activity was severely limited; the Jewish population was subjected to pogroms inspired or tolerated by the government, and to further economic restrictions (for instance, the revocation of the right to distill alcohol); the Ukrainian cultural movement was virtually brought to a standstill as a result of the prohibitions imposed on printing in the Ukrainian language (initiated in the 1870's); the properties of the Armenian church were confiscated by the Viceroy of the Caucasus (1903). It was, however, not accidental that this era of Russification coincided with the period of greatest governmental reaction, during which the Great Russian population itself lost many of the rights which it had acquired in the Great Reforms of Alexander II (1856–1881).

The outbreak of the Revolution of 1905 and the subsequent establishment of a constitutional monarchy brought to a halt the period of national persecution but it did not repair all the damage done in the previous quarter-century. The Dumas, especially the First, in which the minorities were well represented,* gave only slight attention to the national question, though they provided an open rostrum of discussions on that topic. In 1907, the government regained supremacy over the liberal elements; it changed the electoral laws in favor of the Russian upper classes, among whom supporters of the autocracy were strong, depriving the remainder of the population of a proportionate voice in the legislative institutions of the state. The borderlands, where liberal and socialist parties enjoyed a particularly strong following, were hardest hit by the change, and some (Turkestan, for instance) lost entirely the right to representation.

## National Movements in Russia

The paradox — and tragedy — of Russian history in the last century of the *ancien régime* was the fact that while the government clung to the anachronistic notion of absolutism, the country itself was undergoing an extremely rapid economic, social, and intellectual evolution, which required new, more flexible forms of administration. The nineteenth century was a period when capitalism and the industrial revolution penetrated Russia, stimulating the development of some social classes

---

* In the First Duma, the Russians had 59.1 per cent of seats, the Ukrainians 13.8 per cent, the Poles 11.3 per cent, the Belorussians 2.9 per cent, the Jews 2.8 per cent, the Lithuanians 2.2 per cent, the Estonians 0.9 per cent, the Tatars 1.6 per cent, the Latvians 1.3 per cent, the Bashkirs 0.9 per cent, the Germans 0.9 per cent, the Mordvinians 0.4 per cent, the Karaites, Kirghiz, Chechens, Votiaks, Bulgarians, Chuvashes, Moldavians, and Kalmyks had each 0.2 per cent (*Pervaia Gosudarstvennaia Duma*, I [St. Petersburg, 1907], 11).

which had previously been weak (a middle class, an industrial proletariat, and a prosperous, land-owning peasantry), and undermining others (e.g., the landed aristocracy). Western ideas, such as liberalism, socialism, nationalism, utilitarianism, now found a wide audience in Russia. The Russian monarchy, which until the nineteenth century had been the principal exponent of Western ideas in Russia, now lagged behind. The second half of the reign of Alexander I (1815–1825) marked the beginning of that rift between the monarchy and the articulate elements in Russian society which, widening continuously, led to conspiratorial movements, terrorist activity, and revolution, and finally, in 1917, to the demise of monarchy itself.

The national movement among the minorities of the Russian state, which also began in the nineteenth century, represented one of the many forms which this intellectual and social ferment assumed. Because the traditions and socio-economic interests of the various groups of subjects, including the minorities, were highly diversified, their cultural and political development tended to take on a local, and in some cases, a national coloring. Romantic philosophy, which first affected Russia in the 1820's, stimulated among the minority intellectuals an interest in their own languages and past traditions, and led directly to the evolution of cultural nationalism, the first manifestation of the national movement in the Russian borderlands.

Next, in the 1860's and 1870's, the spread of Russian Populism, with its emphasis on the customs and institutions of the peasantry, provided the minority intellectuals with a social ideology and induced them to establish contact with the broad masses of their own, predominantly rural, population. Finally, the development of modern political parties in Russia, which took place about 1900, led to the formation of national parties among the minorities, which in almost all instances adopted either liberal or socialist programs and affiliated themselves closely with their Russian counterparts. Until the breakdown of the tsarist regime, such Russian and minority parties fought side by side for parliamentary rights, local self-rule, and social and economic reforms; but while the Russian parties stressed the general needs of the whole country, the minority parties concentrated on local, regional requirements. The fact that the minorities in Russia developed a national consciousness before their fellow-nationals across the border (the Ukrainians in Austrian Galicia, Armenians in the Ottoman Empire, Azerbaijanis in Persia, and so on), was a result of the more rapid intellectual and economic growth of the Russian Empire.

The refusal of the tsarist regime to recognize the strivings of the minorities was part of the larger phenomenon of its failure to respond to the growing clamor on the part of all its citizens for fundamental reforms, and had equally dire results.

### The Ukrainians and Belorussians

The Ukrainians and Belorussians (22.3 and 5.8 million respectively in 1897) descended from the Eastern Slav tribes which had been separated from the main body of Russians as a result of the Mongolian invasions and Polish-Lithuanian conquest of the thirteenth and fourteenth centuries. For over five centuries, these two parts of Eastern Slavdom developed under different cultural influences. By the end of the eighteenth century, when Moscow had conquered the areas inhabited by the other Eastern Slavic groups, the dissimilarities caused by centuries of separate growth were too considerable to permit a simple fusion into one nation. Through contact with their western neighbors, those peoples had acquired distinct cultural traditions with their own dialects and folklores. Moreover, the steppes of the Black Sea region had for several centuries following the Mongolian invasion remained a no man's land, where runaway serfs, criminal elements, or simply adventurers from Poland, Muscovy, or the domains of the Ottoman Empire had found a haven. In the course of the sixteenth and seventeenth centuries, those groups to which the Turkic name "Cossack" (freebooter) was applied, had formed an anarchistic society with a center along the lower course of the Dnieper, which lived in complete freedom, hunting, fishing, or pillaging. In the course of time, these Cossacks — with their ideal of unlimited external and internal freedom — developed a new socio-economic type of great importance for the future Ukrainian national consciousness.

Tied by the bonds of religion and the memory of common origin, but separated by cultural and socio-economic differences, the Ukrainians and Belorussians did not coalesce completely with their Great Russian rulers. The rapid economic development of the rich Ukrainian agriculture following the liberation of the serfs, especially in the last two decades of the *ancien régime,* when the Ukrainian provinces became one of the world's leading grain exporting regions, created an additional basis for Ukrainian nationalism. There now emerged a prosperous class of independent farmers, without parallel in Russia proper. On the whole, this Ukrainian peasantry knew neither the communal type of land ownership nor the service relationship between peasant and landlord (*barshchina*). Its soil was individually owned, and paid for by money, not by personal labor.

During the eighteenth and part of the nineteenth century, it was still an open question whether the cultural and economic peculiarities of the Ukrainian people would lead to the formation of a separate nation. The absence of a Ukrainian intelligentsia and centripetal economic forces militated against; the Cossack tradition and the interests of the Ukrainian peasants for. Throughout its existence, the Ukrainian movement had to develop in an atmosphere of skepticism in which not only the validity of its demands but the very existence of the nationality it claimed to represent was seriously questioned by persons unconnected with the movement. This accounts, at least in part, for the great vehemence with which Ukrainian nationalists tended to assert their claims.

The cultural phase of the Ukrainian movement began in the 1820's, under the stimulus of the ideas of Western romanticism transmitted through Russia. Scholars began it by undertaking ethnographic studies of the villages of southwestern Russia, where they uncovered a rich and old folklore tradition and the ethos of a peasant culture, the existence of which had been scarcely suspected. On this basis, there arose in Russia and in the Ukrainian provinces a sizable provincial literature which reached a high point with the publication in 1840 of the *Kobzar*, a collection of original poems in Ukrainian by Taras Shevchenko, then a student at the Saint Petersburg Academy of Arts. This began the transformation of a peasant dialect into a literary, and subsequently, a national language. In 1846, a number of writers and students at Kiev founded the Cyril and Methodius Society — a secret organization permeated with the spirit of utopian socialism, German idealism, and the notions of international brotherhood and social equalitarianism. Present also was a strong element of cultural Pan-slavism. This society, like others of similar type in Russia proper, was suppressed in 1847.

In the second half of the century, the Ukrainian movement patterned itself after Populism, prevalent in Russia at the time. It devoted itself to the social problems of the peasantry, and displayed strong sympathy for peasant customs and manners. The cultural movement received a temporary setback in the 1870's when the Russian government, suspecting a liaison between the "Ukrainophiles" (as the Ukrainian Populists were called) and Polish nationalists, issued edicts which for all practical purposes forbade printing in the Ukrainian language. For the next thirty years, its center shifted to Galicia, where it enjoyed greater freedom owing to Vienna's interest in utilizing Ukrainian (Ruthenian) patriotism as a counterbalance to Polish nationalism in this province.

Until the end of the nineteenth century, the Ukrainians had no political parties of their own. In the Ukraine, as in Galicia, there were numerous provincial organizations of a cultural character, the so-called *Hromady* (Communities), devoted to the study of Ukrainian life, but they took no part in political activity. It was only in 1900 that a society of young Ukrainians founded the first political organization, the Revolutionary Ukrainian Party (or RUP for short). This party, established in Kharkov, represented a merger of various groups dissatisfied with the purely cultural activity of the older generation, and determined to give the Ukrainian movement a political expression. The RUP utilized the local Hromady to spread its influence to the provincial towns and villages. Its headquarters were located in Kiev, but the nerve center was abroad, in Lemberg (Lwów, Lviv), where the RUP printed propaganda to be smuggled into Russia, and engaged in other illegal activities. The RUP united several divergent tendencies: separatist, anarchistic, Marxist, Populist, and others. At first the extreme nationalist, irredentist element won the upper hand; the first program of the RUP (1900) demanded unconditional independence for a "greater Ukraine" extending between the Don and the San rivers.[7] But before long, the more moderate elements prevailed and the RUP withdrew the demand for Ukrainian independence from its program, replacing it with a demand for autonomy within the Russian Empire. The RUP played a part in stimulating agrarian disorders in the Ukraine in 1902–1903, and in spreading ideas of Ukrainian nationalism among the masses. It also served as a training ground for many of the future political leaders of the Ukrainian cause.

A few years after its formation, the RUP began to fall apart, as the various groups which it had united stepped out to form independent parties. The first to depart where the separatists (samostiiniki) who, dissatisfied with the gravitation of the party toward Russian socialist organizations, founded the National Ukrainian Party (NUP) in 1902. Next went the extreme left radicals, who, in 1905, joined the Russian Social Democratic Labor Party. The remainder of the RUP adopted the Social Democratic program and renamed itself the Ukrainian Social Democratic Labor Party (USDRP). Its program included the demand for Ukrainian autonomy and the establishment of a regional Seim (Diet) in Kiev. In 1905, the liberal elements of Ukrainian society who had not been associated with the RUP formed a separate Ukrainian Democratic Radical Party (UDRP). Thus within a few years, a large number of Ukrainian parties appeared on the scene — an early manifestation of the extreme factionalism which was to become a characteristic trait of Ukrainian political life. The USDRP and UDRP were the most influential, though none of them seems to have had a numerous following or a very efficient apparatus. The USDRP coöperated closely with the Russian Marxists, whereas the UDRP supported the Russian Kadets.

The Belorussian movement developed more slowly than the Ukrainian. Its cultural phase did not get well under way until the beginning of the twentieth century, with the publication of the *Nasha niva* (Our Land), the first newspaper in the Belorussian language. The first Belorussian national party was the Belorussian Revolutionary Hromada, founded in 1902 in St. Petersburg by a group of students associated with the Polish Socialist Party (PPS), and later renamed the Belorussian Socialist Hromada. The Hromada took over the program of the PPS, adding to it a statement on the national question, which demanded the introduction of federal relations in Russia, with territorial autonomy for the provinces adjoining Vilna and national-cultural autonomy for all the minorities of the region.[8] The Belorussian movement, operating in one of Western Russia's poorest areas, and having to compete with Polish, Jewish, Russian, and Lithuanian parties, remained ineffective and exercised no influence on political developments in prerevolutionary Russia.[9]

### The Turkic Peoples

By 1900 Russia had within its borders nearly fourteen million Turks — several million more than the Ottoman Empire itself. The remaining Moslems were either of Iranian stock, or else belonged to North Caucasian groups whose racial origin is uncertain.

Culturally and economically, the most advanced Turks in Russia were the Volga Tatars (over two million in 1897) who inhabited the regions adjacent to Kazan. Descendants of the Kazan Khanate which had been conquered by Ivan IV, the Volga Tatars had early abandoned the nomadic habits of their ancestors and had settled in the cities and on the soil. Taking advantage of the geographic location of their territory, they developed considerable commercial activity, serving as middle-men between Russia and the East. This economic position they retained after the Russian conquest. A statistical survey undertaken at the beginning of the nineteenth century, revealed that the Tatars owned one-third of the industrial establishments in the Kazan province, and controlled most of the trade with the Orient.[10] The Volga Tatars were the first of the Turks in Russia, or for that matter, anywhere in the world, to develop a middle class. This enabled them to assume leadership of the Turkic movement in Russia.

The Crimean Tatars and the Azerbaijani Turks were next in order of cultural advancement. Both these groups had come relatively late under Russian dominion, the former in 1783, the latter in the first decade of the nineteenth century. The Crimean Tatars were the remnants of the Crimean Khanate which, at one time, had dominated the Black Sea steppes and from the middle of the fifteenth century to the Russian conquest had been under the protection of the Ottoman Sultan. At the time of the Russian occupation, they had numbered, according to contemporary estimates, one half million,[11] but several waves of mass migration to Turkish Anatolia had reduced that number by 1862 to one hundred thousand.[12] In 1897 there were in the Crimea 196,854 Tatars.[13] The Crimean Tatars owed their cultural advance partly to contact with other nations, made possible by their geographic location, and partly to the wealth acquired from subtropical horticulture.

The Azerbaijanis (1,475,553 in 1897) lived along the Kura River valley of Transcaucasia. They formed a smaller part of that branch of the Turks, the majority of whom then, as now, inhabited northwestern Persia. The Azerbaijanis were an agricultural people, consisting of a peasantry and land-owning aristocracy. With the development of the Baku oil industries on their territory, the Azerbaijanis also acquired the beginning of an urban middle class.

The Central Asian Uzbeks (about two million in 1897, not counting those inhabiting Khiva and Bukhara) also were largely settled, and had developed an urban trading and artisan class. At the time of the Russian conquest they were politically and economically the rulers of Turkestan.*

The remaining Turkic groups in Russia consisted largely of semi-nomads: Bashkirs of the southwest Ural region (1,493,000 in 1897); the Kazakhs and Kirghiz (4,285,800), and the Turkmens of Central Asia (281,357 in 1897); and the numerous small tribes of Siberia. The majority of those groups combined cattle-breeding and the tending of sheep with agriculture.

Nearly all the Turkic peoples spoke similar dialects of the same language and had a common racial descent. An observer might have expected, therefore, that "Turkism" or "Pan-Turkism" would provide the basis for a national movement of the Turkic groups in Russia. This, however, did not prove to be the case. The concept of a single Turkic people emerged only at the end of the nineteenth century and, before the Revolution of 1917, had not had an opportunity to affect even the Turkic intelligentsia, let alone the broader masses of the population.

The Turks in Russia, insofar as they felt a sense of unity, were much more conscious of their common Moslem faith than of their common ethnic origin. Since Islam, like most Oriental religions, is not only a set of beliefs but also a way of life, it affects family relations, law, commerce, education, and virtually every other aspect of human existence. This religious bond provided the main basis of the Turkic movement; it was, prior to 1917, always more important than the ethnic element. But it also presented great difficulties to the slowly developing national movement among the Russian Turks which from the first took on an openly westernizing character, and as such was anticlerical. Its leaders found themselves thus in the position of having to uproot the very ideas which provided the *raison d'être* of their movement.

The national awakening of Russian Turks had its beginning in the Crimea. Its leader was Ismail-bey Gasprinskii (Gaspraly or Gaspirali) who, in 1883–84, established in his native city of Bakhchisarai a Turkish-language newspaper, the *Terdzhiman* (*Tercüman*, meaning Interpreter) which before long became the prototype for all Moslem periodical publi-

* The term *Uzbek* is used throughout this study in the Soviet sense; i.e., as consisting of two principal groups: the people known before the Revolution as Sarts, and composed of the descendants of the original Iranian inhabitants of Central Asia, largely urbanized and Turkicized; and the Uzbeks proper, a Turkic people formed in the fourteenth century, who had split away from the main body of the nomadic Turks and who in the course of the sixteenth century had conquered most of Turkestan.

cations in Russia and served as an organ of Moslems throughout the entire country. Gasprinskii also founded a new school system, based on the principles of modern education, to replace the *medresse,* which taught Arabic and restricted instruction to subjects bearing on religion.[14] On the basis of the experience which these efforts provided, there grew up in Russia within one generation a considerable network of periodical publications and "new-method," or so-called *dzhaddidist (jadidist)\** schools. By 1913 Russia had sixteen Turkic periodical publications, of which five were daily newspapers.[15] All except three of those were written in the dialect of the Volga Tatars which was quickly gaining acceptance as the literary language of all Russian Turks. In the same year, there were published in Russia 608 books in Turkic languages in a total edition of 2,812,130 copies, of which 178 titles and 1,282,240 copies were devoted to religious subjects, while the remainder were secular.[16] The reformed school system, which the tsarist government allowed to develop freely, spread to the Volga region and from there to Turkestan. On the eve of the First World War, Russian Turks had access to a considerable number of elementary and several secondary schools of the secular, Western kind which taught youth in their native languages free from government interference or supervision.† From educational institutions of this kind, supported largely by wealthy Kazan or Baku merchants, emerged the intelligentsia which, during the Russian Revolution and the first decade of Soviet rule, was to play a crucial role in the history of the Moslem borderlands.

Beginning with the Russian Revolution of 1905, the political movement among Russian Turks took two parallel courses. There was an All-Russian Moslem movement, and there were local movements of the various national groups. Occasionally the two forms actively supplemented one another, occasionally they conflicted, but they never merged completely. In 1905 and 1906, the leading representatives of the Moslem intelligentsia met in three congresses, the first and third at Nizhnii Novgorod (now Gorkii), the second at Moscow. At those meetings, the principle of unity of all Russian Moslems was asserted through the establishment of a Moslem Union (*Ittifāq-ul-Muslimīn* or *Ittifak*) and agreements for the caucusing of the Moslem deputies in the Russian Dumas. The Third Congress (August 1906) adopted resolutions urging the introduction of regional autonomy into Russia, without specifying whether or not it was to rest on the national principle.[17]

In the First and Second Dumas, in which they had thirty and thirty-nine deputies respectively, the Moslems formed a separate Moslem Faction in which the Volga Tatar Saadri Maksudov (Maksudi) later came to

---

* The term is derived from the Arabic word *jad'īd,* meaning "new."
† Validov, *Ocherk.* Rybakov, "Statistika" states that in 1911 there were in Russia 87 Moslem private institutions, of which 34 were educational.

play a dominant role. The majority of them supported the Russian liberals or Kadets, though small socialist groups were also present within the Faction. The change of electoral laws, effected in 1907 to favor the election of Russian deputies, reduced the number and importance of Moslems in the last two Dumas.

Simultaneously with the All-Russian Moslem movement — which was dominated by liberal elements — there developed regional Turkic parties, generally of a more radical character. The Volga Tatars again led the way. In 1906 two Volga Tatar writers, Fuad Tuktarov and Gaijaz (Ayaz) Iskhakov (Iskhaky), founded a local counterpart of the Russian Socialist Revolutionary Party, which, grouped around the newspaper *Tang* (Dawn), advocated the immediate transfer of all land to the people and, wherever possible, of factories to the workers. The relations of their party, the *Tangchelar* (*Tançelar*), with the pro-Kadet Ittifak were cool and occasionally hostile.[18]

In Azerbaijan a group of young Turkic intellectuals, many of whom had been closely associated with the local Bolshevik organization during the 1905 Revolution, formed in Baku in 1911–12 the Moslem Democratic Party *Mussavat* (*Musavat*). Its original leader was a young journalist, Mehmed Emin Resul-zade. The first program of this Party had a pronounced Pan-Islamic character, expressing the desire for the reëstablishment of Moslem unity throughout the world and the revival of the ancient glories of Islam. It advanced no specific demands for the Azerbaijani people.[19] Indeed, the very concept of a distinct Azerbaijani nation did not come into being until 1917, when local nationalists applied to their people the geographic name of the Persian province inhabited by Turks.

These two parties, established among the leading Turkic peoples in Russia, had no counterparts among the smaller Turkic groups which were to acquire national organizations only during the Revolution of 1917.

### The Peoples of the Caucasus

The term Caucasus (*Kavkaz*) is applied to the territory adjoining the northern and southern slopes of the Caucasian Mountains which stretch between the Caspian and Black seas, a thousand-mile-long chain with elevations surpassing those of the European Alps. Under tsarist administration this area was divided into six provinces or *gubernie* (Baku, Tiflis, Erivan, Elisavetpol, Kutais, and Chernomore), five regions or *oblasti* (Batum, Daghestan, Kars, Kuban, and Terek), and one separate district or *okrug* (Zakataly). Topographically, the Caucasus can be divided into two main parts, separated from each other by the Caucasian range. The Northern Caucasus (*Severnyi Kavkaz*) includes the steppes stretching from the mountains toward the Volga and Don rivers and the northern slopes of the mountains themselves. South of the range is

Transcaucasia (*Zakavkaz'e*), an area covered by mountains of medium height and traversed by three river valleys: the Rion, Kura, and Araks (Aras). The total territory of the Caucasus is 158,000 square miles.

The Caucasian population is extraordinarily heterogeneous. It may safely be said that no other territory of equal size anywhere in the world displays a comparable diversity of languages and races. The mountains of the Caucasus, situated near the main routes of Asiatic migrations into Europe and to the Near Eastern centers of civilization, have offered a natural haven for peoples seeking escape from wars and invasions, and in the course of the past three thousand years nearly every one of the peoples inhabiting or passing through the region has left its mark on the Caucasus' ethnic composition. In 1916 the Caucasus had 12,266,000 inhabitants, divided into the following principal groups:[20]

| | |
|---|---|
| Russians, Ukrainians, Belorussians | 4,023,000 |
| Azerbaijanis and other Moslems | 2,455,000 |
| Armenians | 1,860,000 |
| Georgians | 1,791,000 |
| Caucasian Mountain peoples | 1,519,000 |
| Other European peoples | 140,000 |
| Other indigenous peoples | 478,000 |

The greatest ethnic heterogeneity is to be found in the Northern Caucasus, and especially in its eastern sections, Daghestan and Terek. The term "Caucasian Mountain peoples" (*Kavkazskie gortsy,* or simply *gortsy*) has no ethnic significance; it is merely a general term used to describe the numerous small groups inhabiting the valleys and slopes of the Caucasian range. There one can find living side by side the descendants of the Jews carried into captivity by the Babylonians; of the Avars, who had ravaged Eastern Europe between the sixth and eighth centuries; and of numerous other small peoples, some of whom number no more than a few hundred. In Transcaucasia, on the other hand, in addition to the Azerbaijani Turks, there are two sizable national groups: the Georgians and the Armenians. Their racial origin is still a matter of dispute, but it is certain that they have inhabited their present territories continuously for over two thousand years. Their history has been closely associated with that of the entire Near East, and, at various times, they have been subjected to the dominant powers in that region, the Persians, Greeks, Romans, Arabs, Byzantines, Mongolians, and Turks.

The central factor in the historical development of the Georgians and the Armenians was their adoption of Christianity in the fourth century. As a result of this, they entered into contact with Byzantium, and through it, with Europe. This bond with the West not only brought these two peoples under different cultural influences from those of their neighbors, but also developed in them a consciousness of distinctness, of separateness from the civilization of the Near East, which remained long after they had been cut off from the main body of their co-religionists by the spread of Islam. Surrounded on all sides by Moslems, the Christian Georgians and Armenians always felt themselves drawn to Europe and were susceptible to Western ideas. For the same reason, they passed voluntarily under Russian dominion, and once incorporated into Russia, got along well with their Christian rulers. Eastern Georgia became a vassal of Russia at the end of the eighteenth century to escape Persian misrule; it was not allowed to enjoy the privileges of vassalage for long, however, and in 1801 it was incorporated into the Russian Empire by a tsarist edict. Russian Armenia came under Russian rule as one of the prizes of the victorious wars which the tsars waged with Persia at the beginning of the nineteenth century. Russia ruled only a small part of the Armenian population, the majority of which continued to live on territories of the Ottoman Empire.

The Caucasus is a purely geographic, not a historic or cultural concept. There never was, or could have been, a "Caucasian" national movement. The ethnic, religious, and socio-economic divergencies separating the main groups of the population from each other, not only prevented the emergence of a united cultural or political movement, but actually led to internal frictions and at times to armed conflicts. Instead of one, there were separate national movements of the principal ethnic groups.

The Georgians were primarily a rural people, composed of a largely impoverished ancient feudal aristocracy (5.26 per cent of the entire Georgian population in 1897) and a peasantry. The Georgian urban class was small and insignificant. It was the *déclassé* nobility which, from the beginning, assumed the leadership over the cultural and political life of Georgia. The Georgians possessed nearly all the elements that usually go into the formation of national consciousness: a distinct language, with its own alphabet; an ancient and splendid literary heritage; a national territory; and a tradition of statehood and military prowess. In the 1870's, a cultural movement arose among the Georgian aristocracy, which, with its interest in the newly liberated peasant, assumed forms akin to Russian populism.[21]

The political phase of the national movement in Georgia acquired a somewhat unusual character. Whether it was due to the fact that the carriers of the national ideology in Georgia did not belong to the middle class but to an anti-bourgeois nobility, or whether it was caused by the general receptivity to Western ideas characteristic of the Georgians, or by still other causes, the Georgian movement became from its very inception closely identified if not completely fused with Marxian socialism. Marxism was introduced into Georgia in the 1880's and at once encountered an enthusiastic reception. In the First Duma, six of the seven Georgian deputies were Social Democrats; in the Third, two out of

three. Georgian socialists did not form separate organizations of their
own, but joined the regional branches of the Russian Social Democratic
Labor Party, where they soon attained considerable prominence. They
had no national demands. Noi Zhordaniia, one of the chief theoreticians
of the movement, stated repeatedly that all demands for autonomy were
utopian, and that Georgia would obtain sufficient self-rule as a result of
the anticipated future democratization of Russia.[22] At the beginning of
the twentieth century, a small group of intellectuals, dissatisfied with this
attitude, left the Social Democratic Party and founded a separate organization, *Sakartvelo* (Georgia), which in time transformed itself into
the Georgian Party of Socialists-Federalists. Their program, close in social questions to that of the Russian Socialist Revolutionary Party, called
for the establishment of a Russian Federal Republic with autonomy for
Georgia. Its popular following, however, judging by elections to the
Dumas, was small. About 1910 the Georgian Mensheviks somewhat
modified their views and adopted formulae calling for extraterritorial
cultural autonomy for Georgia.*

The absence of territorial demands in the program of the most powerful party of the Georgian movement need not be interpreted as an indication of the lack of Georgian national sentiment. The national ideals of
the Georgian intelligentsia were identified, ideologically and psychologically, with the goals of Russian and international socialism. As long
as this attitude persisted — that is, as long as Georgian intellectuals
believed Marxist socialism capable of dealing with the problems posed
by the development of the Georgian nation — there was no necessity to
advance territorial demands.

The position of the Armenians was different from that of the Georgians in several important respects: instead of living in a well-defined area
of their own, the Armenians were scattered in small groups among hostile Turkic peoples throughout Eastern Anatolia and Transcaucasia, and
had a numerous, influential middle class. The paramount issue for the
Armenians, ever since the massacres which their population had suffered
in the Ottoman Empire in the 1890's, was Turkey and the Turks. Their
main concern was how to save the defenseless Armenian population
from further massacres engendered by the religious and socio-economic
conflicts between the Armenian bourgeoisie or petty bourgeoisie and the
Turkic land-owning and peasant classes, as well as by the cynical attitude of the central government of Turkey. In this respect, the problems
facing the Armenians were not unlike those confronting the Jews in the
western regions of the Empire. Then there was also the question of de-
vising a political solution which would be suited to the ethnic distribution of the Armenian population and provide its urban classes with com-

* This term will be explained below.

mercial advantages. The Armenian movement acquired early in its history a conspiratorial, para-military character. It was essentially middle and lower middle class in content, and much less socialist in spirit than the political movements in Georgia or in most of the remaining Russian borderlands.

The cultural movement in modern Armenia had begun already in the 1840's, at first under the influence of German and French, and then of Russian, ideas, and was actively supported by Armenian merchants residing in the Levant and Western Europe. Its organization centered around the separate Armenian Church establishments and its head, the Catholicos. In the 1890's there were numerous Armenian schools, as well as many societies and cultural centers, supported by the church in Russian Armenia.[23]

The first Armenian political party was the *Hnchak* (Clarion) founded in 1887 in Switzerland. This party was socialist in character. In the 1890's, some of its members separated and founded the *Dashnaktsutiun* (Federation) which during the next quarter of a century came to occupy a dominant role in Armenian political life. The Dashnaks were, in their social program and in their general reliance on terroristic methods of struggle against the Ottoman government, somewhat akin to the Russian Socialist Revolutionaries, though the latter refused to establish direct relations with the Dashnaktsutiun on the grounds that it was allegedly a petty-bourgeois, nationalistic group which employed socialist slogans only as camouflage.[24] The national program adopted by the Dashnaktsutiun in 1907 made the following demands concerning the Russian Caucasus:

Transcaucasia, as a democratic republic, is to be a component part of the Federal Russian Republic. The former is to be connected with the latter in questions of defense of the state, foreign policy, monetary and tariff systems.

The Transcaucasian Republic is to be independent in all its internal affairs: it is to have its parliament, elected by means of universal, direct, equal, secret, and proportional vote. Every citizen, regardless of sex, is to have the right to vote beginning at the age of twenty.

Transcaucasia is to send its representatives, elected by the same system of universal elections, to the All-Russian Parliament.

The Transcaucasian Republic is to be divided into cantons, which are to have the right to broad local autonomy, and communes with an equal right to self-rule in communal matters.

In determining cantonal borders, it is imperative to take into account the topographical and ethnographical peculiarities of the country in order to form groupings as homogeneous as possible.[25]

The Dashnak program also demanded cultural autonomy, and the right to use local languages in addition to the governmental language of all

Russia. Whereas in Russia the Armenian population was too scattered to permit application of national autonomy, the party did request territorial rights for the Armenians in that part of its program which dealt with the Ottoman Empire.[26]

The North Caucasian peoples had no indigenous national parties despite the fact that they were less assimilated and in many respects more dissatisfied with Russian rule than were the peoples of Transcaucasia. The mountains of the Caucasus had been conquered by Russia in some of the bloodiest and longest campaigns of its entire history. No other acquisition had cost Russia as much effort as that impoverished land inhabited by the wild and independent mountaineers. The forceful expulsions carried on by the tsarist regime, the mass migrations of the people of whole regions following the Russian conquest, punitive expeditions, Cossack encroachments on land, the hostility of the men of the mountains for the inhabitant of the plains, of the Moslem for the Christian — all this created a suitable foundation for national animosities. But it was not sufficient to produce an organized national movement. The North Caucasian mountain peoples possessed no ethnic unity and formed no cultural community; they were isolated from each other by mountain ranges. Moreover, some of the groups feuded among themselves, largely as a result of great discrepancies in the distribution of land.[27]

The Caucasus therefore had not one but several national movements developing side by side. Of unity, there was none. The Georgians had their eyes turned to Russia, to Europe, and to socialism; the chief concern of the Armenians was the Turk on both sides of the frontier; the Azerbaijanis participated in the All-Russian Moslem movement; and the inhabitants of the mountains had developed as yet no definite political orientation.

The national movements among the minorities inhabiting the Russian Empire arose under the stimulus of the same forces which had affected Russian society in the nineteenth century: Romantic idealism, with its glorification of the *Volk* and of historic traditions; Populism, with its idealization on the peasantry; the spirit of Western enlightenment; socialism.

Two features of the minority movements stand out. In the first place, before 1917, among the peoples discussed, there had been in evidence no separatist tendencies. The Russian Empire was considered by most of its inhabitants to be a permanent institution which required not destruction but democratization and social reform. In the second place, in most of the borderlands, there was an alliance between nationalism and socialism. This phenomenon was perhaps due to the fact that the majority of the nationality groups did not possess indigenous middle classes, which in Russia proper, as in other European countries, formed the backbone of the liberal forces. On the other hand, the nationalists could not ally themselves with Russian rightist groups because the Russian rightists automatically opposed them.

### Socialism and the National Problem in Western and Central Europe

Marx and Engels left their followers little guidance in matters of nationality and nationalism. In Western Europe, whence they drew the bulk of the source material for their economic and political studies, the minority problem presented no serious issue: most of the states were nationally homogeneous, without significant minority populations. This appeared to Marx and Engels a normal situation and one fully justified by the progress of historic forces:

> No one will assert that the map of Europe is definitely settled. All changes, however, if they are to be lasting, must be of such a nature as to bring the great and vital European nations ever closer to their *true* natural borders as determined by speech and sympathies; while at the same time the ruins of peoples (*die Voelkertruemmer*), which are still to be found here and there, and are no longer capable of leading a national existence, must be incorporated into the larger nations, and either dissolve in them or else remain as ethnographic monuments of no political significance.[28]

The natural tendency of the capitalist era, in the opinion of Engels, was to form large national states "which alone represent the normal organization of the ruling bourgeoisie of Europe, and which are also indispensable for the establishment of a harmonious international coöperation of peoples, without which the rule of the proletariat is not possible." [29] Both Marx and Engels viewed the small Slav states of Eastern Europe as anachronistic and considered them ever ready to compromise with absolutism in order to realize their selfish national aims; Engels even approved of the medieval German expansion eastward and the conquest of the small Slavic groups, arguing that it was the latter's "natural and inescapable destiny to permit the completion of the process of dissolution and absorption by their stronger neighbors." [30] In the minority problem both founders of modern socialism were in favor of the great powers, of centralism, and of cultural *Gleichschaltung.**

While tending to disregard the minority question, Marx and Engels were not unaware of nationalism as such, which, of course, did exist in Western Europe and on some occasions hindered the development of an international socialist movement. But though conscious of its force, Marx

---

* S. F. Bloom in *The World of Nations* (New York, 1941) demonstrates, however, that Marx neither envisaged nor favored the complete disappearance of national differences.

and Engels saw no reason to fear that in the long run nationalism could prevent the proletarian movement from taking, what they considered, its inevitable course. Such confidence was partly caused by the fact that Marx and Engels shared some assumptions prevalent among liberal thinkers of their day, including the faith in the capacity of capitalism and democracy, with their free trade and opportunities for the expression of popular will, to level national differences and to bring into being a world-wide international civilization. But the confidence in the ability of socialism to overcome nationalism was also inherent in the fundamental tenets of Marxism. The capitalist state, according to Marx, was doomed to disintegrate under the pressure of the economic contradictions which it was constantly engendering. The enrichment of the upper classes and the pauperization of the proletariat inevitably resulted in a realignment of interest groups within every state. It caused a class struggle which was diametrically opposed to nationalism. Either one or the other had to emerge as the victor, and Marx had no doubt which side history had destined for that role. Nationalism could hamper the growth of class consciousness; it could perhaps delay it, and for those reasons, it was important to fight against it. But eventually nationalism had to yield to class rivalries and to the international unity of the proletariat. To admit that under some circumstances the economic interests of a society could coincide with its cultural divisions was essentially contrary to Marx's entire system.

Ethnic isolation and petty states as typical of the feudal era; nationalism and the national state as characteristic of the capitalist era; internationalism and the disappearance of national animosities as proper to the socialist era — such were, in bare outline, the basic views of Marx and Engels on the nationality question. This was the heritage which they bequeathed to their followers.

The principal exponent of the orthodox Marxist views on the nationality question in the early twentieth century was the Polish socialist, Rosa Luxemburg. Early in her career Rosa Luxemburg devoted much attention to the economic development of Poland: her researches led her to the conclusion that Poland's striving for independence had become illusory and retrogressive because economic forces which had been in operation throughout the nineteenth century had tied that country firmly to Russia and to the other two occupying powers. Developing her thesis in a series of articles published in the first decade of the century, she argued that Marx's approval of Polish independence movements, sound for the middle of the nineteenth century, was not valid in the twentieth, partly because of economic factors, and partly because Russia had adopted a constitution and ceased to be the bulwark of European absolutism which it had been in Marx's day. Poland should satisfy herself, consequently, with autonomy within a democratic Russian state. And although Rosa

Luxemburg's views, as her biographer points out, did not lead her to condemn outright all independence efforts of small minorities (she was, for instance, sympathetic to the cause of the nationalities fighting for independence in the Balkans), in Eastern European socialist circles "Luxemburgism" came to be used, in effect, as synonymous with uncompromising hostility toward all national movements in general.[31] Her views gained considerable following among the left-wing Marxist groups in Eastern Europe, especially in Poland.

The post-Marxian socialist movement, identified with the Second International (1889–1914), when socialism enjoyed its golden age, found the strict Marxian approach of the Luxemburg school more of an obstacle than a help in dealing with the challenge of nationalism. At the beginning of the twentieth century the circumstances which had permitted Marx and Engels to disregard the nationality question had changed. First of all, socialism had now left the confines of Western Europe and had penetrated the East, where the minority problem was far from settled. In that region, the Austrian, Russian, and Ottoman Empires had numerous and dynamic minority populations with cultural and historic traditions as old as or older than those of the ruling nations. How were the socialists in these countries to deal with the minority problem? It was impossible to ignore it. To advocate that the subject peoples subordinate themselves to their rulers and, by abandoning their language and cultural traditions, bow to their "inescapable destiny" was, in view of the deep-rooted national loyalties, impractical as well as politically inexpedient. To urge the disintegration of empires into their component national states was contrary to the historical tendencies of capitalism, which favored integration and centralization.

Moreover, the basic assumption on which Marx and Engels had founded their belief in the eventual disappearance of nationalism was obviously considerably incorrect. Side by side with the development of the international socialist movement, and very often in close association with it, there was taking place a development of nationalism in Western Europe and elsewhere. As a result of social legislation initiated by the more advanced Western states, the general rise in living standards of the workers, and other causes, the proletariat was acquiring a greater stake in the well-being of its state than it had had in Marx's time. The poor were in many cases not becoming poorer but richer, and consequently were not as immune to nationalist propaganda as had been expected. The emergence and spread of so-called Revisionism within the Second International, which challenged some of the basic premises of Marxism, reflected socialist realization of these facts. Western socialists, however, did little to find a solution to the problems with which the growth of nationalism had confronted them,* and it remained for their

* See Bibliography, p. 308.

colleagues in the Austrian Empire to evolve a theoretical and practical approach to this vexing question.

The Hapsburg monarchy, the first multinational empire to develop a strong socialist movement, had within its borders several large minority groups (Czechs, Poles, Ukrainians, Italians, Serbians, Croatians, Rumanians) with historical traditions and a developed sense of national consciousness. The Social Democrat there, operating on a mass level and in coöperation with parties from the non-German areas, was compelled to face the national problem much more urgently and in many more forms than the Social Democrat in the West. First of all, he was faced with the question whether the party was to be organized as one for the whole empire or to be divided along territorial or national lines; second, he had to decide how to conduct socialist propaganda among the groups of the population which did not speak German, and how to reconcile the different and often conflicting economic interests of the various nationalities; and, finally, he was required to formulate a constitutional system, satisfactory to all the inhabitants of the empire.

The national problem first came up for discussion at the Bruenn Congress of the Austrian Social Democrats, held in 1899. There two solutions were suggested, both based on the premise that the political unity of the empire was to be preserved.

The first, advanced by the party's Executive Committee, proposed that the empire be divided into provinces corresponding as closely as possible to the ethnographic limits of each nationality, and that within these provinces the numerically dominant ethnic group receive full authority over cultural and linguistic affairs.[32] This proposal was based on the principle of *territorial* national-cultural autonomy.

As a counterproposal, the South Slav delegation suggested a novel scheme of *extraterritorial* national-cultural autonomy. According to this plan, every national group was to have self-rule in linguistic and cultural matters throughout the entire empire regardless of territorial divisions. The state was to be divided not into territories but into nations. In the opinion of its advocates, this project avoided the harmful institutionalization of rigid national-territorial divisions and, furthermore, offered a more practical solution of the national problem in areas where the population was ethnically too mixed to make the customary territorial division feasible.[33]

The Bruenn Congress finally accepted neither the project of the Executive Committee nor the South Slav proposal, but a formula which represented a compromise between the territorial and extraterritorial principles of cultural autonomy:

> 1. Austria is to be transformed into a democratic federation of nationalities (*Nationalitaetenbundesstaat*).

2. The historic Crown lands are to be replaced by nationally homogeneous self-ruling bodies, whose legislation and administration shall be in the hands of national chambers, elected on the basis of universal, equal, and direct franchise.

3. All self-ruling regions of one and the same nation are to form together a nationally distinct union, which shall take care of this union's national affairs autonomously.[34]

At the Bruenn Congress, the Austrian party was reorganized along national lines.

In the next decade the idea of extraterritorial or personal national-cultural autonomy was adopted and further developed by two prominent theoreticians of the Austrian socialist movement, Karl Renner and Otto Bauer. Renner and Bauer endeavored to reconcile the nationalist movement among the minorities of the empire with the socialist striving for proletarian unity. This much appeared certain to them: nationalism had to be faced directly and the nation had to be recognized as a valuable and enduring form of social organization:

Social Democracy proceeds not from the existing states but from live nations. It neither denies nor ignores the existence of the nation but on the contrary, it accepts it as the carrier of the new order, which is visualized not as a union of states but as a community of peoples, as nations . . . Social Democracy considers the nation both indestructible and undeserving of destruction . . . Far from being unnational or antinational, it places nations at the foundation of its world structure.[35]

But this was not enough. If one viewed impartially the development of the preceding century, Bauer asserted, it was impossible to escape the conclusion that nationalism and national differences, instead of disappearing, were actually on the increase. This phenomenon he considered to be inherently connected with the very forces which accounted for the growth of socialism. The rule of the aristocracy or the upper middle class created an illusion of growing cultural internationalization of Europe and the rest of the world, because those ruling circles did possess something resembling an international civilization, be it in the classical heritage, be it in the code of manners of the feudal nobility, or be it in the commercial civilization of the modern era. But this was not true of the lower classes of the population, especially of the rural masses. Illiterate and living in isolation from each other, those groups were deeply rooted in local traditions and preserved the national customs which the upper classes had already lost. They were unaffected by contact with other nations. With the spread of Social Democracy, as those lower classes should obtain control over the instruments of political power, those differences, previously submerged, would come to the surface. Language, the world outlook or ethos of each people, and local interests were destined to assume a greater role in international relations. Nor would those differences vanish. Bauer believed that subjection of individuals or peoples of different mentalities or psychological inclinations to a common experience tended to accentuate their initial differences. He based this belief on the assumption that an identical experience would separate rather than unite people with dissimilar perceptive systems.* The triumph of socialism would therefore "result in an *increasing differentiation of nations* . . . a sharper expression of their peculiarities, a sharper separation of their natures." [36]

The views of the two Austrian socialists — unprecedented and revolutionary in modern socialism — required that Social Democracy find a scheme capable of utilizing what was valuable and permanent in the national movement, and neutralize what was harmful. In the first category were the linguistic and cultural aspects of nationalism; in the latter, the political.

Such a scheme, Renner and Bauer believed, was the principle of extraterritorial autonomy. Each nation, "treated not as a territorial corporation, but as a union of individuals," [37] should be entered, with the names of all the citizens who considered themselves as belonging to it, in a national register (*Nationalkataster*). The subjects thus registered would possess the right to administer their cultural affairs autonomously as one body, regardless of where they happened to reside. Control over the cultural affairs of each nation would be exercised by elective organs which would be given the right to tax their subjects. National culture would thus be placed on the same personal level as religion. The principle *cuius regio, eius natio* would be eliminated, much as the principle *cuius regio, eius religio* had been abandoned in Western Europe several centuries earlier. Coexistent with the extraterritorial organs of cultural autonomy, Bauer and Renner envisaged an elaborate system of territorial organs of administration, partly to take care of political problems which were not connected with nationality questions, and partly to protect the organs of cultural autonomy from encroachments by the central government.

The advantages of this system seemed considerable. By channeling it into the cultural sphere, extraterritorial national-cultural autonomy would neutralize nationalism as a psychological barrier to proletarian coöperation; it would make it unnecessary for the nationalities to seek independent statehood; and finally, by divorcing nationality from territory, such an autonomy would be unaffected by the constant movements

---

* O. Bauer, *Die Nationalitaetenfrage und die Sozialdemokratie* (Vienna, 1907); a criticism of the philosophical assumptions of this viewpoint was undertaken by the Menshevik S. Semkovskii in his *Marksizm i natsional'naia problema*, I (Melitopol, 1924). Semkovskii traced Bauer's theory of "national apperception" to neo-Kantianism.

of population which the expanding industrialization of Central and Eastern Europe was likely to cause. Under this plan, "the advance of the classes shall no longer be hampered by national struggles . . . The field shall be free for the class struggle." *

The so-called Austrian project — of which Renner was the legal and Bauer the social and political theoretician — was a brilliant attempt to analyze and solve the national problem. It marked a clear-cut departure from traditional nineteenth-century socialist views on the national question and provided a solution especially well-suited for the needs of Eastern Europe where the ethnographic map was so heterogeneous as to make a territorial demarcation into national states impractical. Its greatest weakness was perhaps a tendency to oversimplify nationalism. By considering it essentially a cultural phenomenon, Renner and Bauer missed its broader social and economic implications. Their work must be viewed as a compromise between the theories of socialism and the realities of nationalism, and as such, it had an immediate success, particularly in Russia.

The first political party to include the Austrian plan in its program was the Jewish socialist party, the Bund. The Bund arose in the western provinces of Russia in 1897 as the result of a merger of various organizations which had originally been devoted exclusively to the improvement of the economic situation of the Jewish working population. About 1895 these groups decided to abandon their previous concentration on purely economic ends and to engage in political agitation as well. It became apparent at once that this decision made it necessary to assume a definite attitude toward the national question. L. Martov described the change which the party had to undergo in the following words:

> In the first years of our movement, we expected everything from the Russian working class and looked upon ourselves as a mere addition to the general Russian labor movement. By putting the Jewish working-class movement in the background, we neglected its actual condition, as evidenced by the fact that our work was conducted in the Russian language. Desiring to preserve our connection with the Russian movement . . . we forgot to maintain contact with the Jewish masses who did not know Russian . . . Obviously, it would be absurd to further restrict our activity to those groups of the Jewish population already affected by Russian culture . . . Having placed the mass movement in the center of our program, we had to adjust our propaganda and agitation to the masses, that is, we had to make it more Jewish.[38]

The Bund consequently began to employ in its work the Yiddish lan-

---

* Bauer, *Die Nationalitaetenfrage*, 362. The system of extraterritorial cultural autonomy was successfully applied in Estonia in the 1920's; cf. E. Maddison, *Die Nationalen Minderheiten Estlands und ihre Rechte* (Tallinn, 1926).

guage. But it took the party somewhat longer to arrive at a positive national program. As late as 1899, at its Third Congress, the majority of the delegates refused to supplement the party program demanding civil equality with a request for national equality, on the grounds that the class interests of the proletariat must not be distracted by the national question.[39]

Soon afterwards reports reached Russia of the discussions at the Bruenn Congress, and of the project of extraterritorial autonomy advanced there by the South Slav delegation. This news had an immediate effect. No other solution of the national question better met the needs of the Jewish minority in Russia, scattered as it was over large territories without a national home of its own. The Fourth Congress of the Bund, held in 1901, adopted a general statement in favor of the ideas advanced by the South Slav delegation at Bruenn: "The concept of nationality is also applicable to the Jewish people. Russia . . . must in the future be transformed into a federation of nationalities, with full national autonomy for each, regardless of the territory which it inhabits." [40]

Carrying this thesis further, the Bund now demanded that Russian Social Democracy, with which it was affiliated, recognize the Bund as the organization representing the Jewish proletariat in Russia, and consequently grant it the status of a "federal" unit within the party. This request was turned down at the Second Congress of the Russian Social Democratic Labor Party (1903), and, in protest, the Bund temporarily disassociated itself from the Russian party. In the following decade, Bundist theoreticians, outstanding among whom were Vladimir Medem and Vladimir Kossovskii, translated into Russian the principal Austrian works dealing with the problems of nationalism and socialism, in justification of the Bund stand.[41] On the whole, Jewish socialists in Russia were more moderate in their demands and more reserved in their recognition of the permanent values of nationality than were the Austrians. Through their publications, the works of Renner and Bauer first became widely known in Russia and began to exercise influence on other parties.

From the Bund, the idea of extraterritorial autonomy spread to the Armenian Dashnaktsutiun, the Belorussian Socialist Hromada, the Georgian Socialist Federalist Party *Sakartvelo*, and the Jewish SERP, all of which adopted it as supplementary to territorial national autonomy. In 1907, those minority socialist parties met at a special conference at which the majority of the delegates expressed strong preference for the Austrian project.[42]

Thus, in the first decade of the twentieth century socialist parties in the multinational states of Central and Eastern Europe began to grapple with the national question. Theoretical lines were laid down, practical solutions were constructed, and party work was adapted to suit the traditions and peculiarities of the minority populations.

## Russian Political Parties and the National Problem

Russian liberals, represented by the Constitutional Democratic, or Kadet, Party, viewed the entire national problem primarily as a by-product of absolutist oppression and restrictive legislation, and opposed any decentralization of Russia along national lines. In January 1906, when they formulated their formal program, the Kadets made the following provisions concerning the national minorities:

1. All Russian citizens, regardless of sex, religion, and nationality are equal before the law. All class differences and all restrictions of personal rights and property rights of Poles, Jews, and all other separate groups of the population without exception must be changed.

11. In addition to full civic and political equality of all citizens, the constitution of the Russian Empire should also guarantee all peoples inhabiting the Empire the right to free cultural self-determination, such as: full freedom to employ different languages and dialects in public life; freedom to establish and to maintain educational institutions and various gatherings, societies, and institutions which have the purpose of protecting and developing the language, literature, and culture of every people; and so forth.

12. Russian must be the language of the central institutions, the Army, and the Fleet. The use of local languages in governmental and social institutions and schools, maintained at the expense of the government or of organs of self-rule, on a basis of equality with the state language is to be regulated by general and local laws, and within them, by the institutions themselves. The population of every region must be assured of the opportunity to receive elementary, and insofar as it is possible, higher education in the native tongue.

25. Immediately after there is established an All-Empire democratic representative body with constitutional rights, there must be introduced into the Kingdom of Poland an autonomous organization with a *Sejm*, elected on the same basis as the representative body of the whole empire, with the condition that the governmental unity shall be preserved and that [the Kingdom of Poland] shall participate in the central government on the same basis as other parts of the Empire. The frontier between the Kingdom of Poland and the neighboring provinces may be corrected in accordance with the national composition and the desires of the local population; at the same time, there must be established in the Kingdom of Poland general governmental guarantees of civic freedom and the right of nationalities to cultural self-determination; the rights of the minorities must be safeguarded.

26. Finland. The constitution of Finland securing it a special position in the government must be fully reëstablished. All further measures applicable both to the Empire and to the Grand Duchy of Finland must be henceforth agreed upon between the legislative organs of the Empire and the Grand Duchy of Finland.[43]

Kadet opposition to federalism was due not so much to a desire to preserve a centralized, unitary state (for in other sections of their program, the Kadets came out in favor of extensive local self-rule for the provinces of the empire) as to the conviction that Russian conditions made federalism impracticable. Federalism presupposed a certain equilibrium among its constituent units, a balanced distribution of strength. This could not be attained in Russia, where the Great Russian population itself was almost equal in number to all the remaining ethnic groups put together; for this reason alone, the liberals felt, federalism was unsuitable for Russia.[44]

The liberals did little to advance a solution of the nationality problem in the Dumas in which they played an important role. Even the question of Polish autonomy, explicitly formulated in their program, remained in the background, as other more urgent issues of the day occupied the party's attention, to the keen disappointment of Polish deputies.[45] Shortly before the outbreak of the First World War, there emerged in the Kadet party a right wing, which showed great antipathy to the national aspirations of the minorities, and moved close to the views of the conservative parties.[46]

Of the two principal Russian socialist parties, the Socialist Revolutionary Party took an earlier interest in the national problem and assumed a more liberal attitude toward the demands of the minorities than its Social Democratic rival. Within the Social Democratic party itself the Menshevik wing preceded the Bolshevik faction. Neither the SR's nor the SD's, however, devoted much attention to this problem. Russian socialists trusted in the omnipotence of democracy and in its ability to solve of itself all the political ills of the state. The leading socialist theoreticians, particularly among the Marxists, were oriented westward, in the direction of Europe; there they drew their inspiration and their factual material, and there they looked for socialist prototypes valid for the whole world. Except for a brief period following the 1905 Revolution, Russian Marxist socialism remained largely a conspiratorial movement out of touch with the broad masses of the population, inexperienced in the affairs of the state, and unaffected by the practical business of politics, such as had forced Austrian Social Democracy to modify its views.

The Socialist Revolutionary Party, established formally in 1902, continued the traditions of the nineteenth-century Russian populist movement, and inherited its liberal attitude toward the minorities.[47] This heritage helped the SR's to win the support of most of the socialist parties active among the minority nationalities. As the First Congress, held in 1905, they approved a programmatic statement which in addition to full civic equality for all citizens regardless of nationality, included demands for:

A democratic republic with broad autonomy of regions and communities (*obshchiny*) both urban and rural; the widest possible
application of the federal principle to the relations among the individual nationalities; the recognition of their unconditional right
to self-determination . . . the introduction of the native language[s]
in all local, public, and state institutions . . . ; in areas with a mixed
population, the right of every nationality to a part of the budget
devoted to cultural and educational purposes, proportionate to its
number, and to the disposal of such funds on the basis of self-rule.[48]

Coming out in favor of federalism and the principle of national-
cultural autonomy, the Socialist Revolutionary Party became the first to
take into account the existence of a national problem in Russia, and
to present a concrete program for dealing with it. However, the rank
and file of the SR's were far from convinced of the appropriateness of
the solution advocated by the party program. Already at the First Congress the national question caused heated debates, and numerous delegates voiced objections to the resolution, particularly to the statement
granting the nationalities an "unconditional right to self-determination."
Some speakers pointed out that the economic importance of the borderlands for Russia made it impossible to acquiesce in the separation of
the national minorities, while others challenged the wisdom of allowing
the national principle, even by implication, to override the principle of
class revolution.[49]

The ambivalent attitude of the SR's toward the nationality question
emerged in the course of the conference of the so-called national-socialist
parties convened in 1907 on the initiative of the Russian SR's. At that
conference, in which the majority of the representatives of the minority
socialist parties voted in favor of extraterritorial national-cultural autonomy, the Russian SR delegates abstained on the grounds that this principle was not compatible with the national program of their party.[50]
They promised that the party would open a general discussion of the
nationality question and, before long, arrive at a more definitive programmatic statement.

Little was done to carry out this pledge. In 1910 a debate was started
in the Socialist Revolutionary periodical press on the initiative of the
leaders of the Jewish SERP, an affiliate of SR, but its positive results
were negligible.[51] Viktor Chernov, a leader of the SR's, stated that
there could be no general solution of the national problem in Russia,
and, though he personally favored extraterritorial national-cultural autonomy in areas with a mixed population, the national question would need
to be solved separately in each province.[52] The national program, some
SR writers admitted, was the weakest point in the party's platform and
a stumbling block to the spread of socialism in Russia.[53]

Unlike the SR's, whose political philosophy was of native origin and rested on the notion of a free association of communes which made allowance for a federation of nationalities, the Social Democrats were Marxists and shared the Marxist partiality for the great state, for the centralization of political power, and for the world-wide rather than the local aspects of the socialist movement. Believing that Russia's historical development pointed toward a middle-class, national state of the Western type, they looked upon the entire growth of minority movements as a retrogressive process. Their national program was essentially not unlike that of the Kadets.

The program of the original Russian Marxist group, Liberation of Labor (*Osvobozhdenie Truda*), drawn up in the 1880's, contained no mention of the national problem, confining itself to a demand for the establishment of "full equality for all citizens, regardless of religion and national origin." [54] The manifesto of the First Congress of the RSDRP (1898) also made no reference to this question.

The party was for the first time squarely confronted with the national question in 1901, when the Bund demanded that the Jews be recognized as a nation, and the Bund be permitted to function as the exclusive representative of the Jewish working class in Russia. The leaders of the Russian Social Democratic Labor Party reacted to these requests with angry amazement. Martov, writing for the editorial office of the party organ, *Iskra,* branded the request of the Bund as nationalistic, un-Marxian, and completely impractical.[55] Trotsky followed some time later with similar accusations,[56] and Plekhanov was ready to expel the Bund from the party.[57] Lenin jeered: "The Bundists need now only to work out the idea of a separate nationality of Russian Jews, whose language is Yiddish and whose territory is — the Pale of Settlement." [58] The truth of the matter was that the Russian SD's were completely unprepared to deal with the problem which the Bund had brought into the open.

In 1903, at their famous Second Congress, the Social Democrats included in their program the following requests:

> 3. Broad local self-rule; regional self-rule for those localities which distinguish themselves by separate living conditions and the composition of the population.
> 7. Destruction of social orders (*soslovii*) and full equality for all citizens, regardless of sex, religion, race, and nationality.
> 8. The right of the population to receive education in its native tongue, secured by the establishment of schools necessary for that purpose at the expense of the government and of organs of self-rule; the right of every citizen to use his native tongue at gatherings; the introduction of native languages on a basis of equality with the state language in all local social and government institutions.*

* Points 3 and 8 in the program were inserted under the pressure of the Menshevik faction, over the objections of the more centralistically inclined Bolsheviks. Cf. S. M.

9. The right of all nations (*natsii*) in the state to self-determination.[59]

The ninth point of this Social Democratic program requires some clarification because it later became an object of a heated controversy. The principle of "national self-determination" was generally recognized by socialists in Europe and in Russia as a basic democratic right, like, for instance, the principles of equality of the sexes or of freedom of speech. It was adopted from the program of the Second International which had placed this principle in its platform in 1896. Its introduction into the program of the Russian Social Democratic Labor Party put on record the opposition of the Russian Marxists to all forms of discrimination or oppression of one nation by another. It was not a programmatic statement but rather a declaration, and was understood as such at the time.[60]

Until 1912 Menshevik and Bolshevik writers alike rejected the two theoretical solutions which had gained the greatest following among Russian minority parties: federalism on the one hand, and cultural autonomy of the territorial and extraterritorial varieties on the other. Federalism was considered reactionary, because it decentralized the state and delayed the inexorable process of economic unification; cultural autonomy because it strengthened the barriers separating the proletariats of various nationalities, and made it possible for the bourgeoisie to obtain a decisive influence over the cultural development of the people.[61] Nationalism in all its manifestations was viewed as a middle-class, capitalist phenomenon, inimical to the interests of socialism.

Not atypical was the attitude of G. V. Plekhanov, one of the principal theoreticians of the Russian Social Democratic Labor Party. Throughout his long publicistic activity, in the course of which he took the opportunity to deal with virtually every imaginable social and political topic, he found it necessary to write only one article dealing with the questions of nationality and nationalism, and even then only in response to a questionnaire. In this essay, written for the *Revue socialiste* in 1905, he reasserted opinions which were prevalent among socialists in the West in the nineteenth century: the proletariat had literally no fatherland, and if occasionally workers fell under the influence of nationalist emotions it was because class-differentiation in their countries was as yet insufficiently developed.[62] The economic causes of nationalism were disappearing as a result of the world-wide activities of capitalism and the growth of class bonds among the exploited elements of all countries. Hence Plekhanov saw no reason to fear that the national problem in either of its forms could present any serious obstacles to the growth of the socialist movement.

Schwarz, *The Jews in the Soviet Union* (Syracuse, 1951), 25–26. They were lacking in Lenin's original programmatic project; see *LS*, no. 2 (1924), 46, 165.

These premises induced Plekhanov to discourage all attempts on the part of his colleagues to come to grips with the nationality movement. When in 1908, for instance, the Caucasian Mensheviks reported to him on the growth of nationalism in their region and urged the party to devote more attention to that problem, Plekhanov replied with anger that this was not the business of socialists. Genuine Marxists dealt with such phenomena by "advancing a systematic criticism of the nationalistic argumentation." [63] Similar sentiments prevailed among the lesser lights of the party. Indeed at times the vehemence with which Social Democrats attacked the claims of some minorities, such as the Jews or Ukrainians, was no less intense than that displayed by the most reactionary parties of the right.[64]

The Mensheviks were the first to steer away from this uncompromising stand. In the light of the importance which the Social Democratic organizations of the national minorities had acquired in the Menshevik faction (for instance, the Georgians and the Jews), and the general evolution of this section of the party toward the views held by the right (Revisionist) wing of the Second International, such a change was not unexpected. The Mensheviks remained adamant in their hostility to the idea of federalism, but they slowly reconciled themselves to national-cultural autonomy.

In August 1912 a conference took place, in Vienna, of the right-wing elements of the Menshevik fashion, who, because they desired a formal break with the Bolshevik groups, had received from them the nickname of "liquidators." The meeting was attended by some of the outstanding figures of the Russian Marxist movement — Martov, Aleksandr Martynov, Leon Trotsky, Pavel Akselrod, and others — but the majority of the delegates came from the ranks of the non-Russian Social Democratic parties: the Bund, the Latvian Social Democratic Labor Party, the Caucasian parties, and, as guests, the representatives of the Polish Socialist Party and the Lithuanian Social Democratic Labor Party.[65] This meeting — afterwards called the "August Conference of Liquidators" — took the first timid steps in the direction of a national program which the party had heretofore lacked. It asserted in its resolution that national-cultural autonomy was not contrary to the party's program guaranteeing national self-determination.[66] Plekhanov objected to this statement as impractical and "nationalistic," [67] but national-cultural autonomy gained in popularity, and in 1917 it was officially incorporated into the Menshevik platform.[68]

## Lenin and the National Question before 1913

Lenin's changing attitudes toward the national question reflected very clearly the growing importance of this problem in Russian political life: he became more and more aware of national emotions and alive to the need for an acceptable solution. Though Lenin was perhaps the most doctrinaire of all prominent Russian Marxists in his fundamental assumptions, he was also the most flexible in his choice of means. Once he realized the value of the national movement as a weapon for fighting the established order, he stopped at nothing to employ it for his own ends.

There are three clearly distinguishable phases in the development of Lenin's approach to the national problem: from 1897 to 1913, from 1913 to 1917, and from 1917 to 1923. In the first, he formulated his basic views on the problem; in the second, he developed a plan for the utilization of national minority movements in Russia and abroad; and in the third, after having, for all practical purposes, abandoned this plan, he adopted a new scheme derived from his practical experience as ruler of Russia. By 1923 Lenin had undergone another evolution of his views, and was apparently prepared to modify his policy further, but he was prevented by illness and death from carrying out this intention.

Until 1913, Lenin was not well acquainted either with the general and the socialist literature on the national question, or with its political and economic aspects. But with his characteristic sense for political realities, he acknowledged early in his career the possibility of an alliance between the socialists and minority nationalists. The development of socialism, Lenin believed, did not preclude the possibility of the occasional, transitory emergence of various non-proletarian forces. Social Democracy had to be prepared to utilize such forces, whether they expressed dissatisfaction on the part of other classes, or of religious groups, or of national minorities. "Undoubtedly the class antagonism has now pushed the national questions far into the background," he wrote, "but one should not maintain categorically, lest one become a doctrinaire, that the temporary appearance of this or that national question on the stage of the political drama is impossible." [69] When it was useful, socialists also should support nationalist movements, never forgetting that such support was conditional and temporary: "it is the support of an ally against a *given* enemy, and the Social Democrats provide this support in order to speed the fall of the common enemy, but they expect *nothing for themselves* from these temporary allies and concede nothing to them." [70] Here is the key to Lenin's entire treatment of the nationality question formulated as early as 1897–1903.

The party program, Lenin said, quoting Kautsky, was written not only for the present, but also for the future; it had to state not only what was expected of society, but also what was demanded of it. [71] For this reason, it was absolutely necessary to include in the party program a statement concerning the right of all nations to self-determination. If properly interpreted, this statement was in no way contradictory to the general principles of Marxism. The Social Democrats, unlike the Socialist Revolutionaries, did not support the right of nationalities unconditionally, but in a qualified manner, in full dependence on the interests of the proletariat.[72]

> Social Democracy . . . has as its fundamental and principal task to assist the self-determination, not of peoples or of nations, but of the proletariat of every nationality. We must always and unconditionally strive toward the *closest* unification of the proletariat of all nationalities, and only in individual, exceptional cases can we advance and actively support demands for the creation of a new class state, or the replacement of a state's full political unity by the weaker federal bond.[73]

Such were the fundamental views at which Lenin had arrived by 1913. They remained with him until the end of his life. He looked upon the national movement mainly as a force suitable for *exploitation* in the struggle for power. In this respect, he differed from other Russian Social Democrats who considered nationalism an obstacle to the socialist movement and urged either that it be fought directly (Plekhanov), or else that it be neutralized by being diverted into cultural channels (the majority of Mensheviks).

Lenin shared, however, the prevailing Social Democratic hostility to federalism. When, in 1903, the Armenian Social Democratic publicists demanded the establishment of a federal system in Russia, and the introduction of cultural autonomy, Lenin objected: "It is not the business of the proletariat," he wrote, "to *preach* federation and national autonomy . . . which unavoidably lead to the demand for the establishment of an autonomous *class* state." [74] He repeatedly condemned federalism as economically retrogressive, and cultural autonomy as tending to divide the proletariat.

But by late 1912 it became necessary for the Bolsheviks to issue a more specific programmatic statement. All the other major parties in Russia had adopted definite programs for the solution of the minority question. In August of that year, even the Mensheviks who until then had been reticent, began to advocate national-cultural autonomy. Something had to be done. Lenin had moved in the summer to Cracow, and there had the opportunity to witness personally the extent to which the national question had interfered with the development of the socialist movement in the Austrian Empire and in the neighboring provinces of Russian Poland.[75] With great zeal, he applied himself at once to the study of the pertinent literature, which until then he had known only second-hand, principally from the writings of Karl Kautsky. He now read Bauer's chief work and Kautsky's criticism of Bauer, and then several books dealing with the minorities in Russia, especially the Jews and the Ukrainians.[76] He also compiled population statistics and economic data. Before long, he realized that the nationality problem played a much more important role in the life of Russia in general, and of socialism in particular, than he had until then supposed. The potential ally, whose utilization he had posited fifteen years earlier, was immediately available as a weapon against the established regime in Russia. An alliance with the nationality movement — on the conditions previously laid down — was a vital necessity, but such an alliance required a concrete national program with which to approach and to win the sympathy of the minorities.

In the final two months of the year, other events took place which made the need for such a program ever more urgent. On December 10, 1912, a Georgian Menshevik deputy, Akaki Chkhenkeli, made a speech in the Duma in which he demanded the "creation of institutions necessary for the free development of every nationality." [77] This declaration greatly angered Lenin. He considered it a breach of party discipline, and brought up the subject at a conference of his followers held in Cracow in January 1913, at which Stalin was present.[78] At this meeting, Lenin suggested a formal condemnation of Chkhenkeli's speech, and, to provide an immediate answer to the Bundist and Caucasian socialists who had by now become the chief exponents of the Renner-Bauer formula in the Russian Social Democratic movement, he commissioned Stalin to write an article on this topic.

Stalin's appointment was apparently due not so much to his competence in the field — for he had previously written no work on the subject — but to the fact that, being a Caucasian, he was abreast of developments in the area where the Austrian doctrine had gained its greatest following. Far better informed than Stalin was Lenin's able Armenian follower, Stepan Shaumian, who as early as 1906 had written a lengthy work attacking nationalist sentiment in Transcaucasia. But in 1912 Shaumian was in the Caucasus and unavailable to do the job Lenin wanted done.[79] Lenin may well have turned over to Stalin the notebook in which he had kept notes on the reading he had done since the summer, and probably gave other suggestions as well. Had this particular notebook not disappeared, we might be in a better position today to determine the extent of Stalin's indebtedness to Lenin in the writing of the article on "Marxism and the National Question." [80] Lenin expected Stalin to go through all the Austrian and other socialist writings in order to refute the ideas which were gaining prevalence among Russian Marxists.[81] The product of Stalin's efforts, however, hardly fulfilled these expectations.

Stalin's much-publicized essay consists of three principal parts.[82] The first discusses the concept of the nation; the second inadequately describes and criticizes the Austrian project, and the third deals with the theory of cultural autonomy in the Russian socialist movement. The nation is defined as a "historically evolved, stable community arising on the foundation of a common language,* territory, economic life, and psychological makeup, manifested in a community of culture." [83] Stalin argues that Bauer had confused the concept of the nation with that of an ethnic group, and then goes on to characterize nationality movements as essentially bourgeois in character, thus echoing the standard Marxist view before Renner and Bauer had published their studies.

The Austrian project, Stalin asserts, would increase national differences by creating within each state artificial communities of various classes, who were being in reality separated from each other by economic developments. It would thus inevitably lead to a cleavage in the ranks of the proletariat. As proof, Stalin points to Russia, where, in his opinion, the spread of the Renner-Bauer theories had already weakened party unity and assisted the growth of nationalistic tendencies within the Bund and the Caucasian branches of the party. He denies that the Jews are a nation, and condemns the Bund for its efforts to retard the natural process of assimilation of the Jewish population in Russia. In conclusion, he suggests that the only truly Marxist solution of the national problem is that advanced by the Social Democratic program: the right to self-determination (which he does not attempt to clarify), the establishment of civic equality and broad regional autonomy, combined with the protection of minority languages and the creation of minority schools.

Stalin's article added nothing new to the theoretical discussions of the national problem, and represented only a temporary pronouncement of the Bolsheviks on a question which they had previously ignored. An analysis of Stalin's arguments reveals at once their inadequacy. Their greatest weakness was the failure to come to grips with the fundamental assumptions of Renner and Bauer: that nations were the natural formations of human society, that they were worth preserving, and that, far from disappearing with the spread of democracy and socialism, they would grow in importance. The validity of these views determined the soundness of the entire Austrian project, yet Stalin avoided this argument and merely repeated, without substantiation, the shop-worn clichés about the inevitable disappearance of national differences. By failing to place the argument on this level, Stalin missed the main point of disagreement between the supporters and opponents of the Austrian plan.

His analysis of Renner's conception of nationality was faulty, and his own definition of a nation as unoriginal as it was dogmatic. Stalin reproached Bauer for allegedly "confusing the nation, which is a historical

---

* The English translation of Stalin's essay, J. Stalin, *Marxism and the National Question* (New York, 1942), 12, renders the words "stable community arising on the foundation of a common language," as "stable community of language," which, of course, is quite a different concept.

category, with the tribe, which is an ethnic one," [84] whereas Bauer clearly and repeatedly defined the nation as a historical concept.[85] Stalin's assertion that Bauer had divorced "national character" from the economic and other conditions which had produced it, was equally unfounded: Bauer had made it very explicit that he objected to all "fetishism" of the concept of national character, since it was not an independent factor, but one conditioned by economic and other historic forces.[86] Similar faults can be found with other statements of Stalin concerning the ideas of Bauer and Renner. His page references to their works concern pages suspiciously close together, which suggests that he may well have read their books only in part. In some instances, he does not refer to those sections where answers to his charges could be found. The definition of the nation which Stalin employed without any attempt to justify it or to compare it with other existing definitions, was very curious. Odd, from the Marxist point of view, was the word "stable" in reference to the nation; odd also was the statement that a nation was an economic and psychological community. Lenin was before long vehemently to attack such views, because he realized that they constituted the heart of the Renner-Bauer thesis.

Stalin's exposition of the practical aspects of the Austrian program was equally incorrect. He wrongly says that the Austrian Social Democratic Party at its Bruenn Congress had accepted the project of extraterritorial autonomy.[87] Furthermore, his argument that the Austrian scheme was impracticable in Russia because the tsarist government could easily destroy "such feeble institutions as 'cultural' Diets," [88] was completely invalid for two reasons. In the first place, no advocate of the program of extraterritorial cultural autonomy had suggested its introduction into an absolutist state; the entire project was devised for a democracy. In the second place, Renner, desiring to prevent such an eventuality even in a democratic state had actually drawn up an elaborate scheme for the transformation of national institutions into the state's regional administrative apparatus.

The entire attack on the Bund and the Caucasian Mensheviks also rested on a logical fallacy. Stalin's main case against extraterritorial national-cultural autonomy was that it inevitably led to a split of the Social Democratic Party along national lines. As proof, he cited the Austrian experience, where indeed the emergence of the idea of national-cultural autonomy had been followed by a division of the Austrian Social Democratic Party into its national components. Yet the relation between the two events was hardly a causal one. The pressure for the adoption of extraterritorial autonomy and the party reorganization were both effects of one and the same cause: the national aspirations of the Austrian minorities.

Finally, the practical program advanced by Stalin as a solution of

the minority question in Russia contained nothing new. It simply para-
phrased Points 3, 7, 8, and 9 of the party program, adopted jointly by the
Mensheviks and Bolsheviks at the 1903 Congress in London.

Considerable doubt has been thrown by several authorities on Stalin's
authorship of this essay.[89] One biographer of Stalin has even asserted
that Lenin might have provided Stalin with an outline of the article,
as well as the material and the ideas.[90] The direct evidence concerning
the origin of the article is of course very scanty. But a textual analysis,
although it does not reveal the true author, at least indicates that Lenin's
positive participation in its writing was not quite so great. In the essay,
the terms "national culture" and "national psychology" play a prominent
part, both in the definition of the nation and in the subsequent discussion. Lenin, however, always denied the very existence of "national
culture" and labeled those who espoused such concepts victims of
"bourgeois" or "clerical" propaganda.[91] Both these concepts, on the other
hand, were widely employed by Stalin in subsequent speeches and writings of undisputed authorship. Indeed, the entire positive attitude toward the nation permeating this article is very characteristic of Stalin's
attitude toward the national problem. Lenin's approach was more negative, and he certainly never admitted the existence of such a phenomenon
as "psychological national makeup." At the same time, the concept of
national self-determination, in the sense in which Lenin was to develop
it in his own writings of 1913 — that is, as signifying the right to separation — was entirely absent from the essay.*

We have seen that the essay wrongly asserted that the Bruenn Congress of the Austrian Social Democracy had accepted extraterritorial
national-cultural autonomy. Lenin, however, never tired of pointing out
to the Russian followers of Renner and Bauer, as proof of the impracticability of their views, that even the Bruenn Congress had rejected this
proposal.[92] In addition the essay commits some factual blunders of the
most flagrant nature. It is difficult, for example, to conceive how Lenin
could ever have asserted that "at the end of the eighteenth and beginning of the nineteenth centuries . . . North America was still known
as New England." [93]

Thus, on the basis of what is known of Lenin's and Stalin's ideas on
the national question, it is possible to state that the essay on "Marxism
and the National Question," though undoubtedly written under Lenin's
instructions and very likely with some of his assistance, did not, on the

---

* It may be observed that in an article written in 1913, soon after the essay on
"Marxism and the National Question" had been composed, Stalin said that the right
to national self-determination was a general one, and included the right to autonomy
and federation (Stalin, II, 286). Lenin subsequently ridiculed this idea, not only
because he was in principle opposed to federation, but also because he felt that
there could not be any "right" to autonomy and federation from the purely logical
point of view; cf. Lenin, XVII, 427ff.

whole, represent Lenin's opinions.* The character of the work and the ideas expressed in it indicate that in the main it was a work of Stalin's. This essay represented no advance over discussion held by Russian Social Democrats previous to 1913, but rather a not too intelligent restatement of old arguments, replete with errors in fact and in reasoning. It provided no new program for the solution of the minority question. Viewed as a polemical piece, the essay had some passing importance, because it contained an early attack by the Bolsheviks on the Austrian theories, but before long Lenin was to formulate his own views, and neither he nor anybody else bothered to refer to Stalin's article, which would long ago have been relegated to total oblivion, were it not for its author's subsequent career.†

### Lenin's Theory of Self-Determination

Lenin spent a considerable part of the two years preceding the outbreak of World War I continuing his researches into the nationality problem and writing polemical articles on its various aspects. Until 1914, most of his writings were directed against the followers of Renner and Bauer, whom he called "rightists"; thereafter he turned mainly against the "leftists," who included his Bolshevik colleagues, the majority of whom had accepted the ideas of Rosa Luxemburg. Trying to steer a middle course between the two views, neither of which satisfied him, Lenin developed his own national program which centered on a novel interpretation of the concept of national self-determination.

The fundamental weakness of Lenin's new approach to the nationality problem was his endeavor to reconcile two sets of mutually exclusive premises: those derived from Marxism and those supplied by political realities. Renner and Bauer had given up the first; Rosa Luxemburg and her followers had ignored the second. In a sense, each had achieved a consistent program. Lenin, wishing to avoid both pitfalls, created a program which as a solution of the national problem was neither consistent nor practical.

Lenin continued to believe that nationalism, in all its aspects, was

* The point has often been made that Stalin, being ignorant of German, needed help to do his research. This argument is not entirely valid because the principal sources for the essay, such as Bauer, Renner, and the protocois of the Bruenn Congress, had been translated into Russian by Jewish socialists and the footnotes seem to show that Stalin used the Russian translations. Only two of the sources to which reference is made were written in German, and it is possible that Stalin learned of their contents from Lenin's notes or possibly from Bukharin; on the latter see Wolfe, *Three*, 582.

† The Marx-Engels-Lenin Institute in Moscow possesses two letters of Lenin in which reference is made to Stalin's article. Their character can be surmised from the fact that they have never been published in their entirety, and only one sentence from each, taken out of context, has been permitted by Soviet censorship to appear in print. Cf. *Stalin*, II, 402–03.

essentially a phenomenon proper to the capitalist era and destined to vanish with the demise of capitalism itself. Like Marx and Engels, he viewed it as a transitory occurrence whose disappearance the socialists should help speed. He never shared Renner's and Bauer's faith in the intrinsic values of nationality, or in the desirability of preserving the cultural heterogeneity of the world. From the point of view of fundamental assumptions and long-range expectations he belonged in the "leftist" camp of Rosa Luxemburg. But at the same time, Lenin, unlike Rosa Luxemburg, was keenly aware that the force of nationalism was far from spent, particularly in those areas where capitalism was still in its early stages of development. He desired to utilize the national movements emerging in various parts of the Russian Empire and for that reason he refused to adopt the negative attitudes of the leftists. In his awareness of the political implications of the national strivings of the minorities, he came much closer to the position of the "rightists."

According to Lenin, the world, viewed from the aspect of the national problem, could be divided into three principal areas: the West, where the problem had been solved because each nationality had its own state; Eastern Europe, where the process of capitalist development and its inevitable companion, the national state, were only in their formative stage; and the backward, colonial, and semi-colonial areas where capitalism and nationalism have not yet penetrated at all.[94] As far as socialism was concerned, the national problem was therefore one affecting primarily Eastern Europe and the backward areas of the world. Capitalism spreading from Western Europe to the East had to accommodate itself in national states. The large, multinational empires had to transform themselves into national states, and the minor nationalities, incapable of attaining statehood, had to be swept out of their long isolation by the force of industrial development, and had to lose their identity through assimilation in the cities and factories with the industrially more advanced nationalities. Thus, by the time economic development in Eastern Europe should have attained the level existent in the West, Eastern Europe would have lost its multinational character. What economic forces had begun, democracy would complete. By creating equal opportunities for all national groups, and by removing the main causes of national hostility, oppression and persecution, democracy would pave the road for a supra-national world system of government and an international culture of the socialist era.

It is obvious that neither the Renner-Bauer nor the Luxemburg scheme could satisfy these assumptions. The Austrian plan of extraterritorial cultural autonomy was based on what Lenin considered a faulty concept of "national culture," and strove artificially to preserve all those ethnic differences which capitalism was already sweeping away. Culture to Lenin could have only a class character. "Only the clericals and the bourgeoisie can talk of national culture. The toilers can talk only of an international culture of the universal worker movement." [95] What is usually referred to as "national culture" is in reality the culture of the ruling bourgeoisie, and is squarely opposed to the democratic, socialistic culture of the oppressed classes.[96] ". . . the entire economic, political, and spiritual existence of humanity becomes already ever more internationalized under capitalism. Socialism will internationalize it completely." [97] Like Kautsky before him, Lenin argued that extraterritorial autonomy ran contrary to the processes of history. On the one hand, it hindered the process of assimilation; on the other, it ignored the natural tendency of capitalism to form national states and to break up multinational empires.

Since Lenin also remained adamant in his opposition to the federalist project adopted by the Socialist Revolutionaries and their affiliates,[98] he had to find a third solution. But what formula was capable of satisfying the capitalist tendency towards the creation of national states without hindering the process of internationalization of cultures or breaking up the unity of the proletarian movement? Lenin believed that he had found such a formula in the slogan of national self-determination, as defined and limited by him in the summer of 1913.

As had been indicated previously, point 9 in the Russian Social Democratic Labor Party's platform ("the right of all nations in the state to self-determination") had been adopted as a general democratic declaration. It meant, broadly speaking, that Social Democracy was in principle opposed to any form of national oppression and favored the freedom for subjugated peoples. As a statement of principle, it was open to divergent interpretations. It could mean national territorial autonomy, cultural autonomy of a territorial or extraterritorial kind, or the establishment of federal relations. Probably the only interpretation not held by those who had voted this statement into the party's program was that it implied the right to secession and the formation of independent states. With the possible exceptions of Poland and Finland, none of the border peoples of the Empire were considered either willing or ready to separate themselves from Russia.

Casting about for a way out of the dilemma in which his beliefs had placed him, Lenin seized upon Point 9 in the Party's program and reinterpreted it in a way best suited to his purposes. In the summer of 1913, he thus defined what he understood by the right to self-determination: "The paragraph of our program [dealing with national self-determination] cannot be interpreted in any other way, but in the sense of *political* self-determination, that is, as the right to separation and creation of an independent government." [99] Every nation living in the state had, as a nation, one right and one right only: to separate from Russia and to create an independent state. A people who did not desire to take advantage of this right could not ask from the state for any preferential treatment, such as the establishment of federal relations, or the granting of extraterritorial cultural autonomy. It had to be satisfied with the general freedoms of the state, including a certain amount of regional autonomy inherent in "democratic centralism." *

The right of national self-determination, interpreted in this manner, seemed to Lenin to fulfill all the requirements of a good socialist solution of the national problem: it made possible a direct appeal to the nationalist sentiments among Russian minorities for the purpose of winning their support against the autocracy; it was democratic, and as such conducive to the ultimate victory of socialism; it was in harmony with the tendency of capitalism to form national states; and it speeded the assimilation of the minorities.

As Lenin's Bolshevik followers and other socialists were quick in pointing out, however, there was one serious difficulty with this approach. Interpreted in this manner, the right of self-determination seemed to place socialists in a position of giving blanket endorsement to every nationalist and separatist movement in Eastern Europe. Carried to its logical conclusion, such a slogan could lead to the break-up of Eastern Europe into a conglomeration of petty national states. How could this be reconciled with the international character of Marxism, with its striving for the merger of states and the disappearance of national borders? Did it not surpass even the Austrian program in separating the workers of various countries from each other?

Lenin, however, did not believe in the likelihood of Eastern Europe disintegrating into its national components, and felt certain that if his slogan would affect the future political structure of that area at all, it would be in the opposite direction. He had two principal arguments to support this contention. In the first place, he argued, the economic forces — the ultimate determinant in history — worked against the breakup of great states. The centrifugal forces evident in Eastern Europe were mainly psychological in their origin. As long as national oppression was permitted, the victim-nation would remain receptive to nationalist agitation; once this oppression was done away with, the psychological basis for nationalism and separatism would vanish too. And what better way was there of striking at the very root of national antagonism than to guarantee every nation the right to complete political freedom? Lenin was convinced that once the minorities were assured of a right to separate and to form independent states, they would cast off the suspicions which he considered the primary cause of national movements. Then

---

* "The principle of democratic centralism and autonomy of local institutions means namely full and universal *freedom of criticism*, as long as it does not violate the unity of *a specific action* — and the inadmissibility of *any* criticism which undermines or hinders the *unity* of an action decided upon by the party" (*Lenin,* IX, 275).

and only then could economic factors have a free field to accomplish their centralizing, unifying task, unopposed by nationalism. The minorities would find it advantageous to remain within the larger political unit, and thus a lasting foundation for the emergence of large states and an eventual united states of the world would be created.

Lenin's second argument against the charges that his slogan threatened a breakup of Russia, was his qualification of the right to self-determination. To advance the *right* to separation did not mean, Lenin asserted, to condone actual separation. Certainly he had no intention of favoring an "unconditional" right to self-determination, since "unconditional" to him were only the rights of the proletariat. Whether this or that minority should, at a given moment, secede from Russia depended upon any number of unforeseeable factors. Whenever the interests of nationality and the proletariat conflicted, the former had to yield to the latter, and the right to separation had to go overboard. Furthermore, Lenin said, he sponsored the right to self-determination as a general democratic right, much as he favored the right to divorce without actually advocating divorce. The duty of the socialists of the oppressed ethnic groups was to agitate for a union with the democratic elements of the oppressing nation, whereas the socialists of the oppressor nation must guarantee the minorities the right to self-determination.[100]

It is clear, therefore, that Lenin neither desired nor expected the right of national self-determination, in the sense in which he had defined it, to be exercised:

> The freedom of separation is the best and only *political* means against the idiotic system of petty states (*Kleinstaaterei*) and national isolation, which, fortunately for humanity, are inevitably destroyed through the entire development of capitalism.[101]

> We demand the freedom of self-determination, *i.e.*, independence, *i.e.*, the freedom of separation of oppressed nations, not because we dream of economic particularization, or of the ideal of small states, but on the contrary, because we desire major states, and a rapprochement, even a merging, of nations, but on a truly democratic, truly international basis, which is *unthinkable* without the freedom of secession.[102]

> Separation is altogether not our scheme. We do not predict separation at all.[103]

Lenin assumed a similar attitude towards the question of an official state language. Like most Marxists, he desired the eventual transformation of the Russian Empire into a national state, in which the minorities would assimilate and adopt the Russian tongue. But, he warned, this goal could be brought about only voluntarily; it could be made possible only by granting the minorities the right to employ freely their own native tongues. In time, the greatness of Russian culture and the material advantages accruing to those who had mastered its language would bring about cultural and linguistic assimilation.[104]

It was rather difficult to win over other Marxists to these views, and Lenin spent a considerable part of the prewar years writing and speaking publicly in support of his theses. In 1913 and 1914, he delivered a series of lectures on this subject in Switzerland, Paris, Brussels, and Cracow, debating against the proponents of the Renner-Bauer and Rosa Luxemburg views alike.[105]

The outbreak of the war involved Lenin in further theoretical difficulties and forced him to broaden the definition of self-determination. The war caused a well-known cleavage within the ranks of European Social Democracy. Socialists of all the major European powers supported the military efforts of their governments, thus violating repeated pledges of mutual coöperation against future international conflicts. Socialists of the Entente powers argued that the Allied side deserved support as protecting the world from Prussian militarism; those of the Central powers, on the other hand, argued that they were defending the world from the yoke of Russian absolutism and reaction. Whatever the point of their argument, both sides referred to the founders of modern socialism to prove that socialism was not opposed to war as such, but rather imposed upon its adherents the obligation to support the side which was the more progressive. Their disagreements centered around the questions which side represented progress and which would Marx have supported were he alive in 1914.

Lenin, like the whole Zimmerwald left, of which the Bolsheviks were part, disagreed fundamentally with this approach. He argued that the war of 1914 was entirely different from those which had been fought in the nineteenth century. It was not one in which socialists could take sides. This was a new kind of war, an Imperialist war. The capitalist period had entered its final phase, that of finance capitalism, in which, having outgrown national limitations, it struggled for economic control of the entire world. The principal aim of capitalism now was the conquest of new markets, especially in the colonies, and the era of national wars was over. The Allies and the Central powers were equally guilty, equally reactionary, so that the attitudes of Marx, correct for the middle of the nineteenth century, were no longer applicable. The task of the socialists, Lenin and his followers argued, was to bring about a transformation of the international conflict into a civil war and to prepare for an imminent socialist revolution in the belligerent states.

If this was true, however, then one of the main arguments which had induced Lenin to apply to Eastern Europe the right to national self-determination or separation, and to reject the thesis of Luxemburg — namely, the theory that capitalism spreading in the East would accommodate itself in the national state — was invalidated. Nationalism and the national state had become things of the past. Arguing against Lenin, Martov stated the view prevalent among the Social Democrats:

> The *forms* in which this or that national party might wish to realize the right of its people to self-determination may run contrary to the forces of social development and the interests of the proletariat. Let us take, for instance, the Armenian people. The recognition of its right to solve its political destiny does not oblige us to support the slogan of any nation which might wish to realize its right to self-determination through the formation of a separate state with its army, with its tariff wall, etc. If we should find that such a new state would have no economic basis for its development, then, from the point of view of the interests of the proletariat we shall, while asserting the right of free self-determination, demand that the Armenian nation realize this self-determination in another form.[106]

This other form of "free" self-determination which they were going to "demand" was for the majority of Mensheviks national-cultural autonomy. To most Bolsheviks on the other hand, the acceptance of the theory of Imperialism meant the abolition of all borders and the creation of a supra-national state. This was the position taken by Grigorii Piatakov, Nikolai Bukharin, and the overwhelming majority of Bolshevik writers. To them, Lenin's stand appeared entirely inconsistent. If the whole national idea in the era of Imperialism became an empty phantom, devoid of content, how could Marxists support national movements? Early in 1915, using this argument, Piatakov and Bukharin came out openly with a demand for the removal of Point 9 from the party program. When Lenin refused and cited Marx's views of the 1860's to support his views, Bukharin inquired of him, perplexed:

> What? The sixties of the last century are "instructive" for the twentieth century? But this is precisely the *root* of our (logical) disagreements with Kautsky, that they [*sic*] "instruct" us with examples from the pre-Imperialist epoch. Thus you advocate a dualistic conception: in regard to the defense of the fatherland you stand on the basis of the present day, while in regard to the slogan of self-determination, you stand on the position of the "past century." [107]

Bukharin's sentiments were shared by Karl Radek, who also argued that Lenin's slogan attempted to "turn back the wheel of history" and to revive the anachronistic idea of the national state.[108] Late in 1915 Lenin engaged in a bitter argument with the editors of the Bolshevik periodical *Kommunist* over the printing of Radek's attack on the right to self-determination, and when they refused to yield to Lenin's demands that this article be retracted, Lenin caused the journal to be suspended.[109] During 1915 and 1916 most of the outstanding Marxist intellectuals of

Bolshevik leanings, organized around the society *Vpered* (Forward) —
among them the historian Mikhail Pokrovskii and the future Soviet
Commissar of Education Anatolii Lunacharskii — quarreled with Lenin
on this issue.[110] Feliks Dzerzhinskii, the future head of the secret police;
Shaumian, who in 1918 was to serve as Extraordinary Soviet Commissar
for the Caucasus; Aleksandra Kollontai; and many other followers of
Lenin's found themselves unable to accept his stand. Indeed, it is safe
to say that throughout the years of the First World War, Lenin stood
entirely alone in his insistence on the continued validity of the slogan
of national self-determination, against the opposition of all the Zimmerwald groups.

Opposition, however, did not cause Lenin to yield. On the contrary,
after 1914, Lenin reasserted his convictions with increasing vehemence,
although with a significant shift of emphasis.

While gathering materials for his essay on Imperialism, he realized
that the colonial dependencies of the great European powers contained
over a half billion people who were, according to his views, victims not
only of capitalist exploitation but also, in a sense, of national oppression.
He immediately perceived an intimate connection between the problem
of Imperialism and the nationality question. In the African and Asiatic
colonies, which served as the economic foundations of the entire Imperialistic system, there existed a vast reservoir of potential allies of
socialism in its struggle against Imperialism. This struggle could be
effectively undertaken only on a world-wide scale and socialism had to
take full advantage of the forces of popular dissatisfaction by allying
itself with the liberation movements in the colonies. Inasmuch as those
areas had not yet undergone the phase of national development which
Western Europe had already left behind, the struggle in the backward
areas of the world could be expected to assume at first national forms.

Imperialism, therefore, Lenin argued, did not eliminate the national
question or the need for a party statement on self-determination. If
anything, it reëmphasized its importance. Imperialism was basically
national oppression on a new basis.[111] It merely transferred the center
of national movements from Europe to the colonial and semi-colonial
areas of the world. The slogan of self-determination thus became of
greatest importance as a weapon of socialist action and agitation.[112] Moreover, Lenin was careful to point out, this slogan did not lose its validity
in Europe either. Although, by and large, the epoch of national movements was a matter of the past as far as Europe was concerned, nationalism was not entirely out of the question in an Imperialist age even there.
"*If* the *European* proletariat should find itself powerless for a period
of twenty years; *if* the present war were to *end* in victories like those
achieved by Napoleon and in the enslavement of a number of viable

national states . . . then there would be possible a great national war in Europe." [113]

For this eventuality, the socialists had to be prepared.

The connection between Imperialism and national movements in the colonial areas was not an original discovery of Lenin's. He had adopted it freely from the works of several Western socialists such as Rudolf Hilferding and Hermann Gorter.[114] Lenin was, however, the most persistent champion of this idea among Russian socialists, and the first to correlate it with the slogan of national self-determination.

This reasoning explains why, instead of abandoning self-determination during the war, Lenin espoused it ever more vigorously. At the end of the war, he asserted that in the era of Imperialism the slogan of self-determination was assuming the same role which it had played in Europe during the period of the French Revolution, and was acquiring exceptional importance in the Social Democratic platform. Those who persisted in ignoring national movements were waiting for a "pure revolution" instead of a "social revolution," in which the support of non-proletarian groups was essential.[115] At the end of 1916 Lenin started work on a major study of the national question; he was unable to complete it owing to the outbreak of the February Revolution. The existing drafts indicate that, had it been finished, this study would have represented the most exhaustive treatment of the question in all the Russian socialist literature and would have reëmphasized the importance which Lenin by that time attached to national movements.[116]

Lenin's theory of national self-determination, viewed as a solution of the national problem in Russia, was entirely inadequate. By offering the minorities virtually no choice between assimilation and complete independence, it ignored the fact that they desired neither. Underestimating the power of nationalism and convinced without reservation of the inevitable triumph of class loyalties over national loyalties, Lenin looked upon national problems as something to exploit, and not as something to solve. But as a psychological weapon in the struggle for power, first in Russia and then abroad, the slogan of self-determination in Lenin's interpretation was to prove enormously successful. The outbreak of the Russian Revolution allowed the Bolsheviks to put it to considerable demagogic use as a means of winning the support of the national movements which the revolutionary period developed in all their magnitude.

# II

# 1917 AND THE DISINTEGRATION OF THE
# RUSSIAN EMPIRE

### The General Causes

The outbreak of the Russian Revolution had, as its initial consequence, the abolition of the tsarist regime and, as its ultimate result, the
complete breakdown of all forms of organized life throughout Russia.
One of the aspects of this breakdown was the disintegration of the
Empire and the worsening of relations between its various ethnic groups.
In less than a year after the Tsar had abdicated, the national question
had become an outstanding issue in Russian politics.

Immediately after resuming power, the Provisional Government
issued decrees which abolished all restrictive legislation imposed on the
minorities by the tsarist regime, and established full quality of all
citizens regardless of religion, race, or national origin.[1] The government
also introduced the beginnings of national self-rule by placing the administration of the borderlands in the hands of prominent local figures.
Transcaucasia and Turkestan were put under the jurisdiction of special
committees, composed largely of Duma deputies of native nationalities,
to replace the governors general of the tsarist administration. The southwestern provinces were put in charge of Ukrainians, though the government refused to recognize the existence of the entire Ukraine as an
administrative unit until forced to do so under Ukrainian pressure in
the summer of 1917.[2] Those were pioneering steps in the direction of
adapting the governmental machinery to the multinational character
of the Empire and giving the minorities a voice in the administration of
their territories, but unfortunately the local committees to which the
Provisional Government had relegated authority possessed very little
real power, and after the summer of 1917 functioned only nominally.

The Provisional Government considered itself a temporary trustee of
state sovereignty, and viewed its main task as that of preserving unity

and order until the people should have an opportunity to express its own will in the Constituent Assembly. Throughout its existence the government resisted as well as it could all pressures to enact legislation which might affect the constitution of the state. Any such measures it regarded as an infringement on popular sovereignty. This attitude, sound from the moral and constitutional points of view, proved fatal as political practice. The February Revolution had set into motion forces which would not wait. The procrastinating policies of the Provisional Government led to growing anarchy which Lenin and his followers, concentrating on the seizure of power and unhampered by any moral scruples or constitutional considerations, utilized to accomplish a successful *coup d'état.*

The growth of the national movements in Russia during 1917, and especially the unexpectedly rapid development of political aspirations on the part of the minorities, were caused to a large extent by the same factors which in Russia proper made possible the triumph of Bolshevism: popular restlessness, the demand for land and peace, and the inability of the democratic government to provide firm authority.

The growing impatience of the rural population with delays in the apportionment of land which caused the peasantry of the ethnically Great Russian provinces to turn against the government and to attack large estates, had different effects in the eastern borderlands. There the dissatisfaction of the native population was not so much directed against the landlord as against the Russian colonist; it was he who had deprived the native nomad of his grazing grounds and with the aid of Cossack or Russian garrisons had kept the native from the land which he considered his own by inheritance. When the February Revolution broke out, the native population of the Northern Caucasus, the Ural region and much of the steppe districts of Central Asia expected that the new democracy would at once remedy the injustices of the past by returning to them the properties of which they had been deprived. When this did not happen, they took matters into their own hands, and tried to seize land by force. But in doing so they encountered the resistance of Russian and Cossack villages. Thus, in the second half of the year, while a class struggle was taking place in Russia proper, an equally savage national conflict developed in the vast eastern borderlands of the Empire: Chechen and Ingush against Russian and Cossack; Kazakh-Kirghiz against the Russian and Ukrainian colonist; Bashkir against the Russian and Tatar.

In the Ukraine, too, the agricultural question assumed a national form although for quite different reasons. The Ukrainian peasants, especially the rural middle class, found it advantageous, as will be seen, in view of the superiority of the soil in their provinces, to solve the land question independently of Russia proper.

War-weariness was another factor which tended to increase nationalist emotions. Non-Russian soldiers, like their Russian comrades, desired to terminate the fighting and to return home. Uncertain how to go about it, they organized their own military formations and military councils, hoping in this manner to be repatriated sooner, and to obtain by common action a better response to their demands. By the end of the year the formation of such national units had increased to the point where non-Russian troops, abandoning the front, frequently returned to their homes as a body. Once on their native soil, they augmented native political organizations and provided them with military power. The national movement in 1917 had perhaps its most rapid development in the army.

The Bolsheviks, inciting Russian peasants and soldiers against the government, were persuasive in contending that the government did not grant their demands because it had become a captive of the "bourgeoisie." The non-Russian, on the other hand, could be led to believe that the trouble lay not so much in the class-character of the Provisional Government, as in its ethnic composition. Nationalistic parties in some areas began to foster the idea that all Russian governments, autocratic as well as democratic, were inspired by the same hostility toward the minorities and should be equally mistrusted.

Immediately after the fall of the *ancien régime* the minorities, like the Russians, established local organs of internal self-rule. The original purpose of these institutions was to serve as centers of public discussion for the forthcoming Constituent Assembly and to attend to non-political affairs connected with the problems of local administration. Whether called Soviet, Rada (in the Ukraine and Belorussia), *Shura* (among the Turkic peoples), or their equivalents in other native languages, they were originally not intended to infringe upon the authority of the Provisional Government. In time, however, as the authority of the Provisional Government declined, these organs acquired a correspondingly greater voice in local affairs. At first they only assumed responsibility over supply and communication, the maintenance of public order, and, in some cases, the defense of their territories from external enemies — services which Petrograd could not provide. But at the end of 1917, when, as a result of the Bolshevik coup, a political vacuum was created in the country, they appropriated sovereignty itself. While the soviets, largely under the influence of the Bolsheviks and left SR's, proclaimed the overthrow of the Provisional Government and the establishment of rule of the Congress of Soviets, the minority organizations took over the responsibilities of government for their own peoples and the territories which they inhabited. These local organs of administration which arose in the borderlands during the October Revolution and succeeding months were based on the principle of national self-rule and functioned alone or in condominium with the soviets.

For a time it seemed possible that these national organs would co-operate with the new Russian government. In the initial period of Communist rule no one knew how the new regime would treat the minorities. But before long it became apparent that the Soviet government had no intention of respecting the principle of national self-determination and that in spreading its authority it was inclined to utilize social forces hostile to minority interests. In the Ukraine, it favored that part of the industrial proletariat which was, by ethnic origin and sympathy, oriented toward Russia and inimical to the striving of the local peasantry; in the Moslem areas, the colonizing elements and the urban population composed largely of Russian newcomers; in Transcaucasia and Belorussia, the deserting Russian troops. The triumph of Bolshevism was interpreted in many borderland areas as the victory of the city over the village, the worker over the peasant, the Russian colonist over the native.

It was under such circumstances that the national councils, bolstered by sentiments which had matured in the course of the year, proclaimed their self-rule, and in some instances, their complete independence.

## The Ukraine and Belorussia

### The Rise of the Ukrainian Central Rada (February–June 1917)

The news of disorders in Petrograd reached Kiev on March 1. Faced with the prospect of impending civic disorganization, the city officials took the initiative into their own hands and created an Executive Committee of all local social and political organizations, the so-called IKSOOO (*Ispolnitelnyi Komitet Soveta Ob"edinennykh Obshchestven-nykh Organizatsii*: The Executive Committee of the Council of Combined Social Organizations), in the hope that such an institution, representing the forces of public opinion, could maintain order more successfully than the obsolescent bureaucratic machinery of the old regime. The IKSOOO included the political parties, which had formed rapidly in Kiev during the weeks following the outbreak of the Revolution, as well as representatives of the city administration and other organizations of all the nationalities inhabiting the city. The Soviet of Workers' Deputies joined it in the latter part of March.

The Ukrainians also took steps to organize themselves. Their first center was located in the club *Rodina* (Fatherland), where the TUP, the Society of Ukrainian Progressives, had its headquarters. This society was an association of intellectuals of moderate political views, composed mostly of members of the pro-Kadet Ukrainian Democratic Radical Party. On March 4, the leaders of the TUP in association with Ukrainian socialists, who had gathered in Kiev, formed the Ukrainian Central Council or Rada, as a center for Ukrainian affairs in the Kiev region. Originally the Rada consisted of a number of diverse educational and coöperative institutions, which had no definite political or social program except perhaps a general sympathy with the ideal of Ukrainian autonomy. It elected as its chairman *in absentia* the historian, Mikhail Hrushevskii, who was at that moment making his way to Kiev from Moscow. At a period when public opinion, so long repressed by the tsarist regime, was searching eagerly for institutional forms capable of formulating and executing its wishes, when parties and soviets were mushrooming in every part of the country, the creation of an Ukrainian council attracted little attention in Kiev or elsewhere. The predominantly cultural interests of the original founders of the Rada, as well as the modest, conciliatory attitude with which they deferred to the Provisional Government, gave no reason to suspect that the Rada would follow a course of political action capable of endangering the newly established authority. In a telegram to Prince Lvov, the chairman of the Council of Ministers, the Rada stated on March 6: "We greet in your person the first ministry of free Russia. We wish you full success in the struggle for popular rule, convinced that the just demands of the Ukrainian people and of its democratic intelligentsia will be completely satisfied." [3]

Soon, however, more radically inclined Ukrainian political figures, returning from the front and from the tsarist exile, began to arrive in Kiev — men who before the war had been associated with socialist and nationalist movements. They at once assumed effective leadership over the Rada and steered it away from reliance on the Provisional Government toward an independent pursuit of national aspirations. Typical of their sentiments were the remarks made by Hrushevskii upon his arrival in Kiev:

> Nothing is more erroneous than to dig out now old Ukrainian petitions and again to hand them over to the government as a statement of our demands . . . If our demands of five, four, three, and even one year ago had been granted then, they would have been accepted by Ukrainian society with deep gratitude . . . but they can in no way be considered a satisfaction of Ukrainian needs, "a solution of the Ukrainian question" at the present moment! There is no Ukrainian problem any more. There is a free, great Ukrainian people, which builds its lot in new conditions of freedom . . . The needs and claims of the Ukraine are being advanced in all their breadth.[4]

Hrushevskii placed the demand for territorial Ukrainian autonomy in the forefront of the Rada's program, and with his friends applied himself at once to the task of transforming the Rada into a supreme political center of the Ukrainian nation.

To attain this status, the Rada called together at the beginning of April an Ukrainian National Congress, to which it invited all those groups which demanded in their programs the establishment of Ukrainian territorial autonomy. Despite its name, therefore, the Congress represented only one segment of the population and within it only one political tendency. The Congress adopted a series of resolutions, calling for the transformation of Russia into a federal republic, with the Ukraine as an autonomous part, and formulated a representational system for the various provinces populated by Ukrainians, by means of which delegates to the Rada were to be elected in the future. A commission was appointed to work out a project of autonomy for presentation to the All-Russian Constituent Assembly.[5]

Shortly after the formation of the Rada, the old Society of Ukrainian Progressives (TUP), which represented liberal, moderate elements and at the outbreak of the Revolution had been the only active Ukrainian organization remotely resembling a political party, declined in influence. After changing its name to that of the Socialist Federalist Party and losing its leading lights, including Hrushevskii, it gave way to groups with more radical political and economic programs. Two parties, the Ukrainian Social Democratic Labor Party and the Ukrainian Socialist Revolutionary Party, deserve special mention because of the importance which they attained within a short time.

The USD (or USDRP) was a resuscitation of the prerevolutionary party of the same name. At the beginning of April, soon after its reëstablishment, this party decided to abandon its hostility to the national movement, and to climb on the bandwagon of Ukrainian nationalism. At that time it joined the Rada by subscribing to the program of autonomy, to the considerable chagrin of the Russian Social Democratic Labor Party in Kiev, which had hoped to use its Ukrainian counterpart as a weapon against the Rada and its "bourgeois-nationalist" leaders. The USD had in its ranks the most active and experienced leaders of the Ukrainian movement, including several of the original founders of the RUP in 1900: the writer Volodimir Vinnichenko, Simon Petliura, N. Porsh and others. The USD acquired a dominant role in the affairs of the Rada, pursuing a course of nationalism mixed with some elements of socialist radicalism, and vacillating between one and the other depending on the political requirements of the moment.

The USR (or UPSR) was a younger party, which was formally established only after the outbreak of the revolution. Its leaders were young men, mostly students (P. Khristiuk, M. Kovalevskii), less experienced and less well known than their rivals of the USD. The USR, as a consequence, played a much smaller part on the political scene in the first half of 1917. Its influence on the predominantly peasant masses of the Ukrainian population, however, was considerably stronger than a mere survey of the political balance of power in the Rada would indicate. The USR formulae for the solution of the agricultural problem, headed by demands for the nationalization of land and the establishment of a Ukrainian Land Fund, were very popular in the village, and assured the party the sympathy of the peasants.

The USD and the USR, as well as most other, minor, Ukrainian parties of the period, agreed on the need for extensive Ukrainian territorial autonomy. At first they were disposed to wait for the All-Russian Constituent Assembly to formulate and ratify officially the right of the Ukrainians to self-rule, but before long their demands became more urgent. This development was largely due to the pressure of the Ukrainian soldiers and peasants.

As soon as the news of the February Revolution had reached the Western Front, Ukrainian soldiers who previously had had no independent units but had fought side by side with the Russians, began to use the Ukrainian language and to form organizations based on the principle of territorial origin (*zemliachestva*). When the troops learned, a short time later, of the establishment of a Rada in Kiev, many Ukrainian officers and soldiers began to look to it for leadership and in some instances to consider themselves directly bound by orders issued by the Rada. All throughout the second half of March and the first half of April, Ukrainian soldiers stationed in Kiev held impromptu meetings demanding the formation of separate Ukrainian military units and the creation of a Ukrainian national army.[6] In the first half of April an all-volunteer regiment named after Bohdan Khmelnitskii, the Cossack leader of the seventeenth century, was formed in Kiev and sent to the front. The Ukrainian soldiers were strongly influenced by the example of Polish units which began to form at that time on the Southwestern front with the sanction of the Provisional Government, and were permeated with enthusiasm for Cossack ideals.

How violent was the nationalism which had taken hold of the soldiers became evident in the course of the First Ukrainian Military Congress which opened on May 5. During the debates, the speakers attacked the Provisional Government for its failure to treat the Ukraine on equal terms with Poland and Finland, to both of which it had promised independence, and for ignoring demands of the Ukrainians to form military units on their own soil. Some voices were raised in favor of Ukrainian independence and separate representation at the future peace conferences. The general tone of the sessions was so extremely nationalistic that Vinnichenko, the delegate of the Rada and a leading member of the USD, felt forced to plead with the delegates to remain loyal to the Russian democracy which had given the Ukraine its present freedom. Vinnichenko's suggestion that the Congress elect Petliura as its chairman was turned down on the grounds that the Rada, for which he spoke, had taken no part in convoking the Military Congress and consequently had no right to impose candidates on it. The Congress closed on May 8, with the resolution to send a delegation to the Petrograd Soviet to discuss the formation of Ukrainian regiments, and to establish a permanent Ukrainian General Military Committee (UGVK). The delegates recognized the Rada as the organ representing Ukrainian public opinion.[7] Several days after the Congress closed, the Ukrainian delegates to the Kiev Soviet of Soldiers' Deputies separated themselves into a distinct faction.

When the Ukrainian soldiers at the front learned of the decisions of the Military Congress, they too began to form national units, despite the remonstrations of Russian officers' and soldiers' committees. Among them, as among the Kievans, there was hope that the Rada would take care of their interests by terminating the fighting and helping the Ukrainians get their share of the land.[8] The behavior of the soldiers left no doubt about their impatience with the *status quo*. Anxious to win and retain the support of the Ukrainian troops, the Rada included in its platform their demand for the creation of national military units.

The Ukrainian peasantry also displayed nationalist sentiments. The soil in the Ukrainian provinces was better but less plentiful than in the central regions of Russia. The peasantry of these provinces had everything to gain if empowered to dispose of the local land according to its own wishes, and much to lose if compelled to abide by any likely future all-Russian solution of the land question. The Ukrainian village feared most of all having to share the property, which it looked forward to acquiring from the state, church, and large private owners, with the landless peasantry of the north. This desire to apportion the rich Ukrainian black earth independently of Russia, for the sole benefit of the local population, became a powerful factor in the development of nationalist sentiments among the Ukrainian rural masses. Under the influence of the USR they favored a land program providing for the nationalization of all land and the establishment of a Ukrainian Land Fund, with exclusive control over the land and the right to apportion it in accordance with the directives of a Ukrainian Diet (*Seim*). This formula presupposed a fairly wide degree of autonomy. At the Regional Congress of Soviets of Workers', Soldiers' and Peasants' Deputies (Kiev, April 22) the peasant section voted for the introduction of autonomy with provisions for land distribution which would benefit the local inhabitants.[9] At the First All-Ukrainian Peasant Congress (Kiev, May 28– June 2) similar resolutions were adopted, and pressure was applied upon the Rada to undertake more energetic steps toward Ukrainian self-rule.[10]

As the result of the intimate connection between peasant economic aspirations and the slogan of autonomy, the rural restlessness and impatience which in one way or another affected the villages throughout the entire Empire, assumed in the Ukraine nationalistic forms. The more eagerly the peasants demanded land, the more ardently they espoused the slogan of "autonomy now."

Early in June the Rada sent the Provisional Government a note containing a list of demands, calling for the recognition of the principle of Ukrainian autonomy, the separation of the twelve provinces with a predominantly Ukrainian population into a special administrative area, the appointment of a commissar for Ukrainian affairs, and, finally, the formation of a Ukrainian army.[11]

These demands placed the Provisional Government in a difficult position. In principle, most of the cabinet members were not opposed to autonomy for the non-Russian regions of the state. Alexander Kerensky, who had strong influence in the government, was actually identified with pro-Ukrainian sympathies, owing to his defense of Ukrainian rights in the prerevolutionary Dumas.[12] Upon the outbreak of the February Revolution the TUP had singled him out for special favor by sending him an individual message of congratulations, in recognition of his championship of the Ukrainian cause.[13] But the government was loath to make the kind of commitment the Rada had requested because of its general political philosophy, which forbade constitutional changes prior to the convocation of a Constituent Assembly. It also had specific objections. The government considered the Rada neither truly representative of the Ukraine, nor authorized to speak in its name. Furthermore, it feared also that the introduction of the national principle into the army would disorganize and weaken the country's armed forces at the very time when they were being readied for an all-out offensive against the enemy. Moved by such considerations, the Provisional Government turned down the requests of the Rada, suggesting that the questions which it had raised wait for the convocation of the All-Russian Constituent Assembly. Only the demand concerning the army met with a partly favorable reply. Petrograd agreed that something could be done for those Ukrainians who desired to serve under national banners, but on condition that the military authorities of the Kiev district give their approval to any scheme affecting the organization of the army.[14]

This action of the cabinet was favorably received by Russian and Jewish elements in the Ukraine, which were becoming very concerned, if not alarmed, by the behavior of the Ukrainians. The principal non-Ukrainian parties of that region, from the most conservative to the most radical, roundly condemned the actions of the Rada. The IKSOOO and the Kiev Soviet alike expressed approval of the Provisional Government's reply.[15]

On Ukrainian political circles, however, the effect of the cabinet decision was quite different. Infuriated by what they considered an insolent refusal of their modest demands, and convinced that it foreshadowed the attitude of Russian ruling circles toward the whole question of Ukrainian self-rule, they decided to challenge the authority of Petrograd. The government reply had reached Kiev shortly before the Ukrainian Peasant Congress was to close. At the last session Hrushevskii read to the agitated audience the message from the capital and concluded with these menacing words: "We have finished celebrating the holiday of the Revolution, and now we have entered into its most dangerous period, one which threatens with major destruction and disorder. We must prepare to resist effectively any hostile attack . . . I greet you, brothers, and repeat that, come what may, there will be a free autonomous Ukraine." [16] The peasant delegates voted on the spot to disregard the government order and to take steps for the immediate introduction of autonomy.

At the same time as Petrograd turned down the Rada's petition, it refused to grant the UGVK permission to convene a Second Ukrainian Military Congress. Enraged Ukrainian soldiers held protest meetings and urged the Rada to act on its own, without reference to the government. Acting in defiance of Petrograd, the UGVK resolved to proceed with its plans, and set June 5 as the date for the opening of the congress.

On June 10 the Rada issued an official manifesto, the so-called First Universal,* in which, addressing itself to the entire Ukrainian people, it announced that the Ukraine would henceforth decide its own fate and, without separating itself from Russia, take all the necessary measures to maintain order and to distribute the land lying within its borders. The Rada reasserted its claim to the exclusive representation of the Ukrainian national will and imposed upon the Ukrainian society a special tax, the proceeds from which were to be used to pay for the Rada's administrative functions. From the juridical point of view the First Universal was a highly questionable document, but this was a period when juridical considerations were far from uppermost in people's minds, and in Kiev it was received by the Ukrainian population with great emotion, bordering on religious reverence.[17]

During the second half of June the Rada underwent a series of internal structural transformations from which it emerged equipped with the apparatus of a full-fledged government. Its membership was broadened to include not only Ukrainian organizations, such as the Congress of Ukrainian Workers, but also to leave room for the non-Ukrainian population of the region over which it claimed jurisdiction. In this manner, the Rada evolved from a national into a territorial institution. Next a Small Rada, consisting of forty-five members representing the various elements united in the Rada, was formed. The Small Rada

---

* "Universals" were originally decrees issued by Polish monarchs; in the seventeenth century this term was adopted by the Hetmans of the Cossack Host.

was to sit permanently and to perform legislative functions when its parent body was not in session. Finally, a General Secretariat was created: an executive organ similar to a ministry to carry out the decisions of the Rada. Vinnichenko (USD) was appointed its Chairman and Secretary of Interior, with most of the remaining posts going to Ukrainian Social Democrats and Ukrainian Socialist Revolutionaries. Plans were also made to organize a vast network of provincial radas to work with the Central Rada in Kiev and under its aegis.

An anomalous situation was thus created. The Rada, though it professed loyalty to the Russian Government and denied all intention to separate, had in reality disobeyed the regime and established a *de facto* government, which claimed considerable authority over a section of the republic. The precise extent of the Rada's claims was very uncertain, and its leaders did nothing to correct that situation. But it was clear that the authority of the Provisional Government had been seriously challenged.

The developments transpiring in the latter half of June threw panic into the ranks of local non-Ukrainians. For a time rumors that the Rada was planning a coup were circulating in town.[18] The IKSOOO endeavored to sound out Ukrainian politicians about their intentions but it failed to arrive at a *modus vivendi* with the Rada. The Rada delegates insisted that the price for their coöperation was unqualified recognition on the part of the non-Ukrainian groups united in the IKSOOO that the Rada alone represented the Ukrainian people.[19]

After the establishment of the General Secretariat the conflict between the Rada and the Provisional Government had reached a very dangerous point. Since neither of the protagonists, however, felt strong enough to settle the outstanding issues by force, negotiations were opened to seek a solution to the impasse. On June 28 a delegation of governmental leaders composed of Kerensky, Irakly Tseretelli, and M. I. Tereshchenko arrived in Kiev. After three days of prolonged and often acrimonious discussions, an agreement was reached and presented for approval of the government in Petrograd. The terms were embodied in the resolution of the Provisional Government on the Ukrainian Question of July 3, 1917. An excerpt follows:

> Having heard the report of the Ministers Kerensky, Tereshchenko, and Tseretelli on the Ukrainian question, the Provisional Government has accepted the following resolution: to appoint, in the capacity of a higher organ of administration of regional affairs in the Ukraine, a separate organ, a General Secretariat, the composition of which will be determined by the government in agreement with a Ukrainian Central Rada augmented on a just basis with democratic organizations representing other nationalities inhabiting the Ukraine. The Provisional Government will put into effect measures concern-

ing the life of the region and its administration by means of the above defined organ.

While it considers that the questions of the national political organization of the Ukraine and the methods of solving the land question there must be settled by the Constituent Assembly within the framework of a general decree concerning the transfer of land into the hands of the toilers, the Provisional Government views with sympathy the idea of the preparation by the Ukrainian Central Rada of a project concerning the national political status of the Ukraine in accordance with what the Rada itself conceives as the interests of the region, and of a project for the solution of the land question, for presentation to the Constituent Assembly.[20]

This agreement, although in the nature of a compromise, represented a substantial victory for the Rada, above all because it recognized by implication what the Rada had until then in vain claimed: that it was an institution authorized to speak for the Ukrainian people. The majority of the Kadet ministers of the Provisional Government refused to give their approval to the document and resigned from the cabinet in protest.

For the time being an open break between Russian and Ukrainian political circles was avoided. But the rising temper of Ukrainian nationalist emotions and the rapid weakening of the government's ability to resist onslaughts upon its authority made it questionable whether the makeshift solution arrived at in July could last for any length of time.

### From July to the October Revolution in the Ukraine

The Ukrainian national leaders, having compelled the Provisional Government to grant them administrative powers, were now free to demonstrate their political abilities. In fact, however, the Rada and its General Secretariat failed miserably to take advantage of their June triumph. The four months separating the June agreement from the October Revolution was a period of progressive disintegration of the Ukrainian national movement, marked by indecision, by internal quarrels, by unprincipled opportunism, and above all, by an ever-widening gulf between the masses of the population and the politicians who aspired to represent them.

During the first half of 1917 the Ukrainian political parties — the USD's, the USR's, and other groups — were, for all their ideological differences, in close agreement, because the struggle for autonomy against the Provisional Government had provided a bond. But once this struggle was over and positive steps were required, the harmony which had prevailed when the Rada had been in its formative stage gave way to internal wrangling. Furthermore, each party was pulled apart by a progressive hardening of tendencies, by a polarization of left and right wings, which considerably hampered effective action on the part of the Ukrainian national institutions.

It is difficult to obtain a clear picture of the history of the Ukrainian parties during this period. They were of relatively recent origin and had formed under conditions of rapid revolutionary change. Their leaders were for the most part young and inexperienced. They had little contact with public opinion, and, as a consequence, the activities of the parties often reflected not so much the political realities of the country as the personal relations and ideas of the small group of people who took charge of the political organizations. This largely accounts for the confusing vacillations of the Ukrainian parties in the third quarter of 1917.

The USD's continued to maintain effective control over the General Secretariat despite their small organized following. Their aims were primarily political and they paid little attention to the growing agrarian unrest in the Ukraine. Vinnichenko, of the USD, remained Chairman of the General Secretariat throughout most of its existence, and the majority of his colleagues also belonged to this party. The USD's dominated, by their eloquence and organizational skill, the Ukrainian soldiers' and workers' congresses which were held throughout 1917. In the second half of the year the party began to split into two factions: one, led by Vinnichenko, urged a more conciliatory attitude toward the Provisional Government and a policy of moderation; another, dominated by Porsh, demanded a more radical course and closer ties with Russian extreme socialist groups hostile to Petrograd.

As the year progressed, the USR's displayed growing dissatisfaction with USD control of the executive organs of the Rada. They began to charge that the USD influence was much greater than its popular following warranted, and that the party paid lip-service to socialism while in effect concentrating almost exclusively on the attainment of political ends. The USR's were more radically inclined than their rivals, and felt that, with the spread of the revolution, socio-economic activities should take precedence over politics; yet they possessed neither the personnel nor the political skill to wrest control of the Secretariat away from the USD's. The conflict between the two leading parties broke into the open in the middle of July, when the USR's walked out of the USD-dominated Ukrainian Workers' Congress because it had refused to adopt their formula for the solution of the land problem. Relations between the two groups continued to worsen during the latter half of July.

At the beginning of August the growing interparty strife brought about a crisis. Vinnichenko and his colleagues who favored a moderate attitude toward Petrograd resigned from the General Secretariat, and the USR's announced that they would boycott a new Secretariat if it were again formed by the USD's. Until the end of the month frantic attempts were made to find suitable replacements, all of which failed, either because those political figures who were appointed were found unacceptable to the Rada, or because those whom the Rada had found acceptable refused to take the proffered posts. Finally, at the end of August a new cabinet, without USR's, who, while continuing their boycott agreed not to vote against it, was formed by Vinnichenko and approved by Petrograd.

The popular following of the Ukrainian parties in the urban areas was not large enough to render them effective. Elections held in Ukrainian cities and small towns for new city councils (*dumy*) at the end of July, showed that among them they controlled less than one-fifth of the urban electorate. In Kiev itself, the combined USD-USR ticket received 20 per cent of the total vote, as against 37 per cent cast for the ticket of the united Russian socialist parties, 15 per cent for the ticket of "Russian voters," a group hostile to the Ukrainian movement, 9 per cent for the Russian Kadets, and 6 per cent for the Bolsheviks.[21]

In twenty other towns (including Kharkov, Poltava, Ekaterinoslav, and Odessa,) the USD and USR parties, running separately from Russian parties, captured 13 per cent of the seats on the city councils, and on combined tickets with Russian socialist parties, an additional 15 per cent.[22] This showing was far from brilliant, and though their following was stronger in the rural areas, as the elections to the Constituent Assembly three months later were to indicate, the weakness of the Ukrainian parties in the politically crucial urban centers was to have an adverse effect on their whole future history.

One of the salient features of the Ukrainian movement at this period was the fact that its leaders, instead of consolidating their gains and establishing the sorely needed political machinery, preferred to squander their energies on fruitless quarrels with Petrograd over the scope of their authority. As a result of this misguided effort they wasted favorable occasions, lost further contact with the masses, and helped to weaken the liberal and middle-of-the-road socialist Russian forces, with which, in the ultimate analysis, their own interests were closely connected. When the crucial test came, early in 1918, they were quite incapable of defending their authority.

The agreement reached with Kerensky during his visit to Kiev had laid down general principles of the new administration of the Ukraine, but it did not specify with sufficient clarity the division of powers between the Rada and the Provisional Government. In the middle of July, Vinnichenko left for Petrograd to discuss the draft of a constitution which the Small Rada had prepared, and to arrive at a formal and more precise accord.[23] The Rada's interpretation of its powers was broad, considerably broader than Petrograd's. The new coalition government formed in the Russian capital at that time was more conservative than the government with which the Rada had signed the original agreement, and even less disposed to make immediate concessions to the Ukrainian nationalists. The representatives of the Ukrainian General Secretariat found, to their great dismay, that the government jurists appointed to deal with them wanted to limit their authority and interpreted the General Secretariat as a mere administrative organ of the Provisional Government rather than as an autonomous government. Arguments began to develop over the number of secretariats and provinces within the General Secretariat's jurisdiction. Angered by these unexpected difficulties, Vinnichenko returned to Kiev even before the talks were completed. On August 4, Petrograd issued a "Temporary Instruction of the Provisional Government to the General Secretariat of the Ukrainian Central Rada." This document, drafted by Baron B. E. Nolde and A. Ia. Galpern, consisted of nine points:

1. Until the time when the Constituent Assembly decides on the issue of local government, the General Secretariat, which is appointed by the Provisional Government at the suggestion of the Central Rada, shall function as the higher organ of the Provisional Government in matters of local administration of the Ukraine.

2. The authority of the General Secretariat is to extend over the provinces: Kiev, Volhynia, Podolia, Poltava, and Chernigov, with the exception of the counties: Mglinskii, Surazhskii, Starodubskii, and Novozybkovskii. It can also be extended over other provinces or their parts in the event that the provincial administrations (*zemskie upravleniia*) created in these provinces in accordance with directions of the Provisional Government shall express themselves in favor of such an extension.

3. The General Secretariat consists of general secretaries of the following departments: (*a*) internal affairs, (*b*) finances, (*c*) agriculture, (*d*) education, (*e*) trade and industry, (*f*) labor, and also of a General Secretary of nationalities and a General Clerk.

In addition, the General Secretariat includes, for the control of its affairs, a General Controller who participates in the meetings of the Secretariat with a right to a determinative vote.

Not less than four of the secretaries must be appointed from among persons belonging to nationalities other than Ukrainian.

The secretary for nationalities shall have three assistant secretaries, with provisions being made for each of the four of the most numerous nationalities of the Ukraine to have a representative either in the person of the Secretary or in one of his assistants.

4. The General Secretariat considers, works out and presents to the Provisional Government for approval projects which affect the life of the region and its administration. These projects may, prior to their submission to the Provisional Government, be presented for discussion to the Central Rada.

5. The sovereign rights of the Provisional Government in matters of local administration, which enter into the competence of the or-

gans outlined in Article 3, are exercised through the General Secretaries. More specific definition of these matters shall be given in a separate appendix.

6. In all matters, described in the aforesaid article, the local authorities of the region are to get in touch with the General Secretariat which, following communication with the Provisional Government, shall transmit the directives and orders of the latter to the local authorities.

7. The General Secretariat is to submit a list of nominees for the government positions described in Article 5 and they are to be appointed by order of the Provisional Government.

8. The relations between the higher governmental organs and individual civic authorities with the Secretariat and the individual secretaries, as well as the relations of the latter with higher governmental institutions and departments, are to take place through a separate Commissar of the Ukraine in Petrograd, appointed by the Provisional Government. Legislative suggestions and projects concerning only the local affairs of the Ukraine, as well as measures of importance for the whole state, which shall arise in the separate departments or shall be considered by interdepartmental and departmental commissions — when they demand, by virtue of special application to the Ukraine, the participation of the representative of the office of the Commissar on the aforesaid commissions — shall be treated in the same manner.

9. In urgent and unpostponable cases the higher governmental institutions and departments [shall] transmit their orders directly to the local authorities, informing simultaneously the Secretariat.

Prime Minister: Kerensky
Minister of Justice: Zarudnyi.[24]

This Instruction evoked great dissatisfaction in Ukrainian political circles. Many Ukrainians felt that the government had reneged on the July agreement by reducing the General Secretariat to the status of a mere administrative organ of the Provisional Government, and depriving the Rada of the broad powers which they thought the agreement had implied. Specific objections were made to the refusal of Petrograd to grant the Ukrainian organs jurisdiction over military affairs, supply, and means of communications, and to its limitation of Ukrainian rule to a mere five provinces instead of the entire twelve which had been claimed in the First Universal.[25] And yet, in fact the Instruction did not deviate from the June agreement which at the time had been very favorably received by the Rada.[26] It actually represented an important step forward in the development of Russian federalism. For the first time in history a Russian government had recognized the national principle as a basis for the administrative division of the state, and had ceded a part of its authority to an organ of self-rule formed along national-territorial lines.

The cooler heads in the Rada realized the importance of Petrograd's concession and the futility of fighting the Provisional Government for more power. "We have now received more than we had demanded two months ago," Vinnichenko told the Ukrainian critics of the Instruction in the course of debates in the Small Rada.[27] The General Secretariat and then the Small Rada finally accepted the Instruction, though under protest. During the following months, the bitterness over the Provisional Government's action remained, and at the first opportunity the General Secretariat appropriated the functions and territories of which it felt itself unjustly deprived.

The General Secretariat, however, did little if anything to exercise the authority which the Provisional Government through the Instruction had granted it. Above all, it failed to establish contact with the cities and villages of the Ukraine. Nothing came of the intention to establish provincial radas, and instead the countryside was dominated either by soviets, which had no responsibility to the General Secretariat, or by Free Cossack and Haidamak* units, which the rural population began to organize spontaneously for local self-defense and other, less meritorious purposes, such as looting. In August, at the conference of provincial representatives convened by the General Secretariat, nearly every speaker reported the prevalence of civic disorder and the complete collapse of local institutions in his region.[28] Dmytro Doroshenko, a member of the Small Rada and the head of one of the Ukrainian provinces, thus describes the work of the General Secretariat at this time:

> The General Secretary of Finance, Tugan-Baranovskii, left Kiev and did not return for two months, without even bothering to send any information concerning his whereabouts. Most of the secretariats did not know where to start, how to begin. There was not the slightest contact or communication with the provinces, even though this was not difficult to obtain, the more so because all five provincial commissars were our own people — Ukrainians . . . When finally in the middle of August (one and one-half months after the final approval of the General Secretariat!) V. Vinnichenko convened the congress of provincial and county commissars, somebody inquired: whose commissars were they: the Provisional Government's or the General Secretariat's?
>
> None of the General Secretaries ever appeared outside Kiev, despite resolutions of the General Secretariat to the contrary. To the provinces were sent neither orders, nor instructions, nor information, but only proclamations. Kiev would not even answer questions, and

---

* The term *Haidamak*, like many others in the Cossack vocabulary, is of Turkish origin; the Turkish verb *haydamak* means to pillage or ravage. *Haidamachestvo*, a form of banditry prevalent in the so-called Right Bank (i.e., Polish) Ukraine in the eighteenth century, combined violent anti-Catholicism and anti-Semitism with sheer brigandage.

provincial governors, coming to Kiev, could not without much trouble obtain personal interviews on urgent matters with the head of the Secretariat.[29]

Equally critical accounts of the General Secretariat's administrative performance were given by one of the heads of the USR, Khristiuk, and Vinnichenko himself had to admit that his critics were correct, although he attempted to justify himself by pointing to the desperate lack of means and personnel at his disposal.[*]

Moreover, the Ukrainian Rada and its organs were rapidly losing the sympathies of the Ukrainian population itself. Much of the support which the Rada had initially secured among the Ukrainian peasants and soldiers stemmed from popular dissatisfaction with the Provisional Government and especially with its procrastinating land policy. The population urged the Rada to obtain more authority, hoping that it would be utilized to put into effect the desired legislative measures. But since the Rada had failed to act, and by virtue of the June agreement had actually transformed itself into an organ of the Provisional Government, there was no longer the same compelling reason to support it. What could have been the purpose of wresting more authority from Petrograd, if it was to be placed at the disposal of Petrograd's own regional representative? The behavior of the USR's in the Small Rada during August and September, their protests against the General Secretariat's inactivity in the field of socio-economic reform, and their subsequent refusal to participate in the formation of a new Secretariat, reflected the dissatisfaction of the Ukrainian peasantry with the existing state of affairs. Nor were the Ukrainian workers happier. In mid-July the First All-Ukrainian Workers' Congress, convened in Kiev by the Rada, proved to be very critical of the existing Ukrainian institutions, and condemned the Rada for displaying "bourgeois" tendencies. In general, its whole temper was closer to that of the Bolsheviks than to the spirit fostered by the Ukrainian national parties to which most of the delegates belonged.[30] The same situation prevailed at the Third Congress of Peasants of the Kiev area held in September.[31]

Thus the Rada and its General Secretariat drifted aimlessly while the clouds of the impending October storm were gathering ever thicker over the entire country.

The relations of the Rada with the Bolshevik party, which was destined to come to power in Russia, represented a curious mixture of mutual hostility and attraction. From the point of view of long-range objectives the Ukrainian and Bolshevik movements not only had little

---

[*] See Vinnichenko's speech in the Small Rada on August 10, in Manilov, *1917 god,* 205. In later times Vinnichenko placed much of the blame for the inactivity of the Ukrainian institutions on the Provisional Government; see his *Vidrodzhennia natsii,* II (Kiev-Vienna, 1920), 40; Khristiuk, *Zamitky,* I, 110ff.

in common, but were essentially antagonistic. Whereas the Ukrainians, especially the USD's, were interested in promoting their national cause, the followers of Lenin wanted a world-wide revolution based on the principle of proletarian class interests, and fought all those who espoused nationalism. The "betrayal" of the USD in joining the Rada tended to confirm in the minds of the local Bolsheviks the "counterrevolutionary" role of nationalism and to reëmphasize the danger which it presented to their movement.[32] The Bolsheviks alone, of all the major parties in Kiev, refused to enter the Small Rada after the Provisional Government had issued its August Instruction. In other regions of the Ukraine, especially in the industrial areas of the East, where their party was stronger, the Bolsheviks simply did not take the Ukrainian movement into account and disregarded entirely the problems which it posed.[33] Piatakov, the actual boss of the Bolshevik party of the southwestern region centered in Kiev, who even before the Revolution had been known as an opponent of the temporary alliance with nationalism advocated by Lenin, stated bluntly the attitude of the local Bolsheviks in 1917:

> On the whole we must not support the Ukrainians, because their movement is not convenient for the proletariat. Russia cannot exist without the Ukrainian sugar industry, and the same can be said in regard to coal (Donbass), cereals (the black-earth belt), etc. . . .
> We have before us two tasks: to protest against the measures of the government, and especially those of Kerensky, on the one hand, and to fight against the chauvinistic strivings of the Ukrainians on the other.[34]

But the Bolsheviks were willing to use the Ukrainian movement insofar as it weakened the Provisional Government. Thus, as early as June 9, the Kiev Soviet of Workers' and Soldiers' Deputies was startled to hear a Bolshevik orator defend the right of the Ukrainians to seize power. A few days later, during a large parade organized by the Soviet, Bolshevik and Ukrainian participants moved away from the main body of demonstrators and marched side by side in their own separate columns.[35] At the same time, writing in the Russian Bolshevik press, Lenin came out in defense of the Ukrainian nationalists and echoed their charges against the Provisional Government, though he was careful to stress his opposition to separatism.[36]

Reciprocating, the Ukrainian organizations refused to support the Kiev Soviet and the non-Bolshevik parties in their condemnation of Lenin's abortive July coup in Petrograd. The July uprising, Vinnichenko stated at the time, presented no danger for the Ukraine.[37] "One has to admit," he added a few days later, "that if it were not for the Bolsheviks the revolution would not move ahead." [38]

In August and September, when the General Secretariat was functioning as an official organ of the Provisional Government, and the Small Rada admitted into membership various non-Ukrainian groups and parties, including Russian socialists whom the Bolsheviks were fighting, the relations between the two groups were less openly cordial. The Leninists went ahead with their own conspiratorial and demagogic work, but at the same time refrained from stepping on the toes of the Ukrainian nationalists, who were potentially useful to them. At the beginning of August the Bolsheviks even entered the Central Rada, though they still refused to join the more important Small Rada.[39] As is known from the memoirs of a prominent local Bolshevik leader, two attitudes towards the Ukrainians prevailed at that time within the ranks of the Kievan Bolshevik Committee.[40] There was a "left" view, which urged a direct, uncompromising attack on Ukrainian nationalism, and a "right" view, which wanted to exploit it; this was the beginning of a vital split within the Bolshevik movement in the Ukraine on the nationality question, which was to plague it for years to come.

In October, the Bolsheviks and the Ukrainian nationalists moved closer once more, again as a result of altercations between the latter and the Provisional Government.[41] Scarcely had the Small Rada accepted the Provisional Government Instruction (August 9), when the leaders of the Ukrainian parties began to demand a separate Constituent Assembly for the Ukraine. This notion found a lively echo among the masses, for it revived hopes that measures would be taken to apportion the land in a manner satisfactory to the local population and perhaps also to terminate the war.[42] But the more the Ukrainian leaders pressed this project, the worse became their relations with the Russian groups, who saw in it a further step toward anarchy and the decline of legitimate authority. And though nothing came of this idea — the General Secretariat, despite its violent insistence on its right to convene such an Assembly, had no power to bring it about — a new tug-of-war between Petrograd and Kiev got on its way. In the middle of October the government ordered the chairman of the General Secretariat to report to Petrograd to explain its activities. The impending crisis was resolved by the outbreak of the October Revolution.*

The new difficulties with the Provisional Government, as well as the growing radicalism of the populace, induced the USD's to veer left. At the party's Fourth Congress, held in September, the left-wingers, led by Porsh, persuaded the delegates to adopt a series of resolutions essentially identical with those advanced by the Bolsheviks. "In the entire country, as well as in the separate lands," one of the resolutions stated, "there must be established at once a homogeneous revolutionary democratic

* Vinnichenko charges in his memoirs that the Provisional Government wanted to lure the General Secretariat to Petrograd in order to place it under arrest (Vinnichenko, *Vidrodzhennia*, II, 59–60).

rule of the organized proletariat, peasantry, and soldiers." [43] This, in effect, was a demand for the cession of all power to the soviets. Other resolutions called for the termination of the "imperialist war," the transfer of control over public lands and large estates to local peasant committees, the establishment of government and worker control over factories, maximum taxation or confiscation of large capital, and finally, the transformation of the Russian Empire into a Federal Russian Republic.[44]

But it was only on the eve of the Bolshevik coup in Russia that the Ukrainian nationalists came out openly and actively in support of the Bolsheviks. On October 25, when reports from Russia brought the first news of an uprising in Petrograd, the Bolshevik deputies in the Kiev Soviet began to press for the creation of a Revolutionary Committee with which to seize power in the city. At the same time they entered into negotiations with the Ukrainians. The Kievan Bolsheviks were far too weak in Kiev and the remaining areas of the right-bank Ukraine to attempt singlehanded a seizure of power against the forces loyal to the government, and for that reason they felt compelled to arrive at some form of compromise with the Ukrainians. Vladimir Zatonskii, a leading Kievan Bolshevik and a participant in the negotiations, thus describes the agreement:

> The situation was such that the Central Rada was ready at this moment to support what appeared, from its viewpoint, the weaker side: the Petersburg Bolsheviks. Naturally, they wanted to support it cautiously, without compromising themselves in the eyes of the bourgeois world and without strengthening the position of the Bolsheviks in the Ukraine. At the same time the Central Rada was greatly interested in being recognized by the Bolsheviks, as it was obvious that without such recognition the Rada could not really become a regional center.
> The principal purpose of our entering [the Small Rada] was the formation of a united front against the Whites on the following conditions: the Central Rada assumed the responsibility for using its influence with the railroad personnel in order to prevent all the reactionary military units from leaving the confines of the Ukraine, including the Rumanian and southwestern fronts, for the suppression of the uprisings in Petrograd and Moscow. A detachment of Kiev cadets [*iunkers*] already on its way was to be stopped. All work in this direction was to be conducted by the joint efforts of the Rada and the Bolsheviks. We, on our part, agreed not to start an armed rebellion against the [pro-government] Staff in Kiev, but if the latter should initiate an attack, then each side obliged itself to come to the aid of the other against the Whites (no one doubted that in the face of this agreement between the Bolsheviks and the Central Rada, the Staff would not dare to lift a finger). The Central Rada, for its part,

undertook to observe a friendly neutrality towards the Bolshevik uprising in the north, and not to express itself against it anywhere in
any form.[45]

With this agreement in their pockets, the Bolsheviks joined the Small
Rada and sent delegates to the special Revolutionary Committee which
the Rada had formed.

The October agreement between the Reds and Ukrainians afterwards
gave rise to much controversy. Ukrainian nationalist writers prefer to
ignore this embarrassing chapter in their history, and so, perhaps, would
Bolshevik authorities, were it not for the fact that in the latter period of
the Revolution the Bolsheviks in the Ukraine split into two factions,
both of which utilized the record of the October days for purposes of
interparty polemics. On the face of it, the October agreement with the
Rada was extremely advantageous to the Bolsheviks: at the price of a
promise to call off an attack against the military forces loyal to the Provisional Government, which admittedly for lack of strength they could
not have undertaken anyway, they had secured the assistance of the
Rada in neutralizing pro-government troops throughout the southwestern
regions of the Russian Empire.

But as early as the next day (October 26), the right-wing Bolsheviks,
who had conducted the negotiations with the Ukrainians, had reason to
doubt the value of their compact with the Rada. At the meeting of the
Small Rada in which the Bolsheviks now participated, a debate arose
over the events of the previous day. Russian SR's and Mensheviks objected to the presence of the Bolsheviks and demanded to know what
had happened to account for their inclusion in the Revolutionary Committee of the Rada. A spokesman for the Ukrainians replied that the
Leninists had been admitted because they had promised not to seize
power in the Ukraine. Upon hearing these words Zatonskii, the Bolshevik representative, rose to his feet and heatedly protested that the conditions under which his party had agreed to join the Rada the previous
day were entirely different:

> The Central Rada not only did not condemn the Bolshevik move-
> ment but, on the contrary, it spoke of its ideological content, of its
> revolutionary character; it was stated that Bolshevism was the op-
> posite of the counterrevolutionary tendencies of the Provisional Gov-
> ernment. Yesterday it was said that the Central Rada was entirely
> indifferent to what was going on in Petrograd, that it cared only
> about the preservation of order in the Ukraine. I repeat, there was
> no censure. The only thing that had been said then was that the
> Central Rada could not subscribe to the slogan of "all power to the
> Soviets" . . . At yesterday's meeting of the Rada it was definitely
> said that if the Central Rada will not support the Bolshevik move-
> ment, then at any rate it will not oppose it. It was said that the Cen-

tral Rada will take all measures to prevent the sending of troops from the Ukraine for the suppression of the uprising [in Petrograd].[46]

The Bolsheviks, Zatonskii concluded, had joined the Rada only on this basis. No one challenged his memory, but a resolution condemning the Petrograd uprising was adopted, and as a consequence the Bolsheviks left the Small Rada.

The Bolsheviks decided now to proceed on their own with a seizure of power in Kiev. On the twenty-seventh they prevailed on the Soviet of Workers' Deputies (where they enjoyed a majority as they did not in the general Kievan Soviet), to form a separate Revolutionary Committee. But the actual military forces at their disposal were still very small, and it was unlikely that they could win without aid from the Ukrainians. For this reason the Bolsheviks did not completely break with the Rada, but left the door open for further coöperation based on the agreement of two days before, hoping that at a critical moment the Rada would change its mind and come to their assistance.[47]

On October 28, while the rebels were readying for action, pro-government troops surrounded their headquarters, and arrested the entire Bolshevik Revolutionary Committee. Immediately other pro-Bolshevik units, located on the outskirts of the city, began to shoot and attack.

At this critical moment the Rada finally decided to throw its forces into the struggle on the side of the Bolsheviks. On October 29, it issued an ultimatum to the headquarters of the armies of the Provisional Government in Kiev, demanding the immediate release of the arrested Bolshevik leaders from the Revolutionary Committee and the withdrawal from Kiev of all reinforcements which the government had brought into the city during the previous weeks to suppress the anticipated Bolshevik coup.[48] At the same time, Ukrainian patrols occupied strategic points in the city, and prevented pro-government units from liquidating the centers of rebel resistance.

Faced with the hostility of the Ukrainians, the Kievan Staff had no choice but to capitulate. Two days later, representatives of the Staff met with emissaries of the Rada, and accepted their terms.[49] The arrested Bolsheviks were released, and the Staff left the city with its troops. The rule of the Provisional Government in the center of the Ukraine thus came to an end through the joint efforts of the Ukrainian Central Rada and the Bolsheviks.

While the fighting for the city was still in progress, the General Secretariat took steps to enlarge the scope of its authority. Several secretariats, previously vetoed by the Provisional Government, were added, and an announcement was made to the effect that the jurisdiction of the Rada extended over additional provinces.[50]

In other cities of the Ukraine the Rada and its Secretariat did not play the same critical role as in Kiev, because their provincial organizations were insignificant. This was the case in the smaller towns of the Kiev province;[51] in the Kherson province, including the city of Odessa;[52] in the Ekaterinoslav province;[53] and in the Chernigov province.[54] Effective rule over these areas was assumed, soon after the outbreak of the October Revolution, by the local soviets without significant intervention of the Ukrainian groups. In other areas where they were politically more influential, the Ukrainian parties — USD and USR alike — followed the example set by the Kievans and aided the Bolsheviks. In Kharkov, the USD's and USR's entered the Bolshevik-controlled Revolutionary Committee and helped overthrow the local authorities.[55] In Poltava the USD's even suggested a merger with the Bolsheviks in the fall of 1917, and though this idea fell through, they and the USR's sided with the Bolsheviks during the October Revolution.[56] In the city of Ekaterinoslav (Dnepropetrovsk) the USD's reached an agreement with the Bolsheviks, by virtue of which they offered to accept the rule of the local soviet in return for Bolshevik recognition of the Central Rada's Revolutionary Committee.[57]

### Belorussia in 1917

When the February Revolution took place, the Belorussian national movement was still in its embryonic stage. There was only one Belorussian political party: the Hromada, which had a very small organized following and was unknown to the masses of the population. At the time of the first postrevolutionary Belorussian conference, held in Minsk on March 15, 1917, the Hromada mustered only 15 followers.[58] Political life in the Belorussian lands was dominated by Russian and Jewish socialist parties. There is no evidence that in 1917 the peasantry, which composed the mass of the Belorussian people, possessed any consciousness of ethnic separateness.

An important element in the history of this movement in 1917 was the fact that Belorussia was a battleground, with its western half occupied by German and Polish armies, and its eastern half occupied by Russian troops. The political fortunes of the Belorussians were almost entirely dependent on the attitude of the combatants.

In March, at the Belorussian conference, a Belorussian National Committee composed of representatives of all the ethnic groups and all the social classes of the territory, was organized. This committee prepared a statement which was submitted to the Provisional Government for consideration. In its essential points the statement followed the program of the SR's, who had assumed the leadership of the Belorussian cause and exercised within it a dominant ideological influence. The committee demanded the establishment of federal relations in Russia, and the granting of an autonomous status to Belorussia.[59]

In the summer the Hromada gained the upper hand in the National Committee and steered it toward a more radical course. The committee held a second Belorussian conference in July, at which, under the impression of events taking place in the Ukraine, a Belorussian Rada was established.[60] The main goal of the Rada was to realize an agrarian policy modeled after that of the Russian Socialist Revolutionary Party. It specifically excluded landowners from the right to participate in its activities. The Rada took charge of the Belorussian soldier organizations which were being formed at the western front, and early in October, after merging with the Belorussian Military Council, renamed itself the Great Belorussian Rada.

The Bolshevik party on Belorussian territory was inconspicuous in the first half of the year. It was officially organized in Minsk at the end of May[61] by Bolsheviks of prewar standing who had been drafted and served at the time of the Revolution in the ranks of the Western Army.[62] The Bolsheviks concentrated their agitation and propaganda efforts on the Russian soldiers at the western front, and as the soldiers grew more and more war-weary, Bolshevik influence increased. The Leninist slogans of peace had great success among the troops, especially after the failure of the summer offensive undertaken by the Provisional Government in the West. In the fall of 1917, the Bolshevik party in Minsk grew at a meteoric rate: 2,530 members at the end of August; 9,190 in the middle of September; 28,508 members and 27,856 candidates at the beginning of October.[63] The Minsk Committee then reorganized itself as the Northwestern Committee of the Russian Social Democratic Labor Party (Bolshevik), with authority over the party cells located on the territories coinciding with today's Lithuania and Belorussia. The party membership was almost exclusively Russian and military in composition, with some following among the Jewish urban population. It had virtually no contact with the Belorussian inhabitants.[64]

The destruction of the Provisional Government by the Bolsheviks, and the disintegration of the anti-Bolshevik socialist parties which followed it, left the political field in Belorussia to two parties: the Bolsheviks, who controlled large parts of the Russian Army, and the Belorussian Rada, which had some influence among the native soldiers and the intelligentsia.

In early November, the Bolshevik leaders in Petrograd issued directives to the Northwestern Committee to form a Soviet government and to assume power over their territory. Carrying out this order, the local Bolsheviks organized an Executive Committee and a Council of Commissars of the Western Region (*Obliskomzap*), and demanded that all organizations situated in the provinces adjoining Minsk subordinate themselves to those organs.[65] The question of relations with the Rada was left, for the time being, open.

The elections to the Constituent Assembly on Belorussian territory gave the Bolsheviks a considerable victory, owing mainly to the soldier vote. The Belorussian national party failed to elect a single candidate. At the (western) front the Bolsheviks obtained 66.9 per cent, and the SR's 18.5 per cent of the votes. In the Minsk district the Bolsheviks obtained 63.1 per cent, the SR's 19.8 per cent, the Mensheviks and Bundists 1.7 per cent, and the Hromada a mere 0.3 per cent of all the votes.[66] In the city of Minsk the Hromada polled 161 votes out of 35,651 votes cast.[67]

On December 14 the Hromada convened in Minsk a Belorussian National Congress to discuss the problems created by the Bolshevik coup. In attendance were nearly 1,900 deputies, among them a large proportion of anti-Communist Russians. The Congress debated the political future largely from the point of view of the effect which the establishment of the new authority in Petrograd was likely to have on the whole country. Finally, on the night of December 17–18, under circumstances that are completely unclear, the Congress proclaimed the independence of Belorussia.

It may be questioned to what extent this Congress, or that part of it which passed the resolution establishing the republic, represented the wishes of the people over whom it claimed authority. One month earlier the Hromada, participating in the elections to the Constituent Assembly on a platform of autonomy, had polled a mere 29,000 votes in an area populated by several million; how much would it have obtained had its program been nationally more radical? At any rate, the separation of Belorussia in 1917 was an ephemeral act, devoid for the time being of political significance. Unlike the nationalists in the Ukraine and in some other regions of the Russian Empire, the Belorussian nationalists lacked a popular following. Only in the period of the Civil War and the ensuing period of Soviet rule did their movement mature and the act of separation acquire political and psychological importance.

## The Moslem Borderlands

### The All-Russian Moslem Movement

Political life among the Russian Moslems, which matured rapidly in the atmosphere of freedom prevailing in 1917, showed three principal tendencies. On the extreme right were the religious groups, composed of the orthodox Moslem clergy and the wealthiest elements of Moslem society, especially from Turkestan. Their social and political ideas were conservative, paralleling in some respects the views of the Russian Octobrists. These groups were relatively weak on an all-Russian scale, but in some areas, notably the Northern Caucasus and parts of Central Asia, where Moslem orthodoxy was still deeply rooted in popular consciousness and the religious leaders enjoyed great respect, the right wing played an important role. The center group was liberal. Its leaders came from the ranks of the Ittifak; they were westernized, and in their political and social ideologies associated closely with the Russian Kadets, although due to the uncompromising attitude of the Kadets toward the Ottoman Empire, and particularly their insistence on the annexation of the Straits, the Moslem liberals had cooled considerably toward them since the outbreak of the First World War. On the left were the young Moslem intellectuals, who, in addition to subscribing to the secularism and Westernism of the liberals, were also imbued with the ideals of socialism, largely of the Socialist Revolutionary type. At the beginning of the Revolution it was the liberals who assumed leadership over the Moslem movement, partly by virtue of their greater political experience derived from participation in the Dumas. But in the latter half of the year, as the entire country moved toward the left, and as the liberal elements with which the centrists were associated lost authority in Russia, the leadership passed to the radically inclined nationalists.

The All-Russian Moslem movement, which endeavored to unite the sixteen million Moslems in Russia on the basis of religious identity, was from its very inception in the hands of the Moslem liberals. It was essentially a reform movement, whose chief purpose was the secularization and democratization of Moslem life in Russia. Its political aims were moderate and less emphasized.

In April 1917 the Moslem faction of the Russian Duma held a special conference at which it decided to convene an All-Russian Moslem Congress in Moscow at the earliest opportunity. The Duma deputies discussed the norms of representation and issued directives to Moslem organizations throughout the country to make the necessary preparations. In the second half of April, Moslems in all parts of the Russian Empire held provincial conferences and elected deputies for the Moscow session.

The First All-Russian Moslem Congress opened formally on May 1. On hand were about one thousand delegates, including two hundred women. The very first day passed in violent quarrels. Some deputies from Turkestan and the Northern Caucasus objected at the outset to the presence of women, as contrary to the usages of Moslem religion and unbecoming to what they considered the dignity of the occasion. When the subject of female emancipation was presented for discussion, the same deputies, largely clergymen, tried to shout down all speakers advocating legislation in favor of Moslem women, such as equal rights to inheritance, the removal of the veils, enactments prohibiting bigamy and the marriage of minors. But the westernized intelligentsia, with the assistance of the small liberal wing of the clergy, succeeded eventually in defeating the opponents of emancipation, and resolutions proclaiming equal rights for women were passed. This was an event of great historic significance. Russian Moslems were the first in the world to free women from the restrictions to which they had been traditionally subjected in Islamic societies.

The Congress next took steps to form a new religious administration. In tsarist Russia there had been no unified body to serve all the Moslems, and the Mufti of Orenburg, the spiritual head of the so-called Moslems of Inner Russia (i.e., the Volga-Ural region, Siberia, and the central provinces of Russia proper), had traditionally been appointed by the Emperor at the suggestion of the Minister of Interior. This procedure was now changed. The Congress appropriated the right to religious self-rule by appointing a new Mufti, Alimdzhan Barudi, a progressive associated with the jadidist movement and the Ittifak party from the beginning of the century, and by electing a Religious Administration (*Dukhovnoe Upravlenie*) — the nucleus around which the Moslems of the other parts of the Russian Empire were expected with time to gather.

The third topic on the agenda was the national question. Here two divergent viewpoints at once emerged. One group of deputies, dominated by the Volga Tatars, desired the preservation of the administrative unity of the Russian Empire and the solution of the nationality question by means of national-cultural autonomy. This position was taken by the deputies associated with the Russian Kadet and Social Democratic parties, both of which opposed federalism. The prevalence of Volga Tatars in this group can be partly explained by the fact that this nationality had no separate territory of its own, but lived scattered among Russians and Bashkirs: national-cultural autonomy was therefore well suited to meet its particular situation and to preserve the position of leadership which it had attained among Russian Moslems. A contrary proposal was advocated by a leader of the Azerbaijani delegation, Mehmed Emin Resul-zade, with the support of the Bashkirs and the Crimean Tatars. He and his backers favored federalism with territorial self-rule for each nationality. The Congress voted 446 to 271 for the second, the federalist, proposal:

> The form of government which is most capable of protecting the interests of the Moslem peoples is a democratic republic based on the national, territorial, and federal principles, with national-cultural autonomy for the nationalities which lack a distinct territory.
>
> For the regulation of the common spiritual and cultural problems of the Moslem peoples of Russia and for the purpose of coördinating their activities, there is established a central All-Moslem organ for all Russia, with legislative functions in this sphere. The form of this organ, its composition as well as its functions, shall be determined by

a constituent assembly (*Kurultai*) of the representatives of all the autonomous regions.[68]

Before closing, the Congress appointed a National Central Council or *Shura* (*Millî merkezî şûra*) to represent the Empire's Moslems in the Russian capital and to prepare legislative projects resulting from the Congress' decisions for submission to the All-Russian Constituent Assembly. Akhmed Tsalikov (Tsalykkaty), a North Caucasian Menshevik (Ossetin by nationality) was elected to the chairmanship of the Council. In the summer of 1917 the Council prepared a memorandum, in which it urged that the portfolio of agriculture and top positions in several other ministries of a future Russian democratic government be given to Moslems.[69]

The May Congress demonstrated beyond doubt that the leadership of the Moslem movement in Russia was firmly in the hands of westernized, secularized groups of the center and the left, and that, whatever the issues dividing them, Russian Moslems (at least their politically active elements) did have a sense of unity and of a community of interests which made joint activity possible.

The Second Moslem Congress met in Kazan on July 21. The political horizon in Russia was cloudy. This Congress, augmented by delegates of the three other Moslem congresses — Military, Spiritual, and Lay — taking place simultaneously in Kazan, decided to proceed at once with the realization of the second part of the resolution on the nationality question adopted at the First Congress, and to provide Russian Moslems with autonomous cultural organs. A committee was appointed to put all the necessary measures in this direction into effect.[70]

The Second Congress was more radically inclined in social questions than the First. Its platform for elections to the Constituent Assembly included, in addition to the national program of the First Congress, demands for the nationalization of all land and the introduction of an eight-hour working day. The Congress decided that an All-Moslem Democratic Socialist Bloc, which was to compete in the elections on this platform, would form a separate Moslem Faction at the Constituent Assembly.[71]

On November 20, 1917, the Commission, appointed by the Kazan Congress, convened in Ufa a National Assembly, or *Millî Medzhilis* (*Millî Meclis*). This Assembly elected three ministries: religion, education, and finances, to assume responsibility over the three main functions of national-cultural autonomy for the Moslems of Inner Russia. In this manner the first part of the May resolution was realized: the second — federalism — was to await the All-Russian Constituent Assembly.

Thus, by the time the Bolsheviks came to power, Russian Moslems had acquired the rudiments of a state-wide religious and cultural administration. The movement, which had culminated in the Medzhilis, evoked great enthusiasm among Russian Moslem intellectuals, many of whom viewed it as a beginning of a great Islamic revival not only in Russia but outside its borders as well. From the political point of view, however, the All-Russian Moslem movement was weak. With the rapid disintegration of the Russian state, the scattered regions inhabited by Russian Turks were separated one from another. The Crimea, Central Asia, the Northern Caucasus, and Azerbaijan followed their own ways. The Medzhilis and the entire political tendency which it symbolized came to represent, before long, little more than a small group of Volga Tatar political figures. As such, its chances of survival were small, because, unlike other Turks who resided in borderland regions, the Volga Tatars inhabited the center of the Empire, surrounded by Russians and other non-Moslem ethnic groups. To make matters worse for them, the Bashkirs, resenting the domination of the Tatars and their unwillingness to recognize the Bashkirs as a distinct people, separated themselves from the Medzhilis and proclaimed their own republic.[72]

### The Crimea in 1917

The first Crimean Tatar conference met in Simferopol in March 1917. Its resolutions called for the nationalization and distribution of all the so-called vakuf (vakïf) lands (properties given in usufruct to the Moslem clergy) and the establishment of popular control over Moslem religious institutions [73] Chelibidzhan Chelibiev (Celebi Celibiev), a young lawyer educated in Constantinople, who had served as chairman of the conference, was elected Mufti of the Crimean Tatars.* Chelibiev, like many other local Moslem leaders, belonged to the Crimean Tatar National Party (Milli Firka), founded in July 1917 by a group of young intellectuals, most of whom had been educated in Turkey and in Western Europe.[74] The party's program asked for the federalization of Russia, cultural autonomy for the minorities, and the nationalization of all church and private lands.[75] Until 1920, when the Crimea was definitely Sovietized, the Milli Firka enjoyed virtual control over the political life of the Tatar population, which neither the right-wing clergy nor the liberals, the followers of Gasprinskii, could effectively challenge. In September 1917, when the Tatar clergy — which opposed the Milli Firka's land program — held a conference in Bakhchisarai, the Milli Firka ordered it closed.[76]

The relations of the Tatar nationalists with the local Russian elements were not as good as the Tatars might have wished, considering that the

* Since the last decade of the eighteenth century Russia had two Muftis, one in Orenburg, for the Moslems of Inner Russia, and another in the Crimea, for the Moslems of the Taurida Province and the Western regions. For this reason in 1917 the Moslems of those two areas elected their separate Muftis. The Moslems of Central Asia had no common religious leader.

Russians (and Ukrainians) on the peninsula outnumbered them two to one.* The chief source of friction between the two ethnic groups was the fact that, among the Russian inhabitants of the Crimea, the strongest and best organized political party in the first half of 1917 were the Kadets, whom the Tatars disliked for their support of the wartime agreements between Russia and the Entente concerning the Ottoman Empire. In June and July 1917 the Tatars and the Kadet-dominated administration of the Crimea entered into a direct conflict. The Tatars began to demand the immediate transfer to their own organizations of control over all Moslem schools in the Crimea and also asked to be given the right to form a native military regiment. The government refused these demands and arrested Mufti Chelibiev at the end of July, and although the incident was quickly terminated by his release and the granting of both Tatar demands, it did much to alienate the Tatars from the democratic regime.[77]

Relations with the Russian socialist parties were somewhat better, largely because the Milli Firka shared with them some radical ideals, but the cultural gap separating the Russians from the Tatars was too wide to permit friendship. The Crimean Soviets did not interfere in the work of the Milli Firka and its congresses, and the latter, in turn, did not participate in the Soviets. "The Soviet had no definite policy on the nationality question. It conducted no work among the minorities. It had no representatives of the minorities among its personnel. It took no part in the formation of minority organizations whatsoever," wrote one Bolshevik observer.[78]

The Bolsheviks began to play an important role in Crimean politics toward the end of the year. The first Bolshevik organizations in the Crimea were formed in June and July 1917, partly under the influence of Baltic Fleet sailors who had been sent there from Petrograd for purposes of agitation, and partly as a result of the skillful work of an able party organizer, Zhan (Jean) Miller, dispatched to the Crimea by the Bolshevik Central Committee.[79] Bolshevik strength was concentrated in Sebastopol. A port city, serving as the chief naval base for the entire Russian Black Sea Fleet, Sebastopol had a large non-resident population composed of sailors and soldiers responsive to Bolshevik peace slogans. In the middle of the summer, the Bolshevik party there had 250 members, a poor showing in comparison with the 27,000 SR's and 4,500 Mensheviks, but an important nucleus for future revolutionary work.[80] Bolshevik strength in other towns of the peninsula was insignificant; a few railroad

* The Tatars constituted in 1897 34.1 per cent, in 1921 25.7 per cent of the total population of the Crimea; the Russians and Ukrainians (there are no separate statistics for the two groups) 45.3 and 51.5 per cent. The remainder of the population consisted of Jews, Germans, Greeks, Poles, and Armenians (S. A. Usov, *Istoriko-ekonomicheskie ocherki Kryma* [Simferopol, 1925], 29).

workers in Feodosiia, thirty-five members in Yalta, the workers of one factory in Simferopol.[81]

By October 1917 the Russian sailors in Sebastopol and the Tatar military formations presented the only effective force on the peninsula. As Bolshevik influence in Sebastopol increased, the Tatar nationalists moved closer to Russian liberal and socialist groups.

The news of the Bolshevik coup in Russia was unfavorably received by all the Russian socialist parties in the Crimea, including the local Bolshevik organizations, which, at the First All-Crimean Party Conference in November 1917, condemned Lenin's overthrow of the Provisional Government.[82] The Sebastopol Soviet did likewise.[83] At the end of November the Bolshevik Central Committee dispatched to Sebastopol another delegation of heavily armed Baltic sailors who took command of the situation and rallied behind them the more radically inclined local personnel. On December 24 the Bolsheviks loyal to Lenin walked out of the Sebastopol Soviet and organized a Revolutionary Committee. This committee, with the help of the Baltic sailors, arrested and executed summarily a considerable number of naval officers and several of the important SR and Menshevik leaders [84] Several days later it compelled the Executive Committee of the Soviet to resign. This coup against the Soviet gave the Bolsheviks mastery of the city.

In the meantime, the Tatar nationalists, watching anxiously the deterioration of public order in the Crimea, decided to act. On November 26 they convened in Bakhchisarai a Tatar Constituent Assembly (*Kurultai*). Elected on the basis of a broad franchise of all adult male and female Tatars in the Crimea, the Kurultai assumed legislative authority in matters pertaining to the internal administration of Crimean Tatars. It appointed as military commander of all Tatar military units garrisoned in various towns of the peninsula Dzhafer Seidamet (Cafer Seydahmet), a member of the Milli Firka. Next, it adopted a "Crimean constitution," modeled after Western democratic prototypes, which introduced civil equality and secular principles, and abolished, among other things, the inequality of Moslem women and the titles of the Tatar nobility.[85] It also appointed a five-man National Directory, with Chelibiev as Chairman, and Seidamet as Minister of Foreign Affairs and of War. Thus the Kurultai established Tatar territorial self-rule and created a *de facto* Tatar government in the Crimea.

With the Sebastopol Bolsheviks aspiring to authority also, it was only a question of time before the two groups clashed.

*Bashkiriia and the Kazakh-Kirghiz Steppe*

In the steppe regions of the southern Urals and the northern and eastern parts of Central Asia (today's Kirghiz SSR, Kazakh SSR, and Chkalov province) the course of the entire Revolution and Civil War was deeply influenced by a traditional conflict between the native Turks and Russian colonists over land. Nowhere in the Empire did the national struggle assume such violent forms as here, where nationalism merged completely with class and religious antagonisms. From 1917 until 1923, these territories suffered all the horrors of what early Soviet accounts called, with much justice, "a colonial revolution." [86]

The Western Bashkirs, inhabiting the region of the Kama River, were acquired by Russia shortly after the capture of Kazan, in the middle of the sixteenth century; the other Bashkirs, inhabiting the southwestern and southeastern parts of the Ural mountains, came into Russian hands only in the eighteenth century. The Western Bashkirs placed themselves under Russian protection voluntarily, mainly in order to obtain assistance against the neighboring Kazakh-Kirghiz tribes. The Kazakh-Kirghiz, in turn, came under Russian rule in the first half of the eighteenth century. All these inhabitants of the steppe were treated by Russian law as *inorodtsy*, and as such retained a considerable measure of autonomy. But Russian privileges for the inorodtsy applied to the internal life of the people themselves and did not guarantee the integrity of the territory which they inhabited. Before long the Russian conquerors began to encroach upon the domain of the nomads and to enforce a land policy which created great dissatisfaction.

The Bashkirs and Kazakh-Kirghiz were preponderantly semi-nomadic in their habits and stayed so until the early 1930's, when they were subjected to Soviet collectivization. Though in some areas they had already begun to settle and to engage primarily in agricultural pursuits, the bulk of their population continued to graze cattle and sheep, and to change their summer habitat from region to region in accordance with seasonal requirements and the availability of fodder. Their economy was not intensive but extensive, and required great stretches of land, which the nomads had possessed until they had come into direct contact with the Russians, who were an agricultural people and who, having insufficient soil in their homeland, migrated to the sparsely inhabited territories in the East. The Russian population movement, which proceeded in an eastern and southeastern direction,[87] led across the territories of the semi-nomads. The Russians colonized, they built cities and fortresses, and beginning in the early eighteenth century, industrial centers as well. The Turkic tribes, resenting the encroachment of aliens, tried to stem their advance by force, and often rebelled. The Bashkirs were particularly troublesome to the Russian government. In the first half of the eighteenth century, when the Russians began to exploit the mineral deposits of the Urals and to expel the steppe nomads into the mountains and forests, the Bashkirs revolted regularly every few years. They also played a prominent part in the Pugachev rebellion (1773–1774).

The influx of Russians gathered impetus after the liberation of the serfs in Russia (1861), when large numbers of Cossacks and of peasants, freed from bondage, migrated from the central provinces of the state. But the most significant colonizing effort was undertaken by the government itself, during the period of the so-called Stolypin reforms (1907–1911). In an attempt to relieve the pressure on the overcrowded Russian village, and to solve the agrarian unrest which the land shortage had caused, Stolypin undertook an ambitious program of colonization of the eastern steppe regions. The Russian peasants, freed by legislation from the responsibilities of communal land-ownership, were given generous allotments of land suitable for agricultural purposes in one of the steppe provinces, and were assisted by loans and other means to establish themselves permanently in their new homes. This entire operation was conducted by a special Bureau of Resettlement (*Pereselencheskoe Upravlenie*). The land was obtained either by purchase or, more frequently, by a transfer of ownership from the Crown, which claimed for itself most of the territories inhabited by the Turkic nomadic tribes, to the settler. The center of colonization was the Semirechensk province, administratively a part of Turkestan, but settlements were also founded in the adjoining provinces By 1915–16 there were established on the Kazakh-Kirghiz territories 530 Cossack and peasant colonist settlements with 144,000 persons.[88] By 1914 the government had distributed in the Semirechensk province alone 4,200,000 desiatinas (or 11,340,000 acres) of land, of a total of 31 million desiatinas available in that province,[89] including most of the land of agricultural value.

The colonization of the steppe was undertaken without sufficient consideration for the interests of the native population, and it created great hardships, particularly among the Kazakh-Kirghiz. They were in effect expelled from the best grazing lands, and prevented from pursuing their traditional mode of life. As a result, they revolted. The incident responsible for the outbreak of the great nomadic rebellion in 1916 was not directly connected with the tsarist land-policy, but nothing except the great dissatisfaction created among the natives by the colonization could account for the violence and desperation of the rebels. The Kazakh-Kirghiz were, under tsarist rule, traditionally exempt from military service. During the war, however, the Russian government decided it required additional manpower, and in July 1916 ordered the drafting of Kazakh-Kirghiz for noncombatant, rear-line duty. The natives interpreted the new order as the beginning of a new policy toward the steppe nomads, and took to arms. They attacked Russian and Cossack settlements and murdered officials indiscriminately, though the brunt of their wrath was visited upon those connected with the colonial administration. The greatest number of fatalities occurred in the Semirechensk province; of nearly 2,500 Russians and Cossacks who lost their lives in the revolt, almost 2,000 were settled in Semireche.[90] The government, utilizing local army garrisons and colonist detachments, suppressed the rebellion by the end of September, with dire results for the natives. Some 300,000 Kazakh-Kirghiz were expelled from their habitations and forced either to take refuge in the mountains or else to flee across the border into Chinese Sinkiang.[91] Most of their animal stock, including 60 per cent of the cattle, and their unmovable belongings were appropriated by the colonists.[92]

The 1916 Kazakh-Kirghiz revolt was the most violent expression of popular dissatisfaction in the history of Russia between the revolutions of 1905 and 1917. At the time of the downfall of the tsarist regime the relations between Russians and natives in the steppe region were already strained to such an extent that as soon as the state authority had relaxed its hold a national conflict was virtually inevitable.

During the Revolution of 1905 Kazakh-Kirghiz intellectuals began to publish local newspapers, but until 1917 they formed no separate political organizations. In the first two Dumas the deputies of the nomads cooperated with the Moslem Faction and followed Kadet leadership. Among the most active deputies from the Kazakh-Kirghiz regions was Alikhan Bukeikhanov (Ali Khan Bökey Khan or Bükeikhanoglu), whose political career had been temporarily terminated in 1906 when he signed the so-called Viborg Manifesto (a protest issued by members of the First Duma following its dissolution). Bukeikhanov was involved in the 1916 Kazakh-Kirghiz rebellion, and in 1917 was appointed a member of the Provisional Government's Turkestan Committee.[93] Another local political figure was the teacher and writer Akhmed Baitursunov (Baytursun), who edited the newspaper *Kazak*, the leading native publication of the area.

In April 1917 Bukeikhanov, Baitursunov, and several other native political figures took the initiative in convening an All-Kazakh Congress in Orenburg. In its resolutions the Congress urged the return to the native population of all the lands confiscated from it by the previous regime, and the expulsion of all the new (i.e., post-1905) settlers from the Kazakh-Kirghiz territories. Other resolutions demanded the transfer of the local school administration into native hands, and the termination of the recruitment introduced in 1916.[94] Three months later another Kazakh-Kirghiz Congress met in Orenburg. There for the first time the idea of territorial autonomy emerged, and a national Kazakh-Kirghiz political party was formed: the Alash-Orda (the word "Alash" denoting the legendary founder of the local tribes, the word "Orda" the seat of the ancient Kazakh Sultans, and by inference, government in general).[95] The Alash-Orda had as its ultimate purpose the unification of the three principal Kazakh-Kirghiz hordes, Small, Middle, and Great (Kchi Dzhus, Orta Dzhus, and Ulu Dzhus) into one autonomous "Kirghiz" state; the separation of state and religion; and special privileges for the Kazakh-Kirghiz in the distribution of land.[96]

The Bashkirs dispatched a delegation to the First All-Russian Moslem Congress held in Moscow in May 1917, led by a twenty-seven-year-old Orientalist and teacher, Zeki Validov (Ahmed Zeki Velidi, or, as later known, Zeki Velidi Togan). Validov presented to the Congress a project of Bashkir autonomy, suggesting that it be granted either within what he called "Greater Bashkiriia" — a Bashkir-Tatar state of the Volga-Ural region — or else in the form of "Small Bashkiriia," comprising the territories populated by the southern and southeastern Bashkirs alone. The Moslem Congress refused to make such commitments, and Validov, who had a quarrel with the Volga Tatar leadership of the Congress, withdrew from it with fifty Bashkir deputies.[97] Shortly afterwards (July 1917) the Bashkirs held their First Congress in Orenburg, at which they decided to seek territorial autonomy jointly with the Turkic tribes of the east and south, that is, of the steppe region and Turkestan.[98] Indeed, in some respects the Bashkirs had more in common with the semi-nomadic Kazakh-Kirghiz than with the agricultural and commercial Tatars with whom they were geographically connected. Validov, who headed the Bashkir national movement throughout the period of the Revolution, cooperated closely with the Alash-Orda and the Moslem nationalists in Turkestan.

Thus, in July 1917, both the Bashkirs and the Kazakh-Kirghiz had placed the demand for territorial autonomy in the forefront of their political programs. The idea of autonomy was intimately connected with the land question which at that time was the greatest concern of the Turkic tribes. With broad self-rule, they felt, it would be possible to legislate in favor of the natives, and to expel the newcomers.

In the meantime, while political parties were being formed and programs were being formulated, the conflict between the semi-nomads and Russians broke into the open again. In July 1917 the Russian peasants of the Semirechensk province voted at their conference in Vernyi (Alma-Ata) to take all the necessary measures to subdue the natives, including forceful expulsion.[99] In the summer, groups of Kazakh-Kirghiz refugees of the 1916 rebellion began to trek from China back to their homes in Russian Central Asia. The Russian settlers, still bitter over the rebellion and unwilling to yield the properties which they had acquired as loot, had no intention of permitting the natives to return. Detachments of colonists were organized to deal with them. The colonists' brutal treatment of the nearly starved and virtually defenseless returnees, evoked protests throughout Central Asia.[100] There were mass slaughters and in some instances the natives were burned alive. The victims numbered, according to a contemporary Moslem source, 83,000 dead.[101] In September 1917, when the violence reached its peak, the Provisional Government placed the entire Semireche under martial law.[102]

In the neighboring Bashkir regions also, recurrent clashes broke out in the summer and fall of 1917 between Russian and native settlements, though these were not of such dimensions as those of the Kazakh-Kirghiz steppe.[103] There, too, the nomads were particularly hostile to the colonists who had settled under the Stolypin program.

Toward the end of 1917, when the authority of the Provisional Government in the steppe had reached its nadir, the Bashkirs and Alash-Orda leaders established contact with the Orenburg Cossacks, who formed something of a third force in that area. In December the Orenburg Cossacks made an alliance with the natives. The Bashkirs and Kazakh-Kirghiz established their political centers in the city of Orenburg, and there in December they held their respective congresses, at which the autonomies of Bashkiriia and of the Kazakh-Kirghiz steppe were proclaimed.[104] The head of the Orenburg Cossacks, Ataman Dutov, took over the command of the anti-Bolshevik movement in the region and agreed to coöperate with the Bashkir and Kazakh-Kirghiz political leaders.[105]

The Bolsheviks, though they had virtually no party apparatus on this territory (the first formal Bolshevik organizations in the Steppe territory of Central Asia were formed only in 1918), gained strength rapidly at the end of the year. Their following was greatest among the military garrisons, but in time they won support of the railroad workers and of the colonists.[106] A large number of the colonists went over to the Bolsheviks when it became evident that the Communist slogan of "proletarian dictatorship" could be conveniently employed against the natives. Their logic was simple: Bolshevism meant the rule of the workers, soldiers, and peasants; the Kazakh-Kirghiz had no workers, soldiers, or peasants; therefore, the Kazakh-Kirghiz must not rule but be ruled. Numerous among the colonists who, realizing the possibility of exploiting the Soviet system to their own advantage, embraced the Bolshevik cause were the well-to-do peasants (or kulaks) and officials of the tsarist colonizing administration. The latter group, after the collapse of the Provisional Government, had assumed effective authority in the steppe regions and headed the opposition to the native nationalist movement.[107]

### Turkestan and the Autonomous Government of Kokand

Turkestan was the last important territorial acquisition of tsarist Russia. In the 1860's and 1870's Russian armies defeated and subjugated, with relative ease the divided and technologically backward principalities of Bukhara, Khiva, and Kokand, and thence moved into the Transcaspian territories adjoining Afghanistan (Merv captured in 1881). In 1867 the Government General of Turkestan was established with headquarters in Tashkent. The total losses incurred by the Russians in the conquest of Turkestan between 1847 and 1881 were 1,000 killed and 3,000 wounded.[108]

After its conquest Turkestan became both politically and economically a colonial dependency of Russia. The administration of the country was placed entirely in the hands of the military; the Moslem natives did not participate in it. The provinces of Turkestan* were before long found suitable for the cultivation of cotton, and with the help of Russian and foreign capital large-scale cotton plantations were established. On the eve of World War I, Turkestan supplied more than one half of Russia's cotton requirements; during the war, all. The Russians who had settled in Turkestan belonged largely to the privileged urban class. It had been estimated that about 1900 between one-third and one-half of the entire Russian population in that area consisted of noblemen, officials, clergymen, merchants, and other elements connected directly either with the administration or with the commercial establishments which were developing the economy of Turkestan.[109] The Russian newcomers, like the other Europeans who had followed in their wake, lived in separate quarters of the city, and kept apart from the indigenous Moslem population, much as the Western population did in other colonial areas of Asia and Africa.

Unlike the steppe regions inhabited by the Bashkirs and Kazakh-Kirghiz, Turkestan profited considerably from Russian rule. Russian military authorities imposed order and stopped the perpetual warring between the native tribes, while the economic development, made possible by Russian railroad and canal construction, and by Western capital, improved the material condition of the natives. Armin Vámbéry, the Hungarian Orientalist who was strongly anti-Russian in his sentiments, concluded a comparative study of Russian administration in Central Asia and the British rule in India with an appraisal not entirely unfavorable to the former:

> Judging dispassionately and without prejudice, as it is seemly to do in matters of such moment, we must frankly acknowledge that the Russians have done much good work in Asia, that with their advent order, peace, and security have taken the place of anarchy and lawlessness, and that, notwithstanding the strongly Oriental coloring of their political, social and ecclesiastical institutions as representatives of the Western world, they have everywhere made a change for the better, and inaugurated an era more worthy of humanity.[110]

* The General Gubernia of Turkestan consisted of five provinces (*oblasti*): Semirechensk, Syr-Daria, Ferghana, Samarkand, and Transcaspia, and two dependencies, the principalities of Khiva and Bukhara. The statistics which follow do not include the dependencies.

The material benefits which Turkestan derived from Russian rule notwithstanding, the relations between the natives (6,806,085 in 1910) and the Russians (406,607 in 1910) did not rest upon a healthy basis.[111] The Russians formed a privileged caste, and the Moslem population not unnaturally resented this fact; the livelihood of the Russians depended largely upon the preservation of the political and economic preponderance of Russia in Turkestan, and for that reason they were not only disinclined to sympathize with the political strivings of the natives, but were determined to fight tooth and nail for undiminished Russian control of the area. In Turkestan the fight for autonomy on the part of the natives met, in consequence, with the most resolute opposition. In the course of the Revolution and Civil War the latent socio-economic hostilities between the two groups, strengthened by religious animosities, broke into the open, and assumed aspects not unlike those which prevailed in the Bashkir and Kazakh-Kirghiz steppes.

The native political movement in the Turkestan of 1917 consisted of two wings: a religious-conservative wing, organized in the *Ulema Dzhemieti* (*Ulema Cemiyeti;* Association of Clergymen) led by Ser Ali Lapin, and a secular-liberal one, led by Munnever Kari and Mustafa Chokaev (Chokai-ogly). The Ulema had monarchist inclinations and concentrated on the introduction of Moslem courts and the establishment of religious law (*shariat* or *sharī'a*) throughout Turkestan. Its rivals, people connected with the jadidist movement, wanted a westernization of Moslem life in Turkestan and the increased participation of the natives in the political life of the country.[112] The two groups, representing the clerical, orthodox elements, and the middle-class, lay elements respectively, at first were hostile toward each other, but in the latter part of the year, as Russian opposition to native political aspirations solidified, they moved closer and eventually merged. In addition, there was a Moslem socialist movement, organized in the "Union of Toiling Moslems" in Skobelev (Ferghana) and the "Ittihad" in Samarkand. These associations were largely under SR and Menshevik influence, and numerically they were extremely weak, but in the revolutionary period they were exploited with some success by the Bolsheviks.[113]

In 1917 the leadership of the political movement of the Turkestan natives was in the hands of the liberal Moslems, who took the initiative in convening at the beginning of April a Turkestani-Moslem Congress. The resolutions of the Congress demanded the introduction of a federal system in Russia, and the return to the natives of all the confiscated lands. The Congress appointed a Turkestan Moslem Central Council (*Shurai-Islamiye*), with Mustafa Chokaev as its chairman. The Central Council established within a short time a network of provincial organizations in all parts of Turkestan, and endeavored to centralize the political activities of the Turkestan natives.[114] It participated in the May All-Russian Moslem Council, and established contact with the Alash-Orda; but then, as throughout the remainder of the Revolution and Civil War, the Moslem organizations in Turkestan and the steppe regions developed independently of each other.

The Turkestan Committee, composed of nine men (five Russians and four Moslems) appointed by the Provisional Government to replace the tsarist Governor General Kuropatkin, had no power whatsoever. In the summer of 1917, following the withdrawal of the liberal members from the Russian cabinet, the Turkestan Committee, composed largely of Kadets, also tendered its resignation. Petrograd appointed a new Committee under the Orientalist Nalivkin, but it too was ineffective. The actual authority was in the hands of the Tashkent Soviet, headed by a Russian Socialist Revolutionary, the lawyer G. I. Broido, and dominated by SR's and Mensheviks. The Bolsheviks had no separate party organization in Tashkent until December 1917, nor in other parts of Turkestan until 1918, but they did maintain a distinct faction within the Soviet and on a number of occasions advanced Leninist resolutions. In June 1917 the Bolshevik faction in the Tashkent Soviet numbered only five men,[115] and the size of their organized party following at that time can be gauged by the fact that in December 1917 the strongest Bolshevik cell, that of Tashkent, had a mere sixty-four members.[116] The weakness of the Bolsheviks, however, was offset by the growth of a left wing within the SR party, and the ultimate triumph of Communism in Tashkent in late 1917 was made possible largely by the coöperation of the Left SR's with the Bolsheviks. The Tashkent Soviet represented the interests of the European population of Turkestan, especially the soldiers and the skilled workers.

The idea of autonomy was not widely developed among Turkestan Moslems, and certainly it had no such urgency as in the other regions of the Empire inhabited by Turkic peoples. But the necessity for some form of territorial self-rule emerged early in the course of public discussions concerning the elections to the Constituent Assembly in the summer of 1917. The Russians, being outnumbered fifteen to one by the natives, had every reason to fear that if the elections were to be based on the principle of universal, direct vote, they would be completely submerged by the Moslems and possibly lose to them all the nominations. They preferred therefore a *curiae* system of voting, in which Russians and natives balloted separately. Projects to this effect were widely discussed in Russian circles, and one of them was formally accepted by the Tashkent Soviet.[117] At the same time, the Soviet submitted to the Turkestan Committee of the Provisional Government a scheme whereby the administration of the city would be divided into two parts, a Russian and a native.[118]

The Moslem Central Council objected to such legislative projects which would, in effect, preserve the privileges of the Russian population in Turkestan, and on its demand the Tashkent Soviet withdrew the previously accepted electoral plan.[119] To offset the numerical weakness of the Russians without recourse to the system of *curiae*, the Central Council offered to guarantee the Russians a minimum number of deputies in the Constituent Assembly. The discussions concerning the forthcoming elections indicated that the problems of the future administrative status of Turkestan were much more complex than the Moslems had anticipated, and beginning with the summer of 1917, the question of territorial autonomy occupied ever more attention in the discussions of the Central Council. But nothing, perhaps, stimulated autonomist tendencies more than the chauvinistic, colonial mentality of the irresponsible elements who, in the fall of 1917, had gained control over the Tashkent Soviet and had begun to pursue extremely oppressive policies toward the natives.

The revolutionary temper among the Russian soldiers and railroad workers in Tashkent matured more rapidly than it did in other borderlands of the Empire, at least partly because of the shortage of food in Turkestan caused by the reduction of shipments from the Northern Caucasus. As early as September 1917, the Soviet, swayed by Left SR and Bolshevik slogans, proclaimed the overthrow of established authority. It arrested Nalivkin, and tried to take over Turkestan. The Provisional Government reacted at once, dispatching to Tashkent a punitive expedition under General Korovnichenko, whom it also entrusted with the administration of the area. Korovnichenko suppressed the uprising and restored order in Tashkent.[120]

While on his way to Tashkent, the general was met by representatives of the Moslem Central Council, who presented him with a list of demands upon the acceptance of which they conditioned their coöperation with the authorities. Their demands consisted of four points: (1) the termination of the old system of separation of native courts from European courts, and the transfer of the entire judiciary into Moslem hands; (2) the establishment of an autonomous Turkestan Legislative Assembly with authority to vote on all legislative measures applicable to Turkestan; (3) abolition of Russian electoral privileges; (4) the removal of Russian troops from Turkestan and their replacement by Bashkir and Tatar units.[121] The demands of the Central Council apparently represented a compromise of its views with those of the Ulema. General Korovnichenko promised to take those rather extreme and not entirely practical requests into consideration, but before an official reply could be given, Tashkent was taken over by the Soviet.

The October Revolution began in Tashkent at 12 o'clock noon of October 25, when a group of railroad workers opened fire on the Cossack club in the city. Two days later the Soviet, dominated by a Bolshevik and left-SR coalition, obtained control over the Tashkent fortress, and on November 1 it arrested the local representatives of the defunct Provisional Government.[122] In Perovsk (Kzyl-Orda) the Soviet assumed authority on October 30, in Pishpek (Frunze) on November 5.[123] The countryside remained unaffected by the October Revolution. It was Tashkent, the one-time center of the tsarist colonial and military administration, which assumed the role of a fortress of Bolshevism in all of Central Asia.

On November 15, 1917, the new masters of the city assembled the Third Regional Congress of Soviets, which proclaimed the establishment of Soviet rule throughout Turkestan. A Turkestan Council of People's Commissars (*Turksovnarkom*) was appointed to administer the area, under the chairmanship of a Russian army lieutenant, Kolesov; the other cabinet posts were distributed between seven Bolsheviks and eight Left SR's.[124] A Revolutionary Committee was created to deal with the opposition to the new Soviet government.

The Turkestan Moslem Central Council established contact with the new Soviet authorities, and tried to sound them out on the issue of territorial autonomy for Turkestan. Kolesov, speaking in the name of the government, declared himself opposed to this idea.[125] The entire question of Moslem political aspirations came up for discussion at the Congress of Soviets, and the overwhelming majority of the deputies expressed itself not only against any territorial self-rule for Turkestan which might weaken, in any way whatsoever, the authority of Russia, but also against the participation of Moslems in the Soviet government in Central Asia. The remarkable resolution of the Bolshevik faction at the Congress, accepted by a majority vote, read as follows:

> At the present time one cannot permit the admission of Moslems into the higher organs of the regional revolutionary authority, because the attitude of the local population toward the Soviet of Soldiers', Workers', and Peasants' Deputies is quite uncertain, and because the native population lacks proletarian organizations, which the [Bolshevik] faction could welcome into the organ of the higher regional government.[126]

The Congress of Soviets organized a Third Congress of Turkestan Moslems, which was composed largely of members of the socialist Union of Toiling Moslems and Ittihad, in order to secure a formal approval of the Soviet government on the part of the "Moslem population." This task it dutifully fulfilled. The Soviet-sponsored Moslem congress included none of the political parties which in the course of the preceding half a year had identified themselves with the Moslem national cause; it was little more than another rump congress, similar to those which the Bolsheviks were organizing in many other parts of the Empire where their following was weak and the local population was not likely to approve of Soviet rule.

Immediately after the Tashkent Sovnarkom had turned down the Moslem proposal for autonomy, the Central Council opened deliberations whether to wait for the convocation of the Constituent Assembly or to proclaim autonomy at once on its own initiative. The provincial organizations favored the latter course.[127] Some Russian anti-Soviet parties, notably the Right SR's, also fostered the notion of autonomy, hoping in this manner to unseat the Bolsheviks from Tashkent.[128] On December 22, the *Turksovnarkom,* in a last-minute attempt to bridge the ever-widening gulf between the Soviet and the Moslems, is said to have offered Mustafa Chokaev the chairmanship of the Turkestani Soviet government; but Chokaev, apparently convinced that this would place him at the mercy of the Reds, refused.[129] The Central Council instead made preparations for the convocation of a Fourth Extraordinary Congress in December. There was little doubt that this Congress would proclaim the autonomy of Turkestan, and thus challenge the authority of the Tashkent Soviet. The Moslems originally had planned to hold the Congress in Tashkent, but in view of an attack of Russian soldiers on a Moslem crowd celebrating a religious holiday, and the general tension between the old and new town quarters, it was decided to transfer the Congress as well as the seat of the Central Council to the town of Kokand, located in the Ferghana valley, by railroad 220 miles east of Tashkent. In Kokand the population was predominantly (96%) Moslem, and there was less danger of soldier violence.

The Congress opened formally on November 28, 1917, in the old palace of the Kokand Khans. The Soviet's control of the main railroad lines prevented many delegates from arriving on time or at all. Noticeable was the presence of numerous deputies of Bukharan Jews and of anti-Bolshevik Russian parties. The principal question confronting the 180 deputies was that of the future political status of Turkestan. Some voices were raised in favor of independence, others in favor of autonomy within a Russian federation; but all agreed that some form of territorial autonomy was necessary. There were complaints that the advent of Bolshevism had sharpened the colonist appetite for native land, and had placed the Moslems at the mercy of the worst elements of the Russian population.[130] Separatist tendencies were weak, and on the whole, the attitude toward Russia in general and toward the non-Communist Russian political parties in particular, was friendly.[131] In the end the deputies voted in favor of autonomy:

> The Fourth Regional Moslem Congress of Kokand, meeting in an extraordinary session and expressing the will of the peoples inhabiting Turkestan on the matter of autonomy, upon the bases proclaimed by the Great Russian Revolution, declares the territory of Turkestan to be autonomous but united with the Russian democratic federative republic. The task of determining the forms of said autonomy is left

to the Constituent Assembly of Turkestan. The Constituent Assembly must be convened as soon as possible. The Fourth Congress declares solemnly that the rights of the national minorities inhabiting Turkestan will be strictly safeguarded.[132]

The date of the Constituent Assembly of Turkestan was set for March 20, 1918. Before dispersing, the deputies elected a People's Council (*Halk şurası*) of fifty-four members to perform the functions of a Provisional Parliament until March, and also an Executive Committee to serve as a provisional government. Chairmanship of the Council was entrusted to the head of the Ulema, Lapin; whereas the Executive Committee Chairmanship went to leaders of the Central Council, Muhammedzhan Tenichbaev (Tinïshbayoglu, a member of the defunct Turkestan Committee) and after his resignation, to Chokaev. Membership in the Council was divided along national lines: thirty-six seats were apportioned to Moslems, eighteen to Russians.[133] The question of a merger with the Southeastern Union, organized by the Cossacks, which was placed before the Congress by the Bashkir leader Zeki Validov, was left open for the Turkestani Constituent Assembly to decide.[134]

The Kokand Congress created in the Executive Committee a countergovernment to the Soviet regime in Tashkent. The tenacious refusal of the Tashkent Bolsheviks to accede to Moslem demands for some form of territorial self-rule was no doubt a major factor in the split between them and the native political organizations. "Our principal and most serious mistake," a Soviet participant wrote of these events in retrospect, "was our entirely incorrect if not inexplicable political line in the nationality question." [135] Early Soviet historians readily admitted that this mistake was not accidental but was intimately connected with the interests and mentality of the groups which had passed over to the Soviet cause in Turkestan. According to Safarov, Soviet power in Tashkent, in 1917 and early 1918, was largely in the hands of "adventurers, careerists, and plain criminal elements," who were determined by all means to preserve and extend the privileged position enjoyed by the Russian proletariat and the European settlers in Turkestan.[136]

## The Caucasus

### The Terek Region and Daghestan

The Revolution in the Northern Caucasus had a very complex course. The mountain ranges created barriers between adjoining regions, so that their historical development proceeded at times independently of each other. Daghestan, in the eastern sector of the Caucasian chain, and Terek, in its center, though geographically adjacent, followed different courses. Furthermore, in each region different national groups faced different problems and took advantage of the Revolution to realize their own aspirations. The extraordinary geographic and ethnic heterogeneity of the entire area is reflected in its revolutionary history.

The Terek Region (or *oblast'*), with the administrative center in the city of Vladikavkaz (Dzaudzhikau), had in 1912 a population of approximately 1,200,000, composed of the following principal ethnic groups:[137]

| | | |
|---|---|---|
| Russians | | 512,489 |
| Natives of the mountains (*Gortsy*) | | 614,194 |
| Chechens | 245,538 | |
| Ossetins | 139,784 | |
| Kabardians | 101,189 | |
| Ingushes | 56,367 | |
| Kumyks | 34,232 | |
| Others | 37,084 | |
| Nogais | | 35,152 |
| Kalmyks | | 1,792 |
| Armenians | | 24,012 |

The Russian population was divided into two distinct groups: the Terek Cossacks and the so-called *inogorodnye*. The former had inhabited the northeastern foothills of the Caucasian Mountains since the middle of the sixteenth century, when they had been settled as a military guard to protect the domain of the tsars from the incursions of the nomads and the mountain peoples. In the course of the eighteenth century they had lost most of the privileges of self-rule which they had originally possessed, but in a number of respects they still remained a privileged social order. The most important advantage which they enjoyed over the remaining groups of the population, Russian and non-Russian alike, was an abundance of land. Owing to government generosity, the Terek Cossacks possessed more than twice as much land per capita as the native inhabitants of the mountains (13.57 desiatinas to the latter's 6.05).[138] They formed, in other words, something of a landed middle class — a status which in the course of the Revolution was to influence profoundly their relations with the other groups of the region. In 1912 the Terek Cossacks numbered 268,000. They lived in settlements, or *stanitsy*, along the Terek River or the valleys radiating from the river into the mountains.

The inogorodnye ("people from other towns") were, as their name indicates, migrants: newcomers who had arrived in the Northern Caucasus in recent times. They were largely Russians, but among them were also Georgians and Armenians. The first wave of inogorodnye consisted of peasants, who had moved into the rich lands of the North Caucasian steppes from Russia following the liberation of the serfs (1861). Most of these migrants had settled in the western section of the Northern Caucasus, in the Kuban and Don districts, where they rented land from the Cossacks. In the Terek Region there was less land, and consequently the peasant newcomers were less numerous. The second wave of inogorodnye had arrived toward the end of the nineteenth century, in connection with the development of the oil industry (Maikop, Groznyi) and the construction of railroad repair shops; they filled the towns of the Terek Region as laborers, merchants, officials. The term *inogorodnye* had no official sanction, but it was in common use in the Northern Caucasus and it did have certain social significance. In an area where the majority of the population had consisted for several centuries entirely of native tribes and Cossack military settlers, the influx of an urban element and a landless peasantry created a new and distinct class of inhabitants. The inogorodnye and the Cossacks did not get along well. The former disliked the Cossack privileges, wealth, and readiness to help the government to suppress popular resistance against absolutism; the Cossacks resented the fact that the newcomers threatened their privileged position.

The third element in the Terek Region were the natives, or gortsy. These people, however, constituted no unit either in the ethnic, cultural, or socio-economic sense.

The Kabardians were a Cherkess people. At the end of the sixteenth century they had gained complete control over the entire North Caucasian plain, and established dominion over most of the other native peoples. They had acquired possession of much land, and long after the Russians had conquered the Northern Caucasus, the Kabardians remained the richest group in that area. Their per capita ownership of land was 17.5 desiatinas, which was even higher than that of the Terek Cossacks.[139] Owing to this wealth the Kabardians were viewed by some of the poorer mountain peoples with as much hostility as the Cossacks themselves. The Ossetins, who inhabited the central sector of the Terek Region, along the Georgian Military Highway connecting Vladikavkaz with Tiflis, belonged to the Iranian race. Among the indigenous peoples of the Northern Caucasus they were culturally the most advanced. Having in their majority accepted Christianity in the fourth century they had come under the influence of neighboring Georgia, and, after Russian conquest, had adapted themselves far more easily to Western civilization than their Moslem neighbors. At the beginning of the twentieth century the Ossetins had a sizable intelligentsia, educated in Russian schools, and an urban population. The Kabardians and Ossetins both were primarily agricultural peoples.

The Chechens and Ingush presented a special problem. Inhabiting the nearly inaccessible mountain ranges bordering on Daghestan, they were always, from the Russian point of view, a troublesome element. Unassimilable and warlike, they created so much difficulty for the Russian forces trying to subdue the Northern Caucasus that, after conquering the area, the government felt compelled to employ Cossack units to expel them from the valleys and lowlands into the bare mountain regions.

There, faced by Cossack settlements on the one side, and wild peaks on the other, they lived in abject poverty tending sheep and waiting for the day when they could wreak revenge on the newcomers and regain their lost lands. The Ingush and Chechens, with average land allotments of 5.8 and 3.0 desiatinas, were the poorest people in the area. Their hatred was concentrated on the Cossacks.[140]

It is not difficult to perceive that the socio-economic and cultural situation in the Terek Region was conducive to a three-cornered struggle among the Cossacks, the inogorodnye, and the land-hungry mountain peoples. In the course of the Revolution the Cossacks found their principal support among the White Guards; the inogorodnye coöperated with the Bolsheviks; and the natives shifted for themselves, seeking escape from spreading anarchy in independent national activity or in alliances with the Turks, Azerbaijanis, and Bolsheviks.

The population of Daghestan — a region occupying the northeastern end of the Caucasian range — was one of the most primitive in the Empire. Here was the center of extreme religious fanaticism where Sufism and divinely inspired *sheikhs* still held undisputed sway. The Revolution in Daghestan therefore assumed the character of a religious war of the natives against the Christians and westernized Moslems.

The national movement among the inhabitants of the mountains was led, in 1917, by the intelligentsia, the nobility, and the moneyed elements, who strove for the attainment of autonomy within a Russian federation and an improvement of the economic conditions of the native population. The religious tendency, on the other hand, represented an expression of Muridism, a form of Sufism. It stressed the role of God-appointed *imams*, or spiritual leaders, who exercised complete power over their followers. Muridism had enjoyed its greatest popularity in the North Caucasus in the middle of the nineteenth century, at the height of native resistance to Russia. Its hero was Shamil, the leader of the Caucasian wars of the 1830's and 1840's; its ideal, the establishment of a theocratic Mohammedan state; its leaders were the *mullahs*, the clergy. If the nationalistic movement enjoyed greater popularity among the peoples who were culturally and economically more advanced, the religious movement dominated the backward regions, especially Chechnia and Daghestan. Although both these tendencies asserted the principle of unity of the natives and cmploycd Pan-Islamic slogans, they were too divergent in their ultimate goals to merge.

In May 1917, the nationalists convened a congress of gortsy in Vladikavkaz. Advancing no political demands, they asked for free education for all citizens, the continuation of the war, and popular support of the Provisional Government.[141] The Second Congress was to have taken place in the village of Andi, high in the mountains of Daghestan where Shamil had once been active, but the nationalist deputies were scattered by the religious extremists who appeared there in large numbers on the eve of the Congress, and threatened them with violence. Instead, the nationalists met in September in Vladikavkaz, and there formed a Union of Mountain Peoples (*Soiuz Gorskikh Narodov*). The Congress proclaimed the Union an integral part of the Russian Empire, and drew up a constitution regulating the internal relations of its member nations.[142] The intention of the nationalists was to include all the Moslem groups inhabiting the northern as well as southern slopes of the Caucasian range in one autonomous state.

The clergy in the meantime elected as their *imam* a sixty-year-old Arabic scholar and wealthy sheep-owner from Daghestan, Nazhmudin Gotsinskii. The son of a right-hand man of Shamil's, Gotsinskii knew well how to combine the prophetic appeal, popular among the native population, with political expediency. He succeeded in establishing himself as the *de facto* ruler of the high mountain districts of East Caucasus for a major part of the revolutionary period, and in obtaining complete control over the minds and bodies of his fanatical followers. Gotsinskii's assistant, and later chief rival, was Uzun Khadzi, who was even more extreme in his religious views. "I am spinning a rope with which to hang all engineers, students, and in general all those who write from left to right," he once said of his aims.[143]

The Terek Cossacks, who already in March 1917 had elected their own Ataman and formed a Military Government, tried in the autumn to enter into a union with the Cossacks of the Don and Kuban, for the purpose of forming a Southeastern Union (*Iugo-vostochnyi soiuz*). Faced with growing hostility from the urban population; from the inogorodnye, who dominated the soviets; and from the non-Cossack rural population, who refused after the outbreak of the February Revolution to pay rent to the Cossack landowners and demanded that all land be nationalized; the Terek Cossacks offered an alliance to the native nationalists. On October 20, 1917, the Union of the Mountain Peoples and the Terek Military Government united in a Terek-Daghestan Government (*Tersko-Dagestanskoe Pravitel'stvo*), which was to enter the Southeastern Union.[144]

These plans, however, were brought to nought by the outbreak of a full-scale war between the Cossacks and the Chechens and Ingush. Having waited with growing restlessness for nearly a year to regain the lands which they had lost to the Russians in the previous century, the Chechens and Ingush finally lost their patience. In December 1917 they swooped down from the mountains and attacked the cities and Cossack settlements. Vladikavkaz, Groznyi, and the entire Cossack line along the Sunzha River suffered from the blows of the attackers, who looted and pillaged. The Terek-Daghestan Government, whose authority had never extended beyond the confines of Vladikavkaz and which had proved unable even to defend that city from the invaders, dissolved itself in January 1918. The war of the Chechens and Ingush with the population of the plains ended for the time being all possibility of coöperation between the Cossacks and the natives. The Russians — Cossack and inogorodnye alike — now forgot their disagreements and united to defend themselves against the common danger. In the early part of 1918 a bitter national struggle between Moslems and Russians broke out in the Terek Region. The immediate advantage of this struggle accrued to the Bolsheviks, who, supported by a sizable proportion of the inogorodnye and Russian soldiers returning home from the Turkish front, organized the resistance of the Russians against the natives.

### Transcaucasia

Transcaucasia was in 1916 and 1917 under the authority of the Grand Duke Nikolas Nikolaevich, who led Russian troops in successful campaigns against the Turks. When the news of the abdication of Tsar Nicholas II reached the Headquarters of the Caucasian Army he resigned his post. His military functions were assumed by General Yudenich, and his civil powers were taken over by the Special Transcaucasian Committee (*Osobyi Zakavkazskii Komitet*, or *Ozakom* for short). The Ozakom exercised little authority and limited itself during its existence to the introduction of organs of local self-rule (*zemstva*) into Transcaucasia.[145]

Real power in Transcaucasia in 1917 was wielded by the soviets, especially those located in the two principal towns, Tiflis and Baku. Until the end of the year both soviets were dominated by the Mensheviks and the SR's, the former enjoying greater popularity among the industrial workers, the latter among the soldiers. The Tiflis Soviet was a Menshevik stronghold. The Baku Soviet was at first divided equally among SR's, Mensheviks, Mussavatists, and Dashnaks, but by the beginning of 1918, as the result of the influx of deserting soldiers from the front, it inclined more and more to the left, until for a brief time it came entirely under Bolshevik control. The Transcaucasian Soviets were united for the purpose of coördinating their work in a Regional Center (*Kraevoi tsentr sovetov*) located in Tiflis, which passed resolutions on all political and economic measures of general interest for the Caucasus and enforced them through a network of subordinate provincial soviets. The Ozakom did little more than rubber-stamp its decisions. In a sense, therefore, in the spring of 1917 Transcaucasia represented the realization of the Menshevik ideal of a "bourgeois" government (i.e., the Provisional Government and the Ozakom) controlled and directed by "proletarian" organs of self-rule (i.e., soviets).

Largely because of this arrangement and the discipline maintained by the army fighting the Turks, the first year of the Revolution passed in Transcaucasia with relative calm. Neither the anarchy, caused by

*Volodimir Vinnichenko, 1921*

*Mikhail Hrushevskii*

*Simon Petliura, 1917*

*Hetman Skoropadski and Kaiser Wilhelm II
in Berlin, 1918*

*Grigorii Piatakov*

*Vladimir Zatonskii*

**Khristian Rakovskii, 1924**

*Mykola Skrypnik*

*Mehmed Emin'Resul-zade, 1951*

*Mustafa Chokaev, 1917*

*Dzhafer Seidamet and Chelibidzhan
Chelibiev, 1917*

*Zeki Validov (Togan), 1953*

*Joseph Stalin as Commissar of
Nationalities, 1917*

*Mirza Sultan-Galiev*

*Said Alim Khan, last Emir of Bukhara*

*Enver Pasha*

Noi Zhordaniia

Irakly Tseretelli, 1917

Akaki Chkhenkeli

Budu Mdivani, 1922

Filipp Makharadze

Grigorii Ordzhonikidze

Sergei Kirov

Stepan Shaumian

*The General Secretariat of the Ukrainian Central Rada, 1917. Sitting in the center, Vinnichenko; sitting at extreme right, Petliura; standing at extreme left, Pavel Khristiuk.*

*Mikhail Frunze and Ordzhonikidze at Tiflis, 1924*

*Negotiations between Soviet authorities and Basmachi leaders in the Ferghana region, 1921*

the breakdown of political institutions, nor the lootings and attacks on the population by the disintegrating army, which occurred in other parts of the Empire, disturbed the peace. The Revolution in its violent form came to Transcaucasia only in 1918.

In the course of 1917 the political parties of the three principal ethnic groups, the Georgians, Azerbaijanis, and Armenians, emerging from wartime inactivity or suppression, reorganized very quickly and assumed a much more important position in Transcaucasian affairs than they ever had enjoyed in the prerevolutionary period.

The Georgian Mensheviks continued to devote their main efforts not to the pursuit of local aims but to participation in Russian political life. Owing to their influential position in Russian Social Democracy, the Georgians, immediately after the outbreak of the February Revolution, assumed leadership over some of the highest political institutions in the center of Russia. Nikolai Chkheidze and Irakly Tseretelli, both Social Democrats from Georgia, played important roles in the Petrograd Soviet and were in the very center of Russian political life.[146] In the coalition government, established in May, Tseretelli occupied a ministerial chair. By virtue of its intimate relations with the all-Russian socialist movement, Georgian Social Democracy, at least until 1918, was not a "national" party. It advanced no specific demands for the Georgian people, and assumed no specifically "Georgian" attitude on matters pertaining to the Caucasus.

This was not true of the other two parties active among the non-Russian groups in Transcaucasia.

The outbreak of the First World War had placed the leaders of the Azerbaijani national movement in an awkward position. Their pro-Turkish sympathies were generally known. In 1912, in the course of the Balkan War, the Mussavat had even published in Constantinople a manifesto, in which it accused the Russian government, "the Asiatic bear," of being the enemy of all Islam, and urged the Moslems of the Caucasus to support the Ottoman Empire.[147] From 1914 to 1917 the Mussavatists had to suspend open political activity, and to function semilegally under the cover of educational and philanthropic organizations.[148] Although the establishment of democracy in Russia made it possible for them to act in the open again, the Azerbaijani nationalists had to be very cautious as long as Russia remained at war with the Ottoman Empire. Until the spring of 1918, when the Turkish conquest of Transcaucasia became inevitable, the Azerbaijani nationalists coöperated closely with Russian, Georgian, and Armenian groups, and gave no open indication of their pro-Turkish sympathies.

In addition to the Mussavat, two other important Moslem parties were active in Transcaucasia in 1917. The Neutral Democratic Group (NDG) represented the Sunni Moslems of Azerbaijan (the majority of the people were Shiite), but in all other respects it was identical with the Mussavat. The Moslem Union spoke for the conservative clergy and the landowning classes.[149]

In April 1917 the Caucasian Moslems held a conference in Baku. The conference was dominated by the Mussavat, under whose influence it passed resolutions favoring the establishment of a democratic Russian republic, the introduction of federalism, the creation of an all-Moslem organization in Russia, with competence in religious and cultural matters, the conclusion of a peace without annexations or contributions, and the maintenance of friendly relations with the other national minorities.[150] The same program was advanced by the Azerbaijani delegation at the May All-Russian Moslem Congress in Moscow, where it championed the federalist cause against the idea of cultural autonomy sponsored by the Volga Tatars. The Baku Congress also appointed an All-Caucasian Moslem Bureau, with permanent residence in Tiflis, to function as a center for Moslem affairs.

At the end of June the Mussavat merged with the Turkish Federalist Party, newly founded in the heart of the Moslem landowning district in Transcaucasia, Elisavetpol (Gandzha, today Kirovabad). The Federalists, headed by Ussubekov (Nasib bey Yusufbeyli), represented the influential Azerbaijani landed aristocracy. By merging with it, the predominantly urban, middle-class Mussavat gained greatly in strength. At the same time, however, it lost something of its earlier radical social character. The Federalists, while agreeing with the Mussavat on most programmatic issues, strongly opposed the idea of land expropriation as desired by the Mussavatists, and favored government purchase of private estates for distribution to landless peasants. For some time this important question caused disagreements between the Azerbaijani political leaders, but finally in October 1917 the Mussavat gave in and agreed to the Federalist formula.[151] The name of the new party was officially changed to the Turkish Federalist Party Mussavat, though the term *Mussavat* (or *Musavat*) continued in general use.

There can be no doubt that the new Mussavat enjoyed mass following among all elements of the Moslem population in Transcaucasia. In the elections to the Baku Soviet it consistently polled the largest number of votes in the industrial regions of the town, and in October 1917 it received the over-all greatest vote cast in the reëlections to the Baku Soviet, more than twice the number won by the Bolsheviks.[152] In the elections to the Constituent Assembly, the Transcaucasian Turks voted along national lines, giving the Mussavat 405,917 votes, and the other Moslem parties (mainly of a conservative, religious orientation) 228,-889.[153] The total vote of 634,206 thus won by the Moslem parties represented, in round figures, 30 per cent of all the votes cast in the elections throughout Transcaucasia (1,996,263) and corresponded to the proportion of Moslems in the entire population of Transcaucasia. In the Baku province the Mussavat received 90 per cent of the total vote.[154]

To the Armenians the First World War brought a terrible tragedy. Caught in a conflict between Turkey and Russia, they were at first courted by both of the contestants and finally all but annihilated as a result of their choice. The geographical situation of the Armenian population — in the center of the theater of operations — demanded that they pursue a course of strict neutrality, and this was the policy which the Dashnaktsutiun, which by then dominated Armenian political life on both sides of the border, had initially adopted. When in 1914 the Ottoman government, controlled by the Young Turks whom the Dashnaks had helped six years earlier to come to power, offered the Armenians the pledge of autonomy in return for their assistance against Russia, the Dashnaks refused on the grounds of neutrality.[155] Soon after the outbreak of war, however, the leaders of the Dashnaktsutiun changed their mind, and convinced of an Allied victory, threw in their lot with the Russians. They organized Armenian volunteer detachments to fight side by side with the tsarist army, to help them reconnoiter the Eastern Anatolian districts and, after receiving from St. Petersburg vague promises of a unification of all Armenia under a Russian protectorate, they prepared uprisings of the Armenian population in the rear of the Turkish lines.[156] This unwise policy, undertaken by the Russian Dashnaks over the protests of the Constantinople Committee of the party, induced the Turks to take very drastic measures against the Armenian population. An order issued by the Ottoman government in 1915 decreed the expulsion of all Armenians from the eastern border of Turkey to the deserts of Mesopotamia. Carried out with great brutality by front-line troops, the expulsion decree resulted in a massacre of the Armenian population, in the course of which, according to reliable estimates, one million people, or more than one-half of the entire Armenian population of the Ottoman Empire, had perished.[157] The remainder, except for a small group which by hiding saved itself from persecution, fled to the Russian Caucasus.

The massacres of 1915 cast a deep shadow on Armenian politics. In 1917 the Russian Caucasus was crowded with refugees from Anatolia, hungry, impoverished, and desperate. The events of the war brought Armenian-Turkish hostility to a degree of bitterness never before known; the Armenian and Azerbaijani inhabitants of the Caucasus, though not directly involved in the massacres, were ready to pounce upon each other at the slightest provocation. The Armenians were, as a result of this situation, completely dependent upon Russia and favorably inclined to any Russian government, as long as it was anti-Turkish.

Armenian loyalty to the Provisional Government was, therefore, as great as that of the Georgian Social Democracy, but for different reasons.

The Dashnak Regional Conference held in April 1917 voted confidence in the Provisional Government and urged that all nationalities wait with their demands for the convocation of the Constituent Assembly.[158] At the so-called State Conference, organized by the Provisional Government in the fall, Armenian deputies were among the most vociferous defenders of the regime.[159]

By September, however, it became apparent that the Provisional Government in Russia was on the verge of collapse. In order to safeguard the interests of the Armenian population and to have a center capable of administering the needs of the Armenian refugees, the Armenian National Council in Tiflis — formed in the course of the war — decided to form an organ of self-rule by convening an Armenian National Conference.[160] The Armenian Council had at its disposal some three thousand Armenian armed volunteers whom it had organized during the war with the assistance of the tsarist regime. Now it began to press Petrograd for permission to unite under one command all those troops until then serving in small detachments scattered throughout the Russian Army. The Provisional Government, after some hesitation, agreed, and by the end of the year the Council assumed direct command over an Armenian Corps, manned and officered entirely by Armenians.[161]

In the elections to the Constituent Assembly the Dashnaktsutiun polled 419,887 votes, or 20 per cent of all the votes cast in Transcaucasia — the great majority of the whole Armenian vote.[162] Whatever its past mistakes and the terrible price the Armenian population had to pay for them, the Dashnaktsutiun, with its party apparatus and military force, represented the only hope the Armenians had of being saved from utter destruction at the hands of the Moslems.

In November 1917 the Russian army fighting deep in Turkish territory started to disintegrate. Within a few weeks after the news of the October coup in Russia had spread to the rank and file, the excellent fighting body, which only a short time earlier had captured supposedly impregnable Turkish fortresses, threw down its arms and became a motley horde of deserters hastening home by all available means to share in the anticipated distribution of land. This fact completely changed the situation which had prevailed in Transcaucasia since the February Revolution.

The prospect of a Turkish advance on Tiflis and Baku threw indescribable panic into the population. The fear of the Moslem invader in general, and the memory of recent Armenian massacres in particular, caused the political parties of all views to seek a *rapprochement* for the purpose of finding a practical way of preventing the Turks from seizing defenseless Transcaucasia. At the same time steps had to be taken to control the inflow of deserting soldiers, who, in passing across Transcaucasia on the way north, threatened to upset public order. Since there was no institution for coping with such problems, it had to be created.

On November 11 the heads of the leading political parties formed a temporary government under the name Transcaucasian Commissariat (*Zakavkazskii Komissariat*) to replace the defunct Ozakom. The Georgian Menshevik and one time Duma representative, E. P. Gegechkori, became its chairman. He was assisted by another Menhevik, two Socialist Revolutionaries, two Dashnaks, four Mussavatists and one Georgian Federalist. The task of this temporary government was to maintain order until the time when the All-Russian Constituent Assembly had established a new government for the entire Russian state.

After the Bolsheviks had dissolved by force the Constituent Assembly, the Transcaucasian deputies returned home and organized a Transcaucasian Diet (*Zakavkazskii Seim*) with residence in Tiflis. The norms of representation in the Diet were established by tripling the number of candidates elected from each party to the Constituent Assembly, with the addition of representatives of national minorities and of parties which had failed to have any candidates elected.

Thus, at the beginning of February 1918 Transcaucasia possessed a legislative body (*Seim*) and an executive organ (*Komissariat*). As these institutions assumed effective control over the entire area the soviets and their Regional Center relinquished authority. The emergence of these new political bodies, as is evident from the circumstances surrounding their origin, was due not so much to the growth of separatist tendencies (for as yet they did not exist) as to the imperative need for some sort of political authority in a country abandoned to its fate by the former rulers and exposed to dangers which only a formal government could meet. The actual separation from Russia, which took place in April 1918, was to a large extent inspired by similar considerations.

The new organs of self-rule at once tackled the two most pressing dangers threatening the internal security of Transcaucasia, the collapse of the front and the influx of deserters, and a new threat, closely connected with them: Bolshevism. The Commissariat issued orders to local soviets to disarm all soldiers entering the territory of Transcaucasia. This instruction, though necessary, led in some localities to bloody clashes between the native population (which the soviets could not always control) and the soldiers. The worst incident occurred early in January 1918 near the railroad station at Shamkhor, ninety miles east of Tiflis, where a Moslem mob attacked a train full of soldiers and, after disarming them, slaughtered several hundred defenseless Russians.[163] In other areas the enforcement of the Commissariat's directives proceeded more smoothly, since most soldiers were in any case so eager to leave the Caucasus and set out for home that they gladly surrendered their weapons.

The movement of the deserting soldiers gave the Bolshevik party in Transcaucasia its first opportunity to gain a mass following. Despite the fact that at the beginning of the century, and especially during the 1905 Revolution, the Bolsheviks had perhaps won more adherents for their cause in the Caucasus than in any other borderland area of the Empire, at the beginning of 1917 their party was completely disorganized. Arrests by the tsarist police after the 1905 Revolution, exile to remote places in Siberia, and the preference of the Georgian Bolsheviks for working in Petrograd and other cities of Russia proper, destroyed the party apparatus which they had once succeeded in establishing. At the beginning of 1917 there were in Tiflis at the most fifteen to twenty persons, and in Baku twenty-five persons, of definite Bolshevik sympathies, and even they continued to work closely with the Mensheviks.[164] In Baku, the industrial heart of Transcaucasia, the Bolshevik Shaumian was elected Chairman of the Soviet, but entirely because of his personal popularity. When he tried to have the Soviet pass Leninist resolutions condemning the Provisional Government, he was voted out and replaced by a Socialist Revolutionary (beginning of May 1917).[165] At the end of May the Baku Bolsheviks still had no organization of their own. Only in June (June 6 in Tiflis, June 25 in Baku) did they form a separate party.[166]

Unable to break the control of the major indigenous and Russian parties over the population, the Bolsheviks began to concentrate their attention on the soldiers. Bolshevik agitators held meetings in the squares of Tiflis and Baku to attract the attention of the men on leave; they also sent voluminous literature to the garrisons and to the front. Their line of argument was as follows: the Mensheviks and SR's, working hand-in-hand with the bourgeoisie, want to bleed the army to death fighting for their own interests; the soldiers should therefore stop fighting and return home. By adapting their propaganda to the temper of the troops, the Bolsheviks soon gained a considerable following. In November and December 1917, when the soldiers were crossing Transcaucasia on the way home, mainly along the railroad route connecting the Turkish front with Russia via Baku and the Terek region, the Bolsheviks attracted many of them into Red detachments.[167] The dependence of the Bolsheviks upon soldier support was well illustrated by the results of the elections to the Constituent Assembly. In all Transcaucasia the Bolsheviks received 85,960 votes. This represented only 4.3 per cent of the total vote in Transcaucasia.[168] A breakdown of the election figures for Baku (which gave the Bolsheviks the largest number of votes) reveals that the Bolshevik ticket won only 14 per cent of the votes cast in the industrial districts of the city, while gaining 79 per cent of the votes cast by the soldiers.[169]

The Bolsheviks also derived some additional strength in Baku from the fact that the Mussavat throughout 1917 maintained toward them a position of friendly neutrality. The Azerbaijani nationalists favored Bolshevik slogans demanding the termination of the war and considered

Leninist policies to be advantageous to the Ottoman Empire. They came out on a number of occasions in support of Bolshevik resolutions. The Baku Bolsheviks, in turn, spared the Mussavat from the blistering attacks which they were leveling at all other parties in the area, and in general carefully avoided treading on the toes of Azerbaijani nationalists.[*]

In October 1917 the Bolsheviks convened in Tiflis their First Congress to centralize the work of all their organizations, including those of the Northern Caucasus. A total membership of some 8,600 was claimed; 2,600 were from Tiflis, mainly soldiers of the Tiflis garrison; about 2,200 were from Baku, also predominantly men in uniform.[170] The Congress elected a Regional Committee (*Kraevoi Komitet*) under the chairmanship of Filipp Makharadze, an old Georgian Social Democrat and a Leninist since 1905,[171] and adopted resolutions including one on the nationality question which condemned separatism and federalism for Transcaucasia, but supported the idea of Transcaucasian autonomy.[172] Another resolution called for emphasis on agitation in the army.

The Bolsheviks had at first hoped to employ the troops which they had won for their cause to overthrow the Transcaucasian Seim and to seize power.[173] But this project presented great difficulties. The fact that the Georgian Mensheviks in November 1917 had proclaimed the rule of local soviets in Transcaucasia made it impossible for the Bolsheviks to clamor for the transfer of all power to the soviets, as they had done with much success in other parts of the country. Then also the very factors which had induced the troops to sympathize with Bolshevik agitation, war-weariness and the desire to return to the native village, also made them unsuitable for Bolshevik purposes. It was impossible to capture and hold power with people whose chief desire was to disperse and leave the Caucasus. The Red leaders watched with dismay as the principal force which they had secured with much effort dissipated itself and vanished before their very eyes.[174] At the same time the Transcaucasian authorities, headed by people who for over two decades had worked in common conspiratorial organizations with the local Bolsheviks and knew well their tactics, took steps to nip the conspiracy in the bud.

The Bolshevik Regional Committee, in agreement with Petrograd, had set the date of the coup for early December.[175] The plan was to utilize the Tiflis garrison, entirely under Bolshevik control, and one of the pro-Bolshevik infantry regiments stationed in that city to dissolve the Seim and establish the rule of the Council of People's Commissars. But on November 14 the Transcaucasian Commissariat proclaimed martial law in Tiflis, and expelled from the town the regiment which the Bolshe-

---

[*] Ratgauzer, *Revoliutsiia*, 9–10; B. Iskhanian, *Kontr-revoliutsiia v Zakavkaz'e*, I (Baku, 1919), 61–62, 84–85. Iskhanian states that between April and November 1917 not one of the issues of the Bolshevik daily in Baku, *Bakinskii rabochii*, carried criticism of the Mussavat.

viks had intended to use. At the same time a Cossack detachment was sent to Baku to deal with the Bolsheviks active there. Finally, on November 16, a short time before the coup was to have taken place, a group of Georgian workers, organized by the Menshevik-controlled Tiflis Soviet into a "Red Guard," boldly seized the local arsenal and disarmed its garrison. As a consequence of this action the Regional Committee decided to abandon temporarily its plans for a seizure of power in Tiflis.[176] The Bolshevik party was outlawed in Tiflis in February 1918, and soon afterwards its leaders had to leave Georgian territory for Baku and the Northern Caucasus.

Lenin, who had counted much on the success of the Tiflis operation, was furious when the news of the liquidation of the garrison reached him.[177] The failure of the Tiflis Regional Center caused the Bolshevik Central Committee in Petrograd to shift the center of operations for Transcaucasia from Tiflis to Baku. Early in December, Shaumian was appointed Extraordinary Commissar for Transcaucasia and was directed by the Central Committee to seize power.[178]

At the time, however, an even greater threat to Transcaucasian security than the Bolshevik conspiracy was the collapse of the war front. As soon as the Russian armies had left the front lines, the Turks began to advance. One after another fell the fortresses won by tsarist troops in the campaigns of 1915 and 1916: Erzinjan (middle of January 1918); Erzerum (end of February); Trebizond (early March). Soon the Turkish armies approached the prewar borders of Russia. Between them and Tiflis stood only a handful of loyal Russian troops and a few Armenian volunteer detachments.

To stem the Turkish tide the Transcaucasian Commissariat dispatched to Trebizond in the second half of February a delegation headed by the Georgian Menshevik Akaki Chkhenkeli, accompanied by numerous plenipotentiaries of the Azerbaijani and Armenian political parties. The position of the Transcaucasian deputies *vis-à-vis* the Turks was most difficult. A day or two after they had left Transcaucasia for Trebizond, news arrived that the Soviet government had signed a peace treaty with the Central Powers at Brest Litovsk in which, without the slightest regard for the wishes of the local population, it had ceded to the Ottoman Empire most of the territories acquired by Russia in the war of 1877, including Batum, Kars, and Ardahan, with large Armenian and Georgian populations. The Transcaucasian Seim at once denied the validity of the Brest Litovsk Treaty for the Caucasus and voted to seek a separate agreement with Turkey.[179]

But on what legal grounds could Transcaucasia, which had not yet claimed its independence, escape the diplomatic commitments of the Russian government? Chkhenkeli, in answer to this logical question posed to him by the Turks, replied vaguely that Transcaucasia had a *de facto* sovereignty as a result of the collapse of the legitimate Russian government, but, aware of the anomaly of his position, he began to press Tiflis for concessions to the Turks.[180] Inasmuch as the Turks had occupied Ardahan and were beginning to lay siege to Kars, the Transcaucasian Commissariat decided to yield, and on March 28/April 10 officially accepted the Brest Litovsk Treaty as a basis for further negotiations.[181]

But the Turks now posed new demands. On March 31/April 13 they informed the Transcaucasians that in order to make it possible for the representatives of the other Central Powers to take part in the talks, Transcaucasia had to proclaim its independence. This the Seim refused to do. The following day the negotiations in Trebizond were broken off and the delegation recalled.[182] Transcaucasia — still without a sovereign government — was in a state of war with the Ottoman Empire.

The country was placed in a critical situation. On April 1/14, one day after the disruption of diplomatic talks, the Turks marched into the port city of Batum, the third largest town in Transcaucasia. The great fortress of Kars fell ten days later. Logic dictated the acceptance of the Turkish proposal, the more so as the proclamation of independence would have freed Transcaucasia from suffering further unpleasant surprises which continued association with the new Russian regime was bound to bring. But anti-separatist tendencies were very deeply rooted among the majority of Transcaucasian political leaders — Russian, Georgian, and Armenian alike. The Mussavatists alone were not too displeased with the turn which events had taken and with the improvement in their position caused by the Turkish victories, but outwardly they maintained neutrality.

For nearly two weeks the halls of the Seim in Tiflis reverberated with debates on the question of independence.[183] Finally, on April 9/22, over the protests of Kadet and SR members, the independence of the Transcaucasian Federation was proclaimed. The motives were clear:

> The peoples of Transcaucasia are faced with the following tragic situation: either to proclaim themselves at present an inseparable part of Russia, and in this manner to repeat all the horrors of the Russian Civil War and then become an arena of a foreign invasion, in this case Turkish; or to proclaim independence and with their own powers defend the physical existence of the whole country. When the issues boil down to this, then the only solution is the immediate proclamation of political independence and the creation of the independent Transcaucasian Federative Republic.[184]

### The Bolsheviks in Power

The separation of the borderlands previously under the control of the Provisional Government was accompanied by a loss of other Russian territories, some under enemy occupation. Lithuania and Finland proclaimed their independence in December 1917; Latvia followed shortly afterwards. Poland, which was entirely occupied by German troops, enjoyed *de facto* independence recognized officially by the Soviet delegation to the Brest Litovsk Peace Conference. Estonia severed its bonds with Russia in February 1918. In addition vast areas, inhabited by Russians who did not desire to be subjected to the Soviet regime, formed their own governments and proclaimed statehood. Most important in this category was the Siberian Republic created by the SR's, and the Southeastern Union, embracing the Cossack regions of the Northern Caucasus and the Urals, both established in January 1918. It is not far-fetched to assert that at the beginning of 1918 Russia, as a political concept, had ceased to exist.

The disintegration of the Russian Empire confronted the young Bolshevik government with difficulties which it did not anticipate and for which it had made no provisions. Lenin's entire national program was designed to exploit the national problem in Russia in order to weaken tsarist authority and the Provisional Government. The alliance with the minority nationalists in 1917 had provided the Bolsheviks with much assistance, notably in the Ukraine, and there was every reason to expect that in the Civil War, which started almost immediately after the October coup, the slogan of national self-determination could also be successfully employed, this time as a weapon against anti-Soviet forces.

But a breakup of the Russian domain into a conglomeration of small national states was the last thing Lenin desired. Not only was it contrary to his repeatedly stated preference for large states, but it also undermined the economic foundations of the state which the Bolsheviks were attempting to establish. Deprived of its borderlands, Soviet Russia had neither sufficient food, nor fuel, nor raw materials.

The question which confronted Lenin after he had come to power, therefore, was how to reconcile the slogan of national self-determination with the need for preserving the unity of the Soviet state.

First, however, it was necessary to prevent the slogan of national self-determination from doing more harm. Lenin acted quickly. Utilizing Bolshevik organizations established in the borderlands in the days of the Provisional Government, and the Russian troops which to a large extent followed Bolshevik leadership, he overthrew wherever possible the newly formed national republics. The dissolution of the Belorussian Rada; the attempted coup in Transcaucasia; the invasion of the Ukraine; as well as the suppression of the Moslem governments of Kokand, Crimea, the Alash Orda, and the Bashkir republic, which will constitute the subject matter of subsequent chapters of this book, were all a complete violation of the principle of national self-determination. It can scarcely be a subject for wonder that Lenin so flagrantly disregarded his previous pledges.

Having once ventured upon a course of political lawlessness by over-throwing the Provisional Government and by dissolving the popularly elected Russian Constituent Assembly, Lenin could hardly have shown deference to the institutions founded by the minorities. Fundamentally, his disregard of the wishes of the minority populations was not different from his disregard of the will of the Russian people; both had their roots in Lenin's general contempt for democratic procedures and in his convic-tion that the spread of the revolutionary movement required firm, un-hesitant action against all who dared to stand in its way.

The first public indication that the principle of national self-determi-nation (in Lenin's interpretation) required also theoretical change came on December 12, 1917, in an article by Stalin. With no record of having favored this principle, Stalin, at any rate, had previously abstained from criticizing Lenin's views openly, as many other Bolsheviks had done. Now, writing in connection with the Ukrainian crisis, Stalin asserted that the Soviet government could not permit national self-determination to serve as a cloak for counterrevolution. The Council of People's Commissars, he wrote, was ready to recognize the independence of any republic but "upon the demand of the working population of such an area." [185] A month later he restated his case against Lenin's theory even more strongly: "It is necessary to limit the principle of free self-determination of nations, by granting it to the toilers and refusing it to the bourgeoisie. The principle of self-determination should be a means of fighting for socialism." [186]

Such an interpretation of the principle of national self-determination had nothing in common with Lenin's views. It was essentially identical with the argument of the "leftists" whom Lenin had attacked with much vigor during World War I. "Proletarian self-determination" — if one ac-cepts Communist terminology — meant the class struggle and the estab-lishment of the worker's dictatorship by means of soviets and the Bolshevik party. National self-determination rested on the principle of class co-operation and had as its aim the establishment of a national state.

Lenin, occupied at the time with other, more pressing matters, paid no attention officially to Stalin's attempt to reinterpret the slogan of national self-determination, but he took the matter up in March 1919, when the party platform came up for revision at the Eighth Party Congress. Bukh-arin, who belonged to the "leftists" on the national question, was as-signed the task of preparing a draft of a new program. In an attempt to reconcile Lenin's views with those of the "leftists," with whom Stalin also sympathized, Bukharin introduced in his project a double formula: for the advanced nations the slogan of "self-determination of the working classes," for the underdeveloped, colonial areas the slogan of "national self-determination." [187] During the debates at the Congress, both Bukharin and Piatakov criticized the Leninist slogan as impractical. Bukharin asserted that he had adopted Stalin's formula of "proletarian self-determination" as more consistent with Communist doctrines.[188]

Lenin replied to Bukharin — and indirectly to Stalin, who did not speak in defense of his views — that such an attitude was unrealistic and illogical: it drew too neat a distinction between advanced and backward countries. Class differentiation, as experience has shown, had not even taken place in such economically advanced countries as Germany, let alone elsewhere. "Proletarian self-determination" was synonymous with proletarian dictatorship, Lenin argued, and so far had been accomplished only in Russia. It certainly provided no solution for the nationality question. The party program had to take into account realities, and for that reason it was necessary to continue support of national self-determination, even if in a qualified form. Speaking of the proponents of the Bukharin-Piatakov-Stalin line, Lenin said scornfully, "In my opinion, this kind of a Communist is a great Russian chauvinist; he lives inside of many of us, and must be fought." [189]

On Lenin's suggestion the Congress adopted a national program which retained the right to national self-determination, with qualifications:

> 2. In order to overcome the suspicion of the toiling masses of the oppressed countries toward the proletariat of the states which had oppressed these countries, it is necessary to destroy all and every privilege enjoyed by whatever national group, to establish full equality of nations, and to recognize that the colonies and the nations which possess full rights have a right to political secession.
>
> 3. For the same purpose, as one of the transitional forms on the way to full unity, the party proposes a federative unification of states, organized on the Soviet pattern.
>
> 4. As to the question who is the carrier of the nation's will to separation, the Russian Communist Party* stands on the historico-class point of view, taking into consideration the level of historical development on which a given nation stands: on the road from the Middle Ages to bourgeois democracy, or from bourgeois democracy to Soviet or proletarian democracy, and so forth.[190]

The new formula neatly solved the problem which confronted the Communists. It gave them a free hand to agitate for national independence and to attract the sympathies of the nationalists in those areas where the Communists were trying to come into power, without hampering their efforts to overcome nationalist opposition where they were already in

---

* Early in 1918 the Bolsheviks formally adopted the name of the Russian Communist Party (Bolsheviks) (*Rossiiskaia Kommunisticheskaia Partiia [bol'shevikov]*). Henceforth, the terms Bolshevik and Communist are used interchangeably.

control. The double standard which the new formula provided was in the future to prove extremely convenient.

The right to national self-determination, as Lenin had interpreted it before 1917, however, was gone, and with it died the heart of the Bolshevik national program. It was necessary to provide something in its place.

Before November 1917 the Bolsheviks, like the Mensheviks, had opposed the federal idea, but now that the state had fallen apart, the prerevolutionary arguments against this concept were no longer valid. Federalism, which had been a centrifugal factor as long as Russia was one, now became a centripetal force, an instrument for welding together the scattered parts of a disintegrated empire.

For this reason, within a month or two after they had seized power, the Bolsheviks reversed their old stand and took over the Socialist Revolutionary program of a federated Russia.

The first official statement to this effect was drawn up by Lenin in January 1918, in connection with the Bolshevik attack on the Ukraine: "The Central Executive Committee of the Soviets of the Ukraine . . . is proclaimed the supreme authority in the Ukraine. There is accepted a federal union with Russia, and complete unity in matters of internal and external policy . . ." [191] Simultaneously, Lenin prepared a general statement which served as a model for a resolution adopted by the Third Congress of Soviets held at the end of January 1918. "The Soviet Russian Republic," he wrote, "is established on the basis of a free union of free nations, as a federation of Soviet national republics." [192]

At the beginning of April 1918 a Constitutional Commission was appointed to prepare a draft of the fundamental law of the Russian Soviet republic. Headed by Iakov Sverdlov, the commission had, as one of its chief assignments, to determine the nature of the federal system which was to be instituted in the new state. The question was whether the basic units of the federation were to be economic, geographic, ethnic, or historic regions. Each viewpoint had its sympathizers. To reach a decision, the commission appointed two of its members, Mikhail Reisner (of the Commissariat of Justice), and Stalin, to prepare projects for a federal constitution. [193]

Reisner, who presented his draft at the next meeting of the Commission, argued for a federation based on the economic principle. In a socialist republic, he held, the national factor was secondary, and should be limited to cultural matters. It was unwise to create national-territorial units, or to pursue "hidden centralism under the cover of a federal structure." Instead, he proposed that the Russian federation be based on voluntary associations of trade unions, coöperatives, communes, and other local institutions. Reisner's project thus called for a federation of socio-economic groups rather than nationalities, organized extraterritorially rather than territorially, and offering the minorities cultural, in place of political, self-determination.

This project was rejected because the members of the commission felt that it ignored both the centrifugal tendencies in evidence since early 1917, and the fact that the republics which were already in existence on the territory of the defunct Russian Empire were national in character.

Stalin, who was not present when Reisner had read his paper, reappeared at the third session, but without the promised project. He brought with him only a brief statement, which demanded flatly that the federation be based on the principle of national-territorial autonomy, and neither explained nor justified this request. It seems likely that Stalin merely conveyed the wishes of Lenin, who several months earlier had indicated that he desired the Soviet federation to be established along national-territorial lines. Stalin made no other contribution to the work of the commission because a few days later he left for the front. The idea of national-territorial autonomy was accepted by the commission and embodied in the Soviet Russian Constitution of 1918. Soviet Russia thus became the first modern state to place the national principle at the base of its federal structure.

To have an organ capable of dealing with the national question Lenin created in November 1917 a special Commissariat of Nationality Affairs (*Narodnyi komissariat po delam natsional'nostei,* otherwise known as *Narkomnats*). The chairmanship of this commissariat was turned over to Stalin. Its original functions consisted of mediation in conflicts arising among the various national groups in the country and of advising other agencies of the government on problems connected with the minorities.[194] But in time, especially after 1920, it assumed broader responsibilities and became one of the several vehicles which Stalin used to obtain control over the party and state apparatus of the entire country.

The activities of the Narkomnats may be divided into two periods: from its foundation until 1920; and from 1920 until its dissolution in 1924. Until the end of the Civil War the borderland areas were separated from Moscow, and the Narkomnats' field of operations was restricted largely to the minority populations residing in Russia proper. It issued general appeals to the non-Russians, urging them to support the Soviet regime; it conducted propaganda among the prisoners of war; it closed minority organizations of a military or philanthropic nature established during the war in various cities of Russia.*

---

* The Narkomnats suppressed the following organizations: the Caucasian Bureau; all Moslem organizations formed by the All-Russian Moslem Central Council; the Georgian Commissariat of Military-National Affairs; the Higher Lithuanian Council in Russia; the All-Russian Moslem Council; the Armenian National councils; the Union

In the first period the Narkomnats consisted of a chairman, Stalin, a vice-chairman, S. S. Pestkovskii (a Pole, by origin), a collegium, and a number of national sub-commissariats which were created to deal with the individual nationalities. The personnel was selected haphazardly, and was composed largely of "leftists" who opposed Lenin's national policy, including his new idea of federalism and his concessions to the minorities.[195]

In some cases functionaries of this commissariat were placed at the head of the governments which were established by the Soviet authorities in areas conquered from the White Guard. The Narkomnats also endeavored at various times during the Civil War to obtain exclusive control over the Communist underground movements operating in the borderlands, but there is little evidence that it succeeded in realizing this or many other of its claims.* In general, the Narkomnats seems to have exercised in 1918 and 1919 a very limited influence on the course of events in the borderland areas: it acquired importance in Soviet political life only after 1920, when Stalin, having assumed once more personal management of its affairs after his return from the Civil War, changed its personnel and broadened its functions far beyond its original scope.

of Jewish Veterans; and the Central Bureau of Jewish Communities (Narodnyi komissariat po delam natsional'nostei, *Politika sovetskoi vlasti po natsional'nym delam za tri goda* [Moscow, 1920]).

  * E. I. Pesikina, *Narodnyi komissariat po delam natsional'nostei* (Moscow, 1950), 84–89. Pesikina asserts that the Narkomnats actually conducted "all" underground operations in the regions occupied by the enemy (p. 84), but gives no evidence to support this contention.

# III

## SOVIET CONQUEST OF THE UKRAINE

## AND BELORUSSIA

### *The Fall of the Ukrainian Central Rada*

Unlike the pattern in other parts of the old Russian Empire where, following the overthrow of the Provisional Government, authority was, in most cases, vested in the Soviets of Workers', Soldiers' and Peasants' Deputies, the situation in the Ukraine did not permit such a direct transfer of political power. The existence of the Ukrainian Central Rada, which claimed to be the national soviet for the territory, complicated matters. It resulted in an uneasy condominium in which sovereignty was shared between the Rada with its General Secretariat exercising control over the city of Kiev and, to some extent, over the right-bank (i.e., west of the Dnieper) rural districts, and the city soviets, most of which were Bolshevik-dominated, ruling the remaining towns.[1] For a brief time, at the end of October and the beginning of November 1917, it seemed possible for the two governing agencies to coöperate and even to merge, much as they had done during the crucial days of the October Revolution. But with the disappearance of the Provisional Government the fundamental divergence of interests between them came to the fore and led to an armed struggle which finally resulted in the Bolshevik conquest of the Ukraine.

During the first day or two following the liquidation of the Kievan pro-government Staff there was utter confusion in the city. No one knew who was in command: the City Soviet, the Rada, or the newly formed Council of Peoples' Commissars in Petrograd. The Bolshevik Committee in Kiev, especially its right wing, which had favored coöperation with the Ukrainian nationalists and had brought about the establishment of the Rada's Revolutionary Committee, anticipated that the defeat of the pro-Kerensky troops would be followed by the convocation of an All-Ukrainian Congress of Soviets. Its members expected that this congress would appoint a Ukrainian Central Executive Committee and that this committee in turn would assume power over the entire territory of the Ukraine in close liaison with the Petrograd Soviet. Until such time as this operation should have been completed, the Kievan Bolsheviks were ready to recognize the authority of the Rada and of its Revolutionary Committee.[2]

The Ukrainian leaders of the Rada, however, were not quite ready to follow Bolshevik suggestions. The fall of the Provisional Government had caught them unprepared. In the past they had concentrated so strongly on fighting the moderate socialist and liberal groups in charge of the Russian state that they lacked a plan of action now that the old government was gone. Their coöperation with the Bolsheviks had been an opportunist maneuver, but apparently in their planning they had never foreseen that it might bring success. For several days there were heated debates in the Rada, the General Secretariat, and the Ukrainian press. Finally, on November 3, the General Secretariat announced that it was assuming all the power in the territory of the Ukraine (which it interpreted to include, in addition to the five provinces recognized as Ukrainian by the Provisional Government Instruction of July 1917, the provinces of Kharkov, Kherson, Ekaterinoslav, and Taurida, the latter without the Crimean peninsula). In the same declaration the General Secretariat restated its desire to remain part of a Federal Russian Republic, vigorously denying any striving for independence, despite the Bolshevik coup in Russia:

> The central government of Russia has no means of administering the state. Entire regions are left without any centers to govern them; political, economic, and social disorder is spreading. As a consequence the General Secretariat adds the following secretariats: food, military, justice, post, telegraphs, and means of transportation. The authority of the General Secretariat is broadened to include all those provinces in which the majority of the population is composed of Ukrainians . . .
>
> All rumors and discussions about separatism, about the separation of the Ukraine from Russia are either counterrevolutionary propaganda or a result of simple ignorance. The Central Rada and the General Secretariat have announced firmly and clearly that the Ukraine is to be a part of a federal Russian republic, as an equal governmental entity. The present political situation does not alter this decision one bit.[3]

A similar spirit pervaded the Third Universal which the Rada issued on November 6, which proclaimed the Ukraine a People's Republic and a component part of the Russian Federation.[4] Now it was the Bolsheviks who were caught unprepared.[5] The Rada's action added new fuel to the struggle between the two principal factions of the Kievan party organization. Despite their initial disappointment, those who had urged a "soft" policy toward the Ukrainians and the utilization of their political machinery retained control of the Kievan Committee throughout the month of November. They concentrated their efforts now on convoking an All-Ukrainian Congress of Soviets, with the coöperation of the Rada if possible, without it if not. In this they had the support of the newly appointed Commissar of Nationalities, Stalin.[6] In view of the dominant role played by Bolsheviks in the soviets and the pro-Bolshevik sympathies of the left-wing USR's and USD's, there was every reason to expect such a congress to act in accordance with their wishes. The left-wingers on the other hand, who included most of the non-Kievan members of the Regional Committee, took a more intransigent attitude toward the Ukrainian nationalists. Asserting that the alliance with the Rada spread confusion among the Bolshevik rank and file and would result only in further disappointments, they urged a clear break with the Ukrainians.

The only manner in which the Rada could avoid an open conflict with the Bolsheviks and the soviets was to comply with the Bolshevik demand to convoke a Congress of Soviets. This it feared to do, for the simple reason that its own strength lay in the villages, and not in the towns, where the soviets functioned. The soviets were "Russian" institutions and could easily be used to establish the rule of the essentially non-Ukrainian cities over the Ukrainian countryside.[7]

Instead of following the Bolshevik program, the Rada began to concentrate on aiding Russian moderate socialist groups to reëstablish in Russia a coalition socialist government that would replace Lenin's regime and create an All-Russian federation. The Rada refused to recognize the Council of People's Commissars as the legitimate government of Russia and requested that it be replaced by a more representative socialist body.[8] In November the General Secretariat convened in Kiev a conference of nationalities to initiate action leading to the creation of a federal union of Russia. Under the circumstances those were the only sensible lines of policy. The Rada's transfer of support in the short space of a few weeks from the moderate socialists to the Bolsheviks and back again is characteristic of the lack of policy which plagued the Rada throughout its existence.

In November and December the soviets of several cities of the Ukraine, Ekaterinoslav, Odessa, and Nikolaev, joined the Kievan Soviet in recognizing the authority of the Rada and the General Secretariat.[9] The Kharkov Soviet alone refused to do so, and not only pledged its allegiance to the Bolshevik government in Petrograd, but as the month went on, assumed an increasingly hostile attitude toward the Ukrainian political center. The authority of the Rada over the whole country was as ineffective after the proclamation of the Republic as it had been in the days of the Provisional Government. In most towns the Rada had at its disposal volunteer haidamak detachments: an asset of somewhat dubious value, since, as future events were to show, they deserted the Rada in some very critical moments. The rural areas continued to rule themselves in isolation from the rest of the world. The issue between the Rada and the Bolsheviks could be put, therefore, not so much as "who now rules the Ukraine?" — since, in fact, after the fall of the Provisional Government, the answer was "nobody" — but "who will rule it?"

The Ukraine, Belorussia and the Crimea (1922)

In view of the Rada's refusal to convene the All-Ukrainian Congress of Soviets, the Kiev Bolshevik Committee, in coöperation with the City Soviet, decided to proceed on its own. Appealing over the head of the General Secretariat to the soviets located in the towns and villages of the Ukraine, it urged them to send their representatives to Kiev to attend the forthcoming congress, whose date they had set for December 4. At the same time the Bolsheviks made plans for the First Congress of the Bolshevik Party of the Southwestern Territory.

Lenin and his government had every reason to agree with the Kievan Bolsheviks' friendly attitude toward the Rada, and indeed, in the early part of November Petrograd made several courteous gestures in its direction. As late as November 24, Trotsky, about to depart for the Brest Litovsk peace discussions with the Central Powers, offered to include a representative of the Rada in his delegation and voiced his desire that "the Ukrainian toiling masses convince themselves in fact that the All-Russian Soviet government placed no obstacles on the path of Ukrainian self-determination, whatever forms it may take, and that the Russian government recognized the People's Ukrainian Republic fully and most sincerely." [10]

Toward the end of November, however, the relations between Petrograd and Kiev worsened. The main cause of friction lay in relations between the Ukrainian Rada and the Don Cossacks. After the overthrow of the Provisional Government, the region of the Don Cossacks, southeast of the Ukraine, became one of the main centers of anti-Bolshevik activity. Here had gathered a considerable number of high tsarist officers and conservative political statesmen who hoped to utilize the Don Cossack regiments, traditionally loyal to the *ancien régime* because of the privileges which it had bestowed upon them, as the nucleus of an army with which to overthrow the conspirators who had seized power in Petrograd. In November the Don Cossacks, under the headship of Ataman Kaledin, proclaimed a Cossack Republic. When the Ukrainian Rada issued its appeal to the borderlands of the Russian Empire to coöperate with it in the creation of a Russian Federation, they were among the first to respond. The relations between the Ukrainians and their Eastern neighbors were not entirely devoid of friction, especially after Kaledin began to suppress on his territory worker organizations which had considerable Ukrainian membership; they were, however, sufficiently friendly to frighten the Bolshevik High Command in Petrograd with the prospect of a "Vendée" on its vulnerable southern flank. In the eyes of the Bolsheviks, the Rada, in permitting Don Cossack troops to cross Ukrainian territory on their way home from the front, aided the counterrevolution.

Further disagreements arose concerning Ukrainian activities at the front. As long as the Provisional Government had controlled the Russian Army, the Bolsheviks had done everything in their power to disorganize and demoralize the troops fighting the Germans and Austrians, and for that reason had openly welcomed the aid of the Ukrainian nationalists who had demanded the creation of separate Ukrainian military units. But once in the saddle, the Bolsheviks were not inclined to be so friendly to such efforts. Anxious to keep the front as stable as possible, the Bolsheviks objected to Petliura's attempts to separate Ukrainians from the army and to return them home. When Petliura issued instructions to the Ukrainian soldiers serving in the Russian Army to disobey the orders of the Soviet government and to place themselves under his command, the relations between Petrograd and Kiev approached a breaking point. Krylenko, then in charge of the *Stavka* (Russian Army Headquarters) countermanded Petliura's order.[11]

The issue which finally led to an open break were the repressive measures which the Rada took against the Kiev Soviet at the end of November. On receiving information that the Bolsheviks were plotting a seizure of power by the local soviets, the Rada's General Secretariat arrested the leading Bolshevik personalities and expelled from the city the military units loyal to them. This action placed the Rada in complete control of Kiev and removed the possibility of a Red rebellion.[12]

The activities of the Ukrainian Rada made it clear that the Ukrainian nationalists would not continue the policy of sympathetic neutrality which they had adopted during October. Faced with the alternative of violating his program of national self-determination or damaging what he considered the best interests of the proletariat, Lenin without much hesitation chose the former course. Orders were issued to Soviet officers in charge of the recently seized Stavka to prepare for a campaign against the Don Cossacks and if necessary to take action against the forces of the Rada. The Red Commanders worked out a plan calling for the seizure of Kharkov and Ekaterinoslav in the east, and diversionary attacks on Kiev from the north (Chernigov) and west (Podolia).[13]

On December 4 the General Secretariat received a formal protest from Petrograd sent through the Stavka. It charged that the Rada's policy of separating Ukrainian troops from Russian units, of disarming Soviet soldiers on Ukrainian territory (i.e., those troops whom the Bolsheviks had hoped to use in Kiev for the abortive coup at the end of November), and of supporting the separatist tendencies of the Don and Kuban region, was aiding the counterrevolution and would no longer be tolerated. The note ended with the following ultimatum:

1. Will the Central Rada stop its attempts aimed at disorganizing the united front?

2. Will the Central Rada now agree to prevent the movement of all troops to the Don, Ural, or other regions without the approval of the Supreme Commander?

3. Will the Central Rada agree to aid the revolutionary army in its fight against the counterrevolutionary Kadet-Kaledin rebellions?

4. Will the Central Rada agree to stop all attempts to disarm Soviet regiments and the Workers' Red Guard in the Ukraine and to return the arms at once to those who had been deprived of them?

In the event that no satisfactory answer to these questions will be forthcoming within 48 hours, the Council of People's Commissars will consider the Central Rada in a condition of open war against the Soviet government in Russia and the Ukraine.[14]

The General Secretariat replied to Petrograd the following day with a flat refusal. The Ukrainian note stressed the right of the Ukrainians to rule themselves and accused the Bolsheviks of violating their pledges. On the issue of the Don Cossacks, which formed the heart of the Bolshevik charge, the General Secretariat stated that it had permitted the free movement of the Don Cossacks to their homeland for the same reason as it had allowed Russian troops to cross the Ukraine to return home, or had demanded free passage for Ukrainian soldiers to cross Russian territories on their way to the Ukraine. The intervention of Russian Communist troops in the Don Cossack lands, however, was a different matter: this was not demobilization and self-determination as were the other troop movements, but war, and the Ukraine reserved the right not to permit the passage of belligerents across its territory.[15] The note also emphasized that the General Secretariat did not recognize the Council of People's Commissars as the legitimate government of all Russia.

Simultaneously with their ultimatum to Kiev, the Bolsheviks made preparations for the transfer of their forces to the Don and Kuban regions. In the first two weeks of December Russian troops, composed mainly of workers and sailors from Petrograd and Moscow, began to pour into Kharkov, which was selected as the base of operations. V. A. Antonov-Ovseenko, the Bolshevik commander of the Red troops which had seized the Winter Palace in Petrograd during the October coup, arrived in Kharkov in charge of the offensive against Kaledin and the Ukrainians.

The rejection of the Bolshevik ultimatum by the Ukrainians did not result in the immediate outbreak of hostilities. Throughout the month of December Petrograd and Kiev carried on discussions, partly directly, partly through the Ukrainian delegates to the All-Russian Congress of Peasants held in Petrograd. At the beginning of December, Zinoviev arrived in Kiev for talks;[16] a week later a delegation of pro-Bolshevik Ukrainian peasant representatives came there for the same purpose.[17] But all attempts at a peaceful solution of the impending conflict failed, and it is difficult to see how it could have been otherwise, since nothing short of an actual surrender of all sovereign rights on the part of the General Secretariat would have satisfied the Bolshevik demands. While these discussions were still in progress, the Bolshevik press began to lay down a heavy barrage of invective and threat against the Rada, but before taking direct action the Soviet government decided to see what the All-Ukrainian Congress of Soviets would bring.

The Congresses of Soviets, which, according to Bolshevik formulae, performed the functions of constituent assemblies of the new regime, were not institutions with a formal system of organization and representation. There were no fixed norms for selecting the delegates, no standard operating procedures, and no agreed-upon methods of selecting presidia. Consequently, the congresses were generally unrepresentative of the regions which they were supposed to rule. Both in 1905 and in 1917, the majority of socialists, including the followers of Lenin, had regarded the soviets as organs of proletarian opinion or weapons of pressure upon the government, and not as institutions of political rule. Only after Lenin had realized their importance as instruments of attaining power, did they assume a larger role. They were ill-equipped to perform the legislative and executive functions which the Bolshevik coup had thrust upon them. The Bolsheviks took advantage of the irregularities in the structure of the soviets to seize control of the key positions in them in many regions of Russia and to maneuver them to suit their own purposes. The average worker, peasant, or soldier cared little about this constitutional imperfection. He was far more interested in what was done to satisfy his demands than in how it was done or by whom. Such an attitude facilitated the Bolshevik task. But there were instances when a determined opponent of the Bolsheviks could also take advantage of this situation for his own benefit. This occurred in the Ukraine.

The Rada had at first intended to boycott the Bolshevik-sponsored Congress of Soviets, but then it changed its mind and issued instructions to all Ukrainian provincial organizations to dispatch to Kiev as many delegates as possible. Obeying this directive, virtually every Ukrainian coöperative and military and political organization in the country sent at least one representative, with the result that on the appointed day the Ukrainian delegates simply flooded Kiev. When the Congress of Soviets opened, 2,500 delegates demanded admission. The handful of Bolshevik representatives present — a hundred at most — was lost in the crowd of pro-Rada deputies. Unable to prevent them from participating, the Kievan Bolsheviks hoped to attain their ends — the proclamation of Soviet rule in the Ukraine — by means of skillful direction of the Congress, but the Bolshevik self-appointed directing committee had barely taken its seat and opened the meeting, when a group of USR leaders, surrounded by an armed retinue, entered the assembly hall and ejected the Bolshevik chairman bodily from the podium. The direction of the Congress thus passed into the hands of Rada supporters.[18]

The new chairman placed before the Congress the issue of the Bolshevik ultimatum which had arrived in Kiev that same day. The reading of the Petrograd note evoked a storm of protests. Even some Bolsheviks, apparently taken by surprise and unaware of Lenin's intention to bring the crisis with the Rada to a head, apologized before the Congress and called the ultimatum a "misunderstanding." [19] The Congress adopted a strong resolution condemning the action of the Bolshevik government:

> Considering the ultimatum of the Council of People's Commissars an attack on the Ukrainian People's Republic, and declaring that the demands voiced in it violate the right of the Ukrainian people to

self-determination and to a free creation of forms of political life, the All-Ukrainian Congress of Soviets of Peasants', Workers', and Soldiers' Deputies resolves that the centralistic plans of the present government of Moscow (Great Russia), by leading to war between Muscovy and the Ukraine, threaten to break completely the federal relations which Ukrainian democracy strives to establish.

At a time when the democracy of the entire world, led by the vanguard units of international socialism, is fighting for the attainment of general peace, which alone will provide the peasant and proletarian masses with an opportunity to struggle successfully for the interests of the toilers, the threat of a new fratricidal war announced by the Council of People's Commissars to the Ukraine, destroys the brotherhood of the laboring classes of all nations, awakens the manifestations of national animosity, and obscures the class-consciousness of the masses, in this manner favoring the growth of the counterrevolution.

Declaring that the reply of the General Secretariat given on December 17 [New Style] is the proper answer to the attempt of the People's Commissars to violate the rights of the Ukrainian peasants, workers, and soldiers, the All-Ukrainian Congress of Peasants', Workers', and Soldiers' Deputies deems it necessary to take all measures in order to prevent the spilling of brotherly blood and appeals warmly to the peoples of Russia to stop, with all means at their disposal, the possibility of a new shameful war.[20]

This was an unmistakable rebuke to the Bolsheviks. The Bolshevik delegates, enraged by the unexpected turn of events, demanded that the deputies vote on a resolution of their own proclaiming the entire Congress a "meaningless show." When the majority refused to do so, the Bolsheviks walked out of the Congress, followed by some fellow-travelers of the Left USR. The entire group, some 150 delegates, departed for Kharkov, which, with the inflow of Red troops from the north, was being transformed into an alternate capital of the Ukraine, loyal to the Bolshevik regime.

While the Congress of Soviets did not accurately reflect the actual political sympathies of the Ukrainians, since it represented not the population at large but ill-defined political institutions and organizations, there can be little doubt that the Ukrainian parties had a more numerous following in December 1917, than they had had before the October Revolution. One of the main causes for this change was the disintegration of the Russian middle-of-the-road socialist parties in the fall of 1917, and the transfer of a considerable portion of their following to the Ukrainians. The political primacy of the USD's and USR's in the heart of the Ukraine manifested itself in the elections to the All-Russian Constituent Assembly held in December 1917. Those two parties, running on a joint ticket, received the largest number of votes in the provinces of Kiev (600,000 votes of a total 850,000), Podolia (596,000 votes), Poltava, and Ekaterino-slav. In the city of Kiev they received approximately twice the number of votes which they had won in the July elections to the city dumas. In Kherson the USR's, running on a joint ticket with the Russian SR's, also received the largest number of votes. In the province of Kharkov, how-ever, the pro-Ukrainian vote was insignificant.[21]

The "soft" policies of the right-wing factions of the Kievan Bolsheviks having ended in a fiasco, the left wing now took over. Upon their arrival in Kharkov, the Bolshevik deputies who had walked out of the All-Ukrainian Congress of Soviets joined the Bolshevik-controlled Congress of Soviets of the Donets and Krivoi Rog Basins, meeting at Kharkov at the time; and together, on December 11, they formed a new All-Ukrain-ian Congress of Soviets. This rump group appointed a Central Executive Committee, which announced that it was henceforth to be considered as the sole legal government of the entire Ukraine. The new "government," composed of Kiev and Kharkov Bolsheviks, first of all sent a telegram to Petrograd in which it pledged its allegiance to the Soviet government, and declared all the decrees of the Russian Council of People's Commis-sars to be applicable to the Ukraine.[22] On December 12, with the aid of freshly arrived worker and sailor detachments from Moscow, the Kharkov Bolsheviks accomplished a coup against the other socialist groups and seized power in the city. The split between the Bolsheviks and the Ukrainian nationalists was now complete, and the outbreak of an armed conflict was only a matter of time.

The new strategy of the Bolsheviks consisted of raising local rebellions throughout the Ukraine and employing returning soldiers and friendly worker organizations in the seizure of power. In the middle of December clashes between Ukrainian soldiers and pro-Red troops occurred in many towns. The local soviets seized power in Odessa (December 12), Eka-terinoslav (December 26-8), and elsewhere. The only town in which an attempted Bolshevik coup failed was Kiev, where the Rada disposed of strong detachments and the pro-Soviet troops had been expelled at the end of November. Lenin for a time had hoped to acquire Kiev by mak-ing an alliance with a Left USR group which was to take over the Rada and expel the anti-Soviet elements, but this plot failed when the Rada got wind of it and arrested the ringleaders of the conspiracy.[23] The only remaining way to dispose of the Rada was to employ the military forces assembled in Kharkov and to strike directly at the heart of Ukrainian resistance.

The General Secretariat, although well aware of the dangers besetting it, took no definite course of action to meet them. The minutes of a secret session of the General Secretariat held on December 15, several days after a rival Soviet Ukrainian government had been formed in Kharkov, indi-cate that the leaders of the Ukrainian forces were utterly confused and had no notion what to do. There were complaints that the General Secretariat lacked money and consequently could not dispatch agitators with which to keep its own troops in line; that it had no general plan of action; and, above all, that the Ukrainian soldiers were becoming less and less reliable under the influence of Bolshevik propaganda. A Special Commission for the Defense of the Ukraine was formed, but there was little hope of successful resistance.[24]

On January 4/17, 1918, the Kharkov Bolsheviks proclaimed the Rada "an enemy of the people" and the next day a number of detachments of Antonov-Ovseenko's command left Kharkov in the direction of Poltava. They consisted of units of so-called "Red Cossacks," organized by the Kharkov government of pro-Communist Ukrainians; of a Red Guard, formed in Kharkov of various local elements, with criminal groups predominating; and finally of a hard core of Russian workers, soldiers, and sailors sent from the north, who composed the bulk of the invading force.[25] The over-all command of this motley army was entrusted to Lieutenant Colonel Muraviev, an ex-officer of the Tsarist Army of Left SR sympathies whom Antonov-Ovseenko had appointed a member of his staff. The entire group consisted of 600 to 800 men,[26] but its battle strength was greater, for it was preceded by Bolshevik agents dispatched from Kharkov to organize fifth columns in the regions lying on the path of the army.[27] Muraviev, whose ultimate destination was Kiev, took a route leading across the southern fringes of the Chernigov province, where the Bolsheviks had considerable party following in the railroad towns. The march on Poltava presented no difficulties. Only on the very outskirts of the city were the Soviet forces met by small detachments of Ukrainian troops, but those were easily dispersed and on January 6/19, Poltava was occupied. Muraviev lost no time in informing the local citizens of his mission:

> Citizens! The Civil War has started. The Civil War goes on. From the Baltic to the Black Sea across the Danube towards Vienna, Berlin, Paris, and London we shall march with fire and sword, establishing everywhere Soviet power. With fire and sword we shall destroy everything which will dare to stand on our way. There will be no mercy for any of our enemies.[28]

To instill further terror, the Bolshevik Commander issued proclamations reporting fictitious executions of nonexistent people, and dispersed the Poltava Soviet's numerous Socialist Revolutionary and Menshevik members, replacing them with his own soldiers. The Red troops in the captured town went on a wild orgy, which Muraviev himself described as a "drunken bacchanalia." [29]

Such statements and actions on the part of the commander of the Soviet army invading the Ukraine were hardly calculated to win the sympathies of the population for the Soviet cause. But the forces loyal to the Rada were badly demoralized. During the early months of the Civil War the population at large was confused, bewildered, hesitant. A good agitator was worth hundreds of armed men; he could sway enemy troops and thus at times decide crucial conflicts.[30] The Bolsheviks, in preparing to invade the domain of the Rada, were well aware of this, and spared neither money nor personnel to infiltrate into the Ukrainian military units which Petliura had stationed in the northeastern region adjacent to the Kiev province in anticipation of a Red Army strike. The Ukrainian troops were composed entirely of volunteers whose political consciousness was quite undeveloped, and who were easily influenced by propaganda. Bolshevik agitators had considerable success in persuading the soldiers that they could best serve Ukrainian interests by joining the invaders, and many of those who did so were, according to one of the Bolshevik agents, not at all aware "that [the establishment of] the Soviet Ukraine was the result of their own armed struggle in alliance with Soviet Russia, contrary to the wishes of the Central Rada and in opposition to it." [31]

The advance of the Red troops was considerably eased by the work of such agitators. Whole Ukrainian detachments on which the Rada had relied for the defense of Kiev, either passed to the invaders or else refused to move to the front. A large number of units from the two original Ukrainian volunteer regiments, the Bohdan Khmelnitskii and Polubotkovskii, as well as a Taras Shevchenko detachment, went over to the Red Army.[32]

After the capture of Poltava, Muraviev directed the Kharkov Red Guard detachments to turn south and seize Kremenchug. He himself, leading the main Red forces, which were increasing daily with the addition of local Red Guards of soldiers who had deserted Ukrainian units, and of other pro-Bolshevik elements, turned northward, to Grebenka. From there he moved on to Kiev along the Kursk–Kiev railroad line. The Ukrainians, whose troops were concentrated in this area, put up a stiff fight. At the railroad station of Kruty a major battle took place which lasted several days. The Reds finally won and resumed their march on the Ukrainian capital.

While the Red troops were advancing, the General Secretariat issued its Fourth and last Universal (January 9/22, 1918), in which it proclaimed the independence of the Ukraine.[33]

At the same time the remnant of the local Bolshevik party decided to foment an uprising in Kiev, despite orders from the Kharkov Bolsheviks to the contrary.[34] The Communists seized control of the Kiev arsenal on January 16/29, and for several days successfully resisted the Ukrainian troops, but eventually Petliura's men, augmented by units retreating into Kiev from the front, gained the upper hand. The Reds surrendered, and a large majority of them were slaughtered by the Ukrainian soldiers.[35]

On January 26/February 8, 1918, the Red Army marched into Kiev, and the leaders of the Rada with the remaining loyal troops fled. Soon afterwards the Soviet government of the Ukraine moved from Kharkov to Kiev.

### The Communist Party of the Ukraine:
### Its Formation and Early Activity (1918)

The Bolshevik government established in the Ukraine in January 1918 was a failure. First of all, it was a regime founded on sheer military force without the active support or even the sympathy of the Ukrainian people. Muraviev, in his dispatch to Lenin reporting the capture of Kiev, frankly referred to the regime as one "established by means of bayonets." [36] To make matters worse, the behavior of the Red Army conquerors in the Ukraine not only failed to win new adherents for the Soviet cause, but even alienated those groups of the population who at first were not averse to the reëstablishment of Russian rule. The invading army consisted largely of Russian industrial workers — who looked upon rough and ready methods of dealing with opposition, real and imaginary, as the best way of completing the "job" they had been assigned — and of criminal elements, enlisted in the so-called Red Guard, who took advantage of the war to pillage, loot, and murder at will. Discipline was extremely lax. The Red soldiers were frequently drunk, and organized pogroms against the local population which their commanders had no means of curbing. Nor did Muraviev himself help the situation. An unbalanced, sadistic megalomaniac, who, according to Antonov-Ovseenko, delighted in talking without end about "the flow of blood," [37] he issued orders to "annihilate without mercy all officers and junkers, haidamaks, monarchists, and all enemies of the revolution found in Kiev." [38] At a time when there were no courts to distinguish between "friends" of the revolution and its "enemies," this ordinance left much room for the soldiery to exercise freely its vodka-stimulated passions upon the defenseless population.

No one knew better than the Ukrainian Communists who followed the conquering Russian armies how deeply such behavior would alienate the people, but they were powerless to take preventive measures, in part because they had no real strength and were fully dependent on the military to get them to Kiev, and in part because they were hopelessly divided among themselves. The history of the Bolsheviks in the Ukraine is one of endless internal quarrels. There were arguments over the territory within which each group was to operate; there were "deals" between some factions directed against others; there were petitions to the various "bosses" in Moscow and exploitation of rivalries among them for the purpose of gaining local supremacy. In all these controversies the interests of the masses of the population, for whose ultimate benefit the entire Communist effort was allegedly made, were treated as only one of the numerous factors which had to be considered in the struggle for power. It is characteristic of the Bolshevik mentality that, in objecting to the excesses of the invading Red Army, the Ukrainian Communists did not denounce the behavior of Muraviev and his troops as inhuman, but as a tactical mistake which had alienated the population whose support was needed for the proper functioning of the government. Lenin, too, when he intervened, did so for the sake of the smoother operation of the party and its governmental organs, and not out of any concern for the welfare of the inhabitants.

The trouble had started with the arrival in Kharkov of Red troops from Moscow early in December 1917. The Kharkov Revolutionary Committee (*Revkom*), was then dominated by a group of aggressive Bolsheviks, composed largely of Latvian and Russian workers, headed by F. A. Artem (Sergeev), an able and energetic Bolshevik of long standing. The commanders of the Red detachment paid little attention to the local Revkom and proceeded at once to arrest local citizens, exact contributions, disarm Ukrainian troops present in the city, and take other repressive measures against the "counterrevolution," all without so much as consulting the Kharkov Bolsheviks. Artem and his colleagues naturally resented this, and jealous of their authority, made strong remonstrances, but to no avail. Antonov-Ovseenko, contemptuous of the "softness" of the Revkom, ignored pleas that he respect its prerogatives and take into account the "peculiar conditions of the Ukraine." [39]

When the Kievan Bolsheviks arrived in Kharkov following their walk-out from the unsuccessful All-Ukrainian Congress of Soviets, Antonov-Ovseenko, hoping to find a political counterweight to the Kharkov Bolsheviks, established amicable relations with them. Soon, however, they too turned against him. The Kievans were dissatisfied with the slowness of his preparations for an attack against the Central Rada; they were eager to return to Kiev and they voiced objections to the fact that the bulk of the Red forces were being thrown not against the Ukrainian nationalists but against Ataman Kaledin on the Don.[40] The disputes between the Kievans and Antonov-Ovseenko, who in the meantime had been appointed Soviet Commissar of War, came to a head over the behavior of the army in the territory which it conquered from the Rada once the invasion had got underway. The activities of Muraviev, and especially his public speeches, were so distasteful to the Kievan government-in-exile that it published in the Kharkov press official announcements disclaiming any responsibility for his political statements.[41] When the Red officers began to remove officials appointed by the Bolshevik Ukrainian Executive Committee and to replace them with their own personnel, the Kievans took their protests to Lenin himself, and Lenin intervened on their behalf with a telegram "To the People's Commissar, Antonov[-Ovseenko]":

> As a result of complaints of the People's Commissariat [of the Ukraine] concerning friction between you and the Central Executive Committee of the Ukraine, I request that you inform me about your point of view on the matter; on the whole, our interference in the internal affairs of the Ukraine, except as it is imperative for military reasons, is undesirable. It is more convenient to put various measures into effect through organs of local government, and in general, it would be best if all misunderstandings were solved on the spot.[42]

Since Antonov-Ovseenko did not reply, Lenin followed the telegram with a letter, dated January 21/February 3, 1918:

> Comrade Antonov! I have received from the Central Executive Committee (Kharkov) a complaint against you. I regret very much that my request for an explanation on your part did not reach you. Please get in touch with me as soon as possible by direct wire — by [numbers?] one or two through Kharkov — so that we may talk to the point and clear things up. For heaven's sake, apply every effort to *remove all and every friction* with the Central Executive Committee (Kharkov). *This is super-important for the sake of the state.* For heaven's sake, make up with them and grant them *any* sovereignty. I strongly request you remove the commissars whom you have appointed.
>
> I hope very, very much that you will fulfill my request and will attain *absolute* peace with the Kharkov Central Executive Committee. Here there is needed *national super-tact.*
>
> On the occasion of victories over Kaledin and Co. I send you my warmest greetings and wishes and regards. Hurrah and Hurrah! I shake your hand.
>
> Your Lenin.[43]

The friction between Kharkov and Kiev Communists on the one hand, and the Red Commander and his staff on the other, was of brief duration and terminated with the successful close of the Ukrainian campaign. After the seizure of Kiev, Antonov-Ovseenko, confident that the Ukrainian Central Rada was completely destroyed, ordered one part of the troops fighting in the Ukraine to the Don Theater of Operations, and dispatched the remainder, of which Muraviev was made Commander, to the so-called Southwestern or Rumanian front.

Now, however, a new and more serious struggle developed, this time within the Ukrainian Communist organization itself. Its causes lay in certain peculiarities of the Ukrainian historical development. Since the Ukraine had never been an independent state with a definite territory, the name, "Ukraine" was used loosely during the Revolution to denote the region located in the southwestern part of the Russian Empire. Where this country began and where it ended was anybody's guess. Differences of opinion on the subject became strikingly evident under the Provisional Government, in the summer of 1917, when the Rada had defined the Ukraine as a land encompassing nine or even twelve provinces, while Petrograd had thought in terms of a mere five provinces. The disputed areas lay on the left bank of the Dnieper River, in the provinces of Kharkov, Ekaterinoslav, Taurida, and Kherson. These provinces were in part industrialized, and their cities populated with Russians who had migrated from the north relatively recently. The proletarian elements there were almost entirely Great Russian or fully Russified, and although the rural population consisted of Ukrainian-speaking peasants, this entire territory had historically, ethnically, culturally, as well as economically, as much in common with Moscow as with Kiev.

This fact was reflected in the organizational development of the Bolshevik Party. In 1917 there were two Bolshevik Party regional organizations operating in the territory of the later Soviet Ukraine, one in Kiev, another in Kharkov. At All-Russian Bolshevik Party Congresses in 1917, the two groups participated independently of each other. The Kievan group, controlling the Southwestern Region, was the smaller of the two, with approximately 7,800 members, whereas the Kharkov group, with its organizations spread over the industrialized towns of the Donets and Krivoi Rog regions, had more than double that number (15,800).[44] When the majority of the Kievan Bolsheviks had conducted a "soft" policy toward the Ukrainian Rada (fall 1917), the Kharkov Reds had refused to follow them. In December 1917 at the Bolshevik Conference held in Kiev, the two centers formed a joint Regional Party Committee (*Kraevoi Partiinyi Komitet*).[45]

Throughout 1918 and part of 1919 the two groups continued to display divergent tendencies. When the Kievans had arrived at Kharkov in December 1917, the local Revkom had let them know at once that they would not be allowed to interfere in the affairs of the provinces located on the left bank of the Dnieper, and that in general they were unwelcome.[46] The hostility of the Kharkov group toward the Kievan Bolsheviks was mainly motivated by the fear that if a Soviet Ukrainian Republic were actually established, its political center would be located in Kiev, and that subsequently all the remaining party organizations on Ukrainian territory, including those of Kharkov, would be compelled to subordinate themselves to the Kievan Communist apparatus. When the Ukrainian Soviet government had been formed in December, the Kharkov group had consented to join its Executive Committee only on the condition that "its people" were given a proper number of important posts.[47] There were quarrels between the two groups over office space, over the name to be given to the new government (whether to use the word "Ukrainian" or not), and over many other issues, big and small. The arrival of Antonov-Ovseenko had only temporarily swayed the balance of power in favor of the Kievans, with whom the Red Commander made common cause. The Bolshevik Central Committee, anxious to preserve unity, requested the Georgian Communist, Grigorii Ordzhonikidze, on his way to Eka-terinoslav to supervise the collection of food, to stop in Kharkov to recon-cile the warring parties.[48] There is no evidence that he succeeded in carrying out this part of his mission.

In January 1918 the Kharkov Communists, with their colleagues from Ekaterinoslav and the other industrial centers of that territory, decided to terminate the interference of their Kievan comrades, and to free them-selves, once and for all, from the "Ukrainian chauvinism" of the right-bank Communists. They called together a Congress of Soviets of the left-bank provinces, and there, despite protests from Mykola Skrypnyk and some other Ukrainian Communists, founded a separate "Donets-Krivoi Rog Soviet Republic."[49] This meant, in effect, that the Soviet Ukraine was deprived of its industrial territories and divided into two parts with separate governments and separate capitals.

It is difficult to say how long Moscow would have permitted such an anomalous situation to exist. But the two "governments" had barely been established when the territory of the Ukraine proper was occupied by the German and Austro-Hungarian armies, and both groups had to seek refuge in Russia.

The Bolshevik military command, and even the political leaders in Moscow, had been so firmly convinced that the capture of Kiev signified the end of resistance on the part of the Ukrainian Rada that they had not given much thought to the possibility of a Ukrainian-German agree-ment.[50] But this is precisely what happened. The Rada, since December, had had a delegation in attendance at the Brest Litovsk discussions. The diplomats of the Central Powers, sensing the advantages to be derived from splitting the parties sitting across the discussion table from them, had entered into separate negotiations with the representatives of the Ukrainian Rada. On January 26/February 8, 1918, the very day when Red troops occupied Kiev, the Ukrainians reached an agreement with the Central Powers providing for the latter's occupation of the Ukraine. The German and Austro-Hungarian armies marched in a few days later.

The Soviet forces were incapable of offering even token resistance. As soon as news of the occupation had reached Kiev, all government and party organizations began feverishly to evacuate eastward. During the twenty days the Soviet Ukrainian government had been in control of Kiev, it had not had the time to establish its authority over the country. The Germans entered the city on February 18/March 3, 1918, one week after the panic-stricken Communists had departed for Poltava.

The return of the Rada and the military occupation of the Ukraine completely altered the situation, and provided the local Bolsheviks with a subject for renewed disagreements. The Kharkov Bolsheviks were not at all unhappy over the plight of their Kievan comrades. Rather, they applauded their own wisdom in having formed a distinct republic, and interpreted the destruction of the Ukrainian Soviet government as an excellent opportunity for a final break with the Kievans. "Economically our basin is connected with the Petrograd Republic," mused one of their press editorials on March 6, 1918, shortly after the German armies entered the city of Kiev, "politically it is also more convenient for us to join the Russian federation. The conditions of national life in the provinces of Kharkov and Ekaterinoslav also do not tie us to the Ukraine. The proletariat of the Donets Republic must focus all its efforts in the direction of asserting its autonomy and independence from the Ukraine." [51]

In March and April two basic tendencies — left and right — crystallized quite clearly among the Bolsheviks operating in Ukrainian territory. The left was dominated by Kievan Bolsheviks (who in 1917 had belonged to what then was termed the right wing). It desired an active policy of underground work and partisan warfare against the Rada and its German protectors and insisted on the revolutionary potentialities of the Ukrainian population. Its tactics called for an alliance with the peasant masses in that country. The right (which in 1917 had constituted the left wing), on the other hand, argued that the Ukraine, having no proletariat, was incapable of systematic revolutionary activity, and that the reëstablishment of Soviet rule there had to await the outbreak of the world revolution. The latter faction was led by Bolsheviks from Kharkov and Ekaterinoslav. In consequence of their stress on the national revolution, the leftists desired the formation of a united Ukrainian Communist Party, which would merge the organizations of the southwestern territory with those of the Donets-Krivoi Rog Basin, and remain distinct from the Russian Communist Party. The rightists, on the other hand, oriented as they were toward Moscow, opposed such tendencies as separatist.[52] In time the two factions began to reflect ever more clearly the internal contradictions of Ukrainian Bolshevism. The left stood for a peasant-based revolution, and for a certain measure of interparty democracy; the right, for a strictly proletarian movement, and for complete subordination to the central party organs in Moscow.*

The victory, for the time being, went to the left. At the Second All-Ukrainian Congress of Soviets, held in Ekaterinoslav in March 1918, this group succeeded in compelling the right to give up the idea of a separate Donets–Krivoi Rog Republic and agree to the inclusion of their territory and the territories of the two other Soviet republics which had

---

* It is probably no accident that the leader of the left, Piatakov, was "tried" and executed as a Trotskyist twenty years later, while Artem, who headed the right, has been given a prominent place in the Stalinist Pantheon.

arisen since 1917 (Odessa and the Crimea) in a single Ukrainian Soviet Republic. There is some evidence that the influence of Lenin was instrumental in terminating the shortlived but potentially explosive dual regime.[53] At this Congress the Ukraine was also proclaimed an independent Soviet republic. According to early Communist sources this step was taken for purely tactical reasons. The left faction, which dominated the Congress, was opposed to the Brest Litovsk Treaty, and hoped that by proclaiming Ukrainian independence from Soviet Russia it could continue to fight against the German invaders, without involving Russia in a war with the Central Powers.[54]

The left continued to dominate the party apparatus at the Taganrog Conference of Ukrainian Bolsheviks (or Communists, as they formally called themselves henceforth) which met in April 1918. A Communist Party of the Ukraine — KP(b)U — was formed by merging the two separate organizations heretofore operating on Ukrainian territory. This party, in accordance with the resolutions of the Conference, was to be independent of the Russian Communist Party and was to join the Third International.[55] Plans were made to call together an All-Ukrainian Party Congress and to undertake extensive underground work, but before any of those projects could be carried out the Germans had extended their occupation to the left-bank regions of the Ukraine, including Kharkov and Ekaterinoslav. The Ukrainian Communists were compelled to flee to Moscow.

Both factions utilized the period between the Taganrog Conference in April and the First Congress of the Communist Party of the Ukraine, which took place in Moscow at the beginning of June, to win support from the leading members of the Communist hierarchy. The opinion of Lenin was especially important. It is nearly impossible to ascertain now what Lenin's views on this subject really were; for after his death, both sides claimed that they had had his backing.[56] The Kremlin had some reasons to throw its support behind the leftists, because they understood much better the importance of an alliance with the Ukrainian peasantry and stood closer to Lenin on the issue of the minority policy than did the rights. On the other hand, however, the leftists came dangerously near the views of the Russian Left SR's on the question of the Brest Litovsk Treaty and the continuation of the war against Germany. Their policy of active underground movement against the occupants of the Ukraine threatened to lead to the resumption of hostilities with the Central Powers, a danger Lenin wanted at all costs to avoid. In view of the importance of this issue, Lenin perhaps tended on the whole to agree with the rightists. M. Maiorov, one of the leaders of the left, is probably correct in stating that Lenin trusted neither one nor the other faction, considering the rightists to be opportunists, and the leftists hot-heads.[57] Trotsky, according to Maiorov, supported the rights and refused to issue arms and ammunition to the partisans who had been recruited for resistance by the left.[58] Stalin, on the other hand, as far as one can judge on the basis of an article written in March 1918 and some of his actions later in the year, supported the left and urged a "patriotic war" against the invading Germans in the Ukraine.[59]

Whatever his own predilections, Lenin finally settled on a compromise. He approved the demand of the left for the creation of a Central Revolutionary Committee to command the consolidated underground forces operating in the Ukraine, but fully applied the weight of his great prestige in convincing the leftists to act cautiously and to avoid provoking Germany into a resumption of hostilities.[60] He also urged the two factions to come together, and to create a Ukrainian Communist Central Committee composed of representatives of both.[61]

The leftists owed their temporary supremacy not only to the assistance of Lenin on certain crucial issues between them and their rivals, but also to their alliance with some radical, non-Bolshevik parties operating in the Ukraine. This alliance was a direct result of the short-sighted, inconsiderate policy applied by the German occupation forces toward the Ukrainian peasantry.

The main motive which had induced the German High Command to occupy the Ukraine was the prospect of securing large food supplies for their blockaded and hungry homeland. Even before they had signed the treaty with the Ukrainians, they bluntly insisted that the Rada should promise to provide, within a space of several months, one million tons of cereals.[62] The Ukrainian politicians, well aware of the mood of the Ukrainian peasantry, recoiled at the thought of such promises, which were certain to be highly unpopular, but they were in no position to bargain and had to give in.[63] As soon as they had entered the Ukraine, the Germans began to collect large quantities of foodstuffs to dispatch westward. The peasants in many areas resisted them passively and in some areas actively. German units were attacked by angry peasants and disarmed, whereupon the German Command turned to the Rada, demanding that it maintain order and keep the population under control. The Rada was scarcely in a position to do either. Violent quarrels between the more radical elements of the USD and USR, on the one hand, and the nationalist wing, inclined to collaborate with the occupant, on the other, paralyzed the Rada completely.[64] Finally the Germans, disappointed at the impotence and socialist leanings of the Rada, on whose active coöperation they had previously counted, decided to get rid of the useless ally. One day, at the end of April 1918, German soldiers entered the hall where the Central Rada was holding its session, and ordered all those present to disperse.[65] Thus the Ukrainian Central Rada, after one year of stormy history, came to an inglorious end.

The occupying power replaced the disbanded Rada with a puppet government headed by Hetman Pavlo Skoropadski, an ex-officer of the Tsarist Army and a commandant of Free Cossack detachments loyal to the Ukrainian movement. Food-collecting now proceeded more rapidly, unhampered by dissident voices of Ukrainian politicians. But resistance among the peasantry continued, and the Germans took to repressive measures. Collective fines and the shooting of hostages, at times at the rate of ten Ukrainians for one German, became common practice. Field courts were introduced to deal summarily with the local population, when it tried to prevent the troops from carrying out their orders.[66] German civil authorities in the Ukraine protested to Berlin against the brutality of the military command and urged that the interests and moods of the population be taken into account, but with little effect.[67] From the middle of 1918 the entire Ukraine became the scene of a growing peasant rebellion, which was to hold the country in its bloody grip for nearly two years.

The German behavior in the occupied regions provided an excellent opportunity for the Bolsheviks to win a foothold in the Ukraine. In June 1918 there was a further break within the USD and USR parties; the left-wing elements of both passed over to the Bolsheviks and participated in the Second All-Ukrainian Congress of Soviets. The Left USR's even formed a separate party under the name Ukrainian Socialist Revolutionary Fighters (*USR Borotbisty*, or simply *Borotbisty*, as they were henceforth called). In Ekaterinoslav, at the Congress of Soviets which had proclaimed the establishment of the Ukrainian Soviet Republic, there were more Ukrainian and Russian Left SR's in attendance than there were Bolsheviks.[68]

By virtue of their views on the role of the Ukrainian peasantry and the need for active resistance to the German occupation, the leftists in the Ukrainian Communist movement had greater affinities to the radical defectors from the defunct Rada than their rivals. This explains the superiority which the left could attain over the right, dependent as the latter was for its strength on the industrial centers of the occupied territories.

The First Congress of the newly formed KP(b)U met in Moscow at the beginning of June 1918. The debates between the rights and lefts flared up once more, and the leftists again won, though with slender majorities, on the issue of revolutionary activity in the Ukraine. A Central Committee, composed almost exclusively of leftists, was created, and subordinate to it, a Revolutionary Committee to direct the conspiratorial and partisan work.[69] On one very important issue, however, the leftists lost. In April, at the Taganrog Conference they had succeeded in passing a resolution stating that the KP(b)U was an independent Communist party, separate from the RKP(b), and able to join the Third International on a par with foreign Communist parties. Such independence in party matters Lenin would not tolerate. Homogeneity of the Communist movement and strict unity of its command had been cardinal tenets of his long before he had come to power, and perhaps the only principles to which he had remained loyal throughout his life. The summer of 1918 was a period when Moscow undertook to bring into line the numerous provincial Communist party organizations which had grown up in the course of the Revolution and early Civil War, and which had taken advantage of the lack of contact between the center and the borderlands to attain local autonomy.

The long debates over the status of the Ukrainian party took place behind closed doors. When the delegates finally emerged from their meeting, it was announced that the KP(b)U was henceforth to function as a constituent part of the Russian Communist Party, and to carry out all orders emanating from the RKP's Central Committee. The KP(b)U would, as a consequence, have no separate representation at the Third International.[70] This was an unmistakable victory for the rightists.

Unmindful of their defeat on the organizational question, the leftists proceeded at once to prepare for the uprising in the Ukraine. Members of the Revolutionary Committee were dispatched there to get in touch with the peasant partisan leaders.[71] Arms were purchased from German soldiers. Contact was established with the Bolshevik cells that had managed to survive German repression. Everything seemed to proceed smoothly, insuring the success of a mass rebellion, capable of overthrowing the Skoropadski regime and forcing the Germans to evacuate the Ukraine. The Bolshevik underground considered the time ripe:

> The general political conditions at that time were most favorable [sic!]. German rule, violence, and the indemnities which the conquerors widely imposed, tortures, mass executions, punitive expeditions, the burning of villages, the destruction of all peasant and worker organizations, the nullification of all the achievements of the Revolution, starvation wages, ruined enterprises, the high price of all necessities, and, finally, the complete return to the landowners and factory proprietors of all their previous privileges — all this provided splendid soil for the widespread growth of the revolutionary movement and for the development of an active will to fight among the masses.[72]

On August 5, 1918, the Revolutionary Committee of the KP(b)U issued its Order Number 1, calling for a general uprising in the Ukraine.[73]

Despite its favorable prospects the August 1918 Ukrainian rebellion was an utter fiasco. The Bolshevik defeat was even more disastrous than the most determined opponents of the left faction had reason to anticipate. The sporadic, half-hearted uprisings which occurred throughout the country were easily suppressed by the Germans. In the Poltava province, where the Communists had counted on scores of thousands of peasants to take to arms, only one hundred obeyed their call; in most of the remaining regions there was no response at all. In the northern part of the Chernigov province alone did the uprising achieve some success, but not enough to save the situation.[74] The leftists had obviously overestimated their ability to organize the spontaneous peasant disorders which German policies had provoked into a mass rebellion, and their penalty for making this mistake was loss of control over the party apparatus.

In October 1918 the Second Congress of the KP(b)U met in Moscow. This time the rightists, supported by Kamenev, who spoke at the Congress as the representative of the Central Committee of the RKP, won a decisive victory. Kamenev joined the rights in criticizing as highly dangerous the left-wing tactic of dependence on the partisan peasant movement. He also insisted, with the backing of the right, that all Soviet forces presently available in the south, be sent to fight against the Whites concentrating on the Don, and not against the Germans, as Piatakov of the left had demanded. "A Communist is not a man who merely defends his house," said one of the rights at this occasion, "but one who can defend his interests on the Don." [75] In accordance with this dictum all the partisan detachments which the leftists had been able to salvage from the disastrous operations of August 1918, were to be sent far away from the Ukraine, to the North Caucasian front. In this move Moscow saw a practical example of the principle of the subordination of local, national interests to the good of the international socialist cause, as represented by Soviet Russia. A new Central Committee was appointed, with the key positions dominated by rights (Artem, Emmanuil Kviring, and others), though Piatakov was also included, for the sake of interparty unity.[76] Stalin was made a permanent member of the Central Committee of the KP(b)U as a representative of the Central Committee of the RKP. The main tasks of the Ukrainian party were now formulated, in accordance with the wishes of the right faction, "to prepare the Ukraine for the entry of the Russian Soviet Army, [to occur] in connection with the outbreak of the German revolution which is fully ripened and anticipated at any time"; to establish a strong party apparatus in the industrial centers of the Ukraine, and to subordinate them completely to Moscow.[77] The stress was now on the world revolution, on the proletariat, on Russian control and assistance.

In November 1918 the Germans and their allies surrendered in the West, and the war was over. With the evacuation of German and Austrian troops from the Ukraine, the field was again open to a struggle for power.

### The Struggle of the Communists for Power
### in the Ukraine in 1919

The year 1919 in the Ukraine was a period of complete anarchy. The entire territory fell apart into innumerable regions isolated from each other and the rest of the world, dominated by armed bands of peasants or freebooters who looted and murdered with utter impunity. In Kiev itself governments came and went, edicts were issued, cabinet crises were resolved, diplomatic talks were carried on — but the rest of the country lived its own existence where the only effective regime was that of the gun. None of the authorities which claimed the Ukraine during the year following the deposition of Skoropadski ever exercised actual sovereignty. The Communists, who all along anxiously watched the developments there and did everything in their power to seize control for themselves, fared no better than their Ukrainian nationalist and White Russian competitors.

Peasant uprisings, which had already made themselves felt in the summer of 1918 as protests against German food and land policies, grew in intensity in the fall and winter of that year. Throughout the Ukraine there appeared bands of peasant partisans who attacked estates, robbed and killed the Jewish inhabitants, and from time to time launched bold forays on large cities. The whole country was for the larger part of 1919 completely at their mercy. Like peasant rebellions in general, this one too lacked a clearly formulated socio-economic and political program; the peasants definitely did not want the return of the landowners and the reinstitution of tsarist agrarian legislation, which they identified with the German occupants, the Hetman, and the White Armies, but they had no idea what they did want. Lacking a common organization and imbued with a strong spirit of neo-Cossack anarchism, the peasant partisans were utterly incapable of providing the country with anything resembling a firm government, despite the fact that some of their leaders or *bat'ki* attained temporary control over considerable areas.

The heads of the deposed Ukrainian Central Rada began to reëstablish contact with each other early in the fall of 1918, when popular resistance to the Germans and to Skoropadski was gathering momentum. They started at once secret preparations for a return to power. A Ukrainian National Union was founded to replace the defunct Rada, and with it as an executive organ, a Directory of five men, headed by Vinnichenko, was created. The clandestine organizations had their center in Kiev.

The Directory soon did acquire some military forces of its own, but they were not sufficient to cope with the German-supported regiments of Skoropadski. To secure the indispensable assistance for the incipient struggle, the Directory established contact with the Communists. The Soviet government in the spring of 1918 had sent to Kiev a peace delegation headed by the Bulgarian-born Communist, Khristian Rakovskii, and the Ukrainian-born Dmitrii Manuilskii. Ostensibly, the task of this delegation was to sign a peace treaty with the Ukrainian government, at first the Rada, and then with Skoropadski, but in reality it engaged mainly in conspiratorial activity and served as the center for Communist agitation in the Ukraine.[78] In September or October 1918 Vinnichenko, who as the chairman of the Directory and a political figure of known radical social views had been delegated to deal with the Soviet representatives, arrived at an agreement with Manuilskii. The Soviet diplomat pledged that the Red Army would help the Ukrainian forces unseat Skoropadski by diverting German attention, that Moscow would recognize the Directory as the legal government of the Ukraine, and that it would refrain from intervention in Ukrainian affairs. Vinnichenko for his part promised that after the overthrow of the Skoropadski regime and the establishment of the Directory as the Ukrainian government, the Communist Party would be allowed to operate legally on Ukrainian territory.[79] History was repeating itself. Again, as they had done a year earlier, Bolshevism and Ukrainian nationalism joined hands against a common enemy.

After the Germans had evacuated the Ukraine, Hetman Skoropadski made frantic attempts to come to terms with the White Russian generals. From an exponent of Ukrainian national ideals as he now transformed himself into a champion of "Russia, one and indivisible." [80] The clandestine Directory, sensing that the opportunity for a seizure of power had approached, left Kiev and transferred to Belaia Tserkov, fifty miles southwest of the Ukrainian capital, the seat of Bohdan Khmelnitskii's headquarters during his rebellion against Poland in 1648. In the middle of November the Directory announced the deposition of the Hetman and the assumption of power. It issued at once several radical land decrees and proclaimed other socialist measures, calculated to win the sympathies of the peasantry and the worker population of the cities.[81] At the same time the Directory signed an agreement with the newly formed Ukrainian government of Galicia, merging the Russian and the Austrian Ukraine into one state.

The fight against Skoropadski lasted one month. The regiments of the Directory were augmented by peasant partisans, who joined them to help overthrow the detested regime of the Hetman and to prevent the anticipated return of the landowners. The advance on Kiev was a triumphal procession. On December 1/14, 1918, the Ukrainian regiments entered the city, and on the same day the Hetman resigned. There was every reason to expect that a long period of coöperation between the Communists and the Ukrainian nationalists lay ahead: they had the same enemy in General Denikin, who was as hostile to separatist tendencies among Russian national minorities as he was to Bolshevism; they had reached a gentleman's agreement as to future relations; and last but not least, their social and economic slogans had much in common.

Such coöperation probably would have been established, had it not been for the fact that the Communists themselves were quite divided over the Ukrainian policies, and as a result pursued two distinct and contradictory courses of action. The Rakovskii-Manuilskii agreement with the Directory was in harmony with the views of the right. It rested on the assumption that the potentialities for a genuine revolutionary movement in the Ukraine were as yet too small to permit active Communist intervention. In accordance with the right-inspired resolutions of the Second Congress of the KP(b)U, this agreement stressed the task of building a strong Communist apparatus, and of legalizing the party in the Ukraine. But the leftists, who despite their recent defeats still played an important part in Ukrainian Communist circles in exile, were not content to yield to their opponents. From the abortive August rebellion they had managed to salvage some partisan detachments which — apparently contrary to the decisions of the Second Congress of the KP(b)U — were kept in readiness on the northern border of the Ukraine. The leftists were convinced that in the event of a German withdrawal they could accomplish an immediate seizure of power, before the Ukrainian nationalists retook the initiative. The nine-man Revolutionary Committee of the Ukraine, formed earlier in the year, was still in existence, and under the leadership of Piatakov and S. A. Bubnov, was directing from Russian-held territory preparations for an active invasion of the Ukraine at the very time when Rakovskii and Manuilskii were negotiating with the Directory. Its plans called for an alliance with the peasant partisan leaders operating in the left-bank regions and for the seizure of Kiev by means of an internal Communist uprising. In this the leftists had the support of Stalin, who felt that the German evacuation had made it mandatory to abandon the previous cautious policy and to adopt these aggressive plans.[82] In November 1918 Moscow secretly ordered the formation of a Soviet government of the Ukraine under the chairmanship of Piatakov.[83]

The uprising organized by the left in Kiev in mid-November failed to materialize. Instead of accomplishing a coup the Kievan Communists got in touch with the commanders of Petliura's troops and coördinated with the Directory their plans for fifth-column activity. Discussions were also opened concerning the merger of Communist forces with those of the Directory, but they failed, since neither side trusted the other sufficiently.[84]

The Piatakov government, residing in Kursk, was impatiently awaiting Moscow's permission to reveal its existence and to commence hostilities. But Moscow hesitated. The initial victories of the Directory, its ability to secure the support of the peasantry, coupled with a succession of Bolshevik defeats on the Don and in the Baltic areas, made the Communist leaders loath to engage in new adventures. The commanders of the Red Army were definitely opposed to the opening of a new front.[85] The heads of the newly formed Kursk Ukrainian Soviet government sensed that Moscow might change its mind and bombarded the Party Central Committee with telegrams and letters insisting that they be permitted to carry out their original mission. Precious time was passing, the Directory was becoming stronger with every day, and unless the Central Committee realized the urgency of the situation, the whole Ukraine would be lost.[86] "A large number of factors," Zatonskii and Piatakov wired to Stalin at the end of November, "lead us to believe that you are speculating with Petliura's movement." [87]

The impatience of the Ukrainian Soviet government angered Lenin: in one of the numerous direct-wire conversations held between Kursk and Moscow at the end of November, Stalin, who acted as an intermediary, warned Zatonskii and Piatakov to control their tempers lest they incur Lenin's wrath.[88] Finally on November 28 Stalin telegraphed the Kursk Government permission to proceed with its plans.[89] Immediately the existence of the government was proclaimed and overt operations against the Directory began. At its first meeting the government voted to form a Military Soviet of the Ukrainian Soviet Army, provided the Military Soviet of the Russian Republic gave permission.[90] The new Provisional Government of the Ukraine was composed of Piatakov (Chairman), Zatonskii, Kotsiubinskii, Artem, Kliment Voroshilov, and Antonov-Ovseenko.*

The Directory had barely set foot in Kiev when it began to receive disquieting reports from the north and northeast. There was news of Soviet troop movements, of the occupation of various Ukrainian towns by the Red Army, and of anti-Directory proclamations issued by Communists. "Receiving reports of such proclamations, we were so struck and surprised," writes Vinnichenko, "that at first we did not want to believe their authenticity, thinking that those proclamations were forgeries, issued by the followers of the Hetman with the purpose of provoking hostility between Ukrainian democracy and the Russian Communists, and weakening both sides by setting one against the other." [91] Unfortunately for the Directory, its intelligence proved to be correct. The Ukrainian nationalists had a new war with Soviet Russia on their hands.

The Directory protested to Moscow against the invasion, but the

---

* Ravich-Cherkasskii, *Istoriia*, 100. Recent Soviet sources state that this government was "headed" by Artem and Voroshilov, omitting mention of Piatakov and the other commissars; cf. *Istoricheskii zhurnal*, no. 1–2 (1942), 82. This distortion is probably motivated by a desire to obliterate the memory of those who were purged by Stalin in the 1930's.

Soviet Commissar of Foreign Affairs, Chicherin, merely replied that his government was utterly ignorant of any armed conflict with the Ukraine:

We must advise you that your information concerning the advance of our troops into the territory of the Ukraine does not correspond with the facts. The military units which you have perceived are not ours. There is no army of the Russian Soviet Republic on Ukrainian territory. The military operations taking place on Ukrainian territory involve the army of the Directory and the army of Piatakov. Between the Ukraine and Soviet Russia there are at present no armed conflicts. The Directory cannot be unaware that the government of the Russian Socialist Republic has no aggressive intentions against the independence of the Ukraine, and that already in the spring of 1918 our government dispatched a warm greeting to the Ukrainian [Soviet] government, which had come into existence at that time.[92]

Chicherin's reply entirely misrepresented the situation. Piatakov indeed had no army of his own; he was chairman of a revolutionary government which was appointed by the Central Committee of the RKP(b) in Moscow, and the KP(b)U, of whose Central Committee he was a member, was both in name and in fact a mere regional organization of the Russian Communist Party. He was, in a sense, an agent of Soviet Russia. Nor did Moscow's recognition of the first Soviet government of the Ukraine, which was run by self-appointed commissars, fully subservient to the Soviet Russian Council of People's Commissars, have any bearing on the issue of Ukrainian national sovereignty.

According to reports conveyed to Kiev by the Directory's emissary in Moscow, the invasion of the Ukraine was undertaken by Piatakov without the knowledge or approval of Lenin, who supported Rakovskii's and Manuilskii's policies of conciliation toward the Ukrainian nationalists.[93] Could it be that Stalin's backing of the leftists in November 1918 was contrary to the wishes of the Party Central Committee? Vinnichenko states that, at the very time of Piatakov's invasion of the Ukraine, Lenin and the other leaders of the Russian Communist Party had already placed their signatures on the Rakovskii-Manuilskii agreement with the Directory.[94] Be this as it may, sometime in January 1919 Piatakov was deposed from the chairmanship of the Ukrainian Soviet government, and replaced by Rakovskii, who could be better depended on to perform the role of a moderator in the factional struggles within the Ukrainian Communist Party and to follow directives from Moscow. The appointment of a Russified Bulgarian, who only a few months before had represented Soviet Russia in diplomatic negotiations with the Ukraine, and who had publicly expressed extreme skepticism concerning the very existence of the Ukrainian nation, as head of the Soviet government of the very same

Ukraine, was an important step forward in the process of centralization of the political apparatus on Soviet territory.[95] Rakovskii was given two principal directives by Lenin: to win over to the Soviet side the left-wing Ukrainian parties, especially the Borotbisty, and to adopt a more conciliatory policy toward the Ukrainian peasantry.[96]

On January 3, 1919, Soviet troops, composed of partisans and regular Red Army detachments, entered Kharkov. The Directory sent an ultimatum to Moscow, demanding the immediate withdrawal of the Red armies. When this request was turned down on the grounds that the war in the Ukraine was a civil war, and not a war with Russia, the Directory declared war on the Soviet government (January 18, 1919). Petliura was now made the Supreme Commander (*Holovnyi Ataman*) of the Ukrainian armed forces, which consisted of units of Free Cossacks and infantry battalions, officered and largely manned by Ukrainians from Austrian Galicia, who had stayed behind after the armies of the Central Powers had evacuated the Ukraine.

The Directory could offer no serious resistance. First of all, the peasant partisans, with whose help it had come into power, deserted soon after Kiev had been captured and the Hetman removed. The peasants and their leaders had already grown tired of the new government, which, contrary to their expectations, had accomplished no miraculous improvements, and they now went over in droves to the advancing Bolsheviks. In this manner the Directory lost to the enemy the chief partisan leaders — Makhno, Zelenyi, Hryhoryiv — who attached themselves to the invading Soviet army. In the second place, the Directory had never succeeded in establishing effective government. The leaders of the state were actually at the mercy of their military commanders and of the various local Atamans, who ruled their respective regions in a manner which has been aptly compared with that of Chinese war lords.[97] The responsibility for the terrible anti-Jewish pogroms which spread over the entire Ukraine during the reign of the Directory, for the forceful suppression of trade unions, and other acts of violence, must rest most heavily on the shoulders of those unsavory elements; though popular resentment, not unnaturally, was directed against the Directory itself.[98] The internal struggles within the Directory between the socially radical groups led by Vinnichenko and the more nationalistic faction, headed by Petliura, also did not help its cause. Before long, all the socialist groups, including the USR's proper (as distinguished from the Borotbisty) and the Bund had broken openly with the Directory and gone over to the Communists. Having lost the support of the peasantry, of the urban population, and of the most influential political parties, the Directory now transformed itself into a military dictatorship, dominated by Galician officers, whose brutal Ukrainian chauvinism was unpopular with the population. In its last days the Directory tried in vain to maintain itself by seeking support from the Western Allies, who had landed troops in Odessa, and from General Denikin, as well as by appealing to the populace with promises of a quasi-Soviet system of government, in which sovereignty would reside in so-called Toilers Soviets (*Trudovye Sovety*).[99]

On February 6, 1919, almost a year since it had first set foot in the city, the Red Army reëntered Kiev. The second Soviet government which followed in its wake lasted for seven months, until the end of August 1919, when in turn it gave way to the White Armies of General Denikin. It was no more successful than the preceding Ukrainian governments, to a large extent because it failed to follow the instructions which Lenin, with his usual sense for political realities, had given Rakovskii at the beginning of the year. Instead of adopting a moderate policy toward the peasants, the Communists instituted a system of land collectivization, forcing independent peasants into communes and transforming confiscated estates into state farms (*sovkhozy*).[100] The Communists of the Ukraine, and especially the left-wingers, jealous of their own authority, refused to admit the Borotbisty into the KP(b)U, contrary to Lenin's specific directives. Contempt and hostility toward the Ukrainian language on the part of the government also alienated the Ukrainian intelligentsia, who for two years had grown accustomed to free activity. Barely two or three months after its assumption of power, the Soviet Ukrainian government also lost the support of the principal partisan leaders, Makhno and Hryhoryiv, who now turned against the Bolsheviks and under the slogan, "Down with the Communists, Jews, and Russians; long live the rule of true Soviets!" continued to carry out their destructive work.

The remainder of the year passed in continuous civil strife. In the fall of 1919 the White Armies of General Denikin occupied large sections of the Ukraine, including Kiev. They also failed to establish order, and by their unwise attitude toward the peasantry and pogroms against the Jewish inhabitants, incurred the hatred of a large segment of the population. The second Soviet government and the top echelons of the Communist Party of the Ukraine evacuated together with the retreating Red Armies to Russia.

While the territory of the Ukraine was in White hands (fall 1919) and the leaders of the KP(b)U were pounding the pavements of the Russian capital — a general staff without an army — Moscow completed the process of centralizing in its hands all Soviet Ukrainian party institutions.

The defeats suffered by the Ukrainian Communist organization from the very beginning of the Revolution, had considerably weakened the case of those groups within the KP(b)U which had argued that their party should enjoy a certain degree of autonomy. Not that either of the two principal factions in the KP(b)U, or even the center, led by Skryp-

nik and composed largely of Ukrainian nationals, objected to the primacy of Moscow and the Central Committee of the RKP. Piatakov and
Bubnov, who headed the left; Artem and Kviring, who dominated the
right; as well as Skrypnik of the center, were as one in their hostility to
Ukrainian nationalism and shared the conviction that the Ukraine must
remain part of Soviet Russia, subordinating itself entirely to the directives
of Lenin and his chief assistants. Until the end of 1919, at any rate, there
was no evidence in the KP(b)U of a "nationalist deviation"; actually,
the top organs of that party were almost exclusively staffed by Russians.
But there were elements in the KP(b)U, mainly in its left and center
factions, who believed in greater party democracy and in the necessity
of lending the Communist movement an autochthonous character. Those
elements had fought, in vain, at the First Congress of the KP(b)U (June
1918) for the principle of an autonomous Ukrainian organization.

The fact that the KP(b)U was hopelessly divided, that it could not
secure a mass following and in moments of crisis invariably had to appeal
to the Soviet Russian army for assistance, made it difficult to plead with
Moscow for autonomy. The failure of the KP(b)U to contribute to the
defense of the Ukraine against the White forces was the final bit of
evidence attesting to the party's ineffectuality.

On October 2, 1919, Moscow ordered the dissolution of the Central
Committee of the KP(b)U and of the Soviet civil administration in the
Ukraine.[101] Control over the Ukrainian party organizations operating in
Soviet Russia as well as those operating underground on territories oc-
cupied by Denikin, was assumed directly by the Central Committee of
the Russian Communist Party. A year and a half after its foundation, the
Communist Party of the Ukraine had become a mere shadow: an organi-
zation without authority, without influence, without even a formal center.

Following the dissolution of the Central Committee of the KP(b)U
and the simultaneous liquidation of the Ukrainian Council of Defense
which had performed the functions of a civil administration in the
Ukraine, the Ukrainian institutions virtually disappeared from the Soviet
political apparatus. There remained only a three-man *Zafrontovoe biuro*
(literally, "the beyond-the-front bureau") with headquarters in Moscow,
which busied itself largely with the direction of the Communist underground in the Ukrainian areas occupied by the White Armies of General
Denikin. Most of the leaders of the old Ukrainian Soviet apparatus went
into the service of the central and provincial organs of the RKP, while those
who had at one time belonged to the right wing of the KP(b)U, and as
such were opposed even to organizational concessions to Ukrainian nationalism, took advantage of the demise of the KP(b)U's Central Committee to disassociate themselves from Ukrainian affairs once and for all.

Yet not all the persons connected with the Ukrainian Communist
movement took the decision of Moscow with equanimity. A small but

vocal group composed of persons who had at one time belonged variously to the pro-peasant, left wing of the KP(b)U (1918), to non-Communist radical groups such as the Borotbisty or to the left wing of the USD, and even some Communists connected with the central Soviet apparatus who had no sympathies for the Ukrainian national cause but felt that it had been a mistake to dissolve Ukrainian Soviet organizations — all these divergent elements immediately began a struggle for the reëstablishment of the liquidated institutions.

In November 1919 some of the nationally conscious members of the KP(b)U who had taken refuge in Moscow held a series of unofficial meetings to discuss means of reversing the Central Committee's decision on the Ukrainian Party. This decision, viewed by Communists hostile to the Ukrainian cause as a deserved punishment for its weakness and ineffectuality, was interpreted by these groups as an unjust reprisal for the failures stemming from Moscow's own mistakes. Some of the Communists who had remained in the occupied parts of the Ukraine or were serving with the Red Armies on the Ukrainian front shared this latter attitude. In this group was Manuilskii, who was stationed as a Soviet supply commissar in the Chernigov province. Manuilskii sharply criticized Soviet policies in the Ukraine, particularly the unwillingness of the Communists to induce Ukrainians to join the government. In an article published in the Chernigov Communist press at that time, he compared the Communist regime in the Ukraine to a typical colonial administration, and drew parallels between the appointments under both systems of a token number of natives to positions in the government, for the sole purpose of creating the impression that the regime enjoyed local support.[102]

In the latter part of November, when Ukrainian affairs were at their lowest ebb, and indeed the whole Soviet government seemed on the verge of collapse under White blows, fifteen prominent members of the KP(b)U held a special conference in Gomel, close to what had recently been the Ukrainian border. The Central Committee of the RKP somehow learned of the Ukrainian plans and issued a directive which forbade the conference to take place; it even dispatched two trusted Ukrainian Communists to Gomel to see to it that the directive was obeyed. But the Ukrainians chose to disregard the instruction of the center on the grounds that their meeting was an informal one and as such did not require the sanction of the Central Committee. The two emissaries from Moscow not only failed to stop the proceedings, but were themselves prevailed upon to join in the conference.[103]

The Gomel conference agreed quickly on the desirability of reëstablishing a Ukrainian Central Committee and a Ukrainian Soviet government. But on all other issues it was divided. One group, led by G. Lapchinskii, wanted the maximum of independence for the Ukrainian party and state apparatus. Its resolution asked that the Soviet Ukraine, upon its liberation from the Whites, be granted the status of a sovereign republic and be federated with all the other Soviet republics (including those which would presumably arise outside the confines of the old Russian Empire) in matters of defense and economy only. Further it demanded that the government apparatus of the whole Soviet federation be separated from that of the Russian Soviet Federative Socialist Republic (RSFSR), with which until then it had been almost completely merged. This so-called Federalist group represented a new nationalist-communist tendency in Ukrainian Communism. Opposed to it was a group led by Manuilskii, who was also chairman of the Gomel conference. This faction desired the closest possible merger of the Soviet Ukraine and Soviet Russia, and criticized the Federalist proposals as un-Communist in spirit.[104]

The two factions clashed bitterly over the question of whether or not to admit into the future Ukrainian Soviet government representatives of the Borotbisty. The Borotbisty, it will be recalled, were left-wingers of the Ukrainian Socialist Revolutionary Party, who in 1918 had split from the right-wingers and adopted a distinct party name. In March 1919 they once more changed their name, assuming the cumbersome title of the Ukrainian Party of Socialist-Revolutionaries Communists Borotbists (in Russian, *Ukrainskaia Partiia Sotsialistov-Revoliutsionerov Kommunistov Borotbistov*), and five months later, most of them having merged with the dissident radical elements of the Ukrainian Social Democratic Party, formed the Ukrainian Communist Party (Borotbists): *Ukrainskaia Kommunisticheskaia Partiia (Borotbistov)*, or, for short, UKP.* Despite these mergers, the members of these groups continued to be popularly known as Borotbisty. The UKP had a foreign bureau located in Vienna under the direction of Vinnichenko, the onetime chairman of the General Secretariat of the Ukrainian Central Rada (1917) and a leader of the USD. Following repeated disagreements over social policies with the USD's right wing, headed by Petliura, Vinnichenko had broken with the USD's, and allied himself with the Ukrainian crypto-Communists.[105] The UKP was willing to coöperate with the Russian Communist Party on condition that the Ukrainian Red Armies retain their separate status, and that the UKP be permitted to join the Comintern as the principal representative of Ukrainian Communism.[106] Organizationally, the UKP was quite ineffective, but its leaders did enjoy a certain following in the Ukrainian village, a following which the KP(b)U desperately needed.

The swing of such parties as the left USR and left USD to a pro-Soviet position offered the KP(b)U an excellent opportunity to improve

---

* Not to be confused with the Communist Party of the Ukraine, KP(b)U, the official branch of the Russian Communist Party.

its situation, but most of the leaders of the KP(b)U were hostile to the idea of coöperation with them, partly because they disliked the nationalistic flavor of such groups, and partly because they were apprehensive lest an alliance with them water down the Communist spirit of their own party. On April 6, 1919, the Central Committee of the KP(b)U had declared itself opposed to the inclusion of Borotbisty representatives in the Ukrainian Soviet government.[107] The Communist authorities in Moscow, however, especially Lenin, had taken a different view of the matter and immediately issued a directive (signed by Stalin) ordering the KP(b)U "to arrive at an agreement with the USR's in the sense of [allowing] the entrance of representatives of the Ukrainian SR's into the Ukrainian Soviet government." [108] Obedient to orders from above, the KP(b)U had issued appropriate instructions to all its local organizations,[109] but there is no evidence that they had been carried out before the autumn of 1919, when the Communist regime had been expelled from the Ukraine by the White forces.

The Federalists, striving for a broad alliance with non-Communist radical groups, desired the formation of a new Communist Party of the Ukraine, composed of remnants of the KP(b)U, the KPU, and those Borotbist groups which had retained their independent status. The new party was to posses a Bolshevik nucleus, but remain formally separate from the ineffective and virtually defunct KP(b)U.[110] This idea they fostered at Gomel, but with little success. Manuilskii, speaking for the majority, which he headed, stated that the admission of the Borotbisty would not be possible until the latter had changed some of their attitudes, and particularly until they had given up the demand for separate Ukrainian armies.[111] The Federalists were also defeated on their resolutions concerning Russo-Ukrainian relations.

Undaunted by this defeat, the Federalists took their case directly to the Central Committee of the RKP. Sometime in November 1919 they presented it with a memorandum in which they called for a reëvaluation of the party's national policy in the Ukraine. Arguing that the Communists in the Ukraine lacked contact with the village and in the past had depended too much on Moscow, they asserted: "In the struggle for the reëstablishment of Soviet power [in the Ukraine] the leading role must unconditionally belong not to the Moscow center, but to the Ukrainian center." In this connection they also asked for a reconsideration of the party's decision concerning the Ukrainian Central Committee.[112]

The Central Committee of the RKP did not favor this request with a reply, since it obviously ran contrary to all the principles underlying Communist strategy in the borderlands. But this memorandum undoubtedly played a part in inducing Lenin to raise the Ukrainian question at the Eighth Party Conference, held in Moscow December 3–5, 1919. Having been taken to task for his concessions to minority nationalists by

Rakovskii, Manuilskii, Bubnov, and several others present at the Conference, Lenin delivered a scathing attack on Great Russian chauvinism in Communist ranks.* He was especially critical of the policies pursued by his opponents in the Ukraine, and of their unwise handling of the Borotbisty, whose assistance, he believed, was vital for the party's effective operation there.[113]

Lenin's speech produced immediate results. Soon after the Eighth Conference closed, a new party center for the Ukraine was formed in Moscow. It consisted of Rakovskii, Zatonskii, Kossior, Petrovskii, and Manuilskii. At the same time a skeleton Soviet Ukrainian government was created under Rakovskii, Manuilskii, Zatonskii, one Borotbist, and one member of the KPU.[114] The presence of Rakovskii and Manuilskii in both these bodies indicated that they would continue the old centralist, antinationalist policy, while the inclusion of Borotbists in the government signified an effort to attract the non-Communist radicals into active participation in the Soviet administration.

The alliance with the Borotbisty, brought about under Lenin's pressure did not last long in the face of the undiminished hostility of the majority of Communists. The new Soviet organs entered Kharkov late in December 1919, in the wake of the victorious Red Armies. In March 1920, on instructions from Zinoviev, the Chairman of the Comintern, the Borotbisty dissolved their separate organizations and merged with the KP(b)U.[115] The Foreign Bureau of the UKP also disintegrated at this time. Vinnichenko, who had migrated to the Soviet Ukraine in the winter of 1919–20, quickly became disappointed with Communist rule and once more emigrated.[116] The new Soviet regime in the Ukraine thus remained firmly in the hands of centralists who owed all their allegiance to Moscow, and who lacked even those native roots which the leaders of the Communist movement in the Ukraine had possessed in the earlier stages of the revolution.

The history of the Ukraine from 1917, when the old regime had collapsed, until early 1920, when Soviet rule was finally established, reflects a state of rapidly spreading anarchy, which, both in its extent and its duration, is perhaps unique in the history of modern Europe. Over these three years, no fewer than nine different governments attempted to assert their authority over the land. None succeeded. The democracy of the Provisional Government, the moderate socialism of the Rada and its General Secretariat, left- and right-wing Communism, the Cossack Hetmanate and the German occupation armies, the proto-fascist Direc-

---

* The stenographic records of this conference are missing. It is possible, as one of the participants to the Twelfth Party Congress (1923) suggested, that they had been destroyed by the persons whose reputation was likely to suffer from them; see *Dvenadtsatyi s"ezd RKP — Stenograficheskii otchet* (Moscow, 1923), 546.

tory, peasant anarchism, and the military rule of the White Armies — all failed alike. With each year the country disintegrated further, until by 1919 it no longer represented one country, but an infinite number of isolated communities.

The main protagonists in this struggle for power were the Ukrainian nationalists and the Russian Communists.

The Ukrainian movement which emerged in the course of the Russian Revolution was, despite its ultimate failure, a political expression of genuine interests and loyalities. Its roots were manifold: a specific Ukrainian culture, resting on peculiarities of language and folklore; a historic tradition dating from the seventeenth-century Cossack communities; an identity of interests among the members of the large and powerful group of well-to-do peasants of the Dnieper region; and a numerically small but active group of nationally conscious intellectuals, with a century-old heritage of cultural nationalism behind them. All the evidence points to the fact that nationalist emotions during the period of the Revolution received a strong stimulus by having an opportunity to act in the open and to influence directly the masses of the population.

The weakest feature of the Ukrainian national movement was its dependence on the politically disorganized, ineffective, and unreliable village. Despite their numerical preponderance, the peasants provided a most unsatisfactory basis for the development of political action because of their political immaturity, which made them easily swayed by propaganda, and because of their strong inclinations toward anarchism. The fate of the Ukraine, as of the remainder of the Empire, was decided in the towns, where the population was almost entirely Russian in its culture, and hostile to Ukrainian nationalism. The Ukrainian cause was further weakened by the inexperience of its leaders and the shortage of adequate administrative personnel. The political figures came mainly from the ranks of the free professions, with a background of journalism, the law, or university life, but without any knowledge of the actual workings of government. Of course, the same weakness affected the Bolshevik regime in Soviet Russia, but the Communists had the advantage of inheriting from the previous regime large cadres of officials whom they could utilize until proper replacements were available. The Ukrainians had no such reserves because, until 1917, their country had been ruled mainly by Russian bureaucrats, and the natives who had entered the tsarist service were or became Russified. This shortage of personnel with which to administer the country was one of the greatest weaknesses of Ukrainian governments, and forced them eventually into a complete dependence on Galician Ukrainians. And, finally, much of the blame rests directly on the shoulders of the Ukrainian leaders themselves. So overwhelmed were they with the rapid growth of Ukrainian national sentiments among the masses, and so impressed with the ease with which

they had triumphed over the Provisional Government, that they greatly
overestimated their own strength. Instead of concentrating on the task
of establishing good relations with Russian democratic forces and on
winning the support of the non-Ukrainian groups of the population, the
nationalist leaders preferred to engage in the fruitless pursuit of "high
politics," in ridiculous squabbles over the mere appearances of sovereignty, in grandiose acts which bore no relation to political reality. In
the long run this cost them the sympathy of many influential elements on
Ukrainian territory. One cannot fail to notice a certain emotional in-
stability and unrealism on the part of the leaders of the Ukrainian movement. These faults played an important part in their ultimate downfall.

The position of the Communists was in almost every respect opposite
to that of the nationalists. Their strength centered in the towns, not in
the villages; they had a well-organized party apparatus, supplied with personnel and financial resources from Russia; they had a keen sense of
political reality, and a ruthless strategy. Yet they too failed, and after
two years of ups and downs, were completely swept off the political
stage. Their main weakness lay in the fact that they were essentially
foreigners on Ukrainian soil, strangers to its peasant culture, its interests,
and its ambitions.

The Ukrainian national movement did not perish with the termination
of the Revolution and the reëstablishment of Moscow's dominion at the
end of 1919. Rather, it now penetrated into the Communist Party and
state apparatus, with the result that the early 1920's saw a reappearance
of nationalist tendencies, this time within the very Bolshevik ranks.

### Belorussia from 1918 to 1920

Of all the national movements which emerged in the course of the
Revolution, the Belorussian one was perhaps the weakest. Not only was
it very young and out of touch with the masses of the population, but
it had to operate in territories which were for the major part of 1917–
1920 under the occupation of one foreign power or another. The Belorussian national parties could not conduct the kind of political action
which provided their counterparts in other regions of Russia with opportunities to penetrate public consciousness and to secure mass support.
The history of Belorussia during this period was therefore not greatly
affected by a national movement; the latter was confined almost entirely
to diplomatic activity pursued by a numerically small, divided, and
politically ineffective intelligentsia.

Acting on orders from Moscow, the Minsk Bolsheviks commanded the
pro-Soviet troops at the end of December 1917 to disband the Belorussian National Congress which had endeavored to establish an independent
Belorussian Republic, and proclaimed the rule of the Bolshevik-dominated
Soviets.

The first Soviet government of Belorussia — and there were to be three of them — was established by the Communist organs in Minsk with the support of Russian troops of the western front at the end of 1917, and lasted for one hundred days. Its authority extended only to the regions occupied by pro-Communist regiments and to the major cities, such as Minsk, Vitebsk, and Bobruisk, where the local soviets followed Bolshevik leadership. In mid-February 1918 German armies marching eastward began to occupy the Belorussian provinces. At the end of February they entered Minsk, which the Soviet authorities had already cleared a few days earlier. Collaborating with the Germans were troops of the Polish Legion and of the Russian-sponsored Polish army, which had gone over to the Germans following the Bolshevik coup.

On the eve of the German occupation of Minsk, some of the members of the First All-Belorussian Congress of 1917, disbanded by the Communists, emerged from hiding, and hoping to secure German recognition, formed a Provisional Government of Belorussia. The Germans, however, informed the would-be Minsk government that they could not recognize it, because in January another Belorussian Assembly had been established under their auspices in Vilna, which had proclaimed the independence of Belorussia and formed its own administration. Under German prodding, the Minsk and Vilna Belorussian organizations reconciled their claims, and in March 1918 they issued a joint proclamation announcing the establishment of an independent Belorussian National Republic (in Russian, *Belorusskaia Natsional'naia Respublika*).[117] The government of the newly formed state applied to the Kaiser for moral support and material aid.[118] A group of radically inclined Belorussian nationalists, dissatisfied with the policy of collaboration with the Germans, went over to the Communists and sought refuge in Russia.

Neither the Germans nor the Poles paid the slightest attention to the wishes of the Belorussian government, which in effect could do nothing but issue proclamations and appeals. In the spring of 1918 the Germans, displeased with the socialist inclinations of the nationalists in charge of the government, forced some of them to resign and entrusted the leadership of the puppet administration to a one-time conservative Duma representative and wealthy landowner, R. Skirmunt; but he too proved unsatisfactory and was removed. While they did not dissolve the Belorussian Rada, as they had its Ukrainian counterpart, the Germans permitted the Belorussian nationalists even less jurisdiction in their territories than they allowed the Ukrainians.

The repressive policies undertaken by the German armies in the territories under their occupation in the summer of 1918 produced in Belorussia a reaction resembling that which took place in the neighboring Ukraine. Here also the urban proletariat and above all the peasantry became very restless under German rule, and in some areas took to arms.

The 1918 agragrian revolts in Belorussia did not equal in dimension and violence those in the Ukrainian provinces, but they similarly benefited the Communists.

Following the German occupation, those Communists who did not escape eastward went underground. The subterranean Bolshevik cells on Belorussian territory were directed by the Northwestern Regional Committee of the Party, located in Smolensk (then in Soviet hands), which adopted the same tactics as those pursued by the left-wing Communists in command of the KP(b)U: it strove for an alliance with the rebellious peasantry and the partisan detachments arising spontaneously in reaction to German maltreatment. In the middle of July the underground network convened a conference of Communist cells operating in Belorussia. There is evidence that in August 1918 the Belorussian Communists participated in the ill-fated uprising which the Ukrainian left wing had organized in an attempt to overthrow the German occupation.[119]

When in November 1918 the Germans began to evacuate their troops, Belorussia had no nationalist organization capable of assuming political authority, such as existed in the Ukraine in the Directory. The personnel of the German-sponsored Belorussian National Republic quietly departed from Minsk for Germany. When the Red Army reoccupied Belorussia in the latter part of December 1918, the country was in the hands of soviets dominated by Russian and Jewish parties, inclined by seven months of German occupation to be sympathetic to the Communists.

In December 1918 the question of the future status of Belorussia came up for discussions at the congress of the Northwestern Regional Committee of the Russian Communist Party meeting in Moscow. The Soviet government decided that Belorussia was to be made a national republic, and directed the Northwestern Regional Committee to carry out this decision. As the first step in this direction, the Committee was instructed to change its name to that of the Communist Party of Belorussia, KP(b)B.[120] The government of the new republic was to have been composed of members of the KP(b)B and of the left-wing adherents of the Belorussian National Committee who had earlier in the year gone over to the Communists. The Belorussian nationalists were somewhat unhappy over such an arrangement, for they realized full well that as long as the Communist Party in Belorussia remained in the hands of what had been the Smolensk organization, they would have little authority. They requested Moscow for permission to form another, purely Belorussian Communist Party, but this was denied.[121]

Before long the pro-Communist Belorussian nationalists had an open quarrel with their Communist allies. The German retreat had cleared not only Belorussia, but also the adjacent western territories, enabling the Soviet regime to expand beyond the 1917 front line. The Communists hoped to avail themselves of this opportunity by extending the newly created Belorussian Soviet Republic to include Lithuania. In February 1919 the Belorussian republic was merged with Lithuania in a single Lithuanian-Belorussian Soviet Republic (*Litbel*, from the initial letters of their names), and one month later the Communist parties of the two areas were also combined. The government of the Litbel republic was located in Vilna, and headed by K. Mitskevich-Kapsukas, a half-Belorussian, half-Lithuanian Communist serving in the Commissariat of Nationalities. The united party was placed under the chairmanship of the Belorussian nationalist, Z. Zhylunovich.[122] The Belorussians protested against those measures. They resented the fact that Belorussian nationalism had been exploited for tactical reasons, and that their republic was being used as a mere device for Soviet expansion. Before long Zhylunovich resigned his position, and as the Communists began to put into practice measures unpopular with the local population (such as nationalizing for the benefit of the *sovkhozy* all of the confiscated large estates), other nationalists followed his example.[123]

In April 1919 the armies of independent Poland marched into Lithuania and Belorussia, and for the following year most of the territories claimed by Litbel were under Polish occupation. The Poles pursued two contradictory policies in regard to the Belorussian movement. The Warsaw Sejm declared at the beginning of May that Belorussia was historically an inalienable part of the Polish Commonwealth, and decreed the complete integration of the occupied territories with Poland. Marshal Piłsudski, on the other hand, hoping to offset the relative weakness of the new Poland in relation to Russia by forming a union of the small states located along Russia's eastern border, adopted a more conciliatory attitude. At the moment when the Polish Sejm was voting for annexation, Piłsudski offered the Belorussians federal ties with Poland.[124] In general, however, the Polish occupation forces showed little regard either for the social radicalism prevalent among the masses of the population or for the nationalist emotions of a part of the Belorussian intelligentsia. The Poles ordered the return to the landowners of the land confiscated by the Communists and by the peasants themselves, and introduced Polish as the official language on Belorussian territories.[125]

At the end of 1919 Lenin, fearing a possible Polish offensive, at the time when his regime was fighting for its very life against Denikin, put out feelers to Piłsudski, offering to accept what was then the western frontline as the permanent Polish-Russian frontier.[126] Had this proposition been accepted, virtually all of Belorussia would have gone to Poland. But Piłsudski's ambitions were greater. In December 1919 he made an agreement with Simon Petliura, by virtue of which, in return for Galicia, he promised to dislodge the Communists from the Ukrainian territories located on the right bank of the Dnieper River. In April 1920 the Polish armies opened an offensive in the Ukraine against Soviet Russia, which, although initially successful, ended in a Polish defeat and nearly caused the capture by Red Army troops of Warsaw itself. As a result of its defeats, Poland evacuated a major portion of Belorussia.

On August 1, 1920, the Communists, having once more acquired control of Belorussia, reëstablished the Belorussian Soviet Republic. The idea of a combined Lithuanian-Belorussian state was given up. The Treaty of Riga (March 1921) drew the borderline in such a way as to bisect the territories populated by the Belorussians, the western half going to Poland, the eastern to Soviet Russia. Lithuania became an independent republic.

# IV

## SOVIET CONQUEST OF THE MOSLEM BORDERLANDS

*The Moslem Communist Movement in Soviet Russia (1918)*

As has been pointed out earlier, Lenin had stressed prior to 1917 the great importance of the Orient in the struggle for power. He persistently supported the slogan of national self-determination largely because he believed that national movements among the colonial peoples would play a crucial role in a world-wide revolution. This faith — strengthened rather than weakened after Lenin's advent to power — explains the great lengths to which he and his regime were willing to go to win the sympathies of the Eastern peoples residing in the Russian Empire. Pan-Islamism, Pan-Turanianism, religious orthodoxy — all these sensitive areas of Moslem consciousness were played upon by the Soviet government during the Revolution in order to gain a foothold in the Moslem borderlands and to penetrate the Asiatic possessions of the West.

Early in December 1917 the Soviet government issued, over the signatures of Lenin and Stalin, an appeal to Russian and foreign Moslems in which it made extremely generous promises in return for Moslem support:

> Moslems of Russia, Tatars of the Volga and the Crimea, Kirghiz and Sarts of Siberia and of Turkestan, Turks and Tatars of Transcaucasia, Chechens and Mountain Peoples of the Caucasus, and all you whose mosques and prayer houses have been destroyed, whose beliefs and customs have been trampled upon by the Tsars and oppressors of Russia: Your beliefs and usages, your national and cultural institutions are forever free and inviolate. Organize your national life in complete freedom. This is your right. Know that your rights, like those of all the peoples of Russia, are under the mighty protection of the Revolution and its organs, the Soviets of Workers, Soldiers, and Peasants.[1]

The Communist appeal further pledged the annulment of all international agreements concerning the dismemberment of Turkey, including the treaties which had called for the cession of Constantinople to Russia and for the detachment of Turkish Armenia. The entire tone of the proclamation left no doubt that the Soviet regime, by failing to make its customary distinction between "toilers" and "exploiters," was bidding indiscriminately for the support of all Moslem groups.

Among Moslems in Russia, Marxist influence was very limited, and where it did exist (Vladikavkaz, Baku, Kazan), it was Menshevik in character. In general, Moslems had been far more affected by liberal and Socialist Revolutionary thinking than by Marxism. In November 1917 the Soviet government had, for all practical purposes, no basis for political action in the Moslem borderlands. To offset this weakness, the Bolsheviks made an attempt to win over the All-Russian Moslem movement, despite the fact that the ideology of this movement was entirely different from their own, and that in the past its leaders had on more than one occasion displayed hostility to Lenin and his tactics.[2]

By December 1917 there existed, as organs of the All-Russian Moslem movement, a Constituent Assembly, or Medzhilis, sitting in Kazan; three ministries (religion, education, and finance); and an Executive Council, or Shura, in session in Petrograd. The Shura had at its disposal several thousand Moslem troops, composed largely of Volga Tatar veterans of the tsarist armies. In the provinces inhabited by Moslems and in all the major Russian cities, the Shura had established branch offices which endeavored to enlist support for its cause and campaigned for the elections to the Constituent Assembly. The Chairman of the Shura and of all its provincial organizations was the Ossetin Menshevik, Akhmed Tsalikov.

Sometime in December 1917 Stalin got in touch with Tsalikov and offered him an opportunity to join the Soviet government on seemingly very advantageous terms. "In order to coöperate with the [Soviet] regime," Stalin assured him, "the Executive Committee of the Moslems must not at all assume this or that party label; it is sufficient to have a straightforward and loyal relationship, so that their united efforts on behalf of the Moslem toiling masses may proceed at full speed." * If Tsalikov were willing to coöperate on those conditions, Stalin stated, he could have the chairmanship of the Commissariat of Moslem Affairs which the Soviet government intended to establish in the near future.[3] Tsalikov, however, backed by a majority of the Medzhilis, refused the offer and in the Constituent Assembly, where he headed the Moslem

---

* *Pravda* (Petrograd), No. 26, 2/15 December 1917. *Pravda* implies the initiative was taken by Tsalikov, but other sources indicate that it came from Stalin; cf. A Saadi, "Galimdzhan Ibragimov i ego literaturnoe tvorchestvo," *Vestnik nauchnogo obshchestva tatarovedeniia* (Kazan), no. 8 (1928), 29–30.

faction, attacked the Bolsheviks in strong language for their treatment of the minorities.[4]

Balked in his attempt to secure the support of the Moslem Executive Council and with it of the whole apparatus of the All-Russian Moslem movement, Stalin next approached the other Moslem political figures who began to gather in Petrograd for the opening of the All-Russian Constituent Assembly. Early in January he persuaded three deputies to collaborate with him. Among them the most influential figure was Mulla Nur Vakhitov, a twenty-seven-year-old Volga Tatar engineer from Kazan,

Central Asia and the Volga-Ural Region (1922)

to whom Stalin now offered the chairmanship which Tsalikov had refused. In the spring of 1917 Vakhitov with several friends had formed a Moslem Socialist Committee of definite Marxist leanings. Its membership was small, about a dozen persons, but this did not prevent Vakhitov a Pan-Islamist, from entertaining the hope that it would "spread the idea of socialism throughout the entire Moslem world."[5] In 1917 his committee had been pro-Menshevik, disapproving of Lenin's July coup and participating in the elections to the Constituent Assembly on joint tickets with the other Moslem socialist parties, rather than with the Bolsheviks. When, however, he was presented by Stalin with an opportunity to assume the highest post open to a Moslem in the new government — the chairmanship of the Moslem Commissariat — he abandoned his previous associates and went over to the Bolsheviks. The other two deputies whose coöperation Stalin secured were Galimdzhan Ibragimov, a Volga Tatar writer, and Sherif Manatov, a one-time employee of the tsarist secret police and a deputy from the Bashkir regions.[6]

Although the name of the newly created Soviet Moslem center implied the status of a regular ministry, represented in the Council of People's Commissars, it was, in fact, only a subsection of the Commissariat of Nationalities, and as such, responsible directly to Stalin. Its mission was to organize party cells, spread Communist propaganda, and help the Soviet regime destroy independent parties and organizations among Russian Moslems.

Vakhitov tackled his duties with much energy. He dispatched emissaries to the provinces with orders to open local branches of the Commissariat, the so-called Moslem Bureaus or *Musbiuro*. In March and April 1918 he called Moslem conferences in the provinces under Soviet control and opened provincial Moslem Commissariats (*Gubmuskomy*) in Ufa, Orenburg, Kazan, and Astrakhan. Within a few months the Moslem regions and large cities of Soviet Russia were covered with a network of Musbiuro and Gubmuskomy, which agitated among the indigenous Turkic population against the All-Russian Moslem movement and urged the natives to join the ranks of the Red Army. The propaganda efforts of the Commissariat were especially strong among the Turkish prisoners of war captured by the tsarist armies.[7]

The establishment of the Soviet regime and the outbreak of the Civil War had induced the leaders of the All-Russian Moslem movement to accelerate their efforts toward autonomy. The difficulty was that the Medzhilis, which sat in session from November 20, 1917, until the middle of January 1918, could not agree which kind of autonomy was most suitable for the Tatars. One group, called *Toprakçilar Fraksyonu* (i.e., Territorialist faction) wanted an autonomous Volga-Ural state; another, the so-called *Turkcüler Fraksyonu* (Turki faction) wanted a system which would unite all the Turks of Russia. In addition, there was a small leftist group which favored a compromise with the Soviet authorities.[8] Unable to reach an agreement, the Medzhilis appointed a committee to settle this problem, and then dissolved. This committee, functioning in Kazan, decided at the end of February 1918 in favor of a Volga-Ural autonomous state, and issued directives for the convocation of a Constituent Assembly of the region.[9]

The Bolsheviks, however, did not permit the realization of these plans. On February 13/26, having learned of the Committee's resolution, the Soviet authorities in Kazan organized a Revolutionary Staff and arrested several Tatars connected with the local Shura, after which they issued an ultimatum to all the Moslem organizations in the city to subordinate themselves at once to the Kazan Moslem Commissariat. The Tatars rejected this demand, and took cover in the native quarter of Kazan. A brief struggle ensued. Within the native quarter the Bolsheviks had armed a group of Moslem religious mystics, led by one Vaisov, whose "legions" they planned to use against the Shura troops.[10] Vaisov, however, was killed by an angry Tatar mob and his followers were disarmed. The native quarter, therefore, had to be taken from the outside, and this was accomplished a few days later with the help of a detachment of Red sailors newly arrived from Moscow.[11] The Kazan Shura was closed, and all its military detachments dispersed. On April 10/23, 1918, the committee for autonomy was arrested and two days later in Ufa the remaining institutions of the All-Russian Moslem movement were suppressed. By an official order of the Commissariat of Nationalities all the functions and properties claimed by the Medzhilis and its subordinate organizations were transferred to the Moslem Commissariat.[12] Vakhitov and his agency thus served as an instrument with which the Bolsheviks seized control of the All-Russian Moslem movement after its leaders had refused to coöperate.

At the beginning of May 1918 Vakhitov convened a conference of Communists and sympathizers from the Kazan area to discuss the possibility of founding a Tatar-Bashkir state. His intention was to re-create under Soviet auspices the Volga-Ural state which the commission of the defunct Medzhilis had proposed. The conference was pervaded with a strongly nationalistic spirit. Moslem speakers vied with each other in depicting the future glories of Islam and in stressing the importance of a socialistic Tatar republic for all Asia. Despite protests from the Russian delegates, the conference voted to establish an Autonomous Tatar-Bashkir Republic and to include in it not only the areas inhabited by these two peoples, but also those populated by other minority groups, such as the Chuvashes (who were Orthodox Christians but had asked to be admitted to the new Moslem state) and the Marii (also Orthodox Christians). Vakhitov spoke of the resolution as a great step forward in the realization of radical Pan-Islamism. Thanking Stalin and Lenin — in that order — for their support, he concluded the conference on a triumphant note: "We conceive the Tatar-Bashkir Republic as the revolutionary hearth whence the rebellious sparks of the socialist revolution shall penetrate the heart of the East!" [13]

By the end of May, Vakhitov had at his disposal a respectable political machine: a high position in the Commissariat of Nationalities, with the backing of Stalin, its chairman; a network of provincial organizations of the Musbiuro and Gubmuskom types; and the promise of an autonomous Moslem state in the very center of Soviet Russia. All that he still lacked was a separate party organization, and to remedy this deficiency he convened in June 1918 a conference of all the provincial branches of the Moslem Commissariat. At this meeting a Russian Party of Moslem Communists (Bolsheviks), *Rossiiskaia Partiia Kommunistov (b) Musul'man,* and a separate Central Committee, *Tsentral'nyi Komitet Musul'man Kommunistov,* were established.[14] It is not clear whether Vakhitov undertook this bold venture with or without the specific approval of the Central Committee of the Russian Communist Party. At any rate, there was no time for Moscow to intervene; for before Vakhitov's plans could be carried out, the entire party and state apparatus which he had erected since his appointment as chairman of the Moslem Commissariat collapsed.

In the summer of 1918 Czech prisoners of war, who were being transported from Russian camps to the Western front in Europe by way of Siberia, clashed with the Bolsheviks, and took over a number of cities along the railroad lines. The Czech rebellion was of sufficient dimensions for Soviet rule in the Volga-Ural region, tenuous to begin with, to fall. Communists and other elements associated with the Soviet regime hastily evacuated the Kazan province and retreated westward with the Red Armies. The Musbiuro and Gubmuskomy vanished overnight. Vakhitov himself was captured by the Czechs in Kazan and executed, together with a number of other locally prominent Bolsheviks.

Deprived of their leader and of their political machine, the Moslem Communists were completely at the mercy of Moscow, which lost no time in showing its hand. In November 1918 the Central Committee of the Russian Communist Party convened in Moscow a congress of Moslem Communists. Stalin, addressing the delegates, paid them high compliments: "Nobody can bridge the gap between the West and the East as easily and as quickly as you can," he said, "since to you are open the doors of Persia and India, Afghanistan, and China." [15] But at the same time the authorities he represented felt that Moslem Communists should carry out their mission under closer supervision of the Russian Communist Party. The conference had to sign its own death warrant by dissolving the Russian Party of Moslem Communists and subordinating the surviving Musbiuro and Gubmuskomy to the local offices of the RKP. The name of the Central Committee of the dissolved party was changed to read: the Central Bureau of Moslem Organizations of the Russian Communist Party, *Tsentral'noe biuro musul'manskikh organizatsii RKP(b),* and the new body was placed directly under the control of the Russian Central Committee. Stalin was elected the latter's permanent representative in the Moslem Central Bureau.[16]

Behind these administrative changes lay the fact that the young

Moslem Communist movement had ceased to exist as an independent force. Nothing was left of its original status except the fact that it still retained an All-Russian Moslem form, but even that was not permitted to last. In March 1919 the Central Bureau created at the November 1918 Congress was transformed into the Central Bureau of the Communist Organizations of the Peoples of the East, *Tsentral'noe biuro kommunisti-cheskikh organizatsii narodov Vostoka,* which also included non-Moslem nationalities and was headed by Mustafa Subkhi, an Ottoman Turk and a member of the Third International, originally from Constantinople.[17] Shortly afterwards the Moslem Commissariat itself was dissolved and replaced by a Tatar-Bashkir Commissariat with a correspondingly more limited sphere of activity. Alongside of it were created other regional commissariats (e.g., for Turkestan, Transcaucasia).

By the spring of 1919, in other words, not only the organizations of the Moslem Communists in Russia, but the very concept of Islam had disappeared from Soviet political life. Events had shown that it was too dangerous, from Moscow's point of view, to make an indiscriminate use of Pan-Islamist tendencies on Soviet territories, since this had led to the establishment of a separate party organization and had deprived the Bolshevik leaders of full control over their Moslem subjects.

## The Bashkir and Tatar Republics

After the death of Vakhitov, the Soviet government abandoned the idea of a united Tatar-Bashkir state, and instead divided the Volga-Ural region into separate autonomous republics based on the national-territorial principle.

Zeki Validov, the Bashkir leader who had been arrested by the Bolsheviks in Orenburg in February 1918, escaped from confinement soon afterwards, and turned up behind the White lines to organize a Bashkir army. Within a few months he succeeded in forming several native regiments, which were thrown into the battle on the side of the anti-Soviet forces organized by the SR-dominated Committee of the Constituent Assembly (*Komuch*) located in Samara (Kuibyshev).

The collaboration between the Bashkirs and Whites did not last long. It was wrecked by the White leaders' lack of tact and genuine sympathy for the aspirations of the minor nationalities. The Komuch refused to make commitments concerning future self-rule and the Bashkir land demands. Furthermore, friction developed between Validov and the White leaders over jurisdiction in the Bashkir theater of operations, over the billeting of Cossack troops in native villages, over the taxation of the civilian inhabitants, and over the division of military authority. When, in November 1918, Admiral Kolchak overthrew the Komuch and established himself as dictator, the relations between the Bashkirs and the Whites deteriorated even further. Kolchak made no bones about his dislike of the nationalist movement and issued orders to dissolve the separate Bashkir corps and to incorporate its units into the White Army.[18] Disgusted with the treatment which they received from the Whites, and even more apprehensive about their fate in the event of a White victory in the Civil War, the Bashkirs began to discuss the possibility of switching sides. Early in December 1918 Validov convened a secret meeting of Bashkir and Cossack leaders, who were dissatisfied with the fact that their commander, Dutov, had recognized the authority of Kolchak, and suggested the arrest of Dutov; but the plot was betrayed and suppressed.[19]

Through emissaries, covertly dispatched in February 1919 across the battle lines, Validov offered, under certain definite guarantees, to go over to the Reds. He demanded promises of extensive self-rule for the Bashkirs and the creation of a separate Bashkir republic. In March, after one month of negotiations, he reached an agreement with the Communist regime. The agreement stipulated the establishment of an Autonomous Bashkir Republic, located within the boundaries of so-called Small Bashkiriia, as defined by Validov at the 1917 All-Russian Moslem Congress. The Bashkirs were to elect at once a Bashkir Revolutionary Committee (*Bashrevkom*), which was to exercise supreme authority in all matters pertaining to Bashkiriia and its inhabitants until conditions permitted the convocation of a Bashkir Congress of Soviets. The Bashrevkom was to be master of everything within its territory, with the exception of the railroads, factories, and mines, which were to be subordinated to the All-Russian Commissariat of National Economy. The Bashkir armed forces, while retained as a distinct army, were to come under the jurisdiction of the All-Russian Commissariat of War.[20]

On the face of it, this agreement was a far-reaching concession by the Soviet government. It meant the abandonment of the project of a united Tatar-Bashkir republic and the establishment of an autonomous state with far greater political and economic self-rule than Moscow was at that time generally inclined to grant its republics. To the Bashkirs it appeared eminently satisfactory. The agreement gave them an opportunity to realize their national ideals and to enforce their land program.

On February 22, 1919, the Bashkir troops (amounting at the time to 2,000 men) elected a Bashrevkom, which included Validov, and crossed the battle line to join the Reds. Their defection had a serious effect on the morale of the Cossack troops protecting the White front in the Ural region, and on the whole strategic situation in this sector of the Civil War.[21] The leaders of the Kazakh-Kirghiz Alash-Orda, with whom Validov had made common cause in the previous year and a half, decided to continue their association with the White forces, and fought on the side of Dutov and Kolchak until the summer of 1919, when they too, in a large majority, went over to the Communists.

From the beginning of their association with the Bolsheviks the leaders of the Bashkir national movement suffered a series of mishaps, owing partly to the unbridgeable mental gap which separated the two sides, and partly to a fundamental difference of interests between the Russian and Bashkir inhabitants of the area. The Bashkirs, having established contact with the Bolsheviks rather late in the Civil War, had had no experience with Communist methods, and did not realize that the concessions they had been granted were a tactical move to induce their defection from the Whites. They interpreted the March 1919 agreement as granting them political and economic *carte blanche* and drew up a series of measures calling for the compulsory expropriation and resettlement of all non-Moslems who had come to the Bashkir areas during the Stolypin period, and their replacement by Bashkirs residing outside the limits of the republic. At the same time, they began to plan the creation of an autonomous Bashkir Communist Party and the exchange of diplomatic representatives with the other Soviet republics.[22] In the fall of 1919, when the Red Army occupied the Ural area, the Bashrevkom returned to Bashkiriia and announced in a special decree that it was assuming full power and that all the inhabitants of the republic were henceforth to obey its orders.[23]

These aspirations were in basic conflict with the interests and attitudes of the local Bolshevik party and state institutions with which the Bashrevkom had to work. Most Soviet organs in the Ural region, as in the other Moslem regions, were predominantly Great Russian in their ethnic make-up: their personnel consisted largely of workers, soldiers of the military garrisons, and peasant-colonists — all social groups which did not exist among the Bashkirs. It is not surprising, therefore, that the various soviets which emerged throughout the revolutionary period on Bashkir territories were ethnically Russian and fought for the interests of the Russian population. The soviets took the side of the Russian colonists in their struggle for land with the Bashkirs. Bashkirs were, in many instances, excluded from membership in the soviets,[24] and most of the land which the Bolshevik institutions had confiscated in that area from the state, church, or private landowners, was distributed to Russian colonists.[25] "Despite our intentions," wrote the delegate of the central Soviet authorities to Bashkiriia some time later, "we [the Bolsheviks] simply spearheaded the kulak onslaught of our Russian peasantry on Bashkir land."[26] The urban and agricultural Tatar elements in the Bashkir territories also tended to side with the Russians against the natives.

To the Bolshevik party and state institutions functioning on Bashkir territories the very prospect of Bashkir self-rule was distasteful. Time after time, congresses of soviets and provincial or regional revolutionary committees of the Volga-Ural area passed strongly worded resolutions condemning the establishment of an autonomous Bashkir republic.[27] The arguments which they presented to Moscow stated that this region was too important economically to be separated from the Ural industrial centers, that the native population was too weak both physically and morally to uphold Soviet power, that the Bashkirs in general and the leaders of the Bashrevkom in particular had fought on the White side and hence could not be trusted, and finally, that the creation of national republics ran altogether contrary to the international principles of Communism. It may be said without fear of exaggeration that, except for a few influential friends in the center, among them Lenin, the idea of a Bashkir republic found no sympathy whatsoever in Bolshevik circles.* For that reason, as one of the leaders of the Bashrevkom stated later, the main task faced by the Bashrevkom throughout its existence was the fight for the very survival of the young republic.[28]

The difficulties began soon after the Bashrevkom had returned to its homeland in September 1919. It found that during the interval between the reoccupation of the area by Red troops and its own arrival virtually the entire territory of the Bashkir republic had fallen under the control of the Executive Committee of the Ufa province. Even in the capital city of Sterlitamak all the office buildings were taken over by officials from Ufa, who completely ignored the existence of the republic. The thinly scattered but influential Bolshevik Party cells on Bashkir territory were composed mainly of Russian factory workers, who refused to subordinate themselves to the Bashkirs and preferred to obey Red institutions in Orenburg or Ufa.[29] It required a considerable effort, often accompanied by physical force, for the Bashrevkom to assert its authority on its own territory against the hostility of Soviet institutions in the neighboring provinces and Bolshevik organizations within Bashkiriia.

The Bashrevkom was only partly successful, for before long it was faced with another, even more formidable challenge to its authority: the Communist Party. Until the end of 1919 responsibility for party activities in Bashkiriia rested theoretically on the shoulders of the Bashrevkom, which made no attempt either to organize it more effectively or to introduce its personnel and ideology into Bashkir political institutions. For this negligence, which stemmed from the antipathy of the Bashkir leaders toward the elements who filled the local party cells and from their lack of understanding of the place of the party in a Communist society, they were severely criticized by envoys sent from Moscow.[30] In November 1919, under pressure of the same envoys, the first Bashkir regional Communist Party conference was convened. As might have been expected, the conference was heavily dominated by Russians, who succeeded in

* Characteristic was the reply given to a Bashkir delegation in 1920 by Lutovinov, the secretary of the All-Russian Central Executive Committee in Moscow: "That whole autonomous republic, which you take so seriously, is only a game to keep you people busy" (Dimanshtein, "Bashkiriia," 143).

electing a Regional Committee of the Communist Party (*Obkom*) in which their own people held all the key positions. In time this Obkom became a weapon with which local Russians and Tatars, supported by influential persons delegated from the center, destroyed the national autonomy of the Bashkirs.

The first task confronting the Obkom was to strengthen the local Communist Party cells and to centralize the chaotic party organization. This was difficult to do, because there was little contact with the already existing cells, and above all, because the broad masses of the Bashkir population sympathized with the Bashrevkom and displayed undisguised hostility toward Russian Communist officials. The Obkom used a novel and very effective method to overcome those obstacles. It so happened that, at about the same time, the Soviet government in Moscow had created a Society for Aid to Bashkiriia (*Bashkiropomoshch*) in order to alleviate somewhat the starvation and disease which had begun to decimate the peoples of the area. When the chairman of this society — the leader of the right-wing of the Communist Party of the Ukraine, Artem — arrived in Sterlitamak, the Obkom at once perceived the opportunity which had fallen into its hands and made common cause with him. The Obkom and the local agents of the Bashkiropomoshch took advantage of the desperate plight of the native masses, and of their dependence on the material assistance which the Communists alone could provide, to organize among the Bashkirs a powerful network of subordinate Bolshevik cells. A large portion of the 150,000 Bashkirs who received help were formed into so-called Committees of the Poor, and both the personnel and financial resources of the allegedly philanthropic society were used to establish an efficient, centralized party apparatus.[31] Within five months the party membership in Bashkiriia increased fivefold, and Communist organizations, all subordinated to the Bashkir Obkom, were set up in 90 per cent of the counties.[32]

Feeling in a much stronger position, the Russian and Tatar leaders of the Obkom then directly challenged the authority of the Bashrevkom. In January 1920, on the basis of rumors that the Obkom planned to do away with Bashkir autonomy, the leader of the Bashkirs, Kh. Iumagulov (Validov was at the time in Moscow) ordered the arrest of several Tatar members of the Obkom. This provided the Obkom with the opportunity to strike. Urgent appeals for military assistance were sent out by the Obkom to the neighboring provinces of Ufa and Orenburg and to the Turkestan Red Army headed by Frunze, and soon several fortified points under the command of an officer whom the Bashkirs dubbed "Governor General" were established throughout the country. Since most of the Bashkir troops had some time before been dispatched to fight the White Army on the western front, the Bashrevkom had no armed might at its disposal. A meeting of the Obkom which followed this occurrence con-

demned any attempt either in deed or by word of mouth to increase
Bashkir self-rule, and declared that henceforth the Obkom would direct
the work of the Bashrevkom and approve all of the more important political appointments in the republic.[33] The Bashkirs were also deprived
of control over the local secret police (Cheka).

The Bashrevkom found itself in a difficult situation. Its authority was
becoming rapidly undermined and made dependent almost entirely on
the good graces of the central authorities. The leaders of the Bashrevkom
watched with bitterness a group of foreign Russians and Tatars transform themselves from a minority into a ruling power by means of the
principle of Communist Party dictatorship and use their position to further the interests of Russian colonists. The political situation in Bashkiriia grew tense. In March 1920 Trotsky held several conferences in
Ufa with representatives of the Bashrevkom and Obkom in an endeavor
to smooth out their differences. A resolution was drawn up favoring the
Bashrevkom and condemning the interference of Bolshevik party organizations in the affairs of the Bashkir state.[34] The principal political figures
on both sides were recalled to Russia, and a special commission to deal
with any future disagreements was established in Moscow, consisting of
Trotsky (chairman), Stalin, and Kamenev.

Until this time the Bashkir leaders had continued to believe that their
difficulties with the Communist Party and state institutions were due to
the obstinacy and chauvinism of the local Bolsheviks rather than to the
central authorities. On the whole this assumption was not unjustified.
Evidence indicates that the actions which caused friction between Bashkir and Russian institutions were undertaken by the local Bolsheviks on
their own initiative, with little direction from Moscow.[35] Both Lenin and
Trotsky had proven themselves friendly to the Bashkirs, and if Stalin
tended to favor the Tatars, he at least desired that the Bashkirs retain
their autonomy. It was generally accepted that, if it had not been for the
influence of Moscow, local Bolsheviks would have done away with Bashkir autonomy altogether. But the Bashkir leaders failed to perceive that
the support given them by Moscow was neither disinterested nor permanent. In 1920 the Civil War, for all practical purposes, was over, and
the Soviet government was centralizing its political and economic apparatus. It could not tolerate the unique powers which the Bashrevkom had
secured in 1919 — powers which were greater than those enjoyed by
any other political institution on Soviet territory.

On May 22, 1920, the Soviet government published, without having
first consulted the Bashkirs, a new decree on Bashkir autonomy.[36] This
came as a bolt from the blue. The new law was completely centralistic
in spirit and deprived the Bashkir government of most of the rights guaranteed it by the 1919 agreement. Virtually all the political, financial, and
economic organs were now subordinated to the central authorities and

the Bashkirs were left with nothing but minor administrative powers. It was a clear violation of the understanding reached the previous year, and the final blow to Bashkir hopes.

Following the publication of the new decree, the Bashrevkom held a secret meeting, where bitter anger was expressed at this breach of faith, which had made a comedy of Bashkir autonomy. After more than a year of coöperation with the Bolsheviks, none of the plans or hopes of the Bashkir people had been realized: they had neither the land nor the self-rule of which they had expected so much. A strongly worded resolution was adopted:

> In view of the imperialistic tendencies of the Russians, which hinder in every manner the development of the national minorities; in view of the lack of faith of the center toward Bashkir Communists, Bashkir officials are abandoning Bashkiriia and departing for Turkestan, for the purpose of creating there an independent Eastern Communist Party, of which the Bashkir Regional Committee (Obkom) will be a part. The Eastern Communist Party must be admitted into membership of the Comintern. The aim of this exodus is by no means to rouse the national masses against the Soviet government, but rather, through resignations, to protest against Russian chauvinism.[37]

Another complaint, written by Validov, objected to the new autonomy as giving the minorities less self-rule than they had enjoyed under Nicholas II and Stolypin, and accused the Communist Party, especially Stalin, of ignoring their demands and embarking upon a course of out-and-out Great Russian chauvinism.[38] Some time later, in the middle of June, virtually all the Bashkir government officials left their posts and vanished into the Ural mountains.

The departure of the Bashrevkom and the other Bashkir officials soon threw all of Bashkiriia into a civil war which permitted the Russian elements to obtain further advantages. The Obkom immediately requested additional armed help from the neighboring provinces and from the Turkestan Red Army, so that by the end of July 1920 the entire republic was under occupation. The Russian peasants and workers, mobilized to deal with the rebels, eagerly flocked into punitive detachments to revenge themselves on the Bashkirs and to seize the land and cattle which they had long coveted. Under the pretext that they were suppressing a counterrevolutionary uprising, the Russians began a veritable reign of terror, accompanied by the indiscriminate looting and murder of the Bashkir population.[39] The Bashkirs flocked in increasing numbers into the mountains to join the rebels. Thus, in a sense, the Bashkir uprising of 1920 may be viewed as the result of a merger of two separate opposition movements: the initial political opposition of Bashkir officials and intellectuals was strengthened by the outbreak of a popular rebellion of the Bashkirs.

The strength of the mass movement was demonstrated by the fact that it continued for some time after most of the Bashrevkom officials had been either apprehended or forced to flee abroad.

While the rebellion was raging, the Obkom completed its conquest of the political institutions of Bashkiriia. During the summer of 1920, the Bashkirs, who were now considered to have demonstrated their unreliability conclusively, were entirely eliminated from the party and state apparatus. Neither the new Obkom nor the new Bashrevkom, which was appointed to replace the old one, included even a token number of Bashkirs.[40] Moreover, the First Congress of Soviets of Bashkiriia, assembled in the fall of 1920 for the purpose of electing a new government, did not include (at first, at any rate) natives, because all the Bashkir delegates had been arrested as "nationalists." [41] It is not surprising that the government elected by this congress consisted of representatives of all ethnic groups except the Bashkirs.[42] Thus the Bashkir Republic, formally organized in late 1920, had no natives in its government. The party, in close alliance with Tatars and Russian colonists, who now filled the key positions, and in intimate contact with envoys from the center, had emerged victorious.

The suppression of the rebellion was only a question of time. It succumbed to the superior Red forces, to an unusually severe winter, and to hunger. The Bolsheviks granted amnesty to the rebels. Most of the leaders of the old Bashrevkom were captured and returned to minor posts in the republic, while the remainder either fell while fighting in the ranks of the Moslem partisans in Central Asia or else, like Validov, eventually made their way abroad.

All this time, while the Bashkir Republic was experiencing its trials and tribulations, the question of creating a Volga Tatar state had been held in abeyance. The Tatars had played a considerably more important role in the Communist movement than the Bashkirs, and their ambitions were proportionately greater. The idea of an autonomous state, which satisfied the Bashkir nationalists, did not gratify Tatar intellectuals educated in the reformed schools, who had been associated in 1917 with the All-Russian Moslem movement and were steeped in the atmosphere of Moslem radical proselytism. The Tatar Communists were none too eager to speed the cause of a separate Tatar autonomous state. They preferred to wait for the termination of the Civil War, when, they hoped, it would be possible to establish a single Volga-Ural republic, and to resume their activities on an all-Russian scale. Their leader and ideologist at this time was a remarkable Volga Tatar Communist, Mirza Sultan-Galiev.

Sultan-Galiev was born in the Ufa province sometime in the 1880's. He attended the Russo-Tatar Teacher's College in Kazan, and then served as a Russian-language instructor in the reformed Moslem schools in the Caucasus. Before the outbreak of the war he contributed frequently to the Turkic papers in Baku and in St. Petersburg, writing articles about Moslem life in Russia and translating from Russian publications. In the spring of 1917, he was engaged by the Executive Council of the Moscow All-Russian Moslem Congress as a secretary, in which capacity he used his knowledge of languages. Sultan-Galiev had belonged to the left wing of the All-Russian Moslem movement and may have joined the Moslem Socialist Committee founded by Vakhitov. In the elections to the Constituent Assembly, he ran unsuccessfully in Kazan on the same ticket with Vakhitov and Tsalikov. Sometime toward the end of 1917 he went over to the Communists. After the Bolshevik seizure of Kazan, he was appointed Commissar of Education and of Nationalities in the local Soviet government, and in February 1918 he worked with the Revolutionary Staff which suppressed the Kazan Shura. He escaped from Kazan shortly after the Czechs seized the city, and arrived in Moscow at the opportune moment when the Moslem Communist movement had been deprived of its leadership through the death of Vakhitov.

Stalin at once took Sultan-Galiev into his Commissariat of Nationalities and gave him all the support previously lavished on Vakhitov. As Stalin's protégé, Sultan-Galiev rose rapidly. In December 1918 he became Chairman of the Central Moslem Military College, which the Commissariat of Nationalities had recently taken over from Trotsky's Commissariat of War, and in which was vested authority over the Moslem troops fighting on the Red side. Throughout 1919 he traveled extensively on various missions for Stalin and made contacts with Moslem Communists in the borderland areas. In 1920, finally, he was promoted by Stalin to membership in the three-man Small Collegium of the Commissariat of Nationalities, and was made co-editor of the Commissariat's official publication, *Zhizn' natsional'nostei* (The Life of Nationalities). He had become the most important Moslem in the entire Soviet hierarchy and had acquired a unique position from which to influence the Eastern policies of the Communist regime.[43]

Sultan-Galiev and his followers — the so-called right wing of the Tatar Communist Party — had a distinct political ideology. In a series of articles published in the *Zhizn' natsional'nostei* in the autumn of 1919, Sultan-Galiev expressed the belief that the Communist leaders had committed a grave strategic blunder by placing the main emphasis in their revolutionary activity on Western Europe. The weakest link in the capitalist chain was not the West but the East, and the failure of Communist revolutions abroad was directly attributable to the inadequacy of Soviet efforts in the Eastern borderlands. The spread of the revolutionary movement in the Orient, however, required a distinct approach. The Eastern peoples lacked an industrial proletariat, they were much more religious than the Europeans, and hence they should not be subjected to the same revolutionary methods used in the West. Only a very tactful approach, combined with the extensive use of native Moslem Communists, would permit the spread of Communism in the East.[44] The right wing thus placed emphasis on the Eastern instead of the Western revolution, and on the need for conciliatory policies toward the Moslem religion and traditions.

This ideology did not run contrary to Bolshevik strategy of 1919 and 1920, and hence Sultan-Galiev for a time enjoyed the backing of Moscow. If anything, the thinly disguised Pan-Islamic tendencies of the rightists were in harmony with the Kremlin's bid for Moslem support. Owing to the support of Moscow, the rightists dominated the weaker and less numerous left wing. Prominent among the leftists were assimilated Tatars, who had staked their political careers on an alliance with the Russian interests in the Kazan area and who fought against the concessions which the Bolshevik leaders were making to Moslem nationalists of Sultan-Galiev's persuasion. The head of this left faction was also a Tatar, Said Galiev, but the real power behind it consisted of Russian and other European leaders from Kazan: Karl Grazis, the organizer of the 1917 Bolshevik coup in Kazan, and I. I. Khodorovskii, the chairman of the Kazan Soviet government (*Gubispolkom*).[45] The leftists lacked a positive ideology, but they were definitely opposed to national self-rule and were desirous of preserving the privileged position which the Russians and other Europeans enjoyed in the Kazan province. As early as June 1918, when the idea of a Tatar-Bashkir state had first been approved by Moscow, Grazis had attacked the "Eastern orientation" of the government.[46]

As long as the Tatar right did not press for a republic, there was no public conflict between the two factions. But at the end of 1919, the Volga-Ural region had been freed from the White Armies, and Sultan-Galiev with his followers reopened the issue of the Tatar-Bashkir state whose establishment the Czech revolt in August 1918 had prevented. This question was placed on the agenda of the Second Conference of Eastern Communists, held in November 1919. The rightists originally had wanted a republic embracing all the territories in the Volga-Ural region inhabited by non-Russian peoples, but they had had to give up this notion because of Moscow's insistence on the retention of the already existing Bashkir Republic. The rightists therefore came out in favor of a separate Volga Tatar republic. The leftists did not oppose this project directly; they merely expressed the opinion that instead of wasting time and effort on such secondary matters, it would be better to concentrate on the military mobilization of the Moslem population. Moscow, however, backed the right, and resolutions were adopted proclaiming the principle of a Tatar republic.[47] Encouraged by their success, the rightists next tried to persuade Moscow to exclude the city of Kazan from the prospective state. The bad experiences of the Bashrevkom with Soviet authorities in Ufa and Orenburg made it seem desirable to draw the

new state's borders in such a way as to eliminate towns and rural areas
in which the Russians were in a majority. To this, however, Lenin said
no, and the matter was dropped.[48]

The leftists did not give up their opposition to the idea of a Tatar
republic. In April 1920 a group of Communist leaders from Kazan and
its vicinity, attending the Ninth Congress of the Russian Communist
Party in Moscow, visited Lenin and attempted to make him change his
mind. Khodorovskii told Lenin that, in the opinion of the Communists
from Kazan, there were among the Tatar party members no leaders who
could be entrusted with authority, and the creation of a republic would
affect adversely the economy of Soviet Russia. "The Tatar comrades,"
Khodorovskii argued, "will not have either sufficient strength or sufficient
courage to collect grain in their republic in the manner in which we have
been doing it in the Kazan province." [49] Considering the fact that the
Kazan Communists had squeezed from the semi-starved peasantry in the
area ten million *puds* (176,000 short tons) of grain in the preceding year,
this was a potent argument.[50] But Lenin was unimpressed. To him, he
said, it did not seem wise to alienate millions of non-Russian peasants for
the sake of a few million puds of bread; on the contrary, it was necessary
to make special concessions to the Tatar peasants in the matter of grain
collection. Stalin, who was also present at the interview, added that until
better Communist cadres among the Tatars were created, one had to
utilize those that were available.[51] Their mission a failure, the leftists
returned home, and reported on Moscow's decision. The bad news caused
widespread grumbling in local party circles.

The leftists still had one trump card to play. Possessing control of
the state and party apparatus in Kazan, they were in a position to see
to it that if they could not prevent the Tatar Republic from coming into
being, they could at least make certain that its government would fall
into their own hands. In the spring of 1920 they ordered the mobilization
of the Tatar Communists for the Turkestan front, and in this way got rid
of the main body of the opposition.[52] On June 25, 1920, the Kazan
Gubispolkom formally ceded its authority to a Tatar Revkom, especially
created for this purpose; the Revkom in turn convened a Tatar Congress
of Soviets, which met on September 25, 1920, whereupon the Revkom
dissolved itself, and the functions of government over the new Autonomous Tatar Socialist Soviet Republic were assumed by a Tatar Council of
People's Commissars, under the chairmanship of the leader of the left,
Said Galiev.[53]

Once the principle of ethnic division of the Volga-Ural region had
been established, the formation of the other autonomous states in the area
proceeded almost automatically. The Chuvash, who in 1918 had expressed a desire for a union with the Tatars, were directed to organize
a separate state, and the Chuvash Autonomous Region came into being

on June 24, 1920.[54] The Mari and Votiak Autonomous Regions were decreed in November 1920 and January 1921, and were established shortly
afterwards.

Thus, by the end of 1920, Moscow had the situation in the Volga-
Ural region well in hand. The five autonomous republics and regions
created there in the course of 1919 and 1920 were now administered by
elements obedient to the directives of Moscow, and, in addition, there
was a strong Communist Party in the chief towns of the region to supervise and control the local governments.

### The Kirghiz Republic*

The Alash-Orda continued, as had been pointed out earlier, to co-
operate with the Whites even after Kolchak had assumed dictatorial
powers and had done away with the few vestiges of self-rule which the
nationalist organizations had enjoyed under the Committee of the Constituent Assembly. In 1919, however, the affairs of Dutov and Kolchak
went from bad to worse, and before the year was over the Red armies
had occupied considerable areas inhabited by the Kazakh-Kirghiz tribes.
The Soviet government at once took energetic steps to attract the Alash-
Orda to its side, hoping to utilize its prestige and personnel to secure the
support of the native population, as it had done in neighboring Bashkiriia.

As early as January 1919, when Orenburg had fallen and the regular
Red Army had gained a foothold in the Central Asiatic steppes, Mikhail
Frunze, the commander of the Fourth Army of the Eastern Front, called
upon all the Kazakh-Kirghiz fighting for the White cause to change their
allegiance and to side with the Communists, pledging them full amnesty
and complete forgiveness for their past activities.[55] The Soviet government in Moscow reaffirmed this promise by offering safe-conduct to all
the Kazakh-Kirghiz, including those connected with the Alash-Orda, who
wished to attend a Soviet-sponsored Kirghiz Congress in Orenburg.[56] To
administer temporarily the Kazakh-Kirghiz areas, the All-Russian Council
of People's Commissars appointed on July 10, 1919, a Kirghiz Revolutionary Committee or *Kirrevkom*. The Kirrevkom was to rule over the
provinces of Uralsk, Turgai, Akmolinsk, Semipalatinsk, and part of the
Astrakhan province. In the decree establishing the Kirrevkom the government also ordered all the Kirghiz to be subject to military duty in the
Red Army, and all lands owned by Russians on Kazakh-Kirghiz territories to remain in the possession of their present owners.[57] The Kir-

* The Kirghiz republic, established by Soviet Russia in 1920, included areas inhabited by the Kazakh-Kirghiz tribes, and coincided largely with the pre-1917
Steppe General Gubernia and the Uralsk and Turgai provinces. In the mid-1920's
this republic was divided into separate Kirghiz and Kazakh republics. At the time
of the events here described the term "Kirghiz" was in general used by the Soviet
authorities for the tribes for which the term Kazakh-Kirghiz is used by this author.

revkom was composed of seven persons, under the chairmanship of the Pole S. Pestkovskii of the Commissariat of Nationalities.[58]

The Kirrevkom, unlike its Bashkir counterpart, was not in the hands of local nationalists, but of officials selected by Moscow from among trusted Communists, largely non-Moslems, and for this reason it could not serve as an instrument of native opposition as the Bashrevkom had done in Bashkiriia. In the Kazakh-Kirghiz steppe all the organs of political power were, from the beginning of the Soviet occupation in 1919, firmly in the hands of Moscow. The local nationalists were powerless to oppose them even after they had been granted autonomy.

In the summer of 1919 many members of the Alash-Orda, lured by Communist promises and discouraged by the White defeats in the Urals, went over to the Reds. Among them was Akhmed Baitursunov, an old Kazakh-Kirghiz nationalist leader and one of the founders of the Alash-Orda. As soon as he joined the Communists, Baitursunov went to Moscow for a private audience with Lenin.[59] The nature of the interview is not known; but it is not unreasonable to suppose that Lenin made promises to Baitursunov similar to those which he was in the habit of making at the time to other non-Russian nationalists, and that among them were pledges of Kazakh-Kirghiz autonomy and of assistance in the amelioration of the desperate economic situation of the nomads.

At the beginning of January 1920 the Soviet authorities in Aktiubinsk convened a Kirghiz conference, at which a new Kirrevkom was elected to admit members of the Alash-Orda, including Baitursunov. There also approval was given to a resolution calling for the speedy establishment of an autonomous Kirghiz state.[60]

The circumstances surrounding the establishment of the Kirghiz republic so much resembled those which attended the creation of other Moslem states in Soviet Russia, such as the Bashkir and the Tatar republics, that to describe them at length would be redundant. Here too Russian* provincial institutions located in the urban centers (Orenburg, Semipalatinsk) opposed with all means at their disposal and for much the same reasons native autonomy; here too, once an autonomous republic had been created at the insistence of Moscow, the Russians refused to accept its authority and prevented it from functioning properly; here too the split between Russians and natives was clear-cut and led to perpetual friction in party and state organs.[61] In the spring of 1920 the relations between Russians and natives working in local Soviet institutions approached a break. There were constant quarrels over political and economic issues connected with the distribution of food and with the

* In the steppe regions of Central Asia under "Russians" must also be understood the considerable Ukrainian population; unfortunately, the documents do not, as a rule, distinguish between the two groups, and to the native Moslem any Orthodox Slav was a "Russian." For this reason it is necessary here to treat Great Russians and Ukrainians as one.

preparations for the forthcoming Congress of Soviets of Kirghiziia. Finally, the native nationalists headed by Baitursunov decided, out of sheer desperation, to make a direct appeal to the highest authority in Russia, to Lenin himself. In two lengthy telegrams which were sent to Moscow without the knowledge of the local Communists, and which seem to have remained unanswered, Baitursunov and his followers demanded that the leaders of the party help establish genuine self-rule for the natives by restraining what they called "local, provincial, and regional imperialists"; ending the "Bonapartist" tendencies of Communist officials; putting a stop to the stealing and requisitions of native properties; and equalizing the distribution of food.[62] But the Kazakh-Kirghiz nationalists were in no position to do much more than send telegrams. They had no army, no political organizations (the Alash-Orda was never recognized by the Communists, even though its members, as individuals, were welcome), no contacts in Moscow — nothing, in short, with which to transform their dissatisfaction into organized resistance.

In October 1920 the Communist Party's Regional Committee in Orenburg convened the First Kirghiz Congress of Soviets. The congress established an Autonomous Kirghiz Republic with a government consisting of the commissariats of Interior, Justice, Education, Health, Social Security, and Agriculture. On the all-important land question the congress voted to retain the status quo: to stop further colonization of the steppe, but to allow the Russian colonists already settled there to keep their lands, including those which they had seized from the natives in 1916 and 1917.[63]

In 1921 and 1922 the Kazakh-Kirghiz steppe was stricken by famine which made itself felt most heavily among the natives, who had lost their cattle in the course of the 1916 rebellion, and who were slighted in the distribution of food supplies sent in by the government and put at the disposal of local Communist organs.[64] Whole areas were depleted by the lack of nourishment, and instances of cannibalism were not infrequent. In the course of 1921, one million persons perished from hunger in the Kirghiz Republic. Under those circumstances the establishment of the Kazakh-Kirghiz autonomous state, formally decreed in October 1920, was not possible until two years later, when the food situation was normalized. The famine also explains the relative lack during the early 1920's of native popular resistance to the Soviet regime, such as occurred in neighboring Bashkiriia and Turkestan.

### Turkestan

At the end of December 1917 authority over Turkestan was claimed by two rival governments: a Soviet one in Tashkent, backed by Russian railroad workers, soldiers, colonists, and the Communist government in Russia; and a Moslem one in Kokand, supported by the politically conscious elements of the native population, and by some anti-Communist Russian parties.

The news that the natives in Kokand had proclaimed an autonomous state aroused the ire of pro-Soviet groups in Tashkent. The local soldiers, who already in November had arrested and executed General Korovnichenko, the Provisional Government's representative there, now began to round up all the inhabitants whom they suspected of sympathy with the Kokand regime.[65] At the Fourth Regional Congress of Soviets (January 1918) the Communist faction sharply condemned native endeavors to institute self-rule in Central Asia:

> We subordinate entirely the principle of national self-determination to socialism, recognizing the fact that only in the struggle with the counterrevolution is the revolution being shaped — the revolution which will sweep out of its way all obstacles such as the autonomous government of Kokand.[66]

Confronted with such menaces from Tashkent, the Kokand government tried desperately to secure outside assistance with which to augment its weak military forces, but without success. Negotiations with the Cossack Ataman Dutov of Orenburg broke down in the middle of December over the issue of Moslem self-rule; the Alash-Orda was cool to Kokand's offers of coöperation, and in any case it had no important armed forces at its disposal; and the Emir of Bukhara, hostile to the liberals who predominated in Kokand and anxious to preserve neutrality in the Russian Civil War, refused even to receive the emissaries who had been sent to him with requests for help.[67] In January 1918 several small urban centers in the Ferghana valley recognized the sovereignty of Kokand,[68] but the remainder of Turkestan did not follow suit. The Kokand government was unable to back up its assertions of authority even in the city which it had chosen for its residence, because the Russian Soviet in Kokand would not subordinate itself to the autonomous institutions.

In late January 1918, when the crisis in Moslem-Russian relations led to an open conflict, the Kokand government could rely only on a few hundred ill-equipped and inexperienced volunteers against thousands of Russian veterans and mercenaries in the service of the Tashkent Soviet. Its downfall was swift and calamitous.

The struggle which led to the destruction of the autonomous government took place in the city of Kokand.[69] At the end of January the local soviet, persisting in its independent course, took refuge in the fortress, manned by forty-five Russian soldiers. On the night of January 29/February 11, some Moslems penetrated and tried to take over the fortress, but they were expelled. The Russians sent for help to the garrisons of the adjacent towns and to Tashkent. On the following day a small Russian detachment, armed with some heavy weapons, arrived from Skobelev (Fergana), to bolster the soviet's defenses. While the guns were being mounted and the Russian and Armenian inhabitants, fearful of an impending massacre, were moving into the walled enclosure, the Kokand Soviet issued an ultimatum to the Moslem authorities. It called for the surrender of all arms and the punishment of those guilty of the night raid. The Kokand government refused, whereupon the fortress opened fire on the native quarter. The panic-stricken Moslem population began to flee the city and to hide in the mountains.

Through the intercession of Russian civilians, negotiations for a cease-fire were opened. Despite the uncompromising attitude of the Russian soldiers, who insisted on exorbitant contributions from the Moslems, there was good reason to believe that eventually an armistice would have been reached. The Kokand government was too weak militarily to dislodge the Russians, while the fortress had ammunition for no more than one week of fighting. On February 5/18, however, a strong detachment of Russian soldiers, augmented by German and Austrian prisoners of war whom the Tashkent Soviet had hired for this purpose, arrived from Tashkent. Perfilev, the commander of the detachment and at the same time Military Commissar of the Soviet Turkestan government, insisted that negotiations with the Moslems be broken off at once. Early the following day he ordered his troops to assume the offensive by storming the Old City. The outnumbered Moslem defenders were easily dispersed. After gaining control over the entire town, Perfilev allowed his men full freedom. The soldiers, assisted by some Armenians, began to loot the native quarter and to murder the Moslems who had not escaped when the fighting began. After three days of stealing and slaughter, when there was nothing of value left, the soldiers poured gasoline on the houses in the Old City and set them on fire. The Moslem quarter was almost entirely destroyed.* "Kokand is now a city of the dead," wrote a Russian observer a few days after the troops, loaded with loot, had departed; "it resembles a mortuary, from which emanate odors of mold and carrion." [70]

The fall of the city spelled the doom of the Kokand government and of native hopes for self-rule. Some of the leaders of the ill-fated regime were arrested by the conquerors and brought to Tashkent. The head of the government, Mustafa Chokaev, escaped in time to avoid capture. On February 9/22, 1918, the Moslem population of Kokand was compelled to recognize formally the authority of the Tashkent Council of People's Commissars. [71]

Emboldened by their success, the Tashkent Bolsheviks decided to deal next with the Emirate of Bukhara, one of the two independent pow-

---

* Kokand never recuperated from the events of February 1918. Its prerevolutionary population of 120,000 dropped to 69,300 in 1926 and further to 60,000 in 1936.

ers remaining in Turkestan (the other being the Khanate of Khiva). The situation there seemed quite favorable for quick and decisive action. Emir Said Alim Khan of Bukhara was a reactionary and autocratic ruler, who, by resisting all pressures to introduce Western institutions into his domain and by suppressing groups spreading reformist principles, had alienated the liberal jadidist element, which in all other parts of the Russian Empire had supplied the backbone of the Moslem nationalist movement. Sometime at the end of 1917 the Bukharan jadidists, known as the Young Bukharans, established contact with the Soviet authorities in Tashkent. In fighting the Emir, therefore, the Communists enjoyed the advantage of having on their side the local Moslem intelligentsia.

Operations against Bukhara began in the second half of February 1918 under the direction of Kolesov, the chairman of the Turkestan Soviet government. Kolesov moved with his troops to the gates of the capital city and on February 28/March 13, after a conference with the Young Bukharans, presented the Emir with an ultimatum demanding the lifting of all restrictions on freedom of speech, the abolition of the death penalty and corporal punishment, the dissolution of the Emir's advisory body and its replacement by one composed of Young Bukharans, the right of the Young Bukharans to veto all future governmental appointments, and finally the reduction of certain taxes.[72] The Emir for a time was apparently considering the acceptance of these humiliating conditions; but finally, under unknown circumstances, he turned them down. On March 1/14 Kolesov ordered an attack on the walled city. The battle ended in a Russian defeat. The local population, imbued with religious passion, rallied behind the Emir and prevented enemy troops from penetrating Bukhara, and meanwhile massacred several hundred Russian residents of the city. After four days of fighting, Kolesov raised the siege and retreated to Tashkent. With him fled about two hundred Young Bukharans whose lives were endangered by their conspiracy with the Soviets.[73] Shortly after Kolesov's retreat, the Turkestan government formally recognized the independence of Bukhara.[74]

The defeat at Bukhara did not alter the fact that in the spring of 1918 Tashkent's authority extended over the major part of Turkestan. Under its control were the cities and settlements of the Syr-Daria, Ferghana, and Samarkand provinces, as well as the railroad lines and telegraph stations throughout these regions. Only the countryside — the desert areas with their oases and the mountains encircling Turkestan from the south and east — were beyond Tashkent's reach, largely because the maltreatment of the native population by the Turkestan Soviet government and the elements supporting it had alienated the indigenous inhabitants. All through 1918 and most of 1919 the persecutions, expulsions from the land, and looting of the Moslems by the Soviets continued unabated, creating a regime which a contemporary Soviet observer described as "feudal exploitation of the broad masses of the native population by the Russian Red Army man, colonist, and official." [75]

The dissatisfaction of the native population with Soviet rule found expression in partisan warfare, which had its origin in the Ferghana valley, spread to the neighboring provinces, and finally embraced nearly all of Turkestan, including the principalities of Khiva and Bukhara. This popular resistance movement, perhaps the most persistent and successful in the entire history of Soviet Russia, became known as *Basmachestvo,* and its participants as Basmachis.*

The Basmachis were originally ordinary bandits who had preyed on the countryside even before the outbreak of the Revolution. The tsarist regime had never been quite successful in suppressing them. In 1917 their ranks grew rapidly, owing to the amnesty proclaimed by the Provisional Government which released many criminals, and to the curtailment of the cotton industry, which had caused widespread unemployment among the native peasants and had deprived them of their livelihood. The Basmachis were particularly active in the Ferghana valley, the center of the cotton plantations. They were universally feared by the population of this area, Russian and Moslem alike; but since there was no force capable of putting them down, they gradually became stronger and bolder.[76] At the beginning of 1918 the Kokand government made an agreement with one of the most powerful of the local robber leaders, Irgach, appointing him captain of its troops.[77] When Kokand fell, many Moslems connected with the autonomous government and some of the inhabitants of the Ferghana valley who had been maltreated by Soviet troops fled to the mountains and joined the Basmachis, endowing Basmachestvo with the character of a popular resistance movement. The natives of the valley, who previously had dreaded them, now, after the Soviet conquest, often treated the Basmachis as protectors and liberators.

The principal weakness of the Basmachi movement was its lack of unity. The various detachments operated independently of each other under the leadership of ambitious and jealous chieftains, who refused to coördinate their activities and at times engaged in internecine wars. Not infrequently, in critical situations, Basmachi units went over to the Reds. Basmachestvo represented essentially a number of unconnected tribal revolts and exhibited all the shortcomings of such forms of resistance. It never attained its ultimate purpose — the overthrow of Russian rule in Turkestan — because the Russians were infinitely better organ-

* The origin of the term is obscure. Zeki Velidi Togan (quoted in Hayit, *Die Nationalen Regierungen*) traces it from the word "basmak" meaning "to oppress"; the Basmachis would then be "the oppressed." According to some Soviet sources, on the other hand (ZhN, 2 June 1920), it stems from the native term for "robber." Other sources indicate the root of the term to mean in native Turki "to tread underfoot." *Chacun à son goût.*

ized, controlled the cities and the lines of communication, and had at their disposal a more numerous and more experienced armed force. But from 1918 to 1924, and especially in the period 1920–1922 when Basmachestvo was at its height, the revolt drove the Communist rulers of Central Asia to desperation. "The fight against the Basmachis," wrote one Soviet eyewitness, "was a fight with an entirely new, distinct, and unique opponent. The Basmachis were made up of partisan detachments, almost exclusively on horseback. They were elusive and often dissolved in the neighboring villages literally before the eyes of our troops, who would immediately undertake a general search of the villages but without any results." [78] To protect their territories from the rebels, the Soviet authorities had to expend much effort, money, and manpower; late in 1918 a large expeditionary force was dispatched to the mountains to ferret them out.[79] Operating in the mountains and deserts, the Basmachis successfully evaded the regular Soviet forces, and during the Civil War they almost completely controlled the Ferghana valley and the mountains surrounding it.

In the spring of 1918 the Soviet government in Moscow, having received disquieting reports from Turkestan on the general unpopularity of the Bolshevik regime there and on its inability to deal with the Basmachis, decided to intervene. Paramount, in Moscow's eyes, was the question of autonomy. Moscow saw in the persistent refusal of the Tashkent Bolsheviks to grant the natives self-rule the principal reason for the dismal situation. In April 1918 a special emissary was dispatched from Moscow to Tashkent with instructions to proclaim Turkestan an autonomous republic. Shortly afterwards, Stalin, in a confidential report to the Tashkent Communists, confirmed these instructions. Obedient to orders, the Tashkent regime convened at the end of April the Fifth Congress of Soviets — the first at which Moslems and Russians sat together — and reversed the resolutions of the preceding congresses by decreeing the establishment of an Autonomous Republic of Turkestan. To maintain the impression that this resolution was spontaneous and voluntary, the Tashkent government sent a formal note to the Council of People's Commissars in Moscow informing it of the decision. Moscow replied several days later with an acknowledgment and a pledge of full support.[80]

The resolutions of this 1918 Tashkent Congress of Soviets, however, having been imposed from above against the real wishes of the local Communists, remained a dead letter. It was not until two years later that the natives were given the right to participate in the government of Turkestan, or treated on equal footing with the Europeans.[81]

In January 1919 the prestige of the Tashkent government was further weakened by an attempt of its Commissar of War, Osipov, to overthrow Soviet authority in Turkestan. Osipov captured most of the members of the government, whom he speedily shot. He tried to establish contact with the Basmachis and the British, but the Communist officials who had eluded arrest rallied the pro-Soviet forces in Tashkent and suppressed the rebellion before he could carry out these intentions. In reprisal for the plot, the Cheka reportedly executed several thousand persons suspected of hostility to the Communist regime in Turkestan.[82]

At this point a few words may be said about British intervention in Turkestan and the Caucasus. The British expended during World War I considerable effort fighting German and Turkish attempts to penetrate their Middle Eastern possessions and to sever the routes to India. While Russia had been actively engaged in fighting the Central Powers, that is, until the end of 1917, the northwestern approaches to India, leading through the Caucasus and the Transcaspian provinces of Russian Central Asia, were protected by Russian armies. The sudden collapse of the Russian front, however, changed the situation radically to the disadvantage of England, for it opened to the Turks and Germans the roads to the Caspian region and Persia, and thence to Central Asia and Afghanistan. To fill the gap the British were compelled to organize special military missions.

There were two main and several smaller expeditions of this sort. General Dunsterville was sent from India into northwestern Persia, with orders to reach Baku and to prevent the Central Powers from obtaining the Caucasian oil deposits. General Malleson, operating from northeastern Persia, was to keep the Transcaspian province from falling into enemy hands. Colonel Bailey was to make his way to Tashkent. The forces at the disposal of these British officers were quite inadequate for the tasks assigned them. Dunsterville had 900 men, Malleson 2,100 (largely natives recruited for the purpose), while Bailey commanded a mere handful of Indian guards.[83] The British effort was also handicapped by a poor understanding on the part of the commanders of the situation in the territories where they operated. They were in general unclear about the nature of the Civil War in Russia; they tended to treat the Bolsheviks as young hotheads and the non-Russian groups as passive colonial peoples, consistently underestimating the political acumen of the former and the nationalist fervor of the latter.

Considering that the intervention in Russia took place in the borderland areas where most of the population was non-Russian, the British might have been expected to appeal to the national sentiments of the minorities and to collaborate with the national governments which had formed themselves in those areas following the disintegration of the old Empire. This, however, they did not do. For all their importance to India and Britain's Middle Eastern position, the Caucasus and Turkestan were secondary fronts; the World War was being decided in Europe. Britain was not prepared to alienate the Russian Allies — represented during 1918 and 1919 by the Whites — whose assistance in fighting the Central

Powers and in reëstablishing a balance of power in Eastern Europe was important, by supporting minority nationalism and separatism. For better or worse, Great Britain backed the White movement and shared its negative attitude toward the national aspirations of the minorities. Only in 1920, after the White cause had suffered irreparable damage and finally collapsed, did they change their stand and throw their support behind the minorities, but not for long. In 1921 England reconciled itself to the fact that Soviet Russia had established a viable political organism, and began to make approaches to Moscow, abandoning the borderland peoples to their fate.

General Malleson's troops moved into Transcaspia in August 1918 at the request of the Socialist Revolutionary Transcaspian Provisional Government established in Ashkhabad. In August and September they fought, in alliance with Russian White troops and Turkmen detachments, under the leadership of a native nationalist leader, Oraz Serdar, against Red troops trying to penetrate from Tashkent. Malleson had connections with some of the Basmachi chieftains, but, according to Soviet sources, there is no evidence that he supplied them either with money or with arms.[84] In February 1919 British troops received orders from London to evacuate the Transcaspian region, and by early April they were entirely out. In July the Red troops approached Ashkhabad, which was defended by Oraz Serdar and his Turkmen units. After the city had been taken, Oraz Serdar fled to the desert and joined the Basmachi units in the Khiva district.[85] British intervention in Turkestan was thus of brief duration and had no important effect on the course of the Civil War there; at best it delayed somewhat the extension of Soviet rule to the southeastern shore of the Caspian Sea.

In January 1919 Soviet armies captured Orenburg. In the expectation that they would march at once on Tashkent, the Soviet government appointed a special commission for Turkestan (*Kommissia VTsIK po delam Turkestana*) composed of five Communists: Sh. Z. Eliava (chairman), M. V. Frunze (commander of the Fourth Army), V. V. Kuibyshev (political commissar in the Fourth Army), F. I. Goloshchekin, and Ia. E. Rudzutak. It was to replace the Tashkent Communist government and to assume political authority in Turkestan as soon as that area was reunited with Soviet Russia. The five-man commission arrived in Samara in early spring, but because the military authorities considered it more urgent to deal with Kolchak and Dutov than to march on Tashkent, its departure for Turkestan was delayed for more than six months.[86] Finally in the fall the White armies were defeated, and in November 1919 the Turkestan Commission left for Tashkent, to assume there the powers delegated to it by the central authorities.

The first task of the commission after its arrival in Tashkent was to prepare a detailed report on the general situation in that area for the benefit of the central Soviet authorities. Their report painted a most discouraging picture. On the basis of this report, the Central Committee of the Russian Communist Party drew up a "Circular Letter to All Organizations of the Communist Party of Turkestan," a part of which read as follows:

Separated by bands of White Guardists from Soviet Russia almost from the first days of the Revolution, Turkestan had to rely on its own resources. The thin layer of a Russian working class, which was lacking in strong revolutionary traditions and the experience of stubborn class warfare, had naturally enough fallen, in its majority, under the influence of colonially nationalistic hanger-on elements, and had unconsciously conducted a policy hostile to the international interests of the proletarian revolution.

Stimulated by their class and group interests, elements which had nothing in common with the task of liberating toilers, organized themselves under [the Soviet] banner. Old servants of the tsarist regime, adventurers and kulaks, operating under the camouflage of the class struggle, began to persecute the native population in a most brutal manner. Such partial continuation of the old policy under the auspices of Soviet rule could not but repel the poor class of natives from the revolution and push them into the arms of the native magnates. This in fact happened: Soviet rule transformed itself in many parts of Turkestan into a weapon for the national struggle.

The unification of Turkestan with Soviet Russia partly cleared the local atmosphere, which was filled with national hatreds and antagonisms, but nevertheless it could not at once liquidate all the survivals of the past. The colonizing policy had led directly and immediately to the enslavement of the poor class of natives. It was natural that with the termination of that policy the poor class of natives could not at once rise to power and stand up in defense of its interests. Side by side with the colonizing elements, power was acquired also by the exploiting upper classes of the native population, who, instead of helping the toiling masses in the cause of their national-cultural and class self-determination, began to exploit them with ever greater intensity, transferring all the traditional feudal methods of oppression, such as bribery, looting and personal terror, under the "Soviet roof."

So far the Soviet system in Turkestan had not yet been placed on sound foundations. Taking advantage of the decentralized and disorganized conditions of the government, suspicious gangs of hangers-on continue to operate with impunity in the localities. Party organizations are besmirched to an exceptional degree. The toiling masses of the Kirghiz, Sarts, Uzbeks, Turkmens do not as yet know what real Soviet rule and the Communist Party are: the defender of all oppressed and exploited.[87]

Lenin viewed the situation in Turkestan with great anxiety. He feared that Soviet misrule there might have an adverse effect on Communist efforts in the Middle and Far East and alienate those Moslem nationalists whom his regime had won over in the course of the Revolution and Civil War. As soon as he had studied the report, Lenin instructed the Turkestan Commission to take measures to restore order and to gain the sympathies of the local population. "The establishment of correct relations with the peoples of Turkestan," he wrote to Tashkent, "has for the Russian Socialist Federated Soviet Republic at the present time an importance which may be said without exaggeration to be gigantic, all-historical." [88]

On Lenin's instructions the commission adopted policies diametrically opposed to those which had been in force the preceding two years. The native population was permitted to reopen its bazaars, to engage in petty trade and in other commercial activities forbidden to the Russian inhabitants of the area; food distribution, previously favorable to the European urban population, was equalized; natives were urged to join the Communist Party and to participate in the Soviet institutions.[89] All those measures had, as their immediate purpose, the elimination of the dissatisfaction which had engendered and given strength to Basmachestvo. Frunze, arriving in Tashkent in February 1920, admitted publicly that in the past grievous mistakes had been committed as regarded the natives, and promised that henceforth things would be different.[90] He organized "Soviet Basmachi" detachments, and made attempts to liquidate the rebellion by causing mass defections.

This new, "soft" policy had a moderate success and to some extent stopped the further spread of Basmachestvo, but it did not accomplish everything the government had hoped. Some Basmachi chieftains went over to the Reds in the spring of 1920 and helped to build a "Soviet Basmachi" force, only to revolt in September 1920, and take once more to the hills.[91] In Ferghana there were active at the beginning of 1921 nearly six thousand Basmachis, and Soviet authority there, to quote a Soviet observer, "maintained itself only in the form of a few oases in the turbulent sea of Basmachestvo." [92] Moreover, by attacking the Khanate of Khiva and by renewing its offensive against Bukhara, the Soviet government rapidly undid most of the good which its concessions had accomplished, and caused the Turkestan revolt to extend to new regions.

Khiva was seized without great difficulty in February 1920. This state had been torn since 1918 by internal struggles between the Turkmens and Uzbeks over water sources, as well as by a conflict between the conservative orthodox elements, and the liberal jadidist Young Khivans. The military operations against Khiva were brief and, once the city was seized, the Communists recognized the Young Khivans as the legitimate government, signing with them an agreement by virtue of which Khiva, in recognition of its previous status as a semi-independent protectorate of Russia, became the People's Republic of Khorezm (Khorezm being the ancient name for the Khivan Principality).[93]

This conquest opened the northwestern approaches to Bukhara. In May 1920 Frunze began preparations for the conquest of that Emirate by ordering the mobilization of natives in Turkestan, and concentrating his troops on its border. Frunze's plans called for an uprising of the Young Bukharans somewhere within the domain of the Emir, and for a coördinated attack by battle-tried Red Armies from Khiva and Tashkent. A conference of Young Bukharans was called in August 1920 in the town of Chardzhou, seventy miles southwest of Bukhara. Most of the Young Bukharans were not satisfied with the way in which Frunze and the Turkestan Commission were directing the operation, because they themselves had little to say in the planning. But within the Young Bukharan organization there had developed earlier in the year a left-wing faction of Young Bukharan Communists, which, with the support of Moscow, overcame the resistance of the dissatisfied majority. At the Chardzhou conference the Young Bukharans pledged themselves to adopt the Communist platform and to dissolve their organizations in the event of a successful coup against the Emir.[94]

When the conference was finished, the Young Bukharans staged the planned uprising in Chardzhou and requested the Red Army for help. Soviet troops marched in at once, and converged on Bukhara. The battle for the city was bitter. It lasted five days, and for a while it appeared that the Emir might repeat his triumph of 1918. Frunze's troops suffered heavy losses and lacked reserves,[95] but finally, on September 2, 1920, they captured the city. The Emir and his entourage escaped to the eastern, mountainous section of the state, and thence, in 1921, to Afghanistan. Many of his followers, however, stayed behind and under the leadership of Ibrahim Bek organized Basmachi detachments, which soon gave the Soviet authorities as much trouble as those active in the Ferghana region. Thus, the seizure of Bukhara, though it rounded out Soviet possessions in Turkestan, confronted the Communist authorities with added difficulties and new expressions of popular discontent.

### The Crimea

In late December 1917 political strength in the Crimea was divided between Sebastopol and Simferopol. The former was firmly in the hands of the Bolsheviks; the latter in the hands of the Tatar nationalists. The majority of the population of the peninsula, which took neither side, had no forces at its disposal and was compelled to watch helplessly the growing conflict between these two groups.

The Sebastopol sailors were greatly displeased with the activities of the Kurultai. They interpreted the appointment of the Tatar government as an indication that the Moslems intended to take over the Crimea and to impose their rule on the Russian inhabitants. The Bolshevik Executive Committee in the port town exploited the anti-Tatar sentiments of the sailors by spreading propaganda that the peninsula was threatened with "Tatar dictatorship." [96] In the early days of January 1918 small detachments of sailors directed by the Sebastopol Revkom occupied most of the northern half of the Crimea by means of sea-borne landings.

Among the Tatars, the threat of a clash with the Bolsheviks led to a split between the left-wing nationalists, headed by Chelibiev, who wanted a *rapprochement* with the Communists, and the right-wing nationalists, headed by Seidamet, who opposed it. On January 9/22, 1918, the Kurultai held a special meeting at which both viewpoints were discussed. Finally, the decision was taken to approach the Sebastopol Communists with an offer of participation in the All-Crimean government. The Bolsheviks agreed to the proposition, but on the condition that the Kurultai recognize the Soviet government in Petrograd. By a vote of forty-three to twelve the Kurultai turned down this condition, thus eliminating the possibility of a peaceful solution of the conflict. Chelibiev, dissatisfied with the decision, resigned from the Executive Committee, and Seidamet took over his functions.[97]

The direct cause of the armed conflict between Sebastopol and Simferopol which broke out in January 1918 was an agreement between the Tatar nationalists and the Ukrainian Central Rada made in late 1917, which had stipulated that the Tatars would not allow military units hostile to the Rada to move across their territory.[98] When, at the beginning of January, the Bolsheviks in Sebastopol dispatched troops to aid Antonov-Ovseenko in his march on Kiev and the Don, the Tatars tried to disarm them. Sebastopol retaliated by sending a force of 3,000 sailors in the direction of Simferopol with orders to put an end to the "Tatar counterrevolution." On January 13/26 Tatar and Soviet units engaged in battle near the railroad station of Siuren. The Red troops easily dispersed the defenders and entered Simferopol the following day. The Kurultai and other nationalist organizations were at once dissolved. Seidamet, who had commanded the native troops in the ill-fated battle, fled and eventually reached Turkey. Most of the other members of the Milli Firka went into hiding in the Tatar villages. Chelibiev, although he had reason to count on Red sympathy, was arrested and placed in a Sebastopol prison. There, in February 1918, Soviet sailors — very likely without the knowledge of their superiors — shot him and threw his body into the sea.[99]

The first Communist regime in the Crimea lasted for three months, from the end of January until the end of April 1918. It was ineffective, disorganized, and, like the first Soviet government in the neighboring Ukraine, vanished without a trace as soon as German troops had set foot

on its territory. The sailors, whom the Sebastopol Bolsheviks had succeeded in winning over by appeals to their war-weariness and nationalism, quickly grew tired of the new order. Before long, they got out of
hand and began to loot and attack the local population. At the end of
February 1918 they killed 250 citizens in Sebastopol and 170 in Simferopol.[100] Many of the sailors were of Ukrainian origin and refused to fight
in the Bolshevik ranks after learning of the Soviet attack on the Ukraine.
By March 1918 the fleet — the backbone of Soviet power in the Crimea
— was entirely demoralized. Some sailors were deserting for home, others
were going over to the White forces. Thus ended the short-lived coöperation between the Sebastopol fleet and the Communists.

At the beginning of March the Communists convened in Simferopol
the First Regional Congress of Soviets in order to form a Soviet government for the Crimea. Attending, among others, were ninety-one Tatar
deputies, mostly members of the left wing of the disbanded Kurultai.
The Tatars demanded that they be given seats in the Executive Committee, which was to be the government of the peninsula, but the chairman of the congress informed them that before they had a right to ask
for places in the Executive Committee it was incumbent upon them to
join the Communist Party. When the Tatars moved to open a discussion
on the entire national question they again lost, because the non-Moslem
majority voted to refrain from injecting this question into the debates.[101]
The government formed by the congress consisted of twelve Bolsheviks
and eight Left SR's. As a concession to the Tatars a Commissariat of
Crimean Moslem Affairs was created: in this way a lone Tatar received
a post in the Soviet government.[102]

The government had scarcely assumed its duties when the German
armies began to advance into the Ukraine and the Crimea. In an effort
to save the Black Sea fleet from falling into German hands, Moscow
ordered the Crimean Communists to proclaim the independence of the
peninsula, hoping that the Germans might respect the sovereignty of
such a state.[103] In accordance with these directives the Crimean government proclaimed in late March 1918 the Republic of Taurida. (Taurida
is the name of the province of which the Crimean peninsula was a
part.)[104]

This measure, however, failed to preserve the tottering Soviet authority. Not only was it menaced from the outside, but internally it had
also lost all strength. In the elections to the Sebastopol Soviet, held in
the middle of April, the Bolsheviks were heavily outvoted by the SR's
and Mensheviks; in other towns they failed completely.[105] Soon the
Tatars began to raise their heads again. Virtually excluded from the
Soviet government and subjected to the excesses of the sailors, they
awaited with much impatience the arrival of German troops. In the
middle of April some Tatar villages revolted and threw out Communist

officials; here and there Tatar detachments began to reappear. Soon the Sovnarkom left Simferopol secretly, hoping to escape from the Crimea before the arrival of German troops, but it was intercepted by Russian and Tatar units. Four days after the attempted escape, all members of the Soviet government of the Crimea were executed in the vicinity of Yalta.[106] In early May German troops entered Sebastopol unopposed.

The German occupation did not prove itself as beneficial as the Tatars had hoped. As in the Ukraine and Belorussia the Germans vacillated between the desire to support native nationalism in the struggle against the Russians and the will to impose their discipline upon the occupied territories. In May the members of the Kurultai who had emerged from hiding formed a Provisional Crimean Government, with Seidamet as Prime Minister,[107] but the Germans refused to recognize it and instead placed the civil administration in the hands of General Sulkevich, a Lithuanian Moslem who had once served in the Russian armies and during the war had commanded a special Moslem Corps which the Germans had formed in Rumania. Sulkevich's regime, like Skoropadski's in the Ukraine, was a puppet government, serving the interests of the German occupation armies, and out of touch with the Tatar and Russian population. The fact that it assisted the occupants to ship food from the Crimea to Germany, and that it passed legislation returning to the previous owners the land confiscated in the course of 1917 and early 1918, did not increase its popular following. All the efforts of Tatar political figures to use their Turkish connections as a means of exercising pressure on the Germans, proved unsuccessful. The Germans refused to surrender any authority in the Crimea to the Tatars. As soon as the German armies evacuated the peninsula in November 1918, Sulkevich resigned.

After the resignation of Sulkevich, authority over the Crimea was assumed by a Russian government, headed by Solomon S. Krym, a member of the Jewish Karaite sect of the Crimea and a Kadet Deputy in the First Duma. His government drew its principal support from the Russian official and landowning groups, which were strong in the Crimea. Its political and economic orientation was that of the Kadet Party.

In the fall of 1918 three distinct political tendencies emerged among the Tatars. The extreme right wing, composed largely of the clergy and wealthy Moslem landowners, which in 1917 had already had conflicts with the Tatar nationalists over the questions of land and religious administration, supported the Krym government. The Tatar nationalists of the Milli Firka would not coöperate with the Russian liberals. The majority of the Milli Firka preferred to pursue an independent course, hoping sooner or later to secure recognition from both sides engaged in the Civil War, and to regain the authority which the party had enjoyed before being suppressed by the Sebastopol fleet.[108] A minority in the party considered such a course impracticable, and sought conciliation with the Communists. This was the left wing of the Milli Firka, headed by Veli Ibragimov (Ibrahim), which in the winter of 1918–19 established contact with the Communist underground operating in the major cities of the peninsula, and began to work hand in hand with the Communist cells.[109]

When Soviet troops reoccupied the Crimea in April 1919, overthrowing the Krym government, the relations between the Tatar nationalists and the Communists were considerably better than they had been a year earlier, in the days of the Republic of Taurida. With the Soviet armies there arrived numerous Moslem Communists, including the chairman of the Central Bureau of the Communist Organizations of the Peoples of the East, Mustafa Subkhi. Immediately propaganda was started among the Moslem masses, a Crimean Moslem Bureau was opened to handle Moslem affairs, and a considerable effort was made to attract Tatar intellectuals to the Soviet side. In May 1919 the Communists established a Crimean regime, and appointed a government in which several important posts, including the chairmanship of the Commissariat of Foreign Affairs, were given to members of the left wing of the Milli Firka.[110] The Central Committee of the Milli Firka, which had not collaborated actively with the Communist underground, dispatched to the Soviet authorities, shortly after the formation of the republic, a conciliatory note in which it offered to adopt the Communist platform and to support the Soviet regime in return for a share in the administration and the right to function legally on Crimean territory, but this proposition was apparently rejected.[111]

Active collaboration of the Central Committee of the Milli Firka with the Communists dates only from the autumn of 1919. In June 1919 barely one month after it was formed, the government of the Soviet Crimean Republic had to flee before the White armies of General Denikin which had occupied the peninsula. The regime which Denikin had established in the second half of 1919 was perhaps the most reactionary of all to which the Crimea had been subjected since the outbreak of the Revolution; it was also the most hostile to the Tatar nationalist movement. Denikin not only made clear his opposition to Tatar nationalism by dissolving Tatar political organizations which had managed to lead an open, if tenuous, existence from the time of the German occupation, but also alienated the Tatar intellectuals by undoing some of the most important reforms introduced in the Crimea in the spring of 1917. Specifically, he restored the old Vakuf Commission and returned to his post the tsar-appointed Mufti of the Crimea, removed by the March 1917 Crimean conference. Driven underground, the Milli Firka had no choice but to coöperate with the only powerful, well-organized anti-Denikin force — the Communists. The Milli Firka endeavored to reach an agreement with the illegal Communist organizations in the Crimea, but since these organizations were constantly suppressed by the White authorities, its efforts produced no results.[112] Only in the autumn of 1919, when the center of Communist activity was transferred from the Crimean peninsula to Odessa, was it possible for the Milli Firka and the Communist Party to establish regular relations. The two sides agreed at that time to coördinate their anti-White activity in the Crimea.[113]

Baron Wrangel, who succeeded Denikin as leader of the White forces after Denikin resigned in early 1920, attempted to correct the mistakes of his predecessors by making generous promises to the Tatars, including the pledge of autonomy and religious self-rule,[114] but this evidence of good will came too late to bring practical results. In the fall of 1920 the Communists organized a Crimean Revolutionary Committee (*Krymrev-kom*) in Melitopol (Ukraine); in October, they penetrated the White defenses of the Crimea and occupied the peninsula for the third time.

As soon as Soviet rule had been established, the Milli Firka tried to place its relations with the Communists on a more permanent basis. In a formal declaration submitted to the Regional Committee of the Russian Communist Party in the Crimea, the chairman of the Central Committee of the Milli Firka called attention to the fundamental similarities between Communist and Moslem ideals. The Milli Firka, he stated, differed from the Communist party "not in principle, but only in the timing, place, and means of realization [of socialism]"; the Milli Firka believed that, before the socialism for which both parties were striving could be attained, certain reactionary factors, rooted deeply in Moslem life, had to be destroyed. It was ready to coöperate with the Soviet authorities in their fight against international imperialism, religious conservatism, and economic exploitation, provided it was granted the status of a legal party with a right to publish a newspaper and to administer Crimean Moslem religious and educational institutions, including the *vakuf* properties.[115] The Crimean Communists turned down this offer, and branded the Milli Firka an illegal, counterrevolutionary organization.[116]

If the refusal of the Soviet authorities in the Crimea to accept the coöperation offered by the Milli Firka signified their rejection of a large proportion of the Tatar intelligentsia, certainly their agricultural policies incurred the enmity of the Crimean Tatar peasantry. Owing to the fact that Catherine II had distributed very large areas of land in the Crimea to her favorites and other noblemen, the ownership of land there was concentrated in a comparatively few hands. In the second half of the nineteenth century (1877) 1,000 noblemen owned over one-half of all the land in the Crimea.[117] And though this concentration lessened appreciably during the last decades of the *ancien régime*, as small peasant holdings increased, the properties which came within the categories considered subject to confiscation by the Soviet authorities (large estates, church and government lands) still amounted to no less than 50 per cent of all the acreage of the Crimea.[118] Instead of distributing this confiscated property to the peasantry and the landless agricultural laborers, the authorities transferred most of it to gigantic state farms, or *sovkhozy*, which mushroomed throughout the peninsula in 1920 and 1921. In the spring of 1921, there were in the Crimea 987 sovkhozy, owning 25 per cent of all the arable land, and 45 per cent of all the orchards and vineyards.[119] In the setting up of the state farms many irregularities were committed. In fact, the heaviest losers in the new system were the Tatars, because they formed the bulk of the landless peasantry in the Crimea.

Early in 1921 Sultan-Galiev was dispatched by Moscow to the Crimea to report on conditions there, and if necessary, to prepare recommendations for their improvement. Sultan-Galiev's report, published in May 1921 was very critical of Soviet rule in the Crimea. Communist Party work there, he reported, was entirely disorganized and out of touch with the Moslem population; the state farms, run by ex-tsarist and colonial officials directly subordinate to Moscow, ignored the needs of the local population; Tatar education was neglected. He suggested that a Crimean Soviet Socialist Republic be created, that Tatars be admitted in large numbers in Communist organizations, and that the sovkhozy be drastically curtailed.[120] Despite objections from local Communists, and the acceptance of a resolution by the Crimean Regional Communist Party Congress against the creation of a republic,[121] the Bolshevik authorities in Moscow carried out Sultan-Galiev's recommendation and established in November 1921 the Autonomous Crimean Socialist Soviet Republic. The chairmanship of the new government was given to Iurii Gaven, a Bolshevik whose views on the nature of autonomy left no doubt that he would follow closely the directives of Moscow.[122]

The Revolution in the eastern borderlands of the Russian Empire, and particularly in the steppe and desert regions inhabited by Turkic tribes, had a distinct character. Politically and economically, these regions were colonial dependencies of Russia. The cleavage between the native and the immigrant Russian population at the outbreak of the Revolution remained broad, despite progressive Westernization under Russian rule. The overthrow of the tsarist regime loosened the ties connecting the borderlands with the metropolis and removed the mollifying, regulating force which the imperial administration was wont to exercise. Before long the Russian urban inhabitants and colonists entered into a head-on conflict with the natives, which combined all the horrors of class struggle with those of a national war. The natives sought to assert their rights and to correct the injustices of the past by organizing national councils and national political parties, which at first coöperated with the Russian liberal and moderate socialist institutions, and after the

Bolshevik coup, endeavored to establish autonomy. The Russian settlers, anxious to preserve their privileges, found a natural ally in the new Soviet regime. In the Communist ideology, which called for the supremacy of the industrial proletariat, peasantry, and soldiers, the settlers saw the excuse they sought to destroy the political institutions of the natives. Lacking military experience, short of money and personnel, and hampered by the Civil War from securing assistance of their co-religionists in other parts of Russia, the Moslem nationalists were quite powerless against the hostile forces. One by one, the various Kurultais, Madzhilis, and their executive organs were dispersed by Communist-controlled groups.

After the political apparatus of the tsarist regime, the Provisional Government, and the indigenous national organizations had been destroyed, power in most Moslem borderlands passed into the hands of the well-to-do Russian peasantry, the skilled urban proletariat (above all, the railroad workers), the Russian garrisons, and the lower echelons of the old tsarist colonial bureaucracy. Those groups utilized the Soviet government and party machines to intensify the economic and political exploitation of the native population. The Revolution, therefore, brought to the Moslem areas not the abolition of colonialism, but colonialism in a new and much more oppressive form; it established a regime which, for the lack of a more conventional term, may be called "proletarian colonialism." The classes which in Russia proper constituted the lower orders of society formed in the eastern borderlands a privileged order, which itself was engaged in exploitation and oppression. This discrepancy between the effects of the Communist victory in Russia and its effects in the Moslem borderlands was of the utmost importance for the whole history of the national problem in the Soviet Union.

The Russian Revolution and Civil War greatly accelerated the development of nationalism among Russian Moslems. If before 1917 the sense of national consciousness had been in evidence only among a relatively small Moslem middle class and intelligentsia, which had had the advantage of Russian or jadidist schooling, by 1920 it had percolated down to the lowest strata of the population. The nomad or peasant who prior to the revolution had considered himself above all a Moslem now began to think of himself for the first time as a member of a nation, be it Azerbaijani, Kazakh-Kirghiz, Volga Tatar, Bashkir, Crimean Tatar, Uzbek, or some other. The revolutionary upheaval had telescoped into a period of three or four years an ideological and social evolution which under more normal circumstances might have taken an entire generation. The emergence of numerous and diversified political parties among the Moslem minorities, the experience of voting in national elections, the establishment of local territorial governments, and the conduct of military operations under native banners — all these developments advanced the growth of the national movement to a point far beyond that which it had attained in prerevolutionary Russia.

The Soviet regime recognized this fact at once and spared no effort to turn it to its own advantage. In 1917 and 1918, when the Moslem borderlands were largely cut off from Moscow, there was little opportunity to accomplish anything in the regions themselves, but Moscow lost no time in the effort to win over the All-Russian Moslem organizations, and after this move had failed, to pursue the aims of the All-Russian Moslem movement under Communist auspices. In 1919 and 1920, when the borderland areas had been conquered, Moscow made an attempt to reëstablish the equilibrium between the Russians and the natives which the disintegration of the Empire had upset, by exercising pressure upon Soviet organs in these regions to curtail their oppressive policies, and if necessary, to grant the natives concessions. Moscow's alliance with the nationalists defecting from the White side, and its insistence on the establishment of autonomous national states, were in line with this policy.

Toward the Moslems, the Communists therefore pursued a dual course: on the one hand, seizure of power, overthrow of all native institutions which challenged or refused to recognize Soviet authority, and centralization of political power; on the other, a bid for the sympathies of all strata of Moslem society by economic or cultural concessions and an alliance with Moslem nationalists.

# V

## SOVIET CONQUEST OF THE CAUCASUS

### The Transcaucasian Federation

The separation of Transcaucasia from Russia was an act of desperation, undertaken by the local political organizations only after it had become quite apparent that there was no other way of saving this territory from anarchy and enemy occupation. As a remedy it proved to be only of brief effectiveness. Within a few weeks after its formation, the new republic fell apart, and Transcaucasia, torn by internal dissentions, was overrun by Turkish and German troops.

The government of the new state, officially known as the Transcaucasian Federative Republic (*Zakavkazskaia Federativnaia Respublika*), consisted of a coalition of the three principal national parties, presided over by the Georgian Menshevik, Akaki Chkhenkeli. What once had been remarked of the Holy Roman Empire was *mutatis mutandis* applicable here: it was neither Transcaucasian, nor Federative, nor a Republic. Inasmuch as the Turks had occupied portions of the southwest and the Bolsheviks soon seized Baku and the entire eastern half of Transcaucasia, the government controlled no more than the central regions adjoining Tiflis. During its brief existence neither the federal relations nor the republican state institutions had been worked out, and the administration was largely in the hands of the Georgian Menshevik party.

As soon as Transcaucasia had proclaimed its independence, it dispatched a delegation to Batum to reopen negotiations with the Central Powers. Declaring that they needed control over the transportation lines into Northern Persia to expel the British units there, the Turkish negotiators now demanded the railroad line running from Aleksandropol (Leninakan) to Dzhulfa, deep in Armenian territory and beyond the border designated by the Brest Litovsk Treaty. The Transcaucasians protested against this demand and charged that it was a violation of their sovereignty, but disregarding their objections, Turkish troops marched on May 2/15 into undefended Aleksandropol.[1]

While they were fighting a losing battle at the diplomatic table and trying to create an impression of Transcaucasian unity, the Georgians had an uneasy feeling that the Azerbaijanis were not only unwilling to support their efforts, but were actually conniving in secret with the enemy. Indeed, the behavior of the Mussavat since the collapse of the Provisional Government gave reason for suspicion. During all the debates which had taken place in the Transcaucasian Seim prior to the proclamation of independence, the Mussavatists had emphasized the futility of continuing military resistance, and, when pressed for a clear statement of their intentions, admitted that the ties of religion and racial sympathy would prevent them from taking arms against the Turks.[2] At the peace negotiations in Trebizond and Batum, the Mussavat maintained separate delegations which were in close liaison with a mission sent by the North Caucasian nationalists, and seemed much more interested in securing the Porte's assistance in the establishment of an Azerbaijani–North Caucasian state than in stemming the Turkish advance.[3] The negotiations between the Ottoman deputies, and the separate Azerbaijani and North Caucasian missions seemed to indicate the making of a Pan-turanian state.

The Georgians and Armenians were in difficult straits. Every advance of the Turkish armies sent fresh droves of Armenian refugees into the overcrowded cities of Transcaucasia. The prospect of a Turkish state embracing Anatolia, Azerbaijan, and the Northern Caucasus, encircling and cutting off their territories from the remainder of the world, was frightening alike to the Georgian socialists and to the Armenian victims of Moslem violence.

At this critical juncture the Georgians received unexpected assistance from Turkey's ally, Germany. The German Foreign Office, and even more so, the German General Staff wanted to preserve the Brest Litovsk line in the Caucasus and to direct the advance of the Ottoman armies in the general direction of India. The Germans wanted to keep for themselves the Caucasus with its rich mineral resources, which were necessary for their own war effort.[4] For this reason, General von Lossow, the German representative at the Batum negotiations, tended to support the Trans-caucasian delegates, defending them against the seemingly endless territorial demands of the Turks. When the Ottoman delegation requested the Aleksandropol–Dzhulfa railroad, von Lossow sided openly with the Transcaucasians.[5]

In confidential conversations, von Lossow urged the Georgians to secede from the Federation and to proclaim their independence; by so doing they could conclude a separate treaty and place themselves under German protection. Presented with this alternative to certain Turkish occupation, the Georgians accepted the German suggestion. On May 26 they convened the Georgian National Council, which had been established in November 1917 but had not been operative since then, and proclaimed the independence of Georgia.[6] The Azerbaijanis and the Armenians followed suit two days later.[7]

It would be fruitless to take sides in the acrimonious debates of Georgian, Azerbaijani, and Armenian publicists concerning the responsibility for the disintegration of the Transcaucasian Federation. Tseretelli, speaking in the Seim on the day when Georgian independence was proclaimed, placed the blame squarely on the shoulders of the Mussavat, which he accused of conspiring with the Turks against the Federation;[8] the Mussavatists, on the other hand, insisted that it was the Georgians who were at fault in maintaining secret relations with the Germans and "seceding" from Transcaucasia;[9] the Armenians, for once agreeing with the Azerbaijanis, also accused the Georgians, although for different reasons: they charged that the Georgians had made agreements with Turkey before the war.[10] Actually, the Transcaucasian Federation had no *raison d'être* save as a makeshift arrangement to permit the resumption of negotiations with the Turks. The national interests and aspirations of the peoples making up the Federation were too divergent to permit co-existence in one state in a period of violent external pressures. Once Transcaucasia had been separated from Russia, its further disintegration along national lines was almost inevitable.

### Soviet Rule in the North Caucasus and Eastern Transcaucasia (1918)

#### The Terek Region

The Bolsheviks first came into power in the Terek Region and then in Baku by exploiting the national animosities prevalent in those areas. They held power from the spring of 1918 until the early autumn of that year.

The outbreak of the Civil War in December 1917 and the subsequent demise of the so-called Terek-Daghestan state, left the Terek region without a government. A new attempt to create one was made by the Bolshevik organizations of Vladikavkaz and Groznyi, acting in close liaison with the Soviet government in Russia. The Bolsheviks intended their government to rest on a coalition of the *inogorodnye* and Cossacks — a united Russian front against the Moslem natives, which the attacks of the Chechen and Ingush on the inhabitant of the plains had made imperative.

The Bolshevik rise to power in the Northern Caucasus, as in Transcaucasia, was closely connected with the influx of deserting soldiers, who, in transit from the front to their homes in the north, passed through Baku and the railroad towns of the North Caucasus. The Bolsheviks enlisted some of these soldiers, and with their aid, obtained control over the principal soviets in the Terek Region.[11] In the midst of the war, when the towns and Cossack settlements alike were expecting from hour to hour renewed Chechen and Ingush attacks, the Bolshevik organizations with their troops were in a good position to assume leadership. In January 1918 they invited Russian political parties and Cossack representatives to a meeting in the town of Mozdok, for the purpose of combining forces

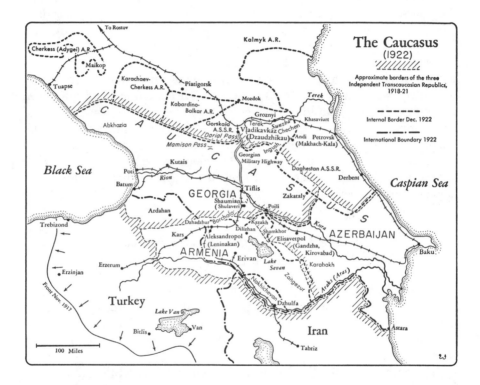

against the invaders from the mountains. At this congress all the Russian political parties of the Terek Region — Mensheviks, SR's, Bolsheviks, as well as some radical Ossetin parties — formed a "socialist bloc" and joined the Cossacks in a new administration: the Terek People's Soviet (*Terskii Narodnyi Sovet*).[12]

The Terek People's Soviet moved in March to Vladikavkaz, where it founded the Terek People's Soviet Socialist Republic (*Terskaia Narodnaia Sovetskaia Sotsialisticheskaia Respublika*). The government of the new republic included representatives of Russian, Cossack, and some native parties (but without the Chechen and Ingush) and was headed by the Georgian Bolshevik, Noi Buachidze. In April the Republic adopted a constitution, which acknowledged the sovereignty of the Russian Soviet Republic and granted Moscow very extensive rights over the Terek Region in matters of finance, foreign affairs, the entry of Russian troops, posts and telegraphs. At the same time, the Terek Region retained broad autonomy in other internal matters, including full legislative, administrative, and judiciary power, on the condition that it did not enact legislation violating the constitution of the RSFSR.[13]

The Terek state represented perhaps the first instance of a "People's Republic," a type of government the Communists were in time to use in other conquered territories where their position was weak. In those areas they satisfied themselves with control of the central organs of political power and with the application of general democratic and socialist measures, postponing the realization of their full Communist program until a more opportune moment. Another characteristic feature of this type of rule was Communist coöperation with socialist and liberal groups.

In May 1918 some deputies of the dissolved Terek-Daghestan administration, who in January had fled Vladikavkaz and had sought refuge in Transcaucasia, proclaimed in Batum the independence of the Northern Caucasus. This step was without practical significance, since the Northern Caucasus was then firmly under the control of the Bolshevik-dominated Terek Republic, but it did open the way for possible Turkish intervention on behalf of the North Caucasian Moslems. The German delegation at the Batum Conference considered the self-styled republic a fiction and refused to grant it recognition.[14]

The Communist-sponsored Terek Republic exercised effective political authority for a brief time only. In the summer of 1918, the traditional animosity between the Cossacks and the inogorodnye led again to an open conflict. Despite specific directives from Lenin to retain an alliance with other socialist parties and to refrain from copying Communist policies in Russia proper, the Terek Bolsheviks, pressed by the land-starved inogorodnye, began to socialize land.[15] The Cossacks would not acquiesce, and quit the government. Moreover, before long the war between the Ingush and the Cossacks, halted in the spring, flared up once more, and the entire region was thrown into complete anarchy. In June violent anti-Soviet demonstrations of Russians dissatisfied with Soviet rule took place in Vladikavkaz, in the course of which Buachidze, the Bolshevik chairman of the republic's government, was killed.[16]

The Georgian Bolsheviks, who had fled to Vladikavkaz at the end of May 1918, after Georgia had proclaimed its independence, found the North Caucasus completely disorganized. "Soviet rule existed only in name, having among the population neither weight nor authority. Either there were no organs of government whatsoever, or else they had no idea what to do." [17]

Early in August the Cossacks attacked and seized Vladikavkaz. The Bolshevik leaders, including Ordzhonikidze, who had been dispatched there in July by the Soviet government from Tsaritsyn (Stalingrad), hid in the mountains, among the Chechen and Ingush. Assuming leadership over the Terek Bolsheviks, Ordzhonikidze made an alliance with the mountain natives and promised them the assistance of the Soviet government in regaining the lands which they had lost to the Cossacks under the tsars. On August 17, Ingush warriors, incited by the Bolshevik exiles, attacked and seized Vladikavkaz. A few days later, the Bolsheviks followed their new allies into the city and reorganized the Terek government. Soviet power now was less popular than it had been at the beginning of the year, when it had enjoyed the support of the Cossacks and non-Communist Russians. Ordzhonikidze admitted that in the fall of 1918 Bolshevik authority in the Terek Region rested exclusively on the assistance of the mountain Moslem groups, especially the Ingush: "I recall the moment before the end of the Fourth Congress [of the Terek Region, held in August 1918] when our fate hung on a hair; this was a moment . . . when we had no following . . . when we were looked upon with timidity . . . when only the Ingush people followed us without hesitation." [18]

The time for the "People's Republic" type of government was past, and Ordzhonikidze, possibly under directives from Stalin (then in Tsaritsyn), with whom he was associated, undertook instead a policy of terror and repression. He organized a secret police, or Cheka, and proceeded to arrest or execute Mensheviks, SR's, and other elements who had expressed dissatisfaction with Communism. "Only then did the population learn the meaning of the Cheka," writes a Communist historian.[19] For the first time the North Caucasus experienced the full horrors of Soviet rule.

The Chechen and Ingush, on the other hand, were handsomely rewarded at the expense of the Cossacks for having saved Soviet rule in the Terek Region. Whole Cossack settlements were expelled, and their land, livestock and household belongings turned over to the Chechen and Ingush.[20] The persecution of the Terek Cossacks and the alliance with the Chechen and Ingush became the cornerstone of Bolshevik policy in the North Caucasus for many years to come. It accounted for the loyalty shown by the Chechen and Ingush toward the Communists during the Civil War. The new regime which the Bolsheviks had established upon their return to Vladikavkaz in August was entirely in their hands and subordinated directly to Moscow. The constitution of April 1918 was altered to eliminate all divergencies from the constitution of

Soviet Russia, and the internal autonomy which the Terek People's Republic had been promised was abolished.[21]

### Baku

Until the middle of March 1918 life in Baku proceeded much as before, despite Communist determination to seize power. Bolshevik inactivity was due primarily to the weakness of the party and its following. The soldiers on whom the Communists had depended at the end of 1917, and who accounted for at least one-third of their following in the city, had dispersed and were gone. The workers, especially the laborers in the oil industry, voted for the SR's if they were Russian, and for their respective national parties if they were not. In such circumstances it was impossible to accomplish an armed seizure of power. The Baku Bolsheviks were compelled to give up their plans for a coup and to concentrate instead on the penetration of the labor unions and other organizations by means of strikes, propaganda, and agitation.[22]

If, despite their numerical weakness, the Communists succeeded in retaining control over the executive organ of the Baku Soviet, the reason must be sought in their effective exploitation of the national animosities which played an important part in local politics. The Baku Soviet reflected in miniature the ethnic and political structure of Transcaucasia: it was composed of Russian, Armenian, and Azerbaijani parties and was torn by the same dissensions which eventually destroyed the Transcaucasian Federation. Throughout 1917 the Bolsheviks and the Mussavatists in the Baku Soviet maintained friendly relations, which aided considerably the weak Bolshevik faction.

In January 1918 Communist-Mussavat relations underwent a change. The city began to suffer from a food shortage, caused by the severance of the railroad connecting Baku with the North Caucasus and by the refusal of the Moslem peasants in Eastern Transcaucasia to deliver produce to the city. The outbreaks of Moslem violence in various parts of Transcaucasia, such as in Shamkhor, which were directed against Russian soldiers and the Russian inhabitants in general, and perhaps above all the threat of a Turkish invasion of the Caucasus, caused the Bolsheviks to turn against the Mussavat, and like their comrades in the Terek Region, to assume the championship of the Russian national cause.[23]

The incident which led to the Bolshevik coup in Baku came unexpectedly, before the Communists were quite prepared to assume power.[24] On March 17/30, 1918 — on the day when the North Caucasian Communists were proclaiming the Terek People's Soviet Socialist Republic in Vladikavkaz — the Executive Committee (*Ispolkom*) of the Baku Soviet, controlled by the Communists, received reports that a ship of repatriated troops of the so-called Savage Division (*Dikaia Diviziia*), composed of

Moslem volunteers in the tsarist service, had entered the Baku harbor. The Russians and Armenians in the soviet, fearing the disembarkation of armed Moslem units would precipitate a national conflict, ordered the troops of the Savage Division to disarm before entering Baku. The troops complied, and were allowed to leave the boat. The action of the Ispolkom soon became known in the Moslem quarter of the city, where it aroused great discontent. Meetings were held and protests voiced against the high-handed methods used by the Russians and Armenians. The Moslem population was enraged that the Russians and Armenians, who had their own armed detachments, had prevented the Azerbaijanis from also acquiring a military force. The next afternoon (March 18/31), a delegation of Baku Moslems appeared at the soviet to demand the return of the confiscated arms; simultaneously shooting broke out in the Moslem quarter. In several sections of the city Russian soldiers were accosted and disarmed by Moslem mobs.

The soviet was convinced that it faced a Moslem "counterrevolution." In any struggle in which the Turkish population was involved, the Armenians were certain to be on the other side of the battle line, and thus on March 18/31 or the following day a coalition was formed between the Communists, Russian SR's, and Armenian Dashnaks. The alliance with the Dashnaks became very embarrassing for the Bolsheviks, partly because of the bad reputation of the Dashnaks among both the Russian socialists and the Moslems, and partly because it was certain to transform any struggle for control of the city into a Moslem-Armenian slaughter.

On March 20/April 2, Dashnak units, directed by the Ispolkom, attacked and disarmed Moslem mobs responsible for the outbreak of violence two days earlier. They met with resistance, but on the morning of the following day the Baku Soviet was in full command of the city.

The defenseless Moslem population was now at the mercy of the Dashnaks and the pro-Communist Russian deserters. For three full days — from March 20 to 23 — the Dashnaks and the deserters massacred Moslems in the city and its industrial suburbs, and then moved into the neighboring countryside to continue the attack on the rural inhabitants. All in all, some three thousand persons, mostly Moslems, lost their lives in the March fighting.[25]

"The March [1918] struggle," wrote a Soviet historian of the Transcaucasian revolution, "consisted without any doubt of the exploitation of two national tendencies against a third national tendency." [26] "The counterrevolution expressed itself through the Turkish national group, whereas the Armenian and Russian national groups actively supported the side of the revolution." [27] The fact that they had come into power in the wake of a purely national clash and with the assistance of the Dashnaks was not easy for the Bolsheviks to justify. Shaumian wrote to Lenin explaining that without the aid of Armenian nationalists Baku with its priceless oil would have been lost;[28] Bolshevik speakers tried to defend the action to the Baku Soviet on the same grounds;[29] and Communist historians ever since have either minimized the role of the Dashnaks in the March events or else ignored it altogether.

In mid-April, the Bolsheviks formed a Soviet government in Baku, composed entirely of Bolsheviks and left-wing Mensheviks (Internationalist), notwithstanding the fact that in the election to the Baku Soviet (April 1918) these parties and their sympathizers had obtained only sixty-seven of a total of 308 seats.[30] The SR's and Dashnaks, who had played a prominent role in the March events and between them had more deputies than the Communists, were excluded from the administration.[31] The new government appointed Shaumian as its chairman and declared as its goal "to be most intimately connected with the All-Russian central government and to execute, in accordance with local conditions, all decrees and directives of the Worker and Peasant Government of Russia." [32]

One of the first measures of the new authority was the suppression of all the Moslem and Menshevik newspapers and societies. An order was also issued to the Dashnaks to disband their separate military detachments and their National Soviet, but the Armenians disregarded it.[33]

During their rule in Baku, the Communists devoted most of their attention to the oil problem. They began at once to dispatch shipments of oil to Russia via the Caspian Sea and Astrakhan, and thence along the Volga northward. During the four months of Soviet control in Baku (March–June 1918) eighty million *puds* (1,440,000 short tons) of oil were shipped to Russia.[34] Having run into difficulties with the oil firms about prices and deliveries, Shaumian decided to seek Moscow's permission to nationalize the industry. His communications with the capital passed through Tsaritsyn, where Stalin acted as intermediary. Soon a reply arrived from Stalin saying that the Council of People's Commissars approved of the request. A few days later, however, a countermanding communication from Lenin and the Commissariat of Fuels informed Shaumian that Stalin's report was not correct, that the decision of the Council was not to nationalize.[35] The Commissariat of Fuels ordered Shaumian to leave the oil industry in private hands in order not to disrupt production; but it was too late to retract the previous directive, and in June the oil industry was nationalized.

The nationalization of the oil industry was one of the prime reasons for the loss of Bolshevik strength in Baku. As the Commissariat of Fuels had anticipated, the production of oil declined considerably after nationalization, and it also resulted in a lowering of workers' wages.[36]

Soviet historians agree that sometime in May the laboring population, traditionally SR and Menshevik in its leanings, had already begun to turn against the Soviet regime, which it had supported for a brief time out of fear of the Turks.[37] Shaumian and his colleagues, so deeply under the spell of the Paris revolution of 1870 that they had called their government the "Baku Commune" and had continually lectured the workers about its Parisian counterpart, tried to stem the unfavorable tide by exhorting the laborers to make ever greater sacrifices and to restrain the appetites for more money which the Communists themselves, while striving for power, had whetted:

> In the struggle with the bourgeoisie the working class had worked out special methods of fighting; it had become used to demanding. This method was once very useful and revolutionary. Now the situation is different. In power is not the bourgeoisie but an organ created by the workers, and for that reason the attitude towards the government should be different. Unfortunately the old psychology has become ingrained, and the workers defend their private interests. Against whom? against the common mass.[38]

In June 1918 the position of the Baku Commune became precarious. The Transcaucasian republics had proclaimed their independence, and the Azerbaijanis were preparing to march with the Turks on Baku, to reclaim the city, and to extort revenge for the massacres of March. From Moscow and Tsaritsyn where Shaumian had sent for help, however, the directives were calm. Stalin relayed the following message on June 25/- July 8:

> [1] Our general policy in the Transcaucasian question is to compel the Germans to acknowledge officially that the Georgian, Armenian, and Azerbaijani questions are internal Russian questions, in the solutions of which they should not participate. It is for this reason that we do not recognize Georgian independence recognized by Germany. (2) It is possible that we might have to yield to the Germans on the Georgian question, but such a concession we shall finally make only on the condition that the Germans pledge non-intervention in the affairs of Armenia and Azerbaijan. (3) The Germans, agreeing to leave us Baku, ask in return to be allotted a certain amount of oil. Of course, we can satisfy this "wish."

Stalin also cautioned Shaumian to avoid a conflict with the Germans by keeping his forces outside of Georgian territory.[39]

Moscow obviously was counting on German-Turkish rivalry to retain a foothold in Transcaucasia and to keep Baku and its oil in Communist hands. As early as February 1918 Lenin had written Shaumian that the salvation of the Soviet regime lay in exploiting internal conflicts among the "imperialist" powers and urged him to play one opponent against the other.[40] But to the non-Moslem population of Baku, faced with the prospect of Turkish occupation, the British units of General Dunsterville, stationed in Northwestern Persia and trying to make their way to the Caucasus, seemed a more attractive ally than the Red Army. Shaumian, realizing the mood of the city, tried to get immediate help from Soviet Russia, but instead of help he received another boastful telegram from Stalin:

> Inform by radio Shaumian in Baku that I Stalin am in the South and will soon be in the Northern Caucasus. The line Khasaviurt-Petrovsk will be straightened out no matter what. Everything has been and will continue to be regularly sent for the help of Baku. To-day a courier is leaving Tsaritsyn with a letter for Shaumian. We shall send bread no matter what. Please straighten out the front at Adzhikabul. Do not lose heart.[41]

Since Stalin was unable to make good his boast, Shaumian established contact with the British, and invited to Baku the troops of the Cossack Colonel G. Bicherakov, a tsarist officer who had commanded Russian military forces in Iran and after the Revolution had joined the British. Bicherakov reached Baku at the beginning of July and was appointed Commander in Chief of the Soviet armies defending the city from the Turks and the Azerbaijanis.

Two weeks after Bicherakov's arrival, the Baku Soviet, in a closed session, voted to ask General Dunsterville also to come to the defense of the city.[42] The Bolsheviks opposed this resolution, arguing that it af-fected the realm of foreign policy, where Moscow alone was competent to decide. In deference to the wish of the Bolshevik group the soviet postponed action until Moscow had given its advice. On July 7/20 a message arrived from Tsaritsyn, signed by Stalin:

> According to the latest information the populist faction of the Baku Soviet demands the calling of the Varangian-British,* allegedly against Turkish conquest . . . In the name of the All-Russian Cen-tral Executive Committee I demand of the entire Baku Soviet, of the army and fleet, complete subordination to the organized will of the workers and peasants of all Russia.[43]

The message also ordered the arrest of all the representatives of foreign firms and military missions. When the Bolshevik faction presented a reso-lution drawn up in this spirit to the Soviet, it was voted down by an overwhelming majority of the deputies. The Soviet decided instead to proceed with its original plan of inviting General Dunsterville.[44] The Communists, too weak to impose their wishes by force, resigned from the Soviet. Charging that the Baku proletariat was "deluded and pre-ferred the forces of England to those of Soviet Russia," Shaumian and

---

* "Varangian" is the Russian equivalent of the term "Norman"; the reference here is to the Norman princes, who, according to Russian Primary Chronicle, were invited by the medieval Kievan state to become the ruling class.

the other Baku Commissars departed at night on a boat for Astrakhan. They were intercepted on the way by war vessels of the Socialist Revolutionary government of Transcaspia, brought ashore, and later executed.[45]

After the departure of the Communists, power in Baku was assumed by the so-called "Centrocaspian Dictatorship," a government dominated by Russian SR's, who had played a large part in swaying public opinion in favor of Great Britain and who had been in contact with General Dunsterville throughout the Soviet regime in Baku.[46] Dunsterville, arriving with his small detachment at the beginning of August, tried to organize the defenses of the city against the besieging Turkish troops, but with little success. The SR's and the Baku Soviet were sorely disappointed with the size of the British detachment, which, thinking wishfully, they had pictured as a substantial army. Dunsterville, on his part, found that the Dashnak units who had to shoulder the main responsibility for the defense of Baku were unreliable. Soon after his arrival Dunsterville had disagreements with the Centrocaspian Dictatorship, and convinced that the city was indefensible, decided to evacuate. British troops embarked on their boats under the cover of night, and barely escaped being shelled by the coast guard of the city which so recently they had come to save.[47] Bicherakov had abandoned Baku some time before.

On September 2/15, 1918, Turkish troops broke through the weakened defenses and captured Baku.

### The Independent Republics (1918–19)

#### Azerbaijan

Shortly after the Transcaucasian Federation had been dissolved (May 1918), the Azerbaijani National Council moved from Tiflis to Gandzha (known before the Revolution as Elisavetpol), which had been occupied in the first half of June 1918 by Turkish troops under Nuri Pasha, the half-brother of Enver. From there the Azerbaijanis hoped, with Turkish help, to reach Baku.

Relations between the Azerbaijanis and their Turkish allies were at first friendly and promised well for the future. Early in June a treaty was signed between the government of the new republic and the Ottoman Empire, which provided, among other things, for Turkish military and economic assistance.[48] The period of harmony was brief. The Azerbaijani National Council (headed by Resul-zade of the Mussavat) and the eight-man government (headed by Fathali Khan-Khoiskii, a one-time liberal Duma deputy and a member of the Neutral Democratic Group) were staffed largely with people associated with parties that espoused socially radical programs. In the Council the socialists had eleven seats, the Mussavat and its affiliate, the NDG, thirty, while the right-wing

Union had only three; in the government all the offices were in the hands of the Mussavat and the socialists.[49] Such a situation did not please the Ottoman commanders, whose own views were conservative. The fact that the Azerbaijani national institutions were committed to the socialization of land in Transcaucasia (the decree passed by the Transcaucasian Seim in December 1917), together with the fact that the program of the Mussavat called for the expropriation of state and church lands and the purchase of large landed estates for distribution among the peasantry, was very unpopular with the Turks. As one of its first acts upon arrival in Gandzha the Azerbaijani National Council postponed the execution of the land nationalization law until the convocation of a national parliament. This, if perhaps not done at the insistence of the Turks, was certainly done for their benefit.[50] Still, in mid-June 1918, Nuri Pasha ordered the dissolution of the Azerbaijani National Council and the resignation of the Azerbaijani government. The new government, appointed with his approval, excluded all socialists, reduced the proportion of the seats held by the Mussavat, and assigned the leading role to the Union. The Mussavatists were despondent over the new turn of events, which shattered their hopes of genuine self rule under Turkish protection.[51]

The Azerbaijanis had played an insignificant part in the military campaign leading to the capture of the oil city. In the summer the Turks ordered the mobilization of Caucasian Moslems, and the Azerbaijanis themselves began to form an army, but the practical results of attempts to utilize the manpower of Azerbaijan were negligible: the local population had no military traditions and could not be used for combat without having undergone a lengthy period of training. The capture of Baku was accomplished by the Turks with the aid of units especially brought for that purpose from the Rumanian front, across the Black Sea. Once the Turks were inside the city, the Moslems took revenge on the Armenians for the massacres of March. In pogroms which lasted for several days an estimated four thousand Armenians perished.[52] Immediately after the capture of the city, the Turkish army proceeded northwest along the Caspian shore toward Daghestan. The ultimate goal of the Turks was the occupation of the Northern Caucasus, but they had got only so far as Derbent, 140 miles from Baku, when the armistice between the Central Powers and the Allies put a stop to their advance.

During their brief stay in Eastern Transcaucasia, the Turks did not make themselves popular. At first they were well received and the masses of the Moslem population, urban as well as rural, greeted them with certain affection. But the enthusiasm waned when the Ottoman command called a halt to the land reform, closed labor unions, suppressed socialist organizations, and in general enforced a policy which deprived the population of the social and political gains which it had made since 1917.[53]

The Armistice of Mudros (November 1918) between the Ottoman Empire and the Allies provided for Turkish evacuation of the Caucasus within one month. On November 17/30, in the wake of the retreating Turks, British troops under General Thomson landed in Baku, and took over the administration. General Thomson permitted the reëstablishment of the labor unions and the socialist parties suppressed by the Turks, but he assumed a hostile attitude to the Azerbaijani nationalists. He informed a delegation which conferred with him shortly after his arrival that the Azerbaijani government was a Turkish product, unrepresentative of the local population, and that his main task in Baku was to make certain that the city was returned to the Russians and contributed to the war effort of General Denikin, the White commander.[54]

To overcome the principal British objection, namely that the government did not reflect the desires of the population of Eastern Transcaucasia, the Azerbaijani National Council, which reassembled after the departure of the Turks, invited not only Moslems but also representatives of other ethnic groups of Eastern Transcaucasia to attend the forthcoming Azerbaijani Parliament. The membership of the Parliament at its opening in December 1918 was:[55]

| | |
|---|---|
| Mussavat | 38 |
| NDG | 7 |
| Unity | 13 |
| Socialists (including one Communist) | 12 |
| Dashnaks | 7 |
| Other Armenians | 4 |
| Other parties | 15 |

The Mussavat and its affiliate, the NDG, thus held something less than one-half of all seats, as contrasted with the three-fourths they had held in the Azerbaijani National Council, which had appointed the first government (May 1918). The new government, created in December, consisted therefore of a coalition of various parties represented in the Parliament, with the exception of the Union. Khan Khoiskii resumed the presidency. General Thomson, apparently convinced that the new government reflected more accurately the wishes of the population, granted it recognition. The Azerbaijani organs created in December 1918 served, except for occasional cabinet changes, for a period of one and a half years.

As long as Baku was occupied by British troops — that is, until August 1919 — political authority in Eastern Transcaucasia was divided between the English command and the Azerbaijani government. The division of authority was apparently never precisely defined, but there can be little doubt that the political power rested ultimately in the hands of the British. The Azerbaijani government concerned itself mostly with internal affairs and administrative matters and the approval of the British command was required for all measures before they could become effective.[56] In the administration, both civil and military, the government had to rely largely on Russians, Georgians, Ottoman Turks, and other non-Azerbaijani residents of the area.

In the winter of 1918–19, a General Staff was formed under the command of General Sulkevich, who had recently escaped from the Crimea, but it was only in the spring of 1919 that an armed force began to take shape. In June, Azerbaijan signed an agreement with Georgia, by virtue of which the latter was to supply it with arms and military instruction.[57] The first units, formed in the summer, were commanded mainly by Russian and Georgian officers, and in some instances by Turks who had remained behind when their armies had evacuated the Caucasus. By the beginning of 1920 Azerbaijan possessed its own armed force, although the goal of an army of 17,000 men, which the government desired, was never realized.

The main problems confronting the republic of Azerbaijan, as well as the other two Transcaucasian states, were a result of the fact that Transcaucasia had developed for over a century as an economic and administrative whole; hence its dismemberment into three parts resulted in a dislocation of its economy and an unsettling of its entire internal life.

Before the Revolution, Eastern Transcaucasia had depended for its food on the North Caucasus and other provinces of Russia. In 1919 those areas were entirely cut off. At the same time the local production of foodstuffs decreased disastrously: in 1919 the cultivated acreage in Eastern Transcaucasia dropped to less than one-fourth of what it had been in 1914.[58] Baku and its adjoining regions suffered, as a consequence, a grave food crisis, which became worse as time went on, although it never reached famine proportions.

The principal source of wealth with which Azerbaijan could augment its food supplies and pay for other functions of government, was oil. The production of oil continued throughout the period of Revolution and Civil War, although at a reduced rate. Unfortunately for Azerbaijan, it could not be marketed. Before 1917 most of the Baku oil had been piped to Batum, on the Black Sea, there refined and then dispatched to Russia; or else shipped to Russia via Astrakhan. In 1919 Batum and its refining facilities were outside the borders of the republic; the transportation facilities for shipping the refined product from Batum and Astrakhan were unavailable as a result of the war; and Russian industry, the nearest and previously principal purchaser, was separated from Transcaucasia by the Civil War. Thus, in early 1920 a full year's production, or four and a half million short tons of crude oil, were lying useless in Baku's storage tanks.[59] Beginning in September 1918 the Baku oil firms and the Azerbaijani government conducted sporadic negotiations with Soviet Russia for a trade agreement, and in early 1920 some shipments of oil did leave for Russia by way of Astrakhan.[60] The bulk of the oil, however, remained unsalable.

The drawing of boundaries was another source of difficulty for the government and a constant cause of friction among the three republics. The population of Transcaucasia was intermingled to such an extent that it was impossible to divide the area along ethnic lines without doing violence to one or another of the groups inhabiting it. The Azerbaijani-Armenian frontier was especially troublesome, not only because the relations between those two peoples were at their worst following the mutual massacres of 1918, but also because the districts which they inhabited could be least successfully separated: Moslem and Armenian villages, located side by side, often used the same regions for cattle and sheep grazing. Since districts inhabited by a mixed Armenian and Azerbaijani population were generally claimed by both sides as their own, throughout 1919 and 1920 there were quarrels and occasional wars between the two states. They seriously weakened the internal stability of the republics and injured their prestige abroad. The main bone of contention were the Zangezur, Nakhichevan, and Karabakh districts.

The territorial aspirations of the Azerbaijani government were of considerable magnitude. In an official petition presented to the Paris Peace Conference in 1919, it claimed not only all of Eastern Transcaucasia, but also Daghestan, Kars, and Batum — an area comprising 60 per cent of Transcaucasia and a portion of the North Caucasus as well.[61] Since neither Georgia nor Armenia were willing to concede these claims, the relations between Azerbaijan and its neighbors remained constantly tense.

### Armenia

The Armenian Republic was an anomalous political organism: two-thirds of its territory was under enemy occupation and nearly one-half of its population consisted of war refugees. It lacked money and food; its administration consisted of people who had devoted the major part of their life to revolutionary or terrorist activity, and were entirely devoid of experience in affairs of government. No territory of the old Russian Empire had suffered greater losses from the First World War, and none was placed in a more desperate situation by the empire's disintegration.

The collapse of the Transcaucasian Federation caused Armenia to be diplomatically isolated. The Azerbaijanis had the Turks; the Georgians, the Germans; the Armenians alone had no one to whom to turn for assistance. All Armenian military resources had been committed to the defense of the central Armenian territories located along the Araks River, and only the fact that the Turks were more interested in seizing

Baku and advancing on the North Caucasus than in turning against the Armenians had saved Erivan from certain capture. In the summer of 1918 the Armenians had dispatched a delegation to Germany, hoping to obtain there help similar to that which had been promised to Georgia, but Berlin was not interested. Armenia had nothing to offer either strategically or economically, and a protectorate over that war-ravaged country was likely to represent a considerable financial liability.[62]

The internal situation of independent Armenia was almost hopeless. Before 1917 the region which became Armenia had imported about one-third of its food requirements from Russia. Not only was supply from this source unavailable, but the population of the republic was, as a result of the refugee influx, twice as large as it was before the war. Armenia was constantly on the brink of famine, which was avoided only because of the assistance extended to that country by the American Relief Mission in 1919 and 1920.[63] The Armenian treasury was empty, and the local currency suffered a catastrophic inflationary decline: from March 1920 to November 1920, alone, the ruble circulating in Armenia declined from 560 to 28,000 for one United States dollar.[64] There was no regular taxation system to pay for the costs of running the government, and the state provided for its needs either by occasional requisitions or by contributions from Armenian colonies abroad. The total expenditures of the state between September 1918 and January 1920 exceeded its income ten times.[65]

At the end of 1919 an American delegation, headed by General James G. Harbord, arrived in Armenia. It was dispatched by the United States government to report on the advisability of establishing an American mandate over Armenia — an idea which was sponsored by the Armenians themselves and which had aroused the sympathy of President Wilson. The Harbord Mission painted in its account a very discouraging picture of internal conditions prevailing in the republic and stated that the majority of the inhabitants desired the reëstablishment of ties with Russia as the only way of attaining economic stability and external security.[66]

The legislative authority in the Armenian Democratic Republic was technically vested in an eighty-man Parliament, but in fact it was firmly in the hands of one party, the Dashnaktsutiun, which controlled the armed forces and possessed the only effective political apparatus on Armenian territory. There is no record of any extensive legislative activity on the part of the government. It limited itself to the founding of Armenian schools and other cultural institutions.[67] The land reform initiated by the Transcaucasian Seim in 1917 was not enforced.

After the German and Turkish evacuation from the Caucasus, Armenia established contact with the staff of General Denikin and until the end of the Civil War collaborated closely with the White forces. In return for Armenian support and certain concessions (such as the Armenian pledge to receive evacuating White armies, given formally in March 1920), Denikin transmitted to Armenia arms and ammunition, and helped the republic financially.[68] In consequence of their pro-Denikin orientation, the Armenians did not participate in the Georgian-Azerbaijani military agreement of June 1919, which was primarily designed to prevent White intervention in Transcaucasia.

The relations between Armenia and the other two Transcaucasian republics were hostile, not only because of Armenia's pro-White policy but also because of its territorial aspirations. As soon as the Turks had left Transcaucasia, Armenia and Georgia engaged in an armed struggle over the Borchalo region (December 1918). The Armenian claim to this territory rested on the fact that the majority of its population was Armenian; the Georgians, on the other hand, asserted that Borchalo was theirs as a part of the pre-1917 Tiflis gubernia, which they claimed in its entirety. The clash was stopped by the intervention of the British occupation authorities in the Caucasus. Both sides agreed to settle the question by plebiscite.[69] In 1919 and 1920 Armenia also fought with Azerbaijan over the Karabakh and Zangezur regions.

Perhaps the worst political mistake of the Armenian republic was to engage in a conflict with a reinvigorated Turkey. Disregarding political realities, and motivated by a desire for revenge, the Armenians undertook to detach from Turkey the provinces which had been populated by their people before the 1915 massacres. In the winter of 1918–19, with British approval, they occupied parts of Eastern Anatolia, and before long Armenian refugees began to trickle back to their ravaged homeland. In May 1919 the Armenian Republic officially proclaimed the annexation of Turkish Armenia.[70] Unfortunately for the Armenians, they overestimated the extent to which Turkish power had been destroyed in World War I and occupied Eastern Anatolia just as a new republican Turkish movement under Kemal Pasha was forming itself in adjacent territories. In July 1919 the followers of Kemal held a conference in Erzerum (on territory claimed by Armenia) and there signed a National Pact, one of the provisions of which called for the return to Turkey of all its old eastern regions, including those annexed by Armenia.[71] Unless one of the sides was willing to give way a clash was inevitable. It finally broke out in 1920 with dire results to the Armenian republic.

### Georgia

Of all the republics which had been separated from Russia and then reconquered by the Communists, Georgia came closest to attaining political stability. Like the other two Transcaucasian republics, it enjoyed certain geographic advantages: the Caucasian mountains permitted it to isolate itself from the Russian Civil War and to weather the first phase of independence, during which many of the other republics formed on the territory of the Russian Empire had been destroyed. But in addition, Georgia also had at its disposal a relatively numerous native intelligentsia with experience in governmental service and grass-roots party work. Georgia's economic situation, although far from sound, was also better than that prevailing in Azerbaijan and Armenia, partly because its communication problems were less serious (Georgia had contact with the outside world through the Black Sea ports, and control of the pivot of the Transcaucasian railroad system in Tiflis), and partly because its internal policies were better planned and more energetically enforced.

Shortly after the independence of Georgia had been proclaimed, German units landed in Batum (June 1918), occupying strategic points along Georgia's border and some towns in the interior of the country. The Germans asked the Georgians not to surrender to the Turks control over the railroad lines, as they were bound to do by the terms of a Georgian-Turkish treaty, signed in Batum at the beginning of June.[72] Instead, the Germans themselves took over the Georgian railroad network. During their stay on Georgian territory the Germans behaved quite correctly, in contrast to their behavior in the Ukraine, Belorussia, and the Crimea. They interfered little with the internal affairs of the republic, respected the authority of the government, and abstained from the brutal methods of food-collecting which they were applying in other parts of old Russia. The Germans undertook to secure Soviet Russia's recognition of Georgian independence, and some progress in that direction was made; but the Communists delayed taking an official stand as long as possible and were still uncommitted in November 1918, when the war was over and the Germans had to evacuate the Caucasus. Certainly, if only by comparing their life under the Germans with the lot of the Azerbaijanis under the Turks, the Georgians had no reason to regret their decision.

Following German and Turkish evacuation, Batum and other points within Georgia were occupied by British troops. The presence of the British, embarrassing as it was to the Georgian government from the point of view of its national prestige, was not unwelcome as protection against the encroachments of neighboring powers, especially the White armies and the Communists. As in Azerbaijan, the British command left the local government some self-rule in internal matters. The original attitude of the British toward the Georgian Social Democrats was as hostile as it was toward the Azerbaijanis; the Georgian Republic, after all, had actively collaborated with the Germans, and, in a sense, had come into being on German initiative. But before long Georgian relations with the British changed for the better. In 1919 London sent as its envoy to Tiflis, Oliver Wardrop, a specialist in Georgian literature and a warm friend of the Georgian cause, who established amicable relations with the local political leaders, and pleaded for a pro-Georgian policy with his superiors in the Foreign Office.[73]

Georgia was governed by a group of Social Democrats who for nearly a quarter of a century had been connected with the Russian and Western European socialist movements. For two and a half years at the helm of the Georgian state they endeavored to realize democratic and socialist ideals. Their efforts, if not always successful, provided a remarkable demonstration of the receptivity of Georgia to Western ideas.

The first Georgian government, headed by Chkhenkeli, and identified with a pro-German policy, relinquished its authority in the fall of 1918. A new cabinet was formed under Gegechkori. In February 1919 elections were held for the Georgian National Assembly, and after the elections a new cabinet was appointed. The elections gave the Social Democrats 105 of a total of 130 seats, the remainder being distributed among the Georgian Socialists-Federalists (nine seats), Georgian National Democrats (eight seats), Socialists Revolutionaries (five seats), and Dashnaks (three seats).[74] Noi Zhordaniia, one of the founders of Georgian Social Democracy, and the chairman of the Tiflis Soviet during the preceding two years, was elected by the National Assembly the President of the Republic. As in Switzerland, whose political system was imitated, the cabinet served directly under the President, and both were responsible to the Assembly. The Georgian government could maintain more than nominal authority over the republic because it had at its disposal a network of provincial party organizations, on whom it could depend to provide administrative personnel and to execute its directives. The Georgian leaders also intended to introduce into Georgia certain other features of the Swiss political system, such as cantonal self-rule.[75] The Georgian constitution, drawn up in 1920 but not ratified until the Soviet armies were approaching the gates of Tiflis a year later, was modeled after Western European democratic constitutions.[76]

The rapid growth of nationalist emotions in Georgia during the period of independence was demonstrated both by repeated border incidents with Armenia and Azerbaijan, and by the manner in which the government met the minority problem within its domain. The Georgian Republic covered a territory corresponding to the two prerevolutionary Russian provinces of Kutais and Tiflis, inhabited by several minority groups: in the north, the Ossetins (an Iranian people); in the west, the Abkhazians (a group of Cherkess origin) and Adzhars (Moslems of Georgian stock); in the south, Armenians. In its endeavor to create a homogeneous national state, the Tiflis government showed little sympathy for the attempts of those minority groups to secure political and cultural autonomy. In early 1919 the Georgian government forcibly closed an Abkhaz National Council which had been convened for the purpose of discussing local grievances and appointing organs of self-rule.[77] The growth of nationalism in Georgia had its parallels in other borderland areas, but its emergence in Georgia was the more remarkable because before the

Revolution Georgia had been among the regions least inclined in that direction.

Of all three Transcaucasian republics Georgia alone tackled the land problem. Because of the mountainous character of the country, only 13.2 per cent of its total surface of approximately fifteen million acres was arable; the peasantry, which formed three-fourths of the republic's entire population owned only a small part (6.2 per cent) of that land, in most cases not enough for sustenance.[78] To alleviate the shortage of land, the government confiscated all the private holdings in excess of forty acres. The confiscated assets were transferred to a special state authority, which at first leased the land to the peasants, and after January 1919 sold it to them for a nominal sum. This reform, which was completed in 1920, gave the state control of nearly one and a half million acres. In addition, the state owned the properties of the tsarist family, of the treasury of the defunct Russian government, and of the church — all of which had been confiscated in December 1917 by the Transcaucasian Seim. The total land at the disposal of the state thus amounted to nine and a half million acres, comprising all the forests, nearly all the pastures and meadows, and one-fourth of all the arable land in Georgia.[79] This reform encountered serious difficulties, such as commonly occur when large agricultural units are divided into small holdings, but it did produce a greater equalization of land distribution. By creating a more numerous class of peasant proprietors who owed their land to the state, the reform strengthened the republic's popular support.

In addition to land, the Georgian government also nationalized the principal industries and the means of communication. In 1920, about 90 per cent of all workers in Georgia were employed in state or coöperative enterprises, and only 10 per cent in privately owned establishments.[80]

The financial situation of the Georgian Republic was precarious. It lacked money in its treasury, a firm currency, and a regular taxation system. At the beginning of 1919 its expenses exceeded its income three and a half fold.[81] One of the main considerations which had induced the government to sell the confiscated land to the peasantry, instead of leasing or distributing it, as would have been more consistent with its socialist doctrine, was the sorry condition of the treasury. It was hoped that with the two hundred million rubles which the sale of the land was expected to bring the state deficit could be liquidated.[82] In the long run, Georgia hoped to improve its economic situation by exploiting the considerable natural wealth of the country (manganese, lumber, coal) and by attracting foreign capital. It planned to exchange its raw materials for food and manufactured goods, and to provide for the needs of the government out of income from the nationalized land and industries, as well as from prospective foreign concessions.

About one-third of Georgia's expenditures was devoted to the upkeep of the republic's armed force. Its nucleus was the Red Guard, which had been formed in Tiflis in November 1917 to suppress the pro-Bolshevik Tiflis Arsenal. The Red Guard, afterwards renamed the Popular Guard, was an all-volunteer reserve unit, run on a democratic basis by elected officers and soldier congresses, and directly subordinated to the President of the Republic. It was an elite militia, composed largely of industrial workers and other urban elements, strongly imbued with the spirit of socialism and nationalism.[83] In addition to the Guard, Georgia also had a regular army, which consisted of draftees and was subordinate to the Minister of War. In the event of mobilization, Georgia could put into the field about fifty thousand men, organized into twenty-three battalions of the Popular Guard, thirty-six battalions of the Regular Army, and some cavalry and artillery units. This army was not large in comparison with those taking part in the Russian Civil War, nor was it well equipped, but as future events were to show, its spirit was good, and by Transcaucasian standards, its combat efficiency high.

## The Prelude to the Conquest

The Soviet republic which the Communists had established in the Terek Region in August 1918 rested primarily on the military support provided by the Eleventh and Twelfth Red Armies, operating in the so-called Caspian-Caucasian Sector of the Southern Front, under the command of A. G. Shliapnikov. Shliapnikov's main assignment was to complete the occupation of the North Caucasus and to spread Soviet power to Azerbaijan by expelling from there the Azerbaijani nationalist authorities and the British military units.[84] At the height of its strength, in December 1918 the Eleventh Army numbered 150,000 men. Political power in the Terek Region during the autumn and winter of 1918–19 was for all practical purposes in the hands of the Revolutionary Committee of this army, in which Ordzhonikidze played a prominent part. The formal government, with its headquarters in Piatigorsk, had little authority.[85]

When in the early months of 1919 the Eleventh and Twelfth Armies melted away, partly as a result of typhus epidemics and partly from mass desertions, Soviet rule in the Terek Region also collapsed. In May and June of that year the White regiments of General Denikin began to move into the North Caucasian regions, occupying first Daghestan and then the Terek. Ordzhonikidze and other local Soviet leaders sought refuge once more in the mountains of Chechnia and Ingushetiia.

Upon his entry into North Caucasian territory, Denikin was for the first time confronted with the national problem, for his armies now operated in a region which was heavily populated by non-Russian groups and which touched directly upon the borders of independent Azerbaijan and Georgia. His handling of this question was likely to determine to a large extent this area's support for the White cause. By his unwillingness to recognize the growth of nationalist sentiments in the borderlands since the outbreak of the Revolution, and by his high-handed treatment of the national republics, Denikin not only failed to win the local sympathies, but actually drove most minority groups into the arms of the Communists. He and his entourage were fundamentally opposed to the existence of independent republics on the territory of what had been the Russian Empire. Whatever other disagreements divided the leaders of the Volunteer Army, Denikin recalled in his Memoirs, the idea of " 'Great Russia, One and Indivisible' sounded clear and distinct to the mind and heart of one and all." [86] Shortly after his troops had reached the borders of the Transcaucasian republics Denikin declared that he would not recognize their independence; and after a number of border incidents with Azerbaijan and Georgia had taken place, he proclaimed, in November 1919, an economic blockade of the two republics: "I cannot permit," he said, "those self-made entities, Georgia and Azerbaijan, which are openly hostile to Russian statehood and have arisen contrary to Russian state interests, to receive food at the cost of Russian territories liberated from the Bolsheviks." [87] General Lukomskii, a high officer connected with the Volunteer Army, stated bluntly that the Whites were tolerating the separation of Transcaucasia only because they were fully occupied fighting the Communists.[88]

In view of Denikin's attitude it is not surprising that the victories of the Volunteer Army in the fall of 1919 created consternation among Georgian and Azerbaijani national leaders. It was obvious to them that regardless of the outcome of the Civil War in Russia, the Transcaucasian republics would be put to a severe test to defend their independence against their northern neighbor once the fighting had ceased.

Denikin placed the administration of the Northern Caucasus in the hands of officers of native origin who were serving in his army, and at first made no effort to interfere with local life or even to extend his dominion into the mountainous backcountry. In August 1919, however, while making the supreme effort to capture Moscow, he issued an order mobilizing the native population of the Northern Caucasus for military service. The natives, traditionally exempt from such duty, refused to obey the order, and in some areas fled to the mountains. Denikin dispatched punitive detachments to deal with these recalcitrants. The natives then organized partisan units which attacked White troops venturing close to their hideouts. By October–November 1919 the White forces were engaged in a full-scale war with the natives of the Northern Caucasus, which, occurring at a decisive moment of the Civil War when the fate of Moscow itself hung in the balance, was without doubt a factor contributing to their ultimate defeat.[89]

The center of anti-Denikin resistance was located in the most inaccessible districts of the Northern Caucasus. It was directed by a Council of Defense (*Sovet Oborony*), in which were allied the diverse elements opposing Denikin, including religious leaders (Ali Khadzhi Akushinskii, and later on, Uzun Khadzi), the North Caucasian nationalists (Kantemir), and the socialists (Tsalikov). The Council of Defense had at its disposal an armed force, composed largely of extremely fanatical religious groups, organized in so-called "Shariat regiments" (*Shariatskie polki*), under the over-all command of Nuri Pasha, the one-time commander of the Ottoman armies invading the Caucasus.[90] Sometime in the fall of 1919 the Bolsheviks, eager to take a part in the direction of the partisan warfare against the White forces, also joined the Council of Defense.[91] At the height of its resistance to Denikin, the Council received some military assistance from Azerbaijan and Georgia. This assistance, small in absolute terms, was significant as an expression of the attitude of the two Transcaucasian republics to the White movement.[92]

The intransigence of the White leaders toward the Caucasian nationalist movements underscored the diplomatic isolation of the two Transcaucasian republics and the vital necessity of obtaining the support of Western powers. In 1919 two delegations arrived in Paris: one from Georgia, composed of Chkheidze and Tseretelli, and one from Azerbaijan, headed by Ali Merdan Bey Topchibashev (Topchibashy), the president of the Azerbaijani National Parliament. The Armenians, too, sent a mission to Paris, consisting of A. Aharonian and Nubar Pasha, the former representing the Armenian Republic, the latter Armenian colonies abroad; the Armenians were not interested in securing Western backing against either the Whites or the Communists, but against the Turks. Those diplomatic missions did not succeed in attaining their ends. The Allies were backing the White movement and did not want to introduce dissension into the anti-Soviet bloc by raising the controversial national question as long as the Whites were holding their own in the Civil War. The Azerbaijani delegation learned from President Wilson that the Paris Peace Conference did not desire to fragmentize the world into small national states: although the Peace Conference was in principle not hostile to the idea of a Caucasian Federation under a mandate of the League of Nations, the ultimate decision on the fate of Azerbaijan had to await the solution of the entire Russian problem.[93] Lord Curzon, the British Foreign Secretary, advised Wardrop in Tiflis that as long as the republics persisted in their animosity toward Denikin and fought among themselves, there was little possibility of greater British effort on their behalf.[94]

After the virtual collapse of the Volunteer Army (winter 1919–20), the Allied Supreme Council in Paris recognized the *de facto* independence of Azerbaijan, Georgia, and Armenia, and prevailed on the defeated Denikin to do likewise (January 1920).[95] But the Western powers were unwilling to commit themselves further, so that the recognition had little, if any, practical significance.

At the end of 1919 the three republics requested the Allied Supreme Council to place them under a League of Nations mandate: Armenia wanted the United States to assume the mandatory power, Georgia and Azerbaijan desired the protection of Great Britain.[96] This idea, however, came to nought; for the United States Senate voted down President Wilson's bill for an American mandate over Armenia, and the British Foreign Office remained cool to the pleas of Tiflis and Baku. The notion of an Italian mandate over Transcaucasia, which was current for a brief time in 1920, also fell through.[97]

Toward the latter part of 1919, the British began to evacuate Transcaucasia. Baku was abandoned in August and Batum in the summer of the following year. The British carried out their decision to withdraw, despite pleas on the part of Georgia and Azerbaijan that they remain in order to reduce the danger of a Communist invasion, which now confronted Transcaucasia in all its magnitude.[98]

Moscow had never given up its claim to Transcaucasia, and on a number of occasions had made it clear that it regarded the separation of that area only as temporary. The importance of the Caucasus for Russia was, in the first place, economic. A book published by the Soviet State Publishing House in 1921 on "The Caucasus and Its Significance for Soviet Russia" pointed out that this region had provided prerevolutionary Russia with two-thirds of its oil, three-fourths of its manganese, one-fourth of its copper, and much of its lead.[99] The separation of the Caucasus had very serious consequences for Soviet industry and transport, which depended heavily on that region for fuel and other mineral resources. The Caucasus was also important as a strategic outpost in the Near East, where the Communists were conducting an active policy at that time. The fact that the Communist Central Committee had issued directives to Sovietize Eastern Transcaucasia to Shaumian (1917) and to Shliapnikov (1918), indicated its continuous interest in that area. Baku, with its oil, was first on the list; the conquest of Georgia and Armenia was somewhat less urgent.

The Soviet offensive against the three Transcaucasian republics (1920–1921) was carried out by methods of internal and external pressure which had been brought to a high degree of perfection in the course of the Civil War. Internally, pressure was brought upon them by the local branches of the Communist Party; externally, by the Red Army and the Commissariat of Foreign Affairs.

To understand the role performed by the Communist Party in the conquest of the Caucasus it is necessary to revert to the year 1918. The arrival of German and Turkish occupation armies on Transcaucasian territory completed the destruction of the Communist Party network, whose disintegration had begun with the outlawing of the party by the Georgian government (February 1918) and the collapse of the Bolshevik-dominated Baku Commune (July 1918). The Regional Committee of the party, located in Tiflis, had departed from Georgia on the eve of the German occupation (May 1918), and had hidden in the Terek Region, which at that time was in Communist hands. From there it had endeavored to weaken the Georgian government by organizing peasant uprisings in the mountainous north and northwestern districts of the republic, inciting the peasantry against the policies of Tiflis, and playing on the national feelings of the non-Georgian peoples. In late 1918 the Regional Committee had succeeded in stimulating among the Ossetins and other borderland peoples of the state a number of local revolts, which they had supplied liberally with money and arms. Those sporadic disorders, however, failed to attain their objective. Disorganization, the absence of good communications, and misunderstandings between the rebellious peasants and the would-be leaders had considerably limited their effectiveness. Georgian punitive expeditions had done the rest. The Tiflis Bolsheviks soon realized the senselessness of their tactics and in early 1919 gave up attempts to come to power by means of peasant rebellions. But by then, as a result of Menshevik arrests and repressions, to quote the leader of the Georgian Communists of that period, "the party work in the cities, and above all, in the villages, had not only subsided, but had come to a virtual standstill." [100] Georgian Communism, and the Regional Committee in command of it, had suffered a defeat.

In Eastern Transcaucasia, the situation was somewhat different. The most influential Communist leaders of Baku, who had proven more successful in their struggle for power than their comrades in Tiflis, had been executed by the Socialist Revolutionaries in Transcaspia after the fall of the Commune. Some of the less important figures had hidden in Northern Persia. At the end of November 1918, following the British evacuation, the latter began to trickle back to the city. Before the month was over, a small group of Baku Communists, largely of Armenian descent (among them Anastas Mikoyan, the future Soviet Minister of Foreign Trade), held a conference which reëstablished the Baku Committee.[101] The Baku Communists concentrated their attention on the industrial proletariat, organizing mass strikes, participating in the struggle for collective bargaining in the denationalized oil industry, and in general exploiting the difficult economic situation in the city. They also tried to gain a foothold among the Moslem workers, who constituted approximately one-half of Baku's labor force, largely in the unskilled categories. For that purpose the Baku Committee used the left wing of the Moslem socialist party, the *Gummet* — which since the summer of 1919 had for all practical purposes been run by the Communists — and the Persian Communist party, *Adalet*.[102]

As soon as the Whites had occupied the Northern Caucasus, the Tiflis Regional Committee, still nominally in control of the entire Transcaucasian party work, slipped back to the Georgian capital, and started to reëstablish its shattered apparatus. At that time the Georgian government, which previously had persecuted the Communists relentlessly, allowed them considerable freedom of activity, since it saw in them an ally against Denikin. In the fall of 1919, Communists began to agitate openly in the streets of Tiflis and to attend meetings of the Social Democratic Party in Georgia.[103]

When the Tiflis Regional Committee, headed by Filipp Makharadze, tried to extend its authority over the Baku Communists, the latter resisted. The Baku organization was numerically stronger and better organized than the Regional Committee, and while the Regional Committee had been located in the Terek Region out of touch with Transcaucasia (June 1918–June 1919), it had enjoyed one year of independent activity. It was accustomed to dealing directly with Moscow and saw no reason to subordinate itself to the Regional Committee whose own record was one of blunders and failures. The two centers engaged in bitter quarrels over a number of issues such as the creation of an Azerbaijani Communist Party and the slogan of a Soviet Azerbaijan Republic, both of which were advocated by Baku and vetoed by Tiflis.[104] The Baku Committee, in turn, objected to the efforts of the Tiflis Communists to instigate internal revolts in Georgia as futile and as leading to further repressive policies on the part of the Georgian government. Finally, at the end of 1919 the Baku Committee requested Moscow to grant it autonomy and independence from Tiflis.[105]

The struggle between the two Communist centers was more than a mere squabble of factions for power. It represented a conflict between two trends within the Communist movement, not unlike that which was taking place at the same time in the Ukraine between the left and the right. In Tiflis were the old Bolsheviks, persons who had been intimately connected with the movement since the early years of the century, who, like the Ukrainian leftists, were inclined to stress the mass character and the democratic aspects of Communism. In Baku, on the other hand, were young, aggressive Bolsheviks (corresponding to the Ukrainian rightists) who had received most of their party experience after the outbreak of the Revolution, and who emphasized the conspiratorial facets of the movement. Tiflis looked for support to the local population, Baku to Moscow.*

In January 1920 the Baku Committee's subordinate and affiliated organizations had three thousand members. The unwieldy loose organ-

* Sergei Kirov, with contempt characteristic of the Baku group, referred to the leaders of the Regional Committee as "our Caucasian orthodox ones, or better yet, old men (stariki)" (Stat'i, I, 201).

ization of the Communist forces made them inefficient for purposes of conspiratorial and para-military action, and for this reason the persons in charge of the committee began in August 1919 to make preparations for reorganization which would tighten the party ranks by unifying all its groups in a single Azerbaijani Communist Party. The Tiflis Regional Committee objected to the idea of an Azerbaijani party on two grounds: it would introduce the national principle into the Communist apparatus in Transcaucasia and thus split the forces which had heretofore acted as a single party; and it would, in effect, remove the Baku cells from the jurisdiction of the Regional Committee. Baku, on the other hand, maintained that the growth of Azerbaijani nationalism made it imperative to organize the party in such a manner.[106] The discussion between the two centers lasted until January 1920, when it was finally settled in favor of Baku, probably with the backing of Moscow.

When Baku began to unite the local cells preparatory to the creation of the Azerbaijani Communist Party, it encountered new difficulties, this time from the Gummet and Adalet, which consented to the amalgamation only on the condition that the Turks and Persians retain their distinct Communist organizations, separate from the Russians.[107] The Baku Committee overcame this difficulty by starting the merger between the Russian Communist Party and the two Moslem parties not at the top, where the Moslems were in a position to resist, but on the lower levels in the factories and local branches. The RKP-dominated Communist cells easily swallowed up the less-numerous and poorly coördinated Adalet and Gummet rank and file, presenting the leadership of these two parties with a *fait accompli*.[108]

In February 1920 the Azerbaijani Communist Party was formally established. Nominally, the new party was subordinate to the Regional Committee, but in fact it was independent of Tiflis. It numbered four thousand members and possessed a widespread network of organizations among trade unions, workers' clubs, and coöperatives. Its money and arms came from Soviet-held Astrakhan, located 525 miles north of Baku, on the Caspian shore.

The Tiflis Communists had less success. In September 1919, when General Denikin was approaching Moscow, the Regional Committee decided to attempt a seizure of power in the hope of diverting his attention. The Georgian government, however, discovered the Communist plan in time, and arrested virtually the entire Regional Committee with nearly two thousand of its followers on the eve of the intended coup.[109] Thus, while the Baku Committee was forging ahead with its organizational work, and patiently waiting for orders from Moscow, the Tiflis Regional Committee had hurried matters, with the result that when the critical moment finally arrived almost its entire leadership was languishing in jail.

In early 1920, when the Red Armies swept to the borders of Azerbaijan, on the heels of the retreating Whites, the Baku organization was poised and ready to strike.

## The Conquest

The Communist coup in Russia and the defeat of the Central Powers in World War I resulted, among other things, in a revolutionary transformation of Near East diplomacy, which altered the traditional pattern of relations between Russia and Turkey, and precipitated the destruction of the independent states of Transcaucasia by the Soviet regime.

One of the more constant factors in European diplomacy of the nineteenth century had been Russo-British rivalry, caused largely by England's sensitivity to Russian expansion in Asia. In its effort to prevent Russia from penetrating the regions close to the imperial life-line connecting London with India, the Foreign Office traditionally made common cause with the Ottoman Empire, whose long frontier with Russia presented it with similar problems. From the 1830's until the end of the nineteenth century, England generally sided with the Sultan in his disputes with the northern neighbor. This Turco-British friendship, one of the mainstays of Near Eastern diplomacy, broke down at the beginning of the twentieth century. Fearful lest a rapidly industrializing and arming Germany upset the balance of power on the European continent, and wishing to bring in Russian military might as a counterweight to the German army, Britain, like France before her, mended her disagreements with St. Petersburg. A few years before the outbreak of the First World War, England, France, and Russia connected themselves by a system of alliances. After the war broke out, Turkey, on the other hand, joined the Central Powers and fought against Russia, not as a friend, but as an enemy of Great Britain.

Russo-British amity lasted only for one decade. Once the Communists had seized power in Petrograd and taken Russia out of the war, the alliances established by the tsarist government with the Western powers lost their *raison d'être*. The revolutionary character of the new Russian regime, its virulent, aggressive hostility toward the economic and political systems of the Allies, as well as its conciliatory policy toward Germany and Austria-Hungary, ended the period of coöperation with the West. By 1918, Britain had lost the ally for whose sake she had abandoned her traditional Near Eastern policy.

After the collapse of the Central Powers and the British occupation of Constantinople, the Kemalist forces, formed in 1919 in the eastern regions of Anatolia in opposition to the England-dominated Sultanate, assumed as their primary task the defense of the Turkish mainland, Asia Minor, against the Western Allies, who had signed among themselves agreements calling for the dismemberment of the entire Ottoman Empire. The Turkish nationalist movement possessed much spirit, intelligent leadership, and a small armed force capable of holding its own on the battlefield. But it was cut off from the remainder of the world and was compelled to draw its strength from a poor, war-ravaged area, which could provide neither armaments nor money.

Force of circumstance impelled Soviet Russia and Kemalist Turkey to arrive at a *rapprochement*. The two were drawn together by mutual hostility toward the Western powers, as well as by need of each other's services: the Kemalists required money and arms, which the Communists alone were in a position to offer, while the Communists desired an ally to secure a beachhead in the Near East. Thus the Russo-Turkish alliance — an unprecedented event in modern diplomatic history — came into being in the winter of 1919–20.

The initiative for the *rapprochement* with Soviet Russia seems to have come from Kemal, whose agents in November 1919 got in touch with the Communist underground in Baku.[110] According to one prominent Baku Communist, the newly formed Azerbaijani Communist Party acted as an intermediary between Kemal and Moscow.[111] Kemal and his emissaries assured the government of Soviet Russia that they shared none of the Panturanian ambitions of the Young Turks who had ruled the Ottoman Empire during the war, and had given up all claim to the North Caucasus and Azerbaijan. As the principal condition for coöperation with the Communist regime, Kemal demanded that the Communists refrain from conducting conspiratorial and propaganda activities on Anatolian territory.[112] Moscow, which as late as September 1919, had issued revolutionary appeals to the Turkish population, readily accepted the offer of friendship extended by the new Turkish leader.[113] In the early months of 1920, Turks and Communists began openly to coöperate in Transcaucasia. Kemalists attended clandestine meetings of the Azerbaijani Communist Party, and assisted in Communist preparations for a coup against the national government of Azerbaijan.[114] Among those most active on behalf of Turco-Soviet amity in the Caucasus were persons who had been prominent in the deposed Young Turk government: Halil Pasha, the uncle of Enver, who had commanded a Turkish army during the war and had escaped from prison in Constantinople in August 1919; Kâzım Karabekir, another high officer, who had led the Fifteenth Army Corps in Turkey at the same time; Nuri Pasha; and others.*

The Russo-Turkish *rapprochement* was for the three Transcaucasian

---

* The coöperation of the Young Turk émigrés with the Kemalists in Soviet Russia indicates that the conflict between the old and the new Turkish regimes was perhaps not as intense as some authorities hold; see, for example, L. Fischer, *The Soviets in World Affairs*, I (London, 1930), 382–94, where the differences between the two regimes are heavily emphasized.

republics nothing short of a calamity. As long as these two great powers were at odds, the republics could stay alive either by playing one power against the other, or else by serving both as a buffer. But the moment Russia and Turkey joined hands, Azerbaijan, Armenia, and Georgia were doomed. Transcaucasia became an obstacle, hindering the exchange of war materials between Ankara and Moscow, and Kemal, who had beforehand renounced all interest in that area, had every reason to welcome its conquest by the Communists.

While initiating relations with Kemal, the Communists reoccupied the North Caucasus. The command of the armies taking over this region was in the hands of General Tukhachevskii, who was put in charge of the entire Caucasian front. Political authority was vested in the North Caucasian Revolutionary Committee, presided over by Ordzhonikidze, an old hand in North Caucasian politics.* Ordzhonikidze continued to pursue the previous Communist policy based on an appeal to the religious and nationalist sentiments prevailing among the natives of the mountains. "Bear in mind, you Dagestantsy," a manifesto issued over the signatures of Ordzhonikidze, Tukhachevskii, and Kirov proclaimed upon Soviet ontry into the North Caucasus, "that the Soviet government and its Red Army have only one goal: to free oppressed nations from enslavement, whatever the state which causes it. The Soviet government leaves religion, customs, your traditions, the internal way of life of the *gortsy* completely intact." [115]

Ordzhonikidze placed local authority in the Terek Region and Daghestan in the hands of partisan leaders and other Communists or quasi-Communists, who had coöperated with the Soviet regime in the course of 1919: D. Korkmasov in Daghestan, Gikalo (a Russian) in Chechnia, I. Ziazikov in Ingushetiia, S. Takoev in Ossetiia, B. Kalmykov in Kabarda, and Katkhanov (a Moslem clergyman) in Balkariia. Although some of these persons had wholeheartedly embraced Communism, most of them were nationalists of radical views who had gone over to the Communists in 1919 largely because the Communists alone had given them promises of national freedom. Initially, both the Terek Region and Daghestan were administratively united in a single Mountain Republic (*Gorskaia Respublika*). This republic soon was split up, mainly as a result of the intense rivalries among the various local leaders, each of whom wanted to have as much authority in his district as possible. First Daghestan was detached to form a separate republic (November 1920),

---

* Ordzhonikidze had left the North Caucasus in the spring of 1919, taking refuge in Georgia. In August 1919 he had made his way to Baku from where he returned by the underground to Soviet Russia. He spent the remainder of the year attached to the Fourteenth Soviet Army operating in the Ukraine. In early 1920 he was sent back to the North Caucasus. Cf. *Entsiklopedicheskii slovar'* . . . *Granat*, XLI, Part 2, pp. 88–89.

and later the remainder of the Mountain Republic was divided into its component parts. The ethnic dismemberment of the area was completed only in 1924.

The decision to conquer Transcaucasia was taken in Moscow no later than March 17, 1920. It was on that day that Lenin wired Ordzhonikidze to organize the invasion:

> It is highly, highly necessary for us to take Baku. Exert all efforts in this direction, but at that same time in your announcements do not fail to show yourself doubly diplomatic, and make as sure as possible that firm local Soviet authority has been prepared. The same applies to Georgia, although in regard to her I advise even greater circumspection. Settle the matter of [troop] transfers with the Commander in Chief.[116]

On March 30, 1920, Ordzhonikidze met in Vladikavkaz with General Tukhachevskii and S. M. Kirov.[117] It was probably intended that the operations against Azerbaijan be directed by Tukhachevskii, but he was recalled to Moscow to participate in the operations against the Poles; and command over the Red Armies in the Caucasus was assigned instead to General A. M. Gekker, a one-time tsarist officer.[118]

Over-all direction of the military and political offensive against the Transcaucasian republics was entrusted to a special Caucasian Bureau (*Kavkazskoe Biuro,* or *Kavbiuro*) formed on April 8, 1920, by the Central Committee of the Russian Communist Party. Its principal tasks were to establish Soviet rule throughout the Caucasus, to accomplish the economic unification of that area, and to proffer assistance to revolutionary movements in the Near East (which meant, in the first place, the Nationalist Turks).[119] The Kavbiuro was attached to the staff of the Eleventh Red Army operating in the North Caucasus. Its chairman was Ordzhonikidze, its vice-chairman Kirov; the Georgian Communists, Budu Mdivani and Aleksandr Stopani completed the staff.* The Kavbiuro was conceived as the central organ for the direction of the conquest of Transcaucasia and its incorporation into Soviet Russia. As such, it performed a crucial role in Communist operations in that area.

Theoretically, at any rate, most of the functions assigned to the Kavbiuro devolved upon the Regional Committee of the Russian Communist Party in Tiflis, which had tried for over two years to seize power in Transcaucasia and to unite that area with Soviet Russia. The establish-

---

* S. M. Kirov (Kostrikov) was a Russian Communist born in the Viatka province. After a period of residence in Siberia he had settled in Vladikavkaz where he worked in printing establishments and participated in Social Democratic activity. He played a minor role in the Terek People's Republic of 1918, and spent most of 1919 in Astrakhan as a Political Commissar in the Eleventh Army (S. M. Kirov, *Stat'i, rechi, dokumenty,* I ([Leningrad], 1936), pp. vii–xlix). Budu Mdivani was an old Bolshevik, who had spent part of the World War in Persia, and after returning in 1917 had worked as a party functionary in various regions of Russia.

ment of a new organ, in competition with the Regional Committee, indicated that Moscow had lost hope that the local Communist organizations
were sufficiently strong or skillful to overthrow the republican governments. Moscow had found it necessary to engineer the conquest from the
outside, from Soviet territory, where it could synchronize it closely with
the activities of the Red Army and of the Commissariat of Foreign Affairs.
The functions of the Regional Committee and of other Communist Party
organizations within Transcaucasia were to be limited to fifth column
activity, and to such other actions as were necessary to lend the conquest
the appearance of an internal revolution. They were not to direct the
coup, but to be directed. Significant also was the fact that the command
of the instruments of conquest was entrusted to Communists who, although connected with the Caucasus by birth or residence, had made
their party careers outside of that region, in various parts of Soviet Russia,
where they had had opportunities of making contact with the highest officials of the Communist Party. Ordzhonikidze, in particular, was friendly
with Stalin, and there is reason to suppose (though there is no direct
evidence) that he owed to Stalin his appointment as chief of the Kavbiuro.

To allay the natural suspicions which the Soviet preparations in the
North Caucasus were causing among the Transcaucasian republics, the
Soviet Commissariat of Foreign Affairs established with them correct and
even friendly diplomatic relations. In January 1920, Grigorii Chicherin
addressed to the Azerbaijani and Georgian governments notes which,
while pleading for coöperation in the war against the White Army, implied Soviet recognition of their independence.[120] When the Azerbaijani
government replied that it welcomed friendly relations with Soviet Russia,
but would not commit itself on the proposal of an alliance against Denikin, Chicherin sent another note at the end of January 1920, in which he
inquired:

> Can [Prime] Minister Khan Khoiskii, in refusing to fight Denikin,
> be unaware that Denikin is an enemy of independent Azerbaijan?
> Does he not realize that a victory for Denikin would signify the end
> of Azerbaijani independence? And, conversely, can the Azerbaijani
> government fail to realize that the Soviet government has recognized
> the independence of Finland, Poland, and other borderland states?
> The Soviet government will also apply to Azerbaijan its general prin-
> ciples of recognition of the independence of peoples.[121]

### The Fall of Azerbaijan

The machinery for the conquest of Azerbaijan was ready at the beginning of April 1920. In the vicinity of Derbent, along the narrow strip of
level land separating the mountains of Daghestan from the shores of the
Caspian Sea, stood assembled the veteran Eleventh Red Army, with its
infantry and armored trains; inside Baku, the Communist underground

had control of a well-armed force of four thousand men, Russian, Armenian, and Moslem. At the same time the Azerbaijani army had been shifted by the Azerbaijani government to the southwestern region of the republic to fight the Armenians, leaving the border with Daghestan entirely unprotected. As early as April 17, 1920, Lenin issued a confidential order appointing Aleksandr Serebrovskii, an official of the Soviet Russian government, director of the future Sovietized Baku oil industries.[122]

The Azerbaijani government, in the final days of its existence, tried to save itself by lodging protests with the Soviet government and negotiating with Ordzhonikidze and the Communist underground, as well as by discussing with Persia plans for a union.[123] The threat of a coup precipitated a split within the Mussavat between a faction headed by M. Hasan Hadzhinskii and Resul-zade, which urged a conciliatory policy toward the Communists, and another, led by Khan Khoiskii, which wanted no concessions whatsoever. The conservative Union, the party of rich landowners and clergymen, was most pro-Communist of all; in part because it was attracted by the Pan-Islamist and Pan-Turanian slogans propagated by the Reds, and in part because its traditional conflict with the Mussavat inclined it to befriend any group which was fighting its rival. At one point in early 1920 the Union even considered a merger with the Azerbaijani Communist Party.[124]

The Mussavatists entered into negotiations with the Red underground, offering the Communists various positions in the government and expressing willingness to make other concessions to preserve the independence of the republic. In these negotiations the Turks, particularly Halil Pasha, played a role as intermediaries. Halil Pasha, who early in 1920 had replaced Nuri Pasha as commander of the Red partisan units in Daghestan, assured the Azerbaijani authorities that the Reds had no evil designs against Azerbaijan and desired merely to facilitate the transmission of military aid to the nationalist forces of Turkey. As evidence of Soviet good will, Halil Pasha cited the fact that the Communist organization had promised him the command of the Eleventh Red Army on its march across Azerbaijan to Turkey.[125]

The lack of radio contact between the Baku underground and the Kavbiuro made it necessary for the Baku Communists to dispatch a special emissary to Ordzhonikidze to receive orders concerning the coup. Early in April the Azerbaijani Communist Party sent the Georgian Communist Kvantaliani for that purpose to Petrovsk. During his absence, plans were laid for great public demonstrations against the government on May 1. But Kvantaliani, returning on April 22, brought word that the Kavbiuro wanted the coup to take place on April 27, so that preparations for the demonstration had to be canceled. According to Kavbiuro directives, the Baku Communists were to present the Azerbaijani government with an ultimatum, and simultaneously to request armed assistance from

Soviet Russia; while the Eleventh Army was marching on Baku, a Revolutionary Committee was to take over Baku.[126]

The Communist campaign developed according to plan. At noon on April 27, 1920, the Central Committee of the Azerbaijani Communist Party, the Baku Bureau of the Regional Committee of the Russian Communist Party, and the Central Workers' Conference of Baku, handed the Azerbaijani government a joint ultimatum demanding that it surrender authority within twelve hours. The government called an extraordinary session of the Parliament to discuss this demand, but before the twelve hours had elapsed news arrived that the Eleventh Red Army had crossed the border the previous night, and was marching on Baku.[127] The government of the republic then capitulated, voicing the hope that the Communist authorities would honor their promises to maintain the independence of Azerbaijan.[128] On April 28, an armored train bearing Ordzhonikidze and Kirov arrived in Baku, and shortly afterwards the troops of the Eleventh Army, having crossed the entire distance from the border virtually without firing a shot, entered the city. (Halil Pasha, who had gone forward to meet the Red forces to claim the military command which he had been promised by the Baku Communists, was told that the Eleventh Army had received no instructions to this effect and was advised to go to Moscow to clear up his claim, which he did.)[129]

Having established himself in Baku, Ordzhonikidze was eager to move on to Georgia and Armenia. His pretext was the desire to come to the assistance of the Georgian Communists who on May 2 staged (possibly at his instigation) an abortive rebellion in Tiflis. On May 3 he wired to Moscow that he expected to be in Tiflis by the middle of the month; at the same time he issued orders to his troops to advance westward along the Kura River. But his request was not approved. At the very time when the Red Army was occupying Baku the anticipated war with Poland had broken out; the Polish-Ukrainian armies struck hard and early in May were approaching Kiev. The prospect of a second front against the relatively well-organized and patriotically inspired Georgians was the last thing the Soviet government desired. In an emergency meeting the Politburo, the Central Committee's Political Bureau, voted against offensive actions in the Caucasus, and passed a resolution which read: "Immediately to send Ordzhonikidze a telegram in the name of Lenin and Stalin forbidding him to 'self-determine' Georgia, and instructing him to continue negotiations with the Georgian government."[130] The situation now called for a "soft" policy toward the two remaining Transcaucasian republics. The Commissariat of Foreign Affairs immediately opened negotiations with Georgia and Armenia. On May 7, 1920, the Soviet Union signed in Moscow a treaty with a representative of the Georgian Republic, which contained in its opening articles an unqualified recognition of Georgian independence:

Art. 1. On the basis of the right of all peoples freely to dispose of themselves up to and including complete separation from the state of which they constitute a part — a right proclaimed by the Socialist Federative Republic of Soviet Russia — Russia recognizes without reservations the independence and sovereignty of the Georgian state and renounces of its own will all the sovereign rights which had appertained to Russia with regard to the people and territory of Georgia.

Art. 2. On the basis of the principle proclaimed in the first article of the present treaty, Russia obliges itself to desist from all interference in the internal affairs of Georgia.

In a secret clause incorporated into the treaty, Georgia promised to legalize the Communist Party and to permit it free activity in its territory.[131]

The Russo-Polish war had saved Georgia and Armenia from certain Soviet occupation. But their doom was not averted; it was merely postponed. On May 29, Moscow appointed Kirov, the vice-chairman of the Kavbiuro, as its envoy to Tiflis, emphasizing by this appointment its continued interest in the conquest of the remainder of Transcaucasia.

Negotiations with Armenia were less fruitful, whether conducted in Moscow or transferred to Erivan.[132]

Although the capture of Baku had been bloodless, the spread of Soviet rule to the remaining regions of Azerbaijan was not completed without a struggle. On the night of May 25/26, 1920, a major rebellion against the Soviet regime broke out in Gandzha; carried out by Azerbaijani soldiers and peasants, with the probable participation of Azerbaijani nationalists, it soon spread to the adjoining areas of Karabakh and Zakataly. Soon most of western Azerbaijan rose in arms against the conqueror. The Red Army units, dispatched with an armored train from Baku to suppress the uprising, captured Gandzha following three days of bitter fighting. Afterwards they looted and pillaged the city for an entire week (May 31 to June 6). Next, the Red detachments fanned out into the countryside to deal with the rebels in the mountainous districts. Not before the end of June did they quell the uprisings and establish Soviet rule firmly throughout Azerbaijan.[133]

The introduction of Soviet rule into Baku was accompanied by severe repressive measures. Ordzhonikidze arrested and executed many persons connected with the Azerbaijani national movement, among them the former Prime Minister Khan Khoiskii and General Sulkevich, who had served in 1919 as Chief of Staff of the Azerbaijani Army. Resul-zade, one of the leaders of the Mussavat, was spared a similar fate by having advocated a pro-Communist course in the final days of independence, and by his personal acquaintance with Stalin and other Caucasian Communists, dating back to the 1905 Revolution when he had belonged to the Bolshevik Party in Baku. Later in the year, Resul-zade was brought to

Moscow by Stalin, who wanted him to join the Soviet government in Azerbaijan; after a year and a half in the Soviet capital, he escaped abroad.[134] The executions carried out by the Communists in Azerbaijan were in sharp contrast to their customary lenient attitude toward nationalist leaders in other conquered borderlands, and served as a prelude to the policy of terror and repression which was to characterize the whole period of Ordzhonikidze's rule in Transcaucasia.

The first Communist government in Azerbaijan consisted almost entirely of Moslems from the left-wing factions of the Gummet and Adalet. Its chairmanship was entrusted to Dr. Nariman Narimanov, an old Social Democrat, who in 1919 and 1920 had served as a Soviet official in Moscow, first as Director of the Eastern Division of the Commissariat of Foreign Affairs and then as one of the heads of the Commissariat of Nationalities.[135] Narimanov had resided in Moscow at the time of the Baku coup and had arrived in Azerbaijan only after it had fallen to the Red Army. The government of the Azerbaijani Soviet Socialist Republic had in fact little voice in the internal affairs of the republic, since its personnel controlled neither the Communist organization of Baku nor the omnipotent Kavbiuro with its army. Once, when Ordzhonikidze had run into difficulties with the Azerbaijani Soviet government and protested to Moscow, Lenin assured him that he had full authority to "direct the entire external and internal policy of Azerbaijan." [136] The appointment of an all-Moslem administration was a purely tactical maneuver, designed to create the impression that the overthrow of the Azerbaijani republic had been brought about by natives. Actual power in Azerbaijan was wielded by the Kavbiuro and by the local Communist party organs run by Ordzhonikidze and his appointees.

### The Fall of Armenia

In August 1920, while the Communist leaders of the Caucasus area were attending the Soviet-sponsored Congress of the Peoples of the East in Baku, a major native revolt broke out in Daghestan. Led by Nazhmudin Gotsinskii and some other local chiefs, the uprising was a reaction against Soviet misrule and against the failure of the Communists to fulfill the promises which they had made upon their entry into North Caucasian territory.[137] The departure of the Soviet army from Daghestan for the Azerbaijani campaign facilitated the spread of the rebellion. As soon as the news from Daghestan reached Baku, Ordzhonikidze relayed it to the Central Bureau of the Communist Party and departed in haste for the North Caucasus.[138]

The outbreak of the rebellion provided Stalin with an opportunity to leave Moscow for a one-month inspection tour of the Caucasus. He arrived in Vladikavkaz on October 21, 1920, and after conferences with party and military officials responsible for the suppression of Gotsinskii's forces, proceeded to Baku. The extent to which Ordzhonikidze had been able to obtain control of the Azerbaijani Communist Party during the half year of his rule in Baku is all too evident in the tone of the official Directive of the Central Committee of the Azerbaijani Communist Party, dated November 4, 1920, and published at the time in the Baku *Kommunist:*

> Our town is host to Comrade Stalin, the worker's leader of exceptional selflessness, energy, and stalwartness, the only experienced and universally recognized expert of revolutionary tactics and the leader of the proletarian revolution in the Caucasus and the East. The Central Committee of the Azerbaijani Communist Party (Bolshevik), realizing the modesty of Comrade Stalin, and his dislike for triumphal official welcomes, had to renounce special meetings in connection with his arrival. The Central Committee of the Azerbaijani Communist Party (Bolshevik) believes that the best welcome, the best greeting which our party, the proletariat of Baku, and the toilers of Azerbaijan can give our beloved leader and teacher, is a new and ever renewed concentration of all efforts for the general strengthening of party and Soviet work. All together for coördinated, militant work, worthy of the hardened proletarian fighter, Comrade Stalin — the first organizer and leader of the Baku proletariat.[139]

Such sycophancy, uncommon at the time even in regard to Lenin, indicated beyond doubt that the Communist apparatus in Azerbaijan was in the hands of people loyal to Stalin.*

Stalin spent nearly two weeks in Baku. On his way back to Moscow he again stopped in Daghestan and the Terek Region, where he participated in conferences connected with the establishment of a separate Daghestan Republic and the revamping of the Communist apparatus in the North Caucasus.† Upon his return to the capital, at the end of November 1920, Stalin published an article in *Pravda* on the situation in the Caucasus, in which he indicated in no uncertain terms that the end of Armenian and Georgian independence was at hand:

> Dashknak Armenia has fallen, without doubt the victim of a provocation of the Entente, which had set it against Turkey and then infamously left it to be harrowed by the Turks. There can be little doubt that Armenia has only one chance of saving itself: a union with Soviet Russia . . .

---

* According to a prominent Communist from Daghestan, the Baku organization in the second half of 1920, was controlled by A. Mikoyan (N. Samurskii, "Krasnyi Dagestan," in V. Stavskii, ed., *Dagestan* [Moscow, 1936], 15).

† Samurskii, 20–21; *Stalin*, IV, 394–407. The revolt in Daghestan continued until May 1921, complicated by the appearance of Said Shamil, a grandson of the famous leader of native resistance to Russian conquest in the mid-nineteenth century. It cost the Red Army five thousand casualties. A. Todorskii, *Krasnaia armiia v gorakh* (Moscow, 1924), is a history of the campaign against the insurgents.

Georgia, which had entangled itself in the snares of the Entente and consequently lost access to Baku oil and Kuban bread; Georgia, which had transformed itself into a principal base of imperialist operations of England and France and for this reason had entered into hostile relations with Soviet Russia — this Georgia completes now the last days of her life . . . There can be little doubt that in a difficult moment Georgia will be abandoned by the Entente, just as was Armenia.[140]

One of the obstacles in planning the campaign against Armenia was the virtual nonexistence there of a Communist Party apparatus. The Communist Party of Armenia, organized formally in Tiflis in 1919, had struck no roots in Armenian soil, largely because the active pro-Turkish policy pursued by the Communists since the end of that year had made it impossible for them to appeal to Armenian sentiments. In early 1920, the Armenian party in Tiflis had conducted a poll among its members to determine whether or not to prepare a coup in the Armenian republic; the majority of the members were of the opinion that such action was premature and at any rate impossible to accomplish without external assistance.[141] An agent dispatched to Erivan to investigate the strength of Communism confirmed the pessimistic outcome of the poll.[142] The Communist Party of Armenia preferred, as a consequence, to bide its time, awaiting the natural collapse of the republic which would inevitably follow the Soviet conquest of Azerbaijan and Georgia.

In May 1920, when the Red Army was marching on Erivan, this hope of the Armenian Communists seemed near realization. The Communist cause secured at that time some following in the western sectors of Armenia, notably among the proletariat of Aleksandropol (most of them unemployed Russian railroad workers who had migrated from Baku after the collapse of the Commune in 1918) and the officers of the Armenian army. On May 10, 1920, a Communist-dominated Revolutionary Committee in Aleksandropol proclaimed the Sovietization of Armenia. But when the Soviet offensive came to a halt and the Red troops withdrew, the Dashnaks quickly regained the upper hand and suppressed the would-be government.[143] During those disorders, the Russian Armenians showed themselves more pro-Soviet, whereas the refugees from Turkish Armenia supported the Dashnaktsutiun.

The actual Sovietization of Armenia, which occurred in December 1920, came as the result of a conflict between the Armenians and the Turks. In late September 1920, the dispute over the Eastern provinces of Anatolia which had kept the two governments at odds ever since the summer of 1919, led to the outbreak of a full-scale war. The tide of battle turned immediately in favor of the Turks, who were more numerous and better armed and who had the support of the Communists. The Armenian Army, according to the then President of the Armenian Republic, Simon

Vratsian, was weakened by Bolshevik propaganda;[144] the rapid advance of Kemalist troops engendered defeatism among the Armenians and made it easy for Communist agitators to spread anti-Dashnak slogans. On October 30, 1920, Turkish troops seized Kars, and a short time later negotiations were opened in Aleksandropol. The Turks posed stiff conditions: the surrender of two thirds of the territory in Eastern Anatolia claimed by the Armenian Republic, the reduction of the Armenian army to 1,500 men, and the renunciation of the Treaty of Sèvres.[*]

While the Armenian regime was negotiating with the Turks, the Kavbiuro prepared to take advantage of the hopeless situation in which Armenia was placed as a consequence of its defeats. On November 27, 1920, Stalin, who had just arrived in Moscow from his Caucasian trip, telephoned Ordzhonikidze in Baku and instructed him to commence operations against Armenia. Lenin also conferred with Ordzhonikidze on the same day.[145] Two days later, Legran, the Soviet diplomat representing Moscow in Erivan at the Armenian-Russian treaty negotiations, handed the Armenian government an ultimatum in which he demanded that it give up its authority to a "Revolutionary Committee of the Soviet Socialist Republic of Armenia," which was located in the Kazakh region of Soviet Azerbaijan.[146] It is likely that this Revolutionary Committee had been formed in Baku in the course of the Congress of the Peoples of the East. Very possibly, too, the plans for the intervention were laid during Stalin's visit to Baku and were held in abeyance until he was able to discuss them with Lenin and the Politburo.

While Legran was dealing with the Armenian government, units of the Eleventh Army crossed the Armenian border from Azerbaijan, occupied Dilizhan, and proceeded along the mountainous road skirting the western shore of Lake Sevan toward the capital of Armenia.[147] There are many indications that the Soviet entry was motivated by a desire to forestall the complete collapse of the Armenian Republic, and to prevent a Turkish occupation of Erivan. The Russian move was directed primarily against Kemal, whose victories had threatened to bring Turkish troops into the heart of Transcaucasia. The readiness with which the Dashnaks consented to the Soviet ultimatum, the establishment of a joint Communist-Dashnak government in the newly Sovietized Armenia, and the silence with which the Armenian diplomatic mission abroad treated the Soviet conquest while loudly protesting Turkish aggrandizement — all

---

[*] The Treaty of Sèvres, between the Entente and Turkey, signed in August 1920 but never ratified, called in Articles 88 and 89 for Turkish recognition of Armenian independence, and the arbitration of the President of the United States in the matter of the Armenian-Turkish frontier. President Wilson's decision, rendered in December 1920, favored the Armenian claims, granting them much of Eastern Anatolia, including Erzerum, Van, Bitlis, and Trebizond. Cf. Mandelstam, La Société des Nations, 72, 99ff; Délégation de la République arménienne, L'Arménie et la question arménienne (Paris, 1922).

these facts indicate that the Armenian government did not consider the Soviet invasion an unfriendly gesture.

On December 2, 1920, Ministers Dro and Terterian of the Armenian Republic and Legran, representing Soviet Russia, signed a treaty in Erivan which provided liberal terms for the defeated Dashnaks:

Article 1. Armenia is proclaimed an independent socialist republic.

Article 2. Until the convocation of the Congress of Soviets of Armenia, all power in Armenia is transferred to a Provisional Military Revolutionary Committee.

Article 3. The Russian Soviet government recognizes [the following areas] as entering undisputably into the territory of the Socialist Soviet Republic of Armenia: the Erivan province with all its counties; a part of the Kars region, which will secure it military control of the railroad line Dzhadzhur-Araks; the Zangezur county of the Elisavetpol province; a part of the Kazakh county of the same province — within the limits of the agreement of August 10 — and those parts of the Tiflis province which had been in Armenian possession until October 23, 1920.

Article 4. The Command of the Armenian army is not subject to any responsibility for actions committed by the army previous to the establishment of Soviet rule in Armenia.

Article 5. Members of the Dashnaktsutiun party and of other socialist parties in Armenia will not be subjected to any repressive measures for their membership in [those] parties.

Article 6. The Military Revolutionary Committee will consist of five members appointed by the Communist Party, and two members appointed by left Dashnak groups with the approval of the Communist Party.

Article 7. The Russian Soviet government shall take measures for the immediate concentration of military forces necessary to the defense of the independence of the Socialist Soviet Republic of Armenia.

Article 8. After the present agreement is signed, the government of the Republic of Armenia is removed from authority; until the arrival of the Revolutionary Committee, power is temporarily transferred to the Military Command, at whose head is placed Comrade Dro. Comrade Silyn is appointed the Commissar of the RSFSR (Russian Socialist Federated Soviet Republic) for the Military Command of Armenia.[148]

After the signature of the treaty, the Armenian army was renamed the Red Army of Armenia, but it was left under the command of Dro, its previous chief and a leading member of the Dashnaktsutiun.

The Revolutionary Committee arrived in Erivan on December 6, 1920, one week after its departure from Azerbaijan. Upon assuming authority, it entirely disregarded the treaty which Legran had signed with the deposed regime. On December 21, 1920, it decreed all laws of the Soviet

Russian government to be in force in Soviet Armenia;[149] no attempt was made to regain for Armenia the territories occupied by the Turks since October 1920, and in March 1921 they were formally ceded to Turkey in the Treaty of Kars; contrary to Articles 5 and 6 of the agreement, the Dashnaks were arrested and before long ejected from the government.[150]

### The Fall of Georgia

In accordance with the secret clause of the treaty of May 1920, the Georgian government immediately released from prisons the Communists whom it had detained since the abortive coup of the previous November. Nearly one thousand Communists benefited from this amnesty. Their own reaction to the sudden liberation was not, as might have been expected, one of gratitude to Moscow for its intercession, but rather one of resentment and anger. Makharadze, who had escaped from a Georgian jail in February 1920 and had assumed leadership of the underground Regional Committee, stated in his memoirs that neither he nor his colleagues had the slightest inkling of the Soviet government's intention to make peace with the Menshevik republic.[151] At the time the treaty was negotiated, the Communist underground apparatus in Tiflis was preparing a new uprising, coincident with the anticipated entry of the Red Army. The May treaty, in which Soviet Russia had recognized the sovereignty of Menshevik Georgia, appeared to the local Communists as an indication that the Party's Central Committee had little regard for their efforts and was prepared to betray the struggle which they had been waging against the Menshevik government for nearly three years.[152]

Their dissatisfaction was only partly softened when Moscow bestowed upon them organizational authority. The secret clause in the Russo-Georgian treaty legalizing the Communist Party on Georgian territory offered opportunities of which the Russian Communist Party intended to take full advantage. In May and June, 1920, the Central Committee of the Russian Communist Party passed a series of resolutions which, among other things, dissolved the old Regional Committee and in its place established a Communist Party of Georgia, charging it with full responsibility for party work on the territory of the Georgian Republic.[153] At the same time it appointed as Soviet ambassador to Tiflis Sergei Kirov, Ordzhonikidze's second in command. Kirov brought with him an enormous staff and tackled the task of assembling the forces with which to undermine and destroy the authority of the republic to which he was accredited. To keep the Georgian government in a state of perpetual tension, he bombarded it with diplomatic protests, in which he charged that the Georgians were violating their treaty with Soviet Russia by arresting Communists, helping the White movement, and intriguing with the Allies. In October 1920, Kirov left his post to attend the Polish-Soviet peace talks and was replaced by A. L. Sheinman.

The Communists made no secret of their intentions. "Our party here," the Tiflis *Kommunist* wrote on June 7, 1920, "must utilize all opportunities and concentrate all efforts on closing its ranks, so that, when the decisive moment comes, we shall be ready and able to achieve the goal which history has placed on the shoulders of the proletariat." [154] "It was a secret to no one," wrote Makharadze a few years later, "that the work of the Communist Party, under the circumstances then [1920] prevailing in Georgia, consisted entirely of the preparation of armed uprisings against the existing government." [155]

After the occupation of Armenia, Georgia was hemmed in on three sides by Soviet Russia. The Red Army, having terminated the war with Poland, was now in position to resume the offensive on the Transcaucasian front.

In preparation for the attack, Ordzhonikidze instructed General Gekker to submit an estimate of the situation. A copy of Gekker's report came into Georgian possession in December, and from it it is possible to reconstruct Soviet military intentions. Gekker stated that from the military point of view the conquest of Georgia could be achieved in six weeks, provided Soviet Russia had the assurance of the friendly neutrality of the Turkish armies stationed along the Georgian and Armenian borders. Without such assurance, the invasion would be at best a precarious adventure, and at worst a disaster, insofar as Soviet troops would be exposed to an attack from the rear. Gekker also suggested that the major offensive aim at southeastern Georgia, where the Azerbaijani border came closest to Tiflis, and that it be supported by diversionary offensives from the North Caucasus.[156] On December 15, 1920, Ordzhonikidze convened a meeting of the Caucasian Bureau to discuss invasion plans, and having secured its approval for an attack on Georgia, wired to Lenin for permission to proceed.[157]

There is considerable evidence that Lenin at first hesitated to approve of the invasion of Georgia advocated by some of his colleagues, especially Ordzhonikidze and Stalin. Much as he wished to establish Soviet rule over Tiflis, whose independence seriously endangered the Communist hold on the Caucasus, he feared adverse effects of the invasion on Soviet Russia's whole international situation. In early 1921 the Civil War had come to an end, and Lenin was anxious to improve Russia's relations with the "capitalist" West, whose help he needed for the reconstruction of the war-ravaged country and the successful launching of the New Economic Policy. A Soviet trade mission, headed by Leonid Krasin, had gone to London and had opened negotiations with the British government: it was a possible prelude to British recognition of the Communist regime and the establishment of regular diplomatic relations between the two countries. Under those circumstances, anything which endangered the good will of the West and frightened it with the specter of further Soviet aggrandizement was harmful to the Soviet cause. The sympathy which the Georgian Mensheviks enjoyed in European socialist circles was an additional reason for circumspection.

From Lenin's point of view, there were also other arguments against an invasion. The Communist movement in Georgia was under close surveillance by the Menshevik police and, after repeated repressions, had lost the power to render the invader effective assistance. The Georgian government was popular and able to defend itself. Then, there was also the uncertainty about Turkey's reaction, the importance of which had been emphasized in Gekker's report. The relations between Soviet Russia and the Kemalists had actually deteriorated in the second half of 1920. A Turkish mission sent to Moscow in June 1920 spent several months in negotiations without coming to an agreement with Russia.[158] The last-minute intervention of the Reds in Armenia also had not contributed to Russo-Turkish amity. In January 1921 the Turks arrested the most important Communist agents operating on their territory and expelled them to Russia; Mustafa Subkhi, who had led the Communist apparatus in Anatolia and tried to return there after being expelled, they executed.[159] In the winter of 1920–21 the Russo-Turkish marriage of convenience showed definite signs of strain, which could have led to catastrophic results if the Kemalists should have decided to intervene on behalf of Georgia.

Finally — and perhaps most importantly — there were military considerations. The Red Army was exhausted from over two years of continuous fighting, and transport facilities were so short that no trains could be spared to ship men and supplies to the Caucasian front. General S. Kamenev, the commander in chief of the Soviet armed forces, was convinced that an attack on Georgia would result in a prolonged war beyond the capacities of the Caucasian army. In three successive reports to Lenin he expressed his opposition to an invasion of Georgia.[160]

Lenin thus had every reason to believe that the limited benefits which he could derive from the acquisition of Georgia would be more than offset by the dangers which forceful expansion at this point held for Soviet Russia's whole internal and external position. He turned down, therefore, Ordzhonikidze's request for permission to invade Georgia; and he remained adamant when, at the beginning of January 1921, Ordzhonikidze repeated his request.[161]

Nevertheless, Lenin was under great pressure and he gradually relented. His resolution may have been somewhat weakened by a memorandum submitted by Chicherin, the Commissar of Foreign Affairs, on January 20, 1921, which painted a very gloomy (from the Menshevik point of view) picture of internal conditions in the Georgian Republic.[162] At the same time Krasin reported a statement made to him by Lloyd George to the effect that Great Britain considered the entire Caucasus within the Soviet sphere of influence and contemplated no intervention there.[163] On the basis of this and other evidence, Lenin presented to the Politburo on January 26, 1921, a policy statement of the Georgian question. This statement, known to us only from incomplete Soviet résumés, seems to have been something of a compromise. On the one hand, it called for the maintenance of regular diplomatic relations with the Georgian Republic. On the other, it made provisions for an eventual rupture of these relations and the overthrow of the Georgian government. Instructions were issued to the Communist Party of Georgia to organize an uprising, and directives were given to the Red Army to come to the assistance of the rebels.[164] Lenin apparently wanted to make very certain before giving his approval to an invasion that the overthrow of the Menshevik government bore all the appearances of an internal uprising. Much of his subsequent displeasure with Ordzhonikidze was caused by the latter's impatience and lack of respect for political decorum.

Preparations for the Communist uprising went ahead at a rapid pace. It broke out on the night of February 11/12. Ordzhonikidze located it in the Borchalo district, which had been contested between Georgia and Armenia over the past three years, and where Georgian authority apparently was not quite established. Direction of the uprising was entrusted to Mamia Orakhelashvili, a Georgian Communist who had been released from Menshevik prison in the May amnesty.

Ordzhonikidze was now very eager to commence military operations and bombarded Moscow with telegrams. Lenin still hesitated to act against the advice of his commander in chief, but finally he yielded. On February 14, the Central Committee agreed to the invasion, and on that day — under conditions of extraordinary security — Lenin dispatched to the Revolutionary-Military Committee of the Eleventh Army and (through Stalin) to Ordzhonikidze the long-awaited but qualified permission:

> The Central Committee is inclined to permit the Eleventh Army to give active support to the uprising in Georgia and to occupy Tiflis provided international norms are maintained and on the condition that all the members of the Revolutionary-Military Committee of the Eleventh Army, after serious appraisal of all the facts, guarantee success. We warn you that we are without bread because of the transport situation, and for this reason we shall not let you have a single train or a single railroad car. We are compelled to limit our shipments from the Caucasus to bread and oil. We demand an immediate reply by direct wire over the signature of all the members of the Revolutionary-Military Committee of the Eleventh Army, as well as Smilga, Gittis, Trifonov, and Frumkin. Until you have our reply to

the wire from all these persons you absolutely must refrain from undertaking anything decisive.[165]

The message ended with the admonition: "Thus, double and redoubled caution, on your responsibility." Instructions were given that General Kamenev, the commander in chief of the Soviet armed forces, be told of the contents of this telegram, but not be shown the text. So secret was the order that Trotsky, then Commissar of War, and absent on the Eastern front, knew nothing of it.[166]

Whether the Revolutionary-Military Committee ever satisfied Lenin's conditions and awaited his definitive word cannot be determined. In any event, having at last secured Lenin's permission in principle, Ordzhonikidze launched his invasion. On February 16, the Eleventh Army crossed the Georgian frontier, ostensibly in order to help the Georgian Revolutionary-Military Committee which Orakhelashvili had set up in the village of Shulaveri two days before, but actually in order to proceed by the shortest route toward Tiflis. When news of the invasion reached Moscow, General Kamenev sent a bitter letter to Lenin accusing the Eleventh Army of having taken the initiative in attacking Georgia despite his warnings, but urging all-out help to the invading units.[167] On February 18, Makharadze, who had been in Moscow all this time, left for the Caucasus to assume chairmanship of the Revolutionary Committee.[168]

Military developments soon vindicated Ordzhonikidze. Following the recommendation of Gekker, he threw his main forces, consisting of infantry regiments of the Eleventh Red Army supported by armored cars and tanks, against the southeastern region of Georgia. On February 17, an armored Red force crossed the border at Poili and made directly for Tiflis. Other Red forces, consisting of cavalry units of the Thirteenth Red Army, under the command of General Budenny, invaded Georgia a few days later from the east.[169]

The Georgians counterattacked in vain. Despite the interception of the Gekker report, which revealed the Soviet campaign plans, Tiflis had failed to work out a sound defensive arrangement. Determined to protect every inch of Georgian soil, it had scattered its forces along the lengthy frontier, too thinly for effective use.* A few days after the start of the invasion, Red tanks reached the gates of Tiflis. Georgian troops, incapable of holding the exposed frontier, retreated from all sides toward the capital. On the night of February 18/19 the Red Army attacked Tiflis and seized Mt. Kodzhori, overlooking the city. At this moment the Georgians rallied and succeeded in temporarily turning the tide of battle in their favor. An attack by a detachment of military cadets recaptured Mt. Kodzhori. Then, for an entire week the Georgians held Tiflis with less

---

* Soviet troops have been estimated in excess of 100,000, whereas the Georgian armies contained no more than one half that number. The Georgians had none of the heavy weapons of the Red Army.

than ten thousand men against Russian forces three times their number, bringing the Soviet offensive to a standstill.

The defenders were aided by a rebellion which broke out behind their enemy's lines in Soviet Armenia on February 19, as a reaction to Soviet misrule. The Armenian anti-Soviet rebels, led by the Dashnaks, seized Erivan and acquired control over considerable areas of Armenia. In effect, they overthrew the Soviet regime in Armenia and reëstablished the government which had been in power before the Communist invasion. The Communists reconquered Armenia only after the Georgian campaign was over, in April 1921.[170]

While the battle for Tiflis was in progress, the Georgian government vainly endeavored to establish contact with Moscow. Moscow denied knowledge of any Soviet attack, while Sheinman, the Soviet representative in Tiflis, asserted that, as far as he was concerned, the war was a conflict between Georgia and Armenia over Borchalo. He could neither interfere nor stop the fighting, but he offered his services as mediator.

The Supreme Allied Council in Paris, which on the eve of the invasion had recognized Georgia *de jure*, did not move in Georgia's defense.

With fresh replacements and new supplies reaching the Red Armies from Baku, Tiflis could not hold out much longer. Georgian troops were shifted by automobiles from one end of the town to another to protect menaced points. The defenders were exhausted from two weeks of constant fighting, and their supplies were running low. On February 24, the Red Army resumed its offensive and nearly closed a ring around the city. The Georgians decided to evacuate Tiflis. During a temporary lull in the battle, Georgian troops disengaged the enemy and pulled out; the government followed shortly afterwards. The long convoys of the retreating Georgians moved in the direction of Kutais and Batum. On February 25, the Red Army entered the capital, and Ordzhonikidze at once sent triumphant telegrams to his superiors, Lenin and Stalin: "The proletarian flag flies over Tiflis!" [171]

While the Georgians were seeking refuge in western Georgia, small detachments of the Ninth Red Army under the command of General Levandovskii (who was in charge of the forces suppressing the rebellion in Daghestan) attacked from the North, after having crossed the icebound Darial and Mamison passes. Other Red units moved toward Batum along the Black Sea coast. These diversionary actions, suggested by Gekker's report, were under the political supervision of Kirov who, upon his return from Riga, had been dispatched to the Northern Caucasus.

When the Georgian government and the remnants of its army had reached Kutais, an ultimatum arrived from the Turks, demanding the surrender of Batum. The Turkish nationalists apparently had no intention of sitting by idly while the Russian Communist conquered all of Georgia. On March 5, without waiting for a reply, Turkish armies occupied the suburbs of Batum and, six days later, the city proper. When, however, on March 17, they attempted to enter the Batum fortress and to disarm the troops garrisoned there, the Georgians resisted. On March 18, the Turkish Parliament in Ankara proclaimed the annexation of Batum. All during that day there was fighting in the city between the Georgian garrison and the Turks.[172]

Turkish intervention ended Georgian hopes of continuing resistance in the western half of the republic. On March 18, the government capitulated to the Russians. The cease-fire agreement which it signed with the Communist Revkom provided for a termination of hostilities, the dissolution of the Georgian army, and full amnesty for all persons connected with the Georgian regime. One of its clauses provided for the advance of Soviet armies across western Georgia to the defense of Batum against the Turks.[173] Having signed the agreement, the Georgian government boarded an Italian steamer and departed for Constantinople. Units of the Red Army, speeding to defend Batum, reached the beleaguered fortress on March 19. Together with the Georgians they threw back the Turkish troops and expelled them from the city. (In the Treaty of Kars Turkey abandoned its claims to Batum.)

Lenin followed the events in Georgia with misgivings. He was convinced that if Ordzhonikidze were to apply in Georgia the methods of administration which he had used in conquered Azerbaijan and Armenia, Georgia would be swept by a wave of popular resistance. Therefore, as soon as Ordzhonikidze had set foot in Tiflis, Lenin sent him a series of directives urging him to adopt a policy of utmost concession to the government and the population of the subjugated country. Lenin wrote him on March 2, 1921:

> Please convey to the Georgian Communists and especially to all members of the Georgian Revkom my warm greeting to Soviet Georgia. I would particularly like them to inform me whether there is between them and us complete agreement on three issues:
> First: it is necessary to arm at once the workers and the poorest peasants, forming a solid Georgian Red Army.
> Second: it is imperative to enforce a special policy of concessions toward Georgian intellectuals and petty traders. It must be understood that it is not only unwise to subject these classes to nationalization, but that it may be necessary to make certain sacrifices to improve their situation and to give them an opportunity to conduct petty trade.
> Third: it is of gigantic importance to seek an acceptable compromise for a block with Zhordaniia and the other Georgian Mensheviks like him, who even before the uprising were not absolutely hostile to the idea of a Soviet government in Georgia on certain conditions.
> I ask you to keep in mind that the internal and external situation of Georgia demands of the Georgian Communists not the application of the Russian pattern, but a skillful and flexible elaboration of a

special original tactic, based on a large-scale concession to all kinds of petty-bourgeois elements.

Please reply. Lenin.[174]

As is apparent from this letter, Lenin's primary concern was with the reaction of the Georgian population to Soviet conquest. He was anxious to minimize the impression that the Soviet Georgian government was a foreign agency (hence his stress on an alliance with Zhordaniia and on the authority of the Georgian Revkom) and fearful that the policies of War Communism might alienate the groups without whose support Soviet rule was possible only on the basis of military occupation (hence his insistence on "concessions"). Lenin reëmphasized these points in two additional messages to Ordzhonikidze and the Caucasian Communists. His telegram to the Revolutionary-Military Soviet of the Eleventh Army (printed March 17, 1921) follows:

> In view of the fact that units of the N [Eleventh] Army are located on Georgian territory, you are requested to establish full contact with the Revkom of Georgia and to conform strictly to the directives of the Revkom, not to undertake any measures which might touch upon the interests of the population without agreement of the Revkom of Georgia, to be particularly respectful toward the sovereign organs of Georgia, to show especial attention and caution in respect to the Georgian population. Give immediately corresponding directives to all organs of the army, including the special section [Secret Police]. Hold responsible all persons violating those directives. Inform [me] of every instance of violation, or even the slightest friction or disagreement with the local population.[175]

In another message to the Caucasian Communists, Lenin elaborated on the differences between the situation in the Caucasus in 1921 and that which had prevailed in Soviet Russia during the period of the Civil War, "A slower, more cautious, more systematic transition to socialism — this is what is possible and necessary for the republics of the Caucasus in contrast to the RSFSR." [176]

How well grounded were Lenin's fears of Ordzhonikidze's ability to rule Georgia became evident in the course of the two years which followed the establishment of Soviet regime there. Ordzhonikidze's failure to follow Lenin's directives led to a complete rupture between the Kavbiuro and the Georgian Communists and brought about one of the most violent internal crises in the early history of the Party.

The seizure of Georgia completed the process of reconquest of the separated borderlands and initiated the last phase in the formation of the Soviet Union: the integration of the conquered territories into a single state.

# V I

## THE ESTABLISHMENT OF THE UNION OF
## SOVIET SOCIALIST REPUBLICS

*The Consolidation of the Party and State Apparatus*

The belief that the socialist state required a centralized administration was common to both wings of the Russian Social Democratic Labor Party, as indeed it was to European Marxism in general. The Marxists viewed the government as an instrument of class warfare and a weapon by means of which the class in power asserted its will, destroyed its opponents, and enacted socio-economic and political legislation which best served its interests. Only a government which had at its disposal complete political and economic authority could accomplish these tasks. The pre-1917 opposition of the Mensheviks and Bolsheviks to federalism, as well as the specific interpretation given by Lenin to the right of national self-determination, were largely inspired by a desire to avoid the evils of a system which permitted hostile elements to find escape from the socialist regime by utilizing the privileges inherent in states' rights.

The Bolsheviks' adoption of the principle of federalism upon their accession to power in no way signified an abandonment of the traditional Marxist hostility to the decentralized state. In the first place, under the circumstances in which it had been adopted, federalism was a step in the direction of centralization, since it gave an opportunity of bringing together once more borderland areas which during the Revolution had acquired the status of independent republics. In the second place, the existence of the Communist Party, with its unique internal organization and extraordinary rights with regard to the institutions of the state, made it possible for the rulers of the Soviet republic to retain all the important features of a unitary state in a state which was formally decentralized.

In Communist political theory the supreme legislative authority belonged to the soviets. "Russia is declared a republic of Soviets of workers', soldiers' and peasants' deputies," stated the Declaration of Rights of the Toiling and Exploited People, issued in January 1918; "All power in the center and locally belongs to these Soviets." [1] According to the Russian Soviet constitution, local soviets delegated their representatives to the All-Russian Congress of Soviets, which in turn appointed an All-Russian Central Executive Committee (VTsIK). The Council of People's Commissars, the supreme executive organ of the state, was in theory responsible to the VTsIK and to the All-Russian Congress of Soviets. In practice, however, the Council of People's Commissars early in the Revolution made itself independent of the VTsIK, which did little more than give formal approval to measures promulgated by the Council of People's Commissars.*

Side by side with the soviets, the Communists recognized another sovereign institution, the Russian Communist Party. The Bolshevik leaders conceived of the Communist Party as the vanguard of the proletarian revolution and as an organization which provided the soviets with intellectual and political leadership. They drew no clear-cut division of authority between the soviets and the party, on the assumption that the interests of the two were in full harmony, but they admitted openly that the chain of command descended from the party to the soviets, and not vice versa. In March 1919, when they drew up their first party program (superseding the general Russian Social Democratic program of 1903), the Bolsheviks stated the relationship between these two institutions in the following words:

> The Communist Party assigns itself the task of winning decisive influence and complete leadership in all organizations of the laboring class: the trade unions, the coöperatives, the village communes, etc. The Communist Party strives particularly for the realization of its program and for the full mastery of contemporary political organizations such as the Soviets . . .
>
> The Russian Communist Party must win for itself undivided political mastery in the Soviets and *de facto* control of all their work, through practical, daily, dedicated work in the Soviets, [and] the advancement of its most stalwart and devoted members to all Soviet positions.[2]

The sovereign legislative powers, theoretically vested in the soviets, were, therefore, absorbed not only by the Council of People's Commissars, which operated on the highest level, but also by the Communist Party, which operated on all levels, down to the smallest town soviets.

The leaders of both the Council of People's Commissars and the Communist Party were in fact the same persons. The intertwining of the personnel and activities of the state and party institutions was so intimate that the process of the integration of the Soviet territory occurred not

---

* The process whereby this condition was brought about is described in E. H. Carr, *The Bolshevik Revolution, 1917–1923,* I (New York, 1951), 147ff.

on one, but on two levels. The evolution of Soviet federalism, therefore, cannot be studied merely from the point of view of the changing relations between the central and provincial institutions of the *state;* it must be approached, first of all, from the point of view of the relations between the central and provincial institutions of the Communist *Party.*

One of the characteristic features of the Bolshevik party organization, the feature which perhaps most distinguished it from the other political organizations of twentieth-century Russia, was its internal discipline. In contrast to the Mensheviks, who thought of the party in terms of a loose association of persons holding similar views, Lenin felt that only an organization which was highly centralized and uncompromising on all matters of party activity, practical as well as theoretical, could perform effective political work. Indeed, the issue of party discipline had been the main cause of the split of Russian Social Democracy into two factions, Menshevik and Bolshevik, at the 1903 Congress. After the Bolsheviks had come to power and assumed the responsibilities of government, their views on this matter were asserted with ever greater emphasis. They were thus enunciated in the program in 1919:

> The party finds itself in a situation in which the strictest centralism and the severest discipline are absolute necessities. All decisions of the higher instance are absolutely binding on the lower ones. Every decision must first of all be carried out, and only later can it be appealed to the proper party organ. In this sense, the party must display in the present epoch virtually a military discipline . . .[3]

The highest organ of the party was its Central Committee; after March 1919, this position was assumed by the Central Committee's Political Bureau (Politburo).

The power which the Communist Party enjoyed in regard to state institutions accounted for the fact that the decisive battles for political control in Soviet-held territories took place within the party organizations. The question of how much authority was to be in the hands of the central organs and how much in the provincial ones was in fact determined by the settlement of relations between the Central Committee and the regional organizations of the Communist Party.

Now, Lenin was firm in insisting that the principles of nationalism and federalism, introduced on his own initiative in the state apparatus, did not apply to the Communist Party. Throughout his life, he remained opposed to the ideas which the Jewish Bund had advocated at the beginning of the twentieth century. During all of 1918 Lenin suppressed repeated efforts of Communists in the republics to win some autonomy from the Central Committee of the RKP, even when such efforts did not go beyond the demand for the right to join the Third International.

His task was facilitated by the fact that nearly all the republican Communist parties were not indigenous, national political organizations, but merely regional branches of the Russian Communist Party. Thus, the Communist Party of the Ukraine was the product of a merger of the Southwestern and Donets-Krivoi Rog Regional Committees of the RKP; the Belorussian Communist Party was the old Northwestern Committee of the RKP under a new name; the Georgian, Armenian, and Azerbaijani Communist parties emerged from the organizational breakup of the Transcaucasian Regional Committee of the RKP; the Turkestan Communist Party came into being through the renaming of the Turkestan Committee of the RKP. Lenin, therefore, did not so much have to centralize the party organization as keep it from falling apart.

In the spring of 1918 the Central Committee of the Communist Party of the Ukraine was compelled to acknowledge the authority of the Central Committee of the RKP and to give up its claims of membership in the Communist International. Late in 1919 it was altogether dissolved. The plan of the Belorussians to institute a separate national Communist Party was vetoed by Lenin. The Moslem Communist Party was first subordinated to the Russian Communist Party and then done away with altogether. Similar steps were taken in the other borderland areas. Lenin had thus made it clear that if he had requested the various regional committees of the RKP to change their designations to correspond to the names of the republics in which they were operating, it was largely a concession to mass psychology; he had no intention of splitting party authority or even of introducing the ideas of nationality and federalism into the party organization. As the Communist Party program of 1919 stated:

> The Ukraine, Latvia, Lithuania, and Belorussia exist at this time as separate Soviet republics. Thus is solved for the present the question of state structure.
>
> But this does not in the least mean that the Russian Communist Party should, in turn, reorganize itself as a federation of independent Communist parties.
>
> The Eighth Congress of the RKP resolves: there must exist a *single* centralized Communist Party with a single Central Committee leading all the party work in all sections of the RSFSR. All decisions of the RKP and its directing organs are unconditionally binding on all branches of the party, regardless of their national composition. The Central Committees of the Ukrainian, Latvian, Lithuanian Communists enjoy the rights of the regional committees of the party, and are entirely subordinated to the Central Committee of the RKP.[4]

If the soviets were to be the supreme legislative organs of the new state; if they, in turn, were to be subjected to *de facto* control by the Communist Party; and if, finally, the Communist Party itself in Russia as well as in the non-Russian Soviet republics, was to be completely subordinated to the Central Committee, then clearly actual sovereignty in all Soviet areas belonged to the Central Committee of the Russian Communist Party. Soviet federalism did not involve a distribution of power between the center and the province; only a corresponding decentralization of the Communist Party would have made the establishment of genuine federal relations possible. If, in 1917, Lenin had accepted state federalism so readily, it was because he knew that the existence of a unified, centralized Communist Party with authority over political institutions throughout the Soviet territories made possible the retention of unalloyed centralized political power.

The Communist leaders, however, were concerned not only with unifying in their own hands the ultimate political authority over the entire Soviet domain, but also with extending the scope of this authority as widely and as deeply as possible. Partly for reasons of dogma (the conviction that in the period of revolution the total resources of society must be brought to bear on the class-enemy), partly for reasons of practical statesmanship (greater efficiency in governing the country and the opportunity for economic planning), they undertook to augment the ultimate policy-making authority — assured them by the party — by assuming control over the entire administrative apparatus of the state.

The integration into a single state of the borderlands conquered in the course of the Civil War began in 1918 and terminated in 1923 with the establishment of the Union of Soviet Socialist Republics (USSR). It was a complex process. Before the Revolution, the Bolsheviks had given little thought to the problems of federalism, and now had to proceed entirely by trial and error. The fundamental incompatibility between the division of powers inherent in federalism and the striving toward the centralization of authority inherent in Communism lent the evolution of the Soviet state a peculiar character. Most of the time it is impossible to tell whether an act involving the transfer of authority from one of the republics to the government of Soviet Russia represented a genuine shift in political power, or only a formal expression of a fact which had been accomplished quietly some time earlier by order of the Party or the Council of People's Commissars. The Communist adherence to democratic terminology in a social order which was authoritarian in the fullest sense of the word also does not contribute to a greater understanding of the growth of Soviet state structure.

For purposes of historical analysis, the territories of the Soviet state which were involved in the process of political consolidation may be divided into three categories: the autonomous regions and republics, the Union Republics, and the People's Republics. It must be borne in mind, however, that such a division is artificial. The centralization occurred in all those areas simultaneously and, even before the formal establishment of the USSR, they were (with the exception of the People's Republics) reduced to a status which was, for all practical purposes, identical.

## The RSFSR

The first Constitution of Soviet Russia (1918), while accepting the general principle of federalism, had made no provisions for the settlement of relations between the federal government and the individual states. Indeed, as one historian points out, the very word "federation" was not even mentioned in the body of the Constitution.[5] During 1918, it was not clear what, if any, difference in status there was between the autonomous regions, the autonomous republics, and the Soviet republics, and all those terms were used interchangeably. Wherever the Communists came into power they simply proclaimed the laws issued by the government of the RSFSR valid on their territory and announced the establishment of a "union" with the Russian Soviet republic.

The first attempt to put into practice the principles enunciated in the Constitution was made in the spring of 1918, when the government of the RSFSR (or, more precisely, its All-Russian Central Executive Committee) ordered the formation of the Tatar-Bashkir and Turkestan republics. As we have seen, these attempts were not successful. The Tatar-Bashkir state never came into being because the Russians evacuated the Volga-Ural region in the summer of 1918; while Turkestan, cut off from Moscow by the enemy, had, until the end of the Civil War, no administrative connection with the RSFSR.

It was only in February 1919, with the signing of the Soviet-Bashkir agreement, that the decentralization of the administrative apparatus along national lines began in earnest. Between 1920 and 1923, the government of the RSFSR established on its territory seventeen autonomous regions and republics.* The autonomous regions (sometimes called "Toilers' Communes") had no distinguishing juridical features even in terms of

---

* They were (in addition to the Bashkir and Turkestan republics): the Autonomous Tatar Socialist Soviet Republic (May 27, 1920); the Autonomous Chuvash Region (June 24, 1920); the Karelian Toilers' Commune (August 6, 1920); the Autonomous Kirghiz Socialist Soviet Republic (August 26, 1920); the Autonomous Region of the Mari People (November 25, 1920); the Autonomous Region of the Kalmyk People (November 25, 1920); the Autonomous Region of the Votiak People (January 5, 1921); the Autonomous Daghestan Socialist Soviet Republic (January 20, 1921); the Autonomous Gorskaia Socialist Soviet Republic (January 20, 1921); the Autonomous Region of Komi (Zyrians) (August 22, 1921); the Autonomous Crimean Socialist Soviet Republic (October 18, 1921); the Autonomous Mongol-Buriat Region (January 9, 1922); the United Karachaev-Cherkess Autonomous Region (January 12, 1922); the United Kabardino-Balkar Autonomous Region (January 16, 1922); the Autonomous Iakut Socialist Soviet Republic (April 20, 1922); the Autonomous Region of the Oirat People (June 1, 1922); the Cherkess (Adyghei) Autonomous Region (July 27, 1922). For this, see D. A. Magerovskii, *Soiuz Sovetskikh Sotsialisticheskikh Respublik* [Moscow, 1923], 16n.

Soviet law and were described by one Soviet authority as "national *gubernii*."[6] The antonomous republics, on the other hand, were regarded as endowed with a certain degree of political competence, although what the limits of this competence were posed a question that troubled the best legal minds of the time.[7]

The common feature of these autonomous units — regions and republics alike — was the fact that they came into being by decree of the All-Russian Central Executive Committee acting alone or in conjunction with the Council of People's Commissars of the RSFSR. The only exception to this rule was the Bashkir Republic founded, as we saw, in February 1919, by agreement between the government of the RSFSR and a group of Bashkir nationalists; but since the 1919 agreement was unilaterally abrogated fifteen months later with the introduction of the new Bashkir constitution on the orders of the Russian Soviet government, this exception cannot be said to have affected the general practice.

The origin of the autonomous states provided additional assurance that they would not infringe in any manner upon the centralized structure of Soviet political authority. "Autonomy means not separation," Stalin told the North Caucasians in 1920, "but a union of the self-ruling mountain peoples with the peoples of Russia."[8] Indeed, the main stress in the Communist interpretation of autonomy was on closer ties between the borderlands and Russia and on the enhancement of the authority and prestige of the Soviet regime in areas where nationalistic tendencies were deeply rooted. As Stalin's statement emphasized, autonomy was considered as an instrument of consolidation, not of decentralization.

As indicated in the sections dealing with the history of the borderlands during the Revolution and Civil War, the government of the RSFSR retained in the reconquered territories full control over the military, economic, financial, and foreign affairs of its autonomous states. These were granted competence only in such spheres of government activity as education, justice, public health, and social security; and even in these realms they were subject to the surveillance of the appropriate commissariats of the RSFSR as well as the local bureaus of the Russian Communist Party. The governments of the autonomous regions and republics, as one Soviet jurist correctly remarked, had more in common, from the point of view of authority and function, with the prerevolutionary Russian organs of self-rule, the so-called Provincial *zemstva*, than with the governments of genuine federal states.[9] There can be little doubt that the tradition of those institutions, introduced during the Great Reforms of the 1860's, had much to do with the evolution of Soviet concepts of autonomy.

The first attempt to consolidate the state apparatus of all the autonomous regions and republics was made in the early 1920's by the Commissariat of Nationality Affairs (Narkomnats or NKN). This commissariat, originally established to serve as an intermediary between the central Soviet organs and the minorities and to assist the government in dealing with problems of a purely "national" nature (which could not be too numerous, in view of the Communist attitude toward the entire problem of nationality and nationalism), had displayed little activity in 1919 and the first half of 1920. Stalin, its chairman, was absent; its vice-chairmen and higher functionaries were called in by the Soviet authorities to fill various posts in the reconquered borderlands; and the remaining borderland areas were largely in the zone of combat or under enemy occupation. As a result, the commissariat led only a nominal existence, publishing a weekly newspaper and occasionally engaging in propaganda activity.

In the spring of 1920 Stalin resumed the active chairmanship of the Commissariat of Nationality Affairs and began to transform it into a miniature federal government of the RSFSR. A decree issued on May 10, 1920, instructed all the national minority groups on the territory of the RSFSR to elect deputies to the Narkomnats.[10] This was intended to give the Commissariat a representative character and, in a sense, was the first step in the abandonment of the purely executive aspect of the Commissariat. On November 6, 1920, the Narkomnats decreed that it would assume jurisdiction over the agencies of the autonomous regions and republics which had been attached to the Central Executive Committee of the All-Russian Congress of Soviets.[11] In December 1920 the government of the RSFSR decreed that the Narkomnats was to open provincial branches and attach them to the Central Executive Committees of the autonomous regions and republics of the RSFSR.[12]

In April 1921 the executive officers of the Narkomnats, and the chairmen of the delegations from the autonomous regions and republics, were constituted into a new body, called the Council of Nationalities (*Sovet Natsional'nostei*).[13]

While undergoing all those important structural changes, the Commissariat of Nationality Affairs claimed for itself ever broader and greater powers. The November 1920 decree stated that no economic and political measures of the Soviet government applicable to the borderlands could become law unless approved by the Narkomnats, and that all the political organizations of the minorities were to deal with the central Soviet government only through their agencies at Narkomnats.[14] When, a month later, the Commissariat established its branch offices in the autonomous states, it gave them authority to participate in the activities of the Central Executive Committees of the autonomous regions and republics.[15] In the summer of 1922, the Narkomnats claimed that it had the right to supervise the other commissariats of the Soviet Russian government insofar as their activities affected the national minorities, that it represented the autonomous republics in all budgetary matters, and that it alone directed the education of the non-Russian party and state cadres.[16] In 1923, the forthcoming dissolution of the Narkomnats was justified by the fact that "it had completed its fundamental task of preparing the formation of the national republics and regions, and uniting them into a union of republics." [17]

Through such measures the Narkomnats was transformed from one of the minor ministries of the RSFSR into a federal government of the autonomous regions and republics of the RSFSR.[18] At least, so it was in theory. In reality, the role of the Narkomnats in the integration of the Soviet state was considerably smaller than its claims implied. The autonomous regions and republics had so little self-rule left that their formal merger in a federal institution had virtually no practical consequences. It was a measure of primarily bureaucratic significance. In 1924 the Commissariat was dissolved and its Council of Nationalities became, through the addition of representatives of the full-fledged Soviet republics, the second chamber of the legislative branch of the government of the USSR.

### Relations between the RSFSR and the Other Soviet Republics

One of the main reasons why the Communists found it necessary to differentiate constitutionally between the various conquered borderlands, forming some into autonomous regions or republics and others into Soviet or Union republics, was the fact that some of the borderlands which had separated themselves from Russia in 1917 and 1918 had entered during the period of their independence into diplomatic or military relations with foreign powers. Thus, the Ukraine had participated in the Brest Litovsk negotiations; Belorussia had dealt with Germany and with Poland; the Transcaucasian republics had signed treaties with Turkey, had maintained diplomatic missions abroad, and had been recognized *de facto* and *de jure* by the most important Western powers. In order to replace the diplomatic representatives of the overthrown borderland republics and to take over their foreign commitments, it was necessary to create the impression that the subjugated lands retained their independence even after Soviet conquest. Hence, a certain distinction was made in Soviet political theory and constitutional law between the non-Russian areas situated inland, out of contact with foreign powers, and those located on the fringes. The inland areas were formed into autonomous regions and republics, while the outlying ones were made into so-called Union republics. Constitutionally, the cardinal difference between the two types of political organization lay in the fact that the Union republics were recognized as sovereign and independent states, with a right to separate from the RSFSR, whereas the autonomous regions and republics were not. But inasmuch as the right to separation was acknowledged by Soviet leaders to apply primarily to nations living in the "capitalist" part of the world, and the mere mention of this right in connection with areas under Soviet control was regarded as *prima facie* evidence of counterrevolutionary activity, this constitutional distinction had no practical consequences whatsoever, although it did have some psychological ones.

Having been conquered from without, the borderland areas in the Union category presented specific problems of integration. In the first flush of the Revolution (1917–18), the Communist regimes which had arisen in the borderland areas such as the Ukraine, Belorussia, and the Baltic states, had assumed all the prerogatives of the governments which they had overthrown. The first Communist government of the Ukraine, for example, had had a Council of People's Commissars composed of thirteen members, including the Commissars of War, Labor, Means of Communication, and Finance.[19] A similar situation had prevailed in the other borderland areas occupied by the Communists at this time. These governments had, therefore, to be absorbed gradually. The spread of authority of the RSFSR over the republics in this category began in the autumn of 1918 and continued virtually without interruption until 1923.

The first move to integrate the administration of the Soviet republics lying outside the RSFSR with that of the RSFSR was taken in connection with the centralization of the Soviet military apparatus. On September 30, 1918, the VTsIK created a Revolutionary-Military Committee (*Revvoensovet*) of the Republic, under the chairmanship of Trotsky, to direct and coördinate the entire Soviet war effort against the White forces. The Revvoensovet was granted extraordinary authority in the combat zones and was empowered, somewhat ambiguously, to utilize all the resources of the Soviet state for the defense of the regime.[20] Its headquarters were in the railroad train which Trotsky used on his rapid inspections of the various sectors of the front endangered by the enemy. From there, Trotsky made requests for manpower and supplies to the vice-chairman of the Revvoensovet, who resided in Moscow and served as a liaison between him and the pertinent government agencies.[21]

To overcome the delays and other difficulties which such an informal arrangement between the military and civil authorities entailed, the Soviet government established on November 30, 1918, an organ which united all the agencies directly concerned with the prosecution of the war: the Council of Workers' and Peasants' Defense (*Sovet Rabochei i Krest'ianskoi Oborony*). This supreme administering body of war mobilization consisted of Lenin, Trotsky, Stalin, and representatives of the Commissariats of Communication (Commissar V. I. Nevskii), Provisions (Deputy Commissar N. P. Briukhanov), and the Extraordinary Commission for the Supply of the Red Army (Chairman L. B. Krasin). The decree establishing the Council instructed all the provincial Soviet institutions to obey the Council's directives.[22] From the point of view of the integration of the Soviet state, the importance of the Council lay in the fact that it exercised authority not only in the RSFSR, but also in Lithuania, Latvia, Belorussia, and the Ukraine; that is, in all those borderland areas where the Communists were in power at that time. The authority of the Council grew rapidly, especially in the Ukraine, which was for the major part of the Civil War an arena of military operations.

The question of formal relations between the government of the Soviet Ukraine and that of the RSFSR was raised in the early part of 1919, shortly after the Communists had dispersed the Directory at the Third Congress of the KP(b)U, held in March 1919 in Kharkov. The majority of the delegates agreed that the Ukraine and Russia should establish as close economic and administrative ties as possible. They also agreed that the Constitution of Soviet Ukraine should in all essential respects resemble that of Soviet Russia (adopted in 1918), with minor alterations to suit local conditions. However, Sverdlov, the representative of the Central Committee of the Russian Communist Party at the Congress, refused to approve even such a moderate view, insisting that the Constitution of the RSFSR was not merely a Russian one, but an international one, and therefore should be adopted by the Ukrainian Soviet Republic without any changes whatsoever.[23]

The relationships between the two governments were actually settled by a decree of the Central Committee of the Russian Communist Party, which was conveyed to the Ukrainian Communists by a directive dated April 24, 1919. According to this directive, the Ukrainian Commissariats of War and of the Means of Communication were to subordinate themselves fully to the corresponding ministries of the RSFSR; the Ukrainian Commissariats of National Economy and Food Supply were to be transferred from Kiev to Kharkov, where they could work under the direct supervision of Moscow and receive necessary funds directly, without requiring the services of the Ukrainian Soviet government; the Commissariat of State Control of the RSFSR was to extend its authority throughout the entire Ukraine; and finally, the Ukrainian railroads were to be directed by the Commissariat of Roads in Moscow.[24]

In May 1919 Trotsky arrived in the Ukraine and took over the government. He did away with the separate Ukrainian Red regiments, merging them with units of the Russian Red Army, and liquidated altogether the Ukrainian Commissariats of National Economy, Finance, and Means of Communications, transferring their functions to the local bureaus of the corresponding Russian commissariats.[25] In place of the Ukrainian Council of People's Commissars, which was, in effect, deprived of its *raison d'être* by the removal of its principal organs, Trotsky formed a local branch of the Russian Council of Workers' and Peasants' Defense. The Ukrainian Council had as chairman Rakovskii, and as deputy chairmen G. I. Petrovskii and A. A. Ioffe — persons unconnected with the Ukrainian Communist movement.[26] The measures put into practice in the Ukraine in the spring of 1919 were given broader validity in a decree of the Central Committee of the RKP of May 1919, which ordered the unification of all the Red Armies and railroad networks on the territories of the Ukraine, Latvia, Lithuania, Belorussia, and the RSFSR under the Council of Workers' and Peasants' Defense.[27]

A further step in the amalgamation of the RSFSR with the conquered borderlands was a decree of the VTsIK of June 1, 1919, called "On the Unification of the Soviet Republics of Russia, the Ukraine, Latvia, Lithuania, and Belorussia for the Struggle against World Imperialism." This decree deprived the enumerated non-Russian republics of their commissariats of War, National Economy, Railroads, Finance, and Labor, in favor of the corresponding commissariats of the RSFSR.[28] The decree broadened the authority which the RSFSR had enjoyed through the Council of Defense and embodied in the Soviet constitution legislation originally introduced as wartime emergency measures. The foundations of the state which eventually became the Union of Soviet Socialist Republics were thus laid not by agreement between the RSFSR and the individual, theoretically independent republics, but by decree of the Russian government. In this respect, therefore, there was little difference in the origins of the RSFSR and the USSR.

Another important similarity between the position of the autonomous states and the Soviet republics vis-à-vis the RSFSR was that in both instances the functions of federal government were vested not in a third power, separate and superior to the federating units, but in one of the states which itself was involved in the act of federation. The government of the RSFSR served as the highest state authority not only on its own territory, but also on the territories of the Ukraine, Belorussia, the Baltic states, Transcaucasia, and whatever other lands were conquered by Soviet troops.[29]

When, in 1920, the Communists conquered Azerbaijan, an area which, save for a brief period in the spring of 1918, had not been previously under their control, they found it desirable to establish interrepublican relations in a more formal manner. The discussions which ultimately led to the signing of a treaty between RSFSR and Azerbaijan were carried on between Lenin, Chicherin, and N. N. Krestinskii on the one side, and M. D. Guseinov and B. Shakhtakhtinskii on the other.[30] The treaty, signed on September 30, 1920, provided for the government of the RSFSR taking over the commissariats of War, Supply, Finance, Means of Transportation, and Communications, as well as all the organs regulating foreign trade and the internal economy. Significantly, it left Azerbaijan the right to retain its own commissariat of Foreign Affairs.[31] The treaty with Azerbaijan thus followed the pattern set by the decree of June 1, 1919.

On December 28, 1920, and January 16, 1921, the government of the

RSFSR signed identical treaties with the governments of Soviet Ukraine and Belorussia. The divisions of authority between the government of the RSFSR and the republican governments was substantially the same as that provided for by the treaty with Azerbaijan. In addition, it stipulated that the two republics would appoint representatives to the commissariats taken over by the RSFSR, and that the exact relationships between the government agencies of the contracting parties would be determined by separate agreements. The two republics were allowed to retain their commissariats of Foreign Affairs and were declared in the preamble to be "independent and sovereign" states. The signatory for the Ukrainian side was Khristian Rakovskii, who two years earlier had served as a representative of the Russian Soviet government in its negotiations with the Ukrainian Rada.[32]

In 1921 and 1922 the republics certainly did not treat the right to the maintenance of diplomatic relations as a formality. Azerbaijan, to mention one example, established full relations with six foreign countries, dispatched its representatives to Turkey and Persia, and accredited diplomatic representatives of Germany and Finland.[33] The other republics also maintained at that time active diplomatic relations and participated in international negotiations either jointly with Soviet Russia or, on occasion, separately.

Such was the situation on the eve of the Soviet conquest of Georgia, which rounded out Communist possessions in Transcaucasia. The integration of Georgia, however, proved a much more difficult task than had been the case with the other borderland areas. The patriotic fervor of the Georgians, as well as the existence in Georgia of a relatively strong and rooted Bolshevik organization, precluded a simple incorporation of that area into Soviet Russia. The Soviet government preferred to accomplish the integration of Georgia and the other Transcaucasian republics in two phases: first, it made them surrender political power to a newly created Transcaucasian Federation and then it made the Federation cede these powers to Moscow. This procedure was in part dictated by economic considerations (Transcaucasia having traditionally functioned as an economic unit) and in part by political ones, namely, the desire to neutralize potential national opposition to "Russification."

In fact, the device of incorporating the republics by means of a federation engendered such bitter resistance, especially in Georgia, that the story of the relations between the Transcaucasian republics and the RSFSR after February 1921 belongs more properly in that part of our narrative which deals with the opposition to centralization.

### The People's Republics

The only political formations under Communist control which, for a time at least, enjoyed self-rule in practice as well as in theory were the so-called People's Republics, of which there were three in 1922: Bukhara, Khorezm (Khiva), and the Far East. The agreement between Soviet Russia and the Khorezmian Soviet People's Republic — which was signed on September 13, 1920, and established the pattern for this type of relationship — granted the RSFSR on the territory of Khorezm certain economic privileges, such as the right to exploit natural resources, to import and export without the payment of tariffs, and to use Russian currency.[34] In all other respects, Khorezm remained an independent republic. A similar agreement was signed on March 4, 1921, with the Bukharan People's Soviet Republic,[35] and on February 17, 1922, with the Far Eastern Republic.[36] In all three of these states the rights of the RSFSR were limited to economic matters.

The self-rule acquired by the Khorezmian, Bukharan, and Far Eastern Republics by virtue of treaties with the RSFSR was not left intact for long. In the case of Khorezm and Bukhara, their autonomy under the Communists was not intended as a permanent deviation from the pattern established in other parts of the country, but rather as a temporary *de facto* recognition of the unique status which these principalities had enjoyed under tsarist rule. The Far Eastern Republic, on the other hand, was quite frankly established as a buffer state intended to keep out the Japanese. Its government was not formally Communistic, but represented an alliance of various "democratic" groups under Communist control. As soon as the Red Army entered Vladivostok in the wake of the evacuating Japanese, the Far Eastern Republic was abolished and its territory incorporated into that of the RSFSR (October–November, 1922).[37] In Khorezm and Bukhara, the Communists gradually increased their authority throughout 1922 and 1923. In 1924, the Soviet government abolished these two People's Republics and later distributed their land among the five new republics created in place of those of Turkestan and Kirghiz: Uzbek, Turkmen, Tajik, Kazakh, and Kirghiz.

### The Opposition to Centralization

The process of integration of the state apparatus encountered serious opposition in the borderlands from groups both inside and outside the Communist Party. This "nationalist deviation" of the early 1920's constituted a stormy chapter in the history of the formation of the Soviet Union. The opposition can be divided into two principal types. There was the resistance of groups which, having collaborated with the Communists for the sake of essentially nationalistic aims, became eventually disillusioned with Communism and turned against it. There was also the opposition of those who had taken seriously the slogans of national self-determination and federalism and, seeing them violated by Stalin and his associates, became defenders of decentralization and states' rights. The former fought for nationalism, the latter for Communism. No collaboration between these two groups was possible, and hence opposition to centralization proved in the end ineffectual.

### Nationalist Opposition: Enver Pasha and the Basmachis

The Soviet conquest of Bukhara (September 1920) reinvigorated the Basmachi movement, which had begun to subside somewhat with the introduction by the Communists of a policy of economic and religious concessions in the first half of 1920. At first the Red Armies had little difficulty in conquering the mountainous sectors of the Bukharan principality, where the population, dissatisfied with the regime of the deposed Emir, was willing to accept a change in rule. But as soon as the Reds began to evacuate Eastern Bukhara, entrusting authority to native militias, various Basmachi chieftains appeared and took those territories back from the Communists. In the fall of 1921 most of Eastern Bukhara was in the hands of rebels. They were supplied with arms and personnel by the deposed Emir, who had fled to Afghanistan to continue from there the struggle for his throne.

Before long the Soviet regime also suffered setbacks in Western Bukhara. The two groups with whose assistance the Communists had come to power and to whom they entrusted the reins of government in the republic — the Young Bukharans and Young Bukharan Communists — disagreed sharply over the relations of the Bukharan Republic with Soviet Russia. The Young Bukharans, composed largely of liberals associated with pre-1917 jadidism, resented Communist penetration into Bukharan institutions and their meddling in local affairs. They complained that the new regime had brought "seven emirs" in the place of one — a reference to the seven commissars (nazirs) who comprised the all-powerful government of the Bukharan Republic.[38] The Young Bukharan Communists, on the other hand, among whom the younger, more radical elements predominated, coöperated fully with the Communists and strove for a closer integration of Bukhara with the Soviet system.

In the fall of 1921, when such internal difficulties threatened to upset Soviet authority in the Bukharan Republic, Enver Pasha, one of the leaders of the defunct Young Turkish government of Turkey, appeared in Turkestan.

Enver, who had acquired great fame throughout the Moslem world for his victories over the Italians in the African War of 1911–12, escaped at the end of World War I from Turkey to Germany. An ambitious man, endowed with a vivid imagination and undaunted personal courage (though quarrelsome and politically unskilled), Enver had little taste for the life of an émigré which the Turkish defeat had imposed on him. After a brief stay in Berlin, he decided to join his one-time associates Nuri Pasha, Dzhemal Pasha, and Halil Pasha, who had gone into the Soviet service. Hostile to England, he found in the anti-British policy pursued by the Soviet regime in 1920 an opportunity to play once more an active part in Middle Eastern politics. Enver arrived in Moscow in the fall of 1920, following a forced plane landing and brief detention in Riga. In September he attended the Baku Congress of Eastern Peoples sponsored by the Third International, where he presented a memorandum, denouncing his own role in the First World War and pledging the Communists his support in the struggle against "Western imperialism." [39]

Enver spent most of 1921 in Transcaucasia, first in Baku and then, after the Communists had conquered Georgia, in Batum. Apparently he desired to reside as near the Turkish frontier as possible, to be in a position to assume leadership in Turkey. In the fall of that year the Soviet government decided to exploit his popularity among Moslems and to send him to Central Asia to help fight the Basmachis. Experience had shown that much success could be achieved by employing one-time Turkish officers to win the sympathies of natives for the Soviet cause.[40] At the same time, Dzhemal Pasha, who had resided in Tashkent since August 1920, was sent on a diplomatic mission to Afghanistan, probably to prevail on the Afghan authorities to stop the Emir of Bukhara and other Turkestani refugees from using that country as a supply base for the Basmachis.*

Enver arrived in Bukhara at the beginning of November 1921. It did not take him long to perceive that he could achieve greater glory by joining the native dissidents than by continuing his ambivalent and uncertain role as a Communist agent. The Basmachi movement was as divided as ever after the failure of an attempt made earlier in the year to unite all the rebel groups under one leader.[41] The Khivan Basmachis were led by Dzhunaid Khan; those of the Samarkand district by Akhil Bek, Karakul Bek, and several other kurbachis; a chieftain named Hamdan ruled the district around Khodzhent; the Ferghana Basmachis were quarreling with each other, and so bitter were the rivalries there that, in some cases, partisan leaders resorted to assassination or went over to the Communists to help destroy their opponents. Even in Eastern Bukhara, where the Emir and his chief lieutenant, Ibrahim Bek, claimed full authority, there were numerous independent partisan leaders, who looked with disfavor upon the deposed monarch.[42] Another source of weakness of the Basmachi rebellion, in addition to the rivalry of individual chieftains, was tribal feuding. Basmachi units of different ethnic origin were at times as busy warring with each other as they were fighting the Communists. Especially bitter was the hostility between the Kirghiz and the Uzbeks, and between the Turkmens and Uzbeks.[43]

It seemed to Enver that all that was needed to transform the genuine

* Der Neue Orient, VI (1922), 1–4. Dzhemal never reached Afghanistan, having been assassinated in Tiflis by an Armenian who sought revenge for the massacres of 1915–16.

and deep-seated dissatisfaction, evident in all parts of Central Asia, into a vast and successful movement for the liberation of all of Turkestan, was the appearance of a personality able to overcome the disunity of Basmachestvo. Enver apparently counted on his personal popularity with the Moslem population and on the appeal of his Pan-Turanian ideology, of which he had long been an avid exponent, to unite the rebel leaders and to stop the intertribal rivalries. With the boldness characteristic of his entire career, he decided, shortly after his arrival in Turkestan, to desert the Communist regime and to defect to the Basmachis. Sometime in November 1921, he left Bukhara with a small retinue, ostensibly to take part in a hunt. In reality he made straight for the headquarters of Ibrahim Bek. With him deserted some of the most prominent members of the Bukharan government, including its chairman, Osman Khodzha, and the Commissars of Interior and of War.[44]

The Basmachis at first received Enver coolly, fearing a Communist snare and suspicious of the jadidist group which accompanied him. But the Emir of Bukhara, with whom Enver had entered into a correspondence, instructed Ibrahim Bek to utilize Enver's military skills and to place him in command of the rebel armies fighting in Eastern Bukhara.[45] Establishing his headquarters in the mountains of Bukhara, Enver began to gather around himself some of the independent chieftains operating in that area. His greatest success occurred early in 1922 when he captured Diushambe. From there he was able to impose his authority on the adjoining towns and villages. In the spring, having built up his force to an army of several thousand men, he began to attack Baisun, which obstructed the road to Western Bukhara and prevented him from spreading to the plains of Turkestan, but despite numerous charges he could not capture it.

Notwithstanding his initial triumphs, Enver failed to rally the bulk of the Basmachi forces to his leadership. He was merely another war lord, ruling a small territory and engaging in fights with neighboring chiefs. Of the sixteen thousand rebels active in Eastern Bukhara no more than three thousand owed him allegiance.[46] Great damage to Enver's cause resulted from his disagreements with the Emir and Ibrahim Bek. Enver was too ambitious to be content with mere partisan warfare, and so he interfered as well with the political life of non-Communist Bukhara. He tried to establish control over all the Basmachi units operating in Eastern Bukhara and incited the native population to expel all the Europeans from Central Asia.[47] In May 1922, he sent an "ultimatum" to the government of Soviet Russia (through Nariman Narimanov, chairman of the government of Soviet Azerbaijan), in which he demanded the immediate withdrawal of all Russian troops from Turkestan, offering in return to assist the Communists in their Middle Eastern activities.[48] Before long he completely lost all political judgment and, when issuing decrees affecting the civil life of Eastern Bukhara without the consent of the Emir, he signed himself "Commander in Chief of all the Islamic troops, son-in-law of the Caliph, and representative of the Prophet." *

Such behavior aroused the suspicions of the Emir, who was altogether none too pleased with the association between the Turkish general and the jadidist defectors from Soviet rule, such as Osman Khodzha, who only recently had been his worst enemies. In the summer of 1922, relations between the headquarters of Enver, located near Diushambe, and those of Ibrahim Bek, situated among the Lakai (a Turkic group, settled among the Iranian Tajiks), came near the breaking point. Soon, the Emir began to withhold support from Enver. On at least one occasion when Enver was hard pressed in combat, Ibrahim Bek refused to come to his assistance.[49] Later in the summer of 1922, the Afghan tribesmen who had been sent to his aid were ordered back to their homeland. Without the wholehearted support of the Emir, Enver was doomed. It is difficult to determine which played a larger part in his failure: his unwise handling of the Emir, or the struggle between the conservatives, represented by the Emir, and the progressive jadidists, of which he had become an unwitting victim. In August 1922, Enver was killed in combat with Red troops, who had surprised him and his small detachment in the mountains. His death ended all hope of a consolidation of the Basmachi forces.

To the Communist authorities the defection of Enver and the spread of the Basmachi revolt to Bukhara demonstrated conclusively that neither the policy of mere military suppression, tried between 1917 and 1920 and in 1921–22, nor the palliative measures tried in 1920–21 were sufficient to bring order to Central Asia. It was necessary to reverse completely the basic economic and political policies of the regime. Consequently, while undertaking a general military offensive against the Basmachis in Bukhara and other parts of Central Asia, the *Turkbiuro* of the Central Committee of the RKP and the *Turkomissia* introduced, in 1922, a series of far-reaching reforms. The most unpopular legislation of the previous rule was abrogated: the *vakuf* lands, previously confiscated for the benefit of the state, were returned to the Moslems; the religious schools, *medresse* and *mektebe*, were reopened; the *shariat* courts were brought back.[50] After these religious concessions, economic concessions were also granted. The New Economic Policy permitted the return of private trade and put an end to the forcible requisitions of food and cotton which had played a considerable part in arousing popular ire against the Communists.[51]

All these concessions had a pacifying effect on Central Asia. The natives, having suffered from the Civil War longer than the other inhabit-

---

* Soloveichik, "Revoliutsionnaia Bukhara," 284. Enver actually was a son-in-law of the Caliph, having married, prior to World War I, the daughter of the Sultan, who was recognized as the Caliph by the Sunni Moslems.

ants of the Soviet state, were eager for peace. As soon as the Communist regime had made it possible for them to return to their traditional ways of life, the Central Asian Moslems gave up the struggle. The entire resistance movement known as Basmachestvo had been not so much an embodiment of a positive political or social philosophy as a desperate reaction to ill-treatment and abuse of authority, and it collapsed as soon as these irritants were removed.

The economic and religious concessions of the Communists deprived the Basmachi movement of its popular support and permitted the authorities first to localize and then to suppress it entirely. In the fall of 1922 the Ferghana rebels were wiped out. Although Ibrahim Bek continued to resist until 1926, when he fled to Afghanistan, the backbone of resistance in Bukhara was also broken by 1923. In Samarkand, however, the Red Army had to fight regular campaigns, supported by airplanes and tanks, as late as 1924.[52] Cut off from the population, the Basmachis reverted once more to brigandage, losing entirely the socio-economic and political character which they had acquired temporarily in the course of the Civil War.*

### Nationalist-Communist Opposition: Sultan-Galiev

Another form of nationalistic opposition occurred within the ranks of the Communist Party itself. Prominent in it were non-Russians of radical views who had joined the Communist movement in the course of the Revolution because of their conviction that the establishment of a socialist economy would more or less automatically lead to the destruction of all national oppression. Their nationalism, though tempered and molded by social radicalism, was not entirely dominated by it. When their faith in the ability of the new order to eliminate national inequalities had been shattered by the experiences of the Civil War period, Communists of this type sought redress in nationalism and independence from Moscow. The most important exponent of this tendency was the Tatar Communist, Sultan-Galiev. His quarrel with the party in 1922–23 became a *cause célèbre*, a test case which opened a heated discussion of the entire national question in the Soviet Union.

Sultan-Galiev had had much opportunity in his capacity as a high official in the Commissariat of Nationality Affairs to observe the effects of Soviet rule on the Moslem population. He was in contact with the Tatar Republic, where, as the leader of the right-wing Communist faction, he enjoyed considerable personal following; he had been sent to

---

* Basmachestvo flared up again in the early 1930's, when it became a rallying point for native opposition to Soviet collectivization. Cf. Ryskulov, *Kirgizstan*, 66–67. Ibrahim Bek, who at that time returned from Afghanistan to lead rebel detachments, was finally captured and executed by the Communists in June 1931; cf. Observer [Jeyhoun Bey Hajibeyli], "Soviet Press Comments on the Capture of Ibrahim Bey," *The Asiatic Review* (London), XXVII, no. 92 (1931), 682–92.

inspect and report on the situation of the Moslem population in the Crimea; and he had had many opportunities to meet and confer with important Moslem Communists and nationalists from Central Asia and other borderland areas. The total impression was so discouraging that Sultan-Galiev began to doubt whether the assumptions which had originally led him to embrace Communism had been sound. As early as 1919, in conversation with his Volga Tatar colleagues, he had expressed doubt whether the world-wide class struggle which the Russian Revolution had unleashed would really improve the lot of the colonial and semi-colonial peoples of the East. The industrial proletariat, he now suspected, was interested less in liberating the exploited colonial peoples from imperialism, than in taking over for its own benefit the entire colonial system. From the point of view of the nonindustrial, colonial peoples, the proletariat's seizure of power would signify a mere change of masters. The English or French proletariats would find it advantageous to retain their country's colonial possessions and to continue the previous exploitation.[53]

Sultan-Galiev did not at first apply those ideas to Soviet Russia and coöperated with the Communist regime for at least two more years after he had first begun to question the inherent ability of the proletariat to solve the national question in the East. It was apparently under the impact of the New Economic Policy that he finally lost all hope in Communism. The NEP, which improved the material situation of the native population, also returned to positions of power the classes which he and other Moslem Communists had identified with the old colonial regime: Russian merchants and officials, as well as Moslem tradesmen and clergymen. Sultan-Galiev viewed the establishment of the NEP as the first formal step in a return to pre-1917 conditions and as the beginning of the liquidation of the socialist revolution in Russia; it increased his skepticism concerning the industrial proletariat's ability to liberate the world's oppressed nations.

He now began to draw broader theoretical conclusions from the evidence provided by four years of Communist rule. The economic inequalities of the world, he argued, could be eradicated not by a victory of the proletariat over the bourgeoisie but by the establishment of the hegemony of the backward areas over the industrialized ones. The war against the imperialism of industrialized societies, not the war against the bourgeoisie: this was the real conflict for universal liberation.

> We maintain that the formula which offers the replacement of the world-wide dictatorship of one class of European society (the bourgeoisie) by its antipode (the proletariat), i.e., by another of its classes, will not bring about a major change in the social life of the oppressed segment of humanity. At any rate, such a change, even if it were to occur, would be not for the better but for the worse . . . In contradistinction to this we advance another thesis: the idea that the mate-

rial premises for a social transformation of humanity can be created only through the establishment of the dictatorship of the colonies and semi-colonies over the metropolitan areas.[54]

Such views struck at the very heart of the Marxist doctrine, but as long as Sultan-Galiev spread them only among his close associates, the Central Committee, which could not have been unaware of the trend of his thought, did not interfere. In the summer of 1921, as a matter of fact, the left-wing faction that had controlled the Volga Tatar Communist party and state apparatus was ousted, and the rightists took over. The chairmanship of the Tatar Council of People's Commissars was assumed by Keshshaf Mukhtarov, a friend and follower of Sultan-Galiev.[55] Soon, however, Sultan-Galiev began to make political demands as well. He advocated the creation of a Colonial International which would unite all the victims of colonial exploitation and would counterbalance the Third International, dominated by Western elements. He also desired the establishment of a Soviet Moslem (or Turkic) republic and the revival of the Moslem Communist Party, destroyed in 1918 by the Central Committee of the RKP.[56] At this point the heavy hand of party discipline fell on his shoulder.*

Sultan-Galiev was arrested in April or May 1923 on the order of Stalin, his immediate superior and former protector.[57] His case was discussed at a special conference of representatives of minorities which gathered in Moscow in June 1923. The charges against him were presented by Stalin, who stated that whereas the shortage of adequate party cadres had compelled the Communists to coöperate with Moslem nationalists in the borderlands, the Soviet regime would not tolerate treason. Stalin specifically accused Sultan-Galiev of collaboration with the Basmachis, with Validov, and with other Moslem nationalists fighting against the Soviet regime. Sultan-Galiev, according to Stalin, "confessed his guilt fully, without concealment, and having confessed, repented." [58] †

Despite his repentance, Sultan-Galiev was expelled from the Communist Party. According to Lev Kamenev, he was the first prominent party member purged on orders from Stalin.‡

* It is impossible to determine from Soviet sources whether Sultan-Galiev had held all of the views here presented before 1923; most of the materials pertaining to his case date from the time of his re-arrest in 1929–30 and fail to indicate the date of his various pronouncements and writings. Nevertheless, the data of the pre-1923 period indicates that at the time of his first arrest he had already held most of the views with which he was charged in 1930. See A. Bennigsen and Ch. Quelquejay, *Les Mouvements nationaux chez les Musulmans de Russie — le "sultan-galievisme" au Tatarstan* (Paris-The Hague, 1960), 126–71.

† In 1934 he was accused of having founded in 1920 with the help of Validov, Baitursunov, and others, an illegal party dedicated to the seizure of political and educational institutions on the territory of Moslem republics, the overthrow of the Soviet government, and the establishment of a "bourgeois pan-Turkic state." *Pravda Vostoka* (Tashkent), 16 and 18 December, 1934, cited in Bennigsen, *Les Mouvements*, 167–68.

‡ Trotsky, *Stalin*, 417. Sultan-Galiev was re-arrested and imprisoned in November

### Communist Opposition: the Ukraine

The characteristic quality of the opposition to centralization in the Ukraine as well as in Georgia derived from the fact that nationalism in both these areas was not so much a cause as a consequence. The leaders of the opposition here were old and tried Bolsheviks, often with a record of outspoken hostility to nationalism in any form. If in 1922 and 1923 they became identified with the ideals of states' rights, it is largely because they perceived behind the process of centralization the growth of a new Russian bureaucracy and the personal ascendancy of Stalin and his coterie. The tenuous guarantees secured by the republics by decree and treaty became for them now bulwarks against the encroachments of a new breed of official whom the Revolution was supposed to have destroyed once and for all. While an Enver Pasha or even a Sultan-Galiev collaborated with Communism because Communism seemed best to further their national goals, men like Mykola Skrypnik, Rakovskii, Mdivani, or Makharadze turned nationalist in order to safeguard Communism.

The "nationalist deviation" in the Ukraine arose principally because of the failure of Moscow to adhere to the terms of the treaty of December 28, 1920. That treaty, it will be recalled, established an economic and military union between the RSFSR and the Soviet Ukraine. The Ukraine surrendered to the RSFSR certain commissariats (Army and Navy, Foreign Trade, Finance, Labor, Means of Communication, Post and Telegraphs, and the Higher Economic Council), but was recognized, in return, as a sovereign and independent republic. The commissariats of the RSFSR had no right to issue directives to their Ukrainian counterparts without the sanction of the Ukrainian Sovnarkom (*Sovet Narodnykh Komissarov* or Council of People's Commissars); nor could they interfere at all with the commissariats left within the competence of the republic. The Ukrainian republic also retained the right to maintain its own commissariat of Foreign Affairs and to enter into diplomatic relations with foreign powers.[59]

It takes no expertise in the theory of federalism to realize that such an arrangement could not work. A country formally recognized as sovereign and independent, and engaged in foreign relations, could hardly allow another power to direct its internal affairs. Conversely, the officials of the government of the RSFSR, accustomed to treating all the territories of the old empire as one, had neither the experience nor the mental habits required to show respect for the intricacies of federal relations. As a result, the elaborate provisions of the 1920 treaty — which at least some officials in the Ukraine interpreted in good faith — remained a dead letter.

---

1929; after that date he vanished. Cf. *Pravda,* November/December 1929, *passim;* *Izvestiia,* 5 November 1929.

The clauses of the treaty, calling for mixed commissions to work out in detail the relations between the Russian and Ukrainian commissariats, were never actually carried out.[60] Throughout 1921 and the first half of 1922, the Sovnarkom and VTsIK of the RSFSR treated the Ukraine as if it were an intrinsic part of the RSFSR. It neither admitted Ukrainian representatives to the commissariats, as provided by the treaty, nor submitted to the Ukrainian Sovnarkom for approval directives to the Ukrainian commissariats.[61] Indeed, in most cases the Russian commissariats did not even trouble to consult their Ukrainian counterparts. The Ukrainians, naturally, protested against such violations of the treaty, but without effect. Their anger increased on occasions when Moscow issued directives to organs which the treaty left fully within the competence of the republic, such as the commissariats of agriculture and justice.[62] And when in May 1922 the Russian Commissariat of Foreign Affairs (probably in connection with the conferences at Genoa or Rapallo) infringed on the international status of the Ukrainian republic, the Ukrainian government sent to Moscow a formal protest, in which it objected to the presumption of the Russian government to speak in its name.[63]

In response to this note, the Central Committee of the Russian Communist Party appointed on May 11, 1922, a mixed commission, headed by Frunze, to investigate the Ukrainian complaint. The commission held two meetings in the course of the month. The main result of its deliberations was a resolution whose lengthy title conveys its contents: "On the inadmissibility of any measures which would lead in practice to the liquidation of the Ukrainian Soviet Socialist Republic, and to the reduction of the powers of its Central Committee, Council of People's Commissars, and central organs." [64] The commission condemned the Russian Commissariat of Foreign Affairs for having violated Ukrainian sovereignty and drafted several agreements between the commissariats of the two republics.[65] But it did not solve the more fundamental problems affecting Russo-Ukrainian relations. Violations of Ukrainian constitutional rights continued. In September 1922, for example, the Commissariat of Education of the RSFSR issued an order applicable to the Ukraine, even though education was entirely within the competence of the latter.[66]

The chief spokesman of the Ukrainian grievances was M. Skrypnik. Little in his background pointed to his becoming the leader of the nationalist opposition in the Ukrainian Communist movement. Although born in the Ukraine, he had moved in 1900, at the age of 28, to St. Petersburg to attend the Technological Institute, and from then until 1917 he had resided in Russia or Siberia. He was an old Marxist, having joined the movement in 1897. After the split in the party in 1903 he had associated himself with the Bolsheviks and had worked for Lenin on various important assignments, including for a time as editor of *Pravda*. In October 1917, he had served on the Revolutionary Committee which directed the

Bolshevik *coup d'état* in St. Petersburg. During 1918 and 1919, as a high Soviet official in the Ukraine, he had taken a "centrist" position between the pro-Ukrainian and pro-Moscow factions. The fact that in 1919 he had been appointed head of the department of the Cheka charged with fighting "counter-revolutionary movements," and in 1920 had been made Commissar of the Interior of the Ukraine, testifies to Lenin's having complete confidence in him.[67]

Skrypnik watched with apprehension and anger the utter disrespect which the Russian party and state apparatus showed for the Ukrainian republic. The violations of the 1920 treaty, related above, convinced him that a powerful faction in the Russian apparatus actually wanted to liquidate his republic and, being an outspoken man, he did not hesitate to make his views known. During the discussion of the nationality question at the Eleventh Party Congress, which met in March 1922, he delivered a brief but very pointed criticism of the party's Ukrainian policy. Referring to Lenin's statement that the Communists would emancipate the oppressed peoples of the whole world, Skrypnik said that they would achieve this aim only if they began to do so at home. The Communist party apparatus, in his opinion, was infiltrated with adherents of *Smena vekh*,* ready to violate the party's solemn pledge proclaiming the Ukraine independent. "The one and indivisible Russia is not our slogan," he exclaimed — at which point a voice from the audience, however, shouted back ominously: "The one and indivisible Communist Party!"[68]

Skrypnik had occasion to make his views heard both at the Twelfth Party Congress (of which later) and at the special party conference which discussed the case of Sultan-Galiev. At this latter meeting, he took issue with Stalin's analysis of what came to be known as "sultangalievshchina." Sultan-Galiev's actions, he said, were a symptom of a grave disease affecting Communism, a disease caused by the failure of the Communists to carry out their national program, and particularly by their inability or unwillingness to check the growth of Great Russian chauvinism in the party and state apparatus. Sultan-Galiev was merely a scapegoat for the failures of others. The proper way to prevent the emergence of nationalist deviations, according to Skrypnik, was to destroy the national inequalities and injustices present in the Soviet system.†

It is not possible to discover in Skrypnik's speeches or writings anything like a concrete ideology. His opposition was that of a convinced Communist who saw nationalism as a legacy of capitalism, and, dis-

---

* *Smena vekh* was a book published in 1921 in Prague by a group of émigrés. It praised the Communist regime for having fulfilled Russia's great national mission.

† M. Skrypnyk, *Stati i promovi* (Kharkov, 1931), II, pt. 2, 15–21. The full stenographic records of this conference, *Chetvertoe soveshchanie TsK RKP s otvetstvennymi rabotnikami natsional'nykh respublik i oblastei — Stenograficheskii otchet* (Moscow, 1923), in which the speeches of Stalin and Skrypnik originally appeared, were unfortunately not available to me.

mayed by its persistence under Communism, fought as best he could for Ukrainian autonomy. His uncompromising position made him many enemies in Moscow. In 1933, threatened with expulsion from the party, he committed suicide.[69]

### Communist Opposition: Georgia

The bitter conflict which broke out in Georgia almost immediately upon the establishment of Soviet rule there, and which lasted until the death of Lenin three years later, involved questions of both policy and personality. On the level of policy the main issue was one of authority: What was the power of the Kavbiuro, as an agency of the Russian Central Committee, over the Central Committees of the republican Communist parties? The leaders of these parties, especially those of the most powerful of them, the Communist Party of Georgia, were quite prepared to subordinate themselves to the directives of Moscow; but they were not willing to do the bidding of the Caucasian Bureau of the Central Committee, headed by the high-handed Ordzhonikidze. Their differences with the Kavbiuro came to a head over the establishment of a Transcaucasian federation, conceived in Moscow and executed by Ordzhonikidze, which threatened to deprive the three Transcaucasian republics of their independence and to transform them into something like the autonomous republics of the RSFSR. It was not long before a dispute over matters of policy transformed itself into a vicious personal feud between two groups of Georgian Communists: the Moscow group, represented by Ordzhonikidze and his supporter, Stalin, and the local, Tiflis group, headed by Mdivani. Lenin at first backed the former, but with time, as we shall see, changed his mind and became so angered by Stalin's and Ordzhonikidze's Caucasian activities that he contemplated taking disciplinary action against them.

On May 21, 1921, the RSFSR and the Georgian Soviet Republic signed a formal treaty modeled on the treaty with Azerbaijan, which recognized Georgia's "sovereignty and independence." The treaty established a military and economic union (but not a political one) between the two republics and provided that the exact arrangements on the merger of commissariats would be worked out by separate agreements. Implicitly, Georgia was allowed to retain its foreign representations, armed forces, and currency.[70]

Yet even before the treaty had been signed, the authorities in Moscow indicated that they were not prepared to respect the sovereignty of the Transcaucasian republics, so solemnly proclaimed on various occasions. Lenin was anxious to achieve quickly the economic unification of Transcaucasia and particularly to integrate the Georgian transport facilities with those of Azerbaijan and Armenia with which they had been traditionally linked. He accordingly instructed Ordzhonikidze on April 9, 1921, to establish a single economic organization for all of Transcaucasia.[71] Ordzhonikidze began by merging the railroad network, the postal and telegraphic services, and the organs of foreign trade. In so doing, he did not consult the Central Committees of the republican parties, causing the Georgian Communists to protest to Moscow.[72]

In the summer of 1921, having concluded that economic integration was not possible without a political one, the Kavbiuro proceeded to lay the foundations for a Transcaucasian federation. To prepare the ground for what promised to be a delicate undertaking, Stalin was dispatched in early July to Tiflis. He was present at the meeting of the Kavbiuro which passed a resolution approving the federation. He also delivered a rather mild, reasonably worded speech in which he pointed out all the reasons for establishing a "certain degree of unity" between the RSFSR and Transcaucasia, but at the same time hastened to assure his audience that there was no intention of depriving the republics of their independence. In his talk he did say a few words, clearly directed at the Georgians, about the dangers of nationalism, but even they were quite conciliatory in tenor; and when some Communists from Baku accused Mdivani and Kote Tsintsadze, members of the Georgian Central Committee, of "nationalist deviationism" Stalin denied that this was the case.[73]

The Georgian Communists were unimpressed by the conciliatory tone of Stalin's words. Convinced that Stalin and Ordzhonikidze, with the support of some Armenian and Azerbaijani Communists, were in fact encroaching upon Georgian sovereignty, they openly disregarded the various measures which the Kavbiuro took to integrate their republic with the rest of the country. On at least one occasion Mdivani and his group sent a personal protest to the TsK (Central Committee) in Moscow.[74]

In view of this situation, it is not surprising that when on November 3, 1921, on instructions from Moscow, the Kavbiuro passed a formal resolution proclaiming the necessity of establishing a Transcaucasian federation, the Georgians protested most violently. The Kavbiuro took its decision without prior consultation of the republican Central Committees — a procedure which was improper as well as tactless. For the federation envisaged by the Kavbiuro was not only a military and economic one, but also a political one. It meant that the three republics surrendered the "independence and sovereignty" guaranteed them by their treaties with the RSFSR, and became in effect transformed into autonomous republics of a federation whose own relations with the RSFSR were not spelled out.[75]

The response was swift. Mdivani, speaking for a growing faction of the Georgian Communists, sent Lenin a personal message in which he predicted that if Ordzhonikidze persisted in forcing through the federation, Transcaucasia would rise in rebellion.[76] This time the opposition was not confined to the Georgians, however. Two young members of the Azerbaijani party, R. Akhundov and M. D. Guseinov, also advised Lenin against carrying out the federation at that time;[77] * and so did M. Frunze, who could not be accused of any local interests.[78] The strength of the opposition was such that Lenin decided to reverse himself. On November 28, 1921, he issued a directive stating that while the Transcaucasian federation was necessary, it seemed premature; and that before being put into effect, it ought to be widely popularized in the Caucasus.[79]

The failure of the projected federation, on which Ordzhonikidze had pinned his hopes of smothering his Georgian opponents, certainly did not improve relations between the Georgian Central Committee and the Kavbiuro. The numerous political intrigues in which the two bodies engaged in their bitter rivalry need not detain us. Suffice it to say that the Kavbiuro, enjoying the support of Moscow, always had the upper hand, and the Georgians had to confine themselves to dilatory tactics.

In line with Lenin's instructions the Kavbiuro undertook in the winter of 1921–22 a propaganda campaign to persuade the population of the advantages of the projected federation. At the very same time, the Georgian government and Central Committee did everything in their power to keep the Kavbiuro from interfering in internal Georgian affairs. Early in January 1922, the Revolutionary-Military Committee of the Georgian Republic issued a decree proclaiming that, until the convocation of the First Congress of Soviets of the Republic, it claimed full and exclusive authority on the territory of the republic.[80] And the First Congress of Soviets of Georgia, meeting toward the end of February, approved a constitution of the republic which stated that "the Socialist Soviet Republic of Georgia was a sovereign state which did not permit any foreign power whatever to exercise equal authority on its territory." On the subject of the relations between Georgia and the other Soviet republics it was pointedly ambiguous. The constitution stated that when the "conditions for its creation came about" Georgia would join the International Socialist Soviet Republic; until then it expected to maintain "close" political and economic relations with the existing Soviet republics.[81]

Notwithstanding Georgian opposition, the Kavbiuro (renamed in February the Transcaucasian Regional Committee, or *Zakraikom*) proclaimed on March 12, 1922, the establishment of the Federal Union of the Soviet Socialist Republics of Transcaucasia (*Federativnyi Soiuz Sovetskikh Sotsialisticheskikh Respublik Zakavkaz'ia*, or FSSSRZ). The constitution of the federation provided that a Plenipotentiary Conference of representatives of the three federating republics elect as its supreme executive organ a Union Council (*Soiuznyi Sovet*). The Union Council had competence over the following spheres of governmental activity: military, finan-

* Both were executed in 1938.

cial, foreign affairs, foreign trade, transport, communications, organized combat against the counterrevolution (i.e., Cheka), and direction of the economy. Absolute control of the economy rested in a Higher Economic Council (*Vysshyi Ekonomicheskii Sovet*), which was to function as a permanent committee of the Union Council. The republics were allowed to retain their foreign legations and certain privileges in matters of tariffs and currency. They also were recognized as remaining legally independent and sovereign. The important matter of relations between the new federation and the RSFSR was to be left to be regulated by a separate agreement.[82]

The proclamation of the Transcaucasian union left little doubt in anyone's mind that the days of Georgian "independence and sovereignty" were numbered. The Central Committee of the Communist Party of Georgia commissioned, in December 1921, its most respected member, Makharadze, to address a memorandum to the Central Committee of the RKP expressing its principal grievances. In it Makharadze charged that the Georgian Communists had not been informed of the intention of Moscow to invade Georgia in February 1921, and for that reason had not been able to stage an internal uprising which would have prevented the entire coup against the Mensheviks from acquiring the character of a foreign invasion. Furthermore he alleged that the Kavbiuro had ignored the Georgian Central Committee and Revkom and thus had failed to win the sympathies of the Georgian population for the Soviet cause; that Ordzhonikidze had disobeyed Lenin's directives concerning the gentle treatment of the population, the creation of a Georgian Red Army, and a moderate economic policy; and that he had refused to take the Georgian Central Committee into his confidence in the matter of the proposed federation. Makharadze urged in conclusion that the process of federating the three Transcaucasian republics be considerably slowed down.*

### Formulation of Constitutional Principles of the Union

The opposition in the Communist apparatus of the Ukraine and Georgia, particularly intense in the spring of 1922, induced the Central Committee to review the system of relations between the RSFSR and the other Soviet republics. This system had so far evolved haphazardly, by means of bilateral treaties. It not only failed to define with the necessary precision the division of authority between the Russian and republican governments, but confused matters by assigning to the government of the RSFSR functions involving at one and the same time the RSFSR

---

* I secured a copy of this report from the Archive of the deposed government of the Georgian Republic. Its authenticity cannot be doubted; charges made in it were repeated by Makharadze at the Twelfth Party Congress of the RKP and also can be verified from other sources.

and the federation as a whole. Soviet Russia's entrance on the international diplomatic scene in the spring of 1922 made the need for normalizing relations between the center and the borderlands more urgent than ever. Clearly, Moscow's international position was not strengthened by its recognition of Ukrainian, Belorussian, and Transcaucasian independence. The time had come to supplement the economic and military unions of 1920–21 with a tighter political one.

Which precise event caused the Central Committee on August 10, 1922, to appoint a constitutional commission is a matter of controversy. Frunze hinted that it was the dispute with the Ukraine over foreign policy.[83] Ordzhonikidze, on the other hand, claimed that the commission was convened on the initiative of Stalin and himself in connection with the Georgian affair.[84] Georgian matters seem to have had something to do with initiating the procedures which eventually led to the formation of the union, for the commission was appointed immediately after the Central Committee had heard a report on Georgia.[85] The commission, whose assignment it was to draft for the Plenum a statement defining the relations between the RSFSR and the republics, was headed by Stalin, and included representatives of both the RKP and the republican parties; but the final report was drafted by a four-man subcommittee consisting of Stalin, Ordzhonikidze, Molotov, and A. F. Miasnikov — all reputed "centralists." [86]

Stalin had never been much impressed either by Lenin's fine distinction between "autonomous republics" and "Soviet republics," or by his high regard for diplomatic niceties in the matter of independence of the republics. This much he had made clear in 1920 in a private letter to Lenin. Commenting on the theses on the national and colonial questions which Lenin had drafted for the Second Congress of the Comintern, Stalin denied that there was a meaningful difference between "autonomous" and "Soviet" republics. "In your theses," he wrote, "you draw a distinction between Bashkir and Ukrainian types of federal union, but in fact there is no such difference, or it is so small as to equal zero." [87] Since by 1921 the position of the Soviet republics had declined as compared to 1920, Stalin had no reason to change his mind; and in drafting his project he proceeded from the same assumption.

In the project Stalin strove to give a straightforward and realistic expression to the constitutional practice that had evolved in the preceding five years under Lenin's personal tutelage. That is to say, he treated the Soviet domain as a unified, centralized state and the government of the RSFSR as the de facto government of all the six Soviet republics. In this manner he hoped to eliminate all those difficulties which the legal fiction of "independence" of the republics had made for those who were running the country.

His draft, called "Project of a Resolution Concerning the Relations between the RSFSR and the Independent Republics," first revealed in 1956, has not yet been published in its entirety, but its main points can be readily reconstructed. The key clause was the first one, calling for the entrance of the five border republics into the RSFSR on the basis of autonomy.[88] If carried out, this clause would have transformed the Ukraine, Belorussia, Georgia, Azerbaijan, and Armenia into autonomous republics of the RSFSR, on a par with the Iakut or the Crimean republics, and would have swept aside the whole elaborate system of relations established by the treaties. The second article provided for the organs of the RSFSR — its Central Executive Committee, Council of People's Commissars, and Council of Labor and Defence — to assume the functions of the federal government for all the six republics. The remaining three articles specified which commissariats were to be taken over by the Russian government, which were to be left to the republics but to function under the control of the corresponding agencies of the RSFSR, and which were to be entrusted entirely to the autonomous republics.[89]

Stalin completed his project at the end of August and dispatched it to the Central Committees of the republics for discussion and approval. It is important to note, however, that even before the republics had reacted, Stalin, on August 29, 1922, sent a wire to Mdivani announcing the extension of the authority of the Russian government: the Sovnarkom, VTsIK, and STO (*Sovet Truda i Oborony*, or Council of Labor and Defence), over the governments of all the republics.[90] The Georgians were so enraged by this unilateral abrogation of the 1921 treaty that they dispatched to Moscow a three-man delegation, which was later joined by Mdivani.[91]

As may be expected, Stalin's draft had no difficulty securing the approval of the Azerbaijani Communist Party, which was under Ordzhonikidze's firm control.[92] But no other republican Central Committee (with the possible exception of the Armenian) followed suit.* The first vocal opposition came from the Georgians. On September 15, 1922, the Georgian Central Committee flatly turned down Stalin's theses, voting unanimously, with one dissent (Eliava) "to consider premature the unification of the independent republics on the basis of autonomization, proposed by Comrade Stalin's theses. We regard the unification of economic endeavor and of general policy indispensable, but with the retention of all the attributes of independence."[93] Ordzhonikidze, who with Kirov attended these proceedings, then decided to overrule the Georgians. On the following day he convened the Presidium of the Zakraikom, which he headed, and had it pass a resolution approving Stalin's project. The Presidium also ordered the Georgian Central Committee, on its personal

---

* It cannot be established definitely whether the Armenian Central Committee approved of Stalin's project. Iakubovskaia (*Stroitel'stvo*, 145 and 149) says that it did, but S. Gililov in his *Lenin* passes over the subject in silence.

responsibility, not to inform the rank and file of its negative decision and to carry out faithfully Stalin's instructions.[94]

The Belorussians responded (on September 16) evasively. First, they asked for territory to be added to their republic; then they stated that as far as relations with the RSFSR were concerned, they would be satisfied with the same arrangement as that made by the Ukraine.[95] The Ukrainians, having procrastinated until October 3, finally passed a resolution which categorically demanded the preservation of Ukrainian independence and the establishment of relations with the RSFSR on the basis of principles formulated by Frunze's commission the previous May.[96]

Stalin's commission reconvened on September 23. It had little to show by way of republican approval, but the lack of enthusiasm in the borderlands apparently did not much trouble either Stalin or his colleagues. There was more discussion of the draft, during which some clauses were criticized and possibly even changed. No one, however, challenged the fundamental premise of "autonomization." [97] Having secured the approval of the commission, Stalin forwarded to Lenin the minutes of its meetings, as well as the favorable resolutions of the Azerbaijani Communist Party and the Zakraikom.[98]

Lenin apparently had not been kept well informed of the commission's work, for the data which Stalin supplied dismayed and angered him. From Lenin's point of view, the project undid the pseudofederal edifice which he had so carefully constructed over the past five years. Worst of all, it threatened to upset the whole fiction of national equality which Lenin counted on to mollify and neutralize the nationalist sentiments of the minorities. He saw no practical advantages to be derived from incorporation of the five independent republics into the RSFSR. Its only consequence would have been to reveal, with brutal frankness, the dependence of all the Communist republics on Russia and to make it very difficult in the future to win nationalist movements for Bolshevism in the so-called colonial and semi-colonial areas.

As soon as he had become acquainted with the commission's materials, Lenin summoned Stalin. He severely criticized his project and exerted on him strong pressure to modify all those points which formalized the hegemony of the RSFSR over the other republics. He wished for an arrangement whereby all the republics, the RSFSR included, constituted a new federation, with a separate government, called the Union of Soviet Socialist Republics of Europe and Asia. Stalin yielded to Lenin on this and agreed to abandon the idea of "autonomization" advocated in the first article of his project in favor of a federal union of equal states. But he refused to concede on the second article. Lenin's demand for the creation of new federal central organs — an All-Union Central Executive Committee, Sovnarkom, and Council of Labor and Defence — to supersede those of the RSFSR seemed to him administratively cumbersome and superfluous. Stalin thought that Lenin's purpose could be achieved as well by the simpler device of renaming the organs of the RSFSR as all-Union ones. But Lenin disagreed and criticized Stalin for being impatient and excessively addicted to administrative procedures. On the conclusion of their interview, both men put down their views in a memorandum which they forwarded to Lev Kamenev, then acting chairman of the Sovnarkom.[99] Stalin's note was surprisingly insolent in tone.

In the end, Stalin had to yield all along the line and, on the basis of Lenin's criticism, to revise his entire project. The project was discussed at a meeting of the Plenum on October 6, 1922. Lenin, suffering from a severe toothache, had to absent himself from this session, but he made his views unmistakably clear in a note which he sent to his colleagues on that day: "I declare war on Great Russian chauvinism; a war not for life but for death. As soon as I get rid of that accursed tooth of mine, I shall devour it with all my healthy ones." [100] He also repeated his insistence that Stalin modify article two of his project. The Plenum accepted Lenin's suggestions, and voted in favor of a new draft calling for the establishment of a Union of Soviet Socialist Republics governed by a newly created Union Central Executive Committee of representatives of the republican Central Executive Committees. The Plenum also appointed a commission of eleven members to translate these principles into a constitutional project.[101] * It may be noted that Mdivani participated as a guest in these deliberations and, however reluctantly, gave his approval in the name of the Georgian party, but only after having insisted that the Georgian republic enter the Union directly, as a full-fledged member.[102]

After its approval by the Plenum, the new draft of constitutional principles was sent to the Central Committees of the non-Russian republics. In Transcaucasia, the Azerbaijani and Armenian parties gave their approval promptly, but the Georgians once more made difficulties. From one point of view, the new statement was preferable to the previous one, which they had so unceremoniously rejected on September 15: the federating republics now entered the Union as formally independent states, equal to the RSFSR. But the new project also had one very serious drawback. Whereas Stalin's old project envisaged the three Transcaucasian republics as entering the RSFSR directly, the new one provided for their joining the Union through the intermediacy of the Transcaucasian Federation. To the Georgian Communists this provision seemed ludicrous and insulting. Why, for instance, should Belorussia have the right to become a full-fledged member of the Union, and not Georgia? And what was the point of creating a federation if the proposed Union would absorb most of the republican commissariats anyway? A double political

---

* The commission consisted of Stalin, Lev Kamenev, Piatakov, A. I. Rykov, Chicherin, M. I. Kalinin, and representatives of the five non-Russian republics (*Bor'ba za uprochenie*, 118).

union — once with the Transcaucasian Federation, and then, through the Federation, with the Union — simply made no sense to them. The Georgians, therefore, protested to Moscow, demanding the abandonment of the projected federation.[103] To this request Stalin replied on October 16 in the name of the Central Committee, stating that it was unanimously rejected.[104]

Tempers in Georgia now reached the point of explosion. Dissident Communist leaders held secret meetings at which they complained of the violation of their rights and criticized the policies of Moscow.[105] They secured at this time the support of the most distinguished Georgian Communist, Makharadze, who on October 19 made a speech in Tiflis pleading for Georgia's direct entrance into the Union.[106] Makharadze was not only the oldest Georgian Bolshevik (like Zhordania he had become a Marxist while attending the university in Warsaw in 1891–92), but he had a well-earned reputation of being an irreconcilable enemy of nationalism. Before the Revolution he had opposed Lenin's slogan of national self-determination from a position which Lenin called "nihilistic"; during the Revolution (at the April 1917 Bolshevik Congress) he had led the faction which demanded the removal of that slogan from the party's program; and in 1921–22, despite some misgivings, he had collaborated with Ordzhonikidze's centralistic measures. That a Communist of such background should have joined the opposition provides evidence of the near unanimity which existed in Georgia at this time.

On October 20, the three members of the Georgian delegation returned from the mission to Moscow on which they had been dispatched at the end of August and reported to the Central Committee. Having heard them, the Committee voted (twelve to three) to appeal to Moscow once more for reconsideration. Accepting now as binding the decision to establish a Transcaucasian federation, it nevertheless requested the abolition of the Union Council and Georgia's direct entrance into the Union, on the same terms as the Ukraine.[107] Simultaneously, Makharadze and Tsintsadze sent strong personal letters to Kamenev and Bukharin complaining about Ordzhonikidze.[108]

Lenin by this time had had his fill of the Georgians. He interpreted their actions as a breach of party discipline as well as a failure to adhere to a decision taken with the concurrence of their representative. On October 21 he dispatched to Tiflis a sharply worded wire in which he rejected their request and stated that he was turning the whole matter over to the Secretariat, that is, to Stalin.[109] Kamenev and Bukharin sent separate wires to Makharadze and Mdivani accusing them of nationalism and insisting that they coöperate in the establishment of the federation.[110] Upon receipt of these dispatches the Central Committee of the Georgian Communist Party on October 22 took the unprecedented step of tendering the Central Committee of the Russian Communist Party its resignation.[111] The resignation was accepted, and a new Georgian Central Committee was promptly appointed by the Zakraikom. It consisted mostly of young converts to Communism who lacked both experience and reputation, and whom Mdivani contemptuously dismissed as "Komsomoltsy." [112] With their support, Ordzhonikidze had no difficulty securing full cooperation and approval of the new constitutional project.[113]

The Georgian affair delayed by several weeks the drafting of the Union agreement. The constitutional committee reassembled again only on November 21, without having accomplished anything in the interval. It now appointed a subcommittee, chaired by the Commissar of Foreign Affairs, G. V. Chicherin, to prepare the draft of a constitution.[114] Chicherin had his draft ready within a week's time.[115] It was at once approved by the constitutional committee and by the Central Committee (Lenin included) and, in the course of December, by the Congresses of Soviets of the four federating republics (Transcaucasia being treated now as a single federal republic).[116] On December 29, 1922, representatives of the republics attended a conference in the Kremlin at which Stalin read the articles of the Union. After some protests, most likely from some Georgians, the majority of those present voted in favor of the act.[117] Next day a joint session of the Tenth Congress of Soviets of the RSFSR and the deputies of the congresses of soviets of the Ukraine, Belorussia, and Transcaucasia took place in Moscow's Bolshoi Theatre. This joint session called itself the First Congress of Soviets of the Union of Soviet Socialist Republics.[118] Its main order of business was to ratify the agreement establishing the Soviet Union — a task which it was confidently expected to fulfill, since 95 per cent of all the deputies were members of the Communist Party and as such were required by party discipline to vote for resolutions passed by the Central Committee.[119] The Congress did not disappoint those expectations.

The agreement stipulated that the supreme legislative organ of the new state was the Congress of Soviets of the USSR and that during intervals between its sessions, the role passed to the Central Executive Committee of the Congress of Soviets. The sessions of the Congress of Soviets were to be held by rotation in the capitals of each of the four republics. The highest executive organ of the Union was to be the Council of People's Commissars of the USSR (Sovnarkom Soiuza), elected by the Central Executive Committee and composed of the following officials: a chairman, a deputy chairman; the Commissars of Foreign Affairs, War and Navy, Foreign Trade, Means of Communications, Post and Telegraphs, Workers' and Peasants' Inspection, Labor, Supply, Finance; the Chairman of the Higher Council of National Economy; and in an advisory capacity, the head of the Secret Police (OGPU). The Union republics were to have their own councils of people's commissars composed of the Commissars for Agriculture, Supply, Finance, Labor, Interior, Justice, Workers' and Peasants' Inspection, Education, Health, Social Security; the Chairman of the Higher Council of National Economy; and as consultants, representatives of the federal commissariats. The Commissariats of Supply, Finance, Labor, Workers' and Peasants' Inspection, and the Higher Council of National Economy of each of the republican governments were to be directly subordinated to the corresponding agencies of the federal government. The agreement thus distinguished three types of commissariats: federal, republican, and joint. Strictly within the competence of the republican governments were only the Commissariats of Agriculture, Interior, Justice, Education, Health, and Social Security. The final article of the agreement guaranteed every republic the right of secession from the Union, despite the fact that, according to the preceding article, only the federal government could effect changes in the Union Agreement — such as, presumably, matters of entering and leaving the Union.[120]

The Presidium of the Central Executive Committee, appointed by the First Congress of Soviets of the USSR, formed on January 10, 1923, six separate commissions to prepare the draft of a constitution based on the articles of the Union Agreement.[121]

### Lenin's Change of Mind

The Georgian opposition, whose history since early 1921 we have traced, was of importance not only for its role in shaping the constitution, but also for its impact on Lenin's attitude toward the nationality question. It provided overwhelming evidence against the basic premise of Lenin's nationality policy: that nationalism was a transitional, historical phenomenon associated with the era of capitalism and bound to dissolve in the heat of intense class struggle. Lenin observed with obvious dismay a new kind of nationalism emerging in the Russian as well as in the minority Communist apparatus — that very apparatus on which he depended to eradicate national animosities. As this evidence accumulated in the winter of 1922–23, Lenin went through a reappraisal of Soviet nationality policy which bore all the marks of a true intellectual crisis. It is likely that had he not suffered a nearly fatal stroke in March 1923 the final structure of the Soviet Union would have been quite different from that which Stalin ultimately gave it.

To understand Lenin's change of mind one must bear in mind the effect which both internal and external events since 1917 had had on his nationality policy. Self-determination interpreted as the right to secession was in fact a dead letter. So was federalism, since the military and economic exigencies of the Soviet state, requiring the merger of the conquered borderlands with the RSFSR, had vitiated the very essence of the federal system which Lenin had been forced to adopt as a substitute for self-determination. The minorities were thus left without any effective guarantees against the encroachments of the central authorities; and yet they needed these more than ever in view of the unlimited authority enjoyed by the Communist party over the citizenry. In the end, Lenin's national program reduced itself to a matter of personal behavior: it depended for the solution of the complex problems of a multinational empire upon the tact and good will of Communist officials. To Lenin such a solution seemed perfectly feasible, in part because he himself was a stranger to national prejudices, and in part because he believed that the establishment of Communism destroyed the soil in which nationalism could flourish.

In fact, however, Lenin's expectations were quite unfounded. Like every staunch realist, he mistook that segment of reality of which he happened to be aware for reality as a whole, and in the end displayed no little naïveté. Nationalism may well have been rooted in psychology, in the memory of wrongs done or in sensitivity to slights; but surely it was more than that. It reflected also specific interests and striving that could not be satisfied merely by tact but required real political and other concessions. Nor could the groups on which Lenin counted to carry out what was left of his nationality program display that reasonableness this program demanded. Before as well as after 1917 even the closest of his followers had rejected his concessions to the nationalities as impractical and incompatible with the Bolshevik ideology. If the Soviet Constitution of 1918 and the Communist program of 1919 had included his formulae calling for a federation based on the national principle and the retention of the slogan of national self-determination (although in a highly qualified form), it was only because of Lenin's tremendous prestige with the Party. The majority of the Bolshevik leaders remained unconvinced, and the numerous new rank and file who had joined the Communists since the Revolution (in 1922 they constituted 97.3 per cent of the active party membership)[122] were even less prepared to assimilate the subtle reasoning which lay behind his national program. To the overwhelming majority of Communists and Communist sympathizers, the goals of the movement — the "dictatorship of the proletariat," the "unity of the anticapitalist front," or the "destruction of counterrevolutionary forces" — were synonymous with the establishment of Great Russian hegemony. The Soviet Russian republic alone had the industrial and military might necessary to accomplish these ends. After the failure of the Communist revolutions in Central Europe, it became the arsenal and fortress of world Communism. The Communist movements in the Russian borderlands had proved themselves weak and incapable of survival without the military assistance of Soviet Russia. The bulk of the membership of the Communist Party came from the urban and industrial centers of the country and hence was predominantly Russian ethnically and culturally. In 1922, 72 per cent of all the members of the Communist Party (including its

## NATIONAL ORIGIN OF COMMUNIST PARTY MEMBERS, 1922

| Nationality | Absolute number | Per cent of RKP | Per 1000 of population of given nationality within the borders of the Soviet state |
|---|---|---|---|
| Great Russians | 270,409 | 72.00 | 3.80 |
| Ukrainians | 22,078 | 5.88 | 0.94 |
| Jews | 19,564 | 5.20 | 7.20 |
| Latvians | 9,512 | 2.53 | 78.00 |
| Georgians | 7,378 | 1.96 | 4.52 |
| Tatars | 6,534 | 1.72 | 1.19 |
| Poles | 5,649 | 1.50 | 10.80 |
| Belorussians | 5,534 | 1.47 | 1.67 |
| Kirghiz | 4,964 | 1.32 | 0.89 |
| Armenians | 3,828 | 1.02 | 2.91 |
| Germans | 2,217 | 0.59 | 1.98 |
| Uzbeks | 2,043 | 0.54 | 0.76 |
| Estonians | 1,964 | 0.53 | 16.30 |
| Ossetins | 1,699 | 0.45 | 8.00 |
| Others | 12,528 | 3.29 | |
| | 375,901 | 100.00 | 2.90 (average for USSR) |

Statistics, based on the 1922 Party Census, from I. P. Trainin, *SSSR i natsional'naia problema* (Moscow, 1924), 26.

regional organizations in the Ukraine, Transcaucasia, and the other borderlands) were Russian by origin, and at least another 10 per cent were Russian by language (see the accompanying table). The administrative personnel of Soviet republics, drawn largely from the bureaucracy of the *ancien régime,* was probably even more heavily dominated by Russian and Russified elements.*

The preponderance of Great Russians in the political apparatus was not in any sense due to a peculiar affinity of members of that nationality for the Communist movement, since, as statistics indicate, the proportion

* A large proportion of the non-Russian Communists were culturally Russified. The Communist Party of the Ukraine — the largest regional subdivision of the RKP — in 1922 had 51,236 members, of whom 53.6 per cent were Russian by nationality, but 79.4 per cent considered Russian their native tongue. The Ukrainian and Jewish members of the KP(b)U formed 23.3 per cent and 13.6 per cent by nationality, and 11.3 per cent and 3.5 per cent by language, respectively. Cf. KP(b)U, *Itogi partperepisi 1922 goda*, I (Kharkov, 1922), p. xii. The Ukrainian data indicates that approximately one half of the Ukrainian and two thirds of the Jewish members were Russian in the cultural sense of the word. A similar situation probably prevailed in neighboring Belorussia. If one applies to the total Ukrainian, Jewish, and Belorussian membership of the RKP the ratios of the KP(b)U, an additional 27,000 members, or 6 per cent of the RKP, will emerge as Russified. The remaining figure of 4 per cent is a low estimate of the proportion of Russified elements among the other national groups.

of Communists among the entire Russian population was only slightly higher than the country-wide average, and there were several national groups whose ratio of Communists was considerably larger. It was rather due to the fact that the industrial and urban population in the country was predominantly of Russian stock, and that a large proportion of the non-Russians likely to engage in political activity were assimilated. In a democratic state such a one-sided ethnic composition of a party would not necessarily have had great practical consequences; it was different in a totalitarian country, where the party was in full control. Already in the course of the Revolution the equation *Communism* = *Russia* had been made in many of the borderlands by both Russians and non-Russians, especially in the eastern regions. As I indicated in the discussion of the 1917–20 period, many elements that had nothing in common with Communist ideology had sided with the Communists because they felt that the regime was essentially devoted to Great Russian interests. This identification of the Communist movement with the Russian cause had inspired much of the opposition in the borderlands to the Soviet government. But it was only after 1920, after the end of the Civil War, that the growth of Great Russian nationalism in the Communist movement became unmistakably evident. At the Tenth Party Congress, held in 1921, a number of speakers called attention to it:

> The fact that Russia had first entered on the road of the revolution, that Russia had transformed itself from a colony — an actual colony of Western Europe — into the center of the world movement, this fact has filled with pride the hearts of those who had been connected with the Russian Revolution and engendered a peculiar Red Russian patriotism. And we now see how our comrades consider themselves with pride, and not without reason, as Russians, and at times even look upon themselves above all as Russians.[123]

Communist writers acquainted with the Soviet Moslem regions pointed to the prevalence of Great Russian nationalism in the eastern borderlands:

> It is necessary to acknowledge the fact that not only the officialdom in the borderlands, which consists largely of officials of the old regime, but also the proletariat inhabiting those areas which actively supports the revolution, consists in its majority of persons of Russian nationality. In Turkestan, for example, Russian workers thought that once the dictatorship of the proletariat had been established, it should work only for *their* benefit, as workers, and that they could fully ignore the interests of the backward agricultural and nomadic population, which had not yet reached their "proletarian" level of consciousness. The same thing had occurred in Azerbaijan, Bashkiriia, and elsewhere. This situation had caused the broad masses

of the native population to think that, when you come right down to it, nothing has changed, and that the *Russian* official has been replaced by a *Russian* proletarian, who, although he talks of equality, in reality, like the previous *Russian* official, takes care only of himself, ignoring the interests of the local population.[124]

The Tenth Congress was the first to take cognizance of the emergence of Great Russian nationalism in the Communist apparatus by including in its resolutions a strongly worded condemnation of what it called "the danger of Great Russian chauvinism." [125]

In view of this development, was Lenin realistic in entrusting the ultimate authority in the controversial matter of relations between the Great Russian majority of the population and its non-Russian minority to the Communist Party? It was psychologically as well as administratively contradictory to strive for the supremacy of the proletariat, and at the same time to demand that this proletariat, which was largely Russian, place itself in a morally defensive position regarding the minorities; to have an all-powerful party, a fully centralized state, and also genuine self-rule in the borderlands; to have the political apparatus suppress ruthlessly all opposition to the regime in Russian proper and adopt a conciliatory attitude toward dissident nationalism in the republics.

Yet if, despite all these factors, Lenin stood fast by his solution of the nationality question, it is because of its bearing on the long-range prospects of Communism. The failure of the revolution in Germany, which he had regarded as essential for the eventual triumph of the Communist Revolution, made Lenin pay even greater attention to the so-called colonial peoples of the East. Here the possibilities of a successful revolution seemed much greater than in Europe. And even though such a revolution would not immediately bring down the capitalist powers, it was expected so to weaken their economic position as to make an ultimate collapse inevitable. But a revolution in Asia and Africa required the use of nationalist slogans, which the Communists could employ only if they proved to be effective champions of national independence. It is for this reason that Lenin considered it of vital importance to dissociate Communism from Great Russian nationalism, with which it had tended to fuse since the end of the Civil War.

Of the three outstanding Communist leaders in the early 1920's, Stalin seems to have realized most clearly the contradictions inherent in the Communist nationality program. The nationalist opposition was divided and ineffective; Lenin approved all the measures giving priority to the Russian apparatus, though he winced at their inevitable consequences; while Trotsky showed little interest in the whole national question. Stalin, however, placed himself squarely on the side of the central apparatus and identified himself with the Great Russian core of the party and state bureaucracy.* He thus stood in the center of Communism's last, and perhaps bitterest, struggle over the national question.

The demoted Georgian Communists kept on sending Lenin telegrams and letters in which they complained of their treatment at the hands of Ordzhonikidze, and requested an impartial inquiry. One such letter particularly attracted Lenin's attention. Written by a prominent figure of the opposition, M. Okudzhava, it accused Ordzhonikidze of personally insulting and threatening Georgian Communists.[126] Lenin turned this letter and other documents over to the Secretariat of the Central Committee, which on November 24 appointed a three-man commission to investigate on the spot the whole Georgian party crisis and in particular the circumstances surrounding the resignation of the old Central Committee. The commission was headed by Dzerzhinskii, and included V. S. Mitskevich-Kapsukas and Manuilskii.[127] Although technically all three were non-Russians, they could hardly have been regarded as representatives of the minority point of view. Manuilskii in particular was known as an outspoken centralist; only three months before he had welcomed enthusiastically Stalin's plan of "autonomization." [128] Dzerzhinskii's close ties with Stalin also did not augur well for the opposition. Lenin must have had some misgivings of this kind, for a few days after the departure of the Dzerzhinskii commission, he asked Rykov to follow it to Tiflis to make an independent inquiry.[129] According to the log of Lenin's secretary, he awaited the return of the emissaries with great impatience.[130]

Rykov came back first and reported to Lenin at Gorki on December 9.[131] What he said we do not know. But how anxious Lenin was to learn all he could is seen from the fact that the instant Dzerzhinskii returned to Moscow (December 12) he departed in haste from Gorki, where he was convalescing, for the Kremlin, and there met with Dzerzhinskii the very same day.[132] Although Dzerzhinskii completely exonerated Ordzhonikidze and Stalin in their dealing with the Georgians,[133] some of the evidence he brought back greatly disturbed Lenin — so much so that from then on he could hardly get the Georgian affair out of his mind. He was troubled most of all by a rather minor incident, to which, for some reason, he attached great importance. It involved a quarrel between Ordzhonikidze and a Georgian Communist named A. Kabakhidze, which ended with Ordzhonikidze giving his opponent a beating.[134] Lenin was infuriated both by Ordzhonikidze's use of physical violence and by Dzerzhinskii's casual treatment of it. He instructed Dzerzhinskii to return to Tiflis to gather more information on this incident, and in the meantime called in Stalin, with whom he had an interview lasting for over two hours.[135] The facts which began to come in from Georgia con-

* It deserves note that in one dispatch, sent to Tiflis in February 1922, Stalin called himself a *Moskvich*, i.e. "Muscovite," (*Bor'ba za uprochenie*, 41).

firmed his worst suspicions, and he became acutely depressed.[136] Having returned to Gorki, he intended the following day (December 15) to write Kamenev a substantial letter on the nationality question,[137] but before he had a chance to do so he suffered another stroke.

While Lenin lay incapacitated, Ordzhonikidze, with Stalin's support, proceeded further to whittle down the powers left the Transcaucasian Federation. The new federation, established in December 1922, as the Transcaucasian Soviet Federative Socialist Republic (*Zakavkazskaia Sovetskaia Federativnaia Sotsialisticheskaia Respublika,* or ZSFSR) was much more centralist than that envisaged in the constitution of the previous March. It also said nothing about the independence of the constituent republics.[138] To reduce anticipated Georgian resistance, the Central Committee of the RKP on December 21 ordered the leaders of the opposition, Mdivani, Makharadze, Tsintsadze, and Kavtaradze, to leave Georgia, justifying its decision by the information which it said Dzerzhinskii's commission had supplied.[139] How powerful Ordzhonikidze's hold on his area was by now may be gleaned from the fact that in December 1922, at the First Congress of Soviets of Transcaucasia, he was hailed by someone as "the leader of the toiling masses of Transcaucasia." [140]

Lenin, having toward the end of December recovered from his stroke, tried at all costs to resume work. He had difficulty with the doctors who would not permit him to do so, until, by threatening to ignore medical advice altogether, he won from them the right to dictate every day, for ten or fifteen minutes, a personal diary.[141] He immediately took advantage of this right to dictate several important memoranda, including one on the nationality question which deserves quotation in full. This memorandum, Lenin's last theoretical contribution on the subject of the national problem, was originally not intended for publication, inasmuch as it contained derogatory remarks about three members of the Central Committee. It became known only because of its involvement in the rivalry between Trotsky and Stalin.

LENIN'S MEMORANDUM ON THE NATIONAL QUESTION[*]

I. The Continuation of Notes, December 30, 1922

Concerning the Question of Nationalities or About "Autonomization":

I am, it appears, much at fault before the workers of Russia for not having intervened with sufficient energy and incisiveness in the

---

[*] Originally published in *Sotsialisticheskii vestnik,* December 1923, pp. 13–15. In the Soviet Union this document was first read at the Twentieth Party Congress, then printed in *Kommunist,* no. 9 (1956), 22–26. The present translation is based on the version in the fourth edition of Lenin's Works, V. I. Lenin, *Sochineniia,* XXXIII (Moscow, 1957), 553–59.

notorious question of "autonomization," which is officially called, it seems, the question of the Union of Soviet Socialist Republics.

In the summer, when this question arose, I was ill, and then, in the fall, I had too great hopes that I would recuperate and have an opportunity of intervening in this question at the October and December Plenums. But, as it turned out, I could attend neither the October Plenum (dealing with this question) nor the December one, and for this reason it had bypassed me almost entirely.

I only managed to exchange a few words with Comrade Zinoviev to whom I conveyed my fears concerning this question. That which I have learned from Dzerzhinskii, who had headed the commission sent by the Central Committee to "investigate" the Georgian incident, only increased my very great fears. If matters have reached the point where Ordzhonikidze could blow up and resort to physical force, as I was informed by Comrade Dzerzhinskii, then one can imagine the rut we have gotten into. Apparently this entire undertaking of "autonomization" was fundamentally incorrect and inopportune.

It is said that we needed a single apparatus. From where come such assertions? Is it not from the same Russian apparatus, which, as I have pointed out in one of the previous numbers of my diary, was borrowed from Tsarism and only barely anointed with the Soviet chrism?

Undoubtedly, we should have waited with taking this measure until we could guarantee for the apparatus as being our own. And we must now, in all conscience, state the opposite: what we call ours is an apparatus still thoroughly alien to us and representing a bourgeois-Tsarist mixture which we had no opportunity of conquering during the five years, in the absence of help from other countries and in view of the pressures of the "business" of war and the fight against hunger.

In such circumstances, it is quite natural that the "freedom of exit from the Union," with which we justify ourselves, will prove to be nothing but a scrap of paper, incapable of defending the minorities in Russia from the inroads of that hundred per cent Russian chauvinist, in reality — the scoundrel and violator, which the typical Russian bureaucrat is. There can be no doubt, that the insignificant per cent of workers who are Soviet or Sovietized will drown in this sea of chauvinism of the Great Russian riffraff like a fly in milk.

It is said in defense of this measure that the Commissariats which concern directly national psychology, national education, are separated. But here arises the question whether it is possible fully to separate those Commissariats, and a second question, whether measures really to protect the minorities from the truly Russian Derzhimorda* have been taken with sufficient care. I think we have not taken those measures, although we could have and should have taken them.

* Derzhimorda is a character in Gogol's *Inspector General.* He symbolizes brutal police mentality and methods.

I think that here a fatal role was played by the hastiness and administrative passions of Stalin, and also by his anger at the notorious "social nationalism." Anger in general plays in politics the worst possible role.

I also fear that Comrade Dzerzhinskii, who journeyed to the Caucasus to "investigate" the "crimes of these social-nationals," distinguished himself in this matter only by his truly Russian attitude (it is known that assimilated non-Russians always overdo in the matter of hundred per cent Russian attitudes) and that the objectivity of his whole commission is sufficiently characterized by the "beating" meted out by Ordzhonikidze. I think that no provocation, not even any offense can excuse such a Russian "beating" and that Comrade Dzerzhinskii is irreparably guilty of having taken a lighthearted view of this beating.

Ordzhonikidze represented the government authority to the remaining citizens in the Caucasus. Ordzhonikidze had no right to this irritability to which he and Dzerzhinskii referred. On the contrary, Ordzhonikidze should have displayed that self-control which is not incumbent upon any average citizen, the more so upon one who is accused of a "political" crime. For, after all, the "social-nationals" were citizens accused of a political crime, and all the circumstances of this accusation could only have qualified it in this manner.

Here arises the principal question: how to understand internationalism.

## II. Continuation of Notes, December 31, 1922

I have already written in my works on the national question, that an abstract formulation of the question of the nationalities in general is worthless. It is necessary to distinguish between the nationalism of the oppressing nation and the nationalism of the oppressed nation, the nationalism of a great nation and the nationalism of a small nation.

In regard to the second nationalism we, the nationals of a great nation, almost always prove in historical practice guilty of an endless amount of coercion and, even more than that, unnoticed to ourselves commit an endless amount of coercions and insults. It is only necessary to bring back my Volga recollections how we slight the minorities. How a Pole is never called anything but a *"Poliachishka,"* how a Tartar is never ridiculed otherwise than as a "Prince," a Ukrainian as a *"khokhol,"* the Georgians and the Caucasian minorities as "Capcasian persons."

For this reason, the internationalism of the oppressing side, or the so-called great nation (though it is great only in its violations, great only as is Derzhimorda), [such an internationalism] must consist not only of the observance of the formal equality of nations but also of that inequality which removes on the part of the oppressing, great nation that inequality which accumulates in actual life. He who does not understand this decidedly does not understand the proletarian attitude toward the national question; he clings essentially to the petty bourgeois viewpoint, and for that reason cannot avoid sliding every minute toward the bourgeois point of view.

What is important for the proletariat? For the proletariat it is not only important but essentially indispensable to win for itself the maximum of confidence of the minorities in the proletarian class struggle. What is necessary for that? For that there is necessary not only formal equality. For that there is necessary the indemnification, in one way or another, by means of behavior or concessions in regard to the minorities, of that mistrust, of that suspicion, of those insults, which the ruling "great" nation had in the historical past brought them.

I think that for Bolsheviks, for Communists, it is unnecessary to elucidate this further. And I think that in this instance, in regard to the Georgian nation, we have a typical example where a genuine proletarian attitude demands from us extraordinary caution, courtesy, and complaisance. That Georgian who treats contemptuously this side of the matter and accuses others of "social-nationalism" (while himself being not only a genuine and veritable "social-nationalist" but also a crude Great Russian Derzhimorda) — that Georgian in reality violates the interests of the proletarian class solidarity, because nothing delays so much the development and consolidation of the proletarian class solidarity as does national injustice, and offended members of minority groups are of all things most sensitive to the emotion of equality and to the violation of that equality by their proletarian comrades, even through carelessness, even in the form of a joke. For this reason, in this case it is better to stretch too far in the direction of concessions and gentleness toward the national minorities, than too little. For this reason the fundamental interest of proletarian solidarity and, consequently, also of the proletarian class struggle, demand that in this case we should never treat the national question formally but should always without fail take into account the difference in the relationship of the oppressed or small nation toward the oppressing or large nation.

### III. Continuation of Notes, December 31, 1922

What practical measures can then be taken in the present situation?

In the first place, the union of socialist republics must be retained and strengthened. About this measure there can be no doubt. We need it, as the world-wide Communist proletariat needs it, for the struggle against the world-wide bourgeoisie and for the defense from its intrigues.

In the second place, it is necessary to retain the union of socialist republics in respect to the diplomatic apparatus. It may be relevant to point out that this apparatus is unique in the body of our state apparatus. We did not allow in it a single influential person from the old Tsarist apparatus. Its entire apparatus, possessed of the slightest authority, consists of Communists. For that reason this whole apparatus (it may be said firmly) has already won for itself the reputation of a proven Communist apparatus, incomparably, immeasurably more purged of the old apparatus, Tsarist, bourgeois and petty bourgeois, than that with which we have had to get along in the other Commissariats.

In the third place, it is necessary to mete out exemplary punishment to Comrade Ordzhonikidze (I say this with that much the greater regret that I personally belong to the circle of his friends, and have worked with him abroad, in emigration), and also to complete the inquiry and to reëxamine all the materials of Dzerzhinskii's commission for the purpose of correcting that enormous number of incorrect and prejudiced judgments which undoubtedly are contained in it. Of course, Stalin and Dzerzhinskii must be held politically responsible for this truly Great Russian nationalistic campaign.

In the fourth place, it is necessary to set the strictest rules concerning the use of the national language[s] in the national republics which enter into our union, and to abide by those rules with especial carefulness. There is no doubt that, under the pretext of the unity of the railroad service, under the pretext of fiscal unity, and so forth, with our present apparatus a mass of abuses of genuinely Russian character shall take place. The struggle with such abuses requires exceptional resourcefulness, not to mention exceptional sincerity from those who shall undertake it. Here will be needed a detailed code, which only the nationals living in the given republic can compile in any successful manner. And we must in no way renounce beforehand having to turn back at the next Congress of Soviets, as a result of all this work, that is, of having to retain the Union of Socialist Soviet Republics only in the military and diplomatic spheres, and in all other respects restoring the full independence of the separate commissariats.

It must be kept in mind that the dispersion of the commissariats and the lack of coördination between them and Moscow and the other centers can be sufficiently paralyzed by party authority, if the latter is applied with the minimum of circumspection and impartiality. The harm which can befall our government from the absence of unification between the national apparatus and the Russian apparatus will be incomparably smaller, infinitely smaller, than that harm which can befall not only us but also the whole International, the hundreds of millions of the peoples of Asia who in the near future are to enter the stage of history in our wake. It would be unforgivable opportunism if, on the eve of this emergence of the East and at the beginning of its awakening, we should undermine our prestige there with even the slightest rudeness or injustice to our own minorities. The necessity for solidarity against the international West which defends the capitalist world is one thing. Here there can be no doubt, and I need not say that I unconditionally approve all those measures. It is another thing when we ourselves fall — even if in trivial matters — into something like imperialistic relations toward the oppressed nationalities, in this manner undermining completely our whole sincerity in matters of principle, our whole principle of defending the struggle against imperialism. And the coming day in world history will be precisely that day, when the peoples, oppressed by imperialism, will have their final awakening, and when the decisive, prolonged and difficult battle for their liberation will get under way.

LENIN

Lenin's analysis of the Georgian incident suffered from all the limitations imposed upon him by the Communist dogma. He was unable to perceive that the failures of the Soviet national policy were due to a fundamental misinterpretation of the entire national problem and followed naturally from the dictatorial system of government which he had established. His mind operated only in terms of class-enemies. Seeking scapegoats, he blamed all national friction on the "bourgeois" elements in the state apparatus, disregarding the fact that in the Georgian crisis the guilty ones, by his own admission, were top members of the Communist Party. His remedies consisted only of reversion to party control of the political apparatus, linguistic measures, and the introduction of "codes of behavior" for Communist officials working in the borderlands — methods which had proved themselves unequal to the task in the previous years of Soviet rule. Nothing illustrated better the confusion which by now pervaded his thoughts on the subject than his contradictory recommendation that the union of republics be both "retained and strengthened" and in effect weakened by restoring to the republics full independence in all but military and diplomatic affairs.[142]

Lenin, hoping to recover from his illness, kept the memorandum to himself, with the intention of basing on it a major policy statement at the forthcoming Twelfth Party Congress. In the meantime he busily gathered evidence against Stalin and Ordzhonikidze. He probably did not realize, however, how quickly power was slipping from his hands. When on January 27, 1923, Dzerzhinskii had returned from his second Caucasian mission and Lenin, through his secretary, demanded to see the materials he had brought back, Dzerzhinskii replied that he had turned all materials over to Stalin. A search for Stalin revealed that he was out of town and unreachable. Upon his return two days later, Stalin flatly refused to surrender the materials and did so only when Lenin threatened to put up a fight for them.[143] There can be little doubt that, although Stalin pretended to be concerned with Lenin's health, in fact he was personally interested in keeping Lenin as much as possible out of the Georgian feud.

Lenin by now could rely only on a few devoted women from his private secretariat. He turned over to them all the materials brought back by Dzerzhinskii and prepared a questionnaire which they were to use in analyzing them. The questionnaire contained the following seven questions: What was the deviation with which the Georgian Central Committee was charged? In what respect did it violate party discipline?

In what ways was it oppressed by the Zakraikom? What instances were there of physical violence used against the Georgians? What was the policy of the Central Committee of the RKP when Lenin was present compared to that when he was absent? Did Dzerzhinskii on his second trip also investigate the charges against Ordzhonikidze? What was the present situation in Georgia?[144] While the secretaries were busy at work preparing the report, Lenin constantly inquired about their progress. According to the diary of his personal secretary, in February 1923 the Georgian question was then uppermost in his mind.[145]

In the meantime, the formation of the Soviet Union was forging ahead. In February 1923 the Plenum of the Central Committee (from which Lenin was also absent) decided to add a second chamber to the Union legislature to represent the national groups. Originally, the Communists had been hostile to the idea of a bicameral legislature, considering it a feature of a "class society" and unnecessary in the "proletarian" state. In November 1922 Stalin had stated that, although some Communists were advocating the creation of a second, upper chamber to provide representation for the nationalities as such, he felt that this view "will undoubtedly find no sympathy in the national republics, if only because the two-chamber system, with the existence of an upper chamber, is not compatible with the Soviet government, at any rate, at the present stage of its development." [146] By February, however, Stalin changed his mind in favor of a bicameral legislature, largely, in all likelihood, because it enabled him to increase his personal control over the Soviet legislature. The Council of Nationalities (Sovet natsional'nostei), which was approved by the party and incorporated into the Constitution, was the same Council of Nationalities that Stalin had formed as part of the Commissariat of Nationality Affairs in April 1921, with the addition of deputies from the three Union republics. The second chamber was, therefore, staffed with people who had Stalin's personal approval.[147] *

Lenin finally received the report on March 3. It must have infuriated him, because he now switched his support completely to the side of the Georgian opposition. His first impulse was to form a new and impartial investigating commission;[148] the second, to entrust the handling of the whole Georgian affair to Trotsky. On March 5, he addressed to Trotsky the following letter:[149]

> Respected Comrade Trotsky! I would very much like to ask you to take upon yourself the defence of the Georgian case in the Central Committee of the Party. The matter is now being "prosecuted" by Stalin and Dzerzhinskii, on whose objectivity I cannot rely. Quite on

---

* It must be noted, however, that the idea of a bicameral legislature was at this time also much advocated by Rakovskii as a means of reducing the preponderance in the government of Great Russians. See his Soiuz Sotsialisticheskikh Sovetskikh Respublik — Novyi etap v Sovetskom soiuznom stroitel'stve (Kharkov, 1923), 4–6.

the contrary. If you agree to assume responsibility for the defence, I shall be at ease. If for some reason you do not agree to do so, please return the materials to me. I shall consider this a sign of your refusal. With best comradely greetings,

Lenin*

With this letter, Lenin forwarded to Trotsky his memorandum on the nationality question.[150]

The following day Lenin sent a brief but significant message to the leaders of the Georgian opposition:[151]

> To Comrades Mdivani, Makharadze, and others: copies to Comrades Trotsky and Kamenev. Respected Comrades! I follow your case with all my heart. I am appalled by the coarseness of Ordzhonikidze, and the connivances of Stalin and Dzerzhinskii. I am preparing for you notes and a speech.
>
> Respectfully,
> Lenin

Simultaneously, Lenin dispatched to Georgia a new investigating commission, consisting of Kamenev and Kuibyshev.

Decidedly, events were taking a dangerous course for Stalin and Ordzhonikidze. They were saved from a public chastisement by Lenin by sheer good fortune. On the day when he had dictated his letter to Mdivani and Makharadze, Lenin suffered his third stroke, which paralyzed him completely and removed him for good from all political activity.†

### The Last Discussion of the Nationality Question

Lenin's third attack deprived the Georgian opposition, and all those who for one reason or another wanted to slow down the inexorable advance of centralization, of their main means of support. It soon became evident that Trotsky neither could nor would assume the task which Lenin had entrusted to him. Instead of taking the issue to the party leadership, he tried first to obtain permission from the entire Central Committee to make public Lenin's memorandum on the nationality question.[152] Whether he failed to secure it, or whether courage deserted him, is not certain. At any rate, Trotsky did not take charge of the anti-Stalinist opposition among the minorities; and thus he failed to take advantage of an excellent opportunity to embarrass his principal rival at a critical phase in their struggle for power. Lenin's note, having passed through

---

* In addition to being angry with Stalin for his handling of the Georgian question, Lenin was on the verge of breaking off personal relations with him because he had insulted Krupskaia.

† Kamenev and Kuibyshev apparently decided in favor of the Georgian opposition, but they did not complete the investigation, being compelled to return to Moscow when Lenin fell ill again. Cf. *Dvenadtsatyi s"ezd*, 151, 157.

the hands of the entire Central Committee, became widely known to the deputies to the Twelfth Party Congress which assembled in Moscow in April 1923. It was behind all the acrimonious debates on the nationality question which took place there.

The nationality question broke into the open at one of the early sessions of the Congress, during the discussions of the report on the party's Central Committee. Mdivani, unable to control his anger, launched a bitter tirade against the policies pursued by the Central Committee and its Caucasian Bureau in Georgia. Makharadze supported him, charging that much of the responsibility for the interparty quarrels in Georgia rested on Ordzhonikidze, who had ignored the old Georgian Bolsheviks in favor of newcomers. He emphatically denied the charge that the Georgian Communists had hindered the unification of Transcaucasia, asserting that they had objected only to the methods and the tempo with which this unification was being accomplished. Ordzhonikidze and Orakhelashvili, speaking for the Stalinist faction, pointed to numerous examples of "nationalist deviations" on the part of the Georgian Central Committee and Georgian government. They also taunted Makharadze with his record as a "nihilist" in the national question and as an opponent of Lenin's national program.[153] Stalin took no pains to conceal his utter contempt for the Georgian oppositions. "I think that some of the comrades, working on a certain piece of Soviet territory, called Georgia," he said, "have apparently something wrong with their marbles." [154]

The discussion on the national question, temporarily shelved after this premature explosion, was resumed at a later session. The principal report was delivered by Stalin. In his report, Stalin skillfully maneuvered between the two extreme views on the problem, stressing simultaneously the danger of Great Russian nationalism under the New Economic Policy and the need for the unification of the Soviet state.[155] But in the course of the discussions, in which he answered criticism leveled at the Soviet treatment of the minorities, Stalin made it unmistakably plain that he was not prepared to go along with Lenin's thesis on the relationship of the Russians toward the minorities:

> For us, as Communists, it is clear that the basis of all our work is the work for the strengthening of the rule of the workers, and only after this comes the second question — an important question, but subordinated to the first — the national question. We are told that one should not offend the nationalities. This is entirely correct, I agree with this — they should not be offended. But to create from this [idea] a new theory, that it is necessary to place the Great Russian proletariat in a position of inferiority in regard to the once oppressed nations, is an absurdity. That which Comrade Lenin uses as a metaphor in his well-known article, Bukharin transforms into a whole slogan. It is clear, however, that the political basis of the proletarian dictatorship

is in the first place and above all in the central, industrial regions, and not in the borderlands, which represent peasant countries. If we should lean too far in the direction of the peasant borderlands at the expense of the proletarian region, then a crack may develop in the system of proletarian dictatorship. This, comrades, is dangerous. In politics it is not good to stretch too far, just as it is not good to stretch too little.[156]

Next, Stalin proceeded to quote from Lenin's previously published works to the effect that the class principle had priority over the national one, and that the Communists from the minority areas were obliged to strive for a close union with the Communists of the nation which had oppressed them. It did not take great subtlety to realize that "the proletarian region," whose hegemony Stalin advocated, meant Russia, and that his references to Lenin's works were inspired by a desire to offset the damage which Lenin's memorandum had done to Stalin's prestige, by indicating the inconsistencies inherent in Lenin's national theory. To Lenin's statement that "it is better to stretch too far in the direction of complaisance and softness toward the national minorities, than too little," Stalin replied that it was not advisable to stretch too far, either.*

The case for the opposition was hopeless. Not only was the Congress packed with Stalinists,[157] but the opposition was also severely handicapped in its choice of arguments. The basic Communist assumptions worked to the advantage of Stalin. The unity, centralization, and omnipotence of the Communist Party, the hegemony of the industrial proletariat over the peasantry, the subordination of the national principle to the class principle — all those Communist doctrines which were in fact responsible for the plight of the minorities — were axiomatic and beyond dispute. By challenging them, the opposition would have placed itself outside the party. The opposition, therefore, had to limit itself to criticism of the practical execution of the Communist national program. One speaker after another of the opposition pointed out the injustices and failures of the Communist regime in the borderlands: the discrimination against non-Russians in the Red Army ("The army still remains a weapon of Russification of the Ukrainian population and of all the minority peoples," Skrypnik stated),[158] in schools, and in the treatment of the natives by officials. But such charges, damning as they were, did not affect the fundamental premises of Stalin's case and were easily brushed aside as exaggerations or minor infractions.

The only attempt to analyze the deeper causes of the crisis in the national policy was made by Rakovskii, who rested his argument on Lenin's thesis of the defective apparatus:

* Both Lenin and Stalin used in the juxtaposed phrases the Russian colloquialisms *"peresolit'"* and *"nedosolit',"* here translated as "stretch too far" and "too little." The allusion thus is obvious.

Comrades, this [national question] is one of those questions which is pregnant with very serious complications for Soviet Russia and the Party. This is one of those questions which — this must be said openly and honestly at a Party Congress — threaten civil war, if we fail to show the necessary sensitivity, the necessary understanding with regard to it. It is the question of the bond of the revolutionary Russian proletariat with the sixty million non-Russian peasants, who under the national banner raise their demands for a share in the economic and political life of the Soviet Union.[159]

Stalin, Rakovskii continued, was oversimplifying the danger of Great Russian nationalism in the party and state apparatus when he called it, in the course of his report, a mere by-product of the New Economic Policy. The real cause of the crisis lay deeper: "[It is] the fundamental divergence which occurs from day to day and becomes ever greater and greater: [the divergence] between our Party, our program on the one hand, and our political apparatus on the other." The state apparatus was, as Lenin said in his memorandum, an aristocratic and bourgeois remnant, "anointed with the Communist chrism." Rakovskii cited a number of instances of the organs of the RSFSR having issued decrees and laws for the other three Soviet republics even before the Union had been formally ratified and the authority of the federal government constitutionally ascertained, and he charged that since December 1922 the Union commissariats had actually governed the entire country, leaving the republics no self-rule whatsoever. To implement Stalin's suggestions on the means for combating the mounting wave of Russian nationalism, Rakovskii concluded, it was necessary to strip the government of the Union of Soviet Socialist Republics of nine tenths of its commissariats.[160]

How weak the opposition really was became painfully evident when Rakovskii placed before the Congress formal resolutions to reduce the preponderance of the Russian republic in the Union government. He had occupied himself much during the previous several months with constitutional questions and even had drafted a constitutional project which vested much more authority in the republics than did the one formulated in Moscow.[161] That Rakovskii should have become a defender of states' rights seemed rather strange in view of his whole record as a "nihilist" on the nationality question. But he was a close and loyal friend of Trotsky and, armed with Lenin's memorandum, he must have felt on solid ground. He now pointed out that, under the existing system, the RSFSR had three times as many representatives in the Soviet of Nationalities as the remaining three republics put together, and suggested a constitutional arrangement which would prevent any one republic from having more than two fifths of the total representation. Stalin, however, brushed aside this motion as "administrative fetishism." It was subsequently voted down.[162] The inability of the opposition to secure acceptance of even such a watered down version of Rakovskii's project (his original idea of granting the republics nine tenths of the commissariats which the articles of Union had given the federal government was whittled down in committee during the discussion of the constitutional question) indicated the extent to which Stalin and the central party apparatus had gained mastery of the situation.

The Twelfth Congress thus rejected all the suggestions which Lenin had made in his article in the hope of healing the breach in the party caused by the national question: it refused to diminish the centralization of the state apparatus of the USSR by granting the republics more organs of self-rule; it vindicated Stalin and Ordzhonikidze; and most important of all, it turned down, through Stalin, the fundamental principle of Lenin's approach, namely the necessity of having the Russians place themselves in a morally defensive position in regard to the minorities. The Twelfth Congress, the last at which the national question was discussed in an atmosphere of relatively free expression, ended in the complete triumph of Stalin. The issue of self-rule versus centralism on the administrative level was decided in favor of the latter. Henceforth nothing could prevent the process of amalgamation of the state apparatus from being brought to its conclusion — the more so, since Lenin, the only person capable of altering its course, was entirely eliminated from active participation in politics.

On July 6, 1923, the Central Executive Committee of the USSR formally approved the Constitution of the USSR, and on January 31, 1924 — ten days after Lenin's death — the Second All-Union Congress of Soviets ratified it.* The process of formation of the Soviet Union was thus brought to an end.

---

* Genkina, *Obrazovanie SSSR*, 122–62, and Iakubovskaia, *Stroitel'stvo*, 217–24, 233–71, describe in detail the steps leading to the ratification of the 1923 Constitution, and analyze the differences between the Constitution and the 1922 agreement establishing the Union.

# CONCLUSION

Although the roots of the national movements which emerged in the course of the Russian Revolution have to be sought in the tsarist period, their anti-Russian and separatist aspects were a direct result of the political and social upheaval which followed the breakdown of the *ancien régime*. Before 1917 the political activities of the minorities were closely integrated with the socialist and liberal tendencies of Russian society itself and represented regional variants of developments which were occurring at the same time on an all-Russian scale. These activities were limited to relatively small groups of intellectuals, who sought to secure for the minorities a greater degree of participation in the government of the Empire through democratization and autonomy. After 1917 the national movements assumed a somewhat different character. The disintegration of political authority and the eruption of violent agrarian revolutions throughout the Russian Empire had severed the bonds between the borderlands and the center and had left the responsibility for the solution of the most urgent social and political problems to the population itself. These groups came to power which were most capable of adjusting themselves to the rapid vacillations of public opinion. In Russia proper and in other areas inhabited by Great Russians, it was the Bolshevik Party which, with its slogans of peace, division of land, and all power to the soviets, temporarily won considerable public support. In most of the borderlands, power was won by the nationalist intelligentsia, which pledged an independent solution of the agrarian problem, the redress of injustices committed by the tsarist regime, and neutrality in the Russian Civil War. In Russia as well as in some of the borderlands, political authority was seized by extremists who had attained mass following only after the outbreak of the Revolution, when the spread of anarchy, confusion, and fear favored groups advocating radical solutions.

But whereas the Bolsheviks had long prepared for a revolution and knew what to do with power once they had attained it, the nationalists did not. They had lacked the opportunities to evolve an ideology, or to secure disciplined party cadres. The nationalist movements after 1917 suffered from profound cleavages among conservative, liberal, and radical tendencies, which prevented them from attaining the unity necessary for effective action. In critical moments, the national governments which had sprung up in the borderlands were weakened from within, torn by dissensions among the divergent groups combined under the banners of nationalism. Another weakness of the nationalists was their inability, and, in some instances, their unwillingness, to win over the predominantly Russian and Russified urban population of the border-lands. They were also far too dependent on the politically immature and ineffective rural population. When in the winter of 1917–18 the Bolsheviks and their followers in the armed forces struck for power in the borderland territories, most of the national governments collapsed without offering serious resistance. The only notable exception was Trans-caucasia, where the existence of strong indigenous parties, especially the Georgian Social Democrats, and the fear of foreign invasion which united the Russian and most of the non-Russian population, gave the local gov-ernments a certain degree of cohesion and strength. The circumstances under which the national republics of what became the Soviet Union emerged were too exceptional and their life span too short for the record to be used as evidence either for or against their viability.

The conflict between the Bolsheviks and the nationalists which broke out in all the borderland areas after the October Revolution, as a result of the Bolshevik suppression of nationalist political institutions, would probably have led to a lasting rupture between them, had it not been for the leaders of the White movement who virtually drove the national-ists into the arms of the Bolsheviks. The White generals proved incapable of grasping either the significance of the national movements or the assistance which they could offer in fighting the Communists. They rejected outright the political claims of the minorities and postponed the solution of the national question to the time when the Bolshevik usurpers should be overthrown and a legitimate Russian government established. In some instances, the White leaders antagonized the minor-ities inhabiting the theater of combat or their own rear lines to the point where armed conflicts broke out.

The Bolsheviks, on the other hand, made determined efforts, through-out the Civil War, to exploit minority nationalism. The entire Bolshevik national program was designed to win nationalist sympathies through generous offers of national self-determination. Whenever expedient, they made alliances with even the most reactionary groups among the minorities, who, fearful of losing the freedom which the collapse of all government authority had given them, lent a willing ear to Bolshevik promises. Though there were some exceptions — notably in Central Asia — the Communists generally succeeded in winning nationalist support at a time when the struggle for power in Russia was at critical stages. In the campaigns against Kolchak in the Urals and against Denikin in the Northern Caucasus, the alliance between the Reds and the nationalists helped tip the scales in favor of the Soviet regime.

The Bolshevik approach, however, although it had brought immediate advantages, also had its shortcomings. It was more useful as a means of fighting for power, than as a program for a party which had acquired power. It was one thing to exploit the mistakes of the opponent by means of promises, and another to make those promises good after the enemy had been overcome. Their entire approach to the national idea, moreover, made the Bolsheviks perhaps the least qualified of all the Russian parties (save for those of the extreme right) to solve the national problem. Not only was their political system based on the dictatorship of a single party, on strict centralism, and on the superiority of the urban, industrial elements over the remainder of the population — doctrines which in themselves precluded an equitable solution of the minority problem — but they also underestimated the viability of nationalism. They were inclined to view it as a mere relic of the bourgeois era, which was bound to disappear once the proletarian class struggle and the world revolution got under way, and they ignored the fact that nationalist movements represented in many cases genuine social, economic, and cultural aspirations. All manifestations of nationalism appearing after the establishment of Soviet power Lenin considered to be due either to the aftereffects of the old regime, or to the alleged influence of functionaries of the tsarist bureaucracy on the Soviet political apparatus. To destroy it once and for all, in Lenin's opinion, it was necessary only to adopt a friendly, conciliatory attitude toward the non-Russian subjects. That nationalism itself represented an aspect of the economic struggle, the Bolsheviks neither could nor would admit. Lenin, the chief architect of Soviet national policy, thus fell victim to his own doctrinairism. The crisis which shook the Communist Party over the national question in the early 1920's, and the Communist confusion over the persistence of national antagonisms in the Soviet Union and even in the party itself, were due largely to the inability of the Communists to recognize the flaw in their monistic class interpretation of world events.

The Soviet Union, as it emerged in 1923, was a compromise between doctrine and reality: an attempt to reconcile the Bolshevik strivings for absolute unity and centralization of all power in the hands of the party, with the recognition of the empirical fact that nationalism did survive the collapse of the old order. It was viewed as a temporary solution only, as a transitional stage to a completely centralized and supra-national world-wide soviet state. From the point of view of self-rule the Communist government was even less generous to the minorities than its tsarist predecessor had been: it destroyed independent parties, tribal self-rule, religious and cultural institutions. It was a unitary, centralized, totalitarian state such as the tsarist state had never been. On the other hand, by granting the minorities extensive linguistic autonomy and by placing the national-territorial principle at the base of the state's political administration, the Communists gave constitutional recognition to the multinational structure of the Soviet population. In view of the importance which language and territory have for the development of national consciousness — particularly for people who, like the Russian minorities during the Revolution, have had some experience of self-rule — this purely formal feature of the Soviet Constitution may well prove to have been historically one of the most consequential aspects of the formation of the Soviet Union.

# CHRONOLOGY OF PRINCIPAL EVENTS

*(All dates are Gregorian, or New Style)*

## 1917

| | |
|---|---|
| March | 12–15: Russian Revolution; establishment of Provisional Government; abolition of all legal disabilities of national minorities. 17: Formation of the Ukrainian Central Rada in Kiev. |
| April | Various Moslem congresses held throughout the Empire. |
| May | 14: Opening of the First All-Russian Moslem Congress in Moscow. |
| June | 23: The Ukrainian Central Rada issues its First Universal. |
| August | 17: The Instruction of the Provisional Government to the Ukrainian Central Rada. |
| November | 7: Bolshevik coup in Petrograd. 8–12: Bolshevik-Rada coup in Kiev. 7–14: Bolshevik–Left SR coup in Tashkent. 24: Establishment of the Transcaucasian Commissariat. |
| December | 6: Finland proclaims its independence. 11: Lithuania proclaims its independence; opening of the Regional Moslem Congress in Kokand. 17: Communist ultimatum to the Ukrainian Central Rada. 19: Opening of the First All-Ukrainian Congress of Soviets in Kiev. 27: Opening of the Belorussian National Congress in Minsk. 30: First Soviet Government of the Ukraine formed in Kharkov. |

## 1918

| | |
|---|---|
| January | 12: Latvia proclaims its independence. 18: Beginning of the Red Army offensive against Kiev. 22: Fourth Universal of the Ukrainian Central Rada proclaiming Ukrainian independence. |
| February | 8: Red Army takes Kiev. 11: Beginning of Moslem-Communist conflict in Kokand. 24: Estonia proclaims its independence. |
| March | 3: German armies march into Kiev. |
| April | 1: Bolshevik-Dashnak coup in Baku. 22: The Transcaucasian Federative Republic proclaims its independence. 29: Germans disband the Ukrainian Central Rada. |
| May | 26: Georgia proclaims its independence. 28: Azerbaijan and Armenia proclaim their independence. |
| July | 10: Ratification of the first Constitution of the RSFSR by the Fifth All-Russian Congress of Soviets. |
| August | 5: Beginning of the abortive Communist uprising in the Ukraine. |
| September | 15: Turkish armies capture Baku. |
| November | 11: End of World War I. 30: Establishment in Moscow of the Council of Workers' and Peasants' Defense. |
| December | 14: Troops of the Directory march into Kiev. |

## 1919

| | |
|---|---|
| January | Armed conflict between Red Army and Directory. |
| February | 6: Red Army captures Kiev. |
| March | 18–23: Eighth Congress of RKP(b) and adoption of new party program. |

October 2: Dissolution of the Central Committee of the KP(b)U. 14: Denikin occupies Orel; high point of his advance on Moscow. 20: Red Army retakes Orel.

## 1920

February 20: Red Army captures Khiva.

April 8: Creation of Caucasian Bureau of RKP(b) (*Kavbiuro*). 25: Outbreak of Soviet-Polish war. 27: Communists invade Azerbaijan and seize Baku.

May 6: Polish armies enter Kiev. 7: Signing of Soviet-Georgian Treaty. 22: New edict on Bashkir autonomy and outbreak of Bashkir rebellion. 25: Outbreak of Azerbaijani rebellion in Gandzha.

August Outbreak of rebellion in Daghestan.

September 2: Red Army captures Bukhara. 30: Treaty with Soviet Azerbaijan.

November 29: Communist ultimatum to Armenia, followed by Turkish-Soviet partition of that country.

## 1921

February 11: Beginning of Red Army operations against the Georgian Republic. 16: Outbreak of rebellion in Soviet Armenia. 25: Red Army captures Tiflis.

November Enver Pasha deserts Communists and joins Basmachis.

## 1922

March 12: Formation of first Soviet Transcaucasian federation (FSSSRZ).

August 4: Death of Enver Pasha. 10: Central Committee appoints committee to formulate principles of union; Stalin's "autonomization" project.

September 27: Lenin intervenes and forces Stalin to abandon "autonomization."

October 6: Plenum of Central Committee approves revised draft of principles establishing the Union. 22: Resignation of the Central Committee of the Communist Party of Georgia.

November 21: G. V. Chicherin heads subcommittee drafting Union constitution.

December 30: First Congress of Soviets of the USSR meets in the Kremlin. 30–31: Lenin writes memorandum on the national question.

## 1923

April 17–25: Twelfth Congress of the RKP(b).

Spring Arrest of Sultan-Galiev.

July 6: The Central Executive Committee of the USSR approves project of Constitution of the USSR.

## 1924

January 21: Death of Lenin. 31: Ratification of the Constitution of the USSR by the Second All-Union Congress of Soviets.

ETHNIC DISTRIBUTION OF THE POPULATION OF THE RUSSIAN EMPIRE
AND THE SOVIET UNION ACCORDING TO THE CENSUSES OF 1897 AND
1926 (*in round figures*)

| Nationality or language group | 1897 | | 1926 | |
|---|---|---|---|---|
| | Total within 1897 borders of Russian Empire (by language) | Total within 1926 borders of USSR (by language) | By nationality | By language |
| Great Russians | 55,667,500 | 54,563,700 | 77,732,200 | 84,129,200 |
| Ukrainians | 22,380,600 | 20,232,500 | 31,189,500 | 27,569,200 |
| Belorussians | 5,885,500 | 3,570,600 | 4,738,200 | 3,466,900 |
| Poles | 7,931,300 | 531,900 | 781,700 | 362,400 |
| Czechs, Slovaks | 50,400 | 20,800 | 27,100 | 25,100 |
| Serbians, Bulgarians | 174,500 | 70,000 | 113,800 | 109,200 |
| Lithuanians, Zmud, Latgals | 1,658,500 | 22,200 | 51,100 | 29,800 |
| Latvians | 1,435,900 | 67,900 | 141,400 | 115,800 |
| Iranian group | 31,700 | 31,100 | 51,300 | 66,600 |
| Tajik group† | 350,400 | 350,400 | 376,400 | 390,100 |
| Talyshes | 35,300 | 35,300 | 77,300 | 80,600 |
| Tats | 95,100 | 95,000 | 28,700 | 87,000 |
| Kurds, Yezidis | 99,900 | 38,400 | 69,100 | 34,100 |
| Ossetins | 171,700 | 171,200 | 272,000 | 266,800 |
| Moldavians, Rumanians | 1,121,700 | 195,100 | 283,500 | 267,600 |
| Germans | 1,790,500 | 1,029,800 | 1,237,900 | 1,192,700 |
| Greeks | 186,900 | 151,500 | 213,700 | 202,600 |
| Gypsies | 44,600 | 31,500 | 59,300 | 40,900 |
| Other Indo-Europeans | 44,000 | 31,800 | 12,500 | 11,000 |
| Jews | 5,063,200 | 2,430,400 | 2,663,400 | 1,883,000 |
| Arabs, Aisors | 7,000 | 6,500 | 15,700 | 16,900 |
| Georgians | 1,352,500 | 1,329,300 | 1,820,900 | 1,908,500 |
| Armenians | 1,173,100 | 1,065,300 | 1,565,800 | 1,472,900 |
| Kabardians | 98,600 | 98,600 | 139,900 ⎫ | 219,300 |
| Cherkesses | 46,300 | 46,200 | 79,100 ⎭ | |
| Abkhazians | 72,100 | 72,100 | 57,000 | 48,100 |
| Chechens | 226,500 | 226,400 | 318,500 ⎫ | 396,300 |
| Ingushes | 47,800 | 47,700 | 74,100 ⎭ | |
| Daghestan Mountain groups | 600,500 | 600,100 | 574,500 | 595,400 |
| Finnish group† | 143,100 | 138,700 | 135,400 | 153,400 |
| Votiaks | 421,000 | 420,100 | 514,200 | 508,700 |

(*continued*)

| Nationality or language group | 1897 | | 1926 | |
|---|---|---|---|---|
| | Total within 1897 borders of Russian Empire (by language) | Total within 1926 borders of USSR (by language) | By nationality | By language |
| Karels | 208,100 | 207,700 | 248,100 | 239,600 |
| Izhoras | 13,800 | 13,300 | 16,100 | —— |
| Chude (Vepsas) | 25,800 | 25,700 | 32,800 | 31,100 |
| Estonians | 1,002,700 | 103,600 | 154,600 | 139,500 |
| Komi (Zyrians) | 153,600 | 153,200 | 226,300 | 220,400 |
| Permiaks | 104,700 | 104,700 | 149,400 | 143,800 |
| Mordvinians | 1,023,800 | 1,020,700 | 1,339,900 | 1,266,600 |
| Marii (Cheremis) | 375,400 | 374,700 | 428,200 | 425,700 |
| Voguls | 7,600 | 7,600 | 5,700 | 5,200 |
| Ostiaks | 19,700 | 19,700 | 22,200 | 18,600 |
| Turco-Tatar group* | 3,767,500 | 3,679,000 | 4,898,800 | 5,444,300 |
| Bashkirs | 1,493,000 | 1,491,900 | 983,100 | 392,800 |
| Karachaevs, Kumyks, Nogais | 174,700 | 174,700 | 186,000 | 173,400 |
| Other Turks | 440,400 | 440,400 | —— | —— |
| Uzbeks, Sarts, Kuramas† | 1,702,800 | 1,702,800 | 2,440,900 | 2,497,200 |
| Taranchi, Kashgars, Uighurs | 71,400 | 71,400 | 108,200 | 67,500 |
| Kara-Kalpaks | 104,300 | 104,300 | 126,000 | 114,900 |
| Kazakhs, Kirghiz | 4,285,800 | 4,285,700 | 4,578,600 | 4,673,300 |
| Turkmens (Turkomans)† | 281,400 | 272,800 | 427,600 | 426,700 |
| Chuvashes | 843,800 | 840,300 | 1,117,300 | 1,104,400 |
| Iakuts, Dolgans | 227,400 | 227,400 | 214,800 | 220,400 |
| Kalmyks | 190,600 | 190,500 | 133,500 | 131,100 |
| Buriats, Mongols | 289,500 | 289,500 | 238,100 | 236,800 |
| Chukchi | 11,800 | 11,800 | 11,100 | 11,300 |
| Chinese, Dungans | 57,400 | 57,300 | 24,800 | 100,700 |
| Koreans | 26,000 | 25,900 | 87,000 | 170,600 |
| Others and unknown | 355,800 | 185,000 | 326,400 | 421,700 |
| Foreign citizens | —— | —— | 387,000 | —— |
| Total population† | 125,666,500 | 103,803,700 | 144,327,700 | |

Based on: Tsentral'noe statisticheskoe upravlenie SSSR, Otdel perepisi, Vsesoiuznaia perepis' naseleniia 17 Dekabria 1926 g., Kratkie svodki, Vypusk IV, *Narodnost' i rodnoi iazyk naseleniia SSSR* (Moscow, 1928), Table I, pp. xxiv–xxvii.

* Includes Volga Tatars, Azerbaijanis, and Crimean Tatars.

† Exclusive of the principalities of Khiva and Bukhara, and Finland. The total population of the territories of Khiva and Bukhara in 1926 was 2,677,700, among them 1,547,200 Uzbeks, 603,700 Tajiks, and 338,500 Turkmens (by nationality).

# THE SYSTEM OF TRANSLITERATION

The Library of Congress system of transliteration is used throughout this book, but without diacritical marks and ligatures.

| Russian | | | Ukrainian | | | Belorussian | | |
|---|---|---|---|---|---|---|---|---|
| А | а | a | А | а | a | А | а | a |
| Б | б | b | Б | б | b | Б | б | b |
| В | в | v | В | в | v | В | в | v |
| Г | г | g | Г | г | h | Г | г | h |
| —— | | | Ґ | ґ | g | Ґ | ґ | g |
| Д | д | d | Д | д | d | Д | д | d |
| Е | е | e | Е | е | e | Е | е | e |
| —— | | | Є | є | ie | | | |
| Ё | ё | e | —— | | | Ё | ё | io |
| Ж | ж | zh | Ж | ж | zh | Ж | ж | zh |
| З | з | z | З | з | z | З | з | z |
| И | и | i | И | и | y | —— | | |
| І | і | i | І | і | i | І | і | i |
| | | | Ї | ї | i | —— | | |
| Й | й | i | Й | й | i | Й | й | i |
| К | к | k | К | к | k | К | к | k |
| Л | л | l | Л | л | l | Л | л | l |
| М | м | m | М | м | m | М | м | m |
| Н | н | n | Н | н | n | Н | н | n |
| О | о | o | О | о | o | О | о | o |
| П | п | p | П | п | p | П | п | p |
| Р | р | r | Р | р | r | Р | р | r |
| С | с | s | С | с | s | С | с | s |
| Т | т | t | Т | т | t | Т | т | t |
| У | у | u | У | у | u | У | у | u |
| | | | | | | Ў | ў | u |
| —— | | | —— | | | | | |
| Ф | ф | f | Ф | ф | f | Ф | ф | f |
| Х | х | kh | Х | х | kh | Х | х | kh |
| Ц | ц | ts | Ц | ц | ts | Ц | ц | ts |
| Ч | ч | ch | Ч | ч | ch | Ч | ч | ch |
| Ш | ш | sh | Ш | ш | sh | Ш | ш | sh |

| Щ щ | shch | Щ щ | shch | | —— |
| Ъ ъ | " | | —— | | —— |
| Ы ы | y | | —— | Ы ы | y |
| Ь ь | ' | Ь ь | | Ь ь | ' |
| Ѣ ѣ | e | | —— | | —— |
| Э э | e | | —— | Э э | e |
| Ю ю | iu | Ю ю | iu | Ю ю | iu |
| Я я | ia | Я я | ia | Я я | ia |

# BIBLIOGRAPHY

For the abbreviations used in the Bibliography see the list facing the first page of Chapter 1. To enhance the usefulness of the Bibliography, the institution where each item can be located is indicated in abbreviated form. The absence of a symbol following the place and date of publication signifies that the source can be found in the Harvard College Library. A book listed as located in a given library, may, of course, in many instances be found in other libraries as well. Periodical publications may be located through the *Union List of Serials*.

# I

# THE NATIONAL PROBLEM IN RUSSIA

## I. GENERAL INFORMATION

### a. The National Minorities

The general literature concerning the minorities in Russia is voluminous. Bibliographies can be found in G. K. Ul'ianov, *Obzor literatury po voprosam kul'tury i prosveshcheniia narodov SSSR* (Moscow-Leningrad, 1930), and G. Teich and H. Ruebel, *Voelker, Volksgruppen und Volkstaemme auf dem ehemaligen Gebiet der UdSSR* (Leipzig, 1942). The latter, however, is replete with errors. D. K. Zelenin, *Bibliograficheskii ukazatel' russkoi etnograficheskoi literatury, 1700–1910* (St. Petersburg, 1913) can be highly recommended as an ethnographic bibliography.

### b. The National Question in General

The journals *Okrainy Rossii* (St. Petersburg, 1906; CSt-H) and *Narody i oblasti* (Moscow, 1914; CSt-H), the former expressing the views of the rightist parties, the latter of the liberal and moderate socialist elements, were devoted exclusively to the discussion of the national problem in Russia. Other sources are:

K. Fortunatov, *Natsional'nyia oblasti Rossii* (St. Petersburg, 1906; Doc. Int.).

E. Haumant, *Le Problème de l'unité russe* (Paris, 1922; NN).

Inorodetz, *La Russie et les peuples allogènes* (Berne, 1917).

M. Langhans, "Die staatsrechtliche Entwicklung der auf Russischen Boden lebenden kleineren Nationalitaeten," *Archiv fuer oeffentliches Recht, Neue Folge*, IX (1925), 173–210 (NN).

C. Lamont, *The Peoples of the Soviet Union* (New York, 1944). Accepts uncritically Communist views.

G. von Mende, *Die Voelker der Sowjetunion* (Reichenau, 1939; NNC), National-Socialist viewpoint.

P. N. Miliukov, *Natsional'nyi vopros* (Prague; 1925).

P. P. Semenov, ed.: *Okrainy Rossii* (St. Petersburg, 1900; CSt-H).

### c. The National Question during the 1917 Revolution

V. B. Stankevich, *Sud'by narodov Rossii* (Berlin, 1921; NN), and E. H. Carr, *The Bolshevik Revolution*, I (New York, 1951), deal at length with the fate of the national minorities during the Revolution and Civil War. G. Semenoff, "Die nationale Frage in der russischen Revolution," *Zeitschrift fuer Politik*, XIV (1924–25), 247–75, contains a reliable historic account. See also:

X. Eudin, "Soviet National Minority Policies, 1918–21," *The Slavonic and East European Review*, XXI (1943), pt. 2, 31–55.

N. N. Popov, *Oktiabr'skaia revoliutsiia i natsional'nyi vopros* (Moscow, 1927; CSt-H).

### d. Soviet National Policy — General Studies

The most thorough and most recent work on this subject is by W. Kolarz, *Russia and Her Colonies* (London, 1952). Other works are:

S. Akopov, *Oktiabr' i uspekhi natsional'nogo stroitel'stva* (Moscow, [1932]; CSt-H).

W. Biehahn, "Marxismus und nationale Idee in Russland," *Osteuropa*, IX (1933–34), 461–76. An early statement of the theory that Marxism is merely a "cover" for Russian nationalism.

——— "Marxismus und Russentum im Bolschewismus," *Osteuropa*, X (1934–35), 492–507. Same view as in previous article.

G. I. Broido, *Natsional'nyi i kolonial'nyi vopros* (Moscow, 1924).

——— "Osnovnye voprosy natsional'noi politiki," *ZhN*, nos. 3–4 (1923), 3–9. An important semi-official statement.

W. H. Chamberlin, "Soviet Race and Nationality Policies," *Russian Review*, V, no. 1 (1945), 3–9.

[S. M. Dimanshtein, ed.], *Natsional'naia politika VKP(b) v tsifrakh* (Moscow, 1930; CSt-H).

W. von Harpe, *Die Grundsaetze der Nationalitaetenpolitik Lenins* (Berlin, 1941)

E. Kantor, *Chto dala sovetskaia vlast' narodam Rossii* (Moscow, 1923; CSt-H).

H. Kohn, *Nationalism in the Soviet Union* (New York, 1933).

L. Mainardi, *USSR — prigione di popoli* (Rome, 1941; DLC).

N. Nurmakov, ed., *Natsional'noe stroitel'stvo v RSFSR k XV godovshchine Oktiabr'ia* (Moscow, 1933; CSt-H).

L. Perchik, *Kak sovetskaia vlast' razreshaet natsional'nyi vopros* ([Moscow], 1932; CSt-H).

R. E. Pipes, "The Genesis of Soviet National Policy" (Ph.D. dissertation, Harvard University, 1950).

N. N. Popov, *Natsional'naia politika sovetskoi vlasti* (Moscow-Leningrad, 1927).

M. Ravich-Cherkasskii, ed. *Marksizm i natsional'nyi vopros* ([Kharkov], 1923; NN). Sources.

P. M. Rysakov, *The National Policy of the CPSU* (Moscow, 1932; NN).

G. Safarov, "Revoliutsionnyi marksizm i natsional'nyi vopros," in Ravich-Cherkasskii, ed., *Marksizm i natsional'nyi vopros*, 305–68.

S. M. Schwarz, *The Jews in the Soviet Union* (Syracuse, 1951).

M. Tougouchi-Gaïannée, *URSS — Face au problème des nationalités* (Liège, [1948]; private).

I. P. Trainin, *SSSR i natsional'naia problema* (Moscow, 1924; NN). Important for numerous statistics.

——— *Velikoe sodruzhestvo narodov SSSR* (Moscow, 1945; DLC).

A. Yarmolinsky, *The Jews and Other Minor Nationalities under the Soviets* (New York, 1928).

### e. The Historical Growth of the Soviet Union

E. B. Genkina, *Obrazovanie SSSR — Sbornik dokumentov, 1917–1924* (Moscow-Leningrad, 1949), is a collection of documents dealing with this topic; careful selection and frequent mutilation of sources demand that it be used with utmost caution. This author's *Obrazovanie SSSR* ([Moscow], 1947), and S. I. Iakubovskaia, *Ob"edinitel'noe dvizhenie za obrazovanie SSSR, (1917–1922)*, ([Moscow], 1947), require the same attitude. Other works are:

W. R. Batsell, *Soviet Rule in Russia* (New York, 1929). Important for its documentation.

S. I. Iakubovskaia, "K voprosu ob obrazovanii SSSR," *Voprosy istorii*, no. 1 (1947), 3–24.

P. A. Miliukov, *Rossiia na perelome* I (Paris, 1927), chapter iv, 202–57.

V. N. L'vov, *Sovetskaia vlast' v bor'be za russkuiu gosudarstvennost'* (Berlin, 1922; CSt-H).

### f. Primary Sources and Periodical Publications

The following works contain important collections of documentary material pertaining to the national problem in Russia: V. N. Durdenevskii, *Ravnopravie iazykov v sovetskom stroe* (Moscow, 1927; NN); G. K. Klinger, ed., *Sovetskaia politika za 10 let po natsional'nomu voprosu v RSFSR* (Moscow-Leningrad, 1928; NN).

The most important periodical dealing with the problem is the newspaper (later journal) *Zhizn' natsional'nostei* (Moscow, 1918–24; CSt-H), published by the Commissariat of Nationalities. The magazine *Revoliutsiia i natsional'nosti* (1933–37) is somewhat less useful. Much information can be obtained from the journals *Proletarskaia revoliutsiia*, *Vlast' sovetov*, and *Kommunisticheskii Internatsional* (CSt-H).

## II. THE RUSSIAN EMPIRE BEFORE 1917

There is unfortunately no systematic study of the historical development and administrative structure of the Russian Empire. A very useful bibliography of pertinent materials can be found in E. Drabkina, *Natsional'nyi i kolonial'nyi vopros v tsarskoi Rossii* (Moscow, 1930), with separate lists for each region. The following surveys can be recommended:

W. Gribowski, *Das Staatsrecht des Russischen Reiches* (Tuebingen, 1912).

V. Ivanovskii, "Administrativnoe ustroistvo nashikh okrain," *Uchenyia zapiski Imperatorskago Kazanskago Universiteta*, LVIII (1891), no. 6, 27–70.

S. V. Iushkov, *Istoriia gosudarstva i prava SSSR*, I (Moscow, 1940).

N. M. Korkunov, *Russkoe gosudarstvennoe pravo*, I (St. Petersburg, 1899; NN) and II (St. Petersburg, 1897; NN).

N. I. Lazarevskii, *Russkoe gosudarstvennoe pravo*, I (Petrograd, 1917) and II (St Petersburg, 1910).

B. E. Nol'de, *Ocherki russkago gosudarstvennago prava* (St. Petersburg, 1911), Part III.

G. B. Sliozberg, *Dorevoliutsionnyi stroi Rossii* (Paris, 1933), 28–96.

Information concerning the national question in the Dumas can be found in the following:

A. R. Lednitskii, "Natsional'nyi vopros v Gosudarstvennoi Dume," *Pervaia Gosudarstvennaia Duma, Sbornik Statei*, I (St. Petersburg, 1907), 154–67.

E. L. Minsky, ed., *The National Question in the Russian Duma* (London, 1915; NN).

N. A. Gredeskul, "Natsional'nyi vopros v Pervoi Dume," *K 10-letiiu Pervoi Gosudarstvennoi Dumy, Sbornik* (Petrograd, 1916), 76–88.

### III. THE NATIONAL MOVEMENTS IN RUSSIA IN MODERN TIMES

A. I. Kastelianskii, ed., *Formy natsional'nago dvizheniia v sovremennykh gosudarstvakh* (St. Petersburg, 1910; DLC) is an unique and absolutely indispensable survey, written by a number of authorities with liberal or socialist leanings; it deals with the national movements among various minority groups in Russia and abroad. Z. Lenskii, "Natsional'noe dvizhenie," *Obshchestvennoe dvizhenie v Rossii v nachale XX-go veka* (St. Petersburg, 1909), I, 349–71, and K. Zalevskii, "Natsional'nyia dvizheniia," *ibid.*, IV, pt. 2 (1911), 149–243, approach the topic from the Social Democratic (Menshevik) point of view. Kommunisticheskaia Akademiia, *Pervaia russkaia revoliutsiia* (Moscow, 1930), contains an excellent bibliography of the literature on the national question which appeared during the revolution of 1905.

Bibliographic information concerning each national group will be found in the bibliography dealing with that group.

### IV. SOCIALISM AND THE NATIONAL PROBLEM IN WESTERN AND CENTRAL EUROPE

#### a. General

S. F. Bloom, *The World of Nations — A Study of the National Implications of the Work of Karl Marx* (New York, 1941).

H. Cunow, "Marx und das Selbstbestimmungsrecht der Nationen," *NZ*, XXXVI, pt. 1 (1917–18), 577–84; 607–17.

—— *Die Marxsche Geschichts- Gesellschafts- und Staatstheorie*, II (Berlin, 1923).

T. G. Masaryk, *Die philosophischen und soziologischen Grundlagen des Marxismus* (Vienna, 1899), chapter viii, "Nationalitaet und Internationalitaet."

*b. The Second International and Some of Its Leaders*

Some idea about the national theories of the leaders of the Second International may be gained from the results of a questionnaire sent out by *La Vie Socialiste* and published in nos. 15–19 (5 June–20 August 1905), which contain replies from seventeen leading European and American socialists. The stenographic reports of the Stuttgart Congress, *Internationaler Sozialisten-Kongress* (Stuttgart, 1907), are also informative. See also:

M. Anim, "Das Nationalitaetsprinzip in der sozialistischen Internationale," *Sozialistische Monatshefte* (Berlin), II (1910), 885–90.

J. Lenz, *Die II Internationale und Ihr Erbe, 1889–1929* (Hamburg, n.d.).

K. Kautsky, one of the chief theoreticians of the Second International wrote much and influenced socialist thinking in Austria and Russia. See:

K. Kautsky, "Die moderne Nationalitaet," *NZ*, V (1887), 392–405; 442–51.

—— *Das Erfurter Programm* (Stuttgart, 1892).

—— "Finis Poloniae?" *NZ*, XIV, pt. 2 (1895–96), 484–91.

—— "Der Kampf der Nationalitaeten und das Staatsrecht in Oesterreich," *NZ*, XVI, pt. 1 (1897–98), 516–24; 557–64; 723–26.

—— "Die Krisis in Oesterreich," *NZ*, XXII, pt. 1 (1903–04), 39–46; 72–79.

—— *Patriotismus und Sozialdemokratie* (Leipzig, 1907).

—— "Nationalitaet und Internationalitaet," *NZ, Ergaenzungsheft No. 1* (Stuttgart, 1908). Kautsky's main work on the subject.

—— *Nationalstaat, Imperialistischer Staat und Staatenbund* (Nuernberg, 1915).

—— "Zwei Schriften zum umlernen," *NZ*, XXXIII, pt. 2 (1915), 71–81.

—— "Nochmals unsere Illusionen," *NZ*, XXXIII, pt. 2 (1915), 230–41.

—— "Noch einige Bemerkungen ueber nationale Triebkraefte," *NZ*, XXXIV, pt. 2 (1916), 705–13.

Bernstein's ideas can be found scattered through the following works:

E. Bernstein, *Die Voraussetzungen des Sozialismus und die Aufgaben der Sozialdemokratie* (Stuttgart, 1899).

—— *Zur Geschichte und Theorie des Sozialismus* (Berlin-Bern, 1901).

—— "Vom geschichtlichen Recht der Kleinen," *NZ*, XXXIII, pt. 2 (1915), 753–59.

—— *Sozialdemokratische Voelkerpolitik* (Leipzig, 1917).

Of interest also are the following essays:

H. Cunow, "Illusionen-Kultus," *NZ*, XXXIII, pt. 2 (1915), 172–81.

L. H. Hartmann, "Die Nationalitaetenfrage und die Sozialdemokratie," *Die Neue Gesellschaft* (1907), 263–72.

H. Heller, *Sozialismus und Nation* (Berlin, 1925).

L. Martin, "Die Nationalisierung der Deutschen Sozialdemokratie," *Gegenwart*, II, no. 37 (1907).

M. Schippel, "Nationalitaets- und sonstiger Revisionismus," *Sozialistische Monatshefte*, II (1907), 712–19.

J. Strasser, *Der Arbeiter und die Nation* (Reichenberg, 1912; DLC). Strasser influenced Lenin.

For the "Austrian theory" the most important works are: Otto Bauer, *Die Nationalitaetenfrage und die Sozialdemokratie*, in *Marx-Studien*, II (Vienna, 1907);

Karl Renner, *Das Selbstbestimmungsrecht der Nationen; Erster Teil: Nation und Staat* (Leipzig-Vienna, 1918). Bauer's work is particularly to be recommended.

F. Austerlitz, "Die Nationalen Triebkraefte," *NZ*, XXXIV, pt. 1 (1915–16), 641–48.

O. Bauer, "Bemerkungen zur Nationalitaetenfrage," *NZ*, XXVI, pt. 1 (1908), 800–802.

——— "Die Bedingungen der nationalen Assimilation," *Der Kampf*, V, no. 6 (March 1912), 246–63. A brief restatement of his views.

A. Kogan, "Socialism in the Multi-National State" (Ph.D. dissertation, Harvard University, 1946).

*Verhandlungen des Gesamtparteitages der Sozialdemokratie in Oesterreich (Bruenn)* (Vienna, 1899).

### V. RUSSIAN POLITICAL PARTIES AND THE NATIONAL QUESTION

The material concerning the national programs and theories of Russian political parties is mainly of a primary nature.

*a. The Right-Wing Parties*

G. Iurskii, *Pravye v Tret'ei Gosudarstvennoi Dume* (Kharkov, 1912).

*Natsionalisty v Tret'ei Gosudarstvennoi Dume* (St. Petersburg, 1912).

*b. The Kadets*

P. D. Dolgorukov, *Natsional'naia politika i Partiia Narodnoi Svobody* (Rostov on Don, 1919; CSt-H).

F. F. Kokoshkin, *Avtonomiia i federatsiia* (Petrograd, 1917; NN). NN).

*Partiia 'Narodnoi Svobody,' Programma* (Moscow, n.d.; NN).

*Programma Partii Narodnoi Svobody (K-D) priniataia na s"ezde v Petrograde 28 Marta 1917 goda* (Odessa, 1917; NN).

*Zakonodatel'nyia proekty i predpolozheniia Partii Narodnoi Svobody, 1905–1907 gg.* (St. Petersburg, 1907; NN).

*c The Socialist Revolutionary Party*

M. Borisov, "Sotsializm i problema natsional'noi avtonomii," *SR*, No. 2 (1910), 227–64.

N. V. Briullova-Shaskol'skaia, *Partiia Sotsialistov-Revoliutsionerov i natsional'nyi vopros* (Petrograd, 1917; CSt-H).

V. Chernov, "Edinoobrazie ili shablon?" *SR*, no. 3 (1911), 147–60.

*Le Parti Socialiste-Révolutionaire et le problème des nationalités en Russie* ([Paris, 1919]; CSt-H).

*Protokoly pervago s"ezda Partii Sotsialistov-Revoliutsionerov* (n.p., 1906; NN).

*Protokoly tret'iego s"ezda Partii Sotsialistov-Revoliutsionerov* (Petrograd, 1917; NN).

*Protokoly konferentsii rossiiskikh natsional'no-sotsialisticheskikh partii* (St. Petersburg, 1908; NN).

A. Savin, "Natsional'nyi vopros i partiia S-R," *SR*, no. 3 (1911), 95–146.

*Stat'i po natsional'nomu voprosu* (Warsaw, 1921; NNC) — B. Savinkov and others.

*d. The Russian Social Democratic Labor Party (General)*

"Iz partii," *Iskra*, no. 7 (August 1901).

V. Leder, "Natsional'nyi vopros v pol'skoi i russkoi sotsial-demokratii," *PR*, nos. 2–3 (1927), 148–208.

RS-DRP, *Vtoroi ocherednoi s"ezd Ross. sots.-dem. rabochei partii-polnyi tekst protokolov* (Geneva, [1903]; NN).

*VKP(b) v resoliutsiakh i resheniakh s"ezdov, konferentsii i plenumov TsK (1890–1932)*, I (1898–1924) (Moscow, 1932; NN).

M. Velikovskii and I. Levin, eds., *Natsional'nyi vopros* ([Moscow], 1931; NN). Important sources.

*e. The Russian Social Democratic Labor Party (Mensheviks)*

G. Geilikman, "Natsionalnyi vopros i proletariat," *Itogi i perspektivy — Sbornik statei* (Moscow, 1906; DLC), 115–39.

D. Markovich, *Avtonomiia i federatsiia* (Petrograd, 1917; NN).

[L. Martov], "Revoliutsionnyi natsionalizm i sotsial-demokratiia," *Iskra*, no. 66 (May 1904).

[L. Martov], "Byt' li sotsializmu natsional'nym?" *Iskra*, no. 72 (August 1904).

G. V. Plekhanov, "Kommentarii k proektu programmy R.S.-D.R.P.," *Sochineniia* (Moscow, [1923]–1927), XII, 205–39.

——— "Otvet nashim neposledovatel'nym sionistam," *Sochineniia*, XIII, 165–68.

——— "Patriotizm i sotsializm," *Sochineniia*, XIII, 263–72.

——— "Eshche odna raskol'nich'ia konferentsiia," *Sochineniia*, XIX, 424–35.

——— "Pis'ma k soznatel'nym rabochim," *Sochineniia*, XIX, 519–29.

*h. The Bund and Other Jewish Socialist Parties*

A. Perelman, "Avtonomizm," *Evreiskaia Entsiklopediia* (St. Petersburg, [1906–1913]), I, 358–67.

V. B—", "Antisemitizm, assimilatsiia i proletarskaia bor'ba," *Iskra*, no. 55 (December, 1903).

[V. Kossovskii], *K voprosu o natsional'noi avtonomii i preobrazovanii Ros. sots.-demokr. rabochei partii na federativnykh nachalakh* (London, 1902).

V. Medem, "K postanovke natsional'nogo voprosa v Rossii," *VE*, XLVII, no. 8 (August 1912), 149–63; no. 9 (September 1912), 149–65.

——— *Sotsialdemokratiia i natsional'nyi vopros* (St. Petersburg, 1906; NN).

——— "Natsional'noe dvizhenie i natsional'nyia sotsialisticheskiia partii v Rossii," in Kastelianskii, *Formy*, 747–98.

M. B. Ratner, Introduction to *Debaty po natsional'nomu voprosu na briunskom parteitage* (Kiev-St. Petersburg, 1906; DLC).

M. Rafes, *Ocherki po istorii "Bunda"* ([Moscow], 1923).

Kh. Zhitlovskii, *Sotsializm i natsional'nyi vopros* (Kiev, 1906; NN).

VI. LENIN AND THE BOLSHEVIKS

*a. Lenin*

Lenin's works on the national question are too numerous to be mentioned individually. The principal essays can be found assembled in V. I. Lenin, *Sobranie sochinenii* (1st ed.; Moscow, 1922–27), XIX, and V. I. Lenin, *Izbrannye stat'i po natsional'nomu voprosu* (Moscow-Leningrad, 1925). Some key sentences from Lenin's writings are selected in P. I. Stuchka, *Leninizm i natsional'nyi vopros* (Moscow, 1926). The most complete and best annotated edition of Lenin's works is the third. V. I. Lenin, *Sochineniia* (30 vols.; Moscow, 1935), which is arranged chronologically, rather than topically. The last volume contains a subject index. Very useful too are Lenin's notes and drafts (many of them not included in the third edition of the *Sochineniia*) found in *Leninskii sbornik*, especially vol. III (1925), 455–87; XVII (1931), 207–318; and XXX (1937).

Among secondary works on Lenin's national theory, many of which are listed in the numbers of *Leniniana* (Moscow, 1926ff.) are:

D. Baevskii, "Bol'sheviki v bor'be za III Internatsional," *IM*, XI (1929), 12–48.

A. Begeulov, ed., *Leninizm i natsional'nyi vopros* ([Rostov on Don, 1931]; CSt-H).
M. Pavlovich, "Lenin i natsional'nyi vopros," *Pod znamenem Marksizma*, I (1924), 164–88 (CSt-H).
N. N. Popov, *Lenin o natsional'nom voprose* (Moscow, 1924).
M. Ravich-Cherkasskii, *Lenin i natsional'nyi vopros* (Kharkov, 1924; NN).
B. D. Wolfe, *Three Who Made a Revolution* (New York, 1948).

*b. Other Bolshevik and Social Democratic Writers*

V. Insarov, "Natsional'nyi vopros i marksizm," *Obrazovanie*, XVI, no. 1 (1907), 153–84; no. 2a (1907), 24–51 (NN).
R. Luxemburg, "Der Sozialpatriotismus in Polen," *NZ*, XIV, pt. 2 (1895–96).
────── Articles on the national question, from the *Przegląd Social-demokratyczny*, in M. Velikovskii and I. Levin, *Natsional'nyi vopros* (Moscow, 1931; NN), 215–41.
K. Radek, "Annexionen und Sozialdemokratie," *Berner Tagwacht*, 28–29 October 1915, quoted extensively in *LS*, XVII (1931), 280–83.
I. V. Stalin, "Marksizm i natsional'nyi vopros," *Sochineniia* (Moscow, 1946ff), II, 290–367.
────── *Marxism and the National Question* (New York, 1942).
L. Trotsky, "Natsional'naia bor'ba i edinstvo proletariata," *Sochineniia* (Moscow, 1924ff), IV, 370–73.
────── "Imperializm i natsional'naia ideia," *Sochineniia*, IX, 207–09.
────── "Natsiia i khoziaistvo," *Sochineniia*, IX, 209–16.
G. Zinov'iev, "O tom, kak bundovtsy razoblachili likvidatorov," *Sochineniia*, (Moscow, 1923ff), II, 261–66.
────── "K natsional'nomu voprosu," *Sochineniia*, IV, 248–57.
────── "Rodnoi iazyk v shkole i natsional'nye uchrezhdeniia," *Sochineniia*, IV, 461–66.


## II

## THE DISINTEGRATION OF THE RUSSIAN EMPIRE

### I. GENERAL

The most important sourcebook for the history of the national problem in 1917 is S. M. Dimanshtein, ed., *Revoliutsiia i natsional'nyi vopros*, III (Moscow, 1930; NN); it contains virtually all the pertinent documents arranged by parties and nationalities. Unfortunately, the other volumes in this series were never published.

Other works pertaining to the national problem in 1917 can be found in the bibliographies for Chapter I and those chapters dealing with the respective regions.

### II. STALIN AND THE COMMISSARIAT OF NATIONALITIES

E. I. Pesikina, *Narodnyi komissariat po delam natsional'nostei i ego deiatel'nost' v 1917–1918 gg.* (Moscow, 1950; NNC) is a recent attempt to magnify the role of the Commissariat by distorting sources and misrepresenting facts which the Soviet reader has no means of verifying; but being the first work to deal with the subject, it has some value. The recollections of Stalin's assistant, S. Pestkovskii, "Kak sozdavalsia Narkomnats," *ZhN*, I (1923), 272–73, and "Vospominaniia o rabote v Narkomnatse," *PR*, no. 6 (1930), 124–31, though very brief, are revealing and trustworthy.

The official publications of the Commissariat of Nationalities bear the character of propaganda material, and contain little information that cannot be obtained elsewhere:

Narodnyi komissariat po delam natsional'nostei, *Politika sovetskoi vlasti po natsional'nym delam za tri goda, 1917-XI-1920"* ([Moscow], 1920; NN).

———— *Natsional'nyi vopros i sovetskaia Rossiia* (Moscow, 1921; DLC).

———— *Otchet narodnogo komissariata po delam natsional'nostei za 1921 god* (Moscow, 1921; Brit. Mus.)

The periodical *Zhizn' natsional'nostei* (Moscow, 1918–1924; CSt-H), the official publication of the Commissariat, contains a wealth of interesting information about its activities in the form of news reports, announcements, etc.

# III

# THE UKRAINE AND BELORUSSIA

### I. GENERAL HISTORIES OF THE REVOLUTION IN THE UKRAINE

The most recent scholarly account of the Revolution in the Ukraine is J. S. Reshetar, Jr., *The Ukranian Revolution, 1917–1920* (Princeton, 1952). Of the partisan histories, the best was written by a professional historian and a member of the Socialist Federalist Party, D. Doroshenko, *Istoriia Ukrainy 1917–1923 rr.* (2 vols.; Uzhgorod, 1930–32; NNC). Also very useful are the accounts of the leaders of the USD Party, V. Vinnichenko, *Vidrodzhennia natsii* (3 vols.; Kiev-Vienna, 1920; NNC), and the USR Party, P. Khristiuk, *Zamitky i materialy do istorii ukrainskoi revoliutsii, 1917–20* (4 vols.; Vienna, 1921–22; NNC). Both works are highly emotional but contain valuable documents and eyewitness reports. Of the Bolshevik accounts, the best are the following: E. G. Bosh, *God bor'by (1917)* (Moscow, 1925; NN); M. G. Rafes, *Dva goda revoliutsii na Ukraine* (Moscow, 1920; CSt-H); and M. Skrypnyk, "Istoriia proletarskoi revoliutsii na Ukraini," *Statti i promovy,* I (Kharkov, 1930; NN), 132–235.

The journal *Letopis'* (later *Litopis*) *revoliutsii* (Kharkov) was the official publication of the Institute of Party History in the Ukraine, and contains a wealth of primary and secondary information.

S. Rozen, ed., "Opyt bibliografii po istorii revoliutsii na Ukraine," *LR,* no. 3–4/18–19 (1926), pp. 236–65; no. 5/20 (1926), pp. 198–208; no. 6/21 (1926), pp. 190–203; is a bibliographical survey of Soviet literature on the history of the Revolution in the Ukraine.

### II. SOME MEMOIR LITERATURE

S. A. Alekseev, ed., *Revoliutsiia na Ukraine po memuaram Belykh* (Moscow-Leningrad, 1930), is an anthology of eyewitness accounts of a non-Communist character. V. A. Antonov-Ovseenko, *Zapiski o grazhdanskoi voine,* I (Moscow, 1924; NNC) is the story of the Commander in Chief of Red Armies invading the Ukraine in early 1918. V. Petriv, *Spomyny z chasiv ukrainskoi revoliutsii (1917–1921)* (3 vols.; (Lwów, 1927–30; NNC), contains recollections of a military officer. See also:

I. Aleksieev, *Iz vospominanii levogo esera* (Moscow, 1922; CSt-H).

V. Andrievskii, *Z mynuloho* (2 vols.; Berlin, 1921; NN).

M. Barthel, *Vom roten Moskau bis zum Schwarzen Meer* (Berlin, [1921]; CSt-H).

D. Doroshenko, *Moi spomyny pro nedavne-mynule (1914–18)* (2 vols.; Lwów, 1923; NN).

C. Dubreuil, *Deux années en Ukraine* (*1917–1919*) (Paris, 1919; CSt-H).
A. A. Gol'denveizer, "Iz kievskikh vospominanii," in Alekseev, *Revoliutsiia*, 1–63.
G. N. Leikhtenbergskii, *Vospominaniia ob 'Ukrainie,' 1917–18* (Berlin, 1921; CSt-H).
O. Nazaruk, *Rik na velikii Ukraini* (Vienna, 1920; CSt-H).
F. Wertheimer, *Durch Ukraine und Krim* (Stuttgart, 1918; CSt-H).

### III. THE YEAR 1917 IN THE UKRAINE

V. Manilov, ed., *1917 god na Kievshchine* ([Kiev], 1928; NN), is a daily chronicle of events from contemporary sources and an invaluable work for the study of that period in the Kiev province. Other works are:

W. Dushnyck, "The Russian Provisional Government and the Ukrainian Central Rada," *Ukrainian Quarterly*, III (1946), 66–79.
I. Kulik, *Ohliad revoliutsii na Ukraini*, I (Kharkov, 1921; NNC).
V. Lipshits, "Khersonshchina v 1917 godu," *LR*, no. 2/17 (1926), 109–16.
M. Ravich-Cherkasskii, "Fevral'–dekabr' 1917 goda v Ekaterinoslave," *LR*, no. 1 (1922), 74–80.
I. Sorokin, "Fevral'skaia revoliutsiia v Khersone," *PR*, no. 2/49 (1926), 101–13.
O. Shulgin, *L'Ukraine contre Moscou, 1917* (Paris, 1935; CSt-H).
A. Zolotarev, *Iz istorii Tsentral'noi Ukrainskoi Rady* ([Kharkov], 1922; NN).

### IV. THE OCTOBER REVOLUTION IN THE UKRAINE

An interesting survey is V. Leikina, "Oktiabr' po Rossii — 2. Ukraina," *PR*, no. 12/59 (1926), 238–54; also N. Popov, *Oktiabr' na Ukraine* (Kiev, 1934; CSt-H). M. Rubach, "K istorii konflikta mezhdu Sovnarkomom i Tsentral'noi Radoi," *LR*, no. 2/11, (1925), 53–85 contains very interesting documents. S. M. Korolivskii, *Pobeda velikoi oktiabr'skoi sotsialisticheskoi revoliutsii i ustanovlenie sovetskoi vlasti na Ukraine* (Kiev, 1951), is a collection of documents of little value. Very important, on the other hand, is a collection of memoirs and eyewitness accounts of Communist leaders of the October revolution in the Ukraine, *Pervoe piatiletie*, (Kharkov, 1922; NN). Most instructive are the local histories of the October revolution in the Ukraine:

#### a. Kiev and Vicinity

E. Bosh, "Oktiabr'skie dni v Kievskoi oblasti," *PR*, no. 11/23 (1923), 52–67.
I. Florovskii, "Vospominanie ob Oktiabr'skom vosstanii v Kieve," *PR*, no. 10 (1922), 520–25.
"K istorii 'Trekhugol'nogo boia' v Kieve," *LR*, no. 4/9 (1924), 186–94.
S. Mishchenko, "Ianvarskoe vosstanie v Kieve," *LR*, no. 3/8 (1924), 20–43.
Patlakh, "Kiev v Ianvare 1918 goda," *LR*, no. 3 (1923), 18–24.
S. Sh[reiber], "Iz istorii Sovvlasti na Ukraine," *LR*, no. 4/9 (1924), 166–85.

#### b. Chernigov

Z. Tabakov, "Oktiabr'skaia revoliutsiia v Chernigovshchine," *LR*, no. 1 (1922), 143–70.

#### c. Ekaterinoslav

V. Averin, "Ot kornilovskikh dnei do nemetskoi okkupatsii na Ekaterinoslavshchine," *PR*, no. 11/70 (1927), 140–70.
E. Kviring, "Ekaterinoslavskii Sovet i oktiabr'skaia revoliutsiia," *LR*, no. 1 (1922), 63–73.
V. Miroshevskii, "Vol'nyi Ekaterinoslav," *PR*, no. 9 (1922), 197–208.

M. Ravich-Cherkasskii, "Fevral'–Dekabr' 1917 g. v Ekaterinoslave," *LR*, no. 1 (1922), 74–80.
I. Zhukovskii, "Podgotovka Oktiabria v Ekaterinoslave," *LR*, no. 1/16 (1926), 7–40.

*d. Kharkov and Donbass*

S. Buzdalin, "Oktiabr'skaia revoliutsiia v Khar'kove," *LR*, no. 1 (1922), 35–38.
"Khar'kovskaia Krasnaia Gvardiia," *LR*, no. 3 (1923), 70–72.
E. Kholmskaia, "Iz istorii bor'by v Donbasse v oktiabr'skie dni," *LR*, no. 1 (1922), 55–58.
E. Medne, "Oktiabr'skaia revoliutsiia v Donbasse," *LR*, no. 1 (1922), 49–54.
G. Petrovskii, "Ocherk iz Oktiabr'skoi revoliutsii v Donbasse," *LR*, no. 1 (1922), 59–62.
S. Pokko, "Organizatsiia i bor'ba Krasnoi Gvardii v Khar'kove," *LR*, no. 1 (1922), 44–48.
N. Popov, "Ocherki revoliutsionnykh sobytii v Khar'kove ot iiunia 1917 g. do dekabria 1918 g.," *LR*, no. 1 (1922), 16–34.

*e. Nikolaev*

I. Kagan, "Partorganizatsiia i oktiabr'skii perevorot v g. Nikolaeve," *LR*, no. 1 (1922), 104–06.
Ia. Riappo, "Bor'ba sil v oktiabr'skuiu revoliutsiiu v Nikolaeve," *LR*, no. 1 (1922), 81–103.

*f. Odessa*

Khristev [Kh. A. Rakovskii], "Rumcherod v podgotovke Oktiabr'skoi revoliutsii," *LR*, no. 1 (1922), 171–83.

*g. Poltava*

S. Mazlakh, "Oktiabr'skaia revoliutsiia na Poltavshchine," *LR*, no. 1 (1922), 126–42.
Smetanich, "Poltava pered 'Oktiabrem,'" *LR*, no. 3/8 (1924), 62–70.

*h. Volhynia*

M. Gendler, "O revoliutsionnykh sobytiiakh v Volynskoi gub. (m. Berezna) 1917–19 gg.," *LR*, no. 1 (1922), 202–05.

V. GERMAN OCCUPATION AND THE HETMANATE

*Die deutsche Okkupation der Ukraine — Geheimdokumente* (Strassbourg, [c. 1937]; CSt-H) is a German translation of a Soviet work containing important documents. V. Manilov, ed., *Pid hnitom nimetskoho imperiializmu*, (1918 r. na Kyiv-shchyni), ([Kiev], 1927; NNC) has much information on Bolshevik tactics in the Ukraine during the German occupation. Other works are:
F. Balkun, "Interventsiia v Odesse (1918–1919 gg.), *PR*, no. 6–7/18–19, (1923), 196–221.
E. Borschak, "La Paix ukrainienne de Brest-Litovsk," *Le Monde Slave*, VI (1929), no. 4, 33–62; no. 7, 63–84; no. 8, 199–225.
A. Bubnov, "Getmanshchina, direktoriia i nasha taktika (1918–1919 gg.)" *PR*, no. 7/66 (1927), 58–77.
S. Dnistrianskyj, *Ukraina and the Peace Conference*, ([Berlin], 1919).
S. Dolenga, *Skoropadshchyna*, (Warsaw, 1934; NNC).
X. Eudin, "The German Occupation of the Ukraine in 1918," *Russian Review*, no. 1 (1941), 90–105.

E. Evain, *Le Problème de l'indépendence de l'Ukraine et la France*, (Paris, 1931; NN).

E. Heifetz, *The Slaughter of the Jews in the Ukraine in 1919* (New York, 1921).

W. Kutschabsky, *Die Westukraine im Kampfe mit Polen und dem Bolshewismus in den Jahren 1918–1923* (Berlin, 1934; NN).

B. Magidov, "Organizatsiia Donetsko-Krivorozhskoi Respubliki i otstuplenie iz Khar'kova," KP(b)U, *Piat' let*, ([Kharkov], 1922); (CSt-H), 65–67.

A. D. Margolin, *Ukraina i politika Antanty* (Berlin, [1921]).

### VI. THE COMMUNIST PARTY OF THE UKRAINE

The most important sourcebook for the history of the KP(b)U is KP(b)U, Institut Istorii Partii, *Istoriia KP(b)U* (2 vols.; Kiev, 1933; NN). There are also two good histories: M. Ravich-Cherkasskii, *Istoriia Kommunisticheskoi Partii Ukrainy* ([Kharkov], 1923; NN) and N. N. Popov, *Ocherk istorii Kommunisticheskoi Partii (bol'shevikov) Ukrainy* (Simferopol, 1929; NN). See also:

E. Bosh, "Oblastnoi partiinyi komitet s-d (b-kov) Iugo-Zapadnogo kraia (1917 g.)," *PR*, no. 5/28 (1924), 128–49.

I. Kapulovskii, "Organizatsiia vosstaniia protiv Getmana," *LR*, no. 4 (1923), 95–102.

T. Khait, "Do protokoliv Kyivskoho Komitetu RSDRP(b) 1917 r.," *LR*, no. 4/49 (1931), 113–38.

M. Khichenko, ed., *Rozoliutsii vseukrainskykh z'izdiv rad* ([Kharkov], 1932; CSt-H).

K.P.(b) Ukrainy, *Pervyi s'ezd K.P.(b)U*. (Kharkov, 1923; CSt-H). Stenographic reports of the congress.

—— *Piat' let* ([Kharkov], 1922; CSt-H). Memoirs of Communists active in the Ukraine.

—— *Itogi Partperepisi 1922 goda*, 2 pts. (Kharkov, 1922; NN). Statistical data.

I. Iu. Kulik, "Kievskaia organizatsiia ot Fevralia do Oktiabria 1917 goda," *LR*, no. 1/6 (1924), 189–204.

V. I. Lenin, *Stat'i i rechi ob Ukraine* ([Kiev], 1936).

M. Maiorov, *Z istoryi revoliutsiinoi borotby na Ukraini, 1914–1919* (Kharkov, 1928; NNC).

"Protokoly Kyivskoi Orhanizatsii RCDRP (bilshovykiv) 1917 roku," *LR*, no. 4/49 (1931), 139–93.

M. Rubach, "K istorii grazhdanskoi bor'by na Ukraine," *LR*, no. 4/9 (1924), 151–65.

V. Zatonskii, "K voprosu ob organizatsii Vremennogo Raboche-Krest'ianskogo Pravitel'stva Ukrainy," *LR*, no. 1/10 (1925), 139–49.

### VII. BELORUSSIA

Among the historical accounts of the history of the Revolution in Belorussia the following deserve particular mention: V. G. Knorin, *1917 god v Belorussii i na Zapadnom fronte* (Minsk, 1925; NN), and V. K. Shcharbakou, *Kastrychnitskaia revoliutsyia na Belarusi i belapol'skaia okupatsyia* (Minsk, 1930; in Belorussian; NN). A collective volume published by the Tsentral'ny Vykanauchy Komitet, BSSR, *Belarus'* (Minsk, 1924; in Belorussian; NN), contains important essays written by Communist participants. Other works are:

S. Agurskii, *Ocherki po istorii revoliutsionnogo dvizheniia v Belorussii (1863–1917)* (Minsk, 1928; NN). Historical background.

A. Charviakou, *Za savetskuiu Belarus'* (Minsk, 1927; NN).

Ia. Dyla, "Sotsyialistychny rukh na Belarusi," in Ts. V. K., BSSR, *Belarus'*, 124–40.

U. Ihnatouski, "Vialiki Kastrychnik na Belarusi," *Belarus'*, 195–214.

—————— "Komunistychnaia partyia Belarusi i belaruskae pytan'ne," *Belarus'*, 229–42.

—————— [V. M. Ignatovskii], *Belorussiia* (Minsk, 1925; NN).

Ie. Kancher, *Belorusski vopros* (Petrograd, 1919; DLC).

A. Kirzhnits, "Sto dnei sovetskoi vlasti v Belorussii," *PR*, no. 3/74 (1928), 61–131.

V. G. Knorin, *Zametki k istorii diktatury proletariata v Belorussii* (Minsk, 1934; NN).

—————— [V. Knoryn], "Komunistychnaia partyia na Belarusi," *Belarus'*, 215–21.

V. Mitskevich-Kapsukas, "Bor'ba za sovetskuiu vlast' v Litve i Zap[adnoi] Belorussii," *PR*, no. 1/108 (1931), 65–107.

V. F. Sharangovich, *15 let KP(b)B i BSSR* (Minsk, 1934; NN).

Z. Zhylunovich, "Liuty-Kastrychnik u belaruskim natsyianal'nym rukhu," *Belarus'*, 182–94.

# IV

# THE MOSLEM BORDERLANDS

### I. GENERAL

As yet, there is no authoritative study of all of Russian Islam. For the Moslem problem in tsarist Russia the best sources are L. Klimovich, *Islam v tsarskoi Rossii* (Moscow, 1936), which is tendentious but has interesting data and a good bibliography, and the scholarly journal *Mir Islama* (Petrograd, 1912–13).

### II. SOVIET POLICY TOWARD THE MOSLEM MINORITIES (GENERAL)

The only work which attempts to deal with the national movements of all Moslem peoples is G. von Mende, *Der nationale Kampf der Russlandtuerken* (Berlin, 1936); it is biased and disorganized but in parts very useful. J. Castagné, "Le Bolchevisme et l'Islam," *Revue du Monde Musulman* (Paris), LI (1922), consists mainly of documents. F. de Romainville, *L'Islam et l'U.R.S.S.* (Paris, 1947; CSt-H), is a popular account, based on Western sources, dealing mainly with post-1940 developments. B. P. L. Bedi, *Muslims in the U.S.S.R.* (Lahore, [1947]), follows Communist propaganda. A. Arsharuni and Kh. Gabidullin, *Ocherki panislamizma i pantiurkizma v Rossii* ([Moscow], 1931), is an invaluable source for the study of Pan-Islamic and Pan-Turanian tendencies among Russian Moslems.

### III. RUSSIA, TURKEY, AND THE PAN-TURANIAN MOVEMENT

G. Aleksinsky, "Bolshevism and the Turks," *Quarterly Review* (London), vol. 239 (1923), 183–97.

H. Jansky, "Die 'Tuerkische Revolution' und der russische Islam," *Der Islam* (Berlin and Leipzig), XVIII (1929), 158–67.

G. Jaeschke, "Der Turanismus der Jungtuerken," *Die Welt des Islams*, XXIII (1941), no. 1–2, pp. 1–54 (NN).

—————— "Der Weg zur russisch-tuerkischen Freundschaft," *Die Welt des Islams*, XVI (1934), 23–38.

J. Lewin, "Die panturanische Idee," *Preussische Jahrbuecher* (Berlin), vol. 231 (1933), 58–69.

"Panislamizm i pantiurkizm," *Mir Islama*, II (1913), 556–71; 596–619. Deals with the influence of both these ideas on Russian Moslems.

"Pantiurkizm v Rossii," *Mir Islama*, II (1913), 13–30.
"W," "Les Relations russo-turques depuis l'avènement du bolchevisme," *Revue du Monde Musulman*, LII (1922), 181–211.
Zarevant, *Turtsiia i Panturanizm* (Paris, 1930; NN).

### IV. THE ALL-RUSSIAN MOSLEM MOVEMENT IN 1917

The most important source are the stenographic reports of the All-Russian Moslem Congress of May 1917, *Bütün Rusya Müsülümanların 1917nci yılda 1–11 mayda Meskevde bulgan Umumî isyezdinin Protokolları* (Petrograd, 1917; Tarih Kurumu Library, Ankara, available to me only in part). The reports of H. Altdorffer, in *Der Neue Orient* (Berlin) for 1917 and early 1918, are useful but not always reliable.

### V. THE CRIMEA

E. Kirimal, *Der Nationale Kampf der Krimtuerken, mit besonderer Beruecksichtigung der Jahre 1917–1918* (Emsdetten, 1952), and M. F. Bunegin, *Revoliutsiia i grazhdanskaia voina v Krymu* ([Simferopol], 1927; CSt-H), are the best works from the viewpoints of the Crimean Turkish nationalists and the contemporary Communists respectively. A good source is the historical journal, *Revoliutsiia v Krymu* (Simferopol, 1924; CSt-H., no. 3 only). See also:
M. L. Atlas, *Bor'ba za sovety* (Simferopol, 1933, CSt-H).
N. Babakhan, "Iz istorii krymskogo podpol'ia," *Revoliutsiia v Krymu*, no. 3 (1924), 3–37.
A. K. Bochagov, *Milli Firka* (Simferopol, 1930; CSt-H).
T. Boiadzhev, *Krymsko-tatarskaia molodezh v revoliutsii* (Simferopol, 1930; CSt-H).
A. Buiskii, *Bor'ba za Krym i razgrom Vrangelia* (Moscow, 1928; NN).
V. Elagin, "Natsionalisticheskie illiuzii krymskikh Tatar v revoliutsionnye gody," *NV*, no. 5 (1924), 190–216; no. 6 (1924), 205–25.
Iu. Gaven, "Krymskie Tatary i revoliutsiia," *ZhN*, no. 48/56, 21 December 1919, and no. 49/57, 28 December 1919.
Grigor'ev [Genker], "Tatarskii vopros v Krymu," *Antanta i Vrangel'*, Sbornik statei (Moscow, 1923; CSt-H), 232–38.
A. Gukovskii, "Krym v 1918–19 gg," *KA*, XXVIII (1928), 142–81; XXIX (1928), 55–85.
S. Ingulov, "Krymskoe podpol'e," in *Antanta i Vrangel'*, 138–71.
S. Liadov, "Zhizn' i usloviia raboty RKP v Krymu vo vremia vladychestva Vrangelia," *PR*, no. 4 (1922), 143–47.
D. S. Pasmanik, *Revoliutsionnye gody v Krymu* (Paris, 1926).
S. Sef, "Partiinye organizatsii Kryma v bor'be s Denikinym i Vrangelem," *PR*, no. 10/57 (1926), 114–55.
D. Seidamet, *La Crimée* (Lausanne, 1921).
——— [J. Seyidamet], *Krym — przeszłość, teraźniejszość i dążenia niepodległościowe Tatarów krymskich* (Warsaw, 1930; in Polish; private).
V. Sovetov, *Sotsial-Demokratiia v Krymu* (1898–1908) (Simferopol, 1933; CSt-H).
V. Sovetov and M. Atlas, *Rasstrel sovetskogo pravitel'stva Krymskoi Respubliki Tavridy* (Simferopol, 1933; CSt-H).
S. A. Usov, *Istoriko-ekonomicheskie ocherki Kryma* (Simferopol, 1925; CSt-H).
V. Utz, *Die Besitzverhaeltnisse der Tatarenbauern im Kreise Simferopol* (Tuebingen, 1911; NNC).
A. Vasil'ev, "Pervaia sovetskaia vlast' v Krymu i ee padenie," *PR*, no. 7 (1922), 3–58.
I. Verner, "Nasha politika v Krymu," *ZhN*, 10 October 1921.
*Ves' Krym, 1920–1925* (Simferopol, 1926; CSt-H).

### VI. THE VOLGA TATARS

B. Spuler, "Die Wolga-Tataren und Baschkiren unter russischer Herrschaft," *Der Islam* (Berlin), XXIX, no. 2 (1949), 142–216, has a good historical account and a rich bibliography. E. Grachev, *Kazanskii Oktiabr'*, I (Kazan, 1926; NN) is a detailed chronicle of the year 1917. The following are important histories of the Revolution and Civil War in the Volga Tatar area: A. I. Bochkov, *Tri goda sovetskoi vlasti v Kazani* (Kazan, 1921; NN); M. Vol'fovich, ed., *Kazanskaia bol'shevistskaia organizatsiia v 1917 godu* (Kazan, 1933; CSt-H), and L. Rubin-shtein, *V bor'be za leninskuiu natsional'nuiu politiku* (Kazan, 1930; CSt-H). A useful list of publications is contained in Tatarskii Nauchno-Issledovatel'nyi Institut, Obshchestvo izucheniia Tatarstana, *Bibliografiia Tatarstana*, Vypusk I, 1917–27 (Kazan, 1930; DLC). The journal *Puti revoliutsii* (Kazan) nos. 1–3 (1922–23) (NN), is devoted to the history of the Revolution in the Kazan region. See also: Abdullah Battal, *Kazan Türkleri* [The Turks of Kazan] (Istanbul, 1341/1925; private), chapter xiii.

I. Borozdin, "Sovremennyi Tatarstan," *NV*, no. 10–11 (1925), 116–37.

N. N. Firsov, *Proshloe Tatarii* (Kazan, 1926; NN).

—— *Chteniia po istorii Srednego i Nizhnego Povolzh'ia* (Kazan, 1920).

Kh. Gabidullin, *Tatarstan za sem' let* (1920–27) (Kazan, 1927; NN).

G. S. Gubaidullin, "Iz proshlogo Tatar," in *Materialy po izucheniiu Tatarstana*, II (Kazan, 1925; NN), 71–111.

S. I. Gusev, "Sviiazhskie dni (1918 g.)," *PR*, no. 2/25 (1924), 100–109.

G. G. Ibragimov, *Tatary v revoliutsii 1905 goda* (Kazan, 1926; NN).

G. G. Ibragimov and N. I. Vorob'ev, eds., *Materialy po izucheniiu Tatarstana*, II (Kazan, 1925).

Istpart; Otdel Oblastnogo Komiteta RKP(b) Tatrespubliki, *Bor'ba za Kazan'*, I (Kazan, 1924; NN).

I. I. Khodorovskii, *Chto takoe Tatarskaia Sovetskaia Respublika* (Kazan, 1920; CSt-H).

D. P. Petrov, *Chuvashiia* (Moscow, 1926).

I. Rakhmatullin, "Mulla-Nur-Vakhitov," *Puti revoliutsii* (Kazan), no. 3 (1923), 35–6.

A. Saadi, "Galimdzhan Ibragimov i ego literaturnoe tvorchestvo," *Vestnik nauchnogo obshchestva tatarovedeniia* (Kazan), no. 8 (1928), 25–50 (DLC).

S. Said-Galiev, "Tatrespublika i t. Lenin," *PR*, no. 9 (1925), 107–17.

M. Sultan-Galiev, *Metody antireligioznoi propogandy sredi Musul'man* (Moscow, 1922; CSt-H).

—— "Sotsial'naia revoliutsiia i Vostok," *ZhN*, nos. 38/46–39/47; 42/50 (1919).

—— "Tatarskaia Avtonomnaia Respublika," *ZhN*, I (1923), 25–39.

B. Spuler, *Idel-Ural* (Berlin, 1942; CSt-H).

A. Tarasov, "Kontrrevoliutsionnaia avantiura tatarskoi burzhuazii (1918 god)," *IM*, no. 7 (1940), 93–100.

Tatarskaia Sotsialisticheskaia Sovetskaia Respublika, *Za piat' let, 1920–25/VI–1925* (Kazan, 1925; NN).

D. Validov, *Ocherki istorii obrazovannosti i literatury Tatar (do revoliutsii 1917 g.)* (Moscow, 1923; NNC).

VKP(b) Tatarskii Oblastnoi Komitet, *Stenograficheskii otchet IX oblastnoi konferentsii tatarskoi organizatsii RKP(b)* (Kazan, 1924; NN).

—— *10-letie Sovetskogo Tatarstana* (Kazan, 1930; CSt-H).

### VII. THE BASHKIRS

A. Adigamov, "Pravda o Bashkirakh," *ZhN*, no. 26/34, 13 July 1919.

S. Atnagulov, *Bashkiriia* (Moscow, 1925; NN).

S. Dimanshtein, "Bashkiriia v 1918–20 gg.," *PR*, no. 5/76 (1928), 138–57.

Kh. Iumagulov, "Ob odnom neudachnom opyte izucheniia natsional'noi politiki v Bashkirii v 1918–19 gg.," *PR*, no. 3/74 (1928), 170–95.

Sh. Manatov, "Bashkirskaia Avtonomnaia Respublika," *ZhN*, no. 1 (1923), 40–45.

P. Mostovenko, "O bol'shikh oshibkakh v 'Maloi' Bashkirii," *PR*, no. 5/76 (1928), 103–37.

M. L. Murtazin, *Bashkiriia i bashkirskie voiska v grazhdanskuiu voinu* ([Leningrad], 1927; CSt-H).

R. E. Pipes, "The First Experiment in Soviet National Policy: The Bashkir Republic, 1917–1920," *The Russian Review*, IX, no. 4 (1950), 303–19.

R. Raimov, "K istorii obrazovaniia Bashkirskoi avtonomnoi sotsialisticheskoi sovetskoi respubliki," *Voprosy istorii*, no. 4 (1948), 23–42.

F. Samoilov, "Malaia Bashkiriia v 1918–1920 gg.," *PR*, no. 11/58 (1926), 196–223; no. 12/59 (1926), 185–207.

—— *Malaia Bashkiriia v 1918–1920 gg.* (Moscow, 1933).

F. Syromolotov, "Lenin i Stalin v sozdanii Tataro-Bashkirskoi Respubliki," *RN*, no. 8/66 (1935), 15–24.

Sh. Tipeev, *K istorii natsional'nogo dvizheniia i sovetskoi Bashkirii* (Ufa, 1929; CSt-H).

### VIII. THE STEPPE REGIONS

S. Brainin and Sh. Shafiro, *Pervye shagi sovetov v Semirech'i* (Alma-Ata–Moscow, 1934; Doc. Int.). G. N. Mel'nikov, *Oktiabr' v Kazakstane* ([Alma-Ata], 1930; CSt-H), and Kazakskaia SSR, S"ezd Sovetov, *Uchreditel'nyi s"ezd sovetov Kirgizskoi (Kazakskoi) ASSR, Protokoly* (Alma-Ata-Moscow, 1936; CSt-H) are among the most important sources for the history of the Revolution in the steppe regions of Central Asia. Other works are:

I. G. Akulinin, *Orenburgskoe Kazach'e voisko v bor'be s bol'shevikami* (Shanghai, 1937; CSt-H).

D. Furmanov, *Miatezh* (Moscow-Leningrad, 1925; Brit. Mus.).

F. I. Goloshchekin, *Partiinoe stroitel'stvo v Kazakstane* (Moscow, 1930; CSt-H).

I. Kuramysov, *Za leninskuiu natsional'nuiu politiku v Kazakstane* (Alma-Ata–Moscow, 1932; CSt-H).

L. Papernyi, "Bluzhdaiushchie oblasti," *VS*, no. 2 (1924), 131–33.

F. Popov, *Dutovshchina* (Moscow-Samara, 1934; CSt-H).

T. R. Ryskulov, *Kazakstan* (Moscow, 1927; NN).

—— "Sovremennyi Kazakstan," *NV*, no. 12 (1926), 105–20.

VKP (b), Kazakhskii Kraevoi Komitet, *Iz istorii partiinogo stroitel'stva v Kazakhstane*, (Alma-Ata, 1936; CSt-H). An important source.

### IX. TURKESTAN, KHIVA, BUKHARA

*a. The Revolution in Turkestan*

The best account of the early period of the Revolution in Turkestan (until the beginning of 1918), despite its extreme anti-Russian bias, is Baymirza Hayit, *Die Nationalen Regierungen von Kokand (Choqand) und der Alasch Orda* (Muenster, 1950; mimeographed; private). J. Castagné, *Le Turkestan depuis la Révolution russe (1917–21)* (Paris, 1922; CSt-H), is mainly valuable for its documentation. Among anti-Soviet works, the following may be mentioned as useful: Mustafa Chokaev [Chokai-ogly], *Turkestan pod vlast'iu sovetov* (Paris, 1935); P. Olberg, "Russian Policy in Turkestan," *Contemporary Review* (London), vol. 122, pt. 1 (1922),

342–47; and R. Olzscha and G. Cleinow, *Turkestan* (Leipzig, [1942]). Of the Communist accounts, the most illuminating is G. Safarov, *Kolonial'naia revoliutsiia* (*Opyt Turkestana*) ([Moscow], 1921; NN). The daily newspaper *Svobodnyi* (later *Novyi*) *Turkestan* (Tashkent, 1918; CSt-H), an organ of Russian Socialist Internationalists, has much data for the early period of the Revolution. P. Antropov, *Chto i kak chitat' po istorii revoliutsionnogo dvizheniia i partii v Srednei Azii* (Samarkand–Tashkent, 1929; NN) is a descriptive bibliography of over one hundred titles. See also the following:

P. Alekseenkov, "Natsional'naia politika Vremennogo Pravitel'stva v Turkestane v 1917 g.," *PR*, no. 8/79 (1928), 104–32.

J. Benzing, *Turkestan* (Berlin, 1943; CSt-H).

S. Bolotov, "Iz istorii osipovskogo miatezha v Turkestane," *PR*, no. 6/53 (1926), 110–37.

F. Bozhko, *Oktiabr'skaia revoliutsiia v Srednei Azii* (Tashkent, 1932; CSt-H).

M. Chokaev [Mustafa Tchokaieff], "Fifteen Years of Bolshevik Rule in Turkestan," *Journal of the Royal Central Asian Society*, XX, pt. 3 (1933), 351–59.

——— [M. Chokayev], "Turkestan and the Soviet Régime," *ibid.*, XVIII, pt. 3 (1931), 403–20.

P. G. Galuzo, *Turkestan-koloniia* (Tashkent, 1935; CSt-H).

F. Gnesin, "Turkestan v dni revoliutsii i Bol'shevizma," *Belyi arkhiv* (Paris), no. 1 (1926), 81–94.

A. Gumanenko, *Shamsi* (Tashkent, 1932; CSt-H). Samarkand in 1917–18.

V. I. Masal'skii, *Turkestanskii krai* (St. Petersburg, 1913). Still the best general description of Turkestan.

Z. Mindlin, "Kirgizy i revoliutsiia," *NV*, no. 5 (1924), 217–29.

S. Muraveiskii [V. Lopukhin], "Sentiabr'skie sobytiia v Tashkente v 1917 godu," *PR*, no. 10/33 (1924), 138–61.

F. Novitskii, "M. V. Frunze na Turkestanskom fronte," *KA*, no. 3/100 (1940), 36–78.

K. Ramzin, *Revoliutsiia v Srednei Azii* (Moscow, 1928; NN); valuable photographic records.

T. R. Ryskulov, *Kirgizstan* (Moscow, 1935; NN).

T. R. Ryskulov and others, *Ocherki revoliutsionnogo dvizheniia v Srednei Azii* (Moscow, 1926; NN).

G. Safarov, "Revoliutsiia i natsional'nyi vopros v Turkestane," *Pravda*, no. 162, 24 July 1920.

E. L. Shteinberg, *Ocherki istorii Turkmenii* (Moscow-Leningrad, 1934; CSt-H).

G. Skalov, "Khivinskaia revoliutsiia 1920 goda," *NV*, no. 3 (1923), 241–57.

Maria Tchokay, ed., *Iash Turkestan* (Paris, 1949–50; CSt-H).

VKP(b)-Istpart Sredazbiuro, *Revoliutsiia v Srednei Azii*, I (Tashkent, 1928; CSt-H).

A. N. Zorin, *Revoliutsionnoe dvizhenie v Kirgizii* (*Severnaia chast'*) (Frunze, 1931; CSt-H).

*b. Bukhara*

O. Glovatskii, *Revoliutsiia pobezhdaet* ([Tashkent, 1930]; CSt-H).

F. Khodzhaev, "O mladobukhartsakh," *IM*, no. 1 (1926), 123–41 (NN).

Said Alim Khan (Emir of Bukhara), *La Voix de la Boukharie opprimée* (Paris, 1929; CSt-H).

D. Soloveichik, "Revoliutsionnaia Bukhara," *NV*, No. 2 (1922), 272–88.

*c. The Basmachi Movement*

The history of the Basmachis remains to be written. The following are some of the principal sources:

J. Castagné, *Les Basmatchis* (Paris, 1925; NN).

Mustafa Chokaev, "The Basmaji Movement in Turkestan," *The Asiatic Review* (London), XXIV, no. 78 (1928), 273–88.

S. B. Ginsburg, "Basmachestvo v Fergane," *NV*, no. 10–11 (1925), 175–202.

V. K[uibyshev], "Basmacheskii front," *ZhN*, no. 16/73, 2 June 1920.

I. Kutiakov, *Krasnaia konnitsa i vozdushnyi flot v pustyniakh — 1924 god* (Moscow-Leningrad, 1930; CSt-H).

A. Maier, ed., *Boevye epizody — Basmachestvo v Bukhare* (Moscow-Tashkent, 1934; CSt-H).

K. Okay (pseud.) *Enver Pascha, der grosse Freund Deutschlands* (Berlin, [1935]; NN). A fictionalized but well-informed account.

G. Skalov, "Sotsial'naia priroda basmachestva v Turkestane," *ZhN*, no. 3–4 (1923), 51–62.

[K.] Vasilevskii, "Fazy basmacheskogo dvizheniia v Srednei Azii," *NV*, no. 29, (1930), 126–41.

*d. The British in Turkestan*

F. M. Bailey, *Mission to Tashkent* (London, 1946).

L. V. S. Blacker, *On Secret Patrol in High Asia* (London, 1922).

V. A. Gurko-Kriazhin, "Angliiskaia interventsiia v 1918–1919 gg. v Zakaspii i Zakavkaz'e," *IM*, no. 2 (1926), 115–40.

W. Malleson, "The British Military Mission to Turkestan, 1918 20," *The Journal of the Royal Central Asian Society*, IX, pt. 2 (1922), 96–110.

F. Willfort, *Turkestanisches Tagebuch* (Vienna, 1930).

J. K. Tod, "The Malleson Mission to Transcaspia in 1918," *The Journal of the Royal Central Asian Society*, XXVII, pt. 1 (1940), 45–67.

# V

# THE CAUCASUS

### I. GENERAL

Among studies dealing with the Revolution on the territory of Transcaucasia, the most recent and most complete is F. Kazemzadeh, *The Struggle for Transcaucasia* (1917–1921) (New York, 1951). S. T. Arkomed, *Materialy po istorii otpadeniia Zakavkaz'ia ot Rossii* (Tiflis, 1923; CSt-H); A. P. Stavrovskii, *Zakavkaz'e posle Oktiabria* (Moscow-Leningrad, 1925; CSt-H), and S. E. Sef, *Revoliutsiia 1917 goda v Zakavkaz'i* ([Tiflis], 1927; DLC), contain documents and other primary materials. Two French secondary works are useful: J. Loris-Mélikov, *La Révolution russe et les nouvelles républiques transcaucasiennes* (Paris, 1920), and E. Hippeau, *Les Républiques du Caucase* (Paris, 1920; Brit. Mus.). The journal *Prométhée* and *La Revue de Prométhée* (Paris; CSt-H and NN) deal largely with the national problem in Soviet Caucasus. See also the following sources:

R. Arskii, *Kavkaz i ego znachenie dlia Sovetskoi Rossii* (Peterburg, 1921; DLC).

O. Baldwin, *Six Prisons and Two Revolutions* (Garden City, 1925).

L. Beria, *On the History of the Bolshevik Organizations in Transcaucasia* (London, 1939).

J. Buchan, ed., *The Baltic and Caucasian States* (London, 1923).

P. G. La Chesnais, *Les Peuples de la Transcaucasie pendant la guerre et devant la paix* (Paris, 1921; DLC).

B. Iskhanian, *Narodnosti Kavkaza* (Petrograd, 1916; CSt-H).

P. Kentmann, *Der Kaukasus — 150 Jahre russischer Herrschaft* (Leipzig [1943], CSt-H).

S. M. Kirov, *Stat'i, rechi, dokumenty*, I ([Leningrad], 1936).

F. S. Krasil'nikov, *Kavkaz i ego obitateli* (Moscow, 1919; CSt-H).

M. D. Orakhelashvili, *Zakavkazskie bol'shevistskie organizatsii v 1917 godu* ([Tiflis], 1927; CSt-H).

G. K. Ordzhonikidze, *Izbrannye stat'i i rechi, 1911–1937* ([Moscow], 1939).

M. E. Rasul-Zade, *O Panturanizme — V sviazi s kavkazskoi problemoi* (Paris, 1930; CSt-H).

A. Sanders [A. Nikuradze], *Kaukasien, Nordkaukasien, Aserbeidschan, Georgien, Armenien — geschichtlicher Umriss* (Munich, 1944; CSt-H).

S. E. Sef, *Bor'ba za Oktiabr' v Zakavkaz'i* ([Tiflis], 1932; NNC).

N. P. Stel'mashchuk, ed., *Kavkazskii kalendar' na 1917 god* (Tiflis, 1916).

K. Zetkin, *Im befreiten Kaukasus* (Berlin, [1926]; NN).

M. Zhakov, S. Sef, and G. Khachapuridze, *Istoriia klassovoi bor'by v Zakavkaz'i*, I (Tiflis, 1930; Doc. Int.).

### II. THE NORTHERN CAUCASUS AND DAGHESTAN

*a.* For the Northern Caucasus the most important works, both containing numerous documents, are: I. Borisenko, *Sovetskie respubliki na Severnom Kavkaze v 1918 godu* (2 vols.; Rostov on Don, 1930; DLC), and N. L. Ianchevskii, *Grazhdanskaia bor'ba na Severnom Kavkaze*, I (Rostov on Don, 1927; NN). Other works are:

A. Avtorkhanov, *K osnovnym voprosam istorii Chechni* ([Groznyi], 1930; CSt-H).

——— *Revoliutsiia i kontrrevoliutsiia v Chechne* (Groznyi, 1933; Doc. Int.).

H. Bammate, *The Caucasus Problem* (Berne, 1919; CSt-H).

N. F. Iakovlev, *Ingushi* (Moscow, 1925; CSt-H).

V. P. Pozhidaev, *Gortsy Severnogo Kavkaza* (Moscow-Leningrad, 1926; NN).

M. Svechnikov, *Bor'ba krasnoi armii na Severnom Kavkaze — Sentiabr' 1918–Aprel' 1919* (Moscow-Leningrad, 1926; Doc. Int.).

*b.* For Daghestan an essential work is A. A. Takho-Godi, *Revoliutsiia i kontrrevoliutsiia v Dagestane* (Makhach-Kala, 1927; DLC). N. Emirov, *Ustanovlenie sovetskoi vlasti v Dagestane i bor'ba s germano-turetskimi interventami, 1917–19 gg.* (Moscow, 1949; DLC), is a recent official history. See also:

N. Samurskii [Efendiev], *Dagestan* (Moscow, 1925).

——— "Grazhdanskaia voina v Dagestane," *NV*, III (1923), 230–40.

——— *Itogo i perspektivy sovetskoi vlasti v Dagestane* (Makhach-Kala, 1927; DLC).

——— "Krasnyi Dagestan," in V. Stavskii, ed., *Dagestan* (Moscow, 1936; NN), 5–32.

——— "Oktiabr'skaia revoliutsiia i dal'neishie etapy ee razvitiia v Dagestane," *PR*, no. 10/33 (1924), 83–104.

TsIK, Dagestanskaia ASSR, *Desiat' let avtonomii DASSR* (Makhach-Kala, 1931; NN).

A. Todorskii, *Krasnaia armiia v gorakh* (Moscow, 1924; Doc. Int.).

### III. AZERBAIJAN

*a. Official*

Claims of the Peace Delegation of the Republic of Caucasian Azerbaidjan Presented to the Peace Conference in Paris (Paris, 1919; NNC) and [The] Economic and Financial Situation of Caucasian Azerbaidjan (Paris, 1919; NNC) are of value.

The journal of the Historical Section of the Azerbaijan Communist Party, Istpart AzKP(b), *Iz proshlogo* (Baku; Doc. Int., incomplete), contains many pertinent articles and memoirs.

*b. Bibliographies*

A. V. Bagrii, *Materialy dlia Bibliografii Azerbaidzhana* (Baku, 1924–26; NN).

*c. Secondary Sources*

The literature on Azerbaijan during the 1917–1923 period is voluminous. S. Belen'kii and A. Manvelov, *Revoliutsiia 1917 g. v Azerbaidzhane* — (*khronika sobytii*) (Baku, 1927; NN), is a detailed chronicle. Ia. A. Ratgauzer, *Revoliutsiia i grazhdanskaia voina v Baku*, I (Baku, 1927; CSt-H), is the most complete history of the subject from the Bolshevik point of view. M. E. Resul-Zade, *Azerbajdžan w walce o niepodległość* (Warsaw, 1938; in Polish; private), and M. Z. Mirza-Bala, *Milli Azerbaycan Hareketi* ([Berlin], 1938; in Turkish; private), represent the anti-Soviet viewpoint. The latter is a valuable history of the Mussavat Party. Other works are:

M. D. Bagirov, *Iz istorii bol'shevistskoi organizatsii Baku i Azerbaidzhana* (Moscow, 1946).

A. Dubner, "Bakinskii proletariat v bor'be za vlast' (1918–20 gg.)," *PR*, no. 9 (1930), 19 45.

———— *Bakinskii proletariat v gody revoliutsii* (1917–1920) (Baku, 1931; CSt-H).

L. C. Dunsterville, *The Adventures of Dunsterforce* (London, 1920).

G. Gasanov and N. Sarkisov, "Sovetskaia vlast' v Baku v 1918 godu," *IM*, no. 5/69 (1938), 32–70.

M.-D. Guseinov *Tiurkskaia demokraticheskaia partiia federalistov 'Musavat' v proshlom i nastoiashchem*, pt. 1 ([Tiflis], 1927; CSt-H).

T. Guseinov *Oktiabr' v Azerbaidzhane* (Baku 1927; NN).

M. S. Iskenderov, *Iz istorii bor'by Kommunisticheskoi partii Azerbaidzhana za pobedu sovetskoi vlasti* (Moscow, 1958).

B. Iskhanian *Kontr-revoliutsiia v Zakavkaz'e* (Baku 1919; CSt-H).

———— *Velikie uzhasy v gorode Baku* (Tiflis 1920; CSt-H).

G. Jaeschke, "Die Republik Aserbeidschan," *Die Welt des Islams*, XXIII, no. 1–2 (1941), 55–69 (NN).

A. G. Karaev, *Iz nedavnego proshlogo* ([Baku, 1926]; NN).

A. Karinian, *Shaumian i natsionalisticheskie techeniia na Kavkaze* (Baku, 1928; CSt-H).

V. N. Khudadov, "Sovremennyi Azerbaidzhan," *NV*, *no.* 3 (1923), 167–89.

M. Kuliev, *Vragi Oktiabria v Azerbaidzhane* (Baku, 1927; NN).

H. Munschi, *Die Republik Aserbeidschan* (Berlin, 1930; NN).

N. Narimanov, *Stat'i i pis'ma* ([Moscow, 1925]; NN).

N. Pchelin, *Krest'ianskii vopros pri Musavate* (1918–1920) (Baku, 1931; Doc. Int.).

A. L. Popov, "Revoliutsiia v Baku," *Byloe*, XXII (1923), 278–312.

———— "Iz istorii revoliutsii v Vostochnom Zakavkaz'e (1917–18 gg.)," *PR*, no. 5/28 (1924), pp. 13–35; no 7/30 (1924), pp. 110–43; no. 8–9/31–32 (1924), pp. 99–116; no. 11/34 (1924), pp. 137–61.

A. Raevskii, *Partiia Musavat i ee kontr-revoliutsionnaia rabota* (Baku, 1929; NN).

———— *Angliiskie 'druz'ia' i musavatskie 'patrioty'* (Baku, 1927; NN).

———— *Bol'shevizm i men'shevizm v Baku v 1904–05 gg.* (Baku, 1930; NN).

———— *Angliiskaia interventsiia i musavatskoe pravitel'stvo* (Baku, 1927), An important source.

Ia. A. Ratgauzer, *Bor'ba za Sovetskii Azerbaidzhan* (Baku, 1928; NN).

Sarkis [N. Sarkisov], *Bor'ba za vlast'* ([Baku], 1930; Brit. Mus.).

S. E. Sef, *Kak bol'sheviki prishli k vlasti v 1917–18 gg. v bakinskom raione* (Baku, 1927; NN).

———— "Bakinskii Oktiabr'," *PR*, no. 11/106 (1930), 67–89.

———— "Iz istorii bor'by za natsionalizatsiiu neftianoi promyshlennosti," *IM*, no. 18/19 (1930), 29–62 (NN).

J. Schafir, *Die Ermordung der 26 Kommunare in Baku [sic!] und die Partei der Sozialrevolutionaere* (Hamburg, 1922; NN).

M. Shakhbazov, "Gandzha do i pri sovetvlasti," *Iz proshlogo* (Baku), no. 2 (1924), 101–07 (Doc. Int.).

S[tepan] G. Shaumian, *Stat'i i rechi* ([Baku], 1924; CSt-H).

S[uren] Shaumian, "Bakinskaia kommuna 1918 goda," *PR*, no. 12/59 (1926), 70–112.

———— *Bakinskaia kommuna* (Baku, 1927; CSt-H).

A. Steklov, *Armiia musavatskogo Azerbaidzhana* (Baku, 1928; Doc. Int.).

———— *Krasnaia armiia Azerbaidzhana* (Baku, 1928; NN).

E. A. Tokarzhevskii, *Ocherki istorii sovetskogo Azerbaidzhana v period perekhoda na mirnuiu rabotu po vosstanovleniiu narodnogo khoziaistva (1921–1925 gg.)* (Baku, 1956).

### IV. ARMENIA

S. Vratsian, *Hayastani Hanrapetouthiun* [The Republic of Armenia], (Paris, 1928; private; in Armenian), is the most thorough account of Armenian history, 1917–1921, from the Dashnak point of view. A. N. Mandelstam, *La Société des Nations et les puissances devant le problème arménien* (Paris, 1926), deals with the foreign relations of the Armenian Republic. B. A. Bor'ian, *Armeniia, mezhdunarodnaia diplomatiia i SSSR* (2 vols.; Moscow-Leningrad, 1928–29), is a badly written but very useful early Soviet account. J. G. Harbord, "American Military Mission to Armenia," *International Conciliation* (New York), no. 151 (June 1920), 275–312, is a non-partisan view of internal conditions in the Armenian Republic written by the head of the American mission there. See also:

A. N., "Kommunizm v Armenii," *Kommunisticheskii Internatsional*, II, no. 13 (1920), 2543–50.

Bakinskii Armianskii Natsional'nyi Sovet, *Armiano-gruzinskii vooruzhennyi konflikt* (Baku, 1919; NN).

H. Barby, *La Débâcle russe* (Paris, [1918]; NN).

———— *Les Extravagances bolcheviques et l'épopée arménienne* (Paris, n.d.; CSt-H).

E. Brémond, *La Cilicie en 1919–1920* (Paris, 1921; private).

Comité Central du Parti 'Daschnaktzoutioun,' *L'Action du Parti S.R. Arménien dit 'Daschnaktzoutioun,' 1914–1923* (Paris, 1923; Brit. Mus.).

Délégation de la République arménienne, *L'Arménie et la question arménienne* (Paris, 1922; private).

A. Gukovskii, "Pobeda sovetskoi vlasti v Armenii v 1920 godu," *IM*, no. 11 (1940), 8–17.

A. P. Hacobian, *Armenia and the War* (New York, [1917]).

L. R. Hartill, *Men Are Like That* (Indianapolis, 1928).

G. Jaeschke, "Urkunden zum Frieden von Gümrü (Alexandropol)," *Mitteilungen des Seminars fuer orientalische Sprachen* (Berlin), XXXVII, pt. 2 (1934), 133–42.

G. Korganoff, *La Participation des Arméniens à la Guerre Mondiale sur le Front du Caucase (1914–1918)* (Paris, 1927).

J. G. Mandalian, *Who Are the Dashnags?* (Boston, 1944; NNC).

A. F. Miasnikov, *Armianskie politicheskie partii za rubezhom* (Tiflis, 1925; NN).

F. Nansen, *Armenia and the Near East* (London, 1928).

A. Poidebard, ed., *Le Transcaucase et la république d'Arménie* (Paris, 1924; DLC).
*Programma armianskoi revoliutsionnoi i sotsialisticheskoi partii Dashnakstutiun* (Geneva, 1908; NNC).
V. Totomiantz, *L'Arménie économique* (Paris, 1920).
M. Varandian, *Le Conflit arméno-géorgien et la guerre du Caucase* (Paris, 1919; DLC).
S. Vratzian, "How Armenia Was Sovietized," *The Armenian Review*, I–II, nos. 1–5 (1948–49), pp. 74–84; 79–91; 59–75; 87–103; 118–27.

### V. GEORGIA

*a. Official Publications of the Georgian Democratic Republic*

The most important publication of the Menshevik-dominated government is Georgia, Ministerstvo Vneshnikh Del, *Dokumenty i materialy po vneshnei politike Zakavkaz'ia i Gruzii* (Tiflis, 1919; CSt-H), which contains a wealth of primary material concerning the foreign relations and domestic policies of the state. Other publications bearing the official seal of the government or the Social Democratic Party both before and after the Bolshevik invasion of 1921 contain, along with much propaganda, some valuable information. Among them are:

Délégation géorgienne a la Conférence de la Paix, *Memoire présenté à la Conférence de la Paix* (Paris, 1919; private).
Assemblée Constituante de la République géorgienne, *La Géorgie sous la domination des armées bolchevistes* (Paris, 1921; NN).
Com. Central du Parti S-D de Géorgie, *L'Internationale socialiste et la Géorgie* (Paris, 1921; Brit. Mus.).
Bureau de Presse géorgien, *Le Prolétariat géorgien contre l'impérialisme bolcheviste* (Constantinople, 1921; Brit. Mus.).
Assemblée Constituante de la République géorgienne, *Le Peuple géorgien contre l'occupation bolcheviste russe* ([Paris, 1922]; CSt-H).
Forcign Bureau, S-D Labour Party of Georgia, *Documents of the Social-Democratic Labour Party of Georgia* (London, 1925; Brit. Mus.).
République de Géorgie, *Documents relatifs à la question de la Géorgie devant la Société des Nations* (Paris, 1925).
*Traité conclu le 7 Mai 1920 entre la République démocratique de Géorgie et la République Socialiste Fédérative Soviétiste Russe* . . . (Paris, 1922).

The daily newspaper *Bor'ba* (Tiflis, 1917–1921; private and CSt-H) which served as the organ of the Central Committee of the Georgian Social-Democratic Party is an extremely useful source.

*b. Non-Communist Secondary Sources*

The most comprehensive study of independent Georgia is W. S. Woytinsky, *La Démocratie géorgienne* (Paris, 1921). Very sympathetic and optimistic accounts are: Karl Kautsky, *Georgia — A Social Democratic Peasant Republic* (London, 1921), and E. Kuhne, *La Géorgie libre* (Geneva, 1920; Brit. Mus.). Z. Avalishvili, *The Independence of Georgia in International Politics (1918–1921)* (London, [1940]), contains a critical account of Georgia's foreign policy. Other general accounts are:
P. Gentizon, *La Résurrection géorgienne* (Paris, 1921).
A. Ibels, *Libérons la Géorgie!* (Paris, 1919).
J. Kawtaradze, *Gruzja w zarysie historycznym* (Warsaw, 1929; NNC).
J. Martin, *Lettres de Géorgie* (Geneva, 1920; Brit. Mus.).
I. Tsérételli, *Séparation de la Transcaucasie et de la Russie et l'indépendance de la Géorgie* (Paris, 1919).

Economic problems and policies are treated in:

V. Babet, *Les Richesses naturelles de la Géorgie* — *Richesses minières* (Paris, 1920; Brit. Mus.).

D. Ghambashidze, *Mineral Resources of Georgia and Caucasia* (London [1919]; Boston Public Library).

A. Hatschidze, *Georgien* (Innsbruck, 1926; Brit. Mus.).

M. Khomériki, *La Réforme agraire et l'économie rurale en Géorgie* (Paris, 1921; CSt-H).

V. Serwy, *La Géorgie coopérative sous le régime bolcheviste* (Brussels, 1922; CSt-H).
Relations with Soviet Russia and other powers are treated in:

[G. Bessedowski], "L'occupation de la Géorgie par la Russie Soviétique," *Prométhée*, V (1930), 12–14.

J. Braunthal, *Vom Kommunismus zum Imperialismus* (Wien, 1922).

K. Chavichvily, "Trotski et la Géorgie," *Prométhée* (Paris), IV, no. 29 (1929), 16–19.

L. Coquet, *Les Héritiers de la 'toison d'or'* (Chaumont, 1930).

R. Duguet, *Moscou et la Géorgie martyre* (Paris, [1927]; CSt-H).

Karibi, *Krasnaia kniga* (Tiflis, 1920; CSt-H).

A. Palmieri, "La Georgia e i Soviety," *Politica* (Rome), XXII (1925), 128–59.

*c. Communist Publications*

The most important account of the events transpiring in Georgia between 1917 and 1921 from the Georgian Bolshevik viewpoint is F. Makharadze, *Sovety i bor'ba za sovetskuiu vlast' v Gruzii, 1917–21* (Tiflis, 1928; CSt-H). The Stalinist history by G. V. Khachapuridze, *Bol'sheviki Gruzii v boiakh za pobedu sovetskoi vlasti* (Moscow, 1951), is of very limited value. The early numbers of the paper of the Central Committee, Communist Party of Georgia, *Zaria vostoka* (Tiflis, 1921; DLC, incomplete) are of much use.

Among works published since 1957 the most informative is a collection of documents on the period following Soviet occupation: Akademiia Nauk Gruzinskoi SSR, *Bor'ba za uprochenie Sovetskoi vlasti v Gruzii* (Tiflis, 1959). G. Zhvaniia, "V. I. Lenin i partiinaia organizatsiia Gruzii v period bor'by za sovetskuiu vlast'," *Zariia Vostoka* (Tiflis), no. 54, 21 April 1961, deals with the invasion of Georgia in 1921. See also: M. Amia, *Put' gruzinskoi zhirondy* (Tiflis, 1926; CSt-H).

V. E. Bibineishvili, *Za chetvert' veka* (Moscow, 1931; CSt-H).

"Demokraticheskoe pravitel'stvo Gruzii i angliiskoe komandovanie," *KA*, XXI (1927), 122–73.

G. Devdariani, *Dni gospodstva men'shevikov v Gruzii* ([Tiflis], 1931; CSt-H).

E. Drabkina, *Gruzinskaia kontr-revoliutsiia* (Leningrad, 1928).

F. Z. Glonti, *Men'shevistskaia i sovetskaia Gruziia* (Moscow, 1923; NN).

V. S. Kirillov and A. Ia. Sverdlov, *Grigorii Konstantinovich Ordzhonikidze* (*Sergo*) — *Biografiia* (Moscow, 1962).

A. Kopadze, *Desiat' let bor'by i pobed* (Tiflis, 1931; NN).

Kommunisticheskaia Partiia (b) Gruzii, *Otchet tiflisskogo komiteta* — *Mart 1923 goda–Mart 1924 goda* (Tiflis, 1924; Doc. Int.).

[F.] Makharadze, *Diktatura men'shevistskoi partii v Gruzii* ([Moscow], 1921).

N. Meshcheriakov, *V men'shevistskom raiu* — *iz vpechatlenii poezdki v Gruziiu* (Moscow, 1921).

G. K. Ordzhonikidze, *Stat'i i rechi*, I (Moscow, 1956).

A. Popov, "Iz epokhi angliiskoi interventsii v Zakavkaz'e," *PR*, no. 6–7 (1923), pp. 222–74; no. 8 (1923), pp. 95–132; no. 9 (1923), pp. 185–217.

RSFSR-Narkomindel, *RSFSR i Gruzinskaia Demokraticheskaia Respublika* — *ikh vzaimootnosheniia* (Moscow, 1921).

Ruben, "V tiskakh men'shevistskoi 'demokratii,'" *PR*, no. 8 (1923), 133–55.

S. E. Sef, *"Demokraticheskoe pravitel'stvo" Gruzii i angliiskoe komandovanie* ([Tiflis], 1928; DLC).

Ia. M. Shafir, *Grazhdanskaia voina v Rossii i men'shevistskaia Gruziia* (Moscow, 1921; NN).

——— *Ocherki gruzinskoi zhirondy* (Moscow-Leningrad, 1925; CSt-H).

L. Trotsky, *Mezhdu imperializmom i revoliutsiei* (Berlin, 1922).

I. P. Vardin, "Smert' gruzinskogo men'shevizma," *Krasnaia nov'* (Moscow), no. 6/16 (1923), 229–51 (NN).

VKP(b) Zakavkazskii Kraevoi Komitet, *Chetvert' veka bor'by za sotsializm* (Tiflis, 1923; NN).

# VI

# THE ESTABLISHMENT OF THE USSR

### I. COLLECTIONS OF DOCUMENTS

Sobranie uzakonenii i rasporiazhenii Rabochego i Krest'ianskogo Pravitel'stva, *Sistematicheskii sbornik vazhneishikh dekretov, 1917–1920* (Moscow, 1920), contains texts of decrees, some of which bear upon the subject of the consolidation of the state aparatus. RSFSR, Narodnyi komissariat po inostrannym delam, *Sbornik deistvuiushchikh dogovorov, soglashenii i konventsii, zakliuchennykh RSFSR s inostrannymi stranami* (2nd ed.; 3 vols.; Moscow-Peterburg 1921–22), and Iu. V. Kliuchnikov and A. Sabanin, *Mezhdunarodnaia politika noveishego vremeni v dogovorakh, notakh i deklaratsiiakh* (3 vols.; Moscow, 1925–29) cite texts of the agreements between the RSFSR and the republics.

The most important publications to have appeared since 1957 bear on the role of Lenin in the formation of the Soviet Union, and his disagreements with Stalin over this matter. The key documents have been published in the fourth edition of Lenin's Works, V. I. Lenin, *Sochineniia*, XXXVI (Moscow, 1957) and *Leninskii Sbornik*, XXXVI (1959). Some of these have appeared earlier outside Soviet Russia.

### II. STENOGRAPHIC REPORTS OF PARTY AND SOVIET CONGRESSES AND RESOLUTIONS

VKP(b), *Desiatyi s"ezd RKP(b)* (Moscow, 1933).

IML, *Odinadtsatyi s"ezd RKP(b) — stenograficheskii otchet* (Moscow, 1961).

RKP(b), *Dvenadtsatyi s"ezd — stenograficheskii otchet* (Moscow, 1923; NN).

TsK, RKP(b), *Rossiiskaia Kommunisticheskaia Partiia (bol'shevikov) v rezoliutsiiakh ee s"ezdov i konferentsii* (1898–1922 gg.) (Moscow–Petrograd, 1923).

*Desiatyi vserossiiskii s"ezd sovetov* (Moscow, 1923).

TsIK, SSSR, *I s"ezd sovetov Soiuza Sovetskikh Sotsialisticheskikh Respublik — stenograficheskii otchet* (Moscow, [1923]).

### III. STUDIES OF SOVIET FEDERALISM IN THE 1920's

Of secondary works, the most important by far is S. I. Iakubovskaia's *Stroitel'stvo soiuznogo Sovetskogo sotsialisticheskogo gosudarstva, 1922–1925 gg.* (Moscow, 1960); based on a rich selection of archival materials, it is quite indispensable despite its faithful adherence to the current official interpretation of historical events. S. S. Gililov, in *V. I. Lenin — organizator Sovetskogo mnogonatsional'nogo gosudarstva* (Moscow, 1960) also uses archival sources. Vital information on Lenin's activities in late 1922 is recorded in the log of his secretary, "Novyi dokument o zhizni i deiatel'nosti

V. I. Lenina," *Voprosy istorii KPSS*, no. 2 (1963), 67–91; cf. L. A. Fotieva, "Iz vospominanii o V. I. Lenine," *Ibid.* no. 4 (1957), 147–67.

I. N. Ananov, *Ocherki federal'nogo upravleniia SSSR* (Leningrad, 1925).

N. N. Alekseev, "Sovetskii federalizm," *Evraziiskii vremennik* (Paris), v (1927), 240–61.

K. Arkhippov, "Tipy sovetskoi avtonomii," *VS*, nos. 8–9 (1923), pp. 28–44; no. 10 (1923), pp. 35–56.

S. N. Dranitsyn, *Konstitutsiia SSSR i RSFSR v otvetakh na voprosy* (Leningrad, 1924).

V. Durdenevskii, "Na putiakh k russkomu federal'nomu pravu," *Sovetskoe pravo*, no. 1/4 (1923), 20–35.

Z. B. Genkina, *Lenin — predsetadel' Sovnarkoma i STO*, (Moscow, 1960).

G. S. Gurvich, "Avtonomizm i federalizm v sovetskoi sisteme," *VS*, no. 1 (1924), 24–29.

———— *Istoriia sovetskoi konstitutsii* (Moscow, 1923).

———— "Printsipy avtonomizma i federalizma v sovetskoi sisteme," *Sovetskoe pravo*, no. 3/9 (1934), 3–39.

———— *Osnovy sovetskoi konstitutsii* (Moscow, 1926).

S. N. Harper, *The Government of the Soviet Union* (New York, [1938]).

V. I. Ignat'ev, *Sovetskii stroi* (Moscow, 1928).

———— *Sovet Natsional'nostei TsK SSSR* (Moscow-Leningrad, 1926).

S. A. Korf, "Vozmozhna-li v Rossii federatsiia?" *Sovremennyia zapiski* (Paris), III (1921), 173–90.

S. B. Krylov, "Istoricheskii protsess razvitiia sovetskogo federalizma," *Sovetskoe pravo*, no. 5/11 (1924), 36–66. A well-documented account.

D. A. Magerovskii, *Soiuz Sovetskikh Sotsialisticheskikh Respublik — (obzor i materialy)* (Moscow, 1923). One of the most valuable studies, important for its source materials.

V. V. Pentkovskaia, "Rol' V. I. Lenina v obrazovanii SSSR," *VI*, no. 3 (1956), 13–24.

B. D. Pletnev, "Gosudarstvennaia struktura RSFSR," *Pravo i zhizn'*, no. 1 (1922), 26–30.

Kh. Rakovskii, "Rossiia i Ukraina," *Kommunisticheskii Internatsional*, no. 12 (1920), pp. 2197–2202.

M. O. Reikhel, ed., *Sovetskii federalizm* (Moscow, 1930; NN).

M. Reisner, "Soiuz Sotsialisticheskikh Sovetskikh Respublik," *VS*, nos. 1–2 (1923), 9–24.

P. I. Stuchka, *Uchenie o gosudarstve i o konstitutsii RSFSR* (Moscow, 1922).

N. S. Timashev, "Problema natsional'nago prava v Sovetskoi Rossii," *Sovremennyia zapiski, XXIX* (1926), 379–99.

B. D. Wolfe, "The Influence of Early Military Decisions upon the National Structure of the Soviet Union," *The American Slavic and East European Review*, IX (1950), 169–79.

# NOTES

## I

## THE NATIONAL PROBLEM IN RUSSIA

1. N. A. Troinitskii, ed., *Pervaia vseobshchaia perepis' naseleniia Rossiiskoi Imperii, 1897 g., Obshchii svod,* II (St. Petersburg, 1905), 1–19.
2. Slavinskii, in *Formy natsional'nago dvizheniia,* 284.
3. Cf. B. E. Nol'de, "Edinstvo i nerazdel'nost' Rossii," *Ocherki russkago gosudarstvennago prava* (St. Petersburg, 1911), 223–554, which contains an excellent historical survey of this problem.
4. Nol'de, "Edinstvo," 468–554; N. M. Korkunov, *Russkoe gosudarstvennoe pravo,* I (St. Petersburg, 1899), 340–50; S. V. Iushkov, *Istoriia gosudarstva i prava SSSR,* I (Moscow, 1940), 478–79.
5. V. Ivanovskii, "Administrativnoe ustroistvo nashikh okrain," *Uchenyia zapiski Imperatorskago Kazanskago Universiteta,* LVIII (1891), no. 6, 31–37.
6. G. B. Sliozberg, *Dorevoliutsionnyi stroi Rossii* (Paris, 1933), 78–79.
7. *Samostiina Ukraina — RUP* (Wetzlar, 1917).
8. *Protokoly konferentsii rossiiskikh natsional'no-sotsialisticheskikh partii* (St. Petersburg, 1908), 94–95.
9. Kastelianskii, *Formy,* 383–95; V. B. Stankevich, *Sud'by narodov Rossii* (Berlin, 1921), 20–37.
10. L. Rubinshtein, *V bor'be za leninskuiu natsional'nuiu politiku* (Kazan, 1930), 30–32.
11. V. Utz, *Die Besitzverhaeltnisse der Tatarenbauern im Kreise Simferopol* (Tuebingen, 1911), 146.
12. S. A. Usov, *Istoriko-ekonomicheskie ocherki Kryma* (Simferopol, 1925), 53.
13. This and all other population statistics for 1897 are from the official Russian census of that year: Troinitskii, *Pervaia vseobshchaia perepis'.*
14. See E. Kirimal, *Der nationale Kampf der Krimtuerken, mit besonderer Beruecksichtigung der Jahre 1917–1918* (Emsdetten, 1952), 9–12; D. Validov, *Ocherki istorii obrazovannosti i literatury Tatar (do revoliutsii 1917 g.)* (Moscow, 1923).
15. S. Rybakov, "Statistika Musulman v Rossii," *Mir Islama,* II, no. 11 (1913), 762–63; see also *Mir Islama,* II (1913), 193–94.
16. N. Ostroumov, "K istorii musul'manskogo obrazovatel'nogo dvizheniia v Rossii v XIX v XX stoletiiakh," *Mir Islama,* II, no. 5 (1913), 312.
17. See stenographic reports of the Third Congress, *Umum Rusya Müsülmanlarının 3ncü Resmî Nedvesi* (Kazan, 1906; Tarih Kurumu Library, Ankara), Resolution V, Articles 28–30.
18. G. G. Ibragimov, *Tatary v revoliutsii 1905 goda* (Kazan, 1926).
19. M. Z. Mirza-Bala, *Millî Azerbaycan Hareketi* ([Berlin], 1938), and M.-D. Guseinov, *Tiurkskaia demokraticheskaia partiia federalistov 'Musavat' v proshlom i nastoiashchem,* pt. 1 ([Tiflis], 1927), 71–78.
20. N. P. Stel'mashchuk, ed., *Kavkazskii Kalendar' na 1917 god* (Tiflis, 1916), 234–37.
21. Z. Avalov, in Kastelianskii, *Formy,* 482–85.
22. K. Zalevskii, "Natsional'nyia dvizheniia," *Obshchestvennoe dvizhenie v Rossii v nachale XX veka,* IV, pt. 2 (St. Petersburg, 1911), 227.

23. S. F. Tigranian in Kastelianskii, *Formy*, 505–06.
24. *Protokoly konferentsii rossiiskikh natsional'no-sotsialisticheskikh partii, passim.*
25. *Programma armianskoi revoliutsionnoi i sotsialisticheskoi partii Dashnaktsutiun* (Geneva, 1908; NNC).
26. *Ibid.*
27. Cf. I. Borisenko, *Sovetskie respubliki na Severnom Kavkaze v 1918 godu*, II (Rostov on Don, 1930), 23; also V. P. Pozhidaev, *Gortsy Severnogo Kavkaza* (Moscow, 1926).
28. F. Engels, *Po und Rhein* (Stuttgart, 1915), 51.
29. F. Engels, "Gewalt und Oekonomie," *NZ*, XIV, no. 1 (1895–96), 679.
30. F. Engels, in 1852; quoted by H. Cunow, *Die Marxsche Geschichts- Gesellschafts- und Staatstheorie*, II (Berlin, 1923), 13; see also K. Marx, *Revolution and Counter-revolution; or Germany in 1848* (London-New York, 1896), 62–64.
31. Articles in *Przegląd Socjaldemokratyczny*, partly printed in M. Velikovskii and I. Levin, eds., *Natsional'nyi vopros* ([Moscow], 1931). Paul Froelich, *Rosa Luxemburg* (London, 1940), 45.
32. *Verhandlungen des Gesamtparteitages der Sozialdemokratie in Oesterreich (Bruenn)* (Vienna, 1899), 74–75.
33. *Ibid.*, 85ff.
34. *Ibid.*, 104.
35. K. Renner, *Das Selbstbestimmungsrecht der Nationen*, I (Leipzig-Vienna, 1918), 23–24.
36. Bauer, *Die Nationalitaetenfrage*, 105.
37. *Ibid.*, 353.
38. L. [*or* Iu.] Martov, *Novaia epokha v evreiskom rabochem dvizhenii* (1895), quoted in M. Rafes, *Ocherki po istorii "Bunda"* ([Moscow], 1923), 32, 35.
39. *Encyclopaedia Judaica* (Berlin, 1928ff), IV, 1208.
40. *Ibid.*
41. V. Medem, *Sotsialdemokratiia i natsional'nyi vopros* (St. Petersburg, 1906), and "Natsional'noe dvizhenie i natsional'nyia sotsialisticheskiia partii v Rossii," in Kastelianskii, *Formy*, 747–98; [V. Kossovskii], *K voprosu o natsional'noi avtonomii i preobrazovanii Ros. sots.-demokr. rabochei partii na federativnykh nachalakh* (London, 1902).
42. *Protokoly konferentsii rossiiskikh natsional'no-sotsialisticheskikh partii.*
43. *Zakonodatel'nyia proekty i predpolozheniia Partii Narodnoi Svobody, 1905–1907 gg.* (St. Petersburg, 1907), pp. xi–xix.
44. F. F. Kokoshkin, *Avtonomiia i federatsiia* (Petrograd, 1917), 7.
45. A. R. Lednitskii, in *Pervaia Gosundarstvennaia Duma*, 154–67.
46. Cf. P. Struve's articles: "Chto zhe takoe Rossiia?" in *Russkaia mysl'*, XXXII (January 1911), 184–87; "Obshcherusskaia kul'tura i ukrainskii partikularizm," *ibid.*, XXXIII (January 1912) pt. 2, 65–86; "Neskol'ko slov po ukrainskomu voprosu," *ibid.*, XXXIV (January 1913), pt. 2, 10–11.
47. On the views of the founders of Russian non-Marxist socialism, see M. Borisov, "Sotsializm i problema natsional'noi avtonomii," *SR*, no. 2 (1910), 227–64.
48. *Protokoly pervago s"ezda Partii Sotsialistov-Revoliutsionerov* (n.p., 1906), 361–62.
49. *Ibid.*, 169–73.
50. *Protokoly konferentsii rossiiskikh natsional'no-sotsialisticheskikh partii*, 58.
51. Borisov, "Sotsializm"; A. Savin, "Natsional'nyi vopros i partiia, S-R," *SR*, no. 3 (1911), 95–146.
52. V. Chernov, "Edinoobrazie ili shablon?" *SR*, no. 3 (1911), 147–60.
53. Borisov, "Sotsializm," 227; Savin, "Natsional'nyi vopros," 126.
54. G. V. Plekhanov, *Sochineniia* (Moscow, 1923ff), II, 360, 403; henceforth referred to as *Plekhanov*.
55. [L. Martov], "Iz partii," *Iskra*, no. 7 (August 1901).
56. L. Trotsky, *Sochineniia* (Moscow, 1924ff), IV, 126.

57. V. I. Lenin, *Sochineniia* (3rd ed.; Moscow, 1935), IV, 21; henceforth referred to as *Lenin*.
58. *Iskra*, no. 51 (22 October 1903).
59. *Programma i ustav RS-DRP* (Paris, 1914; NN), 6–7.
60. Cf. discussions at the April 1917 Bolshevik Party Conference in S. M. Dimanshtein, ed., *Revoliutsiia i natsional'nyi vopros*, III (Moscow, 1930), 21.
61. Cf. D. Markovich, *Avtonomiia i federatsiia* (Petrograd, 1917).
62. *Plekhanov*, XIII, 264, 268.
63. *Ibid.*, XIX, 525.
64. Kastelianskii, *Formy*, 783.
65. *Lenin*, XVI, 709.
66. V. I. Lenin, *Izbrannye stat'i po natsional'nomu voprosu* (Moscow-Leningrad, 1925), 201.
67. *Plekhanov*, XIX, 434–35.
68. Dimanshtein, *Revoliutsiia*, III, 96–97.
69. *Lenin*, V, 341.
70. *Ibid.*, II, 176.
71. *Ibid.*, V, 98–99.
72. *Ibid.*, 338–39.
73. *Ibid.*, 337.
74. *Ibid.*, 243.
75. B. D. Wolfe, *Three Who Made a Revolution* (New York, 1948), 580.
76. For details see *LS*, XXX (1937), where Lenin's reading notes are reproduced.
77. *Lenin*, XVI, 720–21, 729.
78. *Ibid.*, 729ff.
79. A. Karinian, *Shaumian i natsionalisticheskie techeniia na Kavkaze* (Baku, 1928), 7; Shaumian's book (not available to me) bore the title *Natsional'nyi vopros i Sotsial-Demokratiia* (Tiflis, 1906). Cf. Wolfe, *The Three*, 584–86.
80. *LS*, XXX, 7–93.
81. *Lenin*, XVI, 328.
82. Originally published in *Prosveshchenie*, it is reprinted in I. V. Stalin, *Sochineniia* (Moscow, 1946), II, 290–367, henceforth referred to as *Stalin*, and in numerous other editions.
83. *Stalin*, II, 296.
84. *Ibid.*, 301.
85. Bauer, *Die Nationalitaetenfrage*, 125, 127.
86. *Stalin*, II, 301; Bauer, *ibid.*, 138.
87. See above, pp. 24–25.
88. *Stalin*, II, 338.
89. L. Trotsky, *Stalin* (New York [1941]), 157ff; Wolfe, *Three*, 582; B. Souvarine, *Stalin* (New York, 1939), 133ff.
90. Souvarine, *Stalin*, 133.
91. *Lenin*, XVI, 618.
92. *Ibid.*, XVII, 117.
93. *Stalin*, II, 300.
94. *Lenin*, XVII, 427ff.
95. *Ibid.*, XVI, 618.
96. *Ibid.*, XVII, 136ff.
97. *Ibid.*, XVI, 510; also XVII, 65–66.
98. *Ibid.*, XVII, 90, 154; XVIII, 82.
99. *Ibid.*, XVI, 507.
100. The foregoing account is based on a number of articles written by Lenin between the summer of 1913 and the outbreak of the World War; they are conveniently assembled in Lenin, *Izbrannye stat'i*.
101. *LS*, XXX, 128.
102. *Lenin*, XVIII, 328.
103. *Ibid.*, XVII, 90.

104. *Ibid.*, XVIII, 80–83.
105. *LS*, XVII, 213–24.
106. L. Martov, "Chto sleduet iz 'prava na natsional'noe samoopredelenie,'" *Nash golos,* no. 17–18 (January 1916), in *LS*, XVII, 251–52.
107. N. Bukharin to Lenin, November 1915, quoted in D. Baevskii, "Bol'sheviki v bor'be za III Internatsional," *IM*, XI (1929), 37.
108. K. Radek in *Berner Tagwacht*, 28–29 October 1915, cited in *Lenin*, XVIII, 323.
109. *Lenin,* XVII, 179–81.
110. *Ibid.*, 699–701.
111. *LS,* XXX, 102.
112. The foregoing account of Lenin's ideas on the national question in the age of imperialism is based on his articles written during the years of the First World War, chiefly: "Pod chuzhim flagom," *Lenin,* XVIII, 101–16; "Revoliutsionnyi proletariat i pravo natsii na samoopredelenie," *ibid.*, 321–28; "Sotsialisticheskaia revoliutsiia i pravo natsii na samoopredelenie," *ibid.*, XIX, 37–48; "Itogi diskussii o samoopredelenii," *ibid.*, 239–72; "O karikature na Marksizm i ob 'imperialisticheskom ekonomizme,'" *ibid.*, 191–235.
113. *Lenin,* XIX, 182.
114. Cf. *LS,* XVII, 251–52; 300ff.
115. Baevskii, "Bolsheviki," 39ff; *Lenin,* XIX, 271.
116. "Statistika i sotsiologiia," *LS,* XXX, 296–308.

II

## THE DISINTEGRATION OF THE RUSSIAN EMPIRE

1. *Sbornik ukazov i postanovlenii Vremennago Pravitel'stva,* I (Petrograd, 1917 CSt-H). Decree of March 20, 1917, 46–49.
2. See above, pp. 59ff.
3. S. M. Dimanshtein, ed., *Revoliutsiia i natsional'nyi vopros,* III (Moscow, 1930), 132.
4. D. Doroshenko, *Istoriia Ukrainy 1917–1923 rr.,* I (Uzhgorod, 1932), 44–45.
5. Dimanshtein, *Revoliutsiia,* III, 136–37.
6. V. Manilov, ed., *1917 god na Kievshchine,* ([Kiev], 1928), 16, 24.
7. *Visnik Ukrainskoho Heneralnoho Komitetu 1917 r.,* no. 1, (May 1917), in Manilov, *1917 god,* 70.
8. A good description of the mood prevalent among Ukrainian soldiers at that time can be found in V. Petriv, *Spomyny z chasiv ukrainskoi revoliutsii (1917–1921)* (Lwów, 1927–30), I, 8–30.
9. P. Khristiuk, *Zamitky i materialy do istorii ukrainskoi revoliutsii, 1917–20,* I (Vienna, 1921), 44–45. On peasant attitudes toward autonomy, see A. A. Gol'denveizer, "Iz kievskikh vospominanii," in S. A. Alekseev, ed., *Revoliutsiia na Ukraine po memuaram Belykh* (Moscow-Leningrad, 1930), 11.
10. Contemporary newspaper accounts quoted in Manilov, *1917 god.*
11. *Ibid.*, 475–79.
12. On Kerensky's speeches in favor of Ukrainian autonomy in the Duma (1913), see V. Doroshenko, *Ukrainstvo v Rosii* (Vienna, 1917), 107–08.
13. Dimanshtein, *Revoliutsiia,* III, 132.
14. Manilov, *1917 god,* 481–82; *KA,* XXX (1928), 49–55, has an account of discussions of the Ukrainian question in Petrograd.
15. Manilov, *1917 god,* 103ff.
16. *Nova Rada* (Kiev), no. 55 (1917) and *Kievskaia mysl',* no. 137 (1917), in Manilov, *1917 god,* 102.
17. Manilov, *1917 god,* 117.

18. *Kievskaia mysl'*, 6 June 1917, in Khristiuk, *Zamitky*, I, 130–31.
19. Khristiuk, *Zamitky*, I, 86.
20. *Kievskaia mysl'*, no. 162 (1917), in Manilov, *1917 god*, 491.
21. Based on figures reported in *Kievskaia mysl'*, no. 180 (1917), in Manilov. *1917 god*, 179.
22. Based on figures reported in Doroshenko, *Istoriia*, I, 144.
23. The text of the Rada constitution is in Khristiuk, *Zamitky*, I, 96–97.
24. *Kievskaia mysl'*, no. 190 (1917) in Manilov, *1917 god*, 502–03; Ukrainian text in Doroshenko, *Istoriia*, I, 128–29.
25. Khristiuk, *Zamitky*, II, 115–16.
26. Manilov, *1917 god*, 151–52.
27. *Nova Rada*, no. 108 (1917), in Manilov, *1917 god*, 194; Khristiuk, *Zamitky*, I, 146–47.
28. Doroshenko, *Istoriia*, I, 151–52.
29. *Ibid.*, 140.
30. *Rabochaia gazeta* (Kiev), nos. 84–85 (1917); *Kievskaia mysl'*, no. 169 (1917); *Nasha Rada* (Kiev), no. 86 (1917); all in Manilov, *1917 god*, 166–68.
31. *Nova Rada* (Kiev), no. 108 (1917), in Manilov, *1917 god*, 239.
32. Cf. debates on the national question in "Protokoly Kyivskoi Orhanizatsii RSDRP (bilshovykiv) 1917 roku," in *LR*, no. 4/49 (1931), 157–58, 167–68.
33. Dimanshtein, *Revoliutsiia*, III, p. xxxix.
34. K.P.(b)U., Institut Istorii Partii, *Istoriia KP(b)U*, II (Kiev, 1933), 126.
35. *Kievskaia mysl'*, no. 143 (1917), and *Golos sotsial-demokrata*, (Kiev), no. 51 (1917), in Manilov, *1917 god*, 113–14, 125.
36. V. I. Lenin, *Stat'i i rechi ob Ukraine*, ([Kiev], 1936), 266–74.
37. *Kievskaia mysl'*, no. 163 (1917), in Manilov, *1917 god*, 152.
38. *Rabochaia gazeta* (Kiev), nos. 84–85 (1917); *Kievskaia mysl'*, no. 169 (1917); *Nova Rada*, no. 86 (1917), in Manilov, *1917 god*, 166.
39. *Golos sotsial-demokrata* (Kiev), no. 90 (1917), in Manilov, *1917 god*, 504.
40. E. G. Bosh, *God bor'by (1917)* (Moscow, 1925); also E. Bosh, "Oblastnoi partiinyi komitet s-d (b-kov) Iugo-Zapadnogo kraia (1917 g.)," *PR*, no. 5/28 (1924), 131.
41. A. Zolotarev, *Iz istorii Tsentral'noi Ukrainskoi Rady* ([Kharkov], 1922), 20–21.
42. V. Vinnichenko, *Vidrodzhennia natsii*, II (Kiev-Vienna, 1920), 59–60.
43. Manilov, *1917 god*, 520–21.
44. *Ibid.*, 518–21.
45. V. Zatonskii, "Oktiabr'skii perevorot v Kieve," *Kommunist* (Kiev), 7 November 1924, quoted in *LR*, no. 2/11 (1925), 55–56. Other reports on the agreement: Zolotarev, *Iz istorii* 21–25; I. Kulik, *Ohliad revoliutsii na Ukraini*, I (Kharkov, 1921), 23; I. Kulik, in *LR*, no. 1 (1922), 39; M. G. Rafes, *Dva goda revoliutsii na Ukraine* (Moscow, 1920), 47.
46. Quoted from contemporary newspaper accounts in Manilov, *1917 god*, 320.
47. Speech of Piatakov in the Soviet, October 27; *Kievskaia mysl'*, no. 260 (1917), in Manilov, *1917 god*, 324–25.
48. *Rabochaia gazeta* (Kiev), no. 172 (1917), in Manilov, *1917 god*, 344.
49. "K istorii 'trekhugol'nogo boia' v Kieve," *LR*, no. 4/9 (1924), 186–94.
50. Manilov, *1917 god*, 346–47, 349.
51. E. Bosh, "Oktiabr'skie dni v Kievskoi oblasti," *PR*, no. 11/23 (1923), 52–67.
52. V. Lipshits, "Khersonshchina v 1917 godu," *LR*, no. 2/17 (1926), 109–16; Khristev, "Rumcherod v podgotovke Oktiabr'skoi revoliutsii," *LR*, no. 1 (1922), 171–83.
53. M. Ravich-Cherkasskii, "Fevral'–Dekabr' 1917 g. v Ekaterinoslave," *LR*, no. 1 (1922), 74–80.
54. Z. Tabakov, "Oktiabr'skaia revoliutsiia v Chernigovshchine," *LR*, no. 1 (1922), 143–70.
55. *Istoriia KP(b)U*, II, 181.

56. S. Mazlakh, "Oktiabr'skaia revoliutsiia na Poltavshchine," *LR*, no. 1 (1922), 128–29, 136.
57. E. Kviring, "Ekaterinoslavskii Sovet i oktiabr'skaia revoliutsiia," *ibid.*, 67.
58. Z. Zhylunovich, "Liuty-Kastrychnik," *Belarus'* (Minsk, 1924), 186.
59. A. Kirzhnits, "Sto dnei sovetskoi vlasti v Belorussii," *PR*, no. 3/74 (1928), 101–02.
60. V. K. Shcharbakou, *Kastrychnitskaia revoliutsyia na Belarusi i belapol'skaia okupatsyia* (Minsk, 1930), 53.
61. V. G. Knorin, *1917 god v Belorussii i na zapadnom fronte* (Minsk, 1925), 24.
62. V. Knoryn, "Komunistychnaia partyia na Belorusi," *Belarus'*, 215–22; Knorin, *1917 god*, 10.
63. Knoryn, in *Belarus'*, 216–17.
64. *Ibid.*, 217.
65. E. I. Pesikina, *Narodnyi komissariat po delam natsional'nostei* (Moscow, 1950), 55; *Sovetskoe pravo*, no. 1/5 (1924), 96.
66. Kirzhnits, "Sto dnei," 88; V. B. Stankevich, *Sud'by narodov Rossii* (Berlin, 1921), 39.
67. Shcharbakou, *Kastrychnitskaia revoliutsyia*, 50.
68. Dimanshtein, *Revoliutsiia*, III, 294–95; cf. *Bütün Rusya Müsülümanların 1917nci yılda 1–11 mayda Meskevde bulgan Umumî isyezdinin Protokolları* (Petrograd, 1917), 250. I am indebted for many of the details concerning the May 1917 Congress to the kindness of Mr. Ayas Iskhaki Idilli.
69. Second-hand accounts of the May 1917 Congress may be found in the articles of H. Altdorffer in *Der Neue Orient* (Berlin), for 1918, *passim*, and B. Hayit, *Die Nationalen Regierungen von Kokand (Choqand) und der Alasch Orda* (mimeographed, Muenster, 1950), 25ff.
70. E. Grachev, *Kazanskii Oktiabr'*, I (Kazan, 1926), 129–31.
71. *Kazanskoe slovo*, no. 85 (1917), in Grachev, *Kazanskii Oktiabr'*, I, 131.
72. R. E. Pipes, "The First Experiment in Soviet National Policy — The Bashkir Republic, 1917–1920," *Russian Review*, IX, no. 4, (1950), 306.
73. V. Elagin, "Natsionalisticheskie illiuzii krymskikh Tatar v revoliutsionnye gody," *NV*, no. 5 (1924), 194.
74. E. Kirimal, *Der Nationale Kampf der Krimtuerken, mit besonderer Beruecksichtigung der Jahre 1917–1918*, (Emsdetten, 1952), 103.
75. A. K. Bochagov, *Milli Firka*, (Simferopol, 1930), 36.
76. M. F. Bunegin, *Revoliutsiia i grazhdanskaia voina v Krymu* (Simferopol, 1927), 89–90; Kirimal, *Der Nationale Kampf*, 69–70.
77. Elagin, "Natsionalisticheskie illiuzii," 196–98.
78. M. L. Atlas, *Bor'ba za sovety* (Simferopol, 1933), 43.
79. Bunegin, *Revoliutsiia*, 53.
80. *Ibid.*, 54, 77; data for June–July 1917.
81. *Ibid.*, 77–78.
82. *Ibid.*, 81–82.
83. Atlas, *Bor'ba*, 56.
84. *Ibid.*, 59–60.
85. Texts in Kirimal, *Der Nationale Kampf*, 106–14 (Turkish and German); D. Seidamet, *La Crimée*, (Lausanne, 1921) (French).
86. G. Safarov, *Kolonial'naia revoliutsiia (Opyt Turkestana)* ([Moscow], 1921).
87. Slavinskii, in Kastelianskii, ed., *Formy natsional'nago dvizheniia*, 283–84.
88. P. G. Galuzo, *Turkestan — kolonia*, (Moscow, 1935), 139.
89. A. N. Zorin, *Revoliutsionnoe dvizhenie Kirgizii (Severnaia chast')* (Frunze, 1931), 15.
90. Galuzo, *Turkestan*, 209.
91. *Bol'shaia Sovetskaia Entsiklopediia* (Moscow, 1926ff), XXX, 595.
92. Zorin, *Revoliutsionnoe dvizhenie*, 27.
93. Hayit, *Die Nationalen Regierungen*, 89–90.
94. G. N. Mel'nikov, *Oktiabr' v Kazakstane* (Alma-Ata, 1930), 25; Hayit, *Die Nationalen Regierungen*, 87–88.

95. Hayit, 1–2; program taken from S. Brainin and Sh. Shafiro, *Ocherki po istorii Alash-Ordy* (Alma-Ata–Moscow, 1935), quoted by Hayit, 88–89.
96. Dimanshtein, *Revoliutsiia*, III, 363–65.
97. Pipes, "The First Soviet Experiment," 306.
98. Hayit, *Die Nationalen Regierungen*, 91.
99. Zorin, *Revoliutsionnoe dvizhenie*, 25.
100. VKP(b), Kazakhskii Kraevoi Komitet, *Iz istorii partiinogo stroitel'stva v Kazakhstane* (Alma-Ata, 1936), 237–39; Zorin, *Revoliutsionnoe dvizhenie*, 25; T. R. Ryskulov, *Kirgizstan* (Moscow, 1935), 61–63.
101. Dimanshtein, *Revoliutsiia*, III, 321.
102. VKP(b), *Iz istorii*, 239–40.
103. Pipes, "The First Soviet Experiment," 307.
104. VKP(b), *Iz istorii*, 208.
105. Mel'nikov, *Oktiabr'*, 27–29.
106. F. Popov, *Dutovshchina* (Moscow-Samara, 1934), 27–28.
107. Zorin, *Revoliutsionnoe dvizhenie*, 24.
108. V. I. Masal'skii, *Turkestanskii Krai* (St. Petersburg, 1913), 317.
109. VKP(b), Istpart Sredazbiuro, *Revoliutsiia v Srednei Azii*, I (Tashkent, 1928), 16.
110. A. Vambery, *Western culture in Eastern lands* (New York, 1906), 117.
111. The population statistics are from *Aziatskaia Rossiia* (n.p., 1914), Atlas, Table 35; data for Russians includes Cossacks.
112. Hayit, *Die Nationalen Regierungen*, 46–48.
113. P. Alekseenkov, "Natsional'naia politika Vremennogo Pravitel'stva v Turkestane v 1917 g.," *PR*, no. 8/79 (1928), 128–32.
114. Hayit, *Die Nationalen Regierungen*, 23–24.
115. S. Muraveiskii, "Sentiabr'skie sobytiia v Tashkente v 1917 godu," *PR*, no. 10/33 (1924), 139; Istpart, *Revoliutsiia v Srednei Azii*, I, 11, 237.
116. Istpart, *Revoliutsiia v Srednei Azii*, I, 11–13.
117. Hayit, *Die Nationalen Regierungen*, 33.
118. R. Olzscha and G. Cleinow, *Turkestan*, (Leipzig, [1942]), 371.
119. Hayit, *Die Nationalen Regierungen*, 34.
120. Muraveiskii, "Sentiabr'skie sobytiia."
121. *Yaş Turkestan*, no. 89 (April 1937), 17, quoted in Hayit, 36.
122. Mel'nikov, *Oktiabr'*, 32ff.
123. VKP(b), *Iz istorii*, 240–41.
124. Safarov, *Kolonial'naia revoliutsiia*, 70.
125. Hayit, *Die Nationalen Regierungen*, 56.
126. *Nasha gazeta* (Tashkent), 23 November 1917, quoted in Safarov, *Kolonial'naia revoliutsiia*, 70; cf. Istpart, *Revoliutsiia v Srednei Azii*, 26–27.
127. Hayit, *Die Nationalen Regierungen*, 57.
128. *Ibid.*, 57.
129. *Yaş Turkestan*, no. 111 (February 1939), 11, in Hayit, 57.
130. *Svobodnyi Turkestan*, 31 January–1 February 1918 contains stenographic reports of some of the debates.
131. *Ibid.*
132. J. Castagné, *Le Turkestan depuis la Révolution russe* (1917–1921) (Paris, 1922), 23.
133. Hayit, *Die Nationalen Regierungen*, 64.
134. Istpart, *Revoliutsiia v Srednei Azii*, 38.
135. Alekseenkov, in Istpart, 25.
136. Safarov, *Kolonial'naia revoliutsiia*, 71.
137. N. L. Ianchevskii, *Grazhdanskaia bor'ba na Severnom Kavkaze*, I (Rostov on Don, 1927), 53, and I. Borisenko, *Sovetskie respubliki na Severnom Kavkaze v 1918 godu*, II (Rostov on Don, 1930), 21.
138. Ianchevskii, *Grazhdanskaia bor'ba*, I, 56.
139. Borisenko, *Sovetskie respubliki*, II, 23.

140. *Ibid.*, 23. Cf. V. P. Pozhidaev, *Gortsy Severnogo Kavkaza* (Moscow-Leningrad, 1926).
141. Dimanshtein, *Revoliutsiia*, III, 374–76.
142. *Ibid.*, 376–79.
143. A. A. Takho-Godi, *Revoliutsiia i kontr-revoliutsiia v Dagestane* (Makhach-Kala, 1927), 28; there also biographical information concerning Gotsinskii.
144. Dimanshtein, *Revoliutsiia*, III, 379.
145. S. E. Sef, *Bor'ba za Oktiabr' v Zakavkaz'i* ([Tiflis], 1932), 29–30.
146. W. S. Woytinsky, *La Démocratie géorgienne* (Paris, 1921), 86.
147. *Sebilülreşad* (Constantinople), 38–320, p. 226, Year 1328 (1912), quoted in Mehmed-zade Mirza-Bala, *Milli Azerbaycan Hareketi*, ([Berlin], 1938), 66–67.
148. Mirza-Bala, 77–78.
149. *Ibid.*
150. S. Belen'kii and A. Manvelov, *Revoliutsiia 1917 g. v Azerbaidzhane* (Baku, 1927), 35–36.
151. M.-D. Guseinov, *Tiurkskaia demokraticheskaia partiia federalistov 'Musavat' v proshlom i nastoiashchem*, pt. 1 ([Tiflis], 1927), 26–30.
152. Belen'kii and Manvelov, *Revoliutsiia*, 174, 214.
153. Woytinsky, *La Démocratie*, 113.
154. Ia. A. Ratgauzer, *Revoliutsiia i grazhdanskaia voina v Baku*, I (Baku, 1927), 94.
155. B. A. Bor'ian, *Armeniia, mezhdunarodnaia diplomatiia i SSSR*, I (Moscow-Leningrad, 1928), 359.
156. *Ibid.*, 346–83.
157. J. Lepsius, ed., *Deutschland und Armenien, 1914–1918* (Potsdam, 1919) p. lxv.
158. Dimanshtein, *Revoliutsiia*, III, 399–400.
159. *Ibid.*, 403–04.
160. *Ibid.*, 404–05.
161. For a history of the Armenian units during and after the war, cf. G. Korganoff, *La Participation des Arméniens à la Guerre Mondiale sur le Front du Caucase*, (*1914–1918*) (Paris, 1927).
162. Woytinsky, *La Démocratie*, 113.
163. S. Sef, "Pravda o Shamkhore," in *Bor'ba za Oktiabr' v Zakavkaz'i*, 67–91.
164. F. Makharadze, *Sovety i bor'ba za sovetskuiu vlast' v Gruzii, 1917–1921* (Tiflis, 1928), 88, 97; the Baku figure is from A. Dubner, *Bakinskii proletariat v gody revoliutsii (1917–1920)* (Baku, 1931), 13.
165. Belen'kii and Manvelov, *Revoliutsiia*, 47, 50.
166. *Ibid.*, 68–69; Sef, *Bor'ba*, 53.
167. Sef, *Ibid.*, 53–54.
168. Woytinsky, *La Démocratie*, 113.
169. Belen'kii and Manvelov, *Revoliutsiia*, 214.
170. Makharadze, *Sovety*, 97–98; Belen'kii and Manvelov, *Revoliutsiia*, 148.
171. For Makharadze, see *Entsiklopedicheskii slovar'* . . . 'Granat,' XLI, pt. 2, 20ff, which contains an autobiographical sketch.
172. M. Orakhelashvili, *Zakavkazskie bol'shevistskie organizatsii v 1917 godu* ([Tiflis], 1927), 83; Belen'kii and Manvelov, *Revoliutsiia*, 156–62.
173. Makharadze, *Sovety*, 114–15.
174. Sef, *Bor'ba*, 59.
175. Makharadze, *Sovety*, 114–15.
176. Orakhelashvili, *Zakavkazskie*, 52; Sef, *Bor'ba*, 61–62.
177. Orakhelashvili, *ibid.*
178. *Ibid.*
179. Georgia, Ministerstvo Vneshnikh Del, *Dokumenty i materialy po vneshnei politike Zakavkaz'ia i Gruzii* (Tiflis, 1919), 83–86.
180. A. Stavrovskii, *Zakavkaz'e posle Oktiabria* (Moscow-Leningrad, 1925), 16–21.
181. Georgia, *Dokumenty*, 159–61.

182. *Ibid.*, 162–65.
183. *Ibid.*
184. Oniashvili, speaking in the Seim on April 9–22, 1918, in Stavrovskii, *Zakavkaz'e*, 38.
185. *Stalin*, IV, 8.
186. *Ibid.*, 31–32.
187. *LS*, III (1925), 482ff.
188. Vsesoiuznaia Kommunisticheskaia Partiia (bol'shevikov), *Vos'moi s" ezd RKP(b)* (Moscow, 1933), 80–81.
189. *Lenin*, XXIV, 155.
190. TsK RKP(b), *Rossiiskaia Kommunisticheskaia Partiia (bol'shevikov) v rezoliutsiiakh ee s"ezdov i konferentsii (1898–1922 gg.)* (Moscow-Petrograd, 1923), 235–36.
191. *LS*, XI (1929), 24.
192. *S"ezdy Sovetov RSFSR v postanovleniakh i rezoliutsiiakh*, (Moscow, 1939), 44–45.
193. The following account is based primarily on G. S. Gurvich, *Istoriia sovetskoi konstitutsii* (Moscow, 1923).
194. *Izvestiia* (Moscow), 22 May 1920.
195. S. Pestkovskii, "Vospominaniia o rabote v Narkomnatse 1917–1919 gg." *PR*, no. 6 (1930), 124–31.

# III

# THE UKRAINE AND BELORUSSIA

1. I. Kulik, *Ohliad revoliutsii na Ukraini*, I (Kharkov, 1921), 16.
2. Resolutions of the Kievan Soviet of Workers' Deputies and the Kievan Soviet of Soldiers' Deputies, in *Kievskaia mysl'*, nos. 263 and 265, (1917), and *Nova rada*, no. 177 (1917), in V. Manilov, ed., *1917 god na Kievshchine* ([Kiev], 1928), 356.
3. *Kievskaia mysl'*, no. 265 (1917), in Manilov, *1917 god*, 525.
4. D. Doroshenko, *Istoriia Ukrainy, 1917–1923 rr.*, I (Uzhgorod, 1932), 179–81.
5. E. G. Bosh, *God bor'by* (1917) (Moscow, 1925), 46–48.
6. *Pravda* (Petrograd), 24 November/7 December 1917. This article is not reprinted in Stalin's Collected Works.
7. P. Khristiuk, *Zamitky i materialy do istorii ukrainskoi revoliutsii, 1917–20*, II (Vienna, 1921–22), 60.
8. The General Secretariat's resolutions of November 10, in Doroshenko, *Istoriia*, I, 204–05.
9. S. A. Alekseev, ed., *Revoliutsiia na Ukraine po memuaram Belykh* (Moscow-Leningrad, 1930), 397–403.
10. *Pravda*, 26 November/9 December 1917.
11. Khristiuk, *Zamitky*, II, 55; Doroshenko, *Istoriia*, I, 209–10.
12. About Bolshevik plans for an uprising at that time in Kiev, see M. Maiorov, *Z istoryi revoliutsiinoi borotby na Ukraini, 1914–19* (Kharkov, 1928), 48–50.
13. V. A. Antonov-Ovseenko, *Zapiski o grazhdanskoi voine*, I (Moscow, 1924), 22ff; Doroshenko, *Istoriia*, I, 224–25.
14. Doroshenko, *Istoriia*, I, 215.
15. *Ibid.*, 206–09.
16. *Pravda* (Petrograd), 13/26 December, 1917.
17. *Ibid.*, 8/21 December 1917.
18. Doroshenko, *Istoriia*, I, 220.
19. Khristiuk, *Zamitky*, II, 70–71.
20. *Ibid.*, 72–73.

21. The partial results of elections to the Constituent Assembly in the Ukraine can be found in: KP(b)U, Institut Istorii Partii, *Istoriia KP(b)U*, II (Kiev, 1933), 256–57; Doroshenko, *Istoriia*, I, 210–11; *Pravda*, November–December 1917, *passim*.
22. Bosh, *God bor'by*, 88–92; Kulik, *Ohliad*, 30.
23. M. Rubach, "K istorii konflikta . . . . ," *LR*, no. 2/11 (1925), 83–85.
24. *Ibid.*, 79–81.
25. Bosh, *God bor'by*, 127.
26. *Ibid.*
27. Z. Tabakov, "Oktiabr'skaia revoliutsiia v Chernigovshchine," *LR*, no. 1 (1922), 143–70.
28. S. Mazlakh, "Oktiabr'skaia revoliutsiia na Poltavshchine," *LR*, no. 1 (1922), 139.
29. *Ibid.*, 138; Antonov-Ovseenko, *Zapiski*, 139.
30. See Alekseev, *Revoliutsiia na Ukraine, passim*.
31. Tabakov, "Oktiabr'skaia revoliutsiia," 160.
32. *Ibid.*, 159–60; Doroshenko, *Istoriia* I, 225.
33. Khristiuk, *Zamitky*, II, 100ff.
34. Bosh, *God bor'by*, 51–52.
35. S. Mishchenko, "Ianvarskoe vosstanie v Kieve," *LR*, no. 3/8 (1924), 20–43.
36. Antonov-Ovseenko, *Zapiski*, I, 157.
37. *Ibid.*, 85–86.
38. *Ibid.*, 154.
39. *Ibid.*, 53–62.
40. *Ibid.*, 132–33.
41. M. Skrypnyk, "Istoriia proletarskoi revoliutsii na Ukraini," *Statti i promovy*, I (Kharkov, 1930), 177–79.
42. Antonov-Ovseenko, *Zapiski*, 182.
43. *Ibid.*, 182.
44. Skrypnyk, "Istoriia," 144. All figures are for September 1917.
45. E. Bosh, "Oblastnoi partiinyi komitet s-d (b-kov) Iugo-Zapadnogo kraia (1917 g)," *PR*, no. 5/28 (1924), 128–49.
46. Bosh, *God bor'by*, 99.
47. *Ibid.*, 91.
48. Antonov-Ovseenko, *Zapiski*, 184; Bosh, *God bor'by*, 103.
49. B. Magidov, "Organizatsiia Donetsko-Krivorozhskoi Respubliki i otstuplenie iz Khar'kova," in KP(b)U, *Piat' let* ([Kharkov], 1922), 65–67; also Bosh, *God bor'by*, 86, 108.
50. Antonov-Ovseenko, *Zapiski*, 158–59.
51. *Izvestiia Iuga* (Kharkov), quoted in N. N. Popov, *Ocherk istorii Kommunisticheskoi Partii (bol'shevikov) Ukrainy* (Simferopol, 1929), 154–55n.
52. Analyses of the two factions of the Ukrainian Communist Party can be found in Popov, *Ocherk*, and M. Ravich-Cherkasskii, *Istoriia Kommunisticheskoi Partii Ukrainy* ([Kharkov], 1923), *passim*.
53. Maiorov, *Z istoryi*, p. vi.
54. Kulik, *Ohliad*, 38–39.
55. Ravich-Cherkasskii, *Istoriia*, 56–57; Popov, *Ocherk*, 162.
56. Popov, *Ocherk*, 176, claims Lenin supported the rights; Maiorov, *Z istoryi*, p. x, says the opposite.
57. Maiorov, *Z istoryi*, p. xi.
58. *Ibid.*, p. xvi.
59. I. Stalin, *Stat'i i rechi ob Ukraine* ([Kiev], 1936), 40–41.
60. Maiorov, *Z istoryi*, p. xi.
61. *Ibid.*
62. *Die Deutsche Okkupation der Ukraine — Geheimdokumente* (Strassburg, c. 1937), 22–23.
63. *Ibid.*, 22.

64. Khristiuk, *Zamitky*, II, 156–63; V. Vinnichenko, *Vidrodzhennia natsii*, II (Kiev-Vienna, 1920), 297–326; see also German reports in *Die Deutsche Okkupation*, 38–39, 42, where the Rada was called a "pseudo-government."
65. Doroshenko, *Istoriia*, II, 38; Vinnichenko, *Vidrodzhennia*, II, 325.
66. *Die Deutsche Okkupation*, 24.
67. *Ibid.*, 48ff.
68. KP(b)U, *Istoriia KP(b)U*, II, 279.
69. Ravich-Cherkasskii, *Istoriia*, 79–82.
70. The resolutions of the First Congress of the KP(b)U can be found in Ravich-Cherkasskii, *Istoriia*, 197–211.
71. A. Bubnov, "Hetmanshchyna, Dyrektoriia ta nasha taktyka," in V. Manilov, ed., *Pid hnitom nimetskoho imperiializmu* (*1918 r. na Kyivshchyni*), ([Kiev], 1927), 9–25; P. Dikhtiarenko, "V pidpilli za Hetmana ta Dyrektorii," in Manilov, *Pid hnitom*, 26–47; Maiorov, *Z istoryi*, pp. xii–xvi.
72. V. Cherniavskii, "Zi spohadiv pro robotu Oblasnoho Komitetu K.P.(b)U.," in Manilov, *Pid hnitom*, 48.
73. Text in Ravich-Cherkasskii, *Istoriia*, 212.
74. Popov, *Ocherk*, 178.
75. Ravich-Cherkasskii, *Istoriia*, 95.
76. *Ibid.*, 96.
77. *Ibid.*, 217–19; Popov, *Ocherk*, 180.
78. Kh. Rakovskii, "Il'ich i Ukraina," *LR*, no. 2/11 (1925), 7–8.
79. Vinnichenko, *Vidrodzhennia*, III, 158; Khristiuk, *Zamitky*, IV, 29.
80. John S. Reshetar, Jr., *The Ukrainian Revolution, 1917–1920* (Princeton, 1952), 197–98.
81. Vinnichenko, in Alekseev, *Revoliutsiia*, 279.
82. Popov, *Ocherk*, 190.
83. Alekseev, *Revoliutsiia*, 409.
84. "Dopovid Kyivskoho Oblasnoho Komitetu Miskiy Konferentsii Kyivskoi Orhanizatsii K.P.(b)U., z 19-ho sichnia 1919 roku," *Pid hnitom*, 216.
85. V. Zatonskii, "K voprosu ob organizatsii Vremennogo Raboche-Krest'ianskogo Pravitel'stva Ukrainy," *LR*, no. 1/10 (1925), 141.
86. M. Rubach, "K istorii grazhdanskoi bor'by na Ukraine," *LR*, no. 4/9 (1924), 151–65.
87. *Ibid.*, 164.
88. Zatonskii, "K voprosu," 142.
89. *Ibid.*, 148.
90. Rubach, "K istorii," 161–64.
91. Vinnichenko, *Vidrodzhennia*, III, 160.
92. *Rabocha gazeta* (Kiev), January 7, 1919, in Khristiuk, *Zamitky*, IV, 32–33.
93. *Ibid.*, IV, 33; Rakovskii, "Il'ich," 8.
94. V. Vinnichenko, *Rozlad i pohodzhennia* ([Regensburg, 1949]; private), 11.
95. For Rakovskii's views on the Ukraine, cf. *Izvestiia VTsIK*, no. 2/554 January 3, 1919.
96. Rakovskii, "Il'ich," 5–10.
97. Popov, *Ocherk*, 191.
98. A. D. Margolin, *Ukraina i politika Antanty* (Berlin, [1921]), 325, exonerates the Directory of direct participation in pogroms, though he condemns its indifference to them. E. Heifetz, *The Slaughter of the Jews in the Ukraine in 1919* (New York, 1921), 21–56, is more critical of the Directory.
99. Vinnichenko, in Alekseev, *Revoliutsiia*, 282–85.
100. Popov, *Ocherk*, 196–98.
101. Alekseev, *Revoliutsiia*, 114.
102. G. Lapchinskii, "Gomel'skoe soveshchanie," *LR*, no. 6/21 (1926), 40–41.
103. *Ibid.*, 44.
104. *Ibid.*, 44–45, 47–48.
105. Reshetar, *The Ukrainian Revolution*, 307.

106. *Malaia Sovetskaia Entsiklopediia*, II, 47.
107. KP(b)U, *Istoriia KP(b)U*, II, 459.
108. *Ibid.*, 459–60.
109. *Ibid.*, 460.
110. Lapchinskii, "Gomel'skoe soveshchanie," 42.
111. *Ibid.*, 47.
112. Ravich-Cherkasskii, *Istoriia*, 138.
113. *Lenin*, XXIV, 818–19.
114. Ravich-Cherkasskii, *Istoriia*, 139.
115. *Kommunistischeskii Internatsional*, no. 10 (1920), 1655–56. Cf. KP(b)U *Istoriia KP(b)U*, II, 640–45.
116. Reshetar, *The Ukrainian Revolution*, 307.
117. V. K. Shcharbakou, *Kastrychnitskaia revoliutsyia na Belarusi i belapol'skaia okupatsyia* (Minsk, 1930), 59.
118. *Ibid.*, 59.
119. *Ibid.*, 66–73.
120. U. Ihnatouski, "Komunistychnaia partyia Belarusi i belaruskae pytan'ne," in Tsentral'ny Vykanauchy Komitet, BSSR, *Belarus'* (Minsk, 1924), 229.
121. V. Knoryn, "Komunistychnaia partyia na Belarusi," *ibid.*, 219–20.
122. Ihnatouski, "Komunistychnaia partyia," 230.
123. V. G. Knorin, *Zametki k istorii diktatury proletariata v Belorussii* (Minsk, 1934), 29–34; V. Mitskevich-Kapsukas, "Bor'ba za sovetskuiu vlast' v Litve i Zap[adnoi] Belorussii," *PR*, no. 1/108 (1931), 65–107.
124. Shcharbakou, *Kastrychnitskaia revoliutsyia*, 101–02.
125. *Ibid.*, 100–101.
126. *Lenin*, XXV, 58.

# IV

# THE MOSLEM BORDERLANDS

1. *Revue du Monde Musulman*, LI (1922), pt. 1, pp. 7–9.
2. On Lenin's initiative in this policy, see L. Rubinshtein, *V bor'be za leninskuiu natsional'nuiu politiku* (Kazan, 1930), 48.
3. A. Saadi, "Galimdzhan Ibragimov i ego literaturnoe tvorchestvo," *Vestnik nauchnogo obshchestva tatarovedeniia* (Kazan), no. 8 (1928), 25–50.
4. I. S. Mal'chevskii, ed., *Vserossiiskoe Uchreditel'noe Sobranie* (Moscow, 1930), 57–58.
5. I. Rakhmatullin, "Mulla-Nur-Vakhitov," *Puti revoliutsii* (Kazan), no. 3 (1923), 35–30; see also *Izvestiia Vsetatarskogo VTsIK* (Kazan), 12 March 1922 (CSt-H).
6. On Ibragimov, see Saadi, "Galimdzhan Ibragimov." On Manatov, *Die Welt des Islams*, XVI (1934), 30 (NN).
7. Ul'ianitskii, "Cherez god," *ZhN*, 27 April–4 May 1919; "Tatarskii (musul'manskii) otdel Narkomnatsa za tri goda ego sushchestvovaniia," *ibid.*, 24 and 31 December 1920.
8. Abdullah Battal, *Kazan Türkleri* [The Turks of Kazan] (Istanbul, 1341/1925), chapter xiii.
9. *Ibid.*
10. Istpart, Otdel Oblastnogo Komiteta RKP(b) Tatrespubliki, *Bor'ba za Kazan'*, I (Kazan, 1924), 65.
11. A. I. Bochkov, *Tri goda sovetskoi vlasti v Kazani* (Kazan, 1921), 19–21.
12. Narodnyi komissariat po delam natsional'nostei, *Politika sovetskoi vlasti po natsional'nym delam za tri goda, 1917–XI–1920* ([Moscow], 1920), 80–81.
13. *Pravda*, 5/18 May–11/24 May 1918.

14. Rakhmatullin, "Mulla-Nur-Vakhitov," 39–40; Rubinshtein, V bor'be, 51.
15. This speech, not reprinted in Stalin's Collected Works, can be found in ZhN, 24 November 1918.
16. ZhN, 24 November 1918; 22 December 1918.
17. Ibid., 9 March 1919.
18. M. L. Murtazin, Bashkiriia i bashkirskie voiska v grazhdanskuiu voinu (Leningrad, 1927), 202–03.
19. I. G. Akulinin, Orenburgskoe Kazach'e voisko v bor'be s bol'shevikami (Shanghai, 1937), 101–03.
20. Sobranie Uzakonenii — sbornik dekretov 1919 goda (Petrograd, 1920), no. 295/8.
21. Akulinin, Orenburgskoe Kazach'e voisko, 103.
22. F. Samoilov, "Malaia Bashkiriia v 1918–1920 gg.," PR, no. 11/58 (1926), 201ff.
23. ZhN, 21 September 1919; cf. Sobranie Uzakonenii, no. 293.
24. A. Adigamov, "Pravda o Bashkirakh," ZhN, no. 26/34, 13 July 1919.
25. S. Dimanshtein, "Bashkiriia v 1918–1920 gg.," PR, no. 5/76 (1928), 153.
26. P. Mostovenko, "O bol'shikh oshibkakh v 'Maloi' Bashkirii," PR, no. 5/76 (1928), 124.
27. Kh. Iumagulov, "Ob odnom neudachnom opyte," PR, no. 3/74 (1928), 173; Mostovenko, "O bol'shikh oshibkakh," 107; Adigamov, "Pravda"; F. Syromolotov, "Lenin i Stalin v sozdanii Tataro-Bashkirskoi Respubliki," RN, no. 8 (1935), 16–17.
28. Iumagulov, "Ob odnom neudachnom opyte," 172.
29. Ibid., 186.
30. F. Samoilov, Malaia Bashkiriia v 1918–1920 gg. (Moscow, 1933), 21ff.
31. A. Daugel-Dauge, "Opyt 'Bashkiropomoshchi,'" ZhN, 8 December 1920; "Iz Bashkirii," ZhN, 26 January 1921; Samoilov, Malaia Bashkiriia, 35ff.
32. ZhN, 26 January 1921.
33. Sh. Tipeev, K istorii natsional'nogo dvizheniia i sovetskoi Bashkirii (Ufa, 1929), 59.
34. Samoilov, Malaia Bashkiriia, 6ff.
35. Ibid., 91; Mostovenko, "O bol'shikh obshibkakh," passim.
36. Sobranie Uzakonenii 1920 goda, no. 45/203.
37. Murtazin, Bashkiriia, 187.
38. PR, no. 12/59 (1926), 205–07.
39. Mostovenko, "O bol'shikh oshibkakh," 117; Murtazin, Bashkiriia, 188ff.
40. Samoilov, Malaia Bashkiriia, 61, 84, 86ff.
41. Mostovenko, "O bol'shikh oshibkakh," 109.
42. Ibid., 117.
43. Rubinshtein, V bor'be, passim; G. von Mende, Der nationale Kampf der Russlandtuerken (Berlin, 1936), 156ff.
44. Sultan-Galiev, "Sotsial'naia revoliutsiia i Vostok," ZhN, 5 October, 12 October, 2 November 1919; the concluding article to this series was not printed. M. Sultan-Galiev, Metody antireligioznoi propagandy sredi Musul'man (Moscow, 1922).
45. Rubinshtein, V bor'be, 56–59.
46. Ibid., 59.
47. VKP(b), Tatarskii Oblastnoi Komitet, Stenograficheskii otchet IX Oblastnoi konferentsii Tatarskoi Organizatsii RKP(b) (Kazan, 1924), 129.
48. I. Khodorovskii, "Iz vospominanii ob Il'iche," Izvestiia, 22 April 1930; Kh. Gabidullin, Tatarstan za sem' let (1920–27) (Kazan, 1927), 18.
49. Khodorovskii, "Iz vospominanii."
50. Gabidullin, Tatarstan, 16.
51. Ibid.
52. Rubinshtein, V bor'be, 67.
53. Tatarskaia Sotsialisticheskaia Sovetskaia Respublika, Za piat' let, 1920–25/VI–1925 (Kazan, 1925), 18.

54. D. P. Petrov, *Chuvashiia* (Moscow, 1926), 90–92.
55. E. G. Fedorov, "Uchreditel'nyi s" ezd sovetov Kirgizskoi (Kazakhskoi) ASSR," in VKP(b), Kazakhskii Kraevoi Komitet, *Iz istorii partiinogo stroitel'stva v Kazakhstane* (Alma-Ata, 1936), 220.
56. *Izvestiia*, 4 April 1919.
57. "Vremennoe polozhenie o revoliutsionnom komitete po upravleniiu kirgizskim kraem," *Izvestiia*, 17 July 1919.
58. Fedorov, "Uchreditel'nyi s"ezd," 219.
59. *Ibid.*, 218.
60. *Ibid.*, 224.
61. N. Timofeev, "K istorii obrazovaniia Kazakhstanskoi Kraevoi Organızatsii VKP(b)," in VKP(b), *Iz istorii*, 102–71, cites numerous facts to support this contention.
62. *Ibid.*, 151ff.
63. *Izvestiia*, 1 September 1920; Kazakskaia SSR, S"ezd Sovetov, *Uchreditel'nyi s"ezd sovetov Kirgizskoi (Kazakskoi) ASSR, Protokoly* (Alma-Ata–Moscow, 1936).
64. G. N. Mel'nikov, *Oktiabr' v Kazakstane*, (Alma-Ata, 1930), 11ff.
65. J. Castagné, *Le Turkestan depuis la Révolution russe*, (1917–21) (Paris, 1922), 24.
66. *Svobodnyi Turkestan* (Tashkent), no. 9, 25 January 1918.
67. Baymirza Hayit, *Die Nationalen Regierungen von Kokand (Choqand) und der Alasch Orda* (Muenster, 1950), 70–72.
68. *Ibid.*, 77–78.
69. The following account is based on a report from Kokand by B. Ol'ginskii, dated 11. February 1918, in *Svobodnyi Turkestan*, 4/19 March 1918.
70. *Ibid.*
71. *Svobodnyi Turkestan*, 17 February/2 March 1918.
72. *Ibid.*, 18/31 March 1918.
73. O. Glovatskii, *Revoliutsiia pobezhdaet* (Tashkent, 1930), 24.
74. Castagné, *Le Turkestan*, 28ff.
75. G. Safarov, *Kolonial'naia revoliutsiia*, (*Opyt Turkestana*), ([Moscow], 1921), 86; on Soviet treatment of the natives, cf. V. K[uibyshev], "Basmacheskii front," *ZhN*, no. 16/73, 2 June 1920.
76. [K.] Vasilevskii, "Fazy basmacheskogo dvizheniia v Srednei Azii," *NV*, no. 29 (1930), 126–28.
77. S. B. Ginsburg, "Basmachestvo v Fergane," *NV*, no. 10–11 (1925), 183; J. Castagné, *Les Basmatchis* (Paris, 1925), 14–15.
78. F. Novitskii, "M. V. Frunze na Turkestanskom fronte," *KA*, no. 3/100 (1940), 41.
79. Castagné, *Les Basmatchis*, 28–33; Ginsburg, "Basmachestvo," 185–89.
80. E. I. Pesikina, *Narodnyi komissariat po delam natsional'nostei i ego deiatel' nost' v 1917–1918 gg.* (Moscow, 1950), 124–25.
81. Safarov, *Kolonial'naia revoliutsiia*, 85.
82. S. Bolotov, "Iz istorii osipovskogo miatezha v Turkestane," *PR*, no. 6/53 (1926), 110–37; Castagné, *Le Turkestan*, 34; Mel'nikov, *Oktiabr'*, 121.
83. L. C. Dunsterville, *The Adventures of Dunsterforce* (London, 1920), 230; J. K. Tod, "The Malleson Mission to Transcaspia in 1918," *The Journal of the Royal Central Asian Society*, XXVII, pt. 1 (1940), 53; F. M. Bailey, *Mission to Tashkent* (London, 1946).
84. V. K[uibyshev], in *ZhN*, 2 June 1920.
85. Hayit, *Die Nationalen Regierungen*, 104.
86. Novitskii, "M. V. Frunze," 36–37.
87. Safarov, *Kolonial'naia revoliutsiia*, 133.
88. *Lenin*, XXIV, 531.
89. Castagné, *Le Turkestan*, 36.
90. *KA*, no. 3/100, 63–65.
91. Vasilevskii, "Fazy," 132–33; cf. also M. Shkliar in *ZhN*, 17 October 1920.

92. Vasilevskii, "Fazy," 133.
93. G. Skalov, "Khivinskaia revoliutsiia 1920 goda," *NV*, no. 3 (1923), 241–57.
94. Glovatskii, *Revoliutsiia*, 28–29.
95. *KA*, no. 3/100, 74–75.
96. V. Elagin, "Natsionalisticheskie illiuzii krymskikh Tatar v revoliutsionnye gody," *NV*, no. 6 (1924), 212.
97. M. F. Bunegin, *Revoliutsiia i grazhdanskaia voina v Krymu* (Simferopol, 1927), 112; E. Kirimal, *Der Nationale Kampf der Krimtuerken* (Emsdetten, 1952), 151; Elagin, "Natsionalisticheskie illiuzii," *NV*, no. 6 (1924), 214.
98. Kirimal, *ibid.*, 152.
99. Cf. report of the Soviet commander, Iu. Gaven, in *ZhN*, 21 December 1919.
100. Bunegin, *Revoliutsiia*, 126.
101. *Ibid.*, 140; cf. M. L. Atlas, *Bor'ba za sovety* (Simferopol, 1933), 50.
102. Bunegin, *Revoliutsiia*, 122–23, 144.
103. *Ibid.*, 145; A. Vasil'ev, "Pervaia sovetskaia vlast' v Krymu i ee padenie," *PR*, no. 7 (1922), 3–58.
104. Bunegin, *Revoliutsiia*, 145.
105. Vasil'ev, "Pervaia sovetskaia vlast'," 28.
106. V. Sovetov and M. Atlas, *Rasstrel sovetskogo pravitel'stva Krymskoi Respubliki Tavridy* (Simferopol, 1933).
107. Elagin, "Natsionalisticheskie illiuzii," no. 6, 220.
108. Bunegin, *Revoliutsiia*, 224ff.
109. Iu. Gaven, "Krymskie Tatary i revoliutsiia," *ZhN*, no. 49/57, 28 December 1919; I. Verner, "Nasha politika v Krymu," *ZhN*, 10 October 1921.
110. Verner, "Nasha politika."
111. *Ibid.*
112. T. Boiadzhev, *Krymsko-tatarskaia molodezh v revoliutsii* (Simferopol, 1930), 9.
113. Verner, "Nasha politika."
114. Grigor'ev (Genker), "Tatarskii vopros v Krymu," in *Antanta i Vrangel'* (Moscow, 1923), 236–38.
115. A. K. Bochagov, *Milli Firka* (Simferopol, 1930), 64; 115–17.
116. Verner, "Nasha politika."
117. S. A. Usov, *Istoriko-ekonomicheskie ocherki Kryma* (Simferopol, 1925), 69.
118. *Ves' Krym, 1920–1925* (Simferopol, 1926), 65ff.
119. Verner, "Nasha politika."
120. M. P[avlovi]ch, "V Krymu," *ZhN*, 28 May 1921.
121. I. T[rainin], "Dolzhen li byt' Krym Respublikoi?", *ZhN*, 30 July 1921.
122. Cf. Iu. Gaven, "Zadacha sovetskoi vlasti v Krymu," *ZhN*, 1 February 1920.

# V

# THE CAUCASUS

1. Georgia, Ministerstvo Vneshnikh Del, *Dokumenty i materialy po vneshnei politike Zakavkaz'ia i Gruzii* (Tiflis, 1919, 269ff; henceforth referred to as Georgia, *Dokumenty*.
2. A. P. Stavrovskii, *Zakavkaz'e posle Oktiabria* (Moscow-Leningrad, 1925), 15; M. Z. Mirza-Bala, *Milli Azerbaycan Hareketi* ([Berlin], 1938), 121.
3. Mirza-Bala, *Milli*, 121–23; I. Tserétélli, *Séparation de la Transcaucasie et de la Russie et l'indépendance de la Géorgie* (Paris, 1919).
4. F. Kazemzadeh, *The Struggle for Transcaucasia (1917–1921)* (London–New York, 1951), 147.
5. Georgia, *Dokumenty*, 278.
6. The text of the Georgian declaration of independence is to be found in Délégation géorgienne a la Conférence de la Paix, *Mémoire présenté à la Conférence de la Paix* (Paris, 1919), 21–22.

7. The text of the Azerbaijani declaration of independence is in Mirza-Bala, *Milli*, 135.
8. Tsérételli, *Séparation*.
9. Mirza-Bala, *Milli*, 124.
10. M. Varandian, *Le Conflit arméno-géorgien et la guerre du Caucase* (Paris, 1919), 37–52; this source cites the text of an alleged Georgian-Turkish agreement of 1914.
11. N. L. Ianchevskii, *Grazhdanskaia bor'ba na Severnom Kavkaze*, I (Rostov on Don, 1927), 134–36, 189.
12. *Ibid.*, 197–99.
13. I. Borisenko, *Sovetskie respubliki na Severnom Kavkaze v 1918 godu*, II (Rostov on Don, 1930), 231–36, contains the text of this constitution.
14. A. A. Takho-Godi, *Revoliutsiia i kontr-revoliutsiia v Dagestane* (Makhach-Kala, 1927), 61–65.
15. Ianchevskii, *Grazhdanskaia bor'ba*, II, 201–02.
16. Borisenko, *Sovetskie respubliki*, II, 69.
17. F. Makharadze, *Sovety i bor'ba za sovetskuiu vlast' v Gruzii, 1917–1921* (Tiflis, 1928), 175.
18. Speech by Ordzhonikidze in December 1918, quoted by Borisenko, *Sovetskie respubliki*, II, 72–73.
19. Takho-Godi, *Revoliutsiia*, 88–89.
20. *Ibid.*, 89.
21. Borisenko, *Sovetskie respubliki*, II, 79–80.
22. S. E. Sef, *Bor'ba za Oktiabr' v Zakavkaz'i*, ([Tiflis], 1932), 64; see also Suren Shaumian, "Bakinskaia Kommuna 1918 goda," *PR*, no. 12/59 (1926), 77–78.
23. S. E. Sef, *Kak Bol'sheviki prishli k vlasti v Bakinskom raione* (Baku, 1927), 15.
24. Ia. A. Ratgauzer, *Revoliutsiia i grazhdanskaia voina v Baku*, I (Baku, 1927), 144.
25. S. Sef, "Bakinskii Oktiabr'," *PR*, no. 11/106 (1930), 73.
26. S. Sef, *Kak Bol'sheviki prishli k vlasti v Bakinskom raione* (Baku, 1927), 26, quoted in A. Dubner, *Bakinskii proletariat v gody revoliutsii (1917–1920)* (Baku, 1931), p. v.
27. Sef, quoted by Dubner, 25; for other accounts of the March events, see Sef, "Bakinskii Oktiabr'," 70–78; Ratgauzer, *Revoliutsiia*, 147–48.
28. Sef, "Bakinskii Oktiabr'," 79.
29. Ratgauzer, *Revoliutsiia*, 146.
30. *Ibid.*, 168.
31. *Ibid.*, 165.
32. *Ibid.*, 168.
33. Sef, "Bakinskii Oktiabr'," 82.
34. Ratgauzer, *Revoliutsiia*, 174.
35. Stepan Shaumian, *Stat'i i rechi (1908–1918)* (Baku, 1924), 188–90; Sef, *Kak Bol'sheviki*, 33–34; *LS*, XXXV (1945), 24.
36. S. A. Vyshetravskii, *Neftianoe khoziaistvo Rossii za poslednee desiatiletie* (Moscow, 1924), 148–49; Dubner, *Bakinskii proletariat*, 93.
37. Dubner, *Bakinskii proletariat*, 92.
38. Shaumian, speaking on May 16, 1918, in Dubner, 67.
39. Shaumian, *Stat'i*, 224–25.
40. *Ibid.*, 224.
41. Ratgauzer, *Revoliutsiia*, 199.
42. *Ibid.*, 207.
43. *Ibid.*, 212–13; the omissions are in the text.
44. *Ibid.*, 213–15.
45. J. Schafir, *Die Ermordung der 26 Kommunare in Baku und die Partei der Sozialrevolutionaere* (Hamburg, 1922).
46. L. C. Dunsterville, *The Adventures of Dunsterforce* (London, 1920), 182–86.
47. *Ibid.*, 305ff.
48. Mirza-Bala, *Milli*, 135ff.

49. *Ibid.*, 140ff.
50. N. Pchelin, *Krest'ianskii vopros pri Musavate* (*1918–1920*) (Baku, 1931), 21; Ratgauzer, *Bor'ba*, 3.
51. Mirza-Bala, *Milli*, 141–47; A. Steklov, *Armiia musavatskogo Azerbaidzhana* (Baku, 1928), 7.
52. Maj. Gen. J. G. Harbord, "American Military Mission to Armenia," *International Conciliation*, no. 151 (June 1920), 296.
53. Ratgauzer, *Bor'ba*, 14–15; Dubner, *Bakinskii proletariat*, 101.
54. Mirza-Bala, *Milli*, 149; B. A. Bor'ian, *Armeniia, mezhdunarodnaia diplomatiia i SSSR* (Moscow-Leningrad, 1928–29), II, 73–74.
55. M. Kuliev, *Vragi Oktiabria v Azerbaidzhane* (Baku, 1927), 13.
56. A. Raevskii, *Angliiskaia interventsiia i musavatskoe pravitel'stvo* (Baku, 1927), 48–49.
57. Steklov, *Armiia*, 33.
58. Dubner, *Bakinskii proletariat*, 135n.
59. Raevskii, *Angliiskaia interventsiia*, 82.
60. *Ibid.*, 159; R. Arskii, *Kavkaz i ego znachenie dlia Sovetskoi Rossii* (Peterburg, 1921), 45.
61. *Claims of the Peace Delegation of the Republic of Caucasian Azerbaidjan Presented to the Peace Conference in Paris* (Paris, 1919), 28–31.
62. Bor'ian, *Armeniia*, II, 62, 90.
63. S. Vratsian, *Hayastani Hanrapetouthiun* (Paris, 1928), 214ff.
64. Bor'ian, *Armeniia*, II, 83.
65. *Ibid.*, 80
66. Harbord, "American Military Mission to Armenia," 275–312.
67. Vratsian, *Hayastani*, 320–25.
68. *Ibid.*, 330, on agreement; Bor'ian, *Armeniia*, II, 83, on assistance.
69. Raevskii, *Angliiskaia interventsiia*, 108–09.
70. A. N. Mandelstam, *La Société des Nations et les puissances devant le problème arménien* (Paris, 1926), 57.
71. *Ibid.*, 55.
72. M. Varandian, *Le Conflit arméno-géorgien et la guerre du Caucase* (Paris, 1919).
73. E. L. Woodward, ed., *Documents on British Foreign Policy, 1919–1939*, 1st Series, III (London, 1949), *passim*.
74. Makharadze, *Sovety*, 156. W. S. Woytinsky, *La Démocratie géorgienne* (Paris, 1921), 194, and J. Kawtaradze, *Gruzja w zarysie historycznym* (Warsaw, 1929), give slightly different figures.
75. E. Kuhne, *La Géorgie libre* (Geneva, 1920), 57–58.
76. République de Géorgie, *Constitution de la Republique de Géorgie* (Paris, 1922; private).
77. [F] Makharadze, *Diktatura men'shevistskoi partii v Gruzii* ([Moscow], 1921), 71; S. Danilov, "Tragediia abkhazskogo naroda," *Vestnik Instituta po Izucheniiu Istorii i Kultury SSSR* (Munich), I (1951), 124ff.
78. G. Devdariani, *Dni gospodstva men'shevikov v Gruzii* (Tiflis, 1931), 310–311.
79. M. Khoměriki, *La Réforme agraire et l'économie rurale en Géorgie* (Paris, 1921), 17; Woytinsky, *La Démocratie géorgienne*, 210–11.
80. Devdariani, *Dni gospodstva*, 302.
81. Makharadze, *Sovety*, 156–57.
82. *Ibid.*
83. Woytinsky, *La Démocratie géorgienne*, 89ff.
84. M. Svechnikov, *Bor'ba krasnoi armii na Severnom Kavkaze* (Moscow-Leningrad, 1926), 45.
85. *Ibid.*, 102–03.
86. A. Denikine, *The White Army* (London, 1930), 156.
87. Order no. 171, dated 19 November 1919, in *Azerbaidzhan* (Baku), no. 267, quoted in Dubner, *Bakinskii proletariat*, 137.
88. Raevskii, *Angliiskaia interventsiia*, 112.

89. Takho-Godi, *Revoliutsiia*, 118–21.
90. *Ibid.*, 128–29.
91. A. Avtorkhanov, *K osnovnym voprosam istorii Chechni* ([Groznyi], 1930), 57–75.
92. Takho-Godi, *Revoliutsiia*, 114, 127–28; N. Samurskii, "Krasnyi Dagestan," in V. Stavskii, ed., *Dagestan* (Moscow, 1936), 16.
93. Quoted from documents found in the Azerbaijani Historical Archive by Raevskii, *Angliiskaia interventsiia*, 53.
94. Lord Curzon to Wardrop, 4 October 1919, in Woodward, *Documents*, 1st Series, III, 577.
95. Denikine, *The White Army*, 340.
96. Raevskii, *Angliiskaia interventsiia*, 61, on Azerbaijan; Woodward, *Documents*, 1st Series, III, 595, on Georgia; Harbord, "American Military Mission to Armenia," on Armenia.
97. Raevskii, 55–58.
98. *Ibid.*, 58.
99. Arskii, *Kavkaz*.
100. Makharadze, *Sovety*, 193.
101. Sarkis, *Bor'ba za vlast'* ([Baku], 1930), 15; Ratgauzer, *Bor'ba*, 45.
102. A. G. Karaev, *Iz nedavnego proshlogo* [Baku, 1926], 13.
103. Makharadze, *Sovety*, 193–96.
104. Sarkis, *Bor'ba*, 48.
105. *Ibid.*, 93.
106. *Ibid.*, 99–100.
107. *Ibid.*, 97; Karaev, *Iz nedavnego*, 54–55.
108. Dubner, *Bakinskii proletariat*, 145–46; Ratgauzer, *Bor'ba*, 53, 63.
109. E. Drabkina, *Gruzinskaia kontr-revoliutsiia* (Leningrad, 1928), 172; Makharadze, *Sovety*, 197–206.
110. The fullest account of Turco-Soviet relations in this period is by G. Jaeschke, "Der Weg zur russisch-tuerkischen Freundschaft," *Die Welt des Islams*, XVI (1934), 23–38.
111. Karaev, *Iz nedavnego*, 59.
112. Jaeschke, "Der Weg," 27.
113. Iu. V. Kliuchnikov and A. Sabanin, *Mezhdunarodnaia politika noveishego vremeni v dogovorakh, notakh i deklaratsiiakh*, II (Moscow, 1925–29), 384–87.
114. Karaev, *Iz nedavnego*, 88, 121; see also Mirza-Bala. *Milli*, 188ff.
115. Takho-Godi, *Revoliutsiia*, 223.
116. *LS*, XXXIV (1942), 279.
117. S. M. Kirov, *Stat'i, rechi, dokumenty*, I ([Leningrad], 1936), 331.
118. *Entsiklopedicheskii slovar'* . . . 'Granat', XLI, pt. 3, 160–63; *Pravda Gruzii* (Tiflis), 10 March 1922.
119. G. K. Ordzhonikidze, *Izbrannye stat'i i rechi, 1911–1937* ([Moscow], 1939), 113. "Ordzhonikidze, G. K.," *Bol'shaia Sovetskaia Entsiklopediia*, XLIII (1939). G. Zhvaniia, "V. I. Lenin i partiinaia organizatsiia Gruzii v period bor'by za sovetskuiu vlast'," *Zaria Vostoka* (Tiflis), 21 April 1961.
120. Raevskii, *Angliiskaia interventsiia*, 179–80, on Azerbaijan; Kazemzadeh, *The Struggle*, 295, on Georgia.
121. The Azerbaijani State Archive, Deposit of the Ministry of Foreign Affairs, quoted in Raevskii, *Angliiskaia interventsiia*, 185.
122. Steklov, *Armiia*, 66–67; *Izvestiia*, 21 January 1937.
123. Raevskii, *Angliiskaia interventsiia*, 61–64, 185ff; Kazemzadeh, *The Struggle*, 276ff, 283.
124. Karaev, *Iz nedavnego*, 127; Kuliev, *Vragi*, 40.
125. Mirza-Bala, *Milli*, 188–90; Kirov, *Stat'i*, I, 205.
126. Sarkis, *Bor'ba*, 140–41; Karaev, *Iz nedavnego*, 123–34.
127. Raevskii, *Angliiskaia interventsiia*, 190; E. A. Tokarzhevskii, *Iz istorii inostrannoi interventsii i grazhdanskoi voiny v Azerbaidzhane* (Baku, 1957), 268–70.

128. Kazemzadeh, *The Struggle,* 284.
129. Mirza-Bala, *Milli,* 192ff.
130. Zhvaniia, "V. I. Lenin"; cf. *LS,* XXIV, 295–96.
131. *Traité conclu le 7 mai 1920 entre la République démocratique de Géorgie et la République Socialiste Fédérative Soviétiste Russe . . .* (Paris, 1922); RSFSR, Narodnyi komissariat po inostrannym delam, *Sbornik deistvuiushchikh dogovorov, soglashenii i konventsii zakliuchennykh RSFSR s inostrannymi gosudarstvami,* III (Moscow, 1922), 295.
132. Vratsian, *Hayastani,* 410ff.
133. M. Shakhbazov, "Gandzha do i pri sovetvlasti," *Iz proshlogo* (Baku), no. 2 (1924), 101–07.
134. Zarevant, *Turtsiia i Panturanizm* (Paris, 1930); H. Munschi, *Die Republik Aserbeidschan* (Berlin, 1930), 41–46.
135. N. Narimanov, *Stat'i i pis'ma* (Moscow, 1925), pp. x–xiv.
136. *LS,* XXXV (1945), 236. Telegram of Lenin of July 1921.
137. Takho-Godi, *Revoliutsiia,* 142, on Soviet activities in the North Caucasus.
138. On the rebellion, cf. Samurskii, "Krasnyi Dagestan," 18–20.
139. *Kommunist* (Baku), 4 November 1920, quoted in *IM,* no. 11 (1940), 12.
140. *Stalin,* IV, 410–11.
141. Bor'ian, *Armeniia,* II, 96.
142. *Ibid.,* 95.
143. A. N., "Kommunizm v Armenii," pp. 2543–50.
144. Vratsian, *Hayastani,* 417–41.
145. S. I. Iakubovskaia, *Ob"edinitel'noe dvizhenie za obrazovanie SSSR (1917–1922)* ([Moscow], 1947), 99.
146. Bor'ian, *Armeniia,* II, 122.
147. See telegram of Stalin to Ordzhonikidze in V. S. Kirillov and A. Ia. Sverdlov, *Grigorii Konstantinovich Ordzhonikidze (Sergo) — Biografiia* (Moscow, 1962), 140.
148. RSFSR, Narodnyi komissariat po inostrannym delam, *Sbornik deistvuiushchikh dogovorov,* III, 14–15.
149. Vratsian, *Hayastani.*
150. Bor'ian, *Armeniia,* II, 126, 135–36; Vratsian, *Hayastani,* 435ff.
151. Makharadze, *Sovety,* 213.
152. Ruben, "'V tiskakh men'shevistskoi 'demokratii'," *PR,* no. 8 (1923), 146.
153. Zhvaniia, "V. I. Lenin."
154. Quoted in Drabkina, *Gruzinskaia kontr–revoliutsiia,* 175.
155. Makharadze, *Sovety,* 223.
156. The text of the Gekker report can be found in République de Géorgie, *Documents relatifs à la question de la Géorgie devant la Société des Nations* (Paris, 1925), 67–68.
157. Zhvaniia, "V. I. Lenin."
158. Jaeschke, "Der Weg," 29–30.
159. M. Pavlovich, V. Gurko-Kriazhin, and F. Raskol'nikov, *Turtsiia v bor'be za nezavisimost'* (Moscow, 1925), 59–106.
160. Note dated 17 February 1921, Trotsky Archive, Harvard College Library, T–635.
161. Zhvaniia, "V. I. Lenin"; Kirillov and Sverdlov, *Ordzhonikidze,* 143.
162. Zhvaniia, *ibid.*
163. Lloyd George's assurance to Krasin was reported by Chicherin in a speech delivered on 4 March 1925 and cited by I. Tseretelli in *Prométhée* (June, 1928), p. 11 from *Zaria Vostoka* (Tiflis), 5 March 1925.
164. Zhvaniia, "V. I. Lenin."
165. Dispatch by Lenin dated 14 February 1921, Trotsky Archive, T–632.
166. Dispatch by Trotsky from Ekaterinburg (Sverdlovsk), dated 21 February 1921, Trotsky Archive, T–637.
167. Trotsky Archive, T–635.
168. *Entsiklopedicheskii slovar' . . . 'Granat',* XLI, pt. 2, supplement, 20–27.
169. The account of the invasion of Georgia is derived principally from the following

sources: R. Duguet, *Moscou et la Géorgie martyre* (Paris, 1927); République de Géorgie, *Documents;* L. Coquet, *Les Héritiers de la 'toison d'or'*, (Chaumont, 1930); and from contemporary newspaper accounts in *Pravda, The Times* (London), and *New York Times.*

170. Bor'ian, *Armeniia*, II, 125ff.
171. *Pravda*, 2 March 1921.
172. An account of the fight for Batum is given in the report of the commander of the Batum fortress, in Ia. M. Shafir, *Ocherki gruzinskoi zhirondy* (Moscow–Leningrad, 1925), 187–92.
173. Text in Devdariani, *Dni gospodstva*, 226–28.
174. *Lenin*, XXVI, 187–88.
175. *Ibid.* 188.
176. *Ibid.*, 192.

# VI

# THE ESTABLISHMENT OF THE USSR

1. Quoted in E. H. Carr, *The Bolshevik Revolution, 1917–1923*, I (New York, 1951), 117.
2. Program of the Russian Communist Party (1919), in TsK, RKP(b), *Rossiiskaia Kommunisticheskaia Partiia (bol'shevikov) v rezoliutsiiakh ee s"ezdov i konferentsii (1898–1922 gg.)* (Moscow–Petrograd, 1923), 255–56.
3. *Ibid.*, 254.
4. *Ibid.*, 253–54.
5. Carr, *The Bolshevik Revolution*, I, 139.
6. D. Magerovskii, "Soiuz Sovetskikh Sotsialisticheskikh Respublik," *SP*, no. 1/4 (1923), 9.
7. *Ibid.*, 10; V. Durdenevskii, "Na putiakh k russkomu federal'nomu pravu," *SP*, no. 1/4 (1923), 30–33.
8. *Stalin*, IV, 402.
9. B. D. Pletnev, "Gosudarstvennaia struktura RSFSR," *Pravo i zhizn'* (Moscow), no. 1 (1922), 29–30. See also the opinions of D. A. Magerovskii, *Soiuz Sovetskikh Sotsialisticheskikh Respublik (obzor i materialy)* (Moscow, 1923), 20; G. S. Gurvich, *Osnovy sovetskoi konstitutsii* (Moscow, 1926), 149ff; N. N. Alekseev, "Sovetskii federalizm," *Evraziiskii vremennik* (Paris), V (1927), 255, and M. Langhans, "Die staatsrechtliche Entwicklung der auf Russischen Boden lebenden kleineren Nationalitaeten," *Archiv fuer Oeffentliches Recht, Neue Folge*, IX (1925), 195.
10. *Izvestiia*, 22 May 1920.
11. *Ibid.*, 6 November 1920.
12. *Ibid.*, 21 December 1920.
13. *Ibid.*, 27 April 1921.
14. *Ibid.*, 6 November 1920.
15. *Ibid.*, 21 December 1920.
16. *Revue du Monde Musulman*, LI (1922), 26–33.
17. G. K. Klinger, ed., *Sovetskaia politika za 10 let po natsional'nomu voprosu v RSFSR* (Moscow–Leningrad, 1928), 24; cf. I. Trainin, "K likvidatsii Narkomnatsa," *ZhN*, no. 1/6 (1924), 19–30.
18. P. Miliukov, *Rossiia na perelome*, II (Paris, 1927), 249.
19. KP(b)U, Institut Istorii Partii, *Istoriia KP(b)U* (Kiev, 1933), II, 264–65.
20. *Sistematicheskii sbornik vazhneishikh dekretov, 1917–1920* (Moscow, 1921), 63.
21. L. Trotsky, *My Life* (New York, 1931), 411–22.
22. LS, XVIII (1931), 243; *Lenin*, XXVI, 619–20.

23. M. Ravich-Cherkasskii, *Istoriia Kommunisticheskoi Partii Ukrainy* ([Kharkov], 1923), 111.
24. E. G. Bosh, *God bor'by* (*1917*) (Moscow, 1925), 92.
25. B. D. Wolfe, "The Influence of Early Military Decisions upon the National Structure of the Soviet Union," *The American Slavic and East European Review*, IX (1950), 169–79; Ravich-Cherkasskii, *Istoriia*, 131.
26. Ravich-Cherkasskii, *Istoriia*, 131–32.
27. *LS*, XXXIV (1942), 120–21.
28. Magerovskii, *Soiuz*, 68–69.
29. S. I. Iakubovskaia, *Stroitel'stvo Soiuznogo Sovetskogo Sotsialisticheskogo gosudarstva, 1922–1925 gg.* (Moscow, 1960), 123.
30. The background of the Russian-Azerbaijani treaty is discussed by M. S. Iskenderov, *Iz istorii bor'by Kommunisticheskoi partii Azerbaidzhana za pobedu Sovetskoi vlasti* (Baku, 1958), 515–17, and E. A. Tokarzhevskii, *Ocherki istorii Sovetskogo Azerbaidzhana v period perekhoda na mirnuiu rabotu po vosstanovleniiu narodnogo khoziaistva* (*1921–1925 gg.*) (Baku, 1956), 88–90.
31. RSFSR, Narodnyi komissariat po inostrannym delam, *Sbornik deistvuiushchikh dogovorov, soglashenii i konventsii, zakliuchennykh RSFSR s inostrannymi stranami* (Moscow–Peterburg, 1921-22), I, 1–9; henceforth referred to as NKID, *Sbornik*.
32. *Ibid.*, 15–17 and 13–15; cf. above, 137–38.
33. Tokarzhevskii, *Ocherki*, 89.
34. NKID, *Sbornik*, I, 17–27.
35. *Ibid.*, II, 7ff
36. Iu. V. Kliuchnikov and A. Sabanin, *Mezhdunarodnaia politika noveishego vremeni v dogovorakh, notakh i deklaratsiiakh* (Moscow, 1925–29), III, 167ff.
37. "Dalnevostochnaia Respublika (DVR)," *Bol'shaia Sovetskaia Entsiklopediia*, 1st ed., XX (Moscow, 1930), 216–21.
38. *Revue du Monde Musulman*, LI, 224–25.
39. Kommunisticheskii Internatsional i osvobozhdenie Vostoka, *Pervyi s"ezd narodov Vostoka — stenograficheskie otchety* (Petrograd, 1920), 108–12 (NN).
40. D. Soloveichik, "Revoliutsionnaia Bukhara," *NV*, no. 2 (1922), 277.
41. M. Chokaev, "The Basmaji Movement in Turkestan," *The Asiatic Review* (London), XXIV, no. 78 (1928), 284–85.
42. K. Okay, *Enver Pascha, der grosse Freund Deutschlands* (Berlin, [1935]), 387–88.
43. Soloveichik, "Revoliutsionnaia Bukhara," *passim*.
44. *Ibid.*; *Revue du Monde Musulman*, LI, 229.
45. Soloveichik, "Revoliutsionnaia Bukhara," 283; Saïd Alim Khan (Emir of Bukhara), *La Voix de la Boukharie opprimée* (Paris, 1929), 37.
46. [K.] Vasilevskii, "Fazy basmacheskogo dvizheniia v Srednei Azii," *NV*, no. 29 (1930), 134.
47. Soloveichik, "Revoliutsionnaia Bukhara," 283.
48. *Revue du Monde Musulman*, LI, 229–30, cites text of the ultimatum.
49. Soloveichik, "Revoliutsionnaia Bukhara," 284, has Enver's letter to the Emir; cf. Vasilevskii, "Fazy," 134.
50. Vasilevskii, "Fazy," 135; Chokaev, "The Basmaji Movement," 282; J. Castagné, *Les Basmatchis* (Paris, 1925), 34.
51. Vasilevskii, "Fazy," 135.
52. I. Kutiakov, *Krasnaia konnitsa i vozdushynyi flot v pustyniakh — 1924 god* (Moscow–Leningrad, 1930).
53. VKP(b), Tatarskii Oblastnoi Komitet, *Stenograficheskii otchet IX oblastnoi konferentsii tatarskoi organizatsii R.K.P.(b)* (Kazan, 1924), 130.
54. Sultan-Galiev, quoted in A. Arsharuni and Kh. Gabidullin, *Ocherki panislamizma i pantiurkizma v Rossii* ([Moscow], 1931), 78–79; see also A. Arsharuni, "Ideologiia Sultangalievshchiny," *Antireligioznik* (Moscow), no. 5 (1930), 22–29, and M. Kobetskii, "Sultan-Galievshchina kak apologiia Islama," *Antireligioznik*, no. 1 (1930), 12–16, (NN).

55. L. Rubinshtein, *V bor'be za leninskuiu natsional'nuiu politiku* (Kazan, 1930), 75ff.
56. Arsharuni and Gabidullin, *Ocherki*, 78–86; G. von Mende, *Der nationale Kampf der Russlandtuerken* (Berlin, 1936), 158.
57. L. Trotsky, *Stalin* (New York, [1941]), 417.
58. *Stalin*, V, 305.
59. NKID, *Sbornik*, I, 15–16.
60. Magerovskii, *Soiuz*, 24.
61. Iakubovskaia, *Stroitel'stvo*, 130.
62. V. M. Kuritsyn, *Gosudarstvennoe sotrudnichestvo mezhdu Ukrainskoi SSR i RSFSR v 1917–1922 gg.* (Moscow, 1957), 141, 144.
63. S. Gililov, *V. I. Lenin — Organizator Sovetskogo mnogonatsional'nogo gosudarstva* (Moscow, 1960), 145–46.
64. V. V. Pentkovskaia, "Rol' V. I. Lenina v obrazovanii SSSR," *VI*, no. 3 (1956), 14–15; Iakubovskaia, *Stroitel'stvo*, 139–40.
65. Iakubovskaia, *Stroitel'stvo*, 140–41; Pentkovskaia, "Rol' V. I. Lenina," 15; V. Chirko, *Ob"iednavchyi rukh na Ukraini za stvorennia Soiuzu RSR* (Kiev, 1954), 120.
66. Iakubovskaia, *Stroitel'stvo*, 130, 141–42.
67. See his autobiographical sketch in *Entsiklopedicheskii slovar' . . . 'Granat'*, XLI, pt. 3, supplement, 47–59.
68. Institut Marksizma–Leninizma pri TsK KPSS, *Odinadtsatyi s"ezd RKP(b) — stenograficheskii otchet* (Moscow, 1961), 72–75.
69. R. S. Sullivant, *Soviet Politics and the Ukraine, 1917–1957* (New York, 1962), passim.
70. NKID, *Sbornik*, III, 18–19.
71. *Lenin*, XXVI, 191; *LS*, XX (1932), 178.
72. NKID, *Sbornik*, III, 9–13; Akademiia Nauk Gruzinskoi SSR, *Bor'ba za uprochenie Sovetskoi vlasti v Gruzii* (Tiflis, 1959), 347–48; Gililov, *V. I. Lenin*, 157–58; RKP(b), *Dvenadtsatyi s"ezd — stenograficheskii otchet* (Moscow, 1923), 152.
73. *Bor'ba za uprochenie*, 59–61; Gililov, *V. I. Lenin*, 151; Iakubovskaia, *Stroitel'stvo*, 131; *Dvenadtsatyi s"ezd*, 558; *Stalin*, V, 48.
74. Gililov, *V. I. Lenin*, 159; V. S. Kirillov and A. Ia. Sverdlov, *Grigorii Konstantinovich Ordzhonikidze (Sergo) — Biografiia* (Moscow, 1962), 158–59; henceforth referred to as *Ordzhonikidze*.
75. *Bor'ba za uprochenie*, 65; Gililov, *V. I. Lenin*, 161.
76. Iakubovskaia, *Stroitel'stvo*, 48–49; Gililov, *V. I. Lenin*, 160; *Ordzhonikidze*, 162–63.
77. Gililov, *V. I. Lenin*, 160.
78. *Ibid.*, 161.
79. Lenin, *Sochineniia*, 4th ed., XXXIII (1953), 103; Gililov, *V. I. Lenin*, 161.
80. *Bor'ba za uprochenie*, 38.
81. *Ibid.*, 89.
82. Text, *ibid.*, 108–10.
83. *Kommunist* (Kharkov), no. 238 (17 October 1923) in M. V. Frunze, *Sobranie sochinenii* (Moscow-Leningrad, 1926), I, 476–78.
84. Speech cited in *Zaria vostoka*, no. 228, 21 March 1923, reported by E. B. Genkina, *Obrazovanie SSSR*, 2nd ed. [Moscow], 1947), 101; Gililov, *V. I. Lenin*, 151.
85. Gililov, *V. I. Lenin*, 151–52.
86. *Ordzhonikidze*, 171; *Bor'ba za uprochenie*, 117.
87. *Lenin*, XXV, 624; this letter is not reproduced in Stalin's Collected Works.
88. Pentkovskaia, "Rol' V. I. Lenina," 17.
89. My reconstruction rests partly on Iakubovskaia, *Stroitel'stvo*, 144, 148, and Pentkovskaia, "Rol' V. I. Lenina," 17, and partly on Lenin's and Stalin's letters of 27 September 1922, referred to below (see note 99).
90. S. S. Gililov, "Razrabotka V. I. Leninym printsipov stroitel'stva mnogonatsio-

nal'nogo Sovetskogo gosudarstva," Akademiia Obshchestvennykh Nauk pri TsK KPSS, *O deiatel'nosti V. I. Lenina v 1917–1922 gody — Sbornik Statei* (Moscow, 1958), 76; Gililov, *V. I. Lenin,* 165–66; *Ordzhonikidze,* 171.

91. *Bor'ba za uprochenie,* 117.
92. Iakubovskaia, *Stroitel'stvo,* 145.
93. First published in *Sotsialisticheskii vestnik,* no. 2/48 (17 January 1923), 19; reprinted, with a record of the vote, in *Bor'ba za uprochenie,* 116–17.
94. Pentkovskaia, "Rol' V. I. Lenina," 17; Iakubovskaia, *Stroitel'stvo,* 145–46.
95. Gililov, *V. I. Lenin,* 167; Iakubovskaia, *Stroitel'stvo,* 146.
96. Iakubovskaia, *Stroitel'stvo,* 151–52.
97. Pentkovskaia, "Rol' V. I. Lenina," 17; Iakubovskaia, *Stroitel'stvo,* 148–49; Gililov, *V. I. Lenin,* 169.
98. Iakubovskaia, *Stroitel'stvo,* 149.
99. Lenin's memorandum is reproduced in *LS,* XXXVI (1959), 496–98; Stalin's has not been published in full, but can be found in the Trotsky Archive, T–755. Both documents are dated 27 September 1922.
100. Lenin, *Sochineniia,* 4th ed., XXXIII, 335.
101. The revised project, accepted by the Plenum on 6 October, is reproduced in *Bor'ba za uprochenie,* 117–18.
102. *Ordzhonikidze,* 172; Gililov, *V. I. Lenin,* 175.
103. *Dvenadtsatyi s"ezd,* 536; *Stalin,* V, 433.
104. *Sotsialisticheskii vestnik,* 17 January 1923; cf. L. Beriia, *K voprosu ob istorii Bol'shevistskikh organizatsii v Zakavkaz'e,* 7th ed. ([Moscow], 1948), 245.
105. *Dvenadtsatyi s"ezd,* 464.
106. Gililov, *V. I. Lenin,* 175–76.
107. Beriia, *K voprosu,* 243–44; Gililov, *V. I. Lenin,* 174–76; Iakubovskaia, *Stroitel'stvo,* 154; *Ordzhonikidze,* 172–73.
108. *Sotsialisticheskii vestnik,* 17 January 1923, 19; Gililov, *V. I. Lenin,* 176.
109. *Sotsialisticheskii vestnik,* 17 January 1923, 19; Beriia, *K voprosu,* 245–46. L. Schapiro observes (*The Communist Party of the Soviet Union,* London, 1960, 227) that this letter is not reprinted in Lenin's Collected Works; but it should be noted that it is listed in the complete catalogue of Lenin's published writings, Institut Marksizma-Leninizma, *Khronologicheskii ukazatel' proizvedenii V. I. Lenina* (Moscow, 1959–62), II, no. 10,276. See also L. Trotsky, *Stalin* (New York, [1941]), 357.
110. *Sotsialisticheskii vestnik,* 17 January 1923, 19.
111. *Ibid.; Dvenadtsatyi s"ezd,* 156–57; Iakubovskaia, *Stroitel'stvo,* 154–55; Gililov, *V. I. Lenin,* 177.
112. *Sotsialisticheskii vestnik,* 17 January 1923, 19; *Dvenadtsatyi s"ezd,* 158; Gililov, *V. I. Lenin,* 178–79.
113. *Bor'ba za uprochenie,* 118–20.
114. Iakubovskaia, *Stroitel'stvo,* 160.
115. *Ibid.*
116. Carr, *The Bolshevik Revolution,* I, 397.
117. *Pravda,* 30 December 1922; S. I. Iakubovskaia, *Ob"edinitel'noe dvizhenie za obrazovanie SSSR* ([Moscow], 1947), 194.
118. TsIK, SSSR, *I s"ezd sovetov Soiuza Sovetskikh Sotsialisticheskikh Republik — stenograficheskii otchet* (Moscow, 1923).
119. *Ibid.,* 19.
120. *Ibid.,* 8–11.
121. Genkina, *Obrazovanie SSSR,* 123; Iakubovskaia, *Stroitel'stvo,* 193.
122. Based on figures supplied in RKP(b), TsK, Statisticheskii otdel, *RKP(b) v tsifrakh* (Moscow, 1924ff), Vypusk I, table 6, p. 5 (NN).
123. VKP(b), *Desiatyi s"ezd RKP(b)* (Moscow, 1933), 206–07; speech of Zatonskii.
124. I. P. Trainin, "K postanovke natsional'nogo voprosa," *VS,* no. 5 (1923), 29.
125. TsK, RKP(b), *Rossiiskaia Kommunisticheskaia Partiia (bol'shevikov),* 330–31; *Stalin,* V, 40.
126. *Ordzhonikidze,* 174–77.

127. *Dvenadtsatyi s"ezd*, 157; L. A. Fotieva, "Iz vospominanii o V. I. Lenine," *Voprosy istorii KPSS*, no. 4 (1957), 159; "Novyi dokument o zhizni i deiatel'nosti V. I. Lenina," *ibid.*, no. 2 (1963), 71.
128. *Izvestiia*, 17 November 1922; Fotieva, "Iz vospominanii," 158–59; "Novyi dokument," 71.
129. "Novyi dokument," 69.
130. *Ibid.*, 74.
131. *Ibid.*, 76.
132. *Ibid.*, 77; Fotieva, "Iz vospominanii," 150.
133. *Ordzhonikidze*, 177–78.
134. The incident is described in *Ordzhonikidze*, 175–76.
135. "Novyi dokument," 77.
136. Fotieva, "Iz vospominanii," 159.
137. "Novyi dokument," 69, 77.
138. Magerovskii, *Soiuz*, 56–57.
139. *Dvenadtsatyi s"ezd*, 150, 159; *Bor'ba za uprochenie*, 146.
140. G. K. Ordzhonikidze, *Stat'i i rechi* (Moscow, 1956–57), I, 266.
141. Fotieva, "Iz vospominanii," 156, 158.
142. See this book, pp. 285–86.
143. Fotieva, "Iz vospominanii," 161–62.
144. "Novyi dokument," 90–91.
145. *Ibid.*, 84, 91; Fotieva, "Iz vospominanii," 162-63.
146. *Stalin*, V, 143. Cf. Genkina, *Obrazovanie SSSR*, 125ff and V. I. Ignat'ev, *Sovet National'nostei TsIK SSSR* (Moscow–Leningrad, 1926).
147. Cf. J. Stalin, *Marxism and the National Question* (New York, 1942), 134, 142; Iakubovskaia, *Stroitel'stvo*, 198–99.
148. "Novyi dokument," 91.
149. *Sotsialisticheskii vestnik*, no. 23/24 (69/70), 17 March 1923, 15. Copy in Trotsky Archive, T–787. Trotsky's reply is in *Stalin School of Falsification* (New York, 1937), 71.
150. Trotsky Archive, T–794.
151. *Sotsialisticheskii vestnik*, no. 23/24 (69/70), 17 March 1923, 15. Trotsky Archive, T–788.
152. See his circular to the members of the Central Committee of 16 April 1923 in the Trotsky Archive, T–794.
153. *Dvenadtsatyi s"ezd*, 150–59.
154. *Ibid.*, 185–86.
155. Stalin, *Marxism*, 137–57.
156. *Stalin*, V, 264–65.
157. Trotsky, *Stalin*, 357.
158. *Dvenadtsatyi s"ezd*, 523; cf. *ibid.*, 548.
159. *Ibid.*, 529.
160. *Ibid.*, 531–32.
161. See his constitutional project in V. I. Ignat'ev, *Sovetskii stroi*, Vyp. I (Moscow–Leningrad, 1928), 115–19, and his theoretical analysis in *Soiuz Sotsialisticheskikh Sovetskikh Respublik — Novyi etap v Sovetskom soiuznom stroitel'stve* (Kharkov, 1923). The latter contains a critique of the Union constitution.
162. *Dvenadtsatyi s"ezd*, 532–34.

# INDEX

Abkhazians, 212
*Adalet* Party (Persian Communist), 218, 220, 229
Adzhars, 212
Aharonian, Avetis (c. 1864–1948), 216
Akhil Bek, 257
Akhundov, R., 268
Akmolinsk, 172
Akselrod, Pavel Borisovich (1850–1928), 34
Aktiubinsk, 173
Akushinskii, Ali Khadzi, 216
Alash-Orda Party (Kazakh-Kirghiz), 84, 85, 86, 89, 108, 162, 172, 173–175
Aleksandropol, 193, 231, 232
Alexander I, 4, 8
Alexander II, 2, 7
American Relief Mission (Armenia), 209
Anatolia, 12, 101, 221, 231, 236; Eastern, 18, 101, 210, 231
Andi, 96
Ankara, 240
Antonov-Ovseenko, Vladimir Aleksandrovich (1884–purged, died in exile, 1939), 120, 124, 126, 127, 128, 130, 140, 184
Araks River, 16, 208
Ardahan, 106, 107
Armenia, 7, 8, 17, 156, 208–210, 212, 217, 223, 230, 239, 240, 271; establishment of Soviet rule, 227, 230–234; National Conference, 102; National Council (Tiflis), 102; national movement, 18–19, 101, 202; political parties, 19, 101, 102, 106; Provisional Military Revolutionary Committee, 232, 233
Armenian Corps, 102
Armenians, 2, 8, 16–17, 20, 47, 99, 101, 107, 176, 194, 195, 199–200, 201, 205, 206, 208, 209, 216
Armenian Soviet Socialist Republic, *see* Armenia
Artem, Fedor Andreevich (1883–1921), 127, 136, 140, 144, 165
Ashkhabad, 181
Astrakhan, 1, 158, 172, 201, 207–208, 220

Austria, 2, 23, 24, 36; national question, 24–28
"Autonomisation," 270–271, 272, 281, 282–283
Autonomous Regions and Republics, *see* Russia, Soviet
Autonomy, cultural, 24, 25, 31, 33, 34, 37, 40, 42, 77, 78
Avar people, 16
Azerbaijan, 79, 194, 204–208, 210, 212, 214, 216, 217, 221, 223, 224, 253, 254, 266, 279; establishment of Soviet rule, 224, 225–229; foreign relations, 234, integration into USSR, 250, 271; National Council, 204–206; national movement, 20, 99, 100, 104–105, 202; Parliament (December 1918), 206; political parties, 15, 99–100, 106, 204–205
Azerbaijani people, 8, 12–13, 16, 96, 99–101, 194, 195, 199, 200, 202, 203, 205
Azerbaijani Soviet Socialist Republic, *see* Azerbaijan

Bailev, Frederick Marshman, Lieutenant Colonel (1882–1967), 180
Baisun, 258
Baitursunov, Akhmed (1872–?), 84, 173, 174, 262
Bakhchisarai, 13, 79, 81
Baku, 14, 15, 98, 100, 101, 104, 105, 106, 156, 193, 195, 199–204, 217, 218, 225, 230, 231, 257; British occupation, 206–207; establishment of Communist-led Baku Commune (1918), 199–204; Executive Committee of Soviet (Ispolkom), 199, 200; Moslems, 200, 205; oil industries, 13, 201, 202, 207–208, 226; political parties, 199–200, 206; Turkish occupation of, 204, 205, 206; Communist coup (1920), 224, 225–229
Balkariia, 223
Barudi, Alimdzhan, 77
Bashkiriia, 86, 108, 161–168, 170, 247–248, 270, 279; Congress, First (Orenburg, July 1917), 86; Congress of Soviets, First (1920), 168; national

# RUSSIAN RESEARCH CENTER STUDIES

\* Out of print.
† Publications of the Harvard Project on the Soviet Social System.
‡ Published jointly with the Center for International Affairs, Harvard University.